P9-BJQ-218

DISCARD

# URBAN GEOGRAPHY

*Edited by*

*Harold M. Melvin Mayer,* 1916-

*and*

*Clyde F. Kohn*

 *The University of Chicago Press*

*Library of Congress Catalog Number: 59-11973*

THE UNIVERSITY OF CHICAGO PRESS, CHICAGO 37
Cambridge University Press, London, N.W. 1, England
The University of Toronto Press, Toronto 5, Canada

© *1959 by The University of Chicago. Published 1959.*
*Second Impression 1960.*
*Composed and printed by* THE UNIVERSITY OF CHICAGO PRESS,
*Chicago, Illinois, U.S.A.*

# TABLE OF CONTENTS

4,329

Cities are expanding in size and relative importance in many parts of the world. In North America, particularly since the advent of modern highways and automobile transportation, this growth has given rise to many new problems, and old problems have become increasingly difficult of solution. In keeping with this growth of cities, the field of urban geography has become more important both as an academic discipline and as one of the foundations for practical decision-making in governmental, business, and social affairs. City and metropolitan planning agencies, industrial and commercial firms, and many other organizations both public and private are increasingly aware of the urban geographer's contributions toward the solution of their problems.

Location, areal extent, and interaction among the various urban functions are the core of the urban geographer's concern. Knowledge of these factors is a prerequisite for considering such problems as the determination of the number, nature, and location of internal transportation routes and facilities within cities and metropolitan areas, the designation of the amount and location of areas for the appropriate development of each type of land use in the proper places, the location of individual establishments such as factories, shops, schools, and residences to optimize the efficiency of each and of the city as a whole, and the evaluation of a city's economic and physical patterns in relation to the direction and character of its future development.

If urban geography is to be effective in its applications to human affairs, it must rest upon a firm conceptual and theoretical base. The field is now at a stage at which some of its concepts and generalizations have been clearly formulated and a large number of hypotheses stated as bases for further investigation in specific areas and circumstances. There is, however, no systematic presentation of these concepts and hypotheses for the student of geography and others concerned with urban affairs. In lieu of such presentation, this volume of articles and excerpts is designed to facilitate a comprehension of the character and scope of the field of urban geography, both as a scientific discipline and as a body of applied knowledge.

The articles included in this volume provide a sampling of the kinds of work that urban geographers and research workers in closely related fields have been undertaking on modern cities, particularly in North America and western Europe. Limitation of space prevents a broader representation of the field. Many of the topics not included are important to our understanding of cities but have been omitted because little systematic work has been done on them in recent years. Among these are the study of cities as nodes of cultural diffusion and the classification of types of urban sites. Also, few studies of individual cities have been included. This volume is primarily concerned with presenting geographic concepts, principles, and generalizations related to urban functions, forms, distribution, and growth. Those studies of individual cities or metropolitan areas that are included are significant examples of empirical investigations which, when combined with other studies, may lead to advances in methodology or to substantive generalizations.

Urban geography, like most branches of geography, borrows from and contributes to many related fields. Most of the articles in this book were written by geographers. Some of them, however, are contributions to urban geography by scholars and investigators in closely related fields—sociology, economics, planning, marketing, and real estate. Significant contributions are also being made by architects, engineers, political scientists, social psychologists, anthropologists, historians, and many others, examples of whose work are omitted from this volume only because of practical limitations of space and format. Interestingly, much is being done in urban geography today by urban geographers working in collaboration with persons in these other disciplines, both theoretical and practical.

Only a few of the articles in this volume antedate the end of World War II. This is indicative of the accelerating rate at which the field of urban geography is advancing. Many very significant earlier articles have not been included because they have been superseded by more recent contributions containing higher degrees of conceptual formulation and generalization. Many of these more recent articles illustrate the fact that modern urban geographers are drawing more and more upon a wider variety of techniques and are using them in a more sophisticated manner. In addition to the traditional cartographic and other techniques, which have themselves been improved, the urban geographer is using newer techniques involving quantitative and statistical methods. Most of the articles in this volume which antedate World War II represent milestones in the development of generalization about the geography of cities which subsequent empirical work has largely substantiated. An organized review of the field as it existed several years ago is contained in chapter 6 of *American Geography: Inventory and Prospect*, edited by P. E. James and C. F. Jones (Syracuse University Press, 1954).

Many trends in contemporary urban geography are either absent from or underrepresented by the articles selected for this volume. Among these are the areal fragmentation of the political organization of metropolitan areas; the role of cultural differences from place to place in the forms and structures of cities; urbanization in underdeveloped areas; the impact of highway improvements on the structure and growth of cities; urban sites and their characteristics; the defense aspects of urban structure and distribution; and the use of aerial photography in urban studies.

The lack of a suitable textbook in urban geography in the English language including references to contemporary knowledge and methods, together with the rapid growth of interest in the subject, as exemplified by the proliferation of university and college courses and the great demand for the employment of trained urban geographers in industry and government, has motivated the compilation of this book of readings. It is anticipated that one or more systematic treatises suitable for use as textbooks in urban geography will be published in the near future. Prior to the publication of such books, however, the present volume is intended to fill the immediate need for materials useful in classroom instruction and in presenting to persons in related fields something of the objectives, scope, and methodology of present-day urban geography. After a more systematic treatise becomes available, this book will serve a need for collateral reading in those institutions which do not have complete libraries of professional journals and other publications in the field of urban geography or where the use of such publications by large classes is not feasible.

# APPROACHES TO THE STUDY OF URBAN GEOGRAPHY

The study of urban geography is largely a product of the twentieth century. Early writers devoted much of their attention to the physical sites of urban places and to their situation. The emphasis, as in other branches of geography, was on the relation between the location and structure of specific cities and the land they occupied.

Today the urban geographer commonly approaches his study from two different points of view. First, he considers cities as discrete phenomena in the general fabric of settlement of the entire earth, or a major part of it. As such, they can be analyzed geographically in much the same way as any other phenomena similarly distributed. Concepts and generalizations may be formed regarding their distribution, size, function, or rates of growth. Areas served by urban places may be delimited, and the spatial interactions between urban places, inside or outside the delimited tributary areas, may be studied. Within the past few years several papers in urban geography have contributed significantly to theoretical notions regarding the functional base of central places, the size and spacing of cities within selected areas, nodal regions, and other geographic considerations.

Second, the urban geographer studies cities in terms of their morphology, that is, in terms of layout and build considered as expressions of their origin, growth, and function. Studies which have focused on this approach to urban geography have given rise to concepts and generalizations related to the character and intensity of land use within the city and to the spatial interactions of one part of the city with another. These interactions are reflected in the amount, direction, time, and character of movement of persons and goods between the various functional areas that together make up the urban agglomeration. The study of urban transportation, as a result, has become a major concern of geography. So, too, has the areal growth of urban places in recent years, especially the extension of the urban agglomeration into adjacent rural areas. As a result of their interest in morphology, some geographers have recently turned their attention to problems involved in guiding urban growth and development.

Each of the two papers included in this opening section deals with both these approaches to the study of urban places. Harold M. Mayer, in his article "Geography and Urbanism," outlines the major problems with which modern geography deals. Among these he stresses the geographer's interest in the areal association of activities within urban places; the economic base of cities; the areas which cities serve in one way or another; patterns of distribution of cities on the earth as well as the patterns of distribution within cities. He concludes with a discussion of the geographer's growing interest in describing and understanding the spatial frictions existing in cities because of their morphology and the need for interest in planning urban growth.

Robert E. Dickinson, in his paper "The Scope and Status of Urban Geography: An Assessment," elaborates on several of the same problems, especially on the geographic approach to the study of a specific urban settlement. He presents a review of many of the significant contributions that have been made in the field of urban geography. Dickinson states that the task of the geographer in an urban study is to determine the characteristics of the site and situation of the urban settlement, its historical development, and the limits which it has currently attained. The article is also concerned with comparative functional and morphological studies and presents a valuable review of the significant papers that have contributed to a better understanding of the location, spacing, and size of cities, and of their layout and build.

# GEOGRAPHY AND URBANISM

In recent years, geographers have in increasing numbers been turning their attention to the study of urban areas and the problems of cities, and a substantial number have adopted urban geography as their primary field of specialization. Some of them have been attracted to fields of application of their specialization in which geographic concepts have made valuable contributions, as in city planning, public administration, marketing, and local transportation.

Urban geography has a distinctive focus. Its primary concern is the association of activities in urban areas, which are expressed in characteristic associations of land use and occupance features. Thus the center of interest of urban geography, as of all geography, is man, and the reciprocal relationships between man, his works, and the earth. It is concerned with interpreting the patterns and relationships that exist within urban areas, on the one hand, and between urban areas and the non-urban areas that cities serve, on the other.

Many geographers of an earlier generation attributed to the physical environment a deterministic role and an influence precluding the exercise of the wide range of choice of alternative modes and patterns of physical and cultural development which we now know is available to man. Few geographers today hold that the environment determines the form and patterns of culture; most hold firmly the conviction that the most important environmental influence is man himself. They believe that, within very broad limits, the environment can be

Reprinted from *Scientific Monthly*, LXIII (July, 1951), 1–12, with permission of the author and the editor. (Copyright, 1951, by the American Association for the Advancement of Science, Washington, D.C.)

made to serve man rather than be his master; that, with sufficient social and economic motivation, the limitations of the environment which circumscribe man's choice among alternative forms of relation to it are very elastic and flexible.

Modern geographers hold that the activities of man, the physical forms or structures developed for those activities, and their arrangements and associations with one another and with the land are at least as much a reflection of the cultural framework within which they exist and which they are intended to serve as they are a reflection of the relationships with the natural environment. Many geographers ascribe to culture the more important role. It follows, then, that urban geographers must be familiar with the historical, social, economic, and political background of the areas within which cities are located.

Urban geography is concerned with the study of the economic base of cities; with interpretation of the relationships between the city as an important form of man's occupance of the land and the activities within the city's hinterland or economically contributary area which focus upon the city and which give rise to urban occupance. It is not possible, for example, to understand the extent and patterns of industrial and commercial areas within urban agglomerations without an understanding of the nature and distribution of those activities that produce raw materials for the industries, carry the materials to the factories and the products to the markets and the consumers, convert the materials into marketable products, and use the products to secure economic and social advantages.

Cities exist primarily to provide goods and services for the people who live outside the urban boundaries. No city can exist purely as a self-sufficient unit; it is a focus or area of concentration for a variety of activities serving areas beyond the city itself. In return for such activities and services, cities receive, directly or indirectly, sustenance from the areas which they serve. The extent to which any given urban activity serves the people outside the urban area is a measure of the relative importance of that activity as an urbanizing force. The economist devises measures of the relative importance of these activities; the geographer studies them in association with one another. He measures and interprets their relative importance in the various portions of the area the city serves and the location, intensity, and character of occupance of the land within the city itself which is used or is potentially usable for servicing those activities. Thus, studies of the location of industry, of the amount of land used by industry, of the amount of land potentially usable by industry, of the numbers of persons who are, now or potentially, supported by various industries, and the changes that have occurred, are occurring, or may occur among the various industries within a city are vital concerns of the urban geographer. Similarly, the geographer is concerned with the relations between industrial land use in cities and the other forms of occupance of urban land. The relations, for example, between locations of employment (the industrial and commercial areas) and places of living (the residential areas and associated community recreational, educational, shopping, and other service areas) are reflected in the amount, direction, time, and character of movement of persons between the various functional areas that together comprise the urban agglomeration. The study of transportation thus makes possible the differentiation of functional areas characterized by different forms and combinations of forms of occupance. Transportation, therefore, both intraurban and interurban, is a concern of the urban geographer.

A city cannot be considered as an isolated physical or social unit. It must be considered primarily as a focal area for activities—expressed in physical forms such as buildings, streets, and parks and in social forms such as institutions, customs, and mores—for a much larger area, the size and extent of which vary for each urban function. The measure of the extent of these urban relationships, of the differences of extent from one city as compared with another, of the influence of one activity as compared with another from a given city, and the description and interpretation of these differences are concerns of the urban geographer. In such description and interpretation the geographer calls upon many related disciplines, from sociology, anthropology, and political science to engineering, architecture, meteorology, pedology, geomorphology, and even psychology. Specialists in each of these fields may describe and interpret the spatial distribution of those groups of phenomena with which each is especially concerned; only the geographer is concerned with all the interrelationships among them, as they exist within an area and as they differ from one area to another. The urban geographer is thus concerned with the city as a functional as well as a physical entity. He is concerned with the environments of cities as well as with the environments within cities; with the patterns of distribution of cities on the earth as well as with the pattern of distribution of people, buildings, facilities, institutions, and cultures within cities. He is concerned with the interpretations of these distributions and their differences in occurrence and intensity from place to place, insofar as interpretations may be found in the interrelationships among the various phenomena thus distributed. He is particularly, though by no means exclusively, concerned with the study and interpretation of areal differences in the relationships between man and his institutions, on the one hand, and the environment, both physical and social, on the other.

Having concluded that the functions and forms of urban occupance are, to a large extent, within the control of man, and being concerned with the relations among these functions and forms in their spatial arrangement, the urban geographer should logically be concerned with describing and understanding the spatial frictions existing in cities and inhibiting the fulfilment of the maximum social and economic potentialities of urbanism as a form of land occupance and as a way of life. It is a short step from the study of alternative types of spatial relationships to the furnishing of guidance in selecting from among the many alternatives with which man is confronted. The urban geographer, therefore, is concerned with the problem of guiding urban growth and development into such forms and patterns as will further the attainment of a better urban way of life. The guidance of population density in cities through control of land use and the provision of instru-

ments by which the character, density, and distribution of housing and residential areas can be made better to serve the needs of the population; the securing of better relationships spatially and functionally among the various forms of land use in cities; the reduction of the frictions of competition among alternative land uses by proper allocation of land through zoning and other forms of democratic public action; the reduction of the time- and energy-wasting journeys between home and work; the securing of a better physical urban environment through guidance of city growth into forms more acceptable than the sprawl which now characterizes most urban areas —these are objectives that many urban geographers hold to be challenges worthy of the most intense application of geographical knowledge.

ROBERT E. DICKINSON

## *THE SCOPE AND STATUS OF URBAN GEOGRAPHY*
## *AN ASSESSMENT*

THE GEOGRAPHICAL APPROACH

In social surveys and regional town-planning schemes it is invariably assumed that the geographer is primarily concerned with the physical ground plan on which the city rests. It is sometimes further conceded that the geographer follows such appraisal by tracing the effects of this physical ground plan on the growth and character of the city, but as a rule the investigation of these particular aspects is handled by the economist, sociologist, historian, or architect. There are, however, numerous thorough studies of cities by geographers which indicate clearly that urban geography has a well-established scope and special techniques. It seems necessary, therefore, to assess the contribution of geography to the study of the city as revealed in such studies in order to indicate to the geographer the status of the subject and to suggest lines of future investigation. Such a review will also demonstrate to the student of urban problems that the trained geographer, from the new graduate upward, has an equipment and technique that can be applied to the examination of particular problems of social and physical planning.[1]

Economist, historian, sociologist, and

Reprinted from *Land Economics*, XXIV (August, 1948), 221–38, with permission of the author and the editor. (Copyright, 1948, by the University of Wisconsin, Madison, Wis.)

[1] It should be emphasized that this is essentially a bibliographical study and attempts to sum up the general trend in concepts and techniques in urban geography as revealed in a very considerable literature over the last fifty years, and especially in the interwar period. It is in the interest of brevity only that references are confined to works mentioned in the text. It should also be pointed out that the article is written with special reference to Europe.

geographer study the urban settlement from different angles, and it will be well at the outset to define the geographer's conception of such a settlement, since this conditions his particular approach. The urban settlement is regarded by the geographer as a man-made habitat on the earth's surface. The problem of exact definition lies in the smallest urban settlements in any area. With such cases in mind as a basis for discussion, it will be found that size and administrative status are not essential criteria of true urban character. Function and form are the essentials of the matter. The word "urban," as opposed to "rural," implies an activity that is divorced from the cultivation of the soil and that is carried out in close association with kindred activities at fixed places. These activities, in the broadest sense, are cultural (especially religious), commercial, industrial, administrative, and residential (in the sense of non-producers or *rentiers* who are dependent on the urban dwellers and the countryside). Farming, however, is not excluded from the occupations of the urban community. A farming element is particularly characteristic of the towns on the Mediterranean lands and of east central Europe; it was important in the origin of the early medieval towns of western Europe, though it dwindled as trade and industry grew, and it is still not unimportant in many semiurban towns on the Continent.

The specifically urban activities are all located either to serve a surrounding territory or to carry out activities that are tied to certain resources or where such resources can be conveniently assembled. Such activities may be carried out separately at different places. This occurs in the beginnings of permanent settlement and also in thinly populated or backward areas, where such settlement may assume a semipermanent character. In the forested lands of north Sweden there are churches around which cluster timber buildings that are occupied only during the seasonal fairs. The tribal markets of Morocco are temporary settlements. Specialization of urban functions in one place or another is a marked feature in the lands of Western civilization, owing to the development of transport facilities, and takes the form, for example, of an isolated factory, a group of workers' houses in the open country, a mining camp, or a seaside or inland resort. All these may be described as *urban settlements*. When, however, these activities occur in some kind of combination in a permanent and compact settlement with some measure of community organization, the place assumes the character of a *town*. A *city* is a king among towns, enjoying leadership over its neighbors. A fundamental trait of both town and city in all ages has been that they are institutional centers (commercial, cultural, and administrative) for their surrounding territory. It is only in recent times that industry has become a primary cause of urban growth. Upon the basis of regional service and industry there grows a pyramidal structure of secondary occupations, catering to the needs of these specialist occupations and to the personal needs of the inhabitants.

By virtue of its distinct activities, the layout and the buildings of the urban settlement are also distinct from the rural settlement. The urban activities are accommodated in shop, workshop, office, warehouse, and public building and find their mutual and outside contacts by street, road, river, and, more recently, by rail. The dwellings of the workers and their dependents normally take up most of the built-up area. All these are the form-elements of the settlement group. The problem of the geographer is to determine not only the distinctive functions of the urban settlement but also how its form-elements are arranged in relation to each other and to the streets

and places. Generalization cannot safely be applied to all climes and times, and we confine our comments to western Europe. Thus, in England, the simplest urban functions appear in an occasional village in special buildings that are scattered among the houses along the village streets. Even the small English village is primarily a service center for the dispersed farmsteads around it and itself contains very few farmsteads. More of these urban functions are concentrated in the small town, which normally has its nucleus in a market place or a wide main street of medieval origin, on which the urban buildings form a continuous frontage. The larger the town, the more the buildings; these spread from the nucleus along the main streets, and special functions seek special sites. The railway station invariably has become a nucleus of segregation. In the large town the urban functions are so numerous and varied that they compete for space as near as possible to the nucleus so as to form a central district that throbs with activity in the day and is a "deadheart" at night. This core, that is popularly called the "town" or "city" or "downtown," together with the commercial subcenters and the clusters of factories, forms the main areas of work that are separate from the areas of residence in which the workers live. The existence of the core and the marked separation of areas of work and residence is the most distinctive feature of the structure of the large city as opposed to the smaller town.

Finally, these characteristics of urban settlements, their size, functions, spacing, layout, and build, vary regionally with the physical environment, with the density of population, and with the character of the human economies and cultures which they serve and represent. There are vast differences in urban settlement between the English Lowland, the Ganges Plain, and the Australian Riverina. There are also important differences in urban character between different areas of western Europe. Most of these features of settlement are obvious to any careful observer. Their scientific examination and the elucidation of their regional variations both over wide areas and within the urban complex itself are essential problems of urban geography.

The geographical study of an urban settlement is concerned with four main problems: first, the physical and cultural conditions that were involved in the origin of the nucleus of settlement; second, the reactions of this nucleus, in its functional and morphological development, to the impact of historical events; third, the life and organization of the contemporary settlement viewed areally, both as a whole and with respect to the differentiations within it; fourth, the interrelations between the settlement and its surrounding territory. In addition to the study of an individual settlement there is, however, a further important aspect of study, namely, comparison. The size, function, and form of all settlements vary regionally with the development and present social and economic structure of the human groups which they represent and serve, and it is for the geographer to investigate those features of the urban settlement that are really repetitive and significant, just as he studies the rural settlement. In other words, as in the field of geomorphology, the geographical study of human settlements both rural and urban has three aspects. There is the *physical structure* of the settlement—the character and mode of grouping of its buildings and streets; there is the *process* which determines this structure—that is, the social and economic character and traditions of the community; and third, there is the *stage* in the historical development of the settlement. This historical or developmental treatment may lay equal emphasis on each phase of development (especially when different civilizations have produced entirely new structures on the same site), but the final aspect of the study, to which all else should be subordinated, is the depiction and interpretation of the settlement of today, both as a whole and in its component parts.

## SITE AND SITUATION

The first task of the geographer in an urban study is to determine exactly the characteristics of the site and situation of the settlement. The *site* embraces the precise features of the terrain on which the settlement began and over which it has spread. This study demands thorough examination of the initial site that so often has been profoundly modified by human action, especially in the large city. It includes such matters as relief, geology, water supply, the nature of the river that traverses the settlement, the areas liable to flood before embanking, etc. The *situation* is usually taken to mean the physical conditions (as for the site) over a much wider area around the settlement. But of equal importance are the human characteristics of the surrounding country, since these affect the character and fortunes of the urban settlement. The term "nodality" is used by geographers to express the significance of a settlement as a node or focus of routes. Hitherto, the geographer has been prone to assess the position, size, and functions of the urban settlement in terms of the "natural routes" centered on it. The nodality of a settlement is to be measured neither in terms of the physical setting nor simply by the number of man-made routes that radiate from or pass through it but, ultimately, by the traffic of all kinds that uses these routes. In other words, nodality should be measured on the basis of the functions of the settlement as a focus. We need a measure of such centralized or nodal functions in terms of the relations of the settlement with the country and with other settlements around it.

These points may be illustrated by specific references to the towns of western Europe.[2] There is no doubt that the situation of the town, in relation to routes and to the fertility of its surroundings, had a close relation to its size down to the industrial era. Indeed, with a few exceptions, the

[2] Robert E. Dickinson, "The Development and Distribution of the Medieval German Town," *Geography,* XXVII (1942), 9–21 and 47–53.

chief towns at the beginning of the nineteenth century were situated at the junction of the main road and water routes, and these towns and routes almost all date back in origin to the early Middle Ages. Long-distance trade was the primary factor in the development of the early medieval towns. It called into being many mercantile settlements on the main routes, although the chief of these settlements clustered for protection and custom around existing strongholds that already served as seats of defense and administration for their surrounding territories. The growth of handicrafts and of local trade caused these settlements to develop ever closer associations with their surroundings. By 1150 the concept of the town or *civitas* was fully established. It is true that the merchants played a predominant part in the government of the medieval town, but this does not warrant overemphasis of the importance of this element in their origins. Long-distance trade, local market trade, defense, and administration all played their part, and their relative importance varied at different stages in urban development from one region to another.[3]

The development of towns in the early Middle Ages (before 1200) was favored on valley and lowland sites at the junction of valley routes because facilities for trade and for the organization of the populated area and contact with the civilized world were primary factors in their location and growth. In the later Middle Ages (after 1200) the great majority of towns grew as local centers of trade and administration and had only local nodality. Their sites were dictated by the need of defense rather than trade, and either castle or town, or both, were placed on strongly defended natural sites such as hill tops and river spurs. Whatever the origin of these small towns, however, it is quite clear that their survival or growth as active urban centers before

the modern era depended entirely on their ability to function for a tributary area in competition with neighboring towns of similar status.

The advent of the railway in the middle of the nineteenth century added an entirely new element to the nodality factor and radically transformed the structure of the growing urban settlement. The original conditions of the site and situation became of historical significance and were displaced by the new means of communications and the new needs of industry and commerce. But the great majority of towns are still small and have changed little in size from a hundred years ago. The modern city has spread from its original nucleus. Down to the latter half of the nineteenth century the Continental cities were still confined within their fortifications. The walls of many towns were demolished and replaced by boulevards in the early years of the nineteenth century. Others were surrounded by entirely new fortifications to meet the demands of modern warfare or to serve as customs barriers (*octroi*), and these set very real limits to urban expansion until they in turn were replaced by boulevards, buildings, and open spaces. The old town is usually in the heart of the city. In the case of the small towns with defensive sites, the nucleus, be it a castle or town on a hill top or on an island girt by marsh, is separate from the new extension which has grown along a road or near a railway.

## HISTORICAL DEVELOPMENT

Having determined precisely the physical conditions of situation and site which affected the beginnings of the urban settlement, the geographer examines how, with the passage of time, the settlement utilizes, adapts itself to, and transforms these conditions in the process of its formation and expansion. History must be made subsidiary to this main object. This point is important. Many urban studies, especially in Britain, have traced the historical character of the adjustments of the settlement to the physical conditions of its site and

[3] There are numerous careful studies, by both geographers and historians, of the development of urban settlements in different regions of Germany. For bibliography see Dickinson, *op. cit.*

situation and, for that reason, do not give a clear picture of the present physiognomic and functional structure of the settlement as an entity in space, which, as stated above, we believe to be the central object of the study.

A word should be said here about the formation of the individual town in western Europe. The urban geographer's task commences with the appearance of the first traces of permanent settlement. The disputed question of urban origins is obscured by vagueness about what is meant by "urban." The historian is concerned with the emergence of the community as a self-governing body and usually confines his attention to the principal medieval towns. H. Pirenne defined a medieval town as having three characteristics—its population was engaged in industry and commerce, it had a distinct legal constitution and institutions, and it was a center of administration and a fortress.[4] These were certainly true characteristics of the full-fledged town, but such a definition of all urban settlements in selected areas would be quite inadequate and untrue. In attempts to generalize about the origin and character of the medieval town, historian and geographer have failed to realize adequately that single traits of the full-fledged medieval town occur in small towns and villages as separate elements and there is, therefore, no clear-cut distinction between the two. There were, in the Middle Ages, towns without walls, towns without markets, villages with walls, and villages with crafts and tradesmen without the legal constitution of a town.

The route and market place formed the nucleus of the early medieval towns, which usually grew up adjacent to a stronghold from which the developing urban community eventually wrested its independent status. The majority of towns, however, especially west of the Rhine, grew gradually around a castle, a church, or a mon-

astery, whereas in Germany they were founded as self-contained and self-governing communities with planned forms attached to, or independent of, an existing nuclear stronghold. Such founded towns appear also in the numerous *bastide* towns of southwestern France and, more sporadically, in the towns that were founded by the English in the conquered territories of Wales. The expansion of the medieval town was conditioned by the main through and radial routes, by the walls, and by the necessity of adjustment of street and block to the lie of the central monuments, such as castle or cathedral. This growth was the result either of uncontrolled expansion, house by house, or of planned expansion in which the disposition of the houses was fixed by a predetermined street layout.

The broad historical events decisive in the history of urbanism are common to western Europe. The end of the Roman civilization was followed by a period of decadence for over five hundred years. The great phase of medieval growth of the "ecumene" began with the turn of the millennium and by 1500 western Europe was covered by practically all the settlements that exist today. The Renaissance and Baroque periods, from 1500 to 1850, were periods of relative stability. Towns in general grew little but changed much in aspect by the erection of new permanent domestic buildings, new public buildings, gardens, and avenues, and the new bastioned walls that were made necessary by the advent of gunpower. New towns or extensions of old ones were laid out on geometrical designs in accordance with the spirit of the age, as has been so vividly portrayed by Lewis Mumford. The southern steppes of Russia and the lower Danube lands saw the appearance of many towns in the seventeenth and eighteenth centuries and a number also were founded in southern Scandinavia and east central Europe, especially in Poland and Finland.

The "eotechnic" merges into the "paleotechnic" era with the advent of the factory, with machinery driven first by running

[4] H. Pirenne, *Medieval Cities, Their Origin and the Revival of Trade*, trans. F. D. Halsey (Princeton, 1925).

water and later by steam. This era brought the "back-to-back" house to Britain and the tenement to Europe. The end of the nineteenth century ushered in the "neotechnic" era, marked by the decline in the rate of growth of population and of cities, by the advent of the electric dynamo and the internal combustion engine, and by the increased rapidity of municipal transport. These changes have occasioned the "explosion" of the urban aggregate through the expansion of both residence and industry well beyond its administrative limits, and the emergence of particular urban structures on new sites that are apparently unconnected with other urban structures. All these facts form the background to the understanding of the growth and structure of the European city.[5]

These historical phases are evident in the physical structure of almost every west European city as a series of more or less concentric zones. The central zone, the modern business district, is, for the most part, the historic town (medieval and baroque) that is in process of rapid transformation. The middle zone was built up during the latter half of the nineteenth century and is fully occupied by streets and buildings. It is congested with mixed uses near the center but becomes more open and predominantly residential toward the margins. The outer zone has been built up since 1900 on the periphery of the city, where urban structures are widely scattered along the main routes in the midst of rural land. Factories, housing estates, urban open spaces (cemeteries, allotments, playing fields, golf courses, airfields) and noxious industries are its chief urban uses. Expansion outward has been a basic characteristic of urban growth in all eras, and this also implies a succession of types of land use as part of the process. Thus, good residences were initially placed on higher land or on river fronts near the old town. With the expansion of the town the good residences have shifted outward and the old ones have been invaded by other uses and converted to apartment houses or offices.

Recent studies differ considerably in emphasis according to the viewpoint of the particular school. Thus, some German studies depict with equal emphasis the build and activities of the town at each main stage in its development, an approach that is particularly significant in cities that have been completely destroyed and transformed with the passage of different cultures. This approach is well demonstrated in Wilhelmy's study of Sofia.[6] It is more usual to subordinate the study of the past to the understanding of the present, a historical approach that is particularly characteristic of French studies.

## STRUCTURE

It has been stated already that the present urban settlement is the culminating and the central object of the geographical approach. "Après l'étude dans le temps, l'étude dans l'espace," writes (and practices) Raoul Blanchard.[7] There are two aspects of such study, the functional and the demographic structure of the city; and the plan and build or morphological structure of the city. These are intimately interrelated and permit the recognition of homogeneous functional zones or regions. Functional study within the urban complex involves the classification and mapping of land uses, of building types, of industry and commerce, of the density and occupa-

[5] Lewis Mumford, *Culture of Cities* (New York: Harcourt, Brace & Co., 1938), and *Technics and Civilization* (New York: Harcourt, Brace & Co., 1934).

[6] H. Wilhelmy, *Hochbulgarien*, II, *Sofia; Wandlungen einer Grosstadt zwischen Orient und Okzident* (Schriften des Geographischen Instituts der Universität, Kiel, Band 5, 1936).

[7] Raoul Blanchard, *Grenoble: Étude de géographie urbaine* (Grenoble, 1912; reprinted and augmented, 1935), and "Québec: Esquisse de géographie urbaine," *Revue de géographie alpine* (Grenoble) 1934, pp. 216–413, may be referred to as outstanding studies from the French school. From the German school, see H. Bobek, "Innsbruck: Eine Gebirstadt, ihr Lebensraum und ihre Erscheinung," *Forschungen zu deutschen Landes und Volkskunde* (Stuttgart), 1928.

tions of the population, and of the density of traffic on roads and at nodal points. Classification, field methods, and cartographic techniques are essential to all aspects of such study. It is an approach that hitherto has been the peculiar concern of the geographer but is becoming a matter of particular interest today to all those who are interested in the structure of the city.

This geographical approach may be illustrated by a preliminary reconnaissance survey recently carried out under the writer's direction by a group of students in the lower Wye Valley, Monmouthshire, England. The town to be mapped had about 5,000 inhabitants. Three maps were prepared. First, the site and situation were studied in the field and mapped from the Ordnance Survey map with a scale of about 25 inches to one mile, with contours at intervals of 25 feet. The land liable to flood was also determined. Second, the buildings were mapped by age, by marking individual buildings and groups of buildings by periods on the 25-inch map. This was done by inquiry from local authorities, by deduction from building styles, and by the study of old maps that were available. Third, buildings were mapped on the same scale according to use. In such a small town it was found that certain types of structure were recognizable and these were plotted with different colors and digits as follows:

1. Public buildings, with a digit for each type of function.
2. Buildings of three stories and over with two or more stories in commercial use.
3. Buildings with one or two stories with one or both stories in commercial use.
4. Buildings with three stories with one story in commercial use. Digits indicate the type of use in each case (2, 3, and 4), thus: (*a*) shop, (*b*) office, (*c*) bank, (*d*) cafe, (*e*) garage, and (*f*) others.
5. Cottages.
6. Detached or double-fronted residential houses built prior to about 1900.
7. Town houses with three stories.
8. Town houses with two stories.
9. Post-1918 houses.

10. Factories, grouped according to product and indicated by digits.
11. Commercial premises, shown by a special color with digits as follows: (*a*) warehouse, (*b*) mills, (*c*) storage yards, (*d*) garage, (*e*) railway-goods yards, and (*f*) others.

The three provisional maps gave at a glance the site, the layout, and the expansion of the town, while its functional structure and activities were clearly evidenced in the character of the buildings and their uses.

We may turn now to more elaborate studies that obviously demand much labor and, in the case of large cities, team work under central direction. There are many geographical studies of individual cities; but particular attention may be given to a study of Stockholm, a relatively small city with little more than half a million inhabitants, that was prepared in 1934 by a group of geographers in the University of Stockholm on behalf of the municipal authorities.[8] Important examples of mapping technique will be found there. Industry and commerce may be classified and mapped according to the type of building unit (floor space, the number of stories, or transport facilities), the type of product (involving classification on an agreed basis), or the number of employees for each factory unit. The density of population may be mapped for the smallest available unit areas by a graded system of shading or by a dot value—the effective use of the latter, for accurate work, involves mapping block by block. Detailed mapping of ethnic, demographic, and occupational data also demands small statistical units. For all such work the British ward or its equivalent in foreign cities is far too large for research purposes. An example of the unit required is the so-called census tract of the United States Bureau of the Census that covers a few blocks in the urban area. In

[8] H. W. Ahlmann and Others, *Stockholms Inre Differentiering* ("Meddelande fran Geografiska Institutet vid Stockholms Högskola," No. 20 [Stockholm, 1934]). Also W. William-Olsson, "Stockholm: Its Structure and Development," *Geographical Review*, XXX (1940), 420–38.

Chicago, for example, there are 500 census tracts, whereas before 1920 the same city only had 34 wards for statistical analysis. Continental cities have occasionally small districts comparable with these that permit thorough mapping.

The social and economic status of the inhabitants can best be indicated by house rentals, where these are available for sufficiently small districts. Streets may be classified according to the type of shops and traffic. This is determined in the Stockholm study, for example, by adding the shop rents of the street frontage and dividing the total by the length of the frontage; this gives the shop rent per unit of frontage and is a measure of the shopping density of the street. These varied aspects have been examined and mapped in the study of Stockholm mentioned above, and, in order to determine the shifts of urban uses and the processes accounting for them, the distribution of activities was mapped for 1880, the beginning of the rapid development of the modern city and, for 1930, most of the activities being mapped by exact locality by a dot indicating a particular use, such as a bank or office.

Building structures need to be classified and mapped on the lines, for instance, of H. Louis' study of Berlin.[9] In this study, which was undertaken in the field by a group of students, the whole city was mapped as follows: (1) uniform buildings of four stories and over (mainly tenements), (2) varied building structures occurring in both the central and outer areas, (3) villas, housing estates, and gardens, (4) factories, shown in ground plan, (5) allotments (*Laubenkolonien*) and meadows (*Rieselfelder*) fertilized with sewage waste, (6) villages, and (7) the limits of the central business district.

It is now being increasingly realized that this geographical method is essential to the understanding of the anatomy of the urban community preparatory to planning for its

reconstruction. Where such investigations have been undertaken on a large scale in the last twenty years (as in the city inventories of Chicago and New York in the United States) the results are accessible in large publications which, in the case of New York, for example, have been summarized in an admirable geographical essay on that city.[10]

## THE LIMITS OF THE URBAN SETTLEMENT

The urban settlement cannot be interpreted adequately as a mass of materials or in terms of dead patterns. It must be interpreted as an organic part of a social group.[11] In terms of its four functions— dwelling, work, recreation, and transport— every urban settlement forms part of an economic, social, cultural, and political whole, upon which its development depends and all these relations have geographic expression.[12]

Viewed in this way, the urban settlement in general has a two-way relationship with its surroundings that extends beyond its political boundary. First, the countryside calls into being settlements that we call urban to carry out functions in its service. Second, the urban settlement, by the very reason of its existence, influences, in varying degree, its surroundings through the spread of its network of functional relations and the expansion of its settlement area. This regional factor varies greatly. In some cities, like historical regional capitals, market towns, and country capitals, it is highly significant; while in others, especially in specialized urban communities such as industrial settlements and health resorts that owe nothing directly to servicing the countryside, the regional component is at a minimum.

While this is a general urban phenome-

[9] H. Louis, *Die geographische Gliederung von Gross-Berlin* (Stuttgart: Engelhorn, 1936), 26 pp. with two maps.

[10] J. K. Wright, "The Diversity of New York City," *Geographical Review,* XXVI (1936), 620–39.

[11] M. Aurousseau, "Recent Contributions to Urban Geography," *Geographical Review,* XIV (1924), 444–55.

[12] J. L. Sert, *Can Our Cities Survive?* (Cambridge, Mass.: Harvard University Press, 1943).

non, it is particularly true in the United States, where entirely new settlements have grown in recent years around one or more large industrial plants. Endicott in New York and Hershey in Pennsylvania are examples. The urban structures tend to be separate from each other, and urban cohesion develops through the establishment of public utility services (gas, electricity, water, drainage, sewage disposal), and transportation services which are not general in supply or coincident in distribution. The urban settlement has exploded, functions existing separately in separate places, so that new problems arise in providing those common services and institutions that are needed for an efficient and happy community life.

Two problems arise in this connection: first, the assessment of the ways in which the urban settlement acts as a regional focus and how these activities are reflected in its functional structures and its build; and, second, the geographical range and potency of the activities of the urban settlement with its environs. These functional relations are concerned with the housing of workers outside the political limits; with the factories planted on its outskirts; with the inward movement of food supplies (especially perishable foods like milk and vegetables), raw materials and manufactured goods for collection, consumption, and redistribution; with the outward movement of goods, both consumers' goods and producers' goods, and of services—commercial, educational (schools, newspapers, cultural organization), and administrative; and with the range of supply of public utility supplies, which frequently extends beyond the urban area.

The geographer is not so much concerned with the precise analysis of particular service areas, for this is ultimately a problem of marketing for which the economist is more qualified. He is more concerned with the ways in which these relationships are reflected in the functional and physical structure of the town. From this point of view, certain facts are outstanding as fix-

ing the limits of the urban complex. Chief of these is the limit of the urban built-up area. Such an area, when embracing several contiguous administrative districts, was called by Patrick Geddes a "conurbation," and the idea has been elaborated by C. B. Fawcett.[13] This term, however, is inadequate for the geographer, since by definition it is not generally applicable to all large urban settlements; moreover, it implies no minimum limit in area or population. There is no a priori justification for taking 100,000 inhabitants as the minimum limit, and there are many urban areas that lie well inside one political unit. Since the geographer is concerned primarily with the urban settlement as an expression of man's activities on the earth's surface, an alternative term is needed to embrace the whole built-up area, and we suggest the term "urban tract," to equate with Unstead's definition of a tract in a proposed system of regional units.[14] The tract is characterized by the marked differentiation of structures from one area to another just as Unstead's tract, defined in more general terms, contained a number of primary landscape units that he called "stows." Beyond this compact urban tract there is a zone with intimate social and economic relationships with it. It is the area of regular deliveries of consumers' goods and of daily movements of people to the center for business and shopping and to the industrial districts and elsewhere for their daily work. G. Chabot calls it, in reference to Dijon, the *zone du voisinage*.[15] We may refer to it as

[13] P. Geddes, *Cities in Evolution* (London, 1915); and C. B. Fawcett, "British Conurbations in 1921," *Sociological Review*, XIV (1922), 111–22; and "The Distribution of the Urban Population in Great Britain in 1931," *Geographical Journal*, LXXIX (1932), 100–16.

[14] J. F. Unstead, "A System of Regional Geography," *Geography*, XVIII (1933), 175–87.

[15] G. Chabot, "La détermination des courbes isochrones en géographie urbaine," *Comptes rendus du Congrès Internationale de Géographie, 1938*, tome 2: *Géographie humaine*, pp. 110–13. See also H. Hassinger, "Beiträge zur Siedlungs- und Verkehrs-geographie," *Mitt. der K. K. Geog. Ges. in*

the *urban settlement area*. It is marked by a steadily rising population, as opposed to a slow increase or decrease in the urban area and a decrease in the rural areas on its fringes, and by its relatively high density of population in contrast to the rural areas encircling it. A large proportion of its residents are also engaged in daily work in the urban area and in factories in its vicinity.[16] Accessibility is the primary determinant of these areal relations and geographers have paid much attention to the preparation of isochronous maps showing zones of equal time-accessibility to selected points in the city center. Beyond this urban settlement area there is a wider area which is mainly oriented toward its local towns but has occasional contacts with the distant city, which functions as the regional center. This may be called the *city-region*. Many geographical studies on all these aspects of the city have appeared in the interwar period.[17]

COMPARATIVE STUDIES: FUNCTIONAL

The comparative study of the location, spacing, and size of towns as commercial centers was attempted by a German, J. G. Kohl, a hundred years ago.[18] While the works of F. Ratzel and F. von Richthofen, through their refinement of the conception of geography, gave some stimulus to the

---

*Wien*, Band 53 (1910), pp. 5–94, with two maps on a scale of 1:200,000. The latter was a pioneer study.

[16] R. Clozier, *La Gare du Nord* (Paris, 1941), is a thorough study of the *banlieue* of Paris with special reference to the northern districts served by the Gare du Nord.

[17] Robert E. Dickinson, *City, Region and Regionalism* (London: Kegan Paul; and New York: Oxford University Press, 1947). Paris has been studied with particular thoroughness from the point of view of its food supplies. See, for example, R. Dubuc, "L'Apportionnement de Paris en lait," *Annales de géographie*, XLVII (1938), 257–66; P. Gallet, "L'Approvisionnement de Paris en vin," *Annales de géographie*, XLVIII (1939), 359–68; R. Clozier, *op. cit.*

[18] J. G. Kohl, *Der Verkehr und die Ansiedlungen der Menschen in ihrer Abhängigkeit von der Gestaltung der Erdoberfläche* (Leipzig, 1841).

further study of cities, K. Hassert, A. Hettner, and O. Schlüter around 1900 put the subject on a firm footing with regard to its main aims and methods. Hettner (1895 and 1902) stressed the need for functional classification of towns and for mapping the distribution of towns at different epochs according to their functional character. He also emphasized the varying effect of location (*Lage*) and cultural and economic conditions on the character of cities from epoch to epoch and from country to country.[19]

Many attempts have been made by geographers to classify towns according to their functions. One of the most stimulating essays of this type by M. Aurousseau[20] divided towns into six groups classed according to their dominant functions: administration (capital cities and revenue towns), defense (fortress, garrison, and naval towns), culture (university, cathedral, art and pilgrimage centers), production (manufacturing towns and craft centers), communications (classed according to the main function as collection, transfer, and distribution centers), and recreation (health, tourist, and holiday resorts). The communication group was further divided as follows: collection centers—mining, fishing, forest, and depot towns; transfer centers—market, fall-line, break-of-bulk, bridgehead, tidal-limit, navigation-head towns; distribution centers—export, import, and supply towns. But in all urban settlements there is a mixture of two or more primary functions and it is impossible to assess the importance of each consistently on the basis of statistics of occupation, for the selection is based partly on a subjective appraisal of the tone or character of the place. Nevertheless, this method gives a basis for classifying and mapping

[19] A. Hettner, "Die Lage der menschlichen Ansiedlungen," *Geographische Zeitschrift*, I (1895), 361–75, and "Die wirtschaftlichen Typen der Ansiedlungen," *ibid.*, VIII (1902), 92–100.

[20] M. Aurousseau, "The Distribution of Population: A Constructive Problem," *Geographical Review*, II (1921), 563–92.

urban settlements over wide areas, and a first attempt on these lines has been made recently for the United States, in which all the towns with over 10,000 inhabitants are classed on a statistical basis as manufacturing, retail, diversified, wholesale, transport, mining, university, and resort towns.[21]

This method of classification is based upon an estimate of the primary functions of the town. The town, however, owes much of its essential character to the needs of its service area and the functions it performs for it. Thus, attention has been given recently to the assessment of the centralized or regional functions of the town, and the local services which cater primarily to its inhabitants. This idea has been elaborated by W. Christaller, a German scholar,[22] with regard to the distribution, size, and functions of the towns of south Germany, and there are similar studies by other German scholars. A correction to Christaller's rather one-sided conclusions is offered by H. Bobek,[23] who rightly points out that there are big variations in the importance of the centralized functions between town and town, and from one region to another. Further work on this aspect of the functional structure of towns will assist in the planning of new urban communities. Examples are A. E. Smailes's recent studies of towns in England and Wales.[24]

The port is a special class of urban com-

munity, and we wish here to emphasize the close relations that exist between its functions and structure and the territory which it serves and which is vaguely referred to as its hinterland. In an excellent study on hinterlands A. J. Sargent[25] refutes the idea that a hinterland can be bounded by lines. He rightly asserts that it is an economic rather than a geographical concept and that each of the specialized services of the port serves places that may in no sense correspond with each other, just as the places of supply and distribution of the commodities of the manufacturing center are not necessarily coincident in their geographic distribution. Indeed, we would maintain that this wide field of study is geographical economics rather than economic geography and lies within the particular competence of the economist. But it is not fair to assume that the specialized geographer is guilty of such naïve assumptions, for Sargent fails to draw attention to the admirable study of the late Alfred Rühl,[26] a German geographer of repute, on precisely this question with special reference to the German ports, and to L. Mecking's studies of the Japanese ports,[27] as well as to J. H. Schulze's interesting classification of English ports in terms of their predominant functions.[28]

## COMPARATIVE STUDIES: MORPHOLOGICAL

The final aspect of comparative urban geography is one that has received virtually no serious attention from English-speaking geographers. This may be described as

[21] C. D. Harris, "Functional Classification of Cities in the United States," *Geographical Review*, XXXIII (1943), 86–99 [see below, pp. 129–38].

[22] W. Christaller, *Die zentralen Orte Süddeutschlands* (Jena, 1932).

[23] H. Bobek, "Über einige funktionellen Stadttypen und ihre Beziehungen zum Lande," *Comptes rendus du Congrès International de Géographie, 1938*, tome 2: *Géographie humaine*, pp. 88–102.

[24] A. E. Smailes, "The Urban Hierarchy in England and Wales," *Geography*, XXIX (1944), 41–51, "Urban Fields and Their Delimitation," *ibid.*, XXXIII (1948), and "The Urban Mesh in England and Wales," *Transactions of the Institute of British Geographers* (1947); Robert E. Dickinson, "The Commercial Functions of the Nuclei of the English Conurbations," *Sociological Review*, XXI (1929), 38–49.

[25] A. J. Sargent, *Seaports and Hinterlands* (London, 1938).

[26] A. Rühl, *Die Nord und Ostseehäfen im deutschen Aussenhandel*, Berlin ("Veröff. d. Instituts f. Meereskunde," Neue Folge, Heft 3) (Berlin, 1920), 15 maps.

[27] L. Mecking, "Die Seehäfen in der geographischen Forschungen," in *Hermann Wagner Gedächtnisschrift* (Gotha, 1930); and "Die Grosslage der Seehäfen insbesondere das Hinterland," *Geographische Zeitschrift*, Vol. XXXVII (1931).

[28] J. H. Schulze, "Die Häfen als Glieder der Kulturlandschaft," in *Festschrift für Prof. G. W. Zahn* (1931); and *Die Häfen Englands* (Leipzig, 1930).

urban morphology, that is, the study of the layout and build of towns viewed as the expression of their origin, growth, and function. Much work of inferior quality has appeared in this field, because the approach has been empirical rather than genetic, and it is the latter only which permits the recognition of the significant. The study is the precise parallel of the study of rural settlements that has figured so prominently in French and German geographical researches in the last twenty years.

The investigation of the plan and build of towns began to be systematically undertaken about fifty years ago. The relevant aspects of study in an individual town embrace the layout of its streets and blocks considered in relation to public buildings, terrain, and natural (uncontrolled) and planned growth. The precise site and layout of the initial settlement and the mode of its extension from this nucleus are analyzed in close conjunction with historical development. Indeed, historians have found evidence for the mode of growth of a town in its plan which is often far more informative than an ancient document. The buildings are mapped and interpreted from the standpoint of their age, architectural style, and function. It is significant that in Germany most of the work on styles and materials has been done by other specialists, whereas studies of forms or structures have been the particular concern of the geographer.

Comparative study of German towns reveals historic and modern house types. The principal historic types are the gable house (*Gabelhaus*), with gable fronting the street, of several stories, and with narrow street frontage, and the eves house (*Traufenhaus*), with its gable parallel to the street frontage. The origin of these two distinctive house types that still affect the whole aspect of the old towns of Germany is still somewhat obscure. It seems, however, fairly conclusive that they developed during the Middle Ages out of the traditional farmsteads of north, central, and upper Germany in order to meet the needs

of the new urban economy and building requirements. The gable house was the rule in northern Germany and the eaves house in the south. The classic instances of the former are found in the Hanseatic coastal towns. The eaves house was not a postmedieval growth, as has been often asserted, for it was adopted in the initial founding of Freiburg-im-Breisgau in the twelfth century and was in the many other towns in the south German lands that were founded after it, such as Bern and Freiburg in Switzerland. With the appearance of Italian Renaissance influences in the sixteenth century and with the need for increased economy of space and protection from fire, the eaves house was adopted generally, and the house with its gable fronting on the street was actually forbidden in the bylaws of most of the large cities. Among the modern types, the house with a more rectangular ground plan and a mansard roof is characteristic of the Baroque era in the seventeenth and eighteenth centuries. Other types are the *Langhaus*, a long eaves house with saddle roof and small depth, the *Firsthaus*, with two stories, and, like the *Langhaus* except for its greater depth, the lodging house (*Miethaus*), small and rectangular with an adaptation of the mansard roof in the south and west of Germany, a large barrack-like tenement (*Kastenhaus*) in the north and east of Germany, and the better standard apartment house with variously ornamented façades (*Etagenhaus*).[29]

There are many studies of building structures in particular towns. Geisler's early studies of Danzig may be quoted. Houses were mapped in 1918 on a scale of 1:10,000 in three categories, one or two stories, three stories, and four or more stories, and separate colors were used to show transport and administrative buildings, churches, schools, and military buildings, main shopping thoroughfares, warehouses, and factories. In a second study in

[29] W. Geisler, "Die Deutsche Stadt," *Forschungen zu deutschen Lande und Volkskunde* (Stuttgart), 1924.

1922 Geisler mapped four house types, the *Giebelhaus,* with a high gable facing the street frontage (fifteenth to seventeenth centuries), the *Langhaus,* with a high roof (eighteenth to nineteenth centuries), and the *Kastenhaus* and *Etagenhaus* of the late nineteenth century.[30] A similar classification of houses based on roof types will be found in a more recent study of Breslau.[31] H. Hassinger many years ago carried out a survey of the buildings of Vienna in which he recognized seven architectural periods begining with the twelfth century.[32] A particularly interesting French study of houses in the city of Rouen has been undertaken more recently by a specialist in geography and architecture and should stimulate kindred study in other towns.[33] A section on house types appears in most French town studies. Attention is also drawn to studies by American geographers who have taken an increasing interest in recent years in the morphology of settlement, both in the United States and elsewhere. We note, in particular, J. B. Leighley's initial study of the morphology of a group of Swedish towns and his more recent study of the medieval towns of Livonia, that is, of Estonia and Latvia.[34]

Fifty years ago, Otto Schlüter advocated the need for comparative morphological study of towns.[35] He drew attention, for example, to the contrasts between the towns of western Germany that were often the result of gradual, uncontrolled growth and the towns of eastern Germany that were frequently planned entities with rectilinear forms. Such investigation was stimulated directly by the researches of Meitzen into village origins. In this connection mention should be made of the many detailed comparative studies of towns that have been undertaken by German historians and architects for such large areas as Brandenburg,[36] northern Germany,[37] Bohemia,[38] southern Germany,[39] and the state of Brunswick.[40] From such studies, as well as from their independent investigations, German geographers have made a substantial contribution to the understanding of urban morphology. W. Geisler, in a work previously noted, attempted to classify German towns according to site, plan, and build.[41] A more thorough and convincing interpretation on these lines, based on preliminary studies of the towns of Westphalia, is R. Martiny's essay on the morphology of

[34] J. B. Leighley, *The Towns of Mälardalen in Sweden: A Study in Urban Morphology* ("University of California Publications in Geography," Vol. III, No. 1 [1928]), pp. 1–134; and *The Towns of Medieval Livonia* ("University of California Publications in Geography," Vol. VI, No. 7 [1939]), pp. 235–314.

[35] O. Schlüter, "Über den Grundriss der Städte," *Zeitschrift der Ges. f. Erdkunde zu Berlin,* XXXIV (1899), 446–62, "Bemerkungen zur Siedlungskunde," *Geographische Zeitschrift,* V (1899), 65–84.

[36] E. J. Siedler, *Märkischer Städtebau im Mittelalter* (Berlin, 1914), with numerous plans.

[37] Fr. Meurer, *Die mittelalterliche Stadtgrundriss im nördlichen Deutschland in seiner Entwicklung zur Regelmässigkeit* (1914).

[38] A. Honig, *Deutscher Städtebau in Böhmen* (Prague, 1921).

[39] Chr. Klaiber, *Die Grundrissgestaltung der deutschen Stadt im Mittelalter unter besonderer Berücksichtigung der Schwäbischen Lande* (Berlin, 1921).

[40] P. J. Meier, *Niedersächsiecher Städteatlas: Die Braunschweigischer Städte,* Abteilung I (1926) and II (1933), "Veröff. d. Hist. Kom. f. Niedersachsen."

[41] See n. 29.

[30] W. Geisler, *Danzig: Ein Seidlungsgeographischer Versuch* (Inaugural Dissertation, Halle-Wittenberg, 1918); and *Die Weichsellandschaft von Thorn bis Danzig* (Hamburg, 1922); with colored map, scale 1:10,000.

[31] E. Müller, *Die Altstadt von Breslau: City Bildung und Physiognomie,* "Veröff, der Schlesischen Ges. für Erdkunde" (Breslau, 1931).

[32] H. Hassinger, *Kunsthistorischer Atlas von Wien, Oster, Kunsttopographie,* Band 15 (Vienna, 1916); with 19 colored plans; "Kartographische Aufnahme des Wiener Stadtbildes," *Mitt, der K. K. Ges. Wien,* Band 58 (1915), *Kunsthistorischer Plan des I Bezirks der Stadt Wien,* scale 1:10,000 (Vienna, 1912); and *Kunsthistorischer Übersichtsplan von Wien,* scale 1:25,000 (Vienna, 1915).

[33] R. Quenedey, "L'habitation urbaine et son évolution," *Annales d'histoire économique et sociale,* Vol. VI, Nos. 25–26 (1934).

German settlements.[42] He groups all settlements, both rural and urban, into *natural forms*, the result of gradual growth without preconceived planning, and *planned forms*. The natural forms include irregular plans that have emerged by unplanned growth from village origins (*Haufendörfer*) that are characterized by complexity of plan (the type is rare in western and central Europe); the radial and wheel or radial-concentric plans that are usually the result of gradual growth from a nuclear market settlement; and axial plans that grow from a central axis, the main thoroughfare, to form rib, parallel-street, and grid plans. The planned forms fall into five groups—the street market with or without a rib plan; the right-angled street-crossing with the main streets directed to four gates in the town walls—a type that is frequent in southern Germany; the parallel-street plan with long main streets and long blocks separated by very narrow transverse streets; meridianal or spindle plans, a development from the last type in which the streets converge at two gate exits; and, lastly, the grid plan, with a right-angled net of streets of equal width with equal-sized blocks, and a central block in the center reserved for the market place (*Kolonialstadt*). The present writer has examined this whole field of literature in a recent essay.[43]

It is, of course, a short jump from such study of towns to comparative studies in architecture and art, since these are the visible expression of distinctive cultures. This is again a borderline study to which German and French scholars have given some attention. Mention may be made of the detailed study of the history of urbanism by P. Lavedan,[44] now director of the Institute of Urbanism in the University of

Paris, and to the comparative studies of Glück, Gerstenberg, and Pieper.[45]

The foregoing comments and references are primarily concerned with the town in western and central Europe. There are, however, fundamental differences in the character of urban, as of rural, settlements in the neighboring culture areas of Europe, as also in the different culture areas and environments of the world, that still await detailed investigation on similar lines. There are some valuable and stimulating studies, both individual and comparative, of this kind. Mention may be made of Wilhelmy's detailed work on Sofia, interesting for both its method and matter, Whittlesey's study of Kano as a Sudanese capital, H. de Martonne's essay on Buenos Aires, and Clerget's study of Cairo.[46] Among the comparative studies, the importance of which we wish to emphasize for future work, there are brief but suggestive studies

---

[42] R. Martiny, "Grundrissgestaltung der deutschen Siedlungen," *Petermanns Mitteilungen, Ergänzungschaft,* Nr. 197, 1928.

[43] Robert E. Dickinson, "The Morphology of the Medieval German Town," *Geographical Review,* XXXV (1945), 74–97.

[44] P. Lavedan, *Histoire de l'urbanisme: Antiquité et moyen âge* (Paris, 1926), 352 plans and 32 photographs; also by the same author *Qu'est-ce que l'urbanisme? Introduction à l'histoire de l'urbanisme* (1926) and *Géographie des villes* (1936).

[45] H. Glück-Wien, "Das kunstgeographische Bild Europas am Ende des Mittelalters und die Grundlagen der Renaissance," *Monatshefte für Kunstwissenschaft,* ed. G. Biermann (1921), Band 2, pp. 161–73; K. Gerstenberg, *Ideen zu einer Kunstgeographie Europas* ("Bibliothek der Kunstgeschichte," Band 48/9 [1922]); P. Pieper, *Kunstgeographie: Versuch einer Grundlegung* ("Neue Deutsche Forschungen," Abt. Kunstwissenschaft und Kunstgeschichte" [1936]).

[46] Wilhemy, *Hochbulgarien,* Vol. II: Sofia (n. 6 above); H. de Martonne, "Buenos Aires," *Annales de géographie,* XLIV (1935), 281–304; D. Whittlesey, "Kano: A Sudanese Capital," *Geographical Review,* XXVII (1937), 177–99; M. Clerget, *Le Caire: Étude de géographie urbaine et d'histoire économique* (2 vols.; Paris, 1934). See also as examples of recent studies O. H. K. Spate, "Rangoon: A Study in Urban Geography," *Geographical Review,* XXXII (1942), 56–73; C. M. Zierer, "Melbourne. A Functional Center," *Annals of the Association of American Geographers,* XXXI (1941), 251–88; and A. Wagner, *Werden, Leben und Gestalt der Zweimillionenstadt in Südkalifornien* ("Schriften d. Geog. Instituts d. Univ. Kiel," Band 3 [1935]).

by Andrews on the growth and pattern of settlements in the Riverina as characteristic of trends in the newly settled grasslands and, more recently, by Deffontaines on the network of towns in Brazil.[47] We have already suggested that in thinly populated regions, where there is not a continuous spread of human settlement and where civilization is backward, urban character is rudimentary and bears a close similarity to the conditions of western Europe in the Dark Ages; urban studies in such areas are of particular value on the question of urban beginnings in western Europe. In this connection we would note, for example, the studies of W. Fogg on the tribal markets and towns of Morocco and Gourou's study of the Tonkin Delta.[48] Morphological studies are fewer, but mention may be made of the essays edited by S. Passarge on cities in various regions (notably Spain, Japan, and China), and of the studies of the Moslem city, of the cities of Japan, and of the Netherlands East Indies.[49] Broader suggestive works are those of Mukerjee on the settlements of northern India and Gutkind's recent essays on the city in Russia and China, both of which

should stimulate further specific inquiry by geographers.[50]

CONCLUSION

With the ever growing interest in the problems of the modern city—in the problems of its physical growth and reconstruction, in its sociological and economic structure, and in its art and architecture, as well as in its historical development—it is not surprising that there is a great deal of overlap between the approach from slightly different angles of different specialists in the same field. This is as it should and must be. It will be obvious, however, that the trained historian is best fitted to deal with the documentary evidence relevant to the formation of cities and that the art historian can best deal with individual and comparative studies of urban architecture. The geographer has introduced new fields of study in the structure of cities, and it is likely that these will be taken up by other specialists. Indeed, for many years various specialists have shown an interest from their own points of view in the same phenomena.

This consideration is of very great importance in relation to a considerable field of social study which has been taken up in recent years especially in the United States. Since the last war a school of "human ecology" has developed with its seat in the Department of Sociology in the University of Chicago, under the leadership of R. E. Park, E. W. Burgess, and R. D. McKenzie. This school is distinct from that of the geographers in the same university, whose former chairman, Harlan Barrows, defined geography as human ecology in 1923. These sociologists claim that human ecology is the scientific study of the "spatial and temporal relations of human beings as affected by the selective, distributive, and accommodative forces of the environment," and one of its chief concerns is "the effect of position, in time and space, upon human

---

[47] J. Andrews, "The Settlement Net and the Regional Factor," *Australian Geographer,* II (1933–35), 33–48; P. Deffontaines, "The Origin and Growth of the Brazilian Network of Towns," *Geographical Review,* XXVIII (1938), 377–99.

[48] W. Fogg, "Villages, Tribal Markets and Towns: Some Considerations of Urban Development in the Spanish and International Zones of Morocco," *Sociological Review,* Vol. XXXII, Nos. 1 and 2 (1940), and "The Suq: A Study in the Human Geography of Morocco," *Scottish Geographical Magazine,* Vol. LI, No. 3 (1935); P. Gourou, *Les paysans du Delta Tonkinois: Étude de géographie humaine* (Paris: École Publique Française d'Extrême-Orient, 1936).

[49] S. Passarge (ed.), *Stadtlandschaften der Erde* (1930); Busch-Zantner, "Zur Kenntniss der Osmannischen Stadt," *Geographische Zeitschrift,* Vol. XXXVIII (1932); G. T. Trewartha, "Japanese Cities: Distribution and Morphology," *Geographical Review,* XXIV (1934), 404–17; H. Lehmann, "Das Antlitz der Stadt in Niederländisch-Indien," in *Festschrift Norbert Krebs, Landerkundliche Forschung* (1937).

[50] R. Mukerjee, *Man and His Habitation: A Study in Social Ecology* (1940); E. A. Gutkind, *Revolution in Environment* (1946).

institutions and human behavior."[51] This definition is vague, but a formidable research literature indicates its scope and the very valuable results it has achieved in the interwar period. It is the equivalent of what the French sociologist calls "la morphologie sociale."[52] This field has two aspects, the spatial or geographical aspect, and the biological or demographic aspect. The former, in particular, is common ground to geography, sociology, economics, and anthropology.

The social ecologist is concerned with Man in Society. He thinks in terms of social phenomena and social interactions in their distribution in time and space. Such interactions, by a process of competition and selection, are expressed in the physical and social mobility of persons, that is, in "change of residence, change of employment, or change of location of any utility or service."[53] The processes accounting for these distributions in urban growth are referred to by R. D. McKenzie as concentration, centralization, decentralization, segregation, invasion, and succession. Immigrants tend to segregate in areas populated by persons with a similar background of culture and economic status—birds of a feather flock together. In consequence, the city tends to become a sort of mosaic of "cultural and racial islands." Such islands are called by the social ecologists "natural areas," since they grow up by natural (uncontrolled) processes, and each area tends to select certain population types, this selection being based on economic status, racial characteristics, religious beliefs, moral codes, and the like. Thus, to the social ecologist "the natural area as a form

of ecological patterning is primarily a social rather than a geographic phenomenon." In the American city at present, language and customs are especially potent in the formation of natural areas, but, as the immigrant is absorbed and his own language and customs disappear, "social differentiation will manifest itself in other ways—through differences in religion, occupation, education, and income."[54]

The geographer, as distinct from the social ecologist, is concerned with the differentiation of the whole of the urban settlement into its functional areas and social groupings as expressed in the structure and uses and grouping of its building structures. He does not limit his study to the measure of relationships of the settlement to its site and situation. His primary emphasis is on the settlement as a habitat. He is concerned with geographical distributions in the settlement insofar as they represent areal differences in function that are significant for other kinds of phenomena in the same area and for the same population group. The geographer has no established terminology for these component functional units. It is unfortunate that Blanchard refers to them as "natural" regions, but he is using the word, in effect, to define, though with different emphasis, exactly the same thing as the "natural area" of the sociologist and the planner and the economist, that is, as a unit in the urban complex that has emerged through the operation of processes of growth and differentiation.

Many sociological studies of the "natural areas" of American cities have appeared, but what is of most interest to the sociologist is the distribution of social maladjustment in disorganized areas—delinquency (adult and juvenile), vice, suicide, mental disorders, alcoholism, divorce and desertion, poverty, mortality, and disease. The areal interrelationships of such phenomena also have been studied and indexes of social disorganization worked out. In H.

51 R. D. McKenzie, "The Ecological Approach to the Study of the Urban Community," in *The City*, by R. E. Park, E. W. Burgess, and R. D. McKenzie (Chicago, 1925). See also the comprehensive textbook by N. P. Gist and L. A. Halbert, *Urban Society* (New York, 1941), esp. chaps. 6 and 7.

52 M. Halbwachs, *Morphologie sociale* (Paris: Armand Colin, 1938).

53 R. D. McKenzie, "The Scope of Human Ecology," in *The Urban Community*, ed. E. W. Burgess (Chicago, 1926).

54 Quotations from Gist and Halbert, *op. cit.*, chaps. 6 and 7, *passim*.

W. Green's study of Cleveland, Ohio, for example, a map of cultural areas was prepared, based on monthly rental figures as indications of the economic status of the residents, and correlations of social phenomena were made with districts in low- and high-income categories.[55] The sociologists are also more concerned with, and better equipped for, the investigation of social groups in the city, such as "neighborhoods" and the larger "community areas," and here too the principal contributions have come during the interwar period from the United States.

This whole field of study, geographical and ecological, has now become of great importance in western Europe in view of the urgent need for reconstruction. The elaborate social and economic surveys in Britain have neglected this side of study, with a few exceptions, such as the surveys of Merseyside, Southhampton, Sheffield, and the recent County of London Plan. Civic and regional surveys as preliminaries to town and intertown planning have been dominated by the idea of the interrelations of place, work, and folk, which embraces all relevant sciences on a footing of equality in a broad philosophical concept. But this approach fails to canalize and direct research to special problems of social structure in their geographical (or areal) as-

[55] H. W. Green, "Cultural Areas in the City of Cleveland," *American Journal of Sociology*, XXXVIII (1932), 356–67. See also Gist and Halbert, *op. cit.*, chap. 9, "Disorganized Areas."

pects, which is essential for the sound, long-term, physical planning. Significant advances in concept and techniques have been made, however, during the past six years in Britain. We may mention the work sponsored by the Association for Planning and Regional Reconstruction, by the West Midland Group on Post-War Reconstruction and Planning, and by the Nuffield Reconstruction Survey at Oxford. In more direct connection with town planning there are the surveys of Hull and Middlesbrough organized by Max Loch, those of Durham and Exeter organized by Thomas Sharp, and the detailed study of Worcester, undertaken by a group of researchers in the University of Birmingham. There is need, however, for more research workers with adequate training, for the development of techniques of recording, classifying, and mapping data, and for the standardization of terminology. There is no clear-cut line of division between one discipline and another, and the emergence of disciplines in the common pursuit of particular problems is a characteristic of the development of scientific research in our time. In the field of the study of man, there is a real need for institutes of research to investigate all aspects of the problem, for without fundamental researches the planner cannot provide for the optimum use of the land, and the architect cannot build to suit the needs of man, both as an individual and as a member of the community.

## SOME BASIC DEFINITIONS

Although the terms "city" and "urban" are generally understood, the more precise definition of these terms and the delimitation of what constitutes a city are important prerequisites to understanding the concepts of urban geography. The difference between "urban" and "rural" is clear. In former times, and still in many parts of the world, the delimitation of the city and its differentiation from the countryside were fairly simple. Cities had walls or were otherwise sharply bounded. Urban life was different in many respects from rural life; cities were centers from which cultural innovations—ideas, inventions, and organizational control by state and church—spread to the countryside. Nowadays, it is not so easy to define the city. Urban living is not very different from rural living, and with the almost universal availability of radio and television, newspapers and automobiles, the two—city and country—have become a continuum rather than a dichotomy. There are all degrees of urbanization intermediate between the city and the country. The city has broken through its former walls, real or figurative, and has spread itself throughout the countryside. Tentacles of urbanization, in many areas, have reached toward one another, and numerous cities have converged into larger masses: conurbations or megalopolitan concentrations. In recent decades we have become very much aware of the disappearance of the formerly clear-cut distinctions between city and country. Much of the population growth in the United States and in other advanced countries has been on the fringes of cities but beyond the municipal boundaries of the central cities. Metropolitan areas are now the basic urban units in a real geographic sense.

The nations of the world have reached no agreement as to the minimum population which a place must have in order to be considered urban, for statistical and other purposes, or as to the minimum population which an urban agglomeration must have in order to be considered metropolitan. It is therefore not possible to make direct statistical comparisons internationally of the proportion of the population which is urban or metropolitan, or of the numbers and distributions of urban places and metropolitan areas in the respective nations. In the United States, for most purposes, an urban place must have a population of at least 2,500; in Canada, 1,000. In some countries, such as Japan, there are recognized intermediate types of population clusters which are neither urban nor rural. At the other end of the scale of urban size, the conurbation, consisting of one or more central cities with their contiguous urbanized areas, is recognized in England as applying to Greater London and five other areas, each centering upon one or more major cities. This concept is not unlike that of the "Megalopolis" of Jean Gottmann, described in one of the articles in this section.

Not only is there no agreement on the minimum population which a place should have in order to be called "urban"; a fundamental difficulty is that there is no sharp boundary, in most instances, between urban and rural areas. In some countries specific criteria have been used to delimit urban areas; in others the delimitation is quite subjective.

The four articles reproduced in this section indicate clearly the nature of the difficulties found in trying to delimit urban areas. The first is an official publication of the United States Bureau of the Census setting forth the basic definitions adopted, on the one hand, for delimiting urban areas which extend beyond the boundaries of central cities of over a given population (50,000) and, on the other hand, for delimiting the subareas within cities set up for purposes of compiling and publishing statistics which give information necessary to picture the internal patterns of population and development within cities.

The second article, written by a geographer in the Census Bureau, amplifies the definition of the standard metropolitan area and discusses some of the criteria used in bounding such areas. It presents a vivid picture of some of the difficulties that arise when a standard set of criteria, necessary for interarea comparisons, is applied as uniformly as possible to a large number of areas differing from one another in many respects. The third article, written by another geographer who at the time was employed by the Census Bureau, discusses similarly the concept of the urbanized area, which is also used for interarea comparisons of urban concentrations. The standard metropolitan area and the urbanized area serve different purposes. The former has relatively fixed boundaries; the latter's boundaries, by definition, shift as changes in population density occur on the urban periphery. The former is based upon functional interrelations among the parts of an area; the latter is based mainly upon a single criterion: population density.

The fourth article, by a well-known French geographer temporarily resident in the United States, is concerned with a new concept: a supercity formed by the merging of the fringes of many adjacent metropolitan areas. Thus this section presents the problems and results of several attempts to define the sizes and limits of cities in the geographic sense on several different scales.

# CENSUS AREAS OF 1950

This report describes census geographical areas, other than political, for which population and housing statistics are being compiled from the 1950 Census. For the political subdivisions, the basic tabulations and state minor civil division maps are being made available, as in the past. It is the further purpose of this publication to inform the users of census data of the geographical materials, such as maps and boundary descriptions, that are or will be available.

Census areas stressed in this report are standard metropolitan areas, urbanized areas, and state economic areas, which are major geographical units newly established for statistical purposes and included for the first time in the publication plans for a decennial census. Other areas discussed are census tracts, unincorporated places, census enumeration districts, city blocks, and census county divisions in the state of Washington.

The several kinds of census areas are designed to provide users of statistical data with census information in logical arrangement and convenient form, meeting the requirement of adaptability to problems and studies of private and public management. Accordingly, they are basic tools for applying statistical information which must be related to specific areas such as large cities and their suburbs, clusters of contiguous counties with common economic characteristics, and other selected groupings.

## Standard Metropolitan Areas

Standard metropolitan areas have been defined for 168 metropolitan centers in the

Reprinted from *Geographic Reports* ("Series GEO," No. 1, August, 1951), pp. 1–3. (Washington, D.C.: Bureau of the Census, U.S. Department of Commerce.)

United States and 4 in Puerto Rico and Hawaii by a federal interagency committee under the direction of the Bureau of the Budget. These areas are designated as *standard* because the federal statistical agencies represented on the committee have agreed to use these areas insofar as it is feasible.

Each of the new standard metropolitan areas, except in New England, consists of one or more entire counties. While it is recognized that metropolitan areas could be defined more accurately by using minor civil divisions, which were the building blocks of the old metropolitan districts, experience has shown that areas so defined have a limited value because many types of data with which comparisons are desired are available only on a county basis. In New England, where towns rather than counties are commonly the basic geographic units for statistical compilations, the objection applies to a much lesser degree, and mainly for this reason the New England metropolitan areas are defined on a town rather than a county basis.

Each standard metropolitan area includes a city with 50,000 inhabitants or more in 1950 and may include more than one city of such size. Conversely, each city of such size is included in a standard metropolitan area. The county in which the city of 50,000 or more is located is by definition in the standard metropolitan area. Contiguous counties may be included in the area if they meet certain criteria. The general concept adopted is one of an integrated economic unit with a large volume of daily travel and communication between the central city or cities and the outlying parts of the area. This normally results in an area considerably more restricted, especially for the larger cities, than the market or trading area. The details of the criteria are explained in a preliminary 1950 Census release, "Series PC-3, No. 3, Population of Standard Metropolitan Areas." That release presents a complete list of the areas, giving the constituent parts of each one with preliminary population figures for 1950.

The Federal Committee on Standard Metropolitan Areas was set up in the Bureau of the Budget late in 1947 with representatives from the following agencies: the Bureau of the Census, the Bureau of Foreign and Domestic Commerce, the Bureau of Labor Statistics, the Federal Security Agency, the Bureau of Employment Security, the Housing and Home Finance Agency, the Federal Housing Administration, the Federal Reserve Board, and the Bureau of Agricultural Economics. Tentative definitions were discussed with interested local organizations by the Bureau of the Budget or its designated representatives before final approval by the committee.

Areas known as metropolitan districts were used in the 1940 and earlier censuses. They were defined in 1940 for every city of 50,000 or more, two or more such cities sometimes being in one district. In general, metropolitan districts included, in addition to the central city or cities, all adjacent and contiguous minor civil divisions with a population density of 150 or more per square mile. With the 1950 Census, the new concepts of standard metropolitan areas and urbanized areas are replacing the metropolitan districts.

## URBANIZED AREAS

An urbanized area, as defined for the 1950 Census, is an area that includes at least one city with 50,000 inhabitants or more plus the surrounding closely settled urban fringe. Urbanized areas have been established for those cities having 50,000 inhabitants or more in 1940 or at a subsequent special census taken prior to 1950. The following types of areas are included in an urbanized area if they are contiguous to the central city or cities or if they are contiguous to an area already included in the urbanized area:

1. Incorporated places with 2,500 inhabitants or more in 1940 or at a subsequent special census taken prior to 1950
2. Incorporated places of fewer than 2,500 inhabitants each of which includes an area with a concentration of at least 100 dwelling units with a density of 500 or more units per square mile, such density representing approximately 2,000 persons per square mile and being normally the minimum found associated with a closely spaced street pattern
3. Unincorporated area with at least 500 dwelling units per square mile. Boundaries of these areas follow roads, railroads, streams, and other clearly identifiable features
4. Areas devoted to commercial, industrial, transportational, recreational, and other miscellaneous uses functionally related to the central city

Included also are outlying, non-contiguous areas with the required dwelling-unit density located within $1\frac{1}{2}$ miles of the main urbanized part, measured along the shortest connecting highway, and other outlying areas within $\frac{1}{2}$ mile of such non-contiguous areas which meet the minimum residential density rule.

A major objective of the Bureau of the Census in delineating these areas is to provide for a better separation of urban and rural population in the vicinity of our larger cities. It is anticipated that this census improvement will be of value to government organizations concerned with city and regional planning, highways, housing, and vital statistics and also to private organizations concerned with advertising, marketing, utilities, transportation, and social service.

Since the urbanized area outside incorporated places is defined on the basis of housing or population density, its boundaries for the most part are not political but rather follow such features as roads, streets, railroads, streams, and other clearly defined lines which may be easily identified by census enumerators in the field. The urbanized area boundaries were selected after careful examination of all available maps, aerial photographs, and other information sources and then were checked in detail by trained investigators in the field to insure that the criteria were followed and that the boundaries were identifiable.

## STATE ECONOMIC AREAS

New areas called "state economic areas" have been defined by the Bureau of the Census in co-operation with the Department of Agriculture for general statistical purposes and will be used for reporting selected data from the 1950 Censuses of Population and Agriculture. State economic areas are relatively homogeneous subdivisions of states. They consist of single counties or groups of counties which have similar economic and social characteristics or within which a distinctive economy prevails. The 48 states have been divided into 501 state economic areas.

A special class of state economic areas is the metropolitan state economic areas. Outside New England the metropolitan state economic areas are those standard metropolitan areas with a total population of 100,000 or more in 1940, or at a subsequent special census prior to 1950. Where a standard metropolitan area extends across state lines, that segment which lies within each state is designated as a separate state economic area. Standard metropolitan areas in New England, which were defined on a town basis, are approximated on a county basis. According to present plans, when the state economic areas are grouped for agricultural tabulations, the entire nation will be subdivided into 361 areas, recognizing most of the principal type-of-farming areas which have been the accepted unit of analysis by agricultural economists. When the state economic areas are grouped for non-agricultural tabulations, the entire nation will be subdivided into 443 areas of which 150 are metropolitan and 293 are non-metropolitan. The two sets of tabulation areas can be made comparable by appropriate combinations of each.

## CENSUS TRACTS

For the 1950 Census, considerably over 12,000 census tracts were established, which are included in 113 cities with a population of 50,000 or over and in adjacent areas. Census tracts are small areas into which the larger cities and sometimes their adjacent areas are subdivided for statistical purposes by a local census tract committee under rules established by the Bureau of the Census. The tracts are permanently established so that comparisons may be made from census to census. Each tract is defined to have a population of approximately 5,000 and to inclose an area fairly homogeneous in population characteristics. A publication entitled *Census Tract Manual* explains in detail the nature and use of census tracts and outlines the general procedure for their establishment. The Bureau also has prepared a list of the areas which had tracts in 1950 and the names of the local "key persons." Large-scale, detailed maps showing the tract boundaries are available at cost from the Bureau. Tract outline maps generally may be obtained from the local census tract committees through the key persons.

## UNINCORPORATED PLACES

In the 1950 Census, the larger unincorporated places outside the new urbanized areas have been defined, and those with a population of 1,000 or more will be reported in the same manner as incorporated places of equal size. The unincorporated places were delineated concurrently with the urbanized areas as an additional step in providing a better separation of urban and rural population. Each unincorporated place possesses a definite nucleus of residences and has its boundaries so drawn as to include if feasible all the surrounding closely settled area. The actual delimitation of the unincorporated places was accomplished with the use of aerial photographs, the latest state highway planning maps, and other source materials and was supplemented by field inspections made by census personnel. Considerable aid in the way of mapping and field delimitation also was given by many of the state highway departments.

## CENSUS ENUMERATION DISTRICTS

For the 1950 Census, the United States was divided into approximately 230,000 enumeration districts averaging about 700 inhabitants each. An enumeration district is the smallest unit for which census data are tabulated with the exception of city blocks, which were used only in the Census of Housing. The tabulations for the enumeration districts will not be published but may be obtained at cost from the Bureau as they become available. Maps of specific areas showing the enumeration districts and/or the enumeration district boundary descriptions also may be obtained at cost. The charge for maps is related closely to the number of enumeration districts for which limits must be drawn by hand on the maps. On request, estimates of cost will be provided.

## CITY BLOCKS

City blocks are used as areas for the presentation of selected housing data in cities which had a population of 50,000 or more in 1940 or in a subsequent special census prior to 1950. Large-scale city maps identifying the blocks can be furnished at cost. Smaller-scale maps which identify the blocks will be published in the separate bulletins comprising Volume V of the reports of the 1950 Census of Housing.

## CENSUS COUNTY DIVISIONS IN THE STATE OF WASHINGTON

Census county divisions in the state of Washington are newly defined special areas which were used in the 1950 Census and will remain as permanent statistical areas comparable to the minor civil divisions in other states. These divisions were defined by the State Census Board of Washington on the basis of approved criteria and were reviewed by interested state and local groups and the Bureau of Agricultural Eco-

nomics, United States Department of Agriculture. The Bureau of the Census also reviewed and approved the divisions.

The purpose in defining these areas was to provide divisions of the counties which will have relatively permanent boundaries and will be appropriate for the enumeration and presentation of census data for small areas. In many states the minor civil divisions, which are small political subdivisions of the counties, such as townships, serve this purpose satisfactorily. In some states, as in Washington, the minor civil divisions are deficient for statistical purposes because their boundaries change so frequently as to make comparison of data from one period to another impossible.

A total of 642 census county divisions have been established in the state of Washington dividing all the counties. Every effort was made to define areas which have social, economic, and physiographic unity and for which boundaries follow easily recognizable features such as roads, railroads, streams, and the like. Each incorporated place with a population of 2,500 or more, according to a 1948 estimate of the Washington State Census Board, was made a separate census county division, and each place with a population of over 10,000 which was not divided into census tracts was divided into census county subdivisions. Census tracts are established in the cities of Seattle, Tacoma, and Spokane and in the adjacent areas of Seattle and Tacoma. Those tracts which are outside incorporated places with populations of over 10,000 are recognized also as census county divisions.

## AREA SAMPLING

Numerous local governments and private concerns have secured aid from the Bureau of the Census in planning and in preparing materials for the conduct of area sample surveys. This service, which is offered on a reimbursable basis, may include the selection of area samples in accordance with specification supplied and their presentation in map form for field use.

ROBERT C. KLOVE

# THE DEFINITION OF STANDARD METROPOLITAN AREAS

As background for evaluating the definition of standard metropolitan areas, it is well to consider the approach to the problem of defining areas for statistical purposes that is followed by federal agencies, as this approach has been developing over recent decades and particularly in the years preceding the 1950 Census. For the first hundred years of our national existence, statistics were presented for political divisions of the country and almost for them alone. Around the turn of the century it was recognized that statistics for certain non-political areas or special groups of political units might be more useful for certain purposes. The Bureau of the Census, the major statistical agency of the federal government, took the initiative in promoting new types of areas, such as census tracts, industrial areas, and metropolitan districts.

The Census Bureau was not the only federal agency interested in statistical areas, and increasingly in recent years other agencies have taken part in defining special areas. Almost from the beginning local interests also were brought into the picture to assist in determining criteria and defining areas, and in some cases, as, for example, census tracts, they were even given the lead in area delimitation. The increasing participation of other agencies and local interests in the definition of statistical areas, it is believed, is making for greater usefulness of the resulting data.

Following the democratic procedure increases the problem of determining criteria for definitions and applying these criteria. Decisions cannot always be unanimous, and

Reprinted from *Economic Geography*, XXVIII (April, 1952), 95–104, by permission of the author and the editor. (Copyright, 1952, by Clark University, Worcester, Mass.)

the majority rule generally has been observed. It has also been a principle as far as possible to adopt uniform area criteria for the entire country so that data for particular types of areas may be comparable from one part of the country to the other. Statistical areas for government use are designed to satisfy the greatest number of users, and the success of the definitions must be measured in terms of the magnitude of their local acceptance and the minimum local dissatisfaction. Furthermore, it is recognized that statistical areas are subject to a process of change. Not only may the areas change, but the uses of area statistics develop in novel ways. New definition criteria are evolved and new sources of data make possible refinements in the application of the criteria. The purpose of this paper is to show the current status of the metropolitan area definitions.

Standard metropolitan areas have been defined for 172 metropolitan centers in the United States and its territories and possessions by a federal interagency committee under the direction of the United States Bureau of the Budget. These areas are designated as *standard* because the federal statistical agencies represented on the committee have agreed to use these areas insofar as it is feasible. In the Bureau of the Census the standard metropolitan areas are replacing the metropolitan districts, the metropolitan counties, and the industrial areas and are being used for the presentation of statistics of population, housing, manufacturing, and business.

## CRITERIA AND DEFINITION PROCEDURES

Each of the new standard metropolitan areas, except in New England, consists of one or more entire counties. While it is recognized that metropolitan areas could be defined more accurately by using minor civil divisions, which were the building blocks of the old metropolitan districts, experience has shown that areas so defined have a limited value, because many types of data with which comparisons are desired are available only on a county basis. In New England, where towns rather than counties are commonly the basic geographic units for statistical compilations, this objection applies to a much lesser degree; and mainly for this reason the New England standard metropolitan areas are defined on a town rather than a county basis.

Each standard metropolitan area includes a city with 50,000 inhabitants or more in 1950 and may include more than one city of such size. Conversely, each city of such size is included in a standard metropolitan area. The county in which the city of 50,000 or more is located is by definition in the standard metropolitan area. Contiguous counties may be included in the area if they meet certain criteria. The general concept adopted is one of an integrated economic area with a large volume of daily travel and communication between the central city or cities and the outlying parts of the area. This normally results in an area considerably more restricted, especially for the larger cities, than the market or trading area. The following principles were used in determining the eligibility of contiguous counties for inclusion in the standard metropolitan area:

1. Each county must have 10,000 non-agricultural workers, or 10 per cent of the non-agricultural workers in the standard metropolitan area, or more than half of its population residing in contiguous minor civil divisions with a population density of 150 or more per square mile.

2. Each county must have at least two-thirds of its total employed labor force engaged in non-agricultural work.

3. Each county must be economically and socially integrated with the county containing the largest city in the standard metropolitan area. A county is regarded as integrated (*a*) if 15 per cent or more of the workers living in the county work in the county containing the largest city; (*b*) if 25 per cent or more of those working in the county live in the county containing the largest city; or (*c*) if telephone calls from the county to the county containing the largest city average four or more calls per subscriber per month.

In New England, where the city and town rather than the county were used to define standard metropolitan areas, the first and second criteria just mentioned do not apply. In their place, a population density criterion of 150 or more persons per square mile, or 100 or more persons where strong integration is evident, is used.

The Federal Committee on Standard Metropolitan Areas was set up by the Bureau of the Budget late in 1947 with representatives from the following agencies: the Bureau of the Census, the Bureau of Foreign and Domestic Commerce, the Bureau of Labor Statistics, the Federal Security Agency, the Bureau of Employment Security, the Housing and Home Finance Agency, the Federal Housing Administration, the Federal Reserve Board, and the Bureau of Agricultural Economics. After approving the general principles to be followed, the committee requested the Census Bureau to prepare tentative definitions of individual areas. This work was done by a Census Bureau committee, of which the writer was a member, with the active participation of representatives of the Bureau of the Budget and the Bureau of Employment Security and in the later stages with the help of the Bureau of Labor Statistics. These tentative definitions were discussed with interested local organizations by the Bureau of the Budget or its designated representatives. This local review confirmed the tentative definitions in a large majority of the areas. After reconsidering the definitions in the light of information contained in the field reports, the Census Bureau committee prepared final definitions for submission to the federal committee.

## PROBLEMS OF DEFINITION

The problems encountered by the federal committee and its technical subcommittee may be illustrative of the more general problem of area definition, and they also serve to emphasize the difficulties faced in achieving a set of areas comparable over the United States and satisfactory for presenting a wide variety of data. The problems are discussed briefly under three headings: (1) the determination of the criteria; (2) the application of the criteria; and (3) outside pressure for exceptions to the criteria.

*Determination of the criteria.*—Reasons already have been given for the acceptance of the county as the basic unit for defining the standard metropolitan areas. It was recognized that the inclusion of whole counties generally results in the inclusion in the metropolitan area of much territory ordinarily not considered "metropolitan." Since the population of this territory in almost all cases is negligible relative to the total population of the area, its inclusion is of very minor significance for the presentation of economic and demographic statistics.

The requirement that a standard metropolitan area have a city with a population of 50,000 or more is an arbitrary rule. There is nothing magic about exceeding 50,000 that changes the character of a city. A city of 100,000 or a total area population of 100,000 might be more accurate if we knew exactly what "metropolitan" means. However, a very definite rule in terms of population numbers is necessary, and the public has accepted a city population of 50,000 as a mark of metropolitanism. It is a carry-over of the old metropolitan district definition.

The non-agricultural workers criterion is an attempt to measure metropolitan character in terms of either the absolute or the proportionate size of the manufacturing, commercial, and other non-agricultural portions of the labor force. The rule acts to exclude predominantly rural counties. Population density is a similar measure and was almost the single criterion of the extent of the old metropolitan districts. It was retained as one of the measures of metropolitan character in defining the new standard metropolitan areas.

The general requirement that each county in an area must have close economic and social integration with the central city or cities appears to require no defense. The specific rules covering commuting and telephone communication adopted by the committee for demonstrating this integration are subject to question partly because they are empirical, but a more serious objection is the deficiency of adequate data for applying these criteria. They were selected because it appeared that some data along these lines could be secured for most areas.

*Application of the criteria.*—For the purpose of illustration let us assume that we have joined the committee while it is defining the Evansville Standard Metropolitan Area. Evansville is located in southern Indiana on the banks of the Ohio River (Fig. 1). Evansville had a 1940 population of 97,062, so it qualifies for metropolitan area consideration. (The 1950 Census gave it 128,636, so it still qualifies.) No city with a population of 50,000 or more is close to Evansville, so there can be no question that Evansville stands alone as a metropolitan center.

Evansville is in Vanderburgh County, Indiana, which by definition qualifies for inclusion in its standard metropolitan area. Counties contiguous to Vanderburgh which are additional candidates for the standard metropolitan area are Posey, Gibson, and Warrick in Indiana, and Henderson in Kentucky. Each county has less than 10,000 non-agricultural workers according to the latest figures from the Old Age and Survivor Insurance program as collected by the Social Security Administration. Each county also has less than 10 per cent of the non-agricultural employment of Vanderburgh County so obviously would have less than 10 per cent of the non-agricultural employment of any combination of counties selected for the Evansville Standard Metropolitan Area. Contiguous minor civil divisions adjoining Evansville and Vanderburgh County which have a population density of 150 persons or over per square mile are found only in Henderson County, Kentucky. Here, Magisterial Districts 4 and 5 had a population of 27,020 inhabitants in 1940, or 53.8 per cent of the county's population. Therefore, Henderson County, alone, meets the first criterion, which requires a county to have 10,000 non-agricultural workers or 10 per cent of the non-agricultural workers in the standard metropolitan area, or more than half of its population in contiguous minor civil divisions with a population density of 150 or more per square mile.

Henderson County, however, fails to meet the second criterion, since less than two-thirds of its total labor force is in non-agricultural employment. It has only 64.7 per cent. This is a close miss, and it might be that when later census data become available, Henderson County will show better than two-thirds of its labor force in non-agricultural employment; so it is decided to investigate the social and economic integration of Henderson County with Vanderburgh County. All the other coun-

FIG. 1.—Evansville and vicinity, population density per square mile, 1950, for selected minor civil divisions.

ties have failed to meet the two "screening" criteria, so they are no longer given consideration.

Obtaining data to support or deny economic and social integration between counties proved to be difficult. Much of the information on commuting or place of work and place of residence was supplied by the United States Employment Service through its connections with the state employment security agencies and their local labor market analysts. However, much of these data were spotty in distribution, incomplete, and not strictly comparable from one area to another. An example of unusually good data of this type is a survey of Indiana commuting patterns made in 1947 by the state employment service. The accompanying map (Fig. 2) shows that 2.7 per cent of the Evansville employed live in Henderson County, Kentucky. This is approximately 1,500 workers or about 10 per cent of the total employment in Henderson County. It is below the 15 per cent required. No quantitative data on the percentage of workers in Henderson County living in Vanderburgh County was found, but the local labor market analyst is certain that the figure is less than 25 per cent.

Telephone data reveal not more than three calls per subscriber per month from the Henderson exchange area to Evansville, which is less than the four calls required. Accordingly, Henderson County is submarginal in its integration with Evansville and Vanderburgh County and so is excluded from the Evansville Standard Metropolitan Area, which is defined to consist only of Vanderburgh County.

The most frequently encountered problem of definition is the inclusion or exclusion of contiguous peripheral counties which we have already observed in the case of Evansville. Several other examples of counties which gave the committee trouble are here cited to illustrate the variance of conditions.

Monmouth County, New Jersey, was excluded from the New York–Northeastern New Jersey Metropolitan Area, although it met both the non-agricultural workers and population density requirements, on the grounds that its economic and social integration with New York City, Newark, and Jersey City was insufficient (Fig. 3). Monmouth County, you will recall, lies along the Atlantic coast south of Lower New York Bay and contains a chain of seaside resort communities which owe their existence largely to their closeness to the New York urban center. However, most of these places are over fifty miles from Manhattan, and daily commuting and telephone communication are not strong. Other examples may be taken from the San Francisco–Oakland Metropolitan Area (Fig. 6). Marin County lying north of the San Francisco Golden Gate met the screening criteria and was included in the area despite its relatively low population density, because the population there has very close daily commuting ties with San Francisco. Sonoma and Napa counties, north of San Francisco Bay, were excluded for failing to meet the screening criteria. Solano County to the northeast of the Bay met the population density criterion and despite its distance from the central cities was demonstrated to have the minimum integration.

"Split" counties constituted another problem which somewhat to our surprise was found very infrequently. A "split county" is defined here as a county lying between two metropolitan centers and possessing substantial integration with each one. Bucks County, Pennsylvania, is an example which has slight penetration from both Trenton and Allentown–Bethlehem but is predominantly oriented toward Philadelphia (Fig. 4). The outstanding example is Davis County, Utah, located between the Salt Lake and Ogden metropolitan areas (Fig. 5). On the basis of both commuting and telephone data the county is almost evenly divided between the two centers. The decision was to exclude the county from both areas rather than split it and so make impossible the securing of sta-

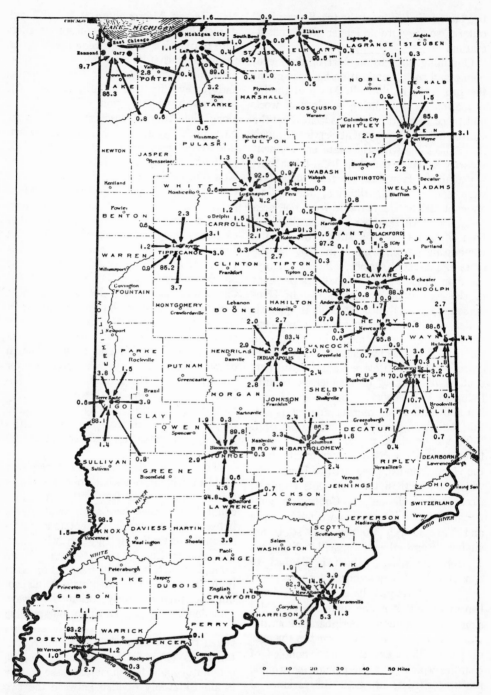

FIG. 2.—Indiana commuting patterns from *The Labor Market,* December, 1947 (periodical published by the U.S. Department of Labor), pp. 9–11. Percentages indicate the distribution of employees by county of residence for major employers in selected industrial areas. Analysis is based on survey of 688 employers in July, 1947.

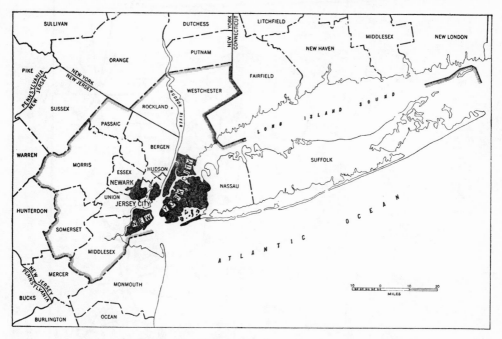

FIG. 3.—New York—Northeastern New Jersey Standard Metropolitan Area

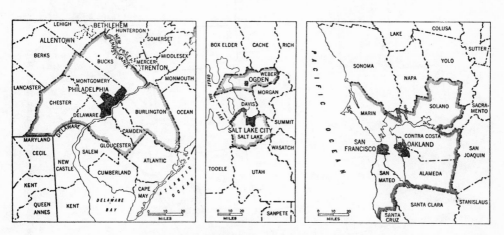

FIG. 4 (*lower left*).—Philadelphia Standard Metropolitan Area
FIG. 5 (*lower center*).—Ogden and Salt Lake City Standard Metropolitan Areas
FIG. 6 (*lower right*).—San Francisco–Oakland Standard Metropolitan Area

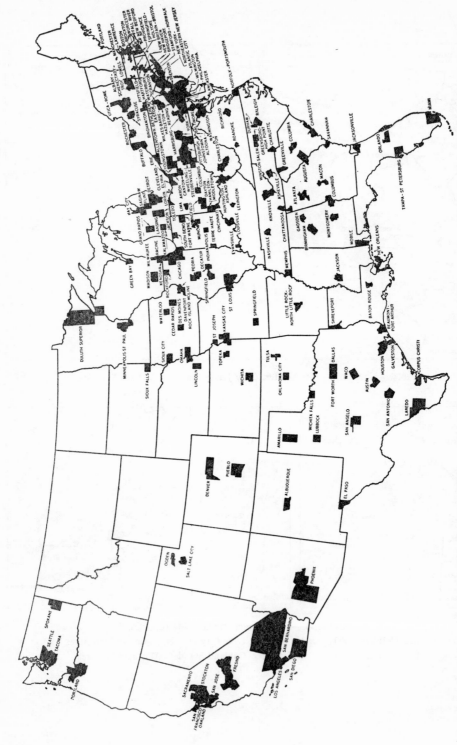

Fig. 7.—The 168 standard metropolitan areas of the United States in 1950 (U.S. Department of Commerce, Bureau of the Census)

tistical data in some fields for these two metropolitan areas.

A more difficult and more frequently met problem was that of competing cities. In the past, metropolitan cities in adjoining counties were in numerous cases included together in one hyphenated metropolitan district as, for example, Scranton–Wilkes-Barre. In defining the new metropolitan areas these combinations as well as others were examined to determine whether integration existed, using the same principles followed for peripheral counties. Integration was demonstrated to be lacking for the following centers which previously had been combined: Scranton and Wilkes-Barre, Boston and Brockton, Lowell and Lawrence and Haverhill, Fall River and New Bedford, Hartford and New Britain, Norfolk–Portsmouth and Newport News, and Racine and Kenosha.

*Outside pressure for exceptions to the criteria.*—The committee, following its field review of the tentative metropolitan area definitions, was asked by local groups to change some of the definitions. In many cases the review resulted in supplying to the committee additional information on population growth in certain areas, decline in agriculture, increase in industrial employment, and evidence of integration or lack of integration between counties. In some cases the committee was urged to make exceptions to the criteria in defining an individual metropolitan area on the grounds that local or regional conditions are unique and require special rules.

In all instances the committee, in reaching a decision on the definition of an area, attempted to apply the criteria without making any exceptions. Naturally not all interests could be satisfied, and in part this was due to the fact that the evidence was not conclusive one way or the other, and close decisions had to be made.

The problem of defining metropolitan areas or regions appears to have received little attention from geographers as revealed in publications, and in only a few instances have geographic studies provided data of either a quantitative or a qualitative nature that would aid in the definitions. Here is a field of inquiry that I believe is worthy of more study by geographers, because if they can contribute to the definition of a better set of metropolitan areas, the data provided for these areas by government surveys will be more useful for the further analysis of metropolitan problems and the attainment of sound conclusions.

ROBERT L. WRIGLEY, JR.

# URBANIZED AREAS AND THE 1950 DECENNIAL CENSUS

As a city outgrows its corporate bound-aries, the social and economic statistics as-sembled for the corporate area cease to give a satisfactory picture of the nature and size of the over-all urban community. This fact has been recognized by the Bureau of the Census since the turn of the century, when it began to delineate metropolitan areas.

At first the Bureau delineated only one type of metropolitan area, but for almost forty years it has defined at least two types of areas for a limited number of cities. It delineated industrial districts for the na-tion's four largest cities in the Census of Manufactures for 1900. Each district in-cluded one or several counties, and the limits in all cases followed county bound-aries. Thus, in most instances, the district was made up of much rural territory as well as urban land. A more restricted metropolitan area based on townships rather than counties and called "metropoli-tan district," was introduced in the Census of Population for 1910. This geographic unit and the industrial district, later called "industrial area," have been used through the years, although the criteria employed in defining them have changed from time to time.

In recent years the "metropolitan" con-cept has become more and more popular. In view of this trend the Census Bureau's treatment of the subject has become more comprehensive. For various reasons the Bureau has stopped using some metropoli-tan units. On the other hand, new metro-politan-type areas have been developed. One metropolitan unit that will not be em-

Reprinted from *Journal of the American Insti-tute of Planners*, XVI (Spring, 1950), 66–70, by permission of the author and the editor. (Copy-right, 1950, by the American Institute of Planners.)

ployed in future census-taking is the indus-trial area, which was last used in the Cen-sus of Manufactures for 1939. In the 1950 Decennial Census, however, the Bureau will again publish a limited amount of sta-tistical material for the old metropolitan districts as they were defined in 1940, al-though they may be discontinued in future censuses after the use of the new standard metropolitan areas becomes established. Each standard metropolitan area is defined as a county or group of counties—except in New England, where groups of towns are employed—with a city of 50,000 or more inhabitants as its center. A selected group of these areas was first used in the Census of Manufactures of 1947. A very significant development in 1950 is the in-troduction of the urbanized area. Since this new metropolitan unit is of great interest to planners, it has been taken as the sub-ject of this paper.

Employing such a geographic unit as the urbanized area is a major innovation in urban census-taking. In a broad sense the urbanized area, as delimited for large cities, includes all incorporated urban commu-nities as well as unincorporated built-up territory either adjoining or located very near the central city or cities. An attempt was made to delimit the urbanized territory of 150-odd population centers and to ex-clude as much vacant or unused land as possible. Segregating urban and rural lands in this fashion gives planners a good pic-ture of the areal extent of metropolitan ur-ban patterns. It also provides a basis for improving the delineation and measure-ment of urban and rural population.

The urbanized area unit will be used in assembling and reporting population sta-tistics for 157 urban agglomerations whose central city has a population of 50,000 or more inhabitants. This includes all cities having a population of 50,000 or more in the 1940 Census plus cities that have reached that population figure since 1940, according to special censuses taken between 1940 and 1950. In several instances two or more cities of this size are in one urbanized area.

Perhaps the best way to describe an urbanized area is to outline the principles used in delimiting it. The original plan was to bound the outer limits of urban residential development beyond incorporated communities; hence, a major consideration in determining urbanized area boundaries has been the number and distribution of residences. However, certain land uses which are closely associated with urban functions but which have little or no residential population also have been included.

After careful study it was agreed that the urbanized area, with some qualifications, should include the following kinds of territory in addition to the central city or cities:

1. All incorporated urban places (i.e., places of 2,500 or more persons) contiguous with the central city—single communities as well as a series of adjoining communities extending out from the main center.
2. All territory adjoining these incorporated places, provided the individual block areas composing this territory each have a housing density equal to 500 dwellings per square mile. From field checks this density appeared to be a satisfactory measure of urbanity; hence, an unincorporated area meeting this criterion has been classed as "urban."
3. Outlying incorporated urban places when connected to the central city or its contiguous incorporated places by unincorporated area with the required housing density.
4. Incorporated places not classified as urban but having a nodal concentration of at least 100 houses and connected to the central city in one of the ways stated above. In such cases the nodal concentration must have a density equal to 500 dwellings per square mile.
5. Outlying incorporated places as well as out-

lying unincorporated area fulfilling housing number and density requirements outlined above, and not attached to the central part of an urbanized area by a solid urban connection, also form part of an urbanized area under special conditions. They are included if they are located within $1\frac{1}{2}$ miles of the main urban development, as measured along a direct highway. Also, those outlying areas within $\frac{1}{2}$ mile of another outlying area, which is within $1\frac{1}{2}$ miles of the main urban development, are included. The sparsely settled territory between these outlying communities and the principal urban settlement is left outside the urbanized area.

6. The following non-residential uses, located outside incorporated places, provided they are contiguous with the urbanized area as delimited under the five points outlined above:
   a) Built-up industrial and commercial districts, including large individual plants located outside the major industrial concentrations.
   b) Railroad yards and shops, airports, large trucking terminals, port areas, and other extensive transportation uses.
   c) Recreational areas—public and private golf courses, municipal parks (but not forest preserves), ball parks, race tracks, amusement parks, and fair grounds.
   d) Municipal facilities, such as water works, sewage disposal plants, and small reservoirs (but not storage reservoirs such as natural or artificial lakes).
   e) Cemeteries $\frac{1}{4}$ square mile or larger.
   f) Public and private educational facilities.
   g) Military installations of 2 square miles or less in area. In some instances those reservations of more than 2 square miles also may be included if their civilian employment is large.
   h) General hospitals as well as all types of municipal institutions. Since county and state hospitals commonly are operated in conjunction with large farms, they are not included in the urbanized area, except in special cases.

In examining this list one may get the impression that a comprehensive land-use survey has been made; that assumption is not true. Detailed mapping and classification of urban land uses is outside the work of the Census Bureau. However, some consideration must be given to all types of land use in order to present fairly complete urbanized area patterns. In some way these patterns are not as complete as many planners and other interested parties would like to have them.

The urbanized areas of some cities include considerable vacant land; on the other hand, some contiguous built-up properties have been excluded. These vagaries stem from a number of conditions that made the job of delineation difficult.

The Geography Division of the Bureau of the Census began delimiting urbanized areas by first making a number of exploratory office and field studies and by discussing the problem in a series of conferences with various interested parties both in and out of the government. In this way the geography staff gained experience and at the same time formulated the principles previously outlined. By using these principles and by employing a small group of trained geographers for the field surveys, a high degree of uniformity in all urbanized area work throughout the country was achieved.

As the main job got under way, the boundary of each urbanized area—the "urban fringe line"—was plotted on maps in the office of the Geography Division. Information was taken from many sources. Maps made by the Sanborn Map Company, the Army Map Service, the United States Coast and Geodetic Survey, and the United States Geological Survey were helpful in many ways. Aerial photographs, housing counts made by the Census Bureau Field Division, special census returns, and local population estimates also were used. These source materials were examined for housing densities, street and highway patterns, railroads, and other information, and a tentative urbanized area or "fringe" line for the various cities and their environs was plotted on the latest available maps or in some instances on aerial photographs.

Since current information was not always available and since there is an ever present possiblility of error in such materials, it was imperative to examine the urbanized area boundary in the field and to check, among other things, housing densities, new construction, and many physical features used as boundaries—primarily streets, railroads, and streams. In the light of this first-hand information, boundary changes were made when necessary to secure easily identifiable limits. This was a factor of great importance.

The urbanized area boundary must be a line that may be followed by the relatively untrained enumerator. Well-defined physical features—streets, railroads, and permanent streams—are used as boundaries, along with the corporate limits, township lines, and other political division boundaries. An imaginary line such as a "point-to-point" connection was seldom employed, and then only under the most favorable circumstances. Because of this fact some blocks of land partially built up with solid urban development but still largely vacant, were brought into the urbanized area simply because a satisfactory boundary could not be found for the built-up portion of the block. In such cases the developed land was considered important enough, and the growth active enough, to bring the entire block into the urbanized area. Problems of this kind were examined and judged on the basis of special rules established to guide the work. As an example, a block of one-half square mile, although largely vacant, was brought into the urbanized area if its closely settled part, incapable of being bounded, possessed at least seventy dwelling units. It is clear from this procedure that considerable vacant land will be found in some urbanized areas.

More vacant land was added to the urbanized area by the policy of including incorporated urban places regardless of how undeveloped the corporate territory might be. This condition is especially striking in New England, where farms and woodland commonly are found within incorporated cities and villages. As a result, the urbanized area map of some New England communities will not truly picture the urban pattern. Although this shortcoming was evident from the outset, the Bureau of the Census always has recognized the integrity of the incorporated urban community and it was felt that this was not an opportune time to change its policy.

In some cases unincorporated marsh land and other territory not suitable for urban development and with an acreage of less than one square mile also was included in the urbanized area. This was done in order to secure a better boundary. If the tract included more than one square mile, it was left out regardless of whether it was surrounded by built-up property, thus leaving a non-urbanized enclave in the urbanized area pattern.

The Bureau of the Census will publish maps and statistics for the urbanized areas. A map of each urbanized area, including a description of the boundary, will appear in one of the census volumes. Statistical data will include tabulations on population and housing. The population and housing data will be published in four general categories: for each incorporated city, for unincorporated area, for the total area outside the central city, and for the entire urbanized area. All these statistics should be of practical value in many fields of work, particularly in planning.

Preparing maps and compiling statistics on urban agglomerations in this manner should focus attention on the metropolitan urban area as a unit. It should help to make people "metropolitan" conscious and thus promote metropolitan planning. Nothing heretofore published will give as realistic a picture of the comparative size of urban areas as well as the relative importance of each center to its surrounding territory. In spite of the shortcomings previously noted, no metropolitan unit has so truly depicted the extent of metropolitan urban development as the urbanized area. Since the Census Bureau plans to revise the urbanized area boundaries for each decennial census, their maps and statistics will provide an interesting and valuable picture of urban expansion. Planners can use this information to study the direction of growth and the shifts in population between the central city and the suburban sections.

In weighing the good points and shortcomings of the urbanized area unit one must bear in mind that it is a pioneer venture. For 1960 the Bureau may broaden the scope of its survey and delimit the urbanized areas of smaller cities. It may find a way to exclude most of the vacant land. In its urbanized area tabulation it may assemble more than just population and housing statistics. Developments of this nature should aid the planner in many ways.

JEAN GOTTMANN

## MEGALOPOLIS, OR THE URBANIZATION OF THE NORTHEASTERN SEABOARD

The frequency of large urban units scattered along the Atlantic seaboard in the northeastern United States was a striking realization to the foreigner who first visited the area, even fifteen years ago. In February, 1942, after a first trip from New York to Washington, the writer, being asked by Isaiah Bowman in Baltimore what was the most striking impression he had had as a geographer in his first months in this country, answered, "The density of great cities along this coast, from Boston to Washington."

In 1950, on the basis of the new census, the Bureau of the Census prepared a map, later published as an illustration in a booklet of statistics on *State Economic Areas*, which showed clearly the continuity of an area of "metropolitan" economy from a little north of Boston to a little south of Washington, more precisely from Hillsborough County in New Hampshire to Fairfax County in Virginia. This seemed to be a first statistical demonstration on the map of the existence of a continuous stretch of urban and suburban areas, the main NE-SW axis of which was about 600 miles long, and within the frame of which dwelt even in 1950 some 30 million people.

In the geography of the distribution of habitat this was a phenomenon unique by its size not only in America but in the world. It resulted obviously from the coalescence, recently achieved, of a chain of metropolitan areas, each of which grew around a substantial urban nucleus. The supermetropolitan character of this vast area, the greatest such growth ever observed, called for a special name. We chose the word *Megalopolis*,[1] of Greek origin and listed in Webster's dictionary as meaning "a very large city."

Indeed, the name "Megalopolis" appears on modern maps of Greece, designating a plateau in the Peloponnesus. A city was established there in ancient times, the founders of which dreamed of a great future for it and of an enormous size. But the Greek town of Megalopolis never grew to be much of a city. What has developed now in the northeastern seaboard surpasses everything dreamers of the past may have visualized. Aristotle, however, wrote in his *Politics:* "When are men living in the same place to be regarded as a single city? What is the limit? Certainly not the wall of the city, for you might surround all Peloponnesus with a wall. Like this, we may say, is Babylon and every city that has the compass of a nation rather than a city" (iii. 3. 1276a, 25).

A few years ago the reviewer of a book

[1] The term *Megalopolis* was preferred to others after careful consideration of various possibilities. We wish to express our appreciation for the help received in this matter from several distinguished classicists at the Institute for Advanced Study, especially from Professors Harold Cherniss, Benjamin Merritt, and the late Jacob Hammer. "Megalopolis" was used by various authors in connection with quite different meanings: ancient philosophers described sometimes by it the "world of ideas"; recently Lewis Mumford used it to describe the whole trend toward large cities. We have felt it appropriate to describe a unique geographical region, characterized more than any other by enormous urban and metropolitan growth, and to assess the present status of a vast region in the northeastern seaboard section of the United States. Our statistical definition as on the maps is based on the map accompanying the Bureau of the Census publication, *State Economic Areas* by Donald J. Bogue (Washington, 1951).

Reprinted from *Economic Geography*, XXXIII (July, 1957), 189–200, by permission of the author and the editor. (Copyright, 1957, by Clark University, Worcester, Mass.)

on the history of eastern railroads referred to the stretch of land along the tracks of the Pennsylvania and the Baltimore and Ohio railroads from New York City to Washington, D.C., as the "Main Street" of the nation. To be quite correct, such a "Main Street" ought to be prolonged along the rail tracks from New York City to Boston. There is, however, some truth in this symbolical expression. This section of U.S. 1 has come to assume within the American nation a special function, or a whole group of intertwined functions, which is hinted at in less urbanized areas by the concept of Main Street.

## WHAT IS THE MEANING OF A STUDY OF MEGALOPOLIS?

Geographers are of course convinced of the value of a study describing a given geographic region endowed with some unity and originality and thus differentiated from neighboring areas. Although such a region may be unique in the world, investigating its features, problems, and structure has generally been recognized as a worthwhile enterprise. As the data describing unique cases piled up, the endeavor developed in the geographical profession to look for general principles and for studies of cases, the outcome of which would be more immediately valuable because they were applicable to some extent in more than one area or place.

Although unique today, Megalopolis obviously has been and still is an extraordinarily interesting laboratory *in vivo* where much of what may well be accepted as the "normalcies" of the advanced civilization of the latter part of the twentieth century is slowly shaping. It is still too early to assess the full meaning of a study of Megalopolis in the frame we have outlined. The study must first be carried out. The many questions it involves could not be listed, let alone discussed, in such a brief article. A few hints may be given, however, of what such a survey could mean and of the main problems it could tackle.

By its size and mass, Megalopolis is both

an exceptional growth and a pioneer area; exceptional, for nowhere else could one find another concentration of population, of industrial and commercial facilities, of financial wealth and cultural activities, comparable to it. However, in several other points in America and on other continents growth of continuously urbanized spaces

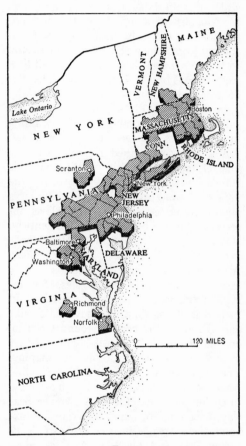

FIG. 1

may be observed. More of such enormous "metropolitan" bodies can be expected to arise as the evolution, already well advanced in and around New York, Philadelphia, Boston, Washington, reaches other cities and their environs. In this sense Megalopolis is a pioneer area: the processes which develop therein will help toward an understanding of, and will forecast ways and obstacles to, urban growth in various other parts.

In fact Megalopolis has already been pioneering in the organization of urban life for quite some time. Such features as skyscrapers, building elevators, city and suburban networks of trains, traffic lights, and one-way streets started here on a large scale to gain later world-wide adoption. Megalopolis grew up from the network provided by the early mushrooming of sea-trading towns along the coast from Boston to New York and then, along the Fall line, from New York to Washington. The size of its principal urban nuclei, especially New York and Philadelphia, caused the subsequent mushrooming of suburbs filling in the spaces between the larger cities. James Madison defined New Jersey as a "barrel tapped at both ends"; that this state's function was essentially to link the area of New York and Philadelphia was apparently understood by such a clever observer at the end of the eighteenth century. But the polynuclear origin of Megalopolis is beginning to be repeated in other regions. A vast urban and suburban area is rapidly expanding around Los Angeles, for instance; inland it has already reached, in fact, San Bernardino; it may unite with San Diego on the coast. Around Chicago, on the shore of Lake Michigan, another impressive urban continuity is shaping. The metropolitan areas stretching in Ohio between Cleveland and Pittsburgh are close to coalescence; and the St. Lawrence Seaway, once opened, may accelerate and expand these trends in the area south of Lakes Erie and Ontario. And as more metropolitan areas are pushing forth suburban tentacles one toward another throughout the nation, additional but smaller Megalopolis-like clusters will be formed. This is a process involving considerable changes in the American modes of living. The trends may become better understood once the case of the largest and most advanced of these areas, the present Megalopolis, is thoroughly analyzed.

## What Are the Problems of Megalopolis?

Within such a vast area the problems are, of course, many and diversified. It may not be necessary, or very useful, to survey all of them, in their local variety, in the different parts of Megalopolis. A few basic questions must, however, be asked: How did Megalopolis happen to arise and with such a shape? What are the present main functions of this area, its role within the American economy and the North Atlantic system of relations? What are the present problems of internal organizations, and what solutions have been attempted?

Here are three sets of questions, each of which requires detailed consideration involving a great deal of research.

Megalopolis' growth in the past sums up a good part of the economic history of the United States. It has not often been examined how the sequence of events and trends in the past growth of the nation affected local developments. Although it is, in area, only a small section of the Northeast, Megalopolis had a crucial part in determining national trends; on the other hand, the main swings of its own history were usually the consequence of shifts in national policies.

Why was Megalopolis' growth throughout its history more rapid and continuous than that of many other urban areas in the world? This question leads into an examination of the factors motivating or determining urban expansion in a given area. In a first inquiry concerning the matter conducted by this writer a few years ago were listed some forty-odd factors that in different ways and at different periods helped the upbuilding of Megalopolis. The two major among these factors appear to be, on the one hand, the polynuclear origin and the part played by the series of northeastern seaboard cities as a *hinge* of the American economy. The federal organization of government and the division of the Atlantic seaboard into so many states (each with access to tidewater) that engaged in a fruitful rivalry made all nuclei compete one with another until their growth joined them together.

The role of the "hinge" is more difficult to perceive but is easily demonstrated by the material accumulated in regional economic history. This seaboard had from the inception of the United States the opportunity and the responsibility of serving both as an oceanic façade for relations abroad and as a springboard for the settlement and development of the continent inland. At different periods the main weight of the northeastern interests oscillated from sea trade to continental development and back again; in New England one of these oscillations in the beginning of the nineteenth century was defined as the period when the main interest shifted "from the wharf to the waterfall." In many towns which, on the Fall line, were later integrated with the area of Megalopolis, wharf and waterfall were very close to one another. Whether the general trends of the American economy threw the door open toward the outside or closed it to turn the main endeavors inland, the hinge remained fixed at the series of eastern cities, extending from Boston to Washington, which alone had the geographical position, the authority, the capital, and the skill to elaborate such policies and put them into application.[2]

The inheritance of the past still heavily influences present situations and trends. Whether the eastern seaboard will keep the monopoly of the "hinge" advantages after the St. Lawrence Seaway is completed remains a burning question. However, the faculty of direct access to the sea was only one of many factors which favored Megalopolis, and the others may still operate in the future. The relative part played by these various factors in shaping the present would be an important and sug-

gestive aspect in the study of Megalopolis' historical background.

The present functions of Megalopolis would be the next step in the proposed research. These functions are several; there is, of course, a residential one expressed in the total figure of the population; but how do the inhabitants make a living and why do they have to be concentrated in this area?

Megalopolis arose as a grouping of the main seaports, commercial centers, and manufacturing activities in the United States. To a large extent the *maritime façade function* still is carried on: most of the seaborne foreign trade of the country goes through Megalopolis' harbors. The *manufacturing function* never stopped developing within the area, although many industries have been brought into operation in other sections of the United States. Megalopolis seems to specialize rather in the more delicate finishing industries and in those involving a great deal of laboratory work and research. However, a good number of large plants (iron and steel, chemical and metallurgical industries) have been erected within the last twenty years in this same area. What the balance is and how much specialization is really shaping up would be interesting to ascertain.

The *commercial and financial functions* remain extremely important for Megalopolis. Despite decentralization trends many times stressed and advocated, this area remains a decisive one for the American economy as well as for international financial relations. If New York City is no longer the financial capital it was earlier in the century, it is because much of that function migrated to Washington, with the increasing role of federal authorities in the management of the nation's business. As a market, for goods as well as for money, Megalopolis as a whole still dominates the rest of the national territory. Not only does it comprise one-fifth of the nation: this fifth is obviously the best paid and the wealthiest. Though other centers of concentrated

[2] See the historical sketch of the "hinge" function in J. Gottmann, "La région charnière de l'économie americaine," *Revue de la porte océane* (Le Havre), VII, No. 71 (March, 1951), 9–14, and No. 72 (April, 1951), 11–20.

wealth have arisen and developed elsewhere, especially on the West Coast and
along the Great Lakes' shores, none can yet
boast a mass approaching that of the Bos-
ton-Washington region. Nor has any had
such a traditional grouping of financial and
social activities as that suggested by some
of New York's thoroughfares: Wall Street,
Park Avenue, or Fifth Avenue, all fractions of the national Main Street.

Whether or not related to the social
stratification and the abundance of money
in the area, Megalopolis acquired and retained a quite remarkable *function of cultural leadership,* despite the American endeavor at decentralization. Here are found
the best-known universities, the better-
equipped laboratories, the greatest density
of learned institutions and large libraries
in North America and probably in the
present world. The vast majority of nationally read periodicals and important
publishing houses have their editorial offices in Megalopolis; some newspapers
from this area have even a nationwide distribution, especially for their Sunday edi-
tions. The concentration of cultural leadership makes it difficult for institutions such
as the Ford Foundation or the R.C.A. Research Laboratories to operate from headquarters located far from Megalopolis.
This leadership is even more evident in the
arts: whether theater, music, or galleries,
the concentration attained in this area has
no match elsewhere in America.

Finally, the question may arise, and
would be more difficult to answer, of the
actual weight of Megalopolis in the political life of the country. Although the national capital is part of it, this region is
only one-fifth of the nation and its votes do
not necessarily make the decision of major
states, parts of which are megalopolitan,
such as New York and Pennsylvania. Nevertheless, Megalopolis has a definite political pattern which differs from that of the
surrounding northeastern country.

Having thus analyzed the past growth
and present functions of Megalopolis, we
come to its actual problems. These are

many. Two categories of problems, particularly pressing in all downtown sections of
modern cities, have attracted attention and
have been given much study: the traffic
difficulties and the slums. Two other problems are nowadays receiving increasing attention in competent quarters: water supply and local government. Both appear inadequately set to answer the present needs
of the huge cities and their quickly expanding suburbs. The rapidly mushrooming
metropolitan commissions and committees
seem to herald already deep changes forth-
coming in the traditional concepts and
practices of local government. Interstate
compacts may arise to help solve transportation problems (such as the Port of New
York Authority); experiments in metropolitan government may be more difficult
to start in parts of Megalopolis because of
the mass and variety of interests at stake—
but the very difficulties make every attempt
more significant.

Megalopolis as a unit has taken shape
only within the last few years. Its laws and
customs will take much longer to evolve
into new forms better adapted to the needs
and resources of such an enormous urban
territory. A survey of the new problems, in
their variety, should nevertheless be of
some help even at this time. While legislation and institutions change slowly, modes
of living evolve far more rapidly. Novelists
have satirized certain aspects of megalopolitan life: a quarter-century after the
"cliff-dwellers" were strongly established
on Fifth and Park Avenues, we hear about
the "exurbanites." The basic fact is the
double trend of the large cities: part of the
population moves out and commutes from
an "outer suburbia" which often extends
fifty miles beyond; and parts of the cities
are converted into immense apartment
house groupings (paradoxically sometimes
called "villages"). These two trends are
particularly clear in Manhattan and in
Washington, but they are gaining other big
nuclei of Megalopolis as well. The threat
of the recent spread of juvenile delinquency
seems to increase the migration of families

to the periphery of metropolitan areas. The new mode of life involves more daily traveling, more traffic jams, and more highways outside the downtown areas; a redistribution of marketing channels (illustrated by proliferating suburban shopping centers and department store branches); some changes in the type of goods needed; an increasing interest in zoning, gardening, and nature conservation.

Because more megalopolitan, the way of life of an increasing proportion of the pop-

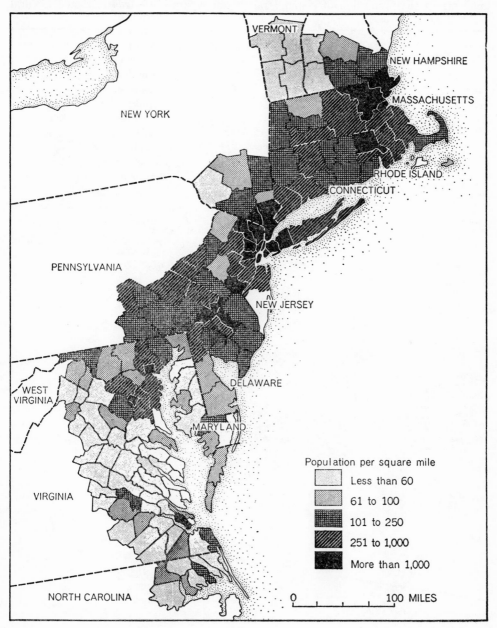

FIG. 2

ulation becomes more country-like although not really rural. The Bureau of the Census has had to revise several times its standards for the definition of metropolitan areas; the criteria of integration with the central urban district include such measurements as the proportion of commuters and the average number of telephone calls per subscriber from a suburban county to the central county of the area, etc. In 1950 the Bureau even had to revise its definition of "urban territory" and introduced the term "urbanized areas" to provide for a better separation between urban and rural

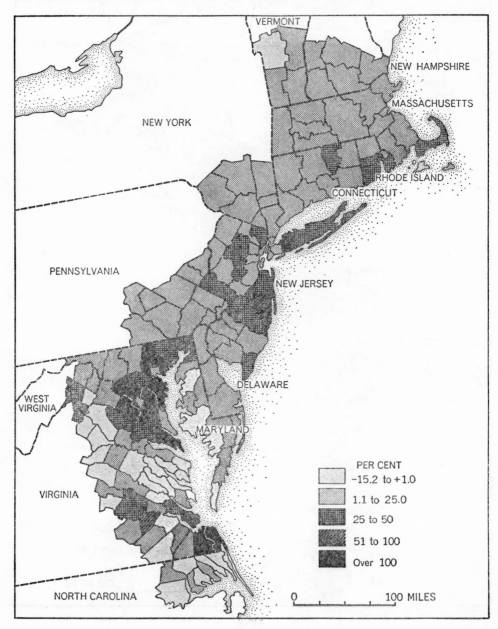

Fɪɢ. 3

territory in the vicinity of large cities, especially within metropolitan areas. New suburban types of farming are also developing, consisting both of a few highly mechanized and specialized large enterprises (such as the truck farming on Long Island) and a scattering of numerous small farms inhabited by people working in the cities and deriving their income from non-agricultural occupations.

The city, in days of yore, was a well-defined, densely settled territory, often surrounded by walls or palisades. Some time ago it broke out of such rigid frames and developed outlying sections, *extra-muros*. In its most recent stage of growth, already characteristic of Megalopolis, it extends out on a rapidly expanding scale, along highways and rural roads, mixing uses of land that look either rural or urban, encircling vast areas which remain "green" (and which some wise endeavors attempt to preserve as recreation space for the future), creating a completely new pattern of living and of regional interdependence between communities.

The coming of age of Megalopolis thus creates, besides problems in legislation, traffic, engineering, marketing, etc., also new psychological problems: people have more difficulty thinking along the traditional lines of division into states when megalopolitan sections of different states are much more integrated in daily life than they could be with upstate areas of the same "Commonwealth"; people have also some difficulty adapting themselves to such a scattered way of life; and officials are often lost when trying to classify according to the traditional categories of urban, rural, rural non-farm, farming, etc. Such are, too briefly reviewed, the various problems of Megalopolis. They are worth analyzing for the conclusions that may follow.

## Lessons from an Analysis of the Megalopolitan Process

A detailed analysis of Megalopolis, as it appears today, seems a worthwhile enterprise despite the present unique character of this region. Its trends acquire immediate national, and sometimes international, significance by the sheer size and weight of Megalopolis in economic and social matters. But it is also, as has been shown, a pioneering area in terms of urbanization. What is observed and experimented with here may serve, though on a smaller scale and in many cases only after some time, to avoid delays and errors in other growing urban areas. It may help improve our management of the intricate process of urbanization.

This process is an old one and has greatly contributed, as many authors have shown, to the growth of Western civilization. Far from having reached its optimum, in the middle of the twentieth century, the process of urbanization accelerated its pace. The United States has demonstrated that enough agricultural commodities of all kinds can be produced for a populous nation, enjoying a high standard of living, by the work of only one-eighth of the total population. This proportion of the farmers within the nation may and probably will be further reduced. Thus 90 per cent of a prosperous nation must live from non-agricultural pursuits, but not in congested slums. This momentous evolution, one of the major American contributions to this century, leading to semiurbanized status, is most advanced in Megalopolis.[3]

The new forms thus attained, the intensity of the problems, the solutions attempted, must be compared to what happens in all these respects in other principal metropolitan areas in the United States and perhaps in Canada. A clearer mode of classification for both problems and possible solutions may thus be worked out, based on factual observation rather than generalized theory. The whole survey may help to evaluate this new expanding frontier of the American economy: the urbanization of the land.

[3] See J. Gottmann, *L'Amérique* (2d ed. rev.; Paris: Hachette, 1954), pp. 170–77 and 244–46; also "La ville américaine," in *Geographia* (Paris), No. 48 (September, 1955), pp. 9–14; and *Virginia at Mid-Century* (New York, 1955), pp. 473–79.

Outside the North American continent many other countries are already faced with a similar acceleration of the process of urbanization. Their policies could greatly benefit from a full analysis of Megalopolis today and its comparison with other urban growths in America. None of the continuous chains of metropolitan areas or conurbations shaping now in other parts of the world is indeed comparable in size or shape as yet to the American Megalopolis. The one most nearly approaching it, which may perhaps coalesce sometime within the next twenty years, would be in our opinion in northwestern Europe, from Amsterdam to Paris, including perhaps a bulge eastward as far as the Ruhr and Cologne along the Rhine and Meuse rivers.

Another possible supermetropolitan system of this kind could well be forming in England. A giant U-shaped urban chain surrounds the southern Pennines, extending from Liverpool and Manchester to Leeds and Bradford, via Birmingham and Sheffield. This U may some day unite southward with the expanding suburbs of Greater London. Then the whole system may enter the megalopolitan family. It would remain, nevertheless, quite different from Megalopolis on the northeastern seaboard. Each large area of such kind will long keep its originality, resulting from its own past and its relation to a given zone of civilization. Large urbanized areas do not need, however, to grow up to megalopolitan size to be able to profit by the lessons in metropolitan organization obtained in Megalopolis.

### How Far Could Megalopolis Grow?

Several important studies of the metropolitan areas around New York City, Philadelphia, etc., are now in progress. These surveys will attempt to forecast future growth, by projecting curves for the next ten to twenty-five years. Urban and suburban territory is expanding at a fast pace in the United States, and this pace has been notably accelerated in recent years. A vast area like Megalopolis would

not have arisen without it. The time has perhaps come to ask once more the question: How far could Megalopolis grow? And in which directions?

In 1955, a group of city planners at Yale University began to speak about a citylike, well-knit system extending from Portland, Maine, to Norfolk, Virginia. Such may be the impression provided by road transportation maps. This writer's observations on completion of a study of Virginia by January, 1955, did not sem to warrant as yet the absorption into Megalopolis of more than a few counties in northern Virginia. Richmond and the Hampton Roads area had not yet been consolidated with the Washington-to-Boston more intensely urbanized system. Beyond eastern Massachusetts northward, urbanization was felt mainly in the summer as a seasonal migration of vacationing or semivacationing people from Megalopolis. However, there could be no doubt that Megalopolis is daily expanding its territorial scope. Our definition (see Fig. 1) based on the Census of 1950 is certainly an underestimation in area for 1957.

Expansion proceeds in many directions, of course, all around the outer fringes. Consolidation of the urban land use within the 1950 limits goes on at the same time. The existing densities of population (see Fig. 2) and the trends of increase of this density by counties in the recent past (see Fig. 3) concur in stressing a relative saturation of most of the areas within Megalopolis between Philadelphia and Boston. Although a great deal of new construction still goes on even in those parts, the more striking increases appear in the southern section of Megalopolis and an expansion in the Virginia Tidewater and northern Piedmont seems unavoidable.

Thus Megalopolis is pushing southward and southwestward. It may indeed reach Richmond and Norfolk some day in the foreseeable future. Another set of directions, this time inland, and breaking away from the fateful axis of U.S. 1, may be inferred from an attentive examination of the distribution already in 1950 of the metropolitan areas in the northeastern section of the United States, between the Atlantic seaboard, the Great Lakes and the Ohio Valley (see Fig. 4). A rather impressive density of such metropolitan areas is found inland along the route of the New York Central Railroad up the Hudson-Mohawk route and the southern shores of Lakes Erie and Ontario. Then from Cleveland southward a little-interrupted chain extends toward Pittsburgh, Pennsylvania. Between Megalopolis and the trans-Appalachian urbanized and industrialized areas, the valleys and ridges of the Appalachian Mountains cause a clear-cut break. But if

the Pittsburgh-Cleveland-Syracuse-Albany chain would come to be consolidated, even mountain ranges could be overcome and an enormous sort of annular megalopolitan system could arise; the St. Lawrence Seaway, if it developed into a major artery of navigation, could precipitate such a trend.

A much smaller but curiously "annular" urban system is already shaping in the Netherlands, as after the coalescence of the cities along the main seaboard axis of Holland, from Amsterdam to Rotterdam, urbanization is gaining inland, along the Rhine from Rotterdam to Arnhem, and along roads and canals from Amsterdam to Utrecht. The coalescence between Arnhem

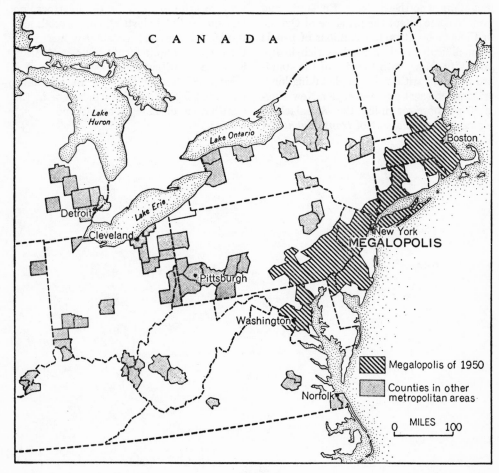

Fig. 4

and Utrecht is on its way. In England the U-shaped chain of the metropolitan type from Manchester to Leeds outlined above has not been filled up between these two cities along the shortest line into another annular formation because of the topographical obstacle of the Pennine range, still an empty area. This obstacle is comparable, though it is on a much smaller scale, to the Appalachian ridges back of Megalopolis.

Other trends of megalopolitan expansion in territory could be discussed either inside the moutainous obstacle itself or northeastward in the seaboard area. But these trends are definitely seasonal. In the past Megalopolis has in fact *emptied* the neighboring mountains, northern New England, and even to some extent the province of Quebec in Canada by attracting millions of people from difficult rural areas, less rich in opportunity. Now, with the rise of the standard of living, with more people taking longer summer vacations, the cooler New England seashore or hills, the Appalachian plateaus, attract a sort of *transhumance* of city folks to summer pastures. This transhumance seems to be constantly on the increase and creates for the summer months long-range commuting problems. If the contiguous areas, where the majority of the permanent population lives from the proceeds of summer residents and tourists, were to be included in the territorial concept of Megalopolis, the limits of our area would have to be rapidly and substantially enlarged.

Urban land utilization is indeed devouring land fast, in many ways. The old habit of considering it as a minor occupant of space will soon have to be revised. Our modern civilization has found the means to grow more and more agricultural products, to raise more and more livestock, on less space; but industrial, commercial, and residential uses are constantly increasing their space requirements. Our generation is probably witnessing the beginning of a great revolution in the geography of land use. Megalopolis heralds a new era in the distribution of habitat and economic activities.

# THE RISE AND GROWTH OF CITIES

In his paper, included in Section 1, Dickinson stresses the point that the geographical study of an urban settlement is concerned, first, with the physical and cultural conditions involved in the origin of the nucleus of settlement and, second, with the reactions of this nucleus, in its functional and morphological development, to the impact of historical events. The literature of urban geography contains numerous studies on the historical development of specific cities, many of them organized in terms of their stages of sequent occupance—a concept introduced into geography by the late Derwent Whittlesey. Few geographers, however, have taken note of the general cultural conditions involved in the origin, growth, and distribution of cities throughout the several epochs of world history. This is understandable in the development of urban geography in America because of the short span of time since the establishment of most urban places here.

An adequate explanation of the distribution, size, function, and growth of cities, as well as their layout and build, calls for an examination of the cultural conditions that were involved in their establishment and subsequent growth. This principle holds true even for the United States, where, in the short span of 150 years, an agricultural society has been replaced by a highly industrialized and urbanized way of life. To explain the present distribution of cities it is necessary, then, to review the physical and cultural conditions under which they were originally established.

Kingsley Davis, in his paper "The Origin and Growth of Urbanization in the World," suggests that it was some time between 6000 and 5000 B.C. that the first cities appeared and that by 3000 B.C. there were in existence what may be called true cities. These early cities, however, went into eclipse, and it was not until Greco-Roman times that a marked gain in city existence developed. From 600 B.C. to A.D. 400 towns and cities became more numerous and the degree of urbanization greater. The full potentialities of the ancient world to support a large city were finally realized with the Romans.

The Dark Ages, from A.D. 400 to about A.D. 1000, witnessed the collapse of cities in Europe, and it was not until the development of trade and the medieval towns after A.D. 1000 that urban centers once again became significant. The appearance of genuine urbanization, however, had to await the Industrial Revolution, when the transformation resulting from the development of industry became a true urban revolution. Since then, urbanization has gone rapidly ahead and is reaching very great proportions today, particularly in northwestern Europe and in those regions where northwestern Europeans have settled and extended their industrial civilization. Davis discusses the growth of urbanization in successive epochs of world history—prehistoric time; the ancient world; the Dark Ages; the Middle Ages; and the Age of Industrialism, which has given rise to our present metropolitan areas.

*The West European City: A Geographical Interpretation,* by Robert E. Dickinson, stands as one of the great contributions of geography to the understanding of urban development within a major part of the earth's surface. The chapter selected for reproduction in this section deals with the growth and spread of the medieval town (A.D. 1000–1500); the development of urban places during the Renaissance and Baroque periods (about 1500–1800); and the distribution of towns in 1830. Dickinson recognizes the period from 1200 to 1400 during the Middle Ages as the period when the overwhelming majority of towns in western Europe came into being. The three hundred years from 1500 to 1800 were relatively stable. Only a few new towns were founded and the proportion of urban and rural population remained fairly constant, although during this time important changes in the character and distibution of industry affected to some extent the location and growth of towns. In 1830 the distribution of towns was the same as it had been for at least five centuries, with urban centers serving primarily as centers of industry, commerce, and administration for their surrounding territories. The selection demonstrates that the present distribution, size, and growth of cities cannot be explained satisfactorily without some knowledge of their historical development.

# THE ORIGIN AND GROWTH OF URBANIZATION
# IN THE WORLD

Urban phenomena attract sociological attention primarily for four reasons. First, such phenomena are relatively recent in human history. Compared to most other aspects of society—e.g., language, religion, stratification, or the family—cities appeared only yesterday, and urbanization, meaning that a sizable proportion of the population lives in cities, has developed only in the last few moments of man's existence. Second, urbanism represents a revolutionary change in the whole pattern of social life. Itself a product of basic economic and technological developments, it tends in turn, once it comes into being, to affect every aspect of existence. It exercises its pervasive influence not only within the urban milieu strictly defined but also in the rural hinterland. The third source of sociological interest in cities is the fact that, once established, they tend to be centers of power and influence throughout the whole society, no matter how agricultural and rural it may be. Finally, the process of urbanization is still occurring; many of the problems associated with it are unsolved; and, consequently, its future direction and potentialities are still a matter of uncertainty. This paper examines the first and last points: the origin, growth, and present rate of progress of urbanization in the world. Since good statistics on urban concentration do not exist even today for substantial parts of the world, and hardly exist for any part during most of the time since cities have been in existence, we are forced to rely on whatever credible evi-

Reprinted from the *American Journal of Sociology*, LX (March, 1955), 429–37, with permission of the author and the editor. (Copyright, 1955, by the University of Chicago.)

dence can be found and so can reach only broad conclusions concerning early periods and only approximations for recent times. Nevertheless, it can be said that our information, both statistical and non-statistical, is much better today than when Adna Weber wrote his classic treatise on comparative urbanization at the turn of the present century.[1]

## THE RISE OF EARLY URBAN CENTERS

Because the archeological evidence is fragmentary, the role of cities in antiquity has often been exaggerated. Archeologists in particular are inclined to call any settlement a "city" which had a few streets and a public building or two. Yet there is surely some point in not mistaking a town for a city. Moreover, what is important is not only the appearance of a few towns or cities but also their place in the total society of which they were a part. Thus, even though in particular regions around the Mediterranean and in southern and western Asia many towns and a few cities arose prior to the Christian Era, there were severe limitations both on the size that such cities could reach and on the proportion of the total population that could live in them.

Speaking generally, one can agree with the dominant view that the diverse technological innovations constituting Neolithic culture were necessary for the existence of settled communities.[2] Yet one should not

[1] Adna F. Weber, *The Growth of Cities in the Nineteenth Century* (New York: Columbia University Press, 1899).

[2] V. Gordon Childe, *Man Makes Himself* (rev. ed.; London: Watts, 1941), chaps. v–vi; *What Happened in History* (London and New York: Penguin Books, 1946 [first printed in 1942]), chaps. iii–iv.

infer that these innovations, which began some 8,000–10,000 years ago, were sufficient to give rise to towns as distinct from villages. Even though the Neolithic population was more densely settled than the purely hunting or food-gathering peoples, it was nevertheless chiefly engaged in an occupation—agriculture—which requires a large amount of land per person. The Neolithic population density was therefore not a matter of town concentration but rather a matter of tiny villages scattered over the land.

What had to be added to the Neolithic complex to make possible the first towns? Between 6000 and 4000 B.C. certain inventions—such as the ox-drawn plow and wheeled cart, the sailboat, metallurgy, irrigation, and the domestication of new plants—facilitated, when taken together, a more intensive and more productive use of the Neolithic elements themselves. When this enriched technology was utilized in certain unusual regions where climate, soil, water, and topography were most favorable (broad river valleys with alluvial soil not exhausted by successive cropping, with a dry climate that minimized soil leaching, with plenty of sunshine, and with sediment-containing water for irrigation from the river itself), the result was a sufficiently productive economy to make possible the *sine qua non* of urban existence, the concentration in one place of people who do not grow their own food.

But a productive economy, though necessary, was not sufficient: high productivity per acre does not necessarily mean high per capita productivity. Instead of producing a surplus for town dwellers, the cultivators can, theoretically at least, multiply on the land until they end up producing just enough to sustain themselves. The rise of towns and cities therefore required, in addition to highly favorable agricultural conditions, a form of social organization in which certain strata could appropriate for themselves part of the produce grown by the cultivators. Such strata—religious and

governing officials, traders, and artisans—could live in towns, because their power over goods did not depend on their presence on the land as such. They could thus realize the advantages of town living, which gave them additional power over the cultivators.

The first cities, doubtless small and hard to distinguish from towns, seem to have appeared in the most favorable places sometime between 6000 and 5000 B.C. From that time on, it can be assumed that some of the inventions which made larger settlements possible were due to towns and cities themselves—viz., writing and accountancy, bronze, the beginnings of science, a solar calendar, bureaucracy. By 3000 B.C., when these innovations were all exercising an influence in Egypt, Mesopotamia, and India, there were in existence what may be called "true" cities. After that there appears to have been, for some 2,000 years, a lull during which the most important innovations, toward the end of the period, were alphabetic writing and the smelting of iron. Curiously, the cities in the regions where city life had originated eventually went into eclipse, and it was not until Greco-Roman times that new principles made possible, in new regions, a marked gain in city existence. The fact that the greatest subsequent cultural developments did not occur primarily in the regions where the first cities arose suggests that cities are not always and everywhere a stimulant of economic and social advance. Childe admits that, if anything, the first cities had a stultifying effect on cultural progress,[3] due perhaps to the unproductive insulation and excessive power of the urban elite. There is no doubt that the religio-magical traditionalism of the early cities was profound.

Why was there so little urbanization in ancient times, and why did it proceed so slowly from that point? The sites of the earliest "cities" themselves show that they were small affairs. The walls of ancient Babylon, for example, embraced an area of

[3] *Man Makes Himself*, p. 227.

very roughly 3.2 square miles,[4] and "Ur, with its canals, harbors, and temples, occupied some 220 acres; the walls of Erech encompass an area of just on two square miles."[5] This suggests that the famous Ur could hardly have boasted more than 5,000 inhabitants and Erech hardly more than 25,000. The mounds of Mohenjo-daro in Sind cover a square mile,[6] and Harappa in the Punjab had a walled area visible in 1853 with a perimeter of 2.5 miles.[7] These were evidently "cities" of 5,000–15,000 inhabitants, yet they were the chief centers for the entire Indus region, an area nearly two-thirds the size of Texas. Less is known about the earliest Egyptian cities, for they were built with mud bricks and have long since disappeared beneath the alluvial soil. Tell el ᶜAmarna, the temporary capital built much later, about 1400 B.C., perhaps held something like 40,000 people. The wall of Hotep-Sanusert, an earlier capital built about 1900 B.C. on the Fayum, measured 350 by 400 meters[8] and inclosed an area of approximately one-twentieth of a square mile. Thebes, at the height of its splendor as the capital of Egypt about 1600, was described by Greek writers as having a circumference of 14 miles. By a liberal estimate it may have contained 225,000 inhabitants.

To the questions why even the largest cities prior to 1000 B.C. were small by modern standards, why even the small ones were relatively few, and why the degree of urbanization even in the most advanced regions was very slight, the answer seems as follows: Agriculture was so cumbersome, static, and labor-intensive that it took many cultivators to support one man in the

[4] Deduced from data given in Marguerite Rutten, *Babylone* (Paris: Presses Universitaires de France, 1948), p. 34.

[5] Childe, *What Happened in History*, p. 87.

[6] Stuart Piggott, *Prehistoric India* (Harmondsworth: Penguin Books, 1950), p. 165.

[7] Childe, *What Happened in History*, p. 118.

[8] Pierre Montet, *La Vie quotidienne en Égypte* (Paris: Hachette, 1946), p. 16.

city. The ox-drawn plow, the wooden plowshare, inundation irrigation, stone hoes, sickles, and axes were instruments of production, to be sure, but clumsy ones. Not until iron came into use in Asia Minor about 1300 B.C. could general improvement in agriculture be achieved. The static character of agriculture and of the economy generally was fostered perhaps by the insulation of the religio-political officials from the practical arts and the reduction of the peasant to virtually the status of a beast of burden. The technology of transport was as labor-intensive as that of agriculture. The only means of conveying bulky goods for mass consumption was by boat, and, though sails had been invented, the sailboat was so inefficient that rowing was still necessary. The oxcart, with its solid wheels and rigidly attached axle, the pack animal, and the human burden-bearer were all short-distance means of transport, the only exception being the camel caravan. Long-distance transport was reserved largely for goods which had high value and small bulk—i.e., goods for the elite—which could not maintain a large urban population. The size of the early cities was therefore limited by the amount of food, fibers, and other bulky materials that could be obtained from the immediate hinterland by labor-intensive methods, a severe limitation which the Greek cities of a later period, small as they remained, nevertheless had to escape before they could attain their full size.

There were political limitations as well. The difficulty of communication and transport and the existence of multifarious local tribal cultures made the formation of large national units virtually impossible. The first urban-centered units were city-states, and when so-called "empires" were formed, as in Egypt, in the Sumerian region, and later in Assyria, much local autonomy was left to the subordinated areas, and the constant danger of revolt prevented the extension of the hinterlands of the cities very far or very effectively. It is symptomatic of the weakness of the early cities that they were constantly threatened and frequently conquered not only by neighboring towns but also by non-urban barbarians. Each wave of barbarians tended to rebuild the urban centers and to become agricultural and sedentary, only to be eventually overwhelmed in turn by new invaders. Other limiting factors were the lack of scientific medicine (which made urban living deadly), the fixity of the peasant on the land (which minimized rural-urban migration), the absence of large-scale manufacturing (which would have derived more advantage from urban concentration than did handicraft), the bureaucratic control of the peasantry (which stifled free trade in the hinterland), and the traditionalism and religiosity of all classes (which hampered technological and economic advance).

The limitations explain why we find, when the sites furnish adequate evidence, that the earliest cities were small affairs, usually no more than towns. Whether in the new or in the old world, even the biggest places could scarcely have exceeded 200,000 inhabitants, and the proportion of the total population living in them must have been not more than 1 or 2 per cent. From 50 to 90 farmers must have been required to support one man in a city.

## Subsequent City Development

If urbanization was to escape its early limitations, it had to do so in a new region, a region more open to innovation and new conceptions. As it turned out, the region that saw a later and greater urban development was farther north, the Greco-Roman world of Europe, flourishing approximately during the period from 600 B.C. to A.D. 400. Iron tools and weapons, alphabetic writing, improved sailboats, cheap coinage, more democratic institutions, systematic colonization—all tended to increase production, stimulate trade, and expand the effective political unit. Towns and cities became more numerous, the degree of urbanization greater. A few cities reached a substantial size. Athens, at its peak in the fifth century

B.C., achieved a population of between 120,000 and 180,000. Syracuse and Carthage were perhaps larger.

The full potentialities of the ancient world to support a large city were realized only with the Romans. Through their ability to conquer, organize, and govern an empire, to put the immediate Italian hinterland to fruitful cultivation, to use both force and trade to bring slaves, goods, food, and culture to the imperial capital, they were able to create in Rome (with the possible exception of Constantinople some centuries later) the largest city that was to be known in the world until the rise of London in the nineteenth century. Yet, despite the fact that Rome and Constantinople came to hold populations of several hundred thousand, they were not able to resist conquest by far less urbanized outsiders. The eclipse of cities in Europe was striking. Commerce declined to the barest minimum; each locale became isolated and virtually self-sufficient; the social system congealed into a hereditary system.[9] When finally towns and cities began to revive, they were small, as the following estimates suggest: Florence (1338), 90,000; Venice (1422), 190,000; Antwerp (sixteenth century), 200,000; London (1377), 30,000;[10] Nuremberg (1450), 20,165; Frankfort (1440), 8,719.[11]

Yet it was precisely in western Europe, where cities and urbanization had reached a nadir during the Dark Ages, that the limitations that had characterized the ancient world were finally to be overcome. The cities of Mesopotamia, India, and Egypt, of Persia, Greece, and Rome, had all been tied to an economy that was primarily agricultural, where handicraft played

[9] Henri Pirenne, *Medieval Cities* (Princeton: Princeton University Press, 1939), pp. 84–85.

[10] Pierre Clerget, "Urbanism: A Historic, Geographic, and Economic Study," *Annual Report of the Smithsonian Institution for 1912* (Washington, D.C.: Government Printing Office, 1913), p. 656.

[11] Henri Pirenne, *Economic and Social History of Medieval Europe* (London: Routledge & Kegan Paul, 1936), p. 172.

at best a secondary role and where the city was still attempting to supplement its economic weakness with military strength, to command its sustenance rather than to buy it honestly. In western Europe, starting at the zero point, the development of cities not only reached the stage that the ancient world had achieved but kept going after that. It kept going on the basis of improvements in agriculture and transport, the opening of new lands and new trade routes, and, above all, the rise in productive activity, first in highly organized handicraft and eventually in a revolutionary new form of production—the factory run by machinery and fossil fuel. The transformation thus achieved in the nineteenth century was the true urban revolution, for it meant not only the rise of a few scattered towns and cities but the appearance of genuine urbanization, in the sense that a substantial portion of the population lived in towns and cities.

## THE WORLD TREND FROM 1800 TO 1950[12]

Urbanization has, in fact, gone ahead much faster and reached proportions far greater during the past century and a half than at any previous time in world history. The tremendous growth in world trade during this period has enabled the urban population to draw its sustenance from an ever wider area. Indeed, it can truly be said that the hinterland of today's cities is the entire world. Contemporary Britain, Holland, and Japan, for example, could not maintain their urban population solely from their own territory. The number of rural inhabitants required to maintain one urban inhabitant is still great—greater than one would imagine from the rural-urban ratio *within* each of the highly urbanized coun-

[12] The writer acknowledges with pleasure the collaboration of Mrs. Hilda Hertz Golden in the statistical work on which this and succeeding sections are based. Such work has been done as part of a continuing program of comparative urban research in the population division of the Bureau of Applied Social Research, Columbia University.

tries. The reason is that much of agriculture around the world is still technologically and economically backward. Yet there can be no doubt that, whether for particular countries or for the entire globe, the ratio of urban dwellers to those who grow their food has risen remarkably. This is shown by the fact that the proportion of people living in cities in 1950 is higher than that found in any particular country prior to modern times and many times higher than that formerly characterizing the earth as a whole.

The rapidity of urbanization in recent times can be seen by looking at the most

TABLE 1

PERCENTAGE OF WORLD'S POPU-
LATION LIVING IN CITIES

|  | Cities of 20,000 or More | Cities of 100,000 or More |
|---|---|---|
| 1800........ | 2.4 | 1.7 |
| 1850........ | 4.3 | 2.3 |
| 1900........ | 9.2 | 5.5 |
| 1950........ | 20.9 | 13.1 |

urbanized country, England. In 1801, although London had already reached nearly the million mark (865,000), England and Wales had less than 10 per cent of their population in cities of 100,000 or more. By 1901 no less than 35 per cent of the population of England and Wales was living in cities of 100,000 or more, and 58 per cent was living in cities of 20,000 or more. By 1951 these two proportions had risen to 38.4 and 69.3 per cent, respectively.

Britain was in the van of urban development. A degree of urbanization equal to that she had attained in 1801 was not achieved by any other country until after 1850. Thereafter the British rate of urbanization began slowly to decline, whereas that of most other countries continued at a high level. By assembling available data and preparing estimates where data were lacking, we have arrived at figures on urbanization in the world as a whole, beginning with 1800, the earliest date for which anything like a reasonable estimate can be obtained. The percentage of the world's population found living in cities is as shown in Table 1. It can be seen that the proportion has tended to do a bit better than double itself each half-century and that by 1950 the world as a whole was considerably more urbanized than Britain was in 1800. As everyone knows, the earth's total population has grown at an extremely rapid rate since 1800, reaching 2.4 billion by 1950. But the urban population has grown much faster. In 1800 there were about 15.6 mil-

TABLE 2

PERCENTAGE OF WORLD'S POPULATION
LIVING IN CITIES, BY REGIONS

| | In Cities of 20,000 Plus | In Cities of 100,000 Plus |
|---|---|---|
| World.................. | 21 | 13 |
| Oceania................. | 47 | 41 |
| North America (Canada and U.S.A.)............ | 42 | 29 |
| Europe (except U.S.S.R.).. | 35 | 21 |
| U.S.S.R................. | 31 | 18 |
| South America........... | 26 | 18 |
| Middle America and Caribbean................. | 21 | 12 |
| Asia (except U.S.S.R.).... | 13 | 8 |
| Africa.................. | 9 | 5 |

lion people living in cities of 100,000 or more. By 1950 it was 313.7 million, more than twenty times the earlier figure. Much of this increase has obviously come from rural-urban migration, clearly the most massive migration in modern times.

In 1800 there were apparently less than 50 cities with 100,000 or more inhabitants. This was less than the number in the million class today and less than the number of 100,000-plus cities currently found in many single countries. By 1950 there were close to 900 cities of 100,000 or more people, which is more than the number of towns and cities of 5,000 or more in 1800.

As yet there is no indication of a slackening of the rate of urbanization in the world as a whole. If the present rate should con-

tinue, more than a fourth of the earth's people will be living in cities of 100,000 or more in the year 2000, and more than half in the year 2050. For places of 20,000 or more, the proportions at the two dates would be something like 45 per cent and 90 per cent. Whether such figures prove too low or too high, they nevertheless suggest that the human species is moving rapidly in the direction of an almost exclusively urban existence. We have used the proportion of the population in cities of 20,000 and 100,000 or more as a convenient index of differences and changes in degree of urbanization. Places of less than 20,000 also fit a demographic definition of "urban." When, therefore, more than a third of the population of a country lives in cities of the 100,000 class (38.4 per cent in England and Wales in 1951), the country can be described as almost completely urbanized (81 per cent being designated as "urban" in the English case in 1951). We thus have today what can be called "urbanized societies," nations in which the great majority of inhabitants live in cities. The prospect is that, as time goes on, a greater and greater proportion of humanity will be members of such societies.

The question may be raised as to how such an extreme degree of world urbanization will prove possible. Who will grow the food and fibers necessary for the enormous urban population? The answer is that agriculture may prove to be an archaic mode of production. Already, one of the great factors giving rise to urbanization is the rather late and as yet very incomplete industrialization of agriculture. As farming becomes increasingly mechanized and rationalized, fewer people are needed on the land. On the average, the more urbanized a country, the lower is its rural density.[13] If,

[13] See Kingsley Davis and Hilda Hertz, "Urbanization and the Development of Pre-industrial Areas," *Economic Development and Cultural Change*, III (October, 1954), 6–26. See also the writer's paper, "Population and the Further Spread of Industrial Society," *Proceedings of the American Philosophical Society*, XCV (February, 1951), 10–13.

in addition to industrialized agriculture, food and fiber come to be increasingly produced by manufacturing processes using materials that utilize the sun's energy more efficiently than plants do, there is no technological reason why nearly all of mankind could not live in conurbations of large size.

## THE REGIONAL PATTERN OF URBANIZATION

The highest levels of urbanization are found today in northwestern Europe and in those new regions where northwest Europeans have settled and extended their industrial civilization. The figures are as shown in Table 2.[14] Oceania is the most urbanized of the world's major regions, because Australia and New Zealand are its principal components. North America is next, if it is defined as including only Canada and the United States. The regions least urbanized are those least affected by northwest European culture, namely, Asia and Africa.

The figures for world regions are less valuable for purposes of analysis than are those for individual countries. The latter show clearly that urbanization has tended to reach its highest point wherever economic productivity has been greatest—that is, where the economy is industrialized and rationalized. This explains why urbanization is so closely associated with northwest Europeans and their culture, since they were mainly responsible for the Industrial Revolution. Of the fifteen most urbanized countries in the world, all but one, Japan, are European in culture, and all but four derive that culture from the northwest or central part of Europe.

The rate of urbanization in the older industrial countries, however, is slowing down. During the twenty years from 1870 to 1890 Germany's proportion in large cities more than doubled; it nearly doubled again from 1890 to 1910; but from 1910

14 From Kingsley Davis and Hilda Hertz, "The World Distribution of Urbanization," *Bulletin of the International Statistical Institute,* XXXIII, Part IV, 230.

to 1940 the increase was only 36 per cent. In Sweden the gain slowed down noticeably after 1920. In England and Wales the most rapid urbanization occurred between 1811 and 1851. Contrary to popular belief, the fastest rate in the United States occurred between 1861 and 1891. Since, as we noted earlier, there has been no slowing-down of urbanization in the world as a whole, it must be that, as the more established industrial countries have slackened, the less-developed countries have exhibited a faster rate. In fact, such historical evidence as we have for underdeveloped areas seems to show that their rates of urbanization have been rising in recent decades. This has been the case in Egypt, where the rate is higher after 1920 than before; in India, where the fastest urbanization has occurred since 1941; in Mexico, where the speed-up began in 1921; and in Greece, where the fastest period ran from 1900 to 1930. Asia, for example, had only 22 per cent of the world's city population in 1900 but 34 per cent of it in 1950, and Africa had 1.5 per cent in 1900 but 3.2 per cent at the later date.

With respect to urbanization, then, the gap between the industrial and the preindustrial nations is beginning to diminish. The less-developed parts of the world will eventually, it seems, begin in their turn to move gradually toward a saturation point. As the degree of urbanization rises, it of course becomes impossible for the rate of gain to continue. The growth in the urban proportion is made possible by the movement of people from rural areas to the cities. As the rural population becomes a progressively smaller percentage of the total, the cities no longer can draw on a noncity population of any size. Yet in no country can it be said that the process of urbanization is yet finished. Although there have been short periods in recent times in England, the United States, and Japan when the city population increased at a slightly slower rate than the rural, these were mere interludes in the ongoing but ever slower progress of urban concentration.

## THE TENDENCY TOWARD METROPOLITAN EXPANSION

The continuance of urbanization in the world does not mean the persistence of something that remains the same in detail. A city of a million inhabitants today is not the sort of place that a city of the same number was in 1900 or in 1850. Moreover, with the emergence of giant cities of five to fifteen million, something new has been added. Such cities are creatures of the

TABLE 3

PERCENTAGE INCREASE IN POPULATION IN 44 METROPOLITAN DISTRICTS IN THE UNITED STATES, 1900–1940

|           | Central Cities | Rest of Districts |
|-----------|---------------|-------------------|
| 1900–1910... | 33.6 | 38.2 |
| 1910–20..... | 23.4 | 31.3 |
| 1920–30..... | 20.5 | 48.7 |
| 1930–40..... | 4.2 | 13.0 |

twentieth century. Their sheer quantitative difference means a qualitative change as well.

One of the most noticeable developments is the ever stronger tendency of cities to expand outward—a development already observed in the nineteenth century. Since 1861, the first date when the comparison can be made, the Outer Ring of Greater London has been growing more rapidly than London itself. French writers prior to 1900 pointed out the dispersive tendency,[15] as did Adna Weber in 1899.[16] There is no doubt, however, that the process of metropolitan dispersion has increased with time. This fact is shown for the United States by comparing the percentage gains in population made by the central cities with those made by their satellite areas in forty-four metropolitan districts for which Thompson could get comparable data going back to 1900. The gains are as shown in Table 3.[17] The difference increases, until in 1930–40 the population outside the central city is growing more than three times as fast as that inside the central city. Furthermore, Thompson has shown that *within the metropolitan area outside the central cities* it was the "rural" parts which gained faster than the urban parts, as the percentage increases per decade shown in Table 4, indicate. Clearly, the metropolitan districts were increasingly dependent on the areas

TABLE 4

PERCENTAGE POPULATION INCREASE OUTSIDE CENTRAL CITIES IN 44 METROPOLITAN DISTRICTS

|           | Urban Parts | Rural Parts |
|-----------|-------------|-------------|
| 1900–1910... | 35.9 | 43.2 |
| 1910–20..... | 30.2 | 34.5 |
| 1920–30..... | 40.6 | 68.1 |
| 1930–40..... | 7.3 | 28.1 |

outside the central cities, and especially upon the sparsely settled parts at the periphery of these areas, for their continued growth. Thompson showed that, the greater the distance from the center of the city, the faster the rate of growth.[18]

The same forces which have made extreme urbanization possible have also made metropolitan dispersion possible, and the dispersion itself has contributed to further urbanization by making large conurbations

15 Paul Meuriot, *Des agglomérations urbaines dans l'Europe contemporaine* (Paris: Bélin Frères, 1898), pp. 249–78. Literature on the movement of industry and people to the periphery of cities is cited, and a theoretical discussion of the subject given, in René Maunier, *L'Origine et la fonction économique des villes* (Paris: Giard & Brière, 1910), pp. 231–314.

16 *Op. cit.*, pp. 458–75.

17 Warren S. Thompson, *The Growth of Metropolitan Districts in the United States, 1900–1940* (Washington, D.C.: Government Printing Office, 1948), p. 5. The picture is much the same for the rest of the metropolitan districts for decades in which comparability could be established.

18 *Ibid.*, p. 9.

more efficient and more endurable. The outward movement of urban residences, of urban services and commercial establishments, and of light industry—all facilitated by improvements in motor transport and communications—has made it possible for huge agglomerations to keep on growing without the inconveniences of proportionate increases in density. In many ways the metropolis of three million today is an easier place to live and work in than the city of five hundred thousand yesterday. Granted that the economic advantages of urban concentration still continue and still push populations in the direction of urbanization, the effect of metropolitan dispersion is thus to minimize the disadvantages of this continued urban growth.

The new type of metropolitan expansion occurring in the highly industrial countries is not without its repercussions in less-developed lands as well. Most of the rapid urbanization now occurring in Africa and Asia, for example, is affected by direct contact with industrial nations and by a concomitant rise in consumption standards. Although private automobiles may not be available to the urban masses, bicycles and busses generally are. Hence Brazzaville and Abidjan, Takoradi and Nairobi, Jamshedpur and New Delhi, Ankara and Colombo, are not evolving in the same manner as did the cities of the eighteenth and nineteenth centuries. Their ecological pattern, their technological base, their economic activity, all reflect the twentieth century, no matter how primitive or backward their hinterlands may be. Thus the fact that their main growth is occurring in the present century is not without significance for the kind of cities they are turning out to be.

## FUTURE TRENDS IN WORLD URBANIZATION

Speculation concerning the future of urbanization is as hazardous as that concerning any other aspect of human society. Following the direction of modern trends, however, one may conclude that, with the Industrial Revolution, for the first time in history urbanization began to reach a stage from which there was no return. The cities of antiquity were vulnerable, and the degree of urbanization reached was so thin in many societies as to be transitory. Today virtually every part of the world is more urbanized than any region was in antiquity. Urbanization is so widespread, so much a part of industrial civilization, and gaining so rapidly, that any return to rurality, even with major catastrophes, appears unlikely. On the contrary, since every city is obsolescent to some degree—more obsolescent the older it is—the massive destruction of many would probably add eventually to the impetus of urban growth.

The fact that the rate of world urbanization has shown no slackening since 1800 suggests that we are far from the end of this process, perhaps not yet at the peak. Although the industrial countries have shown a decline in their rates, these countries, because they embrace only about a fourth of the world's population, have not dampened the world trend. The three-fourths of humanity who live in underdeveloped countries are still in the early stages of an urbanization that promises to be more rapid than that which occurred earlier in the areas of northwest European culture.

How urbanized the world will eventually become is an unanswerable question. As stated earlier, there is no apparent reason why it should not become as urbanized as the most urban countries today—with perhaps 85–90 per cent of the population living in cities and towns of 5,000 or more and practicing urban occupations. Our present degree of urbanization in advanced countries is still so new that we have no clear idea of how such complete world urbanization would affect human society; but the chances are that the effects would be profound.

In visualizing the nature and effects of complete urbanization in the future, however, one must guard against assuming that cities will retain their present form. The tendency to form huge metropolitan aggregates which are increasingly decentralized will undoubtedly continue but probably will not go so far as to eliminate the central business district altogether, though it may greatly weaken it. At the periphery, it may well be that the metropolis and the countryside, as the one expands and the other shrinks, will merge together, until the boundaries of one sprawling conurbation will touch those of another, with no intervening pure countryside at all. The world's population doubles itself twice in a century, becoming at the same time highly urbanized, and as new sources of energy are tapped, the possibility of centrifugal metropolitan growth is enormously enhanced. If commuting to work could be done with the speed of sound and cheaply, one would not mind living two hundred miles from work. Almost any technological advance from now on is likely to contribute more to the centrifugal than to the centripetal tendency. It may turn out that urbanization in the sense of emptying the countryside and concentrating huge numbers in little space will reverse itself—not, however, in the direction of returning people to the farm but rather in that of spreading them more evenly over the land for purposes of residence and industrial work. "Rurality" would have disappeared, leaving only a new kind of urban existence.

ROBERT E. DICKINSON

# THE GROWTH OF THE HISTORIC CITY

THE GROWTH AND SPREAD OF
THE MEDIEVAL TOWN
(*ca.* A.D. 1000–1500)

Europe, as a whole, has experienced four great periods of urban growth, and each gave rise to a special type of city that reflected its civilization. Greek civilization began in the Aegean lands, and there its earliest city-states were located, while the Greek colonial city was founded on the coast lands of the Mediterranean, especially in southern Italy. Roman civilization spread the city idea not only throughout the Mediterranean but also, for the first time, to the mainland of Europe north of the Alps, throughout Gaul as far as the Rhine, throughout southern Europe as far as the Danube, and across the English Channel to the lowland zone of Britain. Then followed the Dark Ages, when urban life and traditions north of the Alps all but disappeared for over five hundred years (*ca.* A.D. 500–1000). The next great phase of urban growth commenced with the turn of the millennium. From A.D. 1000 to 1400 there occurred in western and central Europe on the one hand, and in central Russia on the other, a great expansion of the human habitat and a marked growth of population. The concept of the town developed anew in Gaul and in the Rhineland. By 1400 the whole of western and central Europe was covered with towns and villages. The sphere of western settlement reached north to latitude 60° to the edge of the coniferous forest and the winter frozen seas, and to the east, in the great

Reprinted from *The West European City: A Geographical Interpretation*, chap. 15, pp. 270–300, with permission of the author and publisher. (Copyright, 1951, Routledge & Kegan Paul, Ltd., London.)

borderland of central Europe, it merged into the forested lands of the Slavs and the semiarid steppes of the Magyars and Tatars. The overwhelming majority of the settlements of today, throughout the whole of western, central, and southern Europe, were in existence at the end of the Middle Ages. Thereafter, from about 1500 to 1800, relatively few new towns came into being. The main areas of town building in this period were Poland, Scandinavia, and, above all, the steppes of southern Russia and the middle and lower Danube lands. In western and central Europe this period was one of relative stability, the most marked growth being in the capital and court cities and in the ports.

The second great phase of urban growth took place during the nineteenth century. The Industrial Revolution had its beginnings in England and in the adjacent countries of the Continental mainland in the last decades of the previous century. In the middle of the nineteenth century began the modern phase of coal and iron, the railway, and the steam-driven factory. The great increase of urban population after 1850 reached its peak in western Europe about 1900. By then there were already signs that the rate of increase was slowing down. In the first half of the twentieth century there has been a marked decline in the birth rate in all the countries of western and central Europe, as opposed to the Slav and Magyar lands to the east.

These two latest phases have been named the paleotechnic and neotechnic eras by Patrick Geddes, and he referred to the long preceding era, from about the turn of the millennium to the end of the eighteenth century, as the eotechnic era. This broad classification characterizes the main phases in the development of Western civilization and is based on what Lewis Mumford has called the "technics of civilization."[1] The eotechnic era, characterized in terms of power and its dominant materials, is based on a water and wood complex. It is the era of handicrafts. The paleotechnic era began with the Industrial Revolution and is a coal and iron complex. It is the era of the steam engine. The neotechnic era is an electricity and alloy complex, and began in the last decades of the nineteenth century. It is the era of the dynamo, the electric railway, light and power. Here we shall deal with the spread and growth of the historic city down to the onset of the modern growth of urban populations in the nineteenth century.

With the end of the Roman Empire urban life declined and almost disappeared. This was the case even in the bishops' centers that were huddled within the walls of the Roman *castra* in Gaul and on the Rhine, and on the sites of preceding Germanic settlements in western Germany beyond the Rhine, east as far as the Elbe–Saale rivers. The end of the millennium was marked by great changes heralding the beginning of a new phase of urban growth. The countryside was covered with new fortresses, especially at its more vulnerable route centers, while the existing Roman walls were repaired or extended as a protection from the attacks of Northmen, Huns, and Saracens. Long-distance trade was also revived, and the merchant came into being. He traveled in companies across the continent, seeking depots and protection under the aegis of the stronghold whose lords and clerics he supplied with luxuries. Finally, the great era of forest clearance brought about the spread of farming, and, with it, the growth of crafts and of local trade. Thus there came into being a new type of settlement that consisted of a stronghold of emperor, lord, or bishop, with a mercantile community outside it. The latter, already enjoying special privileges, became the nucleus of the nascent urban community, which was engaged in trade and crafts and sought independence from overlords by demanding the privileges of self-government. The mercantile settlements appeared first in the tenth and early eleventh centuries, on the rivers of northern France and Flanders and on the great west-east routeway in Germany from Cologne to Magdeburg. Gradually during the twelfth century these settlements obtained rights of self-government. By 1150 the term *civitas*, after a long period during which varied meanings had been attached to it, was used to designate the medieval town. According to the historians the medieval town had three essential and universal characteristics—its population was primarily engaged in industry and trade; it had a distinct legal constitution; and it was a center of administration and a fortress.[2]

These early towns were few in number and were situated at the outstanding nodal points, where overland natural routeways and navigable rivers converged. They were particularly numerous in northern France and Flanders, and they had a fairly even distribution in southern France. In the German lands there were two main axes of these towns, along the Rhine and along the northern border of the central uplands from Cologne to Magdeburg. Two other lines of eastward penetration followed by towns were the Main Valley (Würzburg and Bamberg), and the Danube lowland, where

---

[1] Lewis Mumford, *Technics and Civilization* (1934), p. 110.

[2] H. Pirenne, *Les villes du moyen âge* (1927), p. 153. This definition is true for those full-fledged towns which unquestionably enjoyed this stature. But there were hundreds of small towns at the end of the Middle Ages, covering most of the lands, in which these essential traits of the *civitas* did not always occur in combination. Since the historian is primarily interested in the development of institutions, he is concerned mainly with the early and chief towns. But the geographer is concerned with *all* towns and other urban and rural settlements of a region. The traits of the medieval town within the meaning of the above definition varied from region to region in their historical development, and generalizations obscure the realities.

Vienna appeared as the most easterly outpost in 1107.

The overwhelming majority of the towns, however, came into being during the period from about 1200 to 1400. Though often today much smaller in size than their predecessors, they cover and serve directly most of the countryside. These towns drew their law, as a rule, from the pattern of the law of one of the older "parent" cities. They came into being in many ways—as a parasitic settlement around a church or a castle, as a deliberate foundation *de novo*, as a market settlement with elementary rights of self-government, or, much more rarely, as a village that gradually acquired one or more of the privileges of a town. Down to 1200 town life had not reached beyond the Elbe and the Saale, but with the eastward spread of German colonization and trade the overwhelming majority of the towns of eastern Germany, central Europe, and the Baltic shores came into being as deliberate foundations. They derived their law from the chief cities in the west, above all from Lübeck and Magdeburg. Even the towns of indigenous growth in Russia based their law on the German pattern. The smaller towns of western Europe were the result of a slower and more complicated development. Although towns with distinctive rectilinear patterns were founded in all regions, it was in southern France that they were most conspicuous. Here Montauban, founded in 1144, was the prototype of hundreds of *bastides* that were built by both French and English during the Hundred Years' War.

From the end of the twelfth century the overwhelming majority of towns were established on the models of the earlier towns by the grant of *charters*. These charters contained privileges of exemption from feudal dues and rights of self-government. The liberties were at first of an elementary kind but were often followed by advanced liberties of full self-government. The charters were based upon the law of existing old towns, and throughout western and central Europe the law of certain of these old towns served as a standard for new foundations. There was a spread of crafts in the countryside, free from the restrictions of the guilds, and this tended to increase the activities of the towns as local seats for their organization.

The towns of France and England were not usually created *de novo* by deliberate foundation. They acquired rights of self-government gradually, and privileges were often extended to existing communities, many of which were villages, or at any rate semirural in character. More than half the towns of France had their origin in a village, a castle, or an abbey, and grew to be *bourgs* (the French equivalent of a small town or townlet), some of which attained full town status in the Middle Ages. Their origins mostly date back to the early Middle Ages (900–1200), when France bristled with abbeys and feudal castles, and full town status was acquired during the thirteenth century.

In France, Louis VI (1108–37) founded the small town of Lorres in the upper Loire Valley, and its charter became a pattern for many others. The king's charter assured to every settler a house and a lot at a fixed rent, and if he remained there for a year and a day, he was henceforth a free man. The settler was also released from feudal restrictions such as tallage, military service, and forced labor. He could not be brought to trial outside the town and was tried in it by a fixed legal procedure. Fines and punishments were limited. This charter was adopted by later kings and barons in numerous small settlements in northern France. The *bastides* were similarly founded in southern France, and many of them derived their charters from the pattern of the most famous of them all, Montauban.

In England such privileges were granted by charter in the same period. The Normans brought in special laws that were derived from a place called Breteuil. These were granted to a number of new places established along the Welsh frontier and were even carried into Ireland, although many of the places never developed as towns and show little trace of a systematic layout of house lots. About the same time, Henry I (1100–1135) founded several towns, among which were Verneuil in Normandy and Newcastle in England. The king had a castle overlooking the Tyne and granted a group of liberties so as to attract settlers to it. Immigrant peasants were to enjoy freedom after a residence of one year and a day, and these men, known as burgesses, were to be free of servile feudal obligations and to have the right of buying and selling land in the town. Within the town they had special privileges, including a monopoly on the right to trade. They were also to enjoy their own legal privileges. These liberties were extended to many other places in northern England and Scotland.

Town life in England developed slowly in the English lowland. Here developed the English kingdom, and its relative security accounts for the rarity of the strong castle as the seat of crystallization of a town. Very different were the circumstances and character of urban development in the "frontier" lands of Scotland, Wales, and Ireland. The English entered here as conquerors and imposed their civilization upon the native cultures. Law and order had to be maintained among recalcitrant tribes. The Roman *castrum* was established in the nearer border zones of the English Lowland to the north and east. After the Norman Conquest many castles were established in the "marchlands," as elsewhere in the frontier zones of western and central Europe. The Scottish rulers developed an independent pattern of urban life in which the wall and the castle were important elements as means of defense from turbulent neighbors. The conquest of Wales by the English led to the foundation of many small new "towns" adjacent to castles as foreign islands among the Welsh folk. The same story is, in part, true in Ireland and Scotland, except that here the foundation of towns continued in the seventeenth and eighteenth centuries. These are themes that call for further investigation.

The development of small towns in Germany was more tardy than in France and England, and high authority played a more important part in their origins. The first new towns were established during the twelfth century. Freiburg-im-Breisgau was established as a market settlement (*forum*) and was settled by *mercatores* in 1120. It served as a model for many others in south Germany, while Lübeck, originally founded in 1158, served as a model for the Hanseatic towns. In the early Middle Ages imperial power was strong in Germany; the powers of the dukes, bishops, and local lords were very limited, and they were not allowed to erect any independent fortifications. Not until after 1200, with the decline of the imperial power, did feudal anarchy run amok in Germany. Then the land was split up into rags and tatters, and castles and fortress towns were established all over the countryside by the local lords, as castles had been established in France at an earlier date. Between 1200 and 1400, towns appeared in hundreds, serving as centers of local market trade and long-distance trade, and answering to the need for defense and administration of the territories of their petty lords.

To the east of the Elbe and Saale lay the great borderlands between the Baltic and the Black Seas in which western merges into eastern Europe. This zone includes the east Baltic provinces, Poland, and Lithuania, north of the great swirl of the Carpathians and the lands of the Danube basin to the south. Here isolated and backward peoples in the forest and marsh of the north, the Ukraine steppe, and the Danube lands, were affected tardily by culture contacts from both Western and Byzantine cultures. These peoples were the Finns, Esths, Letts, Lithuanians and Poles to the north of the Carpathians, and the Magyars, Rumanians, and Slavs to the south. Western influences, with which we are directly concerned, were those of Roman Catholicism, trade contacts, and the Germanic idea of the town as a self-governing community of traders and craftsmen. The eastern in-

fluences took the form of the Eastern Or-
thodox faith, that was accepted by the
Russian states through Kiev from Constantinople. Here, too, there prevailed the over-
lordship of rulers with their seats in their
"towns," in which clustered castles, nobles'
residences and churches. There was little
economic activity and no independent concept of town government by a homogeneous
economic class except insofar as, in the
later Middle Ages, German traders who
had settled there were granted self-government on the pattern of the German town
law. Poland and Hungary accepted western Catholicism about A.D. 1000. In the
Danube plains, which were controlled by
the Turks from the middle of the fifteenth
century for three hundred years, town development was retarded until the late eighteenth century. Cultural infiltration was
effected from the west throughout this zone
during the Middle Ages, primarily by the
Germans in the center and by the Swedes
in the extreme north, in Finland.

In all these lands there is the same sequence of urban growth. Christianity was
spread by the establishment of bishoprics
in Poland, Bohemia, Hungary and the
northwest of the Balkans, in the eleventh
century. Defense and territorial organization by native rulers gave the first impetus
to the establishment of fixed centers of
settlement, and in some of these the bishoprics were situated. Regular long-distance
and local market trade developed later, and
the spread of the town as a self-governing
entity with German law came at varying
dates after the lapse of about two hundred
and fifty years.

Poland and Bohemia in the early Middle
Ages (ninth to eleventh centuries) had
many periodical markets, places of pagan
worship, and communal strongholds scattered over the countryside. Some of these
were selected as seats of permanent settlement with the introduction of Christianity
and the establishment of permanent trading
centers around cathedral, church, and
castle. This penetration was effected from
the west. But town life in the sense of self-

governing economic communities did not
appear till the middle of the thirteenth
century, especially after the last great in-
cursions of the Mongols. Then towns, large
and small, were founded in the western
provinces. In this period of the mid-thir-
teenth century the foundation of Poznań,
Breslau, Warsaw, Cracow, and many others
took place. Particularly deep was the German penetration along the foreland of the
Carpathians, where Lvov (Lemberg) was
established as the most remote German
town, and into the Carpathians (the Zips
area) and Transylvania (the Siebenbürgen
area), where the towns maintain their remarkably distinctive Germanic character,
in historic architecture and culture traits,
to this day.

Brief reference should be made to the
spread and growth of the town in the lands
around the Baltic Sea, in both Scandinavia
and the east Baltic lands. Here urban life
developed tardily, and the concept of the
town as an economic and self-governing
community was derived in the thirteenth
century from the German lands. Bishoprics
were first established in Denmark in the
middle of the tenth century, and attention
was then directed to the pagan lands across
the waters. Sees appeared at Lund on the
southern tip of the peninsula, and at Trondheim, Bergen, Stavanger, and Oslo, in the
early eleventh century, with a later establishment inland at Hamar. The Goths in
the present provinces of West and East
Gothland early accepted Christianity, and
bishoprics were established at Skara and
Linköping. But the Svears in the region of
Mälardalen clung hard to paganism, and
Christianity did not effectively spread there
until late in the twelfth century, when bishoprics appear at (Gamla) Uppsala, Sträng-
näs, and Västerås. In the east Baltic lands
there was no Christian penetration until
after A.D. 1200.

Trade, like settlement, had its beginnings
on the shores of these northern lands, where
ports collected the furs and skins of the
forested hinterland and engaged in fishing
the herrings of the coasts of southwestern

Norway and southern Sweden.[3] The first seats of urban settlement in Denmark before A.D. 1000 avoided the coasts, seeking the interior of peninsula and islands. Most of the later towns lay on the coasts, at bridgeheads at the heads of the bays, especially on the eastern coast of Jutland, where they were sheltered and lay on the main north-south routes. They also enjoyed the protection of castles against the Wendish pirates of the day. Copenhagen itself enters history in 1013, its castle, built in 1165, being founded by Waldemar the Great as part of this system of coastal defenses.

The principal medieval towns of Norway lay on the southwestern coast: Trondheim, Bergen, Stavanger. Their trade was mainly in fish, and their contacts were almost entirely southward along the coast to the German mainland. Urban growth was much more tardy in the lowlands around the Oslo bay at the head of the Kattegat. Oslo, though it existed as a settlement in the eleventh century, did not develop significantly until the fifteenth, and this seems to have been true of other towns, such as Tönsberg and Porsgrund. Their growth was associated, above all, with the export of timber to the shipbuilding yards of the towns on the European mainland.

Sweden during the Middle Ages looked eastward to the Baltic. The early growth of the towns of the Mälardalen region, the heart of the Swedish state, was associated, above all, with the establishment of bishoprics and the growth of trade. Before 1200 these towns were economically insignificant. Those of central and southern Sweden owed their growth in the thirteenth and fourteenth centuries not only to the establishment of churches and monasteries but also to the development of trade and industry. Of particular importance was the development of metallurgy in the Bergs-

lagen, the district lying northwest of Lake Mälar, which in the later Middle Ages attracted many German mining settlers. The province of Schonen in the extreme southwest of the peninsula belonged to Denmark throughout the Middle Ages and was early brought into the sphere of Christian culture, with its ancient capital at Lund. This place became a bishopric in 1048, an archbishopric in 1104, and was made by Canute the Great into the capital of his eastern empire. Many castles and fortified towns were founded in this territory to preserve the lands for the Danish crown, and ports developed on the southern coast after 1200 to exploit the herring fisheries.

This brief survey of northern Europe brings into the picture only those centers that appeared as outstanding seats of culture and trade in the early Middle Ages and after. In fact the great majority of the small towns of Scandinavia south of latitude 60° appeared later in the fourteenth and fifteenth centuries. They grew up as seats of local market trade, as centers for the felling of timber, mining, and fishing, especially on the southwestern coasts of Sweden (which until the seventeenth century were Danish territories hotly contested by Sweden), and as fortress towns.

The east Baltic lands were occupied by backward pagan peoples—Finns, Esths, Letts, Lithuanians, and Prussians. Here was a field for militant missionary endeavor, that was exploited by the Teutonic Order. These lands, however, were remote from Germany and Scandinavia and were barren lands of marsh and forest. But, more important, they controlled the routeways from the Baltic shores eastward to Russia and the Black Sea. These two factors, the spread of Christianity and of trade, controlled the development of these provinces in the Middle Ages. The earliest towns which (with the exception of Helsinki) became the chief towns of today are all situated on the coast; not one appears, even in its incipient origins, before 1200, and not one was well established before the middle of the thirteenth century.

[3] On early routeways and their relation to urban development see J. B. Leighley, *The Towns of Mälardalen in Sweden: A Study in Urban Morphology* ("University of California Publications in Geography," Vol. III, No. 1 [1928]).

Medieval Livonia corresponded with the modern states of Estonia and Latvia. It derived its name from the fact that it fell to the Livonian Order from Visby at the beginning of the thirteenth century. Occupation by the Order began with the foundation of Riga, which became thenceforth its greatest commercial center. The coastal towns of Riga and Reval commanded the routes eastward to Russia, via the Gulf of Finland, the river Neva, and Lake Ladoga, and via the Duna Valley to Polotsk and Vitebsk, respectively, while Dorpat controlled the routes from Reval and Riga to Pskov and Novgorod. These three Hanseatic cities dominated the remaining urban centers, which were relatively small and quite unimportant. Narva could not rival Reval. Pernau lay aside from the main routes, and Mitau could not rival Riga. All these were German towns.[4]

Town life in Finland was strictly limited to the coastal fringe that was touched at Åbo by the sailing route from Visby and Stockholm and lay in constant contact with Reval. Throughout the Middle Ages the life of Finland was dominated by Sweden, whose influence had its point of penetration and organization in Åbo in the southwestern corner of the fringe. But Åbo did not appear as a full-fledged town until about 1300, and Viborg, the smaller fortress town in the southeastern corner, not until the fourteenth century. These two towns belonged to the net of Hanseatic

[4] "The Livonian towns were not Hansa factories like those in Novgorod itself, in Bruges, London or Bergen. They were settlements of Germans, having the same commercial culture as the north German towns themselves, and having also their own interests independent of Lübeck. They had as well their own political relations to watch over —with the Order, with the bishops, with authorities in Sweden and Finland and in Russian territory. They had their conflicts of interest among themselves. Lacking continuous land connection with the territory on which the north German towns were established, they became Livonian towns first and Hanseatic towns only secondarily" (J. B. Leighley, *The Towns of Medieval Livonia* ["University of California Publications in Geography," Vol. VI, No. 7 (1939)], p. 243).

trade and culture. Low German was their lingua franca, as throughout the Hanseatic realm from Bruges to Novgorod, and the Swedish authorities in these Finnish towns were in constant contact with the town council in Reval. There were only five other medieval towns on this Finnish littoral; these appeared during the latter half of the fourteenth century and were of very little significance.

### THE SIZE OF THE MEDIEVAL TOWN

The emergence of the new mercantile community in the tenth century and the shift of people—merchants, craftsmen, cultivators, nobles, and clerics—from the countryside to the towns to enjoy their manifold privileges, was one of the great revolutionary changes in the economic and social history of Europe. Here we have emphasized the beginnings. During the thirteenth and fourteenth centuries urban life experienced its florescence. Great commercial and industrial emporiums grew. Numerous small towns served as local seats of trade, industry, and defense. In the later Middle Ages long-distance trade grew in the northern lands, under the direction of the Hanseatic League, and in the Mediterranean lands under that of the Italian city-states, especially Venice. The transcontinental trade routes grew in importance, both from the Mediterranean shores across France and across the Alpine passes through Germany, along the Rhine Valley and the Hessian corridor to the cities of Flanders and the Hanseatic ports of north Germany, respectively. East-west routes were also important for trade from western Europe to the Slav lands and the east, through such great emporiums as Cracow, Breslau, Vienna, and Belgrade. It was under such circumstances that the large cities of western and central Europe developed, their size being proportional to the importance of the trade on the routes that centered on them.

Decline did not set in until the fifteenth century, for a variety of complicated causes that we cannot fully discuss here. Suffice it to note that the shift of trade from the land routes to the ocean, the blocking of routes across southeastern Europe and Asia by the Turkish conquests, and, finally, the decline in the efficiency of government in the cities themselves, all contributed to their economic sterility and decline. The founding of villages and towns and the growth of population waned during the fourteenth century,[5] and for the next three centuries there set in a period of relative stability in social and economic life, although there were violent short-period fluctuations. Gustav Schmoller has written of the medieval German Reich:

One can almost say that the picture of the open country and of the towns, at least in its main features, was not changed from 1350 to 1750. There was not much more forest clearance, the number of villages decreased rather than increased and their population grew scarcely at all, and very few new towns appeared. Almost all the towns declined rather than increased in the period from 1250 to 1800.[6]

As for the size of the medieval towns, it has been calculated that at the end of the Middle Ages the population of the Holy Roman Empire was about 12 million, of whom some 10 to 15 per cent lived in towns. There were not far short of 3,000 towns in the Reich, and 12 to 15 of these had over 10,000 inhabitants. Six, according to Sanders,[7] exceeded 20,000, and only Cologne and Lübeck had more than 30,000 inhabitants. From 15 to 20 had between 2,000 and 10,000 inhabitants, and about 150 had from 1,000 to 2,000 inhabitants.

The remainder, some 2,800, had between 100 and 1,000 inhabitants, and 2,500 had less than 500.[8] Thus, again in the words of Schmoller, "One can perhaps say that the increase from A.D. 500 to 1340 of two- or threefold to 12 million was a greater achievement than the increase from 15 million to 64 million from 1700 to 1900."[9]

Stagnation set in toward the end of the Middle Ages, especially after the ravages of the Black Death in 1348, from which it took centuries to recover. Added to this, there was the incredible number of deaths in Germany resulting from the Thirty Years' War, so that the towns often had fewer inhabitants in the eighteenth century than 300 years earlier. Almost all German towns increased till the thirteenth–fourteenth centuries; then came a rapid decrease, often caused by the oppression of a territorial lord, and then in the sixteenth century there was another period of growth. This is clearly revealed in the population curves of such cities as Cologne, Soest, Worms, Basel, and Mainz.[10] In Holland, no town, even at the end of the Middle Ages, exceeded 10,000 inhabitants. Rotterdam and Amsterdam were still small settlements, and the latter did not grow appreciably till the eighteenth century, but then rapidly. In Belgium, the giants among its many industrial and commercial centers were Ghent and Bruges, which probably had about 50,000 inhabitants.[11]

[5] For a discussion of urban economy and demography in the late Middle Ages, see H. Pirenne, *Economic and Social History of Medieval Europe* (1937), chaps. 6 and 7; also H. Bechtel, *Wirtschaftsstil des Deutschen Spätmittelalters: Der Ausdrück der Lebensform in Wirtschaft, Gesellschaft und Kunst von 1350 bis zum 1500* (Munich and Leipzig, 1930).

[6] G. Schmoller, *Deutsches Städtewesen in älterer Zeit*, p. 39. See also K. Frenzel, "Die Deutsche Stadt im Mittelalter als Lebensraum," in *Stadtlandschaften der Erde*, ed. S. Passarge (Hamburg, 1930), pp. 15–28.

[7] P. Sanders, *Geschichte des deutschen Städtewesens* ("Bonner Staatswissenschaftliche Untersuchungen," Heft 6, 1922).

[8] Bechtel, *op. cit.*, pp. 31 ff. At the end of the Middle Ages Cologne had about 30,000–35,000 inhabitants; Strasbourg, Nuremberg, and Ulm about 20,000 each; Augsburg and Hamburg about 18,000, Basel, 9,000, Leipzig, 4,000, and Dresden, 3,000. Lübeck reached 22,000 in 1400, while Frankfurt and Zurich had about 10,000 inhabitants. See B. Heil, *Die Deutschen Städte und Bürger im Mittelalter* ("Aus Natur und Geisteswelt," No. 43 [Berlin, 1921]).

[9] Schmoller, *op. cit.*, p. 59.

[10] Frenzel, *op. cit.*

[11] H. Pirenne, *Histoire de Belgique*, I (1929), 285. Demangeon gives the figure 80,000 for the fourteenth century, with 40,000 for Ypres in 1257, reduced to 6,000 in 1486 (see A. Demangeon, *Géographie universelle*, II, *Belgique—Pays-Bas—Luxembourg* [1927], 101–2).

## The Renaissance and Baroque
## Period (*ca.* 1500–1800)

The network of towns of today was virtually completed by the end of the Middle Ages in western and central Europe, though gaps remained to be filled in, especially in northern Europe. The next 300 years was a period of relative stability, in which only a few new towns were founded and the proportion of urban and rural population remained fairly constant. These general features, however, should not obscure the fact that there were important changes in urban activities which are reflected in the size and structure of the town.

During the sixteenth, seventeenth, and eighteenth centuries there occurred important changes in the character and distribution of industry which were not without effect on the location and growth of towns. Industry in the Middle Ages was almost exclusively concentrated in the towns and controlled by their guilds. Every town had a variety of handicrafts, which, because of the lack of transport facilities, catered primarily to the folk in the surrounding countryside. The large cities alone were seats of specialized industry. Western Europe was traversed in the later Middle Ages by numerous routes which were great arteries of commerce and on which towns were located where materials were collected from, and goods distributed to, distant markets. Already, however, certain minerals and sand (for glassmaking) were worked where these materials were obtained, far from the towns, in remote upland districts which would otherwise have been shunned by settlers who sought to live from the soil. Glassmaking, metal-working (gold, silver, copper, and tin), and porcelain-making were especially important in the uplands of Germany. All these required charcoal as fuel and running water, in addition to their particular raw materials. This brought about a considerable dispersion of industry. This trend affected also the textile industries. Everywhere freedom from the restrictions imposed by the guilds was sought. This was especially true of Flanders, "where

peasant handicrafts were pursued everywhere" so that "the whole of Flanders was one vast workshop."[12] There was a similar widespread distribution of textile-working in the villages of Picardy in the early nineteenth century. The same was true of East Anglia, the Cotswolds, and West Yorkshire in England. This general development was found also in the German states. In Prussia, the heyday of mining in the uplands came in the fifteenth and sixteenth centuries and the Erzgebirge, the high uplands of Saxony, is the only area in western Europe where a considerable number of new towns were founded in this period. The subsequent decline of metal-working released a large labor supply that could not possibly eke out an existence from the impoverished soil of small holdings at high altitudes. The kings of Prussia encouraged the development of the textile industries in these areas as a domestic occupation, and this was organized by merchants (*Verleger*) from town centers. Much the same development took place in the states of southern Germany behind the shelter of their tariff walls. Thus there was a widespread distribution of rural industry in France, the Low Countries, England, and the German lands at the opening of the nineteenth century, and this added to the importance of the town as a commercial center.

This period was one of active urban development in the northern lands of Europe as compared to the German lands. This was the era of Sweden's greatness—the *Storhetstid*—when Finland, and, for a time, the territories of the old Livonian Order, were a part of the Swedish kingdom. The new era was opened by Gustav I early in the sixteenth century. Gustav desired to make Sweden independent politically and economically. He sought, as did the kings of Poland and Hungary at the same time, to transfer the control of trade from the Germans to his own people and to develop commerce and new manufactures. Iron-making was greatly encouraged, the making of wrought bar-iron as well as of finished

[12] Demangeon, *op. cit.*, p. 132.

products. Textile industries were also encouraged and developed in many towns in central Sweden. The traditional method of distributing goods to a widely scattered population through the medium of the wandering peddler was strictly forbidden by royal edict and trade was to be rigidly confined to the towns. New towns were chartered at the seats of the new mining area in the Bergslagen and farther north, and their activities often cut into the trade of existing towns. The properties of the church were confiscated by the crown, and land formerly occupied by the monasteries eventually fell into the public ownership of the towns and favored the development of the towns. The decline in importance of the herring fisheries caused the decline of many small fishing ports. The increasing demand for timber, however, and the growth in size and number of sailing ships—in Sweden as well as in Germany and the Low Countries —led to the exploitation of the Swedish and Finnish forests near the coast where the timber could be delivered to the ports in which the sawmills were located. The need for defense of the frontiers of the state, especially against Russia to the east and Denmark to the south, was a primary consideration in the foundation of fortress towns as both military and naval bases.

Thus many towns appear in this period in northern Europe, especially in the lands controlled by Sweden in the seventeenth century. They appeared either as new towns or as new foundations following on the great devastations wrought by fires, the great scourge of the northern towns, which were, and still are, built almost entirely of timber. Mining towns appear well to the north in the hitherto untouched Norrland. New towns appear, too, on the coasts of the Bothnian Sea north of latitude 60°. Indeed, most of those towns on the shores of the Baltic north of Stockholm and Finnish Åbo and Trondheim were founded in the seventeenth century or later, either as mining centers, or as posts for the assembly and preliminary treatment of ores and timbers, whereas on the Norwegian coast they emerged later as fishing settlements in the nineteenth century. In southern Sweden, the foundation of Göteborg in 1618 as Sweden's window on the west was the prelude to the conquest of the Danish territories to the south between 1645 and 1660. The port of Stockholm was frozen each year for four or five months and was too remote to serve as a naval base for the protection of the Baltic entrances, so Charles XI founded Karlskrona in 1685. Stockholm, the capital, was considerably extended at the same period, as were other European capitals, by additions to the medieval town. Many smaller provincial towns were founded at this time, either as new industrial centers or on the ashes of others that had been ravaged by fire. Most of this planning was the work of military engineers. On the other hand, many towns in Scania were decadent during this period, owing to the incessant wars between Denmark and Sweden, and the decline of the herring fisheries which robbed many small ports of their chief means of existence.

New towns were also founded in Norway. As an example we may cite Oslo. The first sawmills at Oslo are mentioned in the fifteenth century, and at this time the ports in the bay began to develop. In 1618 the town was burned to the ground and Christian IV built a new city, which he called Christiania, near to the site of the old one, which was clustered around the fortified rock of the Akershus. Its growth was slow until after 1850, even though it became the capital of Norway and Sweden in 1815 and has remained the capital of the former country ever since. In 1700 it had 5,000 inhabitants, in 1815, 13,500, but even then it was far exceeded by Bergen.

Finland at this time belonged to Sweden both politically and culturally, and it also experienced a period of prosperity in which many new towns were founded by royal decree and favor. Above all, the port of Helsinki (Helsingfors) was founded on the Gulf of Finland midway between Åbo and Viborg. Its central position, farthest from Swedish and Russian influence, and its favorable location on the Gulf, where it had access to the sea all the year round, favored its growth in the nineteenth century as the national and political capital of Finland. Other towns were founded by Gustavus Vasa, Gustavus Adolphus, Charles IX, and, later in the seventeenth century, by Per Braha, the famous head of the Generalship of Finland, who was responsible for the foundation of Helsinki and a dozen other towns. Particularly significant was the group founded during the first years of the seventeenth century on the coast north of Åbo; the best known is Uleåborg, founded in 1605. Between 1500 and 1800 twenty-three new towns came into being, two of which disappeared, so that at the opening of the nineteenth century there were twenty-eight towns, seven of them dating from the medieval period. In 1805 Åbo had 11,000 inhabitants, Helsinki only 4,000, Viborg 3,000, and Uleåborg 3,000.

In Poland the first phase of town development, through the immigration of German settlers at the invitation of the Polish rulers before 1300, was continued by further foundations in the fourteenth and especially in the seventeenth and eighteenth centuries. Numerous small towns were established, between the existing principal towns which lay at the chief nodal points, with their origins in most cases dating back to the early Middle Ages. The Polish rulers founded these country towns partly to settle new land and partly to foster new industries. In the western provinces, the textile industry and iron-working were encouraged. Many German craftsmen, including large numbers of Protestants, were invited to settle. This migration continued into the nineteenth century, when growth was still further fostered in the western provinces by the infiltration of Germans into such new towns as Lodz and Czestochowa.

Many estimates have been made of the size and growth of the individual European cities during this period prior to the first census returns about 1800. The fact is that while there were no fundamental changes in the social and economic structure of society, the size of towns was affected not only by their ability to function as seats of industry and commerce for distant markets but also by their operation as centers for the commercial organization of regional industries. It was also necessary for the town to draw its food supplies from its immediate environs. In Germany the town was often politically separated from its surrounding area, as was the case, for example, with Cologne, an independent city surrounded by the territory of the bishopric of Cologne. Then again, the continuous growth of a city meant that it had to be supplied with immigrants, for the death rate was abnormally high. Disease and epidemics, as well as famine, often swept the cities like a scourge and reduced their populations. Only immigration could fill the gap. Finally, the guilds and the organization of the town council often fell into the hands of an unscrupulous oligarchy. This is no place to attempt an appraisal of these changes. But it is clear that while many of the chief cities barely maintained themselves, or even declined, others showed a steady but slight increase, while still others developed as active centers of trade and industry.

Among the ports, there was a shift of trade from Bruges, the great emporium in the thirteenth century, to Antwerp in the fourteenth century, when the Merchant Adventurers transferred their headquarters thither. This was followed by the shift of the headquarters of the Hanseatic League in the sixteenth century. The sixteenth century was the peak of Antwerp's prosperity as a center of trade in woolen goods brought from England for distribution on the Continent. Bruges, with 29,000 inhabitants in 1584, was already a shadow of its former self, a *ville morte*, whereas Antwerp in 1560 had reached the 100,000 mark and was one of the largest cities in Europe.[13] The emergence of Holland as a new state, controlling the mouth of the Scheldt, spelt

[13] Demangeon, *op. cit.*, p. 117.

the ruin of Antwerp's trade, and it stagnated until the channel was internationalized by Napoleon in 1793, when the modern development of the city began. In 1750 it had 45,000 inhabitants. The decline of Antwerp was followed by the rise of Amsterdam and Hamburg. Hamburg was a relatively small port in the Middle Ages, having in 1400 about 10,000 inhabitants, but in the seventeenth and eighteenth centuries it took Antwerp's place in European trade and became the leading Hanseatic port and the greatest city in Germany. The Hamburg Bank was established in 1619 and the first Chamber of Commerce in 1665. Severe losses were suffered during the Continental blockade of the Napoleonic wars, but during the nineteenth century growth was rapid. Amsterdam was still a small town in 1300, but by 1400 it was the chief commercial center of Holland and handled the trade with Scandinavia and the coastal trade from Hamburg to Flanders. The coastal trade had hitherto been handled by Utrecht, which lay on the river Vecht and could not be reached by the larger vessels that were being used for the seagoing trade. Amsterdam also grew with the decline of Antwerp in the seventeenth century and acquired a new lease on life with the formation of the independent kingdom of the Netherlands in 1815. In 1800 it had 200,000 inhabitants and was one of the greatest cities in Europe.

The principal ports of France—Rouen, Nantes, Bordeaux, and Marseilles—made similar advances during the seventeenth and eighteenth centuries and profited especially from the trade with the New World and the East. Marseilles had 75,000 inhabitants in 1700 and over 100,000 at the end of the century. New ports were established by Richelieu and Colbert at Le Havre, Dunkirk, Brest, Lorient, La Rochelle, and Sète.

The growth of the chief inland cities of France may be illustrated by several examples. A slow increase is general during the seventeenth and eighteenth centuries. Limoges had 14,000 inhabitants in 1698 and 22,000 in the latter half of the eight-

eenth century. Clermont-Ferrand had about 17,000 inhabitants in 1700, 20,000 in the mid-eighteenth century, and 24,500 in 1791. Grenoble had 10,000 in 1600, 20,000 in 1700, and 29,000 in 1801.[14]

The case of Frankfurt may be taken as an example of the vicissitudes of the German city in this period.[15] Its great prosperity in the sixteenth century was due above all to the large influx of Walloon and Fleming religious refugees and to the commercial activities of the Jews, by virtue of which it became the greatest seat of banking and finance in Europe. In 1387 its population was 10,000; in 1440 it reached 8,000 as compared with 20,000 for Nuremberg at the same date; it had 13,000 in 1578 and 17,000–18,000 in 1590. In 1600 it ranked as one of the chief cities of Europe. It did not reach the size of Cologne (37,000) or Strasbourg and Nuremberg (25,000), but was in the same group as Lübeck, Brunswick, Ulm, and Augsburg. During the seventeenth and eighteenth centuries, disease and famine, and the emigration of some of its religious refugees to the newly founded town of Hanau nearby, caused violent fluctuations in its fortunes. Gley's estimates are as follows: 1640, 18,000; 1700, 29,000; 1725, 30,000 (with 3,000 Jews); 1800, 35,000 (4,000 Jews). During the Thirty Years' War there were huge losses through disease and famine, the deaths during the period 1635–40 amounting to no less than 15,000. In spite of this, there was a slow but general increase in numbers from 18,000 in 1590 to 35,000 in 1800.

## THE DISTRIBUTION OF TOWNS IN 1830

Figure 1 shows the distribution of towns in 1830.[16] This distribution was the same

[14] These figures are taken from studies by Perrier, Arbos, and Blanchard.

[15] Estimates are taken from W. Gley, *Grundriss und Wachstum der Stadt Frankfurt-am-Main*.

[16] A. Welte, "Die Verstädterung Mittel- und Westeuropas im 1830–1930," *Geopolitik*, 1936, pp. 217–26 and pp. 351–58. Similar maps appear in H. Haufe, *Die Bevölkerung Europas*, showing towns with over 5,000 inhabitants.

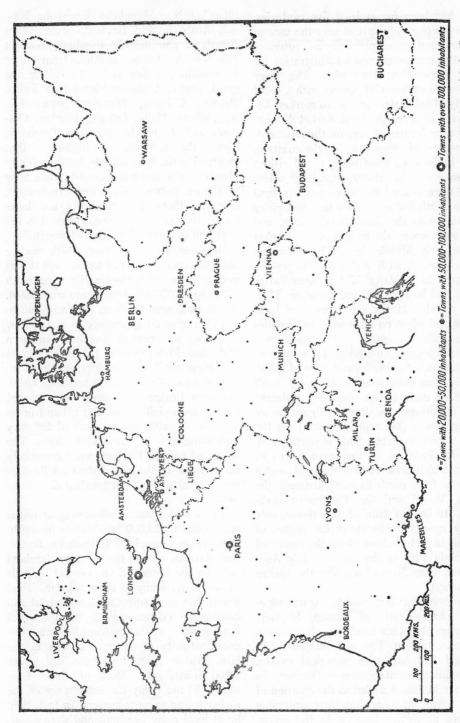

● = *Towns with over 100,000 inhabitants*

◐ = *Towns with 50,000-100,000 inhabitants*

⊙ = *Towns with 20,000-50,000 inhabitants*

Fig. 1.—The distribution of towns in western and central Europe in 1830. (This map is redrawn and modified from A. Welte, article in *Geopolitik*, 1936.)

as it had been for at least five centuries. Towns were evenly spread over the face of the land and served primarily as centers of industry, commerce, and administration for their surrounding territories. The large cities were commercial centers with a great variety of industries catering to markets beyond the limits of the local market district. They were located always on the outstanding avenues of commerce—on the coasts in good harbors (a good tenth of all cities) and on navigable rivers, especially where these were crossed by important overland routes. With few exceptions the chief cities of today were the chief historic cities, and they were among the first towns to develop in the early Middle Ages. The numerous smaller towns, with under 20,000 people, appeared in the later Middle Ages (after 1200) and had less natural nodality. They were situated at the convergence of local routes and often on sites with natural defenses—hilltops, spurs, river meanders—without adequate connection with the surrounding countryside for purposes of trade. Finally, the even spacing of many small towns on main routes obviously reflected their importance as stage or thoroughfare resting places (German, *Rastorte*) on the great overland routes. This is particularly true, for instance, of the small towns of Hesse, which grew on the skein of routes that ran from north to south between the Rhine Massif and the Thuringian highlands. It is also true of the remarkably evenly spaced towns along the routes of Thuringia and of those along the routes of Franconia that in the later Middle Ages radiated from Nuremberg like the spokes of a wheel.

The even distribution of towns was especially characteristic of France. In Germany, on the other hand, the distribution was more uneven. This was due partly to physical and partly to historical causes. The political disintegration of Germany in the later Middle Ages led to the creation of many towns, far more than the countryside required as service centers. In the seventeenth and eighteenth centuries "court

cities" such as Mannheim, Karlsruhe, Kassel, Ansbach, and Bayreuth were established in considerable numbers. Ancient cites were located on the Rhine from source to mouth. Another series lay along the great west-east thoroughfares that linked Bruges, Cologne, Hanover, Brunswick, Magdeburg, Halle, Leipzig, Breslau, Cracow, and Lvov. In southern Germany, along the network of highways that emerged in the later Middle Ages, each city shown on the map was an outstanding node of routes. Between these main routeways, however, there were relatively few large cities; they are also markedly absent in the northern lowland of heath and marsh.

In three areas, however, there was a marked concentration of towns, and this is very pronounced if the smaller towns with 5,000 to 20,000 inhabitants are considered. These areas were northern Italy with southern France as an appendage to it, the Low Countries and central England. Northern Italy and Flanders were the earliest seats of urban medieval development and included some of the greatest medieval cities. Southern France was deeply impregnated with Roman civilization, and urban life revived early with the renewal of industry and commerce in the Middle Ages. The towns of central England were essentially the creation of the new Industrial Revolution that as yet had not touched the Continent.

There was a marked clustering of towns with 5,000 to 20,000 inhabitants in southwestern Germany, in Württemberg, Baden, and Bavaria, and in the northern foreland zone on the border of the central uplands of Germany. Many of these were medieval towns that grew to be small industrial and commercial centers during the industrial development of the mercantilist era. The great majority of towns appeared in the later Middle Ages, but these had under 5,000 inhabitants. Most of these later towns did not enjoy the importance of the earlier towns as route centers. In fact, they lie at local route junctions and were established to serve a local hinterland or to develop local mines. In addition, since many of them were founded primarily as fortresses or were sited next to castles, they were invariably placed on well-protected sites, such as a hilltop, a river meander, or a spur, and were for that reason cut off from easy contact with the country around. Many small towns established at this time have failed to function as real centers of urban activity, for this and other reasons, and are today nothing more than villages. This is characteristic of many of the towns of southern Germany in Württemberg, where they have been described as "speculative failures" from the point of view of their medieval founders. There are many others, as, for example, the hilltop *bastide* settlements, in southern France.

A further point to be made here is that while on the Continent over wide areas, especially in Germany, *all* urban settlements were walled towns, the small unwalled market town was dominant in other areas, either by growth from village origins or, much more usually, by the deliberate act of founding a new market settlement or the concession to a village of the right to hold a market. Areas served almost entirely by such market settlements are Bavaria south of the Danube, much of northwestern Germany, northern France, and the lowland zone of England. Indeed, England is pre-eminently the country of this type of settlement, which the Englishman takes for granted but which is, in fact, a very distinctive settlement form.

## THE ECONOMIC BASE OF CITIES

A major concern of the urban geographer is the reasons why cities exist. People gather in mutual proximity in urban agglomerations in order to carry on certain activities and satisfy certain needs which cannot be performed or satisfied without such proximity. These activities and needs may be social, political, religious, or otherwise not directly related to the process of making a living. Most cities, however, are primarily in existence, and grow, because in cities the opportunities for making a living—employment—are greater in number and variety than in non-urban situations. In other words, most cities depend primarily upon their economic base.

The measurement and the interpretation of the economic base of cities have been the subjects of a major part of the literature of urban geography in recent years. There are many methods that can be used—each with its advantages and limitations—to measure the nature of the economic base of cities, both individually and in relation to one another. Whatever the method selected for a particular study, however, certain premises are fundamental.

Probably the most important premise relating to the urban economic base is that cities exist because within them are performed certain operations—industrial and commercial primarily—which result in the production, transfer, and distribution of goods and services for the population of areas outside the city itself. Cities, in other words, have a focal or nodal character which sets them aside, economically as well as physically, from the area outside. Determination of the extent to which each of the urban functions serves the population outside the city, in contrast to the production of goods and services for consumption inside the city, is an important part of most studies of the urban economic base.

The five articles reproduced in this section of the book together give the reader a picture of the status of present knowledge and experience relating to the economic base of cities. The first article, by John W. Alexander, reviews the history of the concept of the economic base in recent literature and proceeds to a discussion of one of the best-known approaches to the problem: differentiation of the so-called "basic" activities—those producing goods or services for export out of the urban area—from the "nonbasic," or those whose resultant goods and services are consumed within the city or urban agglomeration. This "basic-nonbasic" approach has a number of advantages, and some serious limitations, as the two following articles, by Roterus and Calef and by Tiebout, clearly demonstrate. The principal advantage appears to be that the concept is simple; the disadvantages are the result mainly of not enough experience in the conduct and application of studies using the method, as the questions raised by Alexander in his plea for further research indicate. Roterus and Calef, both geographers, point out the problem, inherent in almost any geographic study, of proper areal delimitation. Tiebout, an economist, relates his criticism to purely economic considerations. Both the critical articles point out, however, that the "basic-nonbasic" approach has important contributions to make to our knowledge of the reasons for the existence of cities.

Alexandersson, in the fourth article in this section, proposes an alternative method for studying the urban economic base: relating the basic-nonbasic ratio —or the proportion of employment in a city producing goods and services for export compared with that in a city producing for internal consumption—to a model or standard representing more or less average conditions.

Isard, one of the authors of the final article in this section, is an economist who has been especially known for his development of the applications of "input-output" techniques of analysis to cities and regions. The "input-output" approach has for some time been applied to national economies, for which data on production, consumption, and movement are more easily available than for cities. The method proposed by Isard appears to have considerable promise as applied to studies of urban economic base, but the amount of data required to apply the method and the general unavailability of some of the requisite information preclude widespread use of the technique in the foreseeable future.

There are many other approaches to the study of the urban economic base. One field which has barely been touched by geographers, except in the special cases of seaports, is the use of measures of actual flow of goods in and out of a city. Here, again, unavailability of data makes such studies impracticable in most cases. The concept of the urban economic base, one of the most important in the entire field of urban geography, requires considerable further testing and development.

JOHN W. ALEXANDER

# THE BASIC-NONBASIC CONCEPT OF URBAN ECONOMIC FUNCTIONS

Among geographers there appears to be an increasing interest in urban geography as evidenced in faculty research and the number of Ph.D. dissertations. The purpose of this paper is to analyze a concept which has particular value in the geographic study of urban settlements. It applies specifically to the economic functions of a city.

The traditional system of studying urban economic functions begins by measuring the livelihood structure. It determines the number of people employed in the city and tabulates them in such categories as trade, manufacturing, and government. This classification is based not on any characteristic of space relationships but rather on type of service performed.

The concept discussed in this paper *is* based on a space relationship; and it recognizes that cities develop in response to demands from other places. Indeed, as Mark Jefferson observed over twenty years ago, "Cities do not grow up of themselves. Countrysides set them up to do tasks that must be performed in central places."[1] No city lives to itself. It serves other areas which can be said to constitute the city's "market region." In turn, the region serves the city. Such functioning is of immediate interest to geographers because the interconnections between city and region are one type of spatial relationship. Thus, one aspect of urban geography is the analysis

Reprinted from *Economic Geography*, XXX (July, 1954), 246–61, by permission of the author and the editor. (Copyright, 1954, by Clark University, Worcester, Mass.)

[1] Mark Jefferson, "The Distribution of the World's City Folks: A Study in Comparative Civilization," *Geographical Review*, XXI (1931), 453.

of those ties which bind a city to its region. For example, how extensive is the region served by a city? How far and in what directions does that region extend? What does the city do for that region? To what degree is the region dependent on that city for goods and services? Answers to these questions constitute useful criteria by which relationships between city and region are measured.

One of the strongest ties between city and region is the economic bond, for the economic life of a city is inextricably interwoven with the economic life of its region. A portion of the economic effort in a city is supported by non-local demands. But these city people in turn have need for local services, and thus a second urban function is discernible—that which caters to the needs of local inhabitants.

The difference between these two economic efforts is of fundamental importance, because the former constitutes the city's economic foundation. As Jefferson observed, the city's life depends upon it. It brings money *into* the city and is termed "basic." By contrast, the second category (serving local demands) is termed "nonbasic" and simply involves an exchange of money which basic efforts have already brought in.

The concept of this basic-nonbasic dualism is recognized in several social sciences, particularly economics and geography. "The primary or 'city building' activities should be identified, i.e., those activities which bring into the community purchasing power from outside."[2] "The support of a

[2] Richard U. Ratcliff, *Urban Land Economics* (New York, 1949), p. 43.

city depends on the services it performs not for itself but for a tributary area. Many activities serve merely the population of the city itself. Barbers, dry cleaners, shoe repairers, grocerymen, bakers, and movie operators serve others who are engaged in the principal activity of the city, which may be mining, manufacturing, trade, or some other activity."[3]

The purpose of this study is principally to analyze the basic-nonbasic concept in terms of its relevance to urban geography. The paper is so organized as to present (1) salient points in the historical development of the concept, (2) an inspection of those qualities which recommend the concept for application by urban geographers, (3) a review of selected case studies in which the concept was applied, and (4) questions which need to be answered or refinements which need to be made in maturing the concept for more fruitful application in geographical studies.

### HISTORICAL DEVELOPMENT OF THE BASIC-NONBASIC CONCEPT

The concept of a city's economic dichotomy has been recognized in theory for more than three decades. Various writers have identified it, often using different terminology such as *primary, urban growth, external, supporting* for "basic," and *secondary, service, internal* for "nonbasic." The first expression of the idea appears to be that of Aurousseau, who wrote in 1921:

It is well known that towns have an extraordinary power of growth. This appears to be due to the relationship between the primary occupations and the secondary occupations of the townsfolk. The primary occupations are those directly concerned with the functions of the town. The secondary occupations are those concerned with the maintenance of the well-being of the people engaged in those of primary nature.[4]

[3] Chauncy D. Harris and Edward L. Ullman, "The Nature of Cities," *Annals of the American Academy of Political and Social Science,* CCXLII (1945) [see below, pp. 277–86].

The first urban analysis explicitly to identify a city's economic dualism was the New York Regional Planning Committee's *Regional Survey of New York and Its Environs* published in 1927. On pages 42–43 of this survey the concept was described in terms of "primary" and "ancillary," as suggested by Frederick L. Olmsted, who described the economic activities of a city as follows:

The multiplicity of their productive occupations may be roughly divided into those which can be considered primary, such as carrying on the marine shipping business of the port and manufacturing goods for general use (i.e., not confined to use within the community itself), and those occupations which may be called ancillary, such as are devoted directly or indirectly to the service and convenience of the people engaged in the primary occupations.

A footnote to the text indicates that Mr. Olmsted first used this terminology in 1921 in a letter to a member of the New York Planning Committee. However, after defining the primary and ancillary components, the study did not proceed to apply the concept in very much detail in analyzing New York's economy, probably because methods had not yet been developed for applying the fledgling idea.

In subsequent years the concept received attention in different disciplines where scholars refined the theory or added new concepts. The most thorough analysis of this historical development is presented in a recent series by Professor Richard B. Andrews.[5]

As far as the author has been able to determine, the first geographer to apply this idea to a specific city was Richard Hartshorne in a study of Minneapolis–St. Paul published in the July, 1932, issue of the *Geographical Review.* On page 437 the author writes:

[4] M. Aurousseau, "The Distribution of Population: A Constructive Problem," *Geographical Review,* XI (1921), 574.

[5] Richard B. Andrews, "Mechanics of the Urban Economic Base," *Land Economics,* XXIX (1953).

The conversion of this particular pair of towns . . . into a metropolitan district of three-quarters of a million in 1930 was based largely on the establishment of that district in the period of rail construction as the one all-important focus of rail lines of the central northwest. This may be readily seen from a brief analysis of the external functions of the urban district. In any city these tend to be obscured somewhat by the large number of functions developed to serve simply the residents of the city itself. In Minneapolis–St. Paul the "internal" functions employed, in 1919, more than half the total number of men workers. Of the remainder, the railroads, including the car shops, employed more than a fourth—by far the largest single group.

The author does not explain how he determined these proportions.

That a city's economy consists of two components was obvious, but nothing appears to have been done to formulate a methodology for applying the concept until Richard Hartshorne worked on the United States manufacturing belt.[6] Hartshorne reasoned that a part of manufacturing in every industrial city produces only for local consumption and that the most meaningful map of a manufacturing region would locate concentrations of industry producing over and above local demands. To arrive at some measurement of this (which actually could be termed "basic" manufacturing) the author mapped industrial wage earners for all cities with over 10,000 population, subtracting from each city's total of industrial wage earners a factor of 10 per cent of the population. The assumption was that 1,000 wage earners in manufacturing would be required to meet the needs of a city of 10,000 people. Hartshorne subsequently concluded[7] that this factor was too high and probably should have been 8 per cent. Nevertheless his study was a pioneer effort to measure what is herein termed "basic" effort, applying it to a single type of endeavor, manufacturing.

The next advance in methodology was an analysis of the economic functions of Oskaloosa, Iowa, by the research staff of *Fortune* magazine.[8] By measuring the balance of payments between Oskaloosa and "the rest of the world" they arrived at a distinction between the city's payments to local creditors and to non-local creditors.

A third advance in methodology was Homer Hoyt's outline of six steps for measuring basic activity which appeared in a book published in 1939.[9] In advancing this method Hoyt also suggested new terminology: "urban growth" for "basic" and "urban service" for "nonbasic." The six steps are as follows:

1. From census reports, or from local sources such as chambers of commerce, local establishments, local trade associations, and employment offices, determine the number of persons engaged in the principal types of employment. It may be necessary to use estimates in some cases, especially in communities for which there are few published statistics.

2. Determine the number engaged in manufacturing, excluding those firms whose production is intended predominantly for the local market.

3. Determine the number engaged in extractive industry obviously intended for the non-local market.

4. Determine the number engaged in non-local governmental, transportation, or communication services and the number employed in lines of work catering to amusement seekers, tourists, or travelers.

5. From published sources (for example, the periodical *Sales Management*) determine the percentage of the national income that is earned by the city being analyzed. Then apply this percentage to the total number of persons engaged

---

[6] Richard Hartshorne: "A New Map of the Manufacturing Belt of North America," *Economic Geography*, XII (1936), 45–53.

[7] Personal conversation with the author.

[8] "Oskaloosa vs. the United States," *Fortune*, April, 1938, pp. 55 ff.

[9] Arthur M. Weimer and Homer Hoyt, *Principles of Urban Real Estate* (New York, 1939). The criteria here quoted appear in the text in chapter vi, "The Future Growth and Structure of Cities." For the background of Hoyt's experience which led to the formulation of his ideas see Andrews, *op. cit.*

in trading, financing, professional, and related activities in the country, as shown by the figures of the Bureau of the Census and the Department of Labor. Assume that the number by which local employment in these lines exceeds this percentage is "urban growth" employment. For example, suppose 15,000,000 persons are employed in these activities in the United States and that the city being analyzed has 1 per cent of the total national income. On this basis, it may be assumed that 150,000 persons will be required to perform the trading and related activities of the city. If 200,000 are so employed, then 50,000 may be considered as representing "urban growth" employment.

6. Total the figures arrived at in paragraphs 2–5 above and compute the percentage which each type of "urban growth" employment represents of this total. These percentages will indicate the relative importance of manufacturing, extractive industry, trading, and the other types of activity in the economic development of the city.

In 1942 Harold McCarty expanded the concept to apply to regional economies as well as community economies. He described basic-nonbasic activities in relation to what he called the *occupational pyramid:*

The base of the pyramid consists of that group of occupations whose presence in the area is not predicated on the existence of other types of production. . . . The base of the pyramid dictates the pattern of the remainder of the structure. . . . The workers in basic industries are not self-sufficing individuals, and the local economic organization must provide them with many types of goods and services including merchandising establishments, as well as transport facilities, business, and personal services, and each of these groups in turn requires workers to care for its needs.[10]

J. H. Jones, in a volume on national planning for Britain's postwar reconstruction of damaged cities, introduced the idea that city planners should give priority to basic activities:

These industries (including services) are the foundation upon which the town has been built,

[10] Harold H. McCarty, "A Functional Analysis of Population Distribution," *Geographical Review,* XXXII (1942), 287–88.

and may therefore be called "basic" industries. Their size will determine the size of the industrial structure and population of the town; no town can grow merely by adding to an already adequate supply of local industries and services. . . . Every area, large and small, must contain some industries that "export" their products to the world outside that area . . . the inhabitants of the towns could not be expected to live by taking in each others' washing.[11]

Robert E. Dickinson directed considerable attention to the concept in a book published in 1947 and pointed out the need for more urban analyses in terms of this economic dichotomy. He went further, to suggest that analyses of cities could be based on this approach:

What is needed is a much more careful analysis of the urban community, not only as a seat of specialized industry and service serving a wide market, but also as a seat of industry and service for the "regional" market over and above "local" needs of the urban community itself. . . .[12]

While granting that in one and the same industrial occupation it is impossible to come to a quantitative measure of the relative importance of the nation-wide and international market, the local urban market, and the wider regional market, this is no reason why the last should not be adopted as a main approach to the study of the occupational structure of towns.[13]

In the past few years, since the publication of Hoyt's "six steps," there has been increasing interest in theoretical aspects of the basic-nonbasic concept. Students in various disciplines find it useful. Several features commend it, particularly to geographers since it is a meaningful expression of a fundamental space-relation between city and supporting areas.

[11] J. H. Jones, "Industry and Planning," in *Creative Demobilization,* Vol. II, *Case Studies in National Planning,* ed. E. A. Gutkind (London, 1944), pp. 126–27.

[12] Robert E. Dickinson, *City Region and Regionalism* (London, 1947), p. 24.

[13] *Ibid.,* p. 36.

### GEOGRAPHIC QUALITIES OF THE BASIC-NONBASIC CONCEPT

Traditional community studies based on employment data published in the census or procured from employment agencies usually are seriously lacking in one respect: they provide no measure of basic activities because such employment data permit no reliable classification of activity in terms of the geographic areas to which the city's

has a definite shortcoming. Much of this can be remedied by application of the basic-nonbasic concept which, by classifying economic endeavor in terms of market location, recommends itself to urban geographers for four reasons:

1. The concept provides a view of economic ties which bind a city to other areas.

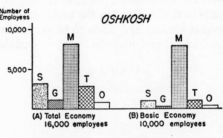

TABLE 1

EMPLOYMENT IN OSHKOSH AND MADISON, WISCONSIN

|  | Oshkosh | Madison |
|---|---|---|
| 1950 population... | 42,000 | 110,000 |
| 1940–50 population growth......... | 5 per cent | 28 per cent |
| Total employment. | 16,000 | 53,500 |
| Basic employment. | 10,000 | 29,000 |
| Leading basic activity.......... | Manufacturing | Government |
| Non-basic employment.......... | 5,900 | 24,300 |
| B/N ratio........ | 100:60 | 100:82 |
| A. Total employment: |  |  |
| 1. Services..... | 3,100 | 14,500 |
| 2. Government. | 1,200 | 14,300 |
| 3. Manufacturing......... | 8,200 | 12,100 |
| 4. Trade....... | 2,700 | 10,200 |
| 5. Others...... | 800 | 2,400 |
| Number of employees........ | 16,000 | 53,500 |
| B. Basic employployment: |  |  |
| 1. Services..... | 900 | 4,500 |
| 2. Government. | 120 | 11,300 |
| 3. Manufacturing......... | 7,880 | 10,100 |
| 4. Trade....... | 950 | 3,000 |
| 5. Others...... | 250 | 300 |
| Number of employees........ | 10,100 | 29,200 |

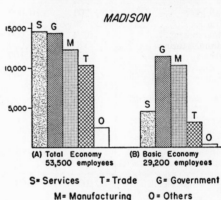

FIG. 1.—Economic structures

The contrast between *total employment* and *basic employment* in this respect is shown in Table 1 (parts A and B) and Figure 1 which give data for two Wisconsin cities, Oshkosh and Madison.[14] The traditional livelihood structure (total employment) for Oshkosh reveals that manufacturing is the leading form of employment, followed by services, trade, and government. But when the nonbasic component is

goods and services are sold. The local component is indistinguishable from the more fundamental (basic) component which supports the settlement. The conventional method of measuring "livelihood structures," informative as far as it goes, thus

[14] John W. Alexander, "Oshkosh, Wisconsin, An Economic Base Study" (1951), and "An Economic Base Study of Madison, Wisconsin" (1953), both published by the Bureau of Business Research, School of Commerce, University of Wisconsin.

removed, the structure of *basic* employment (part B) reveals more clearly the dominance of manufacturing in supporting Oshkosh, with trade displacing services in second place. In the case of Madison the structure of basic employment (part B) is markedly different from the traditional livelihood structure. By total employment, Madison's leading activities are services, government, manufacturing, and trade in that order; but the basic structure reveals services and trade to be far behind government and manufacturing in sustain-

TABLE 2

NONBASIC EMPLOYMENT

| | Oshkosh | Madison |
|---|---|---|
| Services.............. | 2,200 | 10,000 |
| Trade................ | 1,750 | 7,000 |
| Government.......... | 1,080 | 3,000 |
| Manufacturing........ | 320 | 2,000 |
| Others.............. | 550 | 2,100 |
| Number of employees.. | 5,900 | 24,100 |
| *Percentage of non-basic employment:* | | |
| Services.............. | 38 | 41 |
| Trade................ | 30 | 30 |
| Government.......... | 18 | 12 |
| Manufacturing........ | 5 | 8 |
| Others.............. | 9 | 9 |
| Total............ | 100 | 100 |

ing Madison's economy. This is a meaningful distinction producing an entirely different picture, one not revealed by conventional methods of studying livelihood structures. The rationale of the basic-nonbasic concept is that the relationships revealed by data on *basic* employment constitute a more meaningful basis for analyzing a city's economy than do those comprised by *total* employment, that part B of Table 1 and Figure 1 are more significant than part A.

2. Another value of the concept to geographers is that it permits the most satisfactory classification of cities in terms of regional function. Cities are more accurately distinguished by their basic economy

than by their total economy because the basics express a city's service to its region. For such a purpose, the nonbasics "cloud the picture" and therefore should be subtracted from the total economy as one endeavors to distinguish industrial cities from commercial cities from government cities, etc. Harris recognized this and suggested empirical estimates of percentages to achieve such distinctions.[15] However, it would seem that a measurement of basic activity would provide a more accurate method for defining urban regional functions.

Evidence from the Oshkosh and Madison studies reveals that the *nonbasic* employment structures were considerably different from both the *total* and the *basic* structures. (Compare Table 2 and Figure 2 with Table 1 and Figure 1.) Herein lies a corollary reason for subjecting a city's economy to the basic-nonbasic concept: segregation of basic and nonbasic components reveals an entirely different structure for each, a difference which the traditional system (by blending the two into one livelihood structure) fails to reveal.

Indeed, it even may be that the structure of *nonbasic* activities is substantially the same for every city. So far, not much is known about the nonbasic structure of city economies, but data on Oshkosh and Madison reveal that their nonbasic structures are remarkably *similar* in spite of the fact that they are such different types of settlements. Table 1 shows that Madison is much larger than Oshkosh, is growing much faster, and is supported primarily by government while Oshkosh is mostly a manufacturing city. Clearly, these are different types of cities. Yet the nonbasic structure of each is revealed in Table 2 and Figure 2 to consist of the same activities

[15] See Chauncy D. Harris, "A Functional Classification of Cities in the United States," *Geographical Review*, XXXIII (January, 1943), 86–99 [see below, pp. 129–38]. For instance, ". . . only cities with more than 60 per cent of their employment in manufacturing are classified as industrial, whereas cities with only 20 per cent in wholesaling are classified as wholesale centers."

*in order of importance.* In each city the leading nonbasic activity is service, followed by trade, government, and manufacturing. But the similarity is even more remarkable, for although Madison has 24,-300 nonbasic employees and Oshkosh only 5,900, the *percentage* breakdowns are much alike. Table 2 and Figure 2 reveal that in spite of differences in over-all size, each city has exactly the same percentage of nonbasic employment in trade (30 per cent), nearly the same in services (38 per cent compared to 41 per cent), and somewhat similar percentages in government and manufacturing. Thus, Table 2 and the graph of percentage employment in nonbasic activity are remarkably similar. To be sure, evidence from just two cities is insufficient to warrant the conclusion that nonbasic structures are constant from city to city. Nevertheless, the facts on Oshkosh and Madison are presented to suggest that if nonbasic structures *are* similar from city to city, then they definitely should be isolated so that any functional classification of settlements can be based on the basic functions which *do* differ from city to city without being confused with functions which are *not* much different.

In any case, nonbasic activity should be culled out in order to provide an unobstructed view of the city supports, those activities which connect a community with its supporting territory and therefore serve as the best criteria for a geographical classification of cities in terms of function.

3. The basic-nonbasic concept provides a new ratio which may have significance in differentiating types of cities. This is the "basic-nonbasic ratio" which, for short, can be termed the "B/N" ratio. Suppose, for example, that a city has a total of 50,000 people employed, with 25,000 engaged in basic and 25,000 in nonbasic activity. The B/N ratio then is 100:100, which means that for every 100 basic employees there are 100 nonbasic employees. But another city, also with 50,000 employees, might have 30,000 basic and 20,000 nonbasic giving a different ratio: 100:66.

As yet, this concept has not been applied in the analysis of enough cities to produce much evidence about the nature of B/N ratios. Moreover, the few case studies available have employed so many different methods for measuring the basic component that the resulting ratios are scarcely comparable. However, studies by the same analyst employing the same methodology in the case of the two cities already cited (Oshkosh and Madison) revealed that the

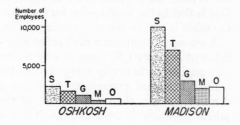

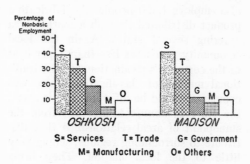

S = Services    T = Trade    G = Government
M = Manufacturing    O = Others

Fig. 2.—Nonbasic employment

B/N ratio varied from 100:60 to 100:82 (Table 1). Madison's nonbasic component is a third greater than that in Oshkosh. Obviously, the ratio can vary considerably. More detail on its variation is presented in the following section, on specific case studies. With the limited information as yet available it seems plausible that urban geographers will find the B/N ratio a useful criterion for the comparative study of cities.[16]

[16] Homer Hoyt, leading student and advocate of the basic-nonbasic concept, says, "I believe that every city has its own distinctive ratio between

4. Provision of the B/N ratio also enables a new classification for individual economic endeavors. To illustrate, a business which makes all its sales to the local market is distinctly different from one which makes all its sales to the outside market. Both businesses might be factories. The traditional method of classifying economic activities would consider them to be in the same category: namely, manufacturing. And yet, in terms of spatial relationships with market areas they are opposites; one is *basic* activity, the other is *nonbasic*. One is tied to the local region for its sales; the other is tied to the surrounding region.

A second illustration: a mail order establishment employs 1,500 people who fill orders originating in nearly every state of the nation. The local community generates a demand for less than 1 per cent of the sales. Elsewhere in that community is a garment factory making work clothes. It also employs 1,500 people who fabricate a product distributed through a market area covering several states. Again the local community purchases less than 1 per cent of the company's production. By the traditional method of classification, these two companies would be different: one is *trade,* the other is *manufacturing.* Yet from the standpoint of areal relationships they distribute to surrounding regions, selling very little to the local market. They bring money into the city and are similar in that both are nearly 100 per cent basic economic activities.

A third illustration: a city has 3,000 employees in *education*—1,500 of them in the local public school system, and 1,500 in a state-supported school of higher learning. The first group constitutes a nonbasic activity, bringing little money into the community; indeed, they are supported by local money. But the second and basic group brings money into the city. Such a distinction between basic and nonbasic can

primary and secondary employment or between basic and nonbasic." (From personal letter to the writer, December 27, 1952.)

divide not only the education category but also manufacturing, trade, governmment, and every other category in the traditional classification system.

Data for such classification are not published but must be procured through personal contact with individual companies and institutions. Organizations providing information can then be classified in terms of basic effort. For example, four categories might be defined as above and illustrated in Figure 3.

Whether the economic activity is a factory or a shoe store or a state university, if over 75 per cent of its service is in response to a demand from the non-local market region it is in category B (Basic). Category Bn (mostly basic, but at least 25 per cent nonbasic) includes stores, factories, theaters, and other enterprises which bring in more money from the outside than from the city but are more dependent on the nonbasic market than is category B. The two remaining categories depend for most of their support upon the local market, category N to a greater degree than category Nb.

An additional entry could indicate type of activity in terms of the traditional classification: "m," manufacturing; "t," trade; "g," government; "s," service, or any of several categories desired. Category "Bnt" would include trading establishments drawing 50–75 per cent of their revenue from basic customers. Obviously, many other variations of this system are possible. Subnumerals could represent "tenths" of basic component: e.g., B1 for 10 per cent basic and B8 for 80 per cent.

The contention in this paper is that a discipline in which spatial relationships are fundamental should, in analyzing urban economies, augment traditional methods by a classification recognizing areal associations. Thus, a factory supported by non-local demands is, in the economic life of the city, more akin to a basic mail-order house, a basic store, a basic educational institution, or a basic government agency than it is to a nonbasic factory, albeit both are "manufacturing." Indeed, insofar as role in a city's economic life is concerned, it often is more important to know whether an enterprise is basic (B) or nonbasic (N) than to know whether it is manufacturing or trade.

By revealing components of the urban economy connecting the city with other areas, by providing a regional service criterion for classifying cities in terms of regional function, by providing the B/N

the present section is not to analyze every case study in which the concept has been applied but rather to select a few which illustrate (a) various methods for measuring basic endeavor and (b) the wide variation in resulting B/N ratios. Readers interested in a comprehensive analysis of several case studies using the concept are reminded of Richard Andrews' series of articles, "Mechanics of the Urban Economic Base" in *Land Economics*.

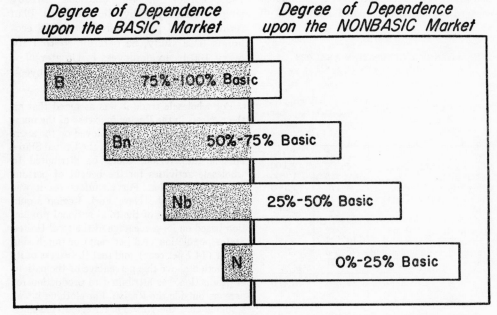

Fig. 3

ratio as another criterion for distinguishing between cities, and by a new method of measuring individual business firms—the basic-nonbasic concept contributes to the geographical understanding of cities.

### APPLICATION OF THE BASIC-NONBASIC CONCEPT IN URBAN STUDIES

Although the concept has existed in theory for more than 30 years, efforts to separate basic and nonbasic parts of a city's economy have been relatively recent. Such studies have been marked by a wide diversity of methodology with a consequential variety of results. The purpose of

The pioneer case study apparently was by the research analysts of *Fortune* magazine who investigated the circulation of money into, through, and out of Oskaloosa, Iowa.[17] By numerous interviews and questionnaires data were gathered from both individuals and business firms as to the amount and source of income. Total business receipts were $13,942,000, of which $8,114,000 came from non-local buyers. This gives a B/N ratio of 100:72. Over $800,000 also came into the city via individual channels—e.g., Oskaloosa residents employed elsewhere. This increases the

[17] See n. 8 above.

basic component so that the ratio becomes 100:65.

Another early effort to measure basic endeavor appears in Harris' study of Salt Lake City. In this, his Ph.D. dissertation at the University of Chicago in 1940, Harris observed:

The important basic occupations of the city are those which serve the hinterland as well as the city. Two measures of the extra-city function in any given occupance are (1) the number engaged beyond the estimated local needs of

TABLE 3

GENERAL OCCUPATION ANALYSIS
OF SALT LAKE CITY*

|  | No. Employed in Salt Lake City | Estimated Surplus over Local Needs† |
|---|---|---|
| Clerical.................. | 8,097 | 3,100 |
| Wholesale trade.......... | 4,137 | 2,000 |
| Retail trade............. | 9,565 | 1,600 |
| Other trade............. | 3,176 | 1,000 |
| Domestic, personal service. | 6,527 | 1,200 |
| Public service........... | 1,813 | 700 |
| Professional service...... | 5,691 | 500 |
| Manufacturing and mechanical industries...... | 13,522 | ......... |
| Transport, communications | 5,656 | ......... |
| Others.................. | 1,821 | ......... |
|  | 54,069 | 10,100 |

* Adapted from Harris, op. cit., p. 4.
† Number actually employed in the city minus the estimated local need for Salt Lake County. The latter is taken arbitrarily as 38.2 per cent of the total state employment on the assumption that the occupational need is proportional to population.

the city and (2) the per cent of the total state employment concentrated in Salt Lake City.

The criterion of employment beyond local needs suggests that about 10,000 of the 54,000 people employed in Salt Lake City are engaged in activities of primary regional significance. ... The other 44,000 are of local or secondary regional significance in that they serve partly the population of the immediate hinterland of Salt Lake County and partly the people of the city or county who are engaged directly in regional activities. [Thus there are at least 10,000 basic employees, and a portion of the remaining

44,000 apparently might be ascribed to basic effort. See Table 3 in this article.]

In each occupational group the relation of the total employed in Salt Lake City to the total employed in the state gives a clue to the regional importance of the city in that occupation. ... [E.g., Salt Lake City contains 28 per cent of Utah's population but 71 per cent of the state's employment in wholesale trade.][18]

In 1944 Homer Hoyt applied to New York City the method he proposed in the 1939 edition of the textbook already cited.[19] Employed by the Regional Plan Association of New York to make an economic base study, he determined that for every 100 basic employees in Greater New York there were 215 nonbasic employees. He explains his method as follows:

For wholesale trade it was assumed that all the workers in the Region in excess of the number of wholesale workers employed on the average by the same population in the United States outside the Region, could be attributed to wholesale activities for the benefit of persons outside the Region. For manufactures it was estimated that the New York Region would consume its share of the total national production based on its percentage of the total United States population (9.8 per cent) or purchasing power (14.7 per cent), and that the excess of its production above this percentage of the national production was attributed to production for persons outside the Region. For clothing it was assumed that the New York Region consumed slightly more than its percentage of the national income, or 15 per cent, because expenditures for clothing tend to increase with income; but for food it was assumed that the New York Region consumed more that its percentage of the total population but less than its percentage of the national income. In this manner, the number of persons working in New York for persons outside the Region, was calculated, and it is estimated ... that approximately 1,500,000 persons, or about 32 per cent of the total number employed in 1940 in the Region, were working on goods or services to be sold outside the Region. This means that for every 100 persons so

18 Chauncy Harris, "Salt Lake City, a Regional Capital," pp. 8–9.

19 See n. 9 above.

engaged, another 215 persons are employed in local manufacture or in service lines.[20]

Hoyt later concluded that the nonbasic component of this ratio was too high because many people were on relief. Since relief payments are a form of basic support, they could be considered to represent the equivalent of a certain amount of basic employment. Thus the 215 nonbasic employees in the foregoing ratio should be linked with a figure exceeding 100 for the basic component. Or, the ratio could be 100: a figure less than 215.[21]

Also in 1944 the Detroit City Plan Commission issued its *Economic Base of Detroit*, which states that for every 100 primary employees in Detroit the city has 117 secondary employees. No specific explanation is made of the method by which these ratios were determined, but it appears that *all manufacturing* is considered to be primary and that all other employment is considered to be secondary.[22] Indeed, "service" activities are specifically declared to be entirely secondary, "Detroit has no primary employment in services."[23]

An analysis of Cincinnati in 1946 sponsored by the City Planning Commission, with Victor Roterus as research director, estimated that the ratio was 100:170 between "urban-growth" (basic) and "urban-serving" (nonbasic) activity. The ratio was derived by much the same technique as that used by Hoyt in New York:

Urban-serving employment for each activity can be calculated by assuming that the population of the area will consume its proportionate share of the national production of goods and services. For example, if in the United States in 1940, 25.2 persons per 1,000 population were

employed in supplying professional services, then professional employment in the same ratio (amounting to 19,830) in the Cincinnati area would be classed as urban-serving. Employment above the figure would be considered urban-growth (serving persons outside the area).

This study made clear that the formula would have to be varied with each activity because urban consumption differs in many instances from the national.[24]

In 1949 Homer Hoyt released *The Economic Base of the Brockton, Massachusetts, Area* in which he identified the two components as "basic" and "service" ("nonbasic") and observed: "Every person employed in a basic industry normally supports approximately one other person in the service or nonbasic activities. Due to the instability of employment and to the number living on unemployment compensation, there were only 21,600 in the service lines in the Brockton area, compared with 26,500 in basic lines."[25] This is a ratio of 100 to 82 in favor of the basic endeavors. The report estimated employment in basic activity apparently on the basis of replies to questions submitted to various economic enterprises.

The analysis of Albuquerque, New Mexico, in 1949, undertaken jointly by the Federal Reserve Bank of Kansas City and the University of New Mexico's Bureau of Business Research, arrived at a ratio of 100:103 between "supporting" and "service" effort. This study actually is of the economic base of Bernalillo County: "Where economic data is concerned, Albuquerque can be considered as synonymous with Bernalillo County since no less than 95 per cent of the population lives in and finds employment in the urban area." The number in supporting employment was estimated by two steps: (*a*) sampling representative business establishments to determine the proportion of business each

[20] Regional Plan Association of New York, *The Economic Status of the New York Metropolitan Region in 1944*, p. 6.

[21] Personal letter to the writer, December 27, 1952. Mr. Hoyt credits Professor Richard U. Ratcliff with observing this discrepancy in the ratio.

[22] Detroit City Plan Commission, *Economic Base of Detroit* (1944), pp. 5, 47.

[23] *Ibid.*, p. 15.

[24] City Planning Commission, Cincinnati, Ohio, *Economy of the Area* (1946), pp. 22–23.

[25] Homer Hoyt Associates, *The Economic Base of the Brockton, Massachusetts, Area* (1949), p. 15.

did with people living outside Bernalillo County and (*b*) pro-rating total employment data for each type of activity (manufacturing, wholesale trade, etc.) according to the percentages determined by the sample.[26]

The "firm-by-firm" approach was used in the economic base study of Oshkosh, Wisconsin.[27] Data tabulation began, not with total employment figures for the city as a whole but with individual business firms each of which reported its total employment and the percentage of sales to local and non-local buyers. Accordingly, employment was pro-rated into basic and nonbasic components. For example, a company with 100 employees depending on the basic market for 70 per cent of its sales would have 70 employees ascribed to basic endeavor. Another company making 90 per cent of its sales to local buyers and employing ten people would have nine ascribed to nonbasic activity. Three-fourths of the city's employment was thus tabulated firm by firm; the numbers of employees in basic and nonbasic categories were accumulated with a final addition, an estimate, for the quarter of the economy not contacted in the survey. By this method, the basic-nonbasic ratio in Oshkosh was determined to be 100:60. The same method applied to Madison, Wisconsin, in 1951 revealed a B/N ratio of 100:82.[28]

It is not the purpose of this paper to review every urban study employing the basic-nonbasic concept, since Andrews' work is a comprehensive digest of these studies. Rather the purpose here is to observe some distinctive methods which have been used and the difference in B/N ratios resulting.

26 Federal Reserve Bank, Kansas City, Missouri, and Bureau of Business Research, University of New Mexico, *The Economy of Albuquerque, New Mexico* (1949), pp. 23 ff.

27 Alexander, "Oshkosh, Wisconsin: An Economic Base Study."

28 Alexander, "An Economic Base Study of Madison, Wisconsin."

It would seem that none of the methods used in the foregoing studies is entirely satisfactory for application to all cities. Tabulation of employment by individual companies is accurate but tedious and generally impractical for large settlements. Use of national proportions as factors for multiplying a community's employment in specific activities is acceptable as a method of estimating but probably permits a large degree of error, since it cannot discriminate well between types of communities. Its application to small cities might result in considerable errors.

The variation in the reported B/N ratios is considerable, from the one extreme of 100:215 (New York) to 100:60 (Oshkosh). Are these cities actually that different in their economic nature? Or were the methods used to determine the ratios that different?

The need is for more case studies which apply the basic-nonbasic concept. Surely the refining of the concept in terms of what should be included in "basic" and "nonbasic" activity, and improvement of the methodology for delimiting the two functions are worthy objectives for urban geographic research.

QUESTIONS FOR FURTHER RESEARCH

After various methods have been tested for measuring basic enterprise and reliable techniques have been proved, answers to the following questions should be available to further the understanding of urban settlements:

1. Is the B/N ratio truly a meaningful characteristic for distinguishing cities? If so, a method for classifying cities could be in terms of B/N ratios. How many cities and what types would have ratios of 100:100? What proportion and what types of settlements would have ratios of 100: less than 100? of 100: more than 100? Or will it be demonstrated that all cities have substantially the same ratio and that variations cited in the foregoing case studies are

coincidental, resulting from flaws in imperfect methodologies?

If the B/N ratio is found to be a meaningful variable, additional questions await investigation.

2. Does the B/N ratio vary with size of settlement? Is there a distinctive ratio for a hamlet, for a small town, for a city of 10,000 people, of 100,000, of 1,000,000? From the case studies cited it would appear that the larger the city, the larger the proportion of nonbasic activity. Communities compared in this study are listed in Table 4 according to population as reported in their analyses. The correlation between size of city and size of nonbasic component in these data is not entirely consistent; perhaps the relationship would have been clearer if there had been uniformity in methods of measuring the ratio. Nevertheless, in the case studies cited, the larger city was found to have the larger proportion of nonbasic employees where: (*a*) the same method was applied, even by different analysts, viz., New York and Cincinnati; (*b*) the same analyst applied different methods, viz., Homer Hoyt in New York and in Brockton; and (*c*) the same analyst applied the same method, viz., Oshkosh and Madison. Not until the same method is applied to numerous cities can evidence be advanced for this hypothesis, but the question can be raised to challenge investigation: Does the B/N ratio vary with population?

3. Does the B/N ratio vary with *type* of settlement? Would a manufacturing city of 50,000 inhabitants have a different ratio than a trading center or a government center of the same size?

4. Does the B/N ratio vary not only with *size* and *type* but also with *location* of settlement? Other things being equal, would a city of 40,000 people located 30 miles from a metropolis have a ratio different from a counterpart located 300 miles from a similar metropolis?

5. Does a city's B/N ratio vary from *time to time?* Would a city's ratio during a depression be different than in a period of prosperity?

6. Does a vigorously growing city have a different ratio than a stagnant city of the same size?

7. Are nonbasic activities similar from city to city? Or is the similarity between Oshkosh and Madison merely a coincidence?

8. How does one delimit an urban community for application of the basic-nonbasic concept? The United States Census provides one useful definition in terms of settlement density, essentially that an "urbanized area" includes not only a municipality of 2,500 inhabitants but also areas with a population density of 2,000 per square mile (as long as the agglomeration

TABLE 4

| Community | Population | B/N Ratio |
|---|---|---|
| New York...... | 12,500,000 | 100:215 |
| Detroit......... | 2,900,000 | 100:117 |
| Cincinnati...... | 907,000 | 100:170 |
| Brockton....... | 119,000 | 100:82 |
| Albuquerque.... | 116,000 | 100:103 |
| Madison........ | 110,000 | 100:82 |
| Oshkosh........ | 42,000 | 100:60 |

has at least 100 dwelling units). However, the economic functions of an urban agglomeration usually are rendered not only by the locally employed inhabitants but also by commuters who reside elsewhere. These people are *not* part of the settlement in terms of residence; they *are* part of its economic function. Conversely, residents of a community working elsewhere are not tabulated with employees in the settlement's economic activities, yet their endeavors bring money into the city. Should an analysis of a settlement's economy be in terms of those who work in it, who live in it, or both? Research endeavors in this field need to clarify the method of delimiting an urban settlement in terms of economic function.

9. What is the best method for applying the basic-nonbasic concept to a settlement,

once it has been delimited? What is the best definition of "basic"? Surely the concept needs refinement and the methodology needs improvement. In any case, the need is for an accurate method for measuring basic activity applicable to a metropolis as well as a small city. Surely, the search for such techniques is a profitable expenditure of a scholar's time.

## SUMMARY AND CONCLUSIONS

For several years students of "urbanology" have recognized a dichotomy in urban economies, based on geographical location of markets for the urban efforts. A city's *basic* activity links the settlement with other portions of the earth's surface; *nonbasic* endeavors link the settlement with itself.

This concept has merit for urban geography because it classifies economic functions fundamentally on the basis of space relationships, it reveals one group of economic ties which bind a city to other areas, it permits a classification of and compara-

tive analysis of settlements, and it provides an additional method for classifying individual economic activities within a city.

Case studies in which the concept has been applied have reported a wide difference in B/N ratios which appear to vary with method of measurement and size of settlement. There is a need for more case studies as a means of improving the methodology.

Urban analysts in a discipline where spatial associations are fundamental can augment their traditional methods of studying urban economies by application of a concept distinguishing between economic endeavors on the basis of location of the demand area. Application of the idea in more case studies should not only improve the methodology but also provide answers to numerous questions, contributing to the body of knowledge about urban settlement. This is a frontier challenging geographic analysts wishing to advance the borders of their discipline toward a mature fruition of economic geography.

VICTOR ROTERUS and WESLEY CALEF

# NOTES ON THE BASIC-NONBASIC EMPLOYMENT RATIO

The concept of basic and nonbasic employment and the notion of the importance of the ratio between them arose during the 1930's. It was developed as an analytical tool in the study of cities, primarily the study of cities for planning purposes. During the ensuing years, however, interest in the concept has become increasingly widespread among planners, economists, geographers, and others concerned with areal matters (particularly urban areas) as evidenced by a gradually increasing volume of studies oriented around the concept[1] and by the lively discussions centering on the basic-nonbasic concept at the last two national meetings of the Association of American Geographers.

Some studies done recently by the authors in connection with the work of the Area Development Division of the United States Department of Commerce have led us to some conclusions about its use as an analytical device for the study of areas. They form the body of these notes.

First of all, we may note that the basic-nonbasic employment ratio has meaning only for a definitely circumscribed area. It is a conceptual device for the study and presentation of certain limited aspects of

Reprinted from *Economic Geography*, XXXI (January, 1955), 17–20, by permission of the authors and the editor. (Copyright, 1955, by Clark University, Worcester, Mass.)

[1] A spate of recent articles includes Homer Hoyt, "Homer Hoyt on Development of Economic Base Concept," *Land Economics*, XXX (1954), 182–91; Richard B. Andrews, "Mechanics of the Urban Economic Base," *Land Economics*, XXIX (1953); John W. Alexander, "The Basic-Nonbasic Concept of Urban Economic Functions," *Economic Geography*, XXX (1954), 246–61 [see above, pp. 87–100]. The Hoyt article contains citations to numerous other studies involving the concept.

the economic life of a definitely delimited area, and any data which we may create (not discover) for any delimited area may change, chameleon-like, if the area is delimited differently. The notion of a definitely circumscribed area is, of course, inherent in the very definitions of basic and nonbasic. Roterus in his study of Cincinnati defined basic employment as that which produces goods and services for export beyond the adopted area. Although some minor variations in terminology have subsequently been suggested, export employment is still the guide to defining basic employment.

The relationship of basic-nonbasic employment to areal delimitation can be made most sharp if we consider the actual process of establishing such a ratio in detail.

Since the basic-nonbasic employment ratio has been almost universally applied to cities, we shall begin by extending the reasoning logically to an extreme case. Let us assume a crossroads hamlet—consisting of a tavern, a filling station, and a grocery store—whose market area is the township. Let us assume further that none of the business owners or their employees trade at any of the other hamlet stores. If we calculate the basic-nonbasic employment ratio we discover that all the gainfully employed represent 100 per cent basic employment; they must, because they all export goods or services from the delimited area. Let us further assume that all other employed people in the larger township area are dairy farmers whose production is sold entirely outside the township. If we take the township as the area of consideration, and again calculate the basic-nonbasic employment ratio, we discover, of course, that the farmers all represent basic employment, but our hamlet businessmen have now become nonbasic workers, because they furnish goods and services to the basically employed farmers. Let us assume further that there is a large city in the county and that all the farmers in the township are dairy farmers who sell fluid milk in the city. If we adopt the county as our study area and calculate our basic-nonbasic employment ratio, we find that our basically employed dairy farmers have now become non-basically employed because they furnish goods for the basic workers of our newly delimited region.

It becomes apparent by proceeding as we have that the numbers of nonbasic employees increase as the size of our delimited area increases. If we take the United States as our circumscribed unit, the ratio of basically employed to nonbasic workers becomes very small, because only workers producing for export out of the country would be basic employees. Clearly the basic-nonbasic proportion is not an absolute; it is a heuristic device for expressing certain relationships.

It has been noted repeatedly that the basic-nonbasic ratio "seems" to show an increase in the proportion of nonbasic workers as the size of cities increases. All the empirical studies indicate this to be the case. However, if the foregoing account of the process of making such employment analyses is correct, we should be astonished if that were not the case. It is a commonplace that large cities perform functions for themselves that smaller cities do not perform for themselves. Clearly, a larger city would have a greater proportion of its employed persons furnishing goods and services for one another than would a small city.

The basic-nonbasic employment ratio, then, is a measure of the degree of economic interdependence existing between the people of a circumscribed area and of persons in all other areas. As the size of the area increases, *ceteris paribus* (including such factors as income levels, level of busi-

ness activity, and cultural levels), the degree of interdependence will decrease.

Whether or not the basic-nonbasic employment ratio is a particularly effective or comparatively crude measure of this interdependence relationship has not been investigated widely. Difficulties in the application of the ratio have been discussed sufficiently so that they are fairly clearly understood. The comparative usefulness of some wholly different measure (such as commodity or monetary flow) needs to be investigated.[2]

What is important here, however, is that the economic base concept is simply a descriptive tool; quantitatively descriptive to be sure, but still merely a description of certain *limited* aspects of the economic functioning of a city or a region. Because it is simply a descriptive device, one wonders what purpose is served by elaborate schemes of data collection for the purpose of attempting extremely accurate proportioning of the employed population between basic and nonbasic groupings. On a priori grounds we would expect, and published studies confirm, that the ratio will vary with city size, and with numerous other circumstances of cities of the same size. For example, a radio plant in Cincinnati may sell 80 per cent of its output outside the metropolitan area one year, and the next year at almost the same level of output and employment sell 70 per cent locally owing to model and consumer preference changes. The Federal Reserve study of Wichita demonstrated the same fact on a city-wide scale.[3]

It appears to us that the important elements in the basic-nonbasic concept are the notion of the multiplier effect or growth-inducing influence of basic (export) industry and the space relationships aspects so

[2] All the matters mentioned in this paragraph and other closely allied issues are discussed in detail in Andrews, *op. cit.*, pp. 164–72.

[3] "The Employment Multiplier in Wichita," *Monthly Review* (Federal Reserve Bank of Kansas City), September 30, 1952.

persuasively pointed out by Alexander.[4] The recognition of these relationships certainly represented a major advance in both theory and practice of urban analysis and planning. "The distinction is useful primarily to indicate the process in urban growth."[5] Neither of these functions of the ratio demands a close determination of the exact ratio in order to accomplish effectively the purposes to which the ratio can be put. To use it in other than a gross way gives a false certitude to its use.

Hoyt's recent article[6] gives two excellent illustrations of our point here. He suggests that the ratio is peculiarly applicable to estimates of future population growth and land-use requirements and gives examples from his own work. In speaking of his population forecasts, he says, "Accordingly I took trends of past (Basic Industrial) growth as an indication of future growth unless I found reasons to expect a reversal of the trend." Again, he predicted land-use requirements "by taking estimated future employment in each type of manufacturing" and relating it to known space requirements. Hoyt is absolutely right in his implication that the use of a multiplier factor (which grows out of the basic-nonbasic idea) will give a more rational prediction of future population or future space requirements than would be made without such a factor. However, it is perfectly clear that the accuracy of his population predictions rests ultimately on the accuracy of his analytical guesses about (*a*) the future structure and size of industry in the community and (*b*) the future basic-nonbasic ratio. Note that we have said more rational, not more accurate. It is easy to imagine situations in which the use of the multiplier factor would increase the predictive margin of error. Basic-nonbasic re-

lationships are so expensive to compute precisely and are subject to so much variation from place to place and, especially, over different periods of time that the ratio is best utilized as a crude general measure. Wherever the concept appears to have utility in prosecuting study or planning of an urban area, it will best be used as a rough, approximate measure of the relationship. Elaborate precautions to establish the ratio with great accuracy will lead to false notions concerning the stability of the findings, and, more importantly, will not repay the effort expended so well as a similar expenditure of time along other lines of investigation.

Another point seems worthy of comment. There is universal agreement that the terms "basic" and "nonbasic" do not imply differences in the relative importance of the two types of activity. Nevertheless, we suspect that there exists a mental construct which, in fact, construes a greater significance to "basic" than to "nonbasic." We quote from a current article,[7] though scores of similar quotations are available. "The support of a city depends on the services it performs not for itself but for a tributary area. Many activities serve *merely* the population of the city itself." And again, "the inhabitants of . . . towns could not be expected to live by taking in one another's washing."

The first quotation undoubtedly reflects an aspect of our national economic life, but to structure our national economy mentally in this way is quite like focusing on the flea and ignoring the elephant on which it rests. With a national income of $305 billion last year, and with farm income representing only about a twentieth ($16.1 billion) of the total national income, we think, nevertheless, that there exists a traditional conception of a hierarchical economy with agriculture at the base, small settlements serving agriculture, larger settlements serving smaller settlements, etc.

[4] *Op. cit.*

[5] Victor Roterus, Cincinnati Metropolitan Master Plan Study "Economy of the Area," Cincinnati Planning Commission, 1946.

[6] *Op. cit.*

[7] Alexander, *op. cit.*

Granted that this is an aspect of our economic structure, the foregoing income figures seem to indicate that it is no longer the fundamental structure. By far the greatest portion of our economy does consist of urban dwellers making their living by "taking in one another's washing." The only way to escape this conclusion is to assign a more "fundamental" aspect to certain functions in our economy than to others; a point of view which all proponents of the basic-nonbasic ratio have been at pains to disclaim. Much more could be said on this point, but in the interests of brevity we will hope that the outlines of the idea are clear.

CHARLES M. TIEBOUT

# THE URBAN ECONOMIC BASE RECONSIDERED

Like old shoes, traditional concepts in economics are more comfortable. New ideas and tools are apt to be upsetting. Eventually, if the concept has merit, the resistance wears and the idea becomes part of the economist's medicine chest, perhaps in modified form. This is one path in the development of doctrine.

In recent years there has appeared the concept of "the urban economic base." Certainly among those people concerned with urban economics, the concept of the base has made some impression. Writers on and users of the base technique do not claim perfection, for both the theoretical concepts and empirical methods are not much past the embryo stage.[1] But the core of the idea seems to be well developed. It is vital that we see how it fits within the general framework of economic analysis before complete acceptance.

This paper will attempt to place the concept of the base within the more conventional framework of modern economic analysis. We believe our analysis will place the base theory in a perspective more valid as a description of urban economic reality and more operational in terms of urban economic research. The paper discusses (1) the objectives of base studies, (2) an analogous situation for the national economy, (3) the theory of the base, and (4) some misgivings about current usage of the base concept.

Reprinted from *Land Economics*, XXXII (February, 1956), 95–99, by permission of the author and the editor. (Copyright, 1956, by University of Wisconsin, Madison, Wis.)

[1] For a fair appraisal of the weakness of the base, conceptually and operationally, see Richard Andrews, "Mechanics of the Urban Economic Base," *Land Economics*, XXIX (May, 1953).

## OBJECTIVES OF BASE STUDY

Properly speaking, there is no single criterion for using the base concept. Any urban investigator is free to use the base for whatever purpose he has in mind, subject only to the restraint that the use makes sense. Yet the use of the base idea, even in modified form, necessarily commits the researcher to certain implicit assumptions about the urban economy. This is merely another way of saying that the urban base approach is a framework of analysis. It is, of course, impossible to study all aspects of the urban economic totality in detail. Some method of aggregation is essential. The simple listing of urban employment by industry types according to the Standard Industrial Classification is one type of aggregation. The conceptual framework of an input-output table is another. The classification according to exports versus local use is still another. Which technique one uses depends on the nature of the study.

The basic versus nonbasic method is one more framework. Supposedly, it is useful because it points up cause-and-effect relations in critical areas of the urban economy. As usually discussed, these areas deal with employment and/or income, somehow measured, in the urban community. These are items which relate to the general health or general economic welfare of the area. Thus it may be argued that the base approach is useful in pointing up the forces determining the level of general economic welfare in the community.

In turn, this leads to the question of just what magnitudes best indicate the level of general welfare. This issue is old hat to economists. It is delightful because it has no solution. Probably, if a vote were taken among economists, some form of income measurement would win. Insofar as other variables—employment, industrial production, and the like—move in the same direction, it does not make too much difference which measure is used. But income, especially per capita, together with some knowledge about its distribution, is probably the best single measure.[2]

Forgetting for the moment the statistical problems involved, we can say that the base approach is a useful framework because it helps to explain the level of income of the economy. Not only does it measure the level of income, when basic and nonbasic activities are added together, but supposedly it helps to explain sources of variation in income. Since so many of the activities of a community, both public and private, are tied to the level of income, this can be a powerful tool.

Yet a word of warning is in order. The base concept cannot explain everything, and in one case is weak in explaining income levels. This is the case of secular growth and factor endowment. By analogy, we know two things happen in the national economy: (1) we grow in possible levels of output, and (2) we do not always produce at capacity—in fact, we rarely do. If one considers the difference between income levels in India and those in the United States, the obvious explanation is poor versus rich factor endowments. On the other hand, if one is concerned with changes in incomes (cycles)—given the factor endowment—the levels of investments, consumption, and so forth are the key variables. A third way of viewing this difference is to consider the level of income in Chicago versus that in some southern city. This is again a question of factor endowment. In Chicago, however, changes in income from year to year may be considered another problem. The base concept is useful in con-

sidering income change but of much less use, as will be shown, in discussing secular income.

In summation, the base concept is useful as a framework of analysis in aggregating urban economic activity. Its advantage over other frameworks is that it points up the interactions of the local economy in a meaningful manner. At least that is what the base technique is supposed to do.[3] The only difficulty is that, as usually formulated, it does not. In order to see why it fails to provide a meaningful aggregation, it will be necessary to look at the same problem at the national level.

## NATIONAL INCOME FORECASTING

One of the favorite hobbies open to economists is that of predicting national income. Obviously, in prediction one must explain something about the nature of the changes which raise or lower the national aggregates. In other words, one must have some idea of how the economic system works. This does not imply that all forecasters use the same method. In general, there are two methods of predicting income levels. One uses selected indexes which seem to show leads in terms of national income. New orders and common-stock prices are examples of the indicators used. A second approach is to set up an econometric model of the economy. These may be simple systems or may involve many equations and unknowns. Implicitly, most discussions of the urban base are simplified econometric models. It is worth a moment to explore the "innards" of these creatures to see their basic ingredients. In this manner base studies can be seen in a new light.

Simply stated, the basic conditions of an econometric model, as used in forecasting, are threefold. (1) The level of some activities depends on the level of other activities in the system. For example, the level of

---

[2] For a discussion of other, but associated, criteria see Richard Andrews, "Mechanics of Urban Base: The Problem of Base Measurement," *ibid.*, XXX (February, 1954), 52–60.

[3] To argue that in order to understand the local economy one must study the demand for its exports is merely carrying the base approach one step further. This is not our concern at this point.

consumption is said to depend, in large part, on the level of income. (2) Some activities are independent of other activities in the economic system; that is, they have their level set by forces outside the system. Insofar as the level of government expenditures is set by Congress, it is an independent variable. (3) The economist, with the help of theory and data, can say something about the stability of the variables. For example, he may feel that the relation between income and consumption is fairly stable over time. On the other hand, he may view investment as unstable and subject to change almost at random.

A simple example will illustrate this point. Suppose we take a simple Keynesian system: (1) income = consumption + investment, (2) consumption = $f$ (income), and (3) investment = autonomous (i.e., set by forces outside the system). Let us further suppose the forecaster feels that, on the basis of historical data, consumption will be 0.8 of income. This, it is assumed, is a stable relation. Further, suppose that, from surveys of intended investment, the level of investment will be at 20. This is the independent variable which is, by assumption, set by forces outside the system postulated. Given the validity of these data we know that the income will be 100.[4] The addition of more equations and unknowns merely serves to elaborate the process and enhance the accuracy of the prediction. We need not fret about this issue. The point involved is that if this setup works and makes sense, then we have stated something about the workings of the economy. Our method of aggregation is useful.

Let us now turn back to the urban scene and see what this same sort of approach yields as a method of explaining income levels in the urban economy.

### THE THEORY OF THE ECONOMIC BASE

The urban economy consists of hundreds of economic units all engaged in the task of creating income. Our problem, as stated above, is to combine these units into mean-

ingful aggregates. The method will be similar to that of the national income forecaster.

First, let us look at those activities with levels set by forces outside the community. Exports, of course, are the biggest item. The forces which determine the demand for exports are outside the control of the urban area. But this does not mean all exports are independent. The exports of the city of New York to suburban towns in the form of retail goods may not be true exports. The reason this is so is that the people who buy these retail goods work in New York. Their level of expenditure is dependent on the income they receive from the city. In effect, the city is selling to itself. This is not true of a shopping center where, say, farmers come to buy. Farm income depends upon the demand for farm products and not upon the income of the shopping center. In the latter case the retail exports are true exports similar to manufactured goods. In the former case they are not. But, in general, it is safe to assume most exports are independent of the local community.

To stop here, as most base studies do, would be a mistake. Other income-creating activities in the urban economy are also more or less independent of the level of income. Residential housing, business investment, and local government expenditures appear to be largely independent of the level of local income. If they are, then they function in the same capacity as true exports. For a small area these may not be of much importance as a percentage of total basic income, but this is not true for larger areas.

On the other side of the base-type division are the nonbasic or dependent activities. As usually pointed out, these activities consist largely of local services, retail trade, and professional as well as other services. The assumption is that these activities have

[4] The three basic equations—(1) $Y = C + 1$, (2) $C = 0.8Y$, and (3) $I = 20$—reduce to (4) $Y = 0.8Y + 20$ by substitution, which yields (5) $Y = 100$.

their level set by the level of community income.

Now all that the theory of the economic base does is bring these two sets of activities together into an urban multiplier. An oversimplified but useful example parallel to our national income example would run as follows: (1) Total urban income = income earned in independent activities + income earned in dependent activities. (2) Income originating in dependent activities = 0.5 total income. (3) Income originating in dependent activities = 20. In this case the income would be 40. In income terms this implies a basic to nonbasic ratio of 1:1. If the function relating dependent activities to total income is constant, an increase of 10 in independent activities will give rise to a total increase of 20 in urban income. This is just a simple form of the well-known economic multiplier. It is the arithmetic of the base approach.

In discussing the forecasting of national income it was pointed out that, in addition to knowing which variables are dependent and which are independent, something should be said about the stability of the variables. If, in the example given in the preceding paragraph, at the same time the basic or independent activities level went up by 10, the function relating dependent or nonbasic activities shifted, independently, from 0.5 to 0.4, any forecast of future income would be quite a way off. Thus it is important to state something about the stability of the variables.

Alexander's study on Madison and Oshkosh gives some support to the a priori assertion that nonbasic to basic ratios are stable.[5] To see this, consider the case of two communities of about the same size and income, located a given distance from the central city. In both communities people possess income and will spend it only on retail goods and services. Our knowledge of the consumers' behavior would in-

dicate that these two sets of consumers will spend their money in roughly the same proportions for various retail and service goods.[6] If this is true, then it follows that the income flowing to dependent activities will be the same in both communities. Further, we would expect the number of employees and firms to be about the same. The ease of entry into retail and service activities, compared with manufacturing, probably accounts for this feature.

This is important. If consumption patterns in the urban economy are stable, as they tend to be for the national economy, then calling some activities dependent or nonbasic is useful. Not only do they depend on the level of urban income, but they depend on the level of urban income in a predictable manner. If empirical studies such as Alexander's can support and quantify this thesis, it will be a major step forward in urban research.

Again on a priori grounds one would look toward the independent activities for sources of instability. Local recessions do not start because of layoffs in the retail sector. Usually it is the manufacturer's business which folds, causing a downturn. Only further studies on the nature of demand for the various independent activities can point up the sources of instability in this area.

In summation, the base is simply a modified form of an old economic concept, the multiplier. Its usefulness is derived from the logic of the assumptions made concerning the behavior of the dependent and independent activities. These are yet to be tested fully by empirical research.

## Current Pitfalls in Base Studies

Using the above analysis as a frame of reference, some attention should be given to the current usage of the base concept. Although many items should be discussed, only four will be mentioned.

[5] John W. Alexander, "The Basic-Nonbasic Concept of Urban Economic Functions," *Economic Geography*, XXX (July, 1954), 246–61 [see above, pp. 87–100].

[6] See the recent *Family Income, Expenditures and Savings in 1950* (Bureau of Labor Statistics Bulletin No. 1097, June, 1953).

The definition of basic activities as the exports of goods, services, and capital beyond the boundaries of the region can be misleading. If the object of a base study is to show the forces determining the level of income, this concept is too limited in its coverage. This follows from the fact that as the boundaries of a region are expanded, exports become less and less. Yet the boundaries are arbitrary, and the wider they are drawn, the less the amount of exports. For the world as a whole there are no exports, but a great deal of income instability exists. This is the danger of equating exports with the source of instability.

Another problem which comes up is the selection of units by which to measure the economic base.[7] For reasons argued above, income may be the best method. But measuring income of a community is a tricky problem, both conceptually and statistically. Conceptually the problem arises as to what is meant by income. The simplest measure is "income accruing to residents." This is the value of the income received by the residents from all sources. Except for some minor adjustments it resembles personal income in the national picture. If factor income is used, all sorts of problems come up. How to allocate corporate profits among residents versus non-residents, rental incomes, and so forth, presents problems. It is not safe to take "value added" in production for an urban economy and use it as the urban income analogous to national income. For the national economy, where all factors are owned by the residents, product and charges against product are good measures. The value of a unit of output must be somebody's income. But for a community the value of the output, of a local steel mill for example, need not be income to local people, even if the concept of value added is used.

7 See Richard Andrews, "Mechanics of the Urban Economic Base," *Land Economics*, XXX (February, 1954), 51–60; Charles Leven, "An Appropriate Unit for Measuring the Urban Economic Base," *Land Economics*, XXX (November, 1954), 369–71.

Thus it seems highly desirable to use income accruing to residents as the measure of urban income. This income can be divided into incomes arising out of dependent and independent activities. In many cases the same individual will have income from both sources. Field surveys are needed to resolve this problem.

Another issue which comes up in base studies is that of secular growth. The concept of the base is essentially a short-run tool of analysis. If the desire is to explain future growth possibilities in terms of both the expansion of existing basic activities and the possibility of attracting new industry, then an approach via location theory and the economics of regional development is called for. All the base type of analysis can do is point out what happens *if* you add more independent activities. It cannot say whether or not you will grow in independent activities. The failure of mining towns to attract new industries with the closing of the mines is evidence supporting this thesis. In like manner, the springing-up of a retail sector around an atomic energy plant supports the thesis of dependent activities. The city planner interested in the possibilities of new manufacturers moving into a zone set aside for industry would do well to consider location theory and forget, in this instance, the economic base approach.

A final word may be in order about urban economic studies in general. The researcher may try to study everything about a community. This usually turns out to be an impossible task. Generally some logical framework is needed. The base approach is a framework. But unless this base approach is modified along the lines suggested above, it may not be very useful. Economics has a theory of the multiplier, both domestic and international, as well as a system of national income accounts. In modified form these can be of invaluable aid as tools of research in helping to understand the urban economy.

GUNNAR ALEXANDERSSON

## CITY-FORMING AND CITY-SERVING PRODUCTION

Within all human groups there is division of labor and specialization associated with an exchange of goods and services. In the family group such a division of labor has occurred in all times and in all cultures. Even between groups an exchange of goods and services has always taken place, indicating also a division of labor. This exchange has reached its fullest development in the modern Western world, where it is now possible for a man to satisfy a varied need for consumption of goods and services in spite of the fact that he may devote all his productive time to such specialized tasks as teaching other people's children or producing details of an automobile motor.

It can be assumed a priori that the exchange between groups will be relatively larger the smaller the groups are. Within a very large group it is possible to obtain a high degree of satisfaction of wants for the individuals even with a limited participation in the intergroup exchange. A division of labor and a specialization can be arranged within the group. Large countries, other things being equal, will have a smaller per capita foreign trade than small ones. It is not a pure coincidence that a large country like the United States, not to mention the Soviet Union, is more protectionist than small countries like Belgium or Sweden. The big country can better afford a protectionist policy because it will not lower the optimum standard of living as much as it would in the small country.

Cities,[1] considered as economic units, are much more dependent than countries on

Reprinted from *The Industrial Structure of American Cities* (Lincoln: University of Nebraska Press, 1956), pp. 14–20, by permission of the author and the publisher. (Copyright, 1956, by University of Nebraska Press.)

[1] The terms "city" and "town" are used in this study as synonyms.

the exchange of goods and services with other groups. A larger per cent of their population can be expected to be engaged in production for the outside world.

As the city is not an autonomous economic unit, there has been no practical need for a distinction between production for the city people and production for the outside world. That there nevertheless is a great interest in such a distinction is evident from the many suggestions of a terminology which have been put forward.[2] An analysis of the industrial structure of a city in order to determine its economic functions can hardly do without this distinction.

In the present study production for the

[2] Here only a few will be mentioned:
Ekstedt suggested "primary city-forming industries" (*primärt stadsbildande branscher*) and "secondary city-forming industries" (*sekundärt stadsbildande branscher*). H. W. Ahlmann, I. Ekstedt, G. Jonsson, W. William-Olsson, *Stockholms inre differentiering* (Stockholm, 1934), p. 40.

William-Olsson made a distinction between "exchange production" (*bytesproduktion*) and "self-production" (*egenproduktion*). Neither Ekstedt nor William-Olsson attempted a quantitative determination of these entities. W. William-Olsson, *Stockholms framtida utveckling* (Stockholm, 1941), pp. 12 ff.

Homer Hoyt and others have distinguished *basic* and *nonbasic* industries, and various ways of measuring them have also been suggested. For exhaustive accounts of the American discussion of the economic bases of cities see Richard B. Andrews, "Mechanics of the Urban Economic Base," *Land Economics* (1953) and John W. Alexander, "The Basic-Nonbasic Concept of Urban Economic Functions," *Economic Geography* (1954) [see above, pp. 87–100].

In a study of the Dutch city of Amersfoort the terms "primary" (*primair*) and "supporting" (*verzorgend*) industries were used, and a method was also worked out to estimate their size. L. H. Klaassen, D. H. van Dongen Torman, L. M. Koyck, *Hoofdlijnen van de sociaaleconomische ontwikkeling der gemeente Amersfoort van 1900–1970* (Leiden, 1949).

city's own inhabitants is referred to as *city-serving production*. Types are grade schools, small bakeries, neighborhood retail stores. Both manufacturing and service industries can be city serving.

The main attention in this study will, however, be directed toward industries which produce for a market outside the geographic city limit.[3] They are the agglomerative element, the *raison d'être* of the city, and might therefore be termed *city-forming industries*. They bring money to the city, which is used to pay for the imports of such goods and services in which the city is deficient.

It is possible to imagine a large, self-sufficient agglomeration in which all industries are city serving. In a primitive, feudal society it would be possible to have a large group of people living together in a city-like agglomeration, growing their food and other raw materials on the surrounding land and trading mostly with each other and very little with the outside world. Agglomerations that come rather close to this type exist in southern Italy, in Spain, and in other parts of the world.[4] Northwest European towns of the period before the Industrial Revolution were also self-sufficient to a degree that is now unknown there. Many citizens were part-time farmers. Much work that now, at least partly, has been taken over by city-forming industries was carried on in the homes.[5] But neither the present-day agricultural agglomerations of southern Europe nor the

northwest European towns of a hundred or more years ago are urban in the modern northwest European and American sense. In America and northwestern Europe of today, cities are highly specialized nodes of production with a very big exchange of goods and services with other urban places and with rural districts.

It is relatively simple to estimate, at least approximately, how large a share of a country's national product goes to the outside world in exchange for imported goods and services. Statistics on foreign trade are available for most countries, and it is usually possible to determine the amount of exports of services such as shipping, tourism, etc. Since internal trade is inadequately covered by statistics, to get an idea of the relative importance of city-forming and city-serving industries, we must resort to indirect methods.[6] Data on "exports" and "total product" of a given city which would allow a direct approach are not available.

An interesting attempt to single out and determine quantitatively the city-forming industries is presented in a study of the Dutch city of Amersfoort. For the eighteen

[3] Note the difference between the administrative city and the (usually larger) geographic city.

[4] They are conspicuously large, say, 10,000–40,000 inhabitants, mostly in areas dominated by one or a few crops, often wheat or wine, requiring the farmers' attention for the work in the most distant fields during a relatively short period of the year. Both wheat and wine are staple foods in these areas and a very large share of the crop is consumed locally.

[5] For example, many food products that were prepared at home in the old days are now furnished in finished or semifinished form by the food-manufacturing industry, to a large extent from out-of-town plants.

[6] The research staff of *Fortune* magazine (Oskaloosa, Iowa), Forbat (Skövde, Sweden), and Alexander (Oshkosh and Madison, Wis.) attempted the direct method by asking the firms of a city what shares of their production were for the city's own population. Interesting as these attempts are, they cannot be applied in a comparative study of cities. It is also doubtful whether they will yield safer results. It is for instance hard to believe that the average retail establishment can judge within reasonable margins of error how much it sells to customers residing in the city, as no records are kept of cash sales. The average businessman may not know the exact location of the city limit, much less the exact residence of his customers.

"Oskaloosa vs. the United States," *Fortune*, April, 1938.

Forbat, "Utvecklingsprognos för en medelstor stad. En studie över näringsliv, befolkning och bostäder i Skövde," *Statens kommitté för byggnadsforskning, rapport nr. 18* (Stockholm, 1949).

Alexander, *op. cit.*, summarizes the results of the Oshkosh and Madison studies, published by the Bureau of Business Research, School of Commerce, University of Wisconsin (1951 and 1953, respectively).

biggest cities in the Netherlands the percentage of people employed in different
manufacturing industries is figured. It is
assumed that the city with the minimum
equipment of a given industry barely has
city-serving (*verzorgend*) production. The
other cities with a smaller or larger "surplus" over this rate, in addition to their
city-serving production, also have a city-
forming (*primair*) portion of the industry
in question. The sizes of the two components are determined by the surplus.

Other methods for measuring the proportion between city-serving and city-forming production have been suggested. Hoyt
and others compare the ratio of a certain
industry in a given city with the ratio for
the country as a whole, the national average. This is convenient in an isolated urban
study, as both ratios are easily computed.
Theoretically, however, it seems to be less
satisfactory. The national average is a statistical abstraction, difficult to interpret.
This is especially true for the sporadic industries. The national average of automobile manufacturing in the United States, to
take one example, is 1.5 per cent, but only
12 per cent of the cities have such a high
ratio of people employed in the automotive
industry. Seventy per cent of the cities
have a rate of 0.2 per cent or lower.

In Detroit 28 per cent of the gainfully
employed population is engaged in automobile manufacturing. One and a half per
cent are, according to Hoyt, needed to supply the city's own population with a normal
number of cars. The 1.5 per cent represents
the city-serving (nonbasic) portion, the remaining 26.5 per cent is the city-forming
(basic) ratio of automobile manufacturing
in Detroit.

The national average is evidently influenced by such irrelevant facts—for the
individual city—as foreign trade and the
configuration of the national boundary. If
Mexico joined the United States, all national averages would change. Or if the
United States were divided into autonomous countries, the national average of au-

tomobile manufacturing with which Detroit
would then be compared would be quite
different from the above ratio. These two
hypothetic changes would, everything else
being equal, have no direct effects on the
industrial structure of Detroit, but they
would definitely influence the city-serving
ratio computed according to Hoyt.

The present study of 864 American
cities with 10,000 or more inhabitants has
been based on the same theory as the
Amersfoort investigation. Accordingly, the
whole of Detroit's automobile manufacturing should be considered as a city-forming
industry. Some of the cars made in Detroit
will undoubtedly be sold to people living in
the city. But all automobile factories in
Detroit were built for a bigger market than
the city itself offers. This is in contrast to
laundries and grade schools, which, even if
they occasionally may have an out-of-town
customer, were built for the city market or
perhaps for only a section of it.

All sporadic industries are of the same
type as automobile manufacturing, whereas
the ubiquitous industries in general are
more complex than the type represented
by laundries and grade schools. Many
ubiquitous industries, like retail shopping
stores, wholesale establishments, etc., are
in most cities based on both the city market
and a wider market, usually the trade area
of the city. They are partly city serving,
partly city forming. In some cases, such as
insurance companies, banks, and public
administration, the industries have both a
sporadic and a ubiquitous component, reflecting the hierarchic structure of all large
organizations. There can also be a sporadic
component in a generally ubiquitous industry for other reasons. Movie production,
the armed forces, and the universities are
examples of such sporadic branches within
ubiquitous industries[7] whose distribution
patterns are shaped by conspicuous advantages of large-scale production similar to
those found in manufacturing. Most ubiq-

[7] Entertainment, public administration, and education, respectively.

uitous industries are both city forming and city serving. Our problem is to determine the ratios of the two components.

The method employed here to determine the ratio of city-serving production will apparently give lower values than methods used by Hoyt and others.[8] Our values answer the question: *What ratios in different industries are a necessary minimum to supply a city's own population with goods and services of the type which are produced in every normal city?*

The following procedure was used to obtain these ratios. For every industry two points on the cumulative distribution diagrams were tentatively chosen, 1 and 5 per cent from the origin, respectively, which represent cities number 9 and 43, as there are 864 cities altogether. These values and not the very lowest ones were chosen to avoid extreme ratios representing such agglomerations as Midway-Hardwick, Georgia, and Kings Park, New York, which are just large hospitals with some settlement around them and are not towns in the ordinary sense. They reach the size of 10,000 inhabitants only because their patients are included. Other agglomerations with very low rates are the two newly built "atom cities," Oak Ridge, Tennessee, and Richland, Washington. They can, however, hardly be considered "normal" yet. Their inhabitants probably go to nearby cities for services which normally would be available in agglomerations of their size and which will probably be available when they have reached a higher degree of maturity.[9]

The values for the two tentative points were tested against actual city structures to find if there are any cities corresponding to the two structure models. It could

---

[8] It is of course perfectly possible to imagine a (large) city with the same industrial structure as the country (with the exception for agriculture), which would give a city-serving percentage of close to 100. Comparisons with the national averages will give by far the highest values for city-serving production; the methods employed by Forbat and Alexander should theoretically give somewhat higher values than the method employed in the present study.

---

a priori be expected that such barely "self-sufficient" cities might be found among extreme manufacturing cities or one-sided service towns in regions with a high city density. They would have a very small trade area, small enough to be considered as a negligible quantity, as people in the neighborhood would prefer to trade in better-equipped cities. On the other side they would have all the service production which normally is available in any city of 10,000 or more inhabitants for its own population. It should be self-sufficient but not deficient in such services.

Among agglomerations which resemble the first tentative model are Kannapolis, North Carolina, and Bristol, Rhode Island. The first one is a company-owned textile-mill town with mills established in 1877,[10] about 22 miles northeast of Charlotte, in a region with an agglomeration density among the highest to be found anywhere in the United States. It is an extremely one-sided textile town with 28,400 inhabitants. The second one, dominated by the manufacturing of saddles, rubber products, and textiles, is located just 12 miles southeast of Providence. After considering the character and location of these agglomerations, they have been judged to be deficient in essential service industries. According to this structure model, city-serving production employs 28.3 per cent of the gainfully employed population of an American city.

If the norm structure is built instead on values 5 per cent from the origin on the cumulative distribution diagrams, city-serving production employs 37.7 per cent. The curves of the ubiquitous industries

---

[9] An indication in this direction is the fact that the small twin cities of Pasco and Kennewick near Richland, which themselves have had their population increased by about 300 per cent to 20,300 inhabitants in the 1940's, have high ratios for "Other retail trade" (12.9 per cent), "Eating and drinking places" (5.1 per cent), etc. The pronounced service centers of Walla Walla and Yakima are within reach for less frequent shopping for the inhabitants of Richland.

[10] *Columbia Lippincott Gazetteer* (New York, 1953).

have all leveled off at this point; the extremely low values are all to the left. It therefore seems that a theoretic minimum structure may be based on these values. Among cities with an industrial structure very similar to that of the second tentative norm structure are Woonsocket, Rhode Island, Tamaqua, Pennsylvania, and Thomasville, North Carolina. Woonsocket is a textile town with 40,100 inhabitants. Tamaqua is a mining town with 11,500 in-

habitants in the Pennsylvanian anthracite region. It is also a railroad and chemical town of B-type. Thomasville is a furniture and textile town with 11,200 inhabitants. All three cities are located in regions with a high density of urban agglomerations.

Local studies of these or similar agglomerations need to be undertaken for a safer testing of the norm structure.

It is evident that even if the values found are valid for cities of 10 to 50 thou-

TABLE 1

INDUSTRIAL STRUCTURE OF SOME TOWNS

| Industry | $k_1$ | $k$ | Kings Park | Rich-land | Kannap-olis | Bristol | Woon-socket | Tama-qua | Thomas-ville |
|---|---|---|---|---|---|---|---|---|---|
| Mining | 0 | 0 | 0 | 0 | 0 | 0 | 0 | 279 A | 0 |
| Construction | 26 | 35 | 31 | 98 C | 35 | 46 | 41 | 29 | 41 |
| Lumber and furniture | 0 | 0 | 0 | 0 | 1 | 1 | 3 | 0 | 295 A |
| Primary metal | 0 | 0 | 2 | 0 | 0 | 77 C | 8 | 7 | 1 |
| Fabricated metal | 0 | 0 | 1 | 0 | 1 | 3 | 2 | 2 | 1 |
| Machinery | 0 | 1 | 1 | 0 | 0 | 5 | 49 | 2 | 2 |
| Electrical machinery | 0 | 0 | 1 | 0 | 0 | 14 | 1 | 0 | 1 |
| Motor vehicles | 0 | 0 | 0 | 0 | 0 | 0 | 1 | 1 | 0 |
| Transport equipment | 0 | 0 | 11 | 0 | 0 | 2 | 0 | 0 | 1 |
| Other durable | 1 | 2 | 4 | 0 | 1 | 45 | 8 | 3 | 16 |
| Food | 3 | 7 | 3 | 2 | 5 | 9 | 8 | 18 | 8 |
| Textile | 0 | 0 | 0 | 0 | 695 A | 196 B | 465 A | 9 | 256 A |
| Apparel | 0 | 0 | 3 | 0 | 1 | 0 | 15 | 46 | 11 |
| Printing | 5 | 7 | 2 | 7 | 6 | 5 | 7 | 8 | 7 |
| Chemicals | 0 | 1 | 1 | 664 A | 0 | 1 | 3 | 115 B | 2 |
| Other non-durable | 0 | 1 | 1 | 0 | 0 | 298 A | 39 | 1 | 1 |
| Railroads | 2 | 4 | 6 | 2 | 2 | 2 | 3 | 127 B | 6 |
| Trucking | 3 | 5 | 2 | 0 | 9 | 6 | 9 | 8 | 4 |
| Other transport | 3 | 5 | 8 | 2 | 9 | 5 | 8 | 4 | 5 |
| Telecommunication | 4 | 6 | 0 | 2 | 3 | 7 | 8 | 8 | 5 |
| Utilities | 6 | 9 | 3 | 2 | 2 | 8 | 10 | 12 | 8 |
| Wholesale | 9 | 14 | 2 | 1 | 4 | 12 | 10 | 15 | 10 |
| Food retail | 23 | 27 | 26 | 14 | 28 | 28 | 29 | 33 | 25 |
| Eating places | 18 | 21 | 18 | 13 | 10 | 19 | 24 | 30 | 21 |
| Other retail | 63 | 80 | 38 | 37 | 65 | 58 | 80 | 77 | 78 |
| Finance | 12 | 18 | 12 | 7 | 12 | 17 | 19 | 18 | 15 |
| Business services | 1 | 2 | 2 | 5 | 1 | 2 | 4 | 2 | 3 |
| Repair services | 8 | 11 | 3 | 2 | 10 | 13 | 15 | 21 | 10 |
| Private households | 10 | 13 | 13 | 13 | 28 | 14 | 9 | 5 | 37 |
| Hotels | 2 | 3 | 6 | 4 | 4 | 3 | 2 | 9 | 2 |
| Other personal services | 17 | 21 | 14 | 13 | 22 | 22 | 18 | 16 | 33 |
| Entertainment | 5 | 7 | 6 | 7 | 6 | 2 | 7 | 7 | 10 |
| Medical services | 13 | 18 | 736 A | 21 | 6 | 11 | 17 | 21 | 13 |
| Education | 22 | 26 | 22 | 43 | 16 | 28 | 22 | 25 | 27 |
| Other professional services | 10 | 12 | 5 | 8 | 10 | 13 | 14 | 14 | 25 |
| Public administration | 17 | 21 | 21 | 43 | 7 | 23 | 40 | 22 | 20 |
| | 283 | 377 | 1,000 | 1,000 | 1,000 | 1,000 | 1,000 | 1,000 | 1,000 |

$k$ = values representing point five per cent from origin on cumulative distribution diagrams.

$k_1$ = same as above for point one per cent from origin.

sand inhabitants, which make up the bulk of the total number in this study, they may not be applicable to larger cities. In New York with its 13 million inhabitants, there will be a relatively larger exchange within the city than is possible within a smaller agglomeration. With increasing size of the town, city-serving production can be expected to increase in relative importance, not to decrease. When it is stated that 37.7 per cent of the gainfully employed population in American cities are engaged in city-serving production, this is to be considered a minimum figure relevant for small cities. In bigger urban agglomerations it can be expected to be higher.[11]

For retail trade the national average of employment should coincide with the $k$-value if this value has been wisely chosen and if there is an "American standard" in the sense that 1,000 average Americans, rural or urban, living in New York or in Mississippi, give employment to the same number of retail trade employees. This must be true as the imports and exports of retail trade services (by tourists, etc.) are infinitesimal in relation to the total retail trade of the United States.

The assumption of an American standard, implied in the present study, is of course an approximation. It is therefore

not surprising that the national average for Other retail trade, 9.2 per cent, differs from the $k$-value, 8.0 per cent. There is a regional difference in the standard of living as well as a difference between rural and urban areas. In California with an above-average urbanization and high standards of living, the per capita retail sales were 26 per cent higher than the United States average in 1948, and the employment in Other retail trade in 1950 was 17 per cent higher than the national average. These differences are mostly due to higher levels of income in California and only in some degree to the presence of a relatively large floating population of non-resident tourists and other visitors.[12]

The high percentage of retail trade employment for some states with high standards of living influences the national average but not the $k$-value. The case of retail trade raises the question whether it would not have been motivated with different $k$-values for different regions. Private households is another industry in which there are at least two different "American standards," one for the South and one for the rest of the country.

The differences between national average and $k$-value for other ubiquitous industries are largely due to the inclusion of sporadic branches in these industries. Thus the national average for education includes college employees, but these do not influence the $k$-value, as most cities do not have a college.

[11] These logical deductions are supported by the results of Alexander's studies on Oshkosh and Madison, Wisconsin, both made with the same methods. For Oshkosh (41 thousand inhabitants) Alexander found a city serving (nonbasic) percentage of 37.5 and for the larger Madison (110 thousand inhabitants), a percentage of 45.1. Alexander, *op. cit.*, p. 251.

[12] "Economic Survey of California," reprint from *California Blue Book* (1950), p. 56.

WALTER ISARD and ROBERT KAVESH

# ECONOMIC STRUCTURAL INTERRELATIONS OF METROPOLITAN REGIONS

The complex internal organization of any given metropolitan region is influenced by the delicately interwoven net of relationships that bind sets of city-regions into a unified whole. It is the purpose of this paper to study certain interurban connections. In setting forth hypotheses concerning spatial flows among metropolitan areas, we shall extend previously developed principles and illustrate with an abstract interdependence model.[1] In the first section a simplified model will be presented. In later sections this model will be qualified in an attempt to make it more realistic.

## I

Assume a large area is meaningfully divided into three regions. Each of the first two has a major focal point at which social and economic activity center, which is a major industrial city. These two are designated Metropolitan Region I and Metropolitan Region II. The third region, specializing in agricultural and extractive pursuits, lacks a single clear-cut focus and is designated Region III.

In addition to a delineation of regions, a classification of various economic and social activities is undertaken. Certain goods and services are marketed only in the region in which they are produced; in contrast, others are marketed not only in the region in which they are produced but also in the other regions, though to different degrees. The former are called "local" activities; the latter, "export."

To avoid cumbersome detail, the numerous economic functions are grouped into nine categories. These are recorded for each region in Table 1. The first for each region represents the characteristic export industry (heavy manufacturing for Metropolitan Region I, light manufacturing for Metropolitan Region II, and agriculture and extractive activity for Region III). The next eight are identical for each region: namely, power and communications; transportation; trade; insurance and rental activities; business and personal services; educational and other basic services; construction; and households.[2] Each of these eight activities is for the moment assumed to be local in nature. None of their output is shipped outside the region in which it is produced. Thus, by definition, it is through export activities alone that the simplified economies of the several regions are interrelated.

Classification of outputs represents only one phase of our problem. Another phase concerns input structures; more specifically, the inputs of each of several factors—raw materials, power, transportation, labor, equipment and other services—required to produce a unit of output. In actuality, much of the output of many industries such as basic steel is absorbed by other industries as inputs rather than by households. Therefore, in order to under-

Reprinted from *American Journal of Sociology,* LX (September, 1954), 152–62, by permission of the authors and the editor. (Copyright, 1954, by the University of Chicago.)

[1] Elsewhere, a model depicting some of the structural interrelationships *within* a given metropolitan region has been sketched (W. Isard, R. A. Kavesh, and R. E. Kuenne, "The Economic Base and Structure of the Urban Metropolitan Region," *American Sociological Review,* XVIII [June, 1953], 317–21). Clearly, however, self-sufficiency is not characteristic of large city-regions.

[2] The output of households roughly corresponds to the value of the services of labor and of capital and land owned by them.

116

# TABLE 1

HYPOTHETICAL INTERMETROPOLITAN TRANSACTIONS TABLE, 19—— CENTS WORTH OF INPUTS PER DOLLAR OF OUTPUT

INDUSTRY PURCHASING

| Industry Producing | (1) Heavy Manufacturing | (2) Power and Communication | (3) Transportation | (4) Trade | (5) Insurance and Rental | (6) Business and Pers. Serv. | (7) Educational and Other Serv. | (8) Construction | (9) Households | (10) Light Manufacturing | (11) Power and Communication | (12) Transportation | (13) Trade | (14) Insurance and Rental | (15) Business and Pers. Serv. | (16) Educational and Other Serv. | (17) Construction | (18) Households | (19) Agriculture and Extraction | (20) Power and Communication | (21) Transportation | (22) Trade | (23) Insurance and Rental | (24) Business and Pers. Serv. | (25) Educational and Other Serv. | (26) Construction | (27) Households |
|---|---|---|---|---|---|---|---|---|---|---|---|---|---|---|---|---|---|---|---|---|---|---|---|---|---|---|---|
| **Metropolitan Region I:** | | | | | | | | | | | | | | | | | | | | | | | | | | | |
| 1. Heavy manufacturing | 33 | 1 | 3 | 1 |  | 9 | 1 | 18 | 3 | 4 | 1 | 2 | 2 | 1 | 14 | 15 | 4 |  | 4 | 1 | 2 | 2 | 1 | 14 | 15 | 4 |  |
| 2. Power and communication | 1 | 11 | 3 | 2 | 8 | 4 | 2 | 4 | 1 |  |  |  |  |  |  |  |  |  |  |  |  |  |  |  |  |  |  |
| 3. Transportation | 2 | 2 | 5 | 1 | 1 | 1 | 2 | 9 | 3 |  |  |  |  |  |  |  |  |  |  |  |  |  |  |  |  |  |  |
| 4. Trade | 1 |  | 2 |  |  | 3 | 5 | 2 | 12 |  |  |  |  |  |  |  |  |  |  |  |  |  |  |  |  |  |  |
| 5. Insurance and rental activities | 1 | 1 | 3 | 5 | 2 | 5 | 4 | 3 | 12 |  |  |  |  |  |  |  |  |  |  |  |  |  |  |  |  |  |  |
| 6. Business and personal services | 1 | 1 | 2 | 7 | 7 | 4 | 2 |  | 3 |  |  |  |  |  |  |  |  |  |  |  |  |  |  |  |  |  |  |
| 7. Educational and other basic services |  |  |  |  | 1 |  | 1 |  | 10 |  |  |  |  |  |  |  |  |  |  |  |  |  |  |  |  |  |  |
| 8. Construction |  | 4 | 6 |  | 10 |  | 1 |  | 1 |  |  |  |  |  |  |  |  |  |  |  |  |  |  |  |  |  |  |
| 9. Households | 34 | 58 | 58 | 63 | 53 | 46 | 50 | 40 | 20 |  |  |  |  |  |  |  |  |  |  |  |  |  |  |  |  |  |  |
| **Metropolitan Region II:** | | | | | | | | | | | | | | | | | | | | | | | | | | | |
| 10. Light manufacturing | 4 | 1 | 2 | 2 | 1 | 14 | 15 | 4 |  | 28 | 1 | 3 | 1 |  | 9 | 1 | 18 | 3 | 4 | 1 | 2 | 2 | 1 | 14 | 15 | 4 |  |
| 11. Power and communication |  |  |  |  |  |  |  |  |  | 1 | 11 | 3 | 2 | 8 | 4 | 2 | 4 | 1 |  |  |  |  |  |  |  |  |  |
| 12. Transportation |  |  |  |  |  |  |  |  |  | 2 | 2 | 5 | 1 | 1 | 1 | 2 | 9 | 3 |  |  |  |  |  |  |  |  |  |
| 13. Trade |  |  |  |  |  |  |  |  |  | 1 |  | 2 |  |  | 3 | 5 | 2 | 12 |  |  |  |  |  |  |  |  |  |
| 14. Insurance and rental activities |  |  |  |  |  |  |  |  |  | 1 | 1 | 3 | 5 | 2 | 5 | 4 | 3 | 12 |  |  |  |  |  |  |  |  |  |
| 15. Business and personal services |  |  |  |  |  |  |  |  |  | 1 | 1 | 2 | 7 | 7 | 4 | 2 |  | 3 |  |  |  |  |  |  |  |  |  |
| 16. Educational and other basic services |  |  |  |  |  |  |  |  |  |  |  |  |  | 1 |  | 1 |  | 10 |  |  |  |  |  |  |  |  |  |
| 17. Construction |  |  |  |  |  |  |  |  |  |  | 4 | 6 |  | 10 |  | 1 |  | 1 |  |  |  |  |  |  |  |  |  |
| 18. Households |  |  |  |  |  |  |  |  |  | 25 | 58 | 58 | 63 | 53 | 46 | 50 | 40 | 20 |  |  |  |  |  |  |  |  |  |
| **Region III:** | | | | | | | | | | | | | | | | | | | | | | | | | | | |
| 19. Agriculture and extraction | 6 | 5 | 4 | 1 | 2 | 14 | 15 | 18 | 6 | 6 | 5 | 4 | 1 | 2 | 14 | 15 | 18 | 6 | 28 | 1 | 3 | 1 |  | 9 | 1 | 18 | 3 |
| 20. Power and communication |  |  |  |  |  |  |  |  |  |  |  |  |  |  |  |  |  |  | 1 | 11 | 3 | 2 | 8 | 4 | 2 | 4 | 1 |
| 21. Transportation |  |  |  |  |  |  |  |  |  |  |  |  |  |  |  |  |  |  | 2 | 2 | 5 | 1 | 1 | 1 | 2 | 9 | 3 |
| 22. Trade |  |  |  |  |  |  |  |  |  |  |  |  |  |  |  |  |  |  | 1 |  | 2 |  |  | 3 | 5 | 2 | 12 |
| 23. Insurance and rental activities |  |  |  |  |  |  |  |  |  |  |  |  |  |  |  |  |  |  | 1 | 1 | 3 | 5 | 2 | 5 | 4 | 3 | 12 |
| 24. Business and personal services |  |  |  |  |  |  |  |  |  |  |  |  |  |  |  |  |  |  | 1 | 1 | 2 | 7 | 7 | 4 | 2 |  | 3 |
| 25. Educational and other basic services |  |  |  |  |  |  |  |  |  |  |  |  |  |  |  |  |  |  |  |  |  |  | 1 |  | 1 |  | 10 |
| 26. Construction |  |  |  |  |  |  |  |  |  |  |  |  |  |  |  |  |  |  |  | 4 | 6 |  | 10 |  | 1 |  | 1 |
| 27. Households |  |  |  |  |  |  |  |  |  |  |  |  |  |  |  |  |  |  | 40 | 58 | 58 | 63 | 53 | 46 | 50 | 40 | 20 |

stand the economic base of metropolitan regions and to anticipate changes within them, it is necessary to know the inter-metropolitan input structures of industries. This requires a table of intermetropolitan[3] interindustrial relations for a base year period, on the order of Table 1.[4]

In Table 1 any one column records the cents' worth of inputs from each industrial category in each region per dollar's worth of output of a given industrial category of a given region where both the given industrial category and the region are specified by the column heading. For example, reading down column 1 furnishes information on the cents' worth of various inputs from the several regions per dollar output of heavy manufacturing in Metropolitan Region I. Thirty-three cents' worth of heavy manufacturing in Metropolitan Region I is fed back as an input into the same activ-

ity in the same region for every dollar's worth of its output (such as Pittsburgh steel, which is fed back to Pittsburgh steel-works). Two cents of transportation services of Metropolitan Region I is absorbed per dollar's worth of heavy manufacturing of Metropolitan Region I. In addition to inputs from other service sectors and the household sector of Metropolitan Region I, the heavy manufacturers of Metropolitan Region I require inputs from the light-manufacturing industry of Metropolitan Region II and from agriculture and extractive activities of Region III. These latter, of course, entail interregional flows.

Consider another column, the fifteenth, which refers to "Business and Personal Services" in Metropolitan Region II. Per dollar of its output nine cents' worth of heavy-manufacturing products from Metropolitan Region I is required. None of the other sectors of Region I furnishes inputs, because these other sectors are defined as local and hence export nothing. Since the business and personal services sector of Metropolitan Region II does not consume

[3] To avoid awkward phrases we use the term "intermetropolitan" as if Region III were a metropolitan region.

[4] Most of the coefficients in Table 1 are based upon a consolidation of the 50 × 50 interindustry flow matrix developed by the Bureau of Labor Statistics (W. D. Evans and M. Hoffenberg, "The Interindustry Relations Study for 1947," *Review of Economics and Statistics*, XXXIV [May, 1952], 97–142). In reducing the B.L.S. 50 industry classification to our three export and eight local industrial categories we crudely defined:

1. *Heavy manufacturing* as the aggregate of iron and steel, plumbing and heating supplies, fabricated structural metal products, other fabricated metal products, agricultural, mining, and construction machinery, metalworking machinery, other machinery (except electric), motors and generators, radios, other electrical machinery, motor vehicles, other transportation equipment, professional and scientific equipment, miscellaneous manufacturing, and scrap and miscellaneous industries.

2. *Light manufacturing* as the aggregate of food and kindred products, tobacco manufactures, textile mill products, apparel, furniture and fixtures, paper and allied products, printing and publishing, chemicals, rubber products, and leather and leather products.

3. *Agriculture and extraction* as the aggregate of agriculture and fisheries, lumber and wood products, products of petroleum and coal, stone, clay, and glass products, and nonferrous metal.

"Service Activities" were expressed in a less aggregative form in order to present some detail on

the internal structural processes of metropolitan regions associated with these activities. The category "Education and Other Basic Services" consists of the services of medical, educational and non-profit institutions, amusement, and eating and drinking places.

Certain activities are omitted from the analysis because their levels of output are not structurally related to the interindustrial matrix of coefficients. These are: inventory change, foreign trade, government, capital formation, and unallocated. Households, generally included with this group, were introduced into the structural matrix in order to catch the local multiplier effect of new basic industry upon a community via the additional income generated.

The actual derivation of a coefficient involves the division of the total value of inputs from a given sector into a second sector by the output of the second sector. That is, if in 1947 the amount of chemicals used in steel production was $99 million and the output of steel was $12.3 billion, the input coefficient representing the cents' worth of chemicals per dollar of steel would be 0.8049.

The data are rounded to the nearest whole figure. Inputs of less than one-half cent per dollar output are not recorded.

any agricultural and extractive products, all its other inputs must come from Region II, as is depicted in Table 1.

Aside from their obvious descriptive value, of what significance are the data of Table 1? In general, input structures are not haphazard; rather they reflect to a large extent stable and meaningful relations. If the output of an efficient aluminum works is doubled, it is reasonable to expect that approximately twice as much power, alumina, carbon electrodes, and other inputs will be required. In short, subject to certain serious qualifications to be discussed later, the input of any service or good into a particular activity may be said within certain limits to vary approximately in direct proportion with the output of that particular activity.

To illustrate the usefulness of input structure information, suppose a resource development program calls for an increase of one million dollars in the output of heavy manufacturing in Region I. How will this affect the output of each activity in each region?

In column 1 of Table 1 are listed coefficients which indicate the cents' worth of various inputs required per dollar output of heavy manufacturing. Multiplying these coefficients by one million gives us the direct inputs required to produce one million dollars' worth of heavy manufactures. These are called the first-round input requirements and are listed in column 1 of Table 2.

But to produce the first-round requirement of $330,000 of heavy manufacturing (item 1 in column 1, Table 2) likewise requires a whole series of inputs. These can be obtained by multiplying column 1 of Table 1 by 330,000. And to produce the $20,000 of transportation (item 3, column 1, Table 2) requires inputs which can be obtained by multiplying column 3 of Table 1 by 20,000. Similarly, the inputs required to produce each of the other items listed in column 1 of Table 2 can be derived. It should be noted that the $340,000, which

is listed in the ninth cell of column 1, Table 2, represents an increment of income received by the households in Metropolitan Region I. This increment results in increases in effective demand for a series of products. On the arbitrary assumption that two-thirds of this new income is spent, these increases in effective demand can be obtained by multiplying column 9, Table 1 (which shows how a dollar spent by households is typically distributed among various products), by 226,667.

Adding together all these inputs (including the new effective demands of households) necessary for the production of the first round of requirements yields the second round of requirements which is recorded in column 2 of Table 2. In turn, the production of the second round of requirements necessitates a third round. This is computed in the same manner as was the second round. Furnishing a third round requires a fourth; a fourth round, a fifth; etc. Each of these rounds is recorded in Table 2. It should be noted that the totals of the rounds converge.[5] After a point it becomes feasible to stop the round-by-round computation and to extrapolate the remaining requirements. However, we have not carried through any extrapolation; as a refinement it implies a degree of accuracy and stability in the data, which, as we shall see in the following section, does not exist in fact.

Thus, we have developed a round-by-round description of how an impulse acting upon one sector of a metropolitan region is transmitted to every sector in the same region and every other region. To derive the total effect, it is merely necessary to sum the rounds horizontally. The totals are recorded in column 8 of Table 2. These totals, of course, can be compared with

[5] The convergence of rounds results from the assumption that only two-thirds of the income received by households in any given round is expenditure in the succeeding round and from the omission of the non-structurally related sectors of inventory change, foreign trade, government, capital formation and unallocated, as noted in n. 4.

## TABLE 2

### Input Requirements (Hypothetical), by Round, for $1 Million Output of Heavy Manufacturing in Metropolitan Region I

| Industry Grouping | First-Round Input Requirements (1) | Second-Round Input Requirements (2) | Third-Round Input Requirements (3) | Fourth-Round Input Requirements (4) | Fifth-Round Input Requirements (5) | Sixth-Round Input Requirements (6) | Seventh-Round Input Requirements (7) | Sum of Rounds (8) |
|---|---|---|---|---|---|---|---|---|
| **Metropolitan Region I:** | | | | | | | | |
| 1. Heavy manufacturing | $330,000 | $118,810 | $47,793 | $23,417 | $13,407 | $8,559 | $5,884 | $550,870 |
| 2. Power and communication | 10,000 | 8,670 | 7,763 | 4,614 | 2,858 | 1,667 | 994 | 36,566 |
| 3. Transportation | 20,000 | 14,910 | 7,417 | 4,508 | 2,516 | 1,475 | 871 | 51,697 |
| 4. Trade | 10,000 | 31,440 | 15,687 | 11,021 | 6,042 | 3,573 | 2,060 | 79,823 |
| 5. Insurance and rental activities | 10,000 | 32,940 | 18,965 | 12,612 | 7,135 | 4,155 | 2,430 | 88,237 |
| 6. Business and personal services | 10,000 | 11,810 | 8,159 | 4,860 | 2,906 | 1,664 | 983 | 40,382 |
| 7. Educational and other basic services | | 22,700 | 10,077 | 7,463 | 3,945 | 2,359 | 1,344 | 47,888 |
| 8. Construction | | 2,600 | 4,759 | 2,731 | 1,789 | 1,031 | 622 | 13,532 |
| 9. Households | 340,000 | 148,070 | 110,102 | 57,920 | 34,886 | 19,773 | 10,805 | 721,556 |
| **Metropolitan Region II:** | | | | | | | | |
| 10. Light manufacturing | 40,000 | 75,600 | 60,601 | 47,894 | 34,849 | 25,264 | 18,115 | 302,323 |
| 11. Power and communication | | 400 | 971 | 1,182 | 1,190 | 1,056 | 856 | 5,655 |
| 12. Transportation | | 800 | 1,781 | 1,821 | 1,601 | 1,309 | 1,016 | 8,328 |
| 13. Trade | | 800 | 2,364 | 3,044 | 2,858 | 2,470 | 1,963 | 13,499 |
| 14. Insurance and rental activities | | 400 | 1,696 | 2,689 | 2,706 | 2,490 | 1,972 | 11,953 |
| 15. Business and personal services | | 800 | 1,825 | 1,954 | 1,772 | 1,479 | 1,159 | 8,989 |
| 16. Educational and other basic services | | | 670 | 1,387 | 1,394 | 1,275 | 1,033 | 5,759 |
| 17. Construction | | | 104 | 325 | 446 | 455 | 391 | 1,721 |
| 18. Households | | 10,000 | 20,747 | 20,643 | 18,918 | 15,744 | 12,381 | 98,433 |
| **Region III:** | | | | | | | | |
| 19. Agriculture and extraction | 60,000 | 60,220 | 50,741 | 39,365 | 29,244 | 21,250 | 15,387 | 276,207 |
| 20. Power and communication | | 600 | 1,122 | 1,402 | 1,386 | 1,229 | 1,019 | 6,758 |
| 21. Transportation | | 1,800 | 2,430 | 2,360 | 2,085 | 1,673 | 1,310 | 11,658 |
| 22. Trade | | 1,200 | 3,226 | 3,541 | 3,481 | 2,922 | 2,385 | 16,755 |
| 23. Insurance and rental activities | | 2,400 | 4,646 | 4,962 | 4,701 | 3,917 | 3,156 | 23,782 |
| 24. Business and personal services | | 600 | 1,256 | 1,490 | 1,463 | 1,260 | 1,032 | 7,101 |
| 25. Educational and other basic services | | | 1,600 | 1,876 | 1,969 | 1,680 | 1,397 | 8,522 |
| 26. Construction | | | 372 | 664 | 719 | 581 | 581 | 3,018 |
| 27. Households | | 24,000 | 27,936 | 28,508 | 25,037 | 20,595 | 16,189 | 142,265 |
| Total | $830,000 | $571,570 | $414,810 | $284,253 | $211,303 | $151,006 | $107,335 | $2,583,277 |

other sets of totals which reflect impacts of other types of impulses.[6]

## II

The simplified model presented above may now be qualified and fashioned somewhat more realistically.[7]

First, re-examine the problem of industrial classification. The categorization of an activity exclusively as local or export is, in many instances, unjustified. There is no provision for those industries, by far the majority, in which both local and export elements are coexistent. As an instance, most educational services are local in character; yet on the university level some are definitely national in that they perform services for persons whose permanent residences are in all parts of the country. As another example, the products of the cotton industry are for the most part export; yet the by-product, cottonseed, which is typically considered part of the cotton industry, is consumed almost entirely locally by various vegetable-oil mills.[8]

[6] E.g., if instead of $1 million of new heavy manufacturing, an equivalent amount of new agricultural and extractive output is required, the impact will be more localized and confined to the region of initial expansion (Region III). For full details and other contrasts see R. Kavesh, "Interdependence and the Metropolitan Region" (unpublished doctoral dissertation, Harvard University, 1953), chap. iii.

[7] Because of limitation of space, we shall discuss only briefly the several important points which are raised. Full discussion of these points is contained in W. Leontief, *The Structure of the American Economy, 1919–1939* (New York: Oxford University Press, 1951); W. Leontief *et al.*, *Studies in the Structure of the American Economy* (New York: Oxford University Press, 1953); W. Isard, "Interregional and Regional Input-Output Analysis: A Model of a Space Economy," *Review of Economics and Statistics*, XXXIII (November, 1951), 318–28; W. Isard, "Regional Commodity Balances and Interregional Commodity Flows," *American Economic Review*, XLIII (May, 1953), 167–80; W. Isard, "Location Theory and Trade Theory; Short-Run Analysis," *Quarterly Journal of Economics*, LXVIII (May, 1954), 305–20; and various papers on input-output analysis at the Conference on Research in Income and Wealth, November, 1952.

In theory a fine enough classification of industries could be adopted so as to circumvent this shortcoming. In practice, however, such an industrial grouping would be infeasible in terms of the tremendous number of computations to be performed. Hence, whatever the classification finally chosen, some imperfection will exist which in turn will restrict the validity of the analysis.

Examination of the classification of Table 1 immediately discloses an oversimplification. In general, the exports of any metropolitan region do not fall into one category alone. Characteristically, exports consist of diverse outputs, ranging from agricultural and mining products to light and heavy manufactures. Therefore, the export sectors should be specified by component parts (subject to computational resources), particularly since disaggregation of any industrial category into finer parts is usually desirable where such is feasible.[9] On the other hand, one should not overlook the definite tendencies for metropolitan regions to assume definite specializations as implied by the oversimplified model.[10]

Second, reconsider the problem of the stability of input coefficients—the assumption that from round to round the cents' worth of any input per unit of a given output remains constant, or the equivalent, namely, that the amount of any input sup-

[8] The pattern of gasoline sales by metropolitan regions presents another interesting case of overlap. For the most part, gasoline is sold in neighborhood stations for local consumption. To this extent it is a local good. However, many service stations are situated along major intermetropolitan highways and sell gasoline for transient automobiles and trucks. In this sense, the consumption of gasoline takes place on a supraregional basis; thus there is a distortion of the local balance of production and consumption.

[9] See M. Holzman, "Problems of Classification and Aggregation," in W. Leontif *et al.*, *op. cit.*, chap. ix. However, see qualifications below.

[10] See, e.g., Colin Clark, "The Economic Functions of Cities in Relation to Size," *Econometrica*, XIII (April, 1945), 97–113; and G. M. Kneedler, "Functional Types of Cities," *Public Management*, XXVII (July, 1945), 197–203.

plied an industry varies proportionally with the output of that industry. As the output of an industrial activity expands, new combinations of the various inputs and new technical processes may become economically feasible. These new combinations and processes would require different percentage increases in the various inputs into the production process; this would be inconsistent with the basic assumption. For many industries such changes might involve minor substitutions of one type of input for another and hence not significantly bias the results. In other industries there may be major substitution effects.[11] However, to the extent that these effects can be anticipated, they can be incorporated into the model by the appropriate alteration of coefficients in the relevant rounds.

Associated with the above shortcoming are the restraints which limited resources impose. For example, as the demand for coal rises, veins of an inferior quality may need to be exploited. This in turn would lead to greater consumption of coal per unit of output of a coal-consuming industry. At the extreme, where there are fixed limits to a given resource (including human labor services), entirely new production techniques and/or locations may be dictated to realize increments of output.[12]

Again, to the extent that resource limitations and associated changes in production techniques can be anticipated, to the same extent the coefficients for the several rounds can be altered to incorporate into the analysis relevant information on these factors.

Still more critical a qualification stems from changes in consumption patterns incident to income changes.[13] Simple cents' worth of inputs per dollar of income, which are listed in columns 9, 18, and 27 of Table 1, are misleading. Consumers' studies are required in which households are broken down by occupation, ethnic grouping, fam-

ily size, rural-urban location, and other key indicators to reveal how expenditure patterns are related to changes in the level of income and associated occupational shifts. Once obtained, relevant information can be injected into the model to yield more valid results.

Another major set of qualifications is linked to the resource limitations already noted. As long as there is vacant housing in a metropolitan region, excess capacity in the transit and power systems, available space for expansion at the center, the calculated growth of the area can be effected. However, where vacant housing does not exist and where streets are congested and transit and power systems overloaded, additional capacity must be constructed to permit expansion in the various industries and service trades. Therefore, in addition to the inputs that are required to produce expanded outputs from existing and new

[11] See J. S. Duesenberry, "The Leontief Input-Output System" (Harvard Economic Research Project, Harvard University; Cambridge, Mass., 1950). (Mimeographed.)

[12] The data presented in the above tables are expressed in dollars and cents. Yet they can be easily translated into physical units. For example, consider the labor problem in a given market area (metropolitan region). It is possible to introduce new rows in Table 1, where each row corresponds to a particular type of labor (skilled, semiskilled, manual, etc.), the nature of the problem determining the particular breakdown of labor to be adopted. Reading down any column would denote the requirements of each type of labor (in terms of man-hours) to produce a unit of output corresponding to the industry and region listed at the head of the column. Thus, in studying the impact of any given resource development program, we can derive the additional requirements of various types of labor by regions; this in turn throws light not only on the short-run feasibility of a given resource development program but also upon the likely long-run interregional labor migrations (given information on reproduction rates and other population characteristics). In similar fashion, a conversion of the table into physical terms could supply insights on the adequacy of actual power facilities, housing, and transportation networks of various metropolitan regions.

[13] The socioeconomic data basic to Engel's law indicate this tendency. For discussion of this law see, among others, Carle C. Zimmerman, *Consumption and Standards of Living* (New York: D. Van Nostrand Co., 1936), and S. J. Prais, "Nonlinear Estimates of the Engel Curves," *Review of Economic Studies*, XX (1952–53), 87–104.

facilities, a whole series of inputs is required to construct the new facilities.

Here, too, appropriate modification of the model can be made. For example, given a knowledge of the capacity of an existing housing complex (together with information on the doubling-up effect and other cultural adaptations to shortage known to be feasible, the nature of the demand for diverse types of housing, and the input structures of the several sectors of the housing industry), it is possible to allow for the phenomenon of housing expansion in our analytic framework. It should be borne in mind, however, that to the extent to which a particular resource in short supply is diverted from producing output on current account to building up plant equipment and other capacity to produce, then to a similar extent the expansion of the non-capacity-building activities are curtailed.

In effect, the initial, highly simplified linear model—linear in the sense that each input varies in direct proportion to the output—has been molded into a less hypothetical, non-linear model which does recognize important non-proportionalities in interactivity relations.

### III

In the previous section a number of considerations were introduced to lend more reality and validity to the simplified model of Section I. However, granted that data can be obtained to describe meaningfully non-linear interrelations, to the extent that such a three-regional construct does not exist, the model remains hypothetical. Let us now re-examine this hypothetical characteristic.

It is a commonplace that social science has not yet reached the stage where it can explicitly consider every variable in a given problem. Those investigators who attempt to obtain results applicable to policy questions concentrate upon what they consider to be the relatively few important variables. Even though this procedure suffers from omission and oversimplification, it

still may afford the most useful results for practice. This, too, must be our way of implementing the above model.

Let the problem be an attempt to project various economic magnitudes in the Greater San Juan Metropolitan Region, Puerto Rico. Immediately the problem of demarcating the boundaries of this region arises. Some sociologists might stress the rural-urban dichotomy and draw the line where the influences of the city proper become subordinate to those of the smaller settlements and rural communities. A strict economist might include only those contiguous areas trading extensively with San Juan. An ecologist might attempt to identify the dominant-subdominant-influent-subinfluent relationships of the core and the various sectors of the hinterlands.[14]

For our purposes, no single orientation suffices. If we imagine the Puerto Rican economy in 1975, we anticipate that improvements in transportation and communications will co-ordinate the entire island into one major region, with its focus at San Juan. This is not to deny that there will be major satellite cities such as Ponce and Mayagüez; but the bonds of these cities to the San Juan area will be so strong and connections so closely interwoven that it will be feasible to recognize the whole of Puerto Rico as one "Greater" metropolitan region. Such a metropolitan region would be akin to the Greater New York Metropolitan Region, which includes such major satellite cities as Bridgeport, New Brunswick, and Norwalk.[15]

Consider the external relations of this

[14] Among others, see Stuart A. Queen and David B. Carpenter, *The American City* (New York: McGraw-Hill Book Co., 1953), and Donald J. Bogue, *The Structure of the Metropolitan Community* (Ann Arbor: University of Michigan Press, 1949).

[15] The 3,423 square miles of the Greater San Juan Metropolitan Region (the entire island) contrast with the 4,853 square miles included in the Census Los Angeles Metropolitan Area and with the 6,914 square miles included in the Greater New York Metropolitan Region as currently defined by the New York Regional Plan Association.

Greater San Juan Metropolitan Region. Currently the major ties are with the metropolitan construct embracing the Greater New York–Philadelphia–Baltimore urban-industrial region. A lesser economic connection is with the Gulf Coast. Recognizing the difficulties of establishing new ties, and that institutional resistances and entrepreneurial inertia are among several forces tending to keep incremental economic activities within the framework of existing transportation and communication channels, one is inclined to anticipate that these two regions of the United States will continue to dominate the external relations of the Greater San Juan Metropolitan Region.

There is a second ground for such belief. From a transport-cost standpoint, Greater San Juan is closer to both the Gulf Coast and New York–Philadelphia–Baltimore urban-industrial region than to any other region of the United States. Even though in terms of physical distance the South Atlantic region is nearest Puerto Rico, at best the likelihood is small that a sufficient volume of commodity movement will be generated between the South Atlantic region and Puerto Rico to realize the economies of scale, both in handling costs and in use of transport facilities, which are achieved in the Gulf Coast and New York–Philadelphia–Baltimore trade. This signifies that from an economic standpoint the South Atlantic region is considerably more distant.

Moreover, Greater San Juan, as a growing economy, is likely to find that the sale of additional industrial output through displacing existing suppliers in a well-established market is more difficult than through capitalizing on new market demand. Because the Gulf Coast and the New York–Philadelphia–Baltimore areas will be among the most rapidly expanding regions of the United States, it does not appear unreasonable to expect that Puerto Rican businessmen will concentrate for the most part on these two regions for new sales outlets.

Hence, if the problem is to project the interrelations between Greater San Juan and the mainland and if we are given techniques of analysis which can treat only a relatively few variables, the Gulf Coast and the New York–Philadelphia–Baltimore urban-industrial complex may be considered the most significant external regions for our analysis. This lends a partial justification for our three-regional model.

The specific situation of Greater San Juan has still another point of contact with our model. As indicated above, in general no region specializes in one export product alone. Each usually produces a number of goods for export, although frequently with distinct specialization. For our particular problem, the Gulf Coast, with its extensive agricultural production as well as its emphasis on oil-refining, natural gas production, and other extractive industries, may be taken as Region III. This is especially relevant in the case of Puerto Rico, since her chief imports from the Gulf Coast are lumber, petroleum products, rice, wheat flour, and mixed dairy and poultry feeds.[16]

Furthermore, the presence of heavy manufacturing in the greater New York–Philadelphia–Baltimore complex, with the corresponding shipments of finished goods to Puerto Rico, justifies treating this area as Metropolitan Region I. This judgment is reinforced by the major steel development program currently being undertaken in the Delaware River Valley. The heavy metal output of this area may by 1975 attain proportions comparable in magnitude to the present Pittsburgh complex.[17]

Finally, consider the human and natural endowment of Puerto Rico. Mineral and agricultural resources are of a very low or-

[16] S. E. Eastman and D. Marx, Jr., *Ships and Sugar: An Evaluation of Puerto Rican Offshore Shipping* (Rio Piedras: University of Puerto Rico Press, 1953).

[17] W. Isard and R. Kuenne, "The Impact of Steel upon the Greater New York–Philadelphia Urban-Industrial Region," *Review of Economics and Statistics*, XXXV (November, 1953), 289–301.

der.[18] In contrast, population is excessive, which, together with the expectation of continued high reproduction rates, suggests the continuance of relatively depressed wage rates. Those industries migrating to Puerto Rico tend, therefore, to be both labor-oriented and of such a nature that the assembly of required raw materials and shipment of product incur relatively low transport costs. Textiles are a good example. Therefore, Greater San Juan may be taken to conform with our light-manufacturing economy, Metropolitan Region II.

## IV

We have now converted a simplified model into one which though still hypothetical is of more practical significance. The initial 9-industry classification takes on added meaning when it is disaggregated into a 50-industry or even a 192-industry classification. This operation is currently feasible. Too, the recent input-output study of Puerto Rico permits a similar meaningful disaggregation for Metropolitan Region II (Greater San Juan).

At this point it is appropriate to reexamine the problem of substituting nonlinearities for linearities and non-proportionalities for proportionalities, with special reference to the input structures of the existing and potential industrial activities of Puerto Rico.

Consider the input structure of any particular industry of Puerto Rico. Since the area is still relatively underdeveloped, the stability of coefficients can be seriously questioned. It is quite likely that, as plants take root in Puerto Rico, new techniques will be used, especially since incipient industrialization has a significant effect on the attitudes of the working force, which in turn is reflected in labor productivity.[19] As

a result, it is necessary to secure for such new plants the set of inputs which prospective management may expect to be required for current operation and/or to approximate from social science research studies the effects of the introduction of new industry upon labor productivity and in turn upon the set of inputs and techniques utilized. Obviously, where no adequate information is available, it becomes necessary to rely heavily upon individual judgment.

Another set of non-linearities is introduced when we consider the problem of effective demand in underdeveloped countries such as Puerto Rico. In many cases the justification for erecting a plant in a given industry is lacking because the potential market is inadequate to absorb the output of a plant of a minimum technically feasible size. However, as development proceeds and effective demand mounts, a stage may be reached where demand does become adequate for a particular market-oriented operation, such as cement production. When effective demand does reach such a level, it becomes necessary to alter the entire set of technical coefficients relating the input of the given commodity, say, cement, from any given metropolitan region into each industrial activity of every metropolitan region. This and similar alterations can be effected in round-by-round computations if, beforehand, information relating to such potential shifts is available.

As indicated, another extremely important set of non-linearities arises in attempting to anticipate consumption habits. Data are relatively sparse on how industrialization, increasing urbanization, rising incomes, and intensified contact with the mainland will influence cultural patterns of the island. Additionally, more research is required on how such institutional factors as entrepreneurial vigor and savings schedules will be modified. Obviously, in any attempt at a determination of the extensive ramifications of new industrial expansion,

18 H. S. Perloff, *Puerto Rico's Economic Future* (Chicago: University of Chicago Press, 1950), chap. iv.

19 See, e.g., W. E. Moore, *Industrialization and Labor* (Ithaca: Cornell University Press, 1951).

reliance upon the considered judgment of social scientists as well as local residents for pertinent information is necessary, the more so when relevant data are sharply limited.

## V

To conclude, a model has been developed, which, it is hoped, will have some validity for purposes of projection, either in its present or in a less comprehensive form. The model has many shortcomings. Since they are fully discussed elsewhere, we have treated them here only cursorily. Further, there are serious problems arising from the inadequacies of the data, the unpredictability of changes in behavioral patterns and culture, and the uncertain direction and magnitude of technological development. Nevertheless, we feel that where decisions on metropolitan community development and regional welfare must be made *now* for planning for the future, this procedure is useful, especially as a complement to our existing set of analytical tools and techniques.

## CLASSIFICATION OF CITIES

A classification of cities involves the development of a taxonomy in which urban settlements are described according to certain characteristics considered pertinent for the purpose at hand. In some instances classifications have been developed in terms of attributes, as, for example, classifications of cities according to their sites. Thus, cities located on rivers have been classified according to their location relative to the mouths of rivers, to the junction of two or more rivers, to the head of navigation on rivers, and so on. In other instances, on the assumption that differences are relative, not absolute, classifications have been developed in terms of variables. Examples of such classifications include those based on size of population and on functions.

Classification of urban places according to size of population implies more than a numerical distinction. It implies a relationship between population and urban functions; that is, with growing size the urban settlement becomes more complex, more differentiated, and increasingly multifunctional. Classes of urban settlements, according to size, have commonly been referred to as villages, towns, cities, and metropolises, with the implication that for each class additional functions are encountered, or establishments become differentiated.

Of particular significance for the geographer are the several classifications which distinguish cities according to the principal functions which they perform. Two papers dealing with functional classifications are presented in this section. The first of these is Chauncy D. Harris' oft-quoted article, "A Functional Classification of Cities in the United States." Harris describes his method as a "quantitative method of functional analysis." He assigns a city to a functional type on one quantitative criterion: the type of economic activity measured in terms of occupation and employment in which the residents are engaged. Because employment figures furnish a critical index of the relative importance of manufacturing and trade, and because such figures were available for all the cities classified, they formed the main basis of the classification. In order to arrive at a meaningful classification of cities, Harris employs different ratios for different types of functions. Thus, on the basis of empirical evidence, only cities with more than 60 per cent of their employment in manufacturing were classified as manufacturing, whereas cities with only 20 per cent in wholesaling were classified as wholesale centers. Where mapped, metropolitan districts were used rather than the political cities.

It must be recognized that any classification based on variables rather than attributes presents certain problems. As Harris points out, all large cities (and, one might add, most cities) are multifunctional. The classification of a city as manufacturing does not imply the absence of trade. There are all shades of gradations between and among the types proposed, and some cities are borderline. The differences between classes of cities based on functions are, in other words, relative rather than absolute.

Howard J. Nelson, in his paper "A Service Classification of American Cities," attempts to overcome some of these difficulties by using a classification based on stated statistical procedures. By calculating standard deviations from the mean for each of nine activity groups, Nelson groups his cities according to three degrees of variation from the mean.

In his classification a city may provide more than one type of service in outstanding proportions. Thus Jacksonville, Florida, is described by the following symbols: TPsPbFW, which means that its employment is 1 standard deviation above the mean for the nation's cities in five services—transportation and communication, personal service, public administration, finance and wholesale. Maps included in the article show the distribution of cities classified according to the system outlined.

CHAUNCY D. HARRIS

# A FUNCTIONAL CLASSIFICATION OF CITIES
# IN THE UNITED STATES

That cities differ in function has long been recognized. Functional types such as industrial, commercial, mining, university, and resort towns have been differentiated by numerous writers, and outstanding examples of each have been cited.[1] However, the literature on the functions of cities, although suggestive, is sadly deficient in studies of criteria for distinguishing types and in classifications including more than a few well-known type examples.[2] The present paper attempts to remedy these deficiencies by proposing a quantitative method of functional analysis and by submitting a classification of American cities based on that method.

## THE METHOD

The classification is based on the activity of greatest importance in each city. All

Reprinted from the *Geographical Review*, XXXIII (January, 1943), 86–99, with permission of the author and the editor. (Copyright, 1943, by the American Geographical Society, New York.)

[1] W. S. Tower, "The Geography of American Cities," *Bulletin of the American Geographical Society*, XXXVII (1905), 577–88; R. D. Salisbury, H. H. Barrows, and W. S. Tower, *The Elements of Geography* (New York, 1912), pp. 595–601; Nels Anderson and E. C. Lindeman, *Urban Sociology* (New York, 1928), pp. 19–21; Niles Carpenter, *The Sociology of City Life* (New York, 1931), pp. 10–17; L. D. Stamp and S. H. Beaver, *The British Isles* (London, New York, Toronto, 1933), pp. 567–75; "Our Cities: Their Role in the National Economy" (Report of the Urbanism Committee to the National Resources Committee, Washington, 1937), pp. 2–3, 8, 38; Eugene Van Cleef, *Trade Centers and Trade Routes* (New York and London, 1937), pp. 6–12; E. E. Muntz, *Urban Sociology* (New York, 1938), pp. 8–18; S. A. Queen and L. F. Thomas, *The City* (New York and London, 1939), pp. 13–15; N. P. Gist and L. A. Halbert, *Urban Society* (2d ed.; New York, 1941), pp. 15–24.

large cities are more or less multifunctional, and the classification of a city as industrial does not imply the absence of trade. There are all shades of gradations between and among the types proposed, and some cities are borderline, but the general types are distinct. It should be noted also that the original function of a city may be no guide at all to the most important activity at the present time; a state capital that owes its chief growth to manufacturing is here classed as an industrial center.

Two sets of available figures aid in the determination of the principal activities in each city: occupation figures and employment figures. Occupation figures, obtained by asking each person what he does, are available for the 377 cities of the United States that had more than 25,000 population in the 1930 Census.[3] Occupations are divided into ten principal groups. Occupation figures, although comprehensive, furnish poor indexes for the two principal urban activities—manufacturing and trade. The usefulness of the category of manu-

[2] See, however, Homer Hoyt, "Economic Background of Cities," *Journal of Land and Public Utility Economics*, XVII (1941), 188–95.

[3] Fifteenth Census of the United States, 1939, *Population*, Vol. IV, *Occupations by States* (Washington, D.C.: U.S. Bureau of the Census, 1933). See the tables for the individual states: Tables 3 and 4 give the figures and percentages for the 93 cities with more than 100,000 inhabitants. Table 5 gives the figures for the 284 cities with 25,000 to 100,000 inhabitants. In this case, figures for men and women were added to give the total in each occupation, and the percentage in each major division was then calculated on a slide rule. The Sixteenth Census will provide figures by useful-industry groups and for retail and wholesale trade for the 1,079 cities of more than 10,000 population in 1940.

129

facturing and mechanical occupations is blurred by the inclusion of carpenters, painters, electricians, mechanics, and other local service groups with workers in industrial establishments. The value of trade figures is lessened by failure to distinguish between retail and wholesale trade. Furthermore, the large number in domestic

ments and since they separate retail and wholesale trade.

As employment figures furnish a critical index of the relative importance of manufacturing and trade, and as such figures are available for all the cities classified, they form the main basis of the classification (Table 1). Occupation figures are used to

## TABLE 1
### CRITERIA USED IN CLASSIFYING CITIES

*Manufacturing cities M' subtype.*—Principal criterion: Employment in manufacturing equals at least 74 per cent of total employment in manufacturing, retailing, and wholesaling (employment figures).

Secondary criterion: Manufacturing and mechanical industries contain at least 45 per cent of gainful workers (occupation figures). NOTE: A few cities with industries in suburbs for which no figures were available were placed in this class if the percentage in the secondary criterion reached 50.

*Manufacturing cities M subtype.*—Principal criterion: Employment in manufacturing equals at least 60 per cent of total employment in manufacturing, retailing, and wholesaling.

Secondary criterion: Manufacturing and mechanical industries usually contain between 30 per cent and 45 per cent of gainful workers.

*Retail centers (R).*—Employment in retailing is at least 50 per cent of the total employment in manufacturing, wholesaling, and retailing and at least 2.2 times that in wholesaling alone.

*Diversified cities (D).*—Employment in manufacturing, wholesaling, and retailing is less than 60 per cent, 20 per cent, and 50 per cent, respectively, of the total employment in these activities, and no other special criteria apply. Manufacturing and mechanical industries with few exceptions contain between 25 per cent and 35 per cent of the gainful workers.

*Wholesale centers (W).*—Employment in wholesaling is at least 20 per cent of the total employment in manufacturing, wholesaling,

and retailing and at least 45 per cent as much as in retailing alone.

*Transportation centers (T).*—Transportation and communication contain at least 11 per cent of the gainful workers, and workers in transportation and communication equal at least one-third the number in manufacturing and mechanical industries and at least two-thirds the number in trade (occupation figures). (Applies only to cities of more than 25,000, for which such figures are available.)

*Mining towns (S).*—Extraction of minerals accounts for more than 15 per cent of the gainful workers. (Applies only to cities of more than 25,000, for which such figures are available.) For cities between 10,000 and 25,000 a comparison was made of mining employment available by counties only with employment in cities within such mining counties. Published sources were consulted to differentiate actual mining towns from commercial and industrial centers in mining areas.

*University towns (E).*—Enrolment in schools of collegiate rank (universities, technical schools, liberal-arts colleges, and teachers colleges) equaled at least 25 per cent of the population of the city (1940). (Enrolment figures from *School and Society*, LII [1940], 601–19.)

*Resort and retirement towns (X).*—No satisfactory statistical criterion was found. Cities with a low percentage of the population employed were checked in the literature for this function.

service in southern cities invalidates some comparisons with northern cities.

Employment figures, obtained by asking each industrial and trading establishment how many it employs, are available for the 984 cities of the United States that had more than 10,000 inhabitants in 1930.[4] Employment figures are of high value, since they include only true industrial establish-

[4] Census of Business, 1935, *Retail Distribution,* Vol. II, *County and City Summaries, 1936; Wholesale Distribution,* Vol. III, *Cities and Counties, 1937;* Biennial Census of Manufactures, 1935 (mimeographed press releases for each state) (U.S. Bureau of the Census). Fortunately these figures are available grouped by cities in B. P. Haynes and G. R. Smith, *Consumer Market Data Handbook* (1939 ed., "U.S. Bureau of Foreign and Domestic Commerce, Domestic Commerce Series," No. 102 [1939]), lines 18, 20, and 22.

supplement the interpretation in all types and to distinguish two functional types. Other methods are utilized in recognizing two minor types. To facilitate comparisons, all figures are reduced to percentages: occupations as percentages of total gainful workers; employment as percentages of total workers employed in manufacturing, wholesaling, and retailing only.

One problem has been to rule out local service employment in activities that exist merely to serve workers employed in the primary activities of the city. On the basis of an analysis of cities of well-recognized types, an empirical solution has been evolved by assigning higher percentages to some functions than to others; on this basis only cities with more than 60 per cent of their employment in manufacturing are classified as industrial, whereas cities with only 20 per cent in wholesaling are classified as wholesale centers.

The cities are classified not as political units but as functional units. As metropolitan districts are the nearest approach to true functional units defined and mapped on a uniform national scale, they are adopted in this study for all areas so recognized. In addition, 9 small clusters are treated as single units.[5] The 605 functional units classified contain 988 cities.[6] Each of the 140 metropolitan districts contains at least one city of more than 50,000 population, and altogether they contain 510 cities of more than 10,000. The 9 smaller clusters contain 22 cities of 10,000–50,000 population. Each of the 456 other units contains only one city of more than 10,000, but, in 66 of these, industries located in suburbs are im-

[5] The clusters are Lewiston–Auburn, Maine; Gloversville–Johnstown, N.Y.; Pottsville and Shenandoah, Mahanoy, Tamaqua, Mt. Carmel, and Shamokin, Pa.; Muskegon–Muskegon Heights, Mich.; Marinette, Wis.–Menominee, Mich.; Manitowoc–Two Rivers, Wis.; Champaign–Urbana, Ill.; Texarkana, Ark.–Tex.; and Aberdeen–Hoquiam, Wash.

[6] The 988 cities consist of 984 with more than 10,000 population in 1930 plus 4 educational centers with fewer than 10,000 in 1930 but more than this number in 1940.

portant enough to affect the classification. Figures by metropolitan districts and for the smaller clusters have been obtained by addition of figures for all counties or small towns in each district or cluster. The presence of industrial suburbs in other cities has been recognized chiefly by statistical checks.

## THE FUNCTIONAL CLASSIFICATION

In the classification nine principal types of cities are recognized and each type is designated by a letter (Fig. 1). Cities classified as manufacturing (M), retailing (R), and diversified (D) are the most numerous. Other groups are wholesaling (W), transportation (T), mining (S), educational (E), resort or retirement (X), and others (including political, P). The distribution of each type is shown in Figures 2–10.

*Manufacturing cities.*—Manufacturing cities are the most numerous functional type, comprising 44 per cent of the metropolitan districts and 43 per cent of the smaller centers. In view of the large number of cities in this type, two subtypes have been recognized, M′, with 118 cities, and M, with 140 cities; the former are cities overwhelmingly manufacturing, and the latter are manufacturing cities with other functions important but definitely secondary (Fig. 2).

In the M′ cities retail and wholesale trade, transportation, and other activities exist largely for the service of people employed directly in manufacturing. The largest city of this group is Detroit. Smaller, but more notable for dominance of manufacturing, are Lowell–Lawrence, Fall River–New Bedford, Waterbury, Reading, Flint, and Winston-Salem among the metropolitan districts. The smaller cities with heaviest dominance of manufacturing are Vandergrift, Pennsylvania, Fulton, New York, and Thomasville, North Carolina.[7]

[7] Other cities with unusual dominance of manufacturing are Biddeford, Me.; Nashua, N.H.; Leominster and Gardiner, Mass.; Torrington, Conn.; Little Falls and Gloversville–Johnstown, N.Y.; Ellwood City, Berwick, Hanover, and Mead-

M cities are less dominantly manufacturing than M' cities but more numerous. Philadelphia is the largest city of this type. Pittsburgh, Buffalo, Rochester, Syracuse, Albany–Schenectady–Troy, and Springfield –Holyoke are other examples from the metropolitan districts.

As is indicated by Figure 2, the manufacturing cities show a close correspondence to the manufacturing belt as outlined by Sten De Geer, Hartshorne, Strong, A. J.

employment structure of cities within the belt. Even in many cities that started as trading centers, manufacturing now overshadows other activities. Manufacturing cities outside this belt are of a raw-material type, treating products whose bulk or perishability is reduced by manufacture.[9]

*Retail centers.*—Retail centers are mostly smaller cities outside the manufacturing belt and its border zone (Fig. 3). They include 20 per cent of the smaller centers

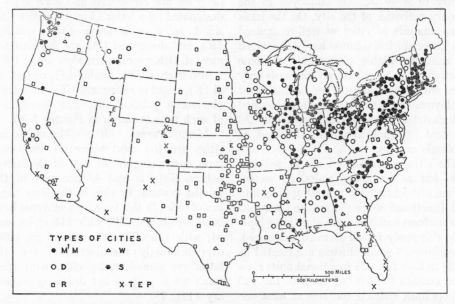

Fig. 1.—A functional classification of 605 cities in the United States. See Table 1 for types and criteria and Figs. 2–10 for separate mappings. Washington is the only political (*P*) center shown here. A mimeographed list of the cities may be obtained on request from the American Geographical Society.

Wright, and C. F. Jones.[8] Most of these cities lie within a well-marked belt east of the Mississippi and north of the Ohio, with two narrow extensions stretching through the southeastern United States along the Piedmont and in the Great Valley. That most cities within this belt are classified as manufacturing is evidence of the extent to which industry has come to dominate the

ville, Pa.; Lorain, Ohio; Elwood, Connersville, and Anderson, Ind.; Hopewell, Va.; High Point and Concord, N.C.; and Kingsport, Tenn.

[8] For a critical review see *Geographical Review*, XXIX (1939), 137–38.

but less than 10 per cent of the metropolitan districts. Of the five largest R cities, none over 200,000, three (Tulsa, Wichita,

[9] Lumber mills are located in Bogalusa, La., Beaumont–Port Arthur, Tex., Eureka, Calif., Klamath Falls and Astoria, Ore., and Longview, Aberdeen–Hoquiam, Tacoma, Everett, and Port Angeles, Wash.; fruit and vegetable canneries in San Jose, Calif., and Aberdeen–Hoquiam and Everett, Wash.; salmon canneries in Astoria, Ore., and Aberdeen–Hoquiam and Everett, Wash.; smelters in Pueblo, Colo. (iron), Anaconda, Mont., and Tacoma, Wash. (copper); and oil refineries in Beaumont–Port Arthur, Tex. These comprise all the cities in the western United States classified as M or M'.

and Shreveport) are partly supply and office centers for oil regions, and one (Austin) is a political, educational, and residential as well as a retail center. All other retail centers have fewer than 100,000 inhabitants.

About half of the 104 R cities lie within

veloped but neither is clearly dominant. As would be expected, diversified cities form a larger percentage of metropolitan districts than of smaller centers (about 25 per cent, as compared with 20 per cent), and four of the five largest cities in the country fall into this class.

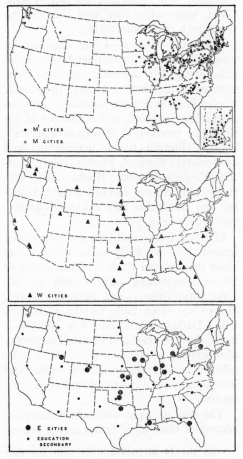

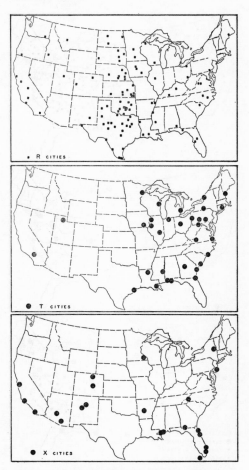

FIGS. 2 (Manufacturing cities), 5 (Wholesale centers), and 8 (Educational centers).

FIGS. 3 (Retail centers), 6 (Transportation centers), and 9 (Resort and retirement centers).

a single conspicuous band between the 95th and 100th meridians, near the eastern margin of the Great Plains, and near the western limit of safe arable agriculture. Other R cities are mostly small centers in the South or West.

*Diversified cities.*—In diversified cities both trade and manufacturing are well de-

Diversified cities are well distributed, but they are particularly numerous in the broad transitional area between the manufacturing belt and the band of retail centers (Fig. 4). Within the manufacturing belt diversified cities are cities with a large amount of trade; within the band of retail centers they are cities that have become centers of local industries; in the transitional zone manufacturing has become an important but not dominant factor in many cities.

In the manufacturing belt are New York, Chicago, and Boston—great trading cities in which a trading core is balanced by important and numerous industrial suburbs.

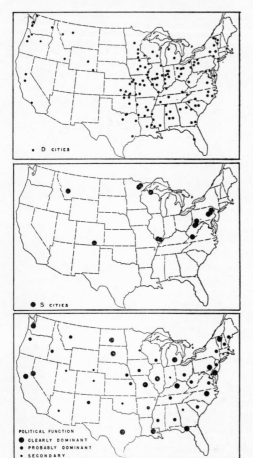

FIGS. 4 (Diversified cities), 7 (Mining towns), and 10 (State capitals).

Similar but smaller diversified cities in this belt include the five state capitals—Springfield, Indianapolis, Columbus, Charleston, and Richmond.

In the transitional zone, cities near the manufacturing belt, such as St. Louis, Nashville, and Birmingham, lean toward manufacturing, and those at a greater dis-

tance, such as Minneapolis–St. Paul, Des Moines, Kansas City, Little Rock, Montgomery, and Tampa–St. Petersburg, reveal a greater importance of trade.

The diversified cities within the retail band are mostly oil-refining and flour-milling centers.[10] In Los Angeles, Sacramento, Portland, and Spokane, on the Pacific Coast, wholesaling has been balanced by the growth of manufacturing.

*Wholesale centers.*—Cities classified as wholesale are of two distinct types: small cities engaged in assembly and large cities engaged in distribution. Most of the smaller wholesaling centers are associated with the assembling, packing, and marketing of agricultural products.[11] Riverside and Redlands, California, handle oranges (as well as tourists); Sanford, Florida, celery; Suffolk, Virginia, peanuts; Hopkinsville, Kentucky, and Wilson, North Carolina, tobacco; and Wenatchee and Yakima, Washington, apples (Fig. 5).

Cities of the second type are usually the largest cities in a wide region, whether port cities such as San Francisco and Seattle or inland distributing centers such as Salt Lake City, Denver, and Memphis. Fargo, Sioux City, Sioux Falls, Omaha, Oklahoma City, Dallas, Waco, and San Antonio—large cities in the band of retail centers—also perform wholesaling functions. Wholesale and retail cities are closely related and have usually been grouped together as trade centers.

The two principal wholesale distribution centers of the United States are, of course,

[10] Of the 24 diversified cities with less than 100,000 population west of the eastern boundaries of Kansas–Texas, 20 are diversified chiefly because of the presence of a single industry or type of industry: 9, by oil refineries; 4, railroad shops; 3, flour mills; and 2 each, canneries and lumber mills.

[11] Breakdown of wholesaling by types is available only for cities of more than 20,000 population. Riverside, Calif., and Yakima, Wash., the only assembly wholesaling centers of this size, each have more than 70 per cent of wholesale employment in "farm products–consumer goods" (Census of Business, 1935; *Wholesale Distribution*, Vol. III, Table 12B, pp. 81 and 96).

the two largest cities, New York and Chicago, but in them wholesaling employs only 15 per cent and 13 per cent of total employment, respectively; wholesaling is but one of many important activities associated with these great diversified metropolitan centers. If one included only the political city (omitting industrial suburbs), New York, Boston, Atlanta, Kansas City, Missouri, and Houston would be considered wholesale centers rather than diversified. Other diversified centers with important wholesaling are Los Angeles, Portland, Spokane, St. Louis, St. Joseph, Minneapolis–St. Paul, Richmond, Nashville, and Birmingham. In addition, a group of large Middle Western manufacturing cities have an important but secondary emphasis on wholesaling: Cleveland, Cincinnati, Louisville, Toledo, and Milwaukee. Also, some port cities such as New Orleans and Portland, Maine, that have been classified as transportation centers could as well be considered wholesale centers.

*Transportation centers.*—Of the 32 cities classified as transportational, 18 are railroad centers and 14 ports (Fig. 6). All are more than 25,000 in population, merely because figures on transportation are not available for smaller cities; undoubtedly many cities of 10,000–25,000 population should be classed with this group.[12] New Orleans is the largest city classified as transportational. Although half a dozen other ports of this functional type have more than 100,000 population, only three railroad cities are as large. In all the larger centers other activities have also been important in the growth of the population.

The railroad towns are important division points. Several are associated with passes through mountains. Altoona, Cumberland, and Roanoke are the outstanding examples, though Elmira, Harrisburg, Ogden, and San Bernardino are similar.[13] Railroad centers within the manufacturing

belt—such as Altoona, Harrisburg, Roanoke, and Elkhart—are manufacturing cities of some importance; such centers outside the belt—Ogden, Monroe, Louisiana, Meridian, Mississippi, and Macon, for example—are diversified.

Manufacturing is less important in the ports than in the railroad centers. Only New London, Connecticut, and Norfolk, Virginia, are strongly industrial, and both are naval bases also. Wholesaling, more than manufacturing, characterizes most American ports. New Orleans and Portland, Maine, are virtually wholesale centers, and Mobile, Jacksonville, and Duluth–Superior have important wholesaling.

*Mining towns.*—In the United States there are only 14 urban areas of more than 10,000 population in which mining is the dominant activity (Fig. 7). Butte, Montana, is a copper-mining town, and Hibbing and Virginia, Minnesota, and Ironwood, Michigan, are iron-mining centers. The other ten are coal-mining towns: Trinidad, Colorado; West Frankfort and Harrisburg, Illinois; Bluefield, Fairmont, and Morgantown, West Virginia; and Connellsville, Pottsville, Hazleton, and Scranton–Wilkes-Barre, Pennsylvania. All are bituminous centers except the last three, which are anthracite.

In general, the larger centers even in mining districts are largely commercial, manufactural, or transportational in function. Mining must of necessity be carried on at the source of the raw material and does not, therefore, ordinarily give rise to large centers. Much coal mining is carried on in towns too small to be included in the present classification. The importance of mining as an urbanizing influence is therefore inadequately represented in the mere number of these centers. The Pittsburgh metropolitan district, for example, contains 109 incorporated places of less than 10,000 population; many of these are mining centers, yet the Pittsburgh area as a whole

12 For example, Ashtabula, Ohio, Logansport, Ind., Centralia, Ill., and Pocatello, Idaho, classified as diversified, and probably Bluefield, W.Va., classified as mining.

13 Pueblo, Cheyenne, Laramie, Missoula, Spokane, Reno, and Sacramento also have similar functions in part.

functional unit employs more in manufacturing than in mining. With increasing distance south and east from Pittsburgh, manufacturing becomes less important and coal mining assumes dominance,[14] but even within this border area the three largest centers, Johnstown, Charleston, and Clarksburg, are manufacturing and trading centers with only 2–5 per cent of the gainful workers in mining.

Although manufacturing is important in the anthracite region, mining is dominant. There are many cities of more than 10,000 population, but they lie so close together that they have been grouped in three urban units containing 19 cities of more than 10,000—12 in the Scranton–Wilkes-Barre metropolitan district, 6 in the Pottsville cluster, and 1 in Hazleton.

Unfortunately, the figures in the present study have not permitted a study of oil towns, but doubtless the larger centers are refining towns and supply and office centers rather than mining towns.

*University towns.*—Most of the 17 university towns in the United States are small centers dominated by great state universities of middle western states (Fig. 8). Ann Arbor, Michigan, Lafayette and Bloomington, Indiana, Champaign–Urbana, Illinois, Columbia, Missouri, Iowa City and Ames, Iowa, Lawrence and Manhattan, Kansas, and Stillwater and Norman, Oklahoma, are the seats of state universities with an average enrolment of nearly 8,000 students

each.[15] State institutions also dominate Logan, Utah, Boulder, Colorado, Denton, Texas,[16] Baton Rouge, Louisiana, Gainesville, Florida, and Ithaca, New York.[17]

Many institutions of collegiate rank are in towns too small to be included in the present classification: 52 towns with fewer than 10,000 inhabitants contain institutions with enrolments of more than 1,000. Corvallis, Oregon, Pullman, Washington, Moscow, Idaho, College Station, Texas, Chapel Hill, North Carolina, Athens, Oxford, and Oberlin, Ohio, State College, Pennsylvania, and Hanover, New Hampshire, are well-known smaller university towns.

In addition to the 17 university towns, Figure 8 shows 32 cities in which universities and colleges, although culturally important, are not large enough to dominate the city economically.[18] Examples of such cities are Lexington, Kentucky, Durham, North Carolina, Athens, Georgia, Tuscaloosa, Alabama, Lubbock, Texas, and Eugene, Oregon.[19]

*Resort and retirement towns.*—Most of the 22 resort cities included in the classification are either summer or winter resorts, though a few are year-round residential and retirement centers.[20]

---

[14] Thus in Allegheny County 15,000 are employed in mining but 115,000 in manufacturing; in the three counties to the south and east (Washington, Fayette, and Westmoreland), mostly within the Pittsburgh metropolitan district, there are about 45,000 in mining and the same number in manufacturing; in the next three counties east (Indiana, Somerset, and Cambria, exclusive of the city of Johnstown) there are 35,000 in mining as compared with only 3,000 in manufacturing, but there is no city of more than 10,000 population. In West Virginia (exclusive of a few non-mining counties on the eastern and western edges) the employment in mining is 110,000, as compared with 35,000 in manufacturing, and much of the latter is in Charleston and Clarksburg. Only three mining towns in West Virginia are large enough to ʰᵉ included in this classification.

[15] The state universities of Ohio, Wisconsin, Minnesota, Nebraska, and Texas average even larger in size, but as all are located in state capitals, they are relatively less important in the growth of their cities.

[16] Texas State College for Women and North Texas State Teachers College. No teachers college by itself is large enough to dominate any of the cities classified.

[17] Cornell is only partly a state institution; the New York State College of Agriculture is affiliated with the privately endowed university.

[18] Cities in which college enrolments equal between 5 and 25 per cent of the population of the city.

[19] Of the 16 functional units in the United States with the highest percentages in professional service, 7 are university towns (shown on Fig. 8), 7 are political capitals, 3 are retirement centers, and only 2 do not fall into one of these categories (including duplications).

[20] As no criterion has been found for the relative importance of the resort function of cities, some

In warm southern climates on the tempering seacoast are such winter resorts as St. Augustine, Daytona Beach, Palm Beach, Miami, and Key West in Florida, Biloxi and Gulfport in Mississippi, and San Diego and Santa Barbara in California. Inland centers include Thomasville, Georgia, Santa Fe and Albuquerque, New Mexico, and Phoenix and Tucson, Arizona.

Summer resorts are near cool mountains, ocean, or lakes. Atlantic City is the largest and most famous, but along the North Atlantic, around the Great Lakes and the numerous glacial lakes of Michigan, Wisconsin, and Minnesota, and in the forested coolness of the Appalachians and Rockies are scores of summer resorts too small to be classified.

The United States, in contrast with Europe, has relatively few health resorts associated with mineral springs. Saratoga Springs, New York, Hot Springs, Arkansas, and Colorado Springs, Colorado, are the only ones large enough to be included in this classification.[21]

Some towns are residential centers, in contrast with holiday, tourist, or health resorts. Fort Collins, Colorado, seems to be of this type.[22] Most residential towns, however, are specialized suburbs of large cities and not independent functional units.

---

centers in which other functions are more important have probably been grouped with resorts. On the other hand, Los Angeles, the greatest retirement center of all, is classified as a diversified city because of its many other activities. Similarly, St. Petersburg, grouped with Tampa in a metropolitan district, has also been classified as diversified. Resort towns and university towns have a high percentage of gainful workers in domestic and personal service.

[21] A group of smaller spas is discussed by W. D. Thornbury, "The Mineral Waters and Health Resorts of Indiana," *Proceedings of the Indiana Academy of Sciences, 1940,* L (1941), 154–64.

[22] Many small towns with universities serve an important residential function. County-seat towns in the Middle West often serve as minor residential and retirement towns. In the West the families of many ranchers live in towns during the winter while the children are in school.

*Other types of cities.*—The foregoing classification does not, of course, recognize and map all known types of cities. Regional capitals, political capitals, army bases (garrison towns), naval bases, professional centers, and financial centers have not been differentiated on a statistical basis. Towns concerned with primary production, such as fishing towns, logging camps (as distinct from towns with lumber mills, which are classified as industrial), and farming towns, are similar to mining towns in that they usually have less than 10,000 population. Cathedral, pilgrimage, and fortress towns are not represented in this country.

Regional centers are a clear type of American city. Such a center is a large, centrally placed city dominating and serving a wide tributary region. In general, these cities are important wholesale, financial, and office centers. A high percentage of their gainful workers are engaged in professional and clerical occupations. One good criterion of such a center is newspaper circulation. Of the 41 regional centers defined by metropolitan newspaper circulation,[23] all except 4 have important wholesaling functions.[24] These centers comprise 9 wholesale centers,[25] 19 diversified cities (all with a strong seconday emphasis on wholesaling), 8 manufacturing cities, and 5 other types.

Political capitals are represented in Figure 1 by Washington, D.C., only. Although the establishment of cities as state capitals gave many of them an early leadership that resulted in important commercial and industrial growth, political functions have

[23] R. E. Park and Charles Newcomb, "Newspaper Circulation and Metropolitan Regions," in *The Metropolitan Community,* ed. R. D. McKenzie (New York and London, 1933), pp. 98–110. Cf. R. E. Dickinson, "The Metropolitan Regions of the United States," *Geographical Review,* XXIV (1934), 278–91.

[24] Helena and Albuquerque are small centers without important wholesaling, and Detroit and Knoxville are large cities in which wholesaling is overwhelmed in importance by manufacturing.

[25] They include all the metropolitan districts classified as wholesale centers except San Antonio and Waco.

been subordinate to other activities in many of the state capitals. Providence, Denver, and Salt Lake City each contain more than a third of the population of their states; it is inconceivable that political functions could have been the primary cause of such growth. In the last decade political functions have been expanding rapidly in the national capital, in the state capitals, and in various regional centers for federal offices. Such functions are undoubtedly of major importance to state capitals such as Harrisburg, Frankfort, Springfield, Lansing, Jefferson City, Bismark, Raleigh, Tallahassee, Baton Rouge, Austin, Sacramento, and Olympia, which have been put in other classes, and to Pierre, Dover, Carson City, and Montpelier, too small to be classified.[26] The state capitals are shown in Figure 10. In 16 the political function is clearly dominant. In 20 the political function is probably dominant. In 12, political activities are overshadowed by trade or industry. This last group includes Annapolis, put in the Baltimore metropolitan district by the census. Political capitals are not included in the general classification presented in Figure 1 because no satisfactory criterion has been found to measure the relative importance of the political function.

Related to political capitals as centers of government functions are army-garrison towns and naval bases. In normal peacetime there are no army-garrison towns in the United States, but during the present crisis [World War II] many centers have felt the imprint of large army concentrations. Among larger cities San Antonio is probably the nearest American approach to a garrison town. Naval bases are major factors in the life of New London, Norfolk, and San Diego. Pensacola is a naval air-training base.

Professional centers are closely related to retirement or resort towns. Rochester, Minnesota, with its Mayo Clinic, should

perhaps be considered a professional center, but it has been grouped with retirement towns. Colonies of artists and writers sometimes develop in or near resort towns.

No large American cities are primarily financial centers, but Hartford, the great insurance center, is the nearest approach. Des Moines and Canton, among other cities, are minor insurance centers, but in them insurance is clearly subordinate to other activities.

A number of small towns are engaged in fishing, lumbering, or farming. Gloucester is famous as a fishing center. Ephemeral logging camps have in turn arisen in Maine, the Lake States, the South, and the Pacific Northwest. The farm village is familiar in New England and in irrigated regions, particularly in Utah, Texas, and California.

## LOCATION OF CITIES

The different functional types of cities exhibit differences in the factors affecting their location.[27] The central-location theory, in which centrality within a productive hinterland is stressed, is illustrated best by the distribution of wholesaling centers, which are usually large cities centrally placed within a wide area, and of retail centers, centrally placed within a smaller area.[28] By way of contrast, in the rise of mining and resort centers site factors, either mineral resources or climate, are of greater importance than central location. Industrial cities are intermediate in that both location factors of convenience to markets and raw materials and site factors of power and labor are important; they exhibit diffusion within a clearly defined manufacturing belt.

[26] The city of Albany would come in this class, but the metropolitan district of Albany–Schenectady–Troy is perhaps better considered a manufacturing center.

[27] Factors in the location of cities of various functional types are discussed particularly in Tower, *op. cit.;* Carpenter, *op. cit.,* pp. 33–61; and Gist and Halbert, *op. cit.,* pp. 75–96. For an analysis of the interplay of factors affecting the location of a single city see C. D. Harris, "Location of Salt Lake City," *Economic Geography,* XVII (1941), 204–12.

[28] The central-location theory is reviewed and developed in Edward Ullman, "A Theory of Location for Cities," *American Journal of Sociology,* XLVI (1940–41), 853–64 [see below, pp. 202–9].

HOWARD J. NELSON

# A SERVICE CLASSIFICATION OF AMERICAN CITIES

Everyone is aware that modern cities are performing more and more of the services necessary to the functioning of society. There is an awareness, too, that these vital services are not performed in the same proportions by all cities. Almost every geographer would classify Detroit as a manufacturing city; Rochester, Minnesota, as a professional town; and Hartford, Connecticut, as an insurance center; thereby indicating that one city does more than its share of the nation's manufacturing, another provides professional services in outstanding proportions, and the third specializes in serving the insurance needs of society.

But perhaps this classification is done more by faith or intuition than on the basis of exact knowledge. At what point does an economic activity become important enough in a city to be of special significance? Can criteria be devised that will determine which cities should be labeled insurance centers or retail trade cities or centers of public administration? It is the purpose of this article to present a method that will form a basis for such a classification.

## PROCEDURE

The best practical source of recent statistical data for a study involving a large number of American cities is the 1950 Census of Population. Here is available raw material gathered from every settlement in the United States, broken down in generous detail for urban places with populations of 10,000 or more. As we are interested in "geographic" or "functional" cities rather than political entities, urbanized areas,

Reprinted from *Economic Geography*, XXXI (July, 1955), 189–210, with permission of the author and the editor. (Copyright, 1955, by Clark University, Worcester, Mass.)

which take in the entire built-up area, are used whenever available—where the central city had at least 50,000 persons in 1940. (For example, the Los Angeles Urbanized Area is considered one functional unit, instead of using the 45 political entities within it—Los Angeles, Pasadena, Long Beach, and so on—as 45 separate cities.) Urban places, mainly political cities but occasionally isolated unincorporated concentrations of population, are used for the smaller centers. After the urban places within urbanized areas are excluded to eliminate duplication, some 897 individual urban concentrations of over 10,000 persons remain for consideration.

The proportion of the labor force of a city engaged in performing a service is perhaps the best means of measuring the distribution of that activity. It is one of the few measures that are easily comparable from activity to activity or from year to year. Furthermore, the proportion of the labor force actually employed in a service is of much more direct significance to the economy of the city than the value or volume of sales of goods or of services performed, or similar measures for the manufactured products in a city.

The Census of Population breaks down the services performed by the labor force of a city into twenty-four major industry groups. These are listed in the first column of Table 1. In considering the broad categories of services performed by urban areas for society, however, condensations and omissions seem called for. Agricultural workers, for example, who may simply reflect farm land within loosely drawn city limits, were omitted. So, arbitrarily, were the categories of utility and sanitary services, construction, and personal service in private households (though all other categories of personal service were included), on the grounds that these are not essentially services performed by urban areas for society as a whole. The following nine major categories of services were chosen for investigation in this study: mining; manufacturing; transportation and communication; wholesale trade; retail trade; finance, insurance, and real estate; personal serv-

of Table 2 indicates the average percentage of those gainfully employed in various activity groups for the total of 897 cities.

It is obvious from Table 2 that the average proportions of the labor force in each of the activity groups differ greatly. The performance of manufacturing service occupies the largest proportion of the labor force in the 897 American cities of 10,000

TABLE 1

MAJOR ECONOMIC ACTIVITIES

| Census Classification by Industry Groups* | Service Classification |
|---|---|
| Agriculture, forestry, and fisheries......... | Omitted |
| Mining................................. | Mining |
| Construction........................... | Omitted |
| Manufacturing......................... | Manufacturing |
| Railroads and railway express service...... | Transportation and communication |
| Trucking service and warehousing | |
| Other transportation | |
| Telecommunications | |
| Utilities and sanitary services............. | Omitted |
| Wholesale trade........................ | Wholesale trade |
| Food and dairy produce stores, and milk retail................................. | Retail trade |
| Eating and drinking places | |
| Other retail trade | |
| Finance, insurance, and real estate........ | Finance, insurance, and real estate |
| Business services....................... | Omitted |
| Repair services | |
| Private households...................... | Omitted |
| Hotels and lodging places................ | Personal service |
| Other personal services | |
| Entertainment and recreation | |
| Medical and other health services......... | Professional service |
| Educational services, government | |
| Educational services, private | |
| Other professional and related services | |
| Public administration................... | Public administration |
| Industry not reported................... | Omitted |

* U.S. Census of Population, 1950, Vol. II, Table 35, "Economic Characteristics of the Population...."

ice; professional service; and public administration (see Table 1).

After the nine categories indicated by Table 1 had been decided upon, the percentages of the total labor force in each activity group for each of the 897 cities were calculated. Table 2 illustrates the procedure for several selected cities. However, as individual percentages are almost meaningless without some point of reference, the arithmetic averages for each activity group were computed. The final column

or more, 27.07 per cent. Another sizable fraction, nearly 20 per cent, is concerned with retail trade. Thus, over 45 out of every 100 workers in our cities are engaged in providing these two essential urban services—the fabrication of products and the distribution of goods at the retail level. The professional services necessary to society utilize about 11 per cent of the urban labor force—doctors, lawyers, teachers, engineers, etc. The other six categories of urban services are performed by a relatively small fraction of urban workers. Transportation and communication account for 7.12 per cent; personal service, 6.2 per cent; public administration, 4.58 per cent; wholesale trade, 3.85 per cent; finance, insurance, and real estate, 3.19 per cent; and mining, 1.62 per cent.

Doubts might logically arise at this point —surely cities with variations in size of from 10,000 to 13,000,000 must vary considerably in the proportions of the labor force employed in the different services.

How valid are averages taking in all of these differently sized cities? To shed some light on this question the 897 cities were broken down into seven arbitrarily selected groups by size as shown in Table 3. This table indicates that though there is some correlation between size of city and the proportions of the labor force in each activity, no constant or regular change is in evidence. However, there is variation in some of the percentages, and where they are small this may be quite significant.

TABLE 2

PROPORTION OF LABOR FORCE IN SELECTED ACTIVITIES*
(Sample Cities)

| | New York | | Detroit | | Kearney, Neb. | | Rochester, Minn. | | Average of 807 Cities (Per Cent) |
|---|---|---|---|---|---|---|---|---|---|
| | In 000's | Per Cent | In 000's | Per Cent | In 000's | Per Cent | In 000's | Per Cent | |
| Population................ | 12,296 | ....... | 2,659 | ....... | 12.11 | ....... | 29.88 | ....... | ....... |
| Labor force.............. | 6,099 | ....... | 1,068 | ....... | 3.28 | ....... | 13.0 | ....... | ....... |
| Manufacturing........... | 1,573 | 25.8 | 501 | 46.9 | 0.27 | 8.3 | 0.81 | 6.1 | 27.07 |
| Retail trade............. | 822 | 13.5 | 164 | 15.3 | 1.18 | 36.2 | 2.72 | 20.7 | 19.09 |
| Professional service...... | 448 | 7.3 | 73 | 6.9 | 0.84 | 25.6 | 4.39 | 33.3 | 11.09 |
| Transportation and comm. | 475 | 7.8 | 71 | 6.7 | 0.32 | 9.7 | 0.73 | 6.3 | 7.12 |
| Personal service......... | 361 | 5.9 | 59 | 5.5 | 0.36 | 11.0 | 1.40 | 10.6 | 6.20 |
| Public administration..... | 227 | 3.7 | 36 | 3.4 | 0.20 | 6.1 | 0.41 | 3.1 | 4.58 |
| Wholesale trade.......... | 274 | 4.5 | 33 | 3.1 | 0.22 | 6.6 | 0.42 | 3.1 | 3.85 |
| Finance, insurance, and real estate................ | 353 | 5.8 | 36 | 3.4 | 0.13 | 3.9 | 0.39 | 2.9 | 3.19 |
| Mining................. | 3 | 0.05 | 0.3 | 0.01 | 0.005 | 0.15 | 0.01 | 0.09 | 1.62 |

* Source: Census of Population, 1950, Vol. II, Table 35.

TABLE 3

AVERAGE PERCENTAGE OF THOSE GAINFULLY EMPLOYED IN SELECTED ACTIVITY GROUPS

| | Manufacturing | Retail | Professional Service | Wholesale | Personal Service | Public Admin. | Trans. and Comm. | Finance, Insurance, Real Estate | Mining | Total No. of Cities |
|---|---|---|---|---|---|---|---|---|---|---|
| In cities of from | | | | | | | | | | |
| 10,000 to 24,999... | 26.65 | 19.66 | 11.34 | 3.72 | 5.79 | 4.39 | 7.03 | 2.96 | 2.11 | 550 |
| 25,000 to 49,999... | 26.07 | 19.07 | 11.98 | 3.87 | 7.09 | 4.80 | 6.98 | 3.22 | 1.03 | 166 |
| 50,000 to 99,999... | 29.31 | 18.56 | 9.76 | 4.24 | 6.47 | 4.79 | 7.75 | 3.39 | 0.48 | 59 |
| 100,000 to 249,999.. | 29.77 | 18.07 | 9.50 | 4.21 | 6.61 | 5.22 | 7.14 | 3.74 | 0.71 | 71 |
| 250,000 to 499,999.. | 28.10 | 17.81 | 9.22 | 4.40 | 6.86 | 6.40 | 7.58 | 4.38 | 1.24 | 25 |
| 500,000 to 999,999.. | 27.21 | 18.16 | 9.17 | 5.10 | 6.72 | 4.96 | 8.83 | 5.06 | 0.41 | 14 |
| 1,000,000 and over. | 30.86 | 16.32 | 8.97 | 4.15 | 6.42 | 6.92 | 7.35 | 4.75 | 0.16 | 12 |
| Average......... | 27.07 | 19.23 | 11.09 | 3.85 | 6.20 | 4.58 | 7.12 | 3.19 | 1.62 | 897 Total |

Generally speaking, the proportions of the labor force in retail trade, professional service, and mining vary inversely with city size, that is, the percentages decrease as the cities get larger. Most of the other activities seem to be performed in greater nroportions in the larger cities. However, in almost every case the trend is marked by several exceptions.

## FREQUENCY VARIATIONS

To portray graphically the distribution of economic services among American cities the frequency graphs shown in Figure 1 were constructed. These nine graphs show the frequency with which a given percentage of the labor force employed in an activity occurs in the 897 cities under consideration. In these graphs the vertical axis indicates the number of cities involved and the horizontal axis the percentage of the labor force in each service.

Striking variations in the distribution of the nine different services among our urban centers are apparent in Figure 1. A unique type of distribution is illustrated by manufacturing service. Retail trade exemplifies a second, quite different, type. The seven remaining services might be considered together as a third type, somewhat similar to type two.

The manufacturing services provided by American cities display a greater variation, in terms of percentage of labor force employed, than any other activity. Unlike the distribution of any other activities, manufacturing shows no sign of "peaking" or grouping around some "typical" percentages. No city is without some manufacturing, but a few cities get by with less than 5 per cent of the labor force in this service. On the other hand, some cities have more than 65 per cent of their employed persons in this activity, and 91 cities have over 50 per cent of their labor force in manufacturing. Obviously, less that is meaningful can be said about an average or "normal" amount of manufacturing in a city than about any other activity. How much manu-

facturing should a city have to consider itself "balanced," for example?

Retail trade, perhaps because of its general necessity wherever concentrations of population are found, presents a distribution closer to a theoretical "normal curve" than any other service. In no city does less than 6 per cent of the working force serve the retail needs of the people. In some others 30 per cent and more, up to an extreme of 36.22 per cent, make their living providing this service. However, in about 120 cities the average is present, and there are almost the same number of cities with proportions below the average as there are with percentages above it.

The seven remaining activities fall into what may be considered a third general type of frequency distribution. Typically, most of the cities have a fairly common, rather low percentage of their labor force in a given activity. Then, in each case, there are a few cities in which the service is performed in outstanding amounts. Professional service, for example, commonly is supplied by from 6 to 12 per cent of the labor force. However, in a few cities these percentages rise many times above normal, with 30, 40, and, in several cases, nearly 60 per cent of the labor force employed in professional service. Generally speaking, transportation and communication, personal service, wholesale trade, finance, insurance, and real estate, and public administration follow a similar type of frequency distribution.

Mining perhaps warrants some special comments. This activity, which of course can exist only in the presence of minerals, is highly localized. This is the only activity which is not reported at all in a number of our cities. In 673 cities less than 1 per cent of the labor force is engaged in this activity. These, presumably, are workers in sand, gravel, and clay pits, limestone quarries, and the like. On the other hand, where minerals are present the percentage may go up appreciably. For example, 14 cities have more than 25 per cent of their workers in

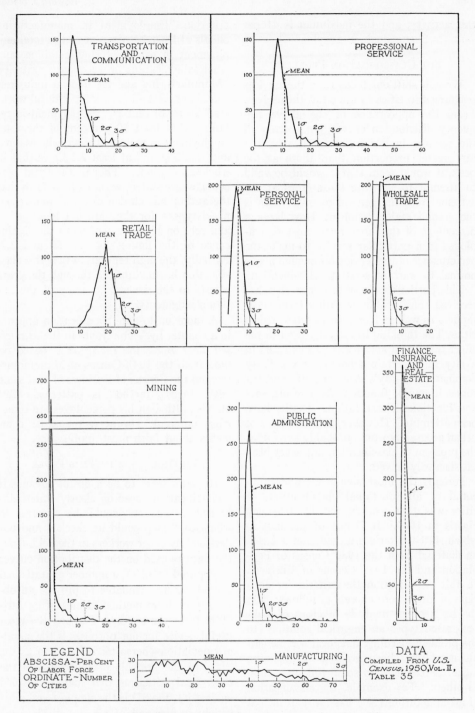

Fig. 1.—Distribution of economic services among American cities

this activity, and the maximum is 41 per cent (in Shenandoah, Pennsylvania).

## THE CLASSIFICATION PROBLEM

We now shift our focus from the services performed in cities to the cities themselves. From the appearance of the above frequency distribution curves, particularly of the services in which some cities have a far greater proportion than those at the peak, it would seem that it would be valid to attempt to separate those cities at the extreme from the general average. This is the second major problem: How large a percentage of the labor force must be employed in a particular service to make the performance of the service far enough above normal to warrant separate classification?

This particular question is one that has received considerable attention from geographers as well as from others interested in cities. The thinking has usually been to the effect that, if an activity is concentrated in a city in a certain amount, this activity dominates the city's economic life and becomes its major function. As a result, several functional classifications of cities have been attempted. However, most students of urban geography would probably agree that the problem of classification has never been satisfactorily solved.

Perhaps the most significant and influential of all functional classifications of cities was that worked out by Chauncy Harris in 1943.[1] It is one of the first in which stated criteria are used, and is based on material from the 1930 Census of Population and the 1935 Census of Business. In this classification the criteria for each class of cities were chosen as follows: "On the basis of an analysis of cities of well-recognized types an empirical solution [to the problem of ruling out local service employment] has been evolved by assigning higher percentages to some functions than to others." For example, the classification of manufacturing (M′) has for its principal

criterion "Employment in manufacturing equals at least 74 per cent of the total employment in manufacturing, retailing, and wholesaling," plus a secondary criterion "Manufacturing and mechanical industries contain at least 45 per cent of gainful workers." In retail centers, "Employment in retailing is at least 50 per cent of the total employment in manufacturing, wholesaling, and retailing and at least 2.2 times that in wholesaling alone." Though the exact percentages are stated, we must have faith that the author has chosen cities of well-recognized types—for they are not identified—and rely on his judgment as to the significance of the figures 74, 45, 50 and 2.2. Actually, the high reputation that this classification has maintained through the years attests to the general accuracy of the author's judgments.

A more up-to-date classification appears in a chapter by Victor Jones in the *Municipal Year Book* for 1953.[2] It is based on data from the 1948 Census of Manufacturing and the Census of Business of that same year. Jones's method is patterned after Harris', although his percentages are somewhat different. However, the same comments about faith must apply.

## METHOD USED IN THIS PAPER

It would seem to be a useful advance if a classification based on clearly stated statistical procedures could be devised in which each step could be checked and understood by other workers in the field. Once the data plotted on the distribution curves is prepared (Fig. 1), a number of statistical procedures are available to provide an objective, uniform method of measuring variation from the average. Perhaps the most useful device for our purposes is the standard deviation (hereafter referred to as the SD). In the first place (regardless of the theoretical criticisms that may be leveled against it), the SD is the simplest and most widely understood of all statistical meas-

---

[1] Chauncy D. Harris, "A Functional Classification of Cities in the United States," *Geographical Review*, XXXIII (1943), 86–99 [see above, pp. 129–38].

[2] Victor Jones, "Economic Classification of Cities and Metropolitan Areas," *Municipal Year Book*, 1953, pp. 49–54, 69, and Table IV.

ures of variation. Second, the *degree* of variation can be compared by use of the SD even if in some cases we are dealing with large percentages (as in manufacturing) or with small numbers (as in wholesale trade). This would seem to be an advantage over the simple percentage deviation used by Pownall.[3]

Standard deviations from the mean were therefore calculated for each of the nine activity groups and are presented in Table 4. The SD's are also indicated on the frequency curves in Figure 1 by the letter $\sigma$. Three degrees of variation from the average were recognized, and the cities grouped

divisions are made and why they are made at that point.

When applied to the 897 American cities chosen for this study, the method just described is not mutually exclusive; that is, a city may provide more than one type of service in outstanding proportions. This would seem to be an asset to the classification rather than a weakness, fitting observed reality.

Many cities high in professional service, for example, are also high in personal service. Thus Boulder, Colorado, is classified Pf3Ps2, indicating that the city is three or more SD's above the average in

TABLE 4

AVERAGES AND STANDARD DEVIATIONS FOR SELECTED ACTIVITY GROUPS

|  | Manu-facturing | Retail Trade | Profes-sional Service | Trans. and Comm. | Per-sonal Service | Public Admin. | Whole-sale Trade | Finance, Insur-ance, and Real Estate | Mining |
|---|---|---|---|---|---|---|---|---|---|
| Average................. | 27.07 | 19.23 | 11.09 | 7.12 | 6.20 | 4.58 | 3.85 | 3.19 | 1.62 |
| S.D..................... | 16.04 | 3.63 | 5.89 | 4.58 | 2.07 | 3.48 | 2.14 | 1.25 | 5.01 |
| Average plus 1 S.D........ | 43.11 | 22.86 | 16.98 | 11.70 | 8.27 | 8.06 | 5.99 | 4.44 | 7.63 |
| Average plus 2 S.D........ | 59.15 | 26.47 | 22.87 | 16.28 | 10.34 | 12.54 | 8.13 | 5.69 | 12.64 |
| Average plus 3 S.D........ | 75.26 | 30.12 | 28.16 | 20.86 | 12.41 | 16.02 | 10.27 | 6.94 | 17.65 |

in their appropriate categories. Cities that are over $+1$ SD from the average in manufacturing were given a Manufacturing 1 (or Mf1) rating, over 2 SD's an Mf2 rating, over 3 *or more* SD's an Mf3 rating. A similar procedure was followed for each activity group.

Inspection of Figure 1 indicates the point of the frequency curve at which the $+1$, 2, and 3 SD's occur. In a number of instances this point coincides fairly well with a "natural break" in the frequency curve. In other instances, as in the case of manufacturing, where a "natural break" would be difficult to determine, it provides a standard, objective division point. But, in any case, it is always clear where the

professional service and over two SD's above the average in personal service. Occasionally, a city may be far enough above the average to receive a rating in three, and even, rarely, in four categories.

Some cities do not rank high enough in any service to come under any of the above nine categories. These are lumped together in a single "diversified" group, although this is a somewhat misleading term. What is meant is that they are simply not unusually high in any service.

THE SERVICE CLASSIFICATION

All cities that were more than one SD above the average for any of the nine service categories were then classified, and plotted on maps included as Figures 2 to 10. Cities which were not outstanding in any category, as defined above, appear as

[3] L. L. Pownall, "Functions of New Zealand Towns," *Annals of the Association of American Geographers*, XLIII (1953), 332–50.

diversified cities in Figure 11. The following abbreviations were used to indicate the categories:

Manufacturing....................Mf
Retail trade......................R
Professional service..  .............Pf
Transportation and communication. .T
Personal service...................Ps
Public administration..............Pb
Wholesale trade...................W
Finance, insurance, and real estate...F
Mining........................Mi
Diversified......................D

A classification of 897 American cities appears as an appendix to this article.[4]

*Manufacturing.*—Cities that provide manufacturing service in outstanding amounts are more numerous than those of any other category, according to this classification. More than one-fifth—183 out of 897—of the cities are in this class. This is in spite of the fact that in order to be classified as a manufacturing center, over 43 per cent of a city's labor force must be employed in some type of manufacturing activity (average plus 16.04). In fact, over half the labor force in some 93 cities finds employment in manufacturing, a much higher concentration than is found in any other category.

As Figure 2 indicates, cities in which manufacturing service is significantly above the average are strongly localized in the area north of the Ohio and east of the Mississippi, the general area recognized as a "manufacturing belt" by many geographers. Five-sixths of the Mf cities are in this area. Two-thirds of the remainder, some 19 cities, are located on either flank of the Appalachian Mountains. In no other category are cities so highly localized.

Manufacturing cities located outside of the above two areas deserve special mention. Some, such as Antioch, Pittsburg, and Costa Mesa, California, and St. Charles, Missouri, are small cities, located outside large urbanized areas but adjacent to them.

[4] A mimeographed table giving the SD values for all except the diversified cities is available upon request from the author.

Hoquiam and Longview, Washington, are lumber centers, while Richland, in the same state, is an atomic center. In the Middle West, Austin, Minnesota, is a meat-packing center, and Newton, Iowa, is famous for washing machines. In addition there are Anaconda, Montana—copper; Bastrap, Louisiana—paper; Port Arthur and Baytown, Texas—petroleum.

Only one city has a large enough proportion of its labor force in manufacturing to fall into the Mf3 category. It is the unincorporated area of Brandon–Judson, South Carolina (textiles), with 76.21 per cent of its labor force in manufacturing. There are 29 cities in the Mf2 group, only 3 of which are outside the traditional "manufacturing belt." They are Kannapolis (textiles) and Thomasville (furniture), North Carolina, and Richland, Washington (atomic energy).

There are a few large cities in the manufacturing group. Detroit is the only urban area of over 1,000,000, and Providence, Rhode Island (583,000), is the next largest city in this group.

*Retail trade.*—The distribution of the 137 cities which provide retail services in outstanding proportion is considerably different from that of manufacturing cities, as is evident from Figure 3. Very few retail cities are found in areas in which manufacturing cities are concentrated. The largest concentration of the retail centers is a broad belt between the Rockies and the Mississippi River. California and Florida also contain important concentrations.

Six cities fall into the R3 category— where the number employed in retailing is more than 3 SD's from the average number in retailing. These cities are Kearney, Nebraska (36.22); Harlingen, Texas (34.25); Binghampton, New York (33.4); and three California cities—El Centro (30.95), Hanford (30.5), and Tulare (30.34). Miami, Florida, is the largest city, 459,000 persons, to have a retail classification.

*Professional service.*—Eighty-one cities in the United States are outstanding in the

Fig. 2.—Manufacturing

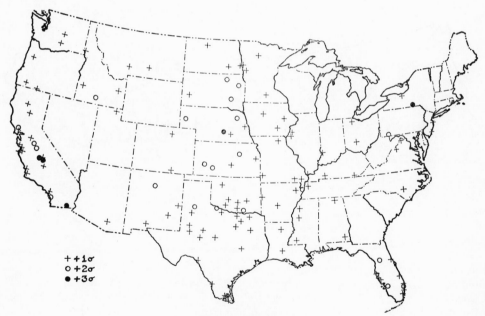

Fig. 3.—Retail trade

147

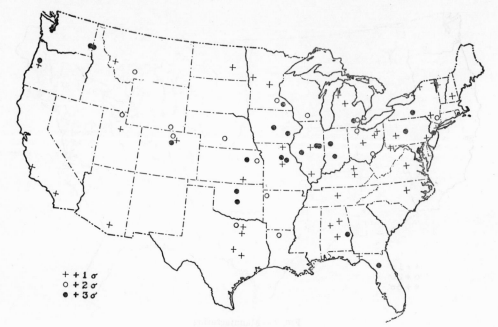

FIG. 4.—Professional service

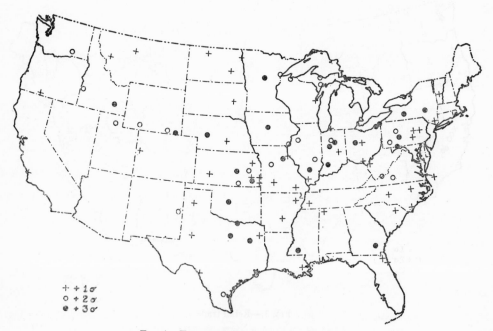

FIG. 5.—Transportation and communication

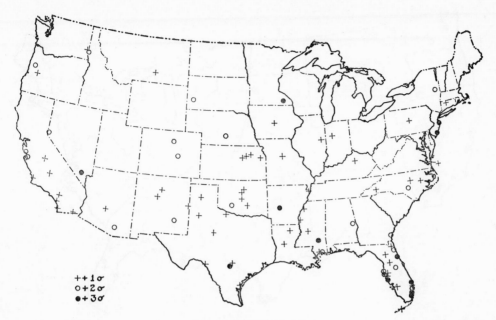

FIG. 6.—Personal service

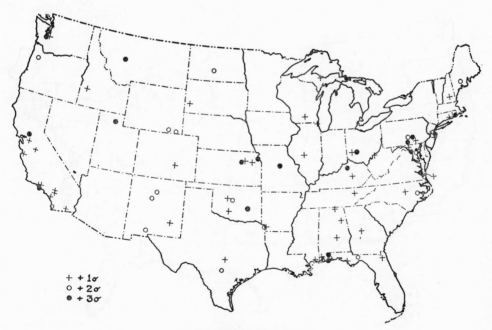

FIG. 7.—Public administration

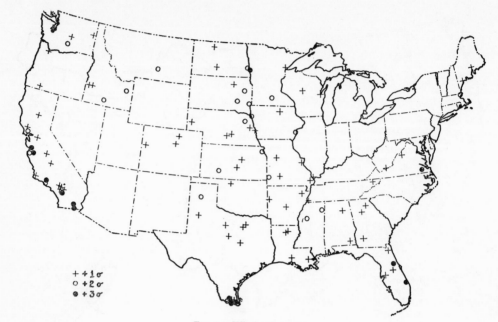

FIG. 8.—Wholesale trade

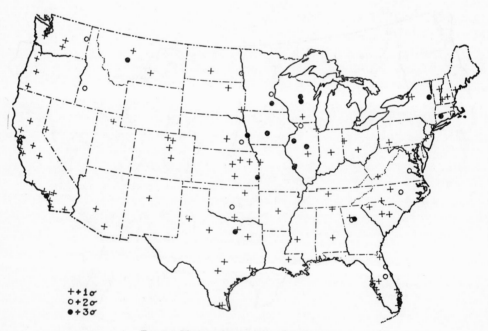

FIG. 9.—Finance, insurance, and real estate

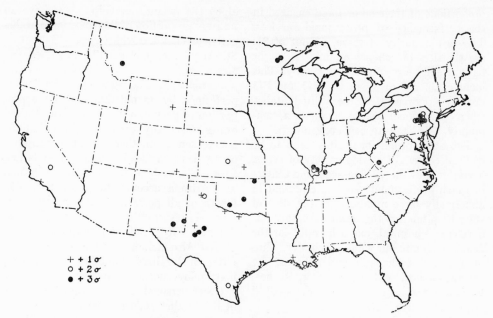

FIG. 10.—Mining

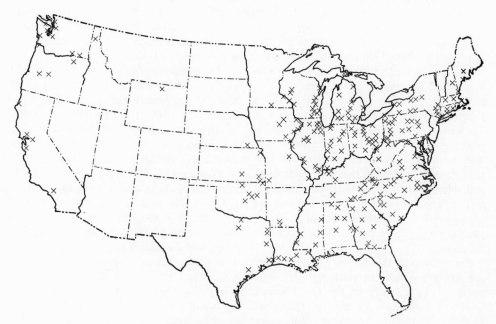

FIG. 11.—Diversified cities

151

proportions of their labor force engaged in the performance of professional services. The vast majority of these, 62 out of 81, are the sites of colleges or universities, or have a college or university nearby. This includes 34 out of 39 in the Pf2 and Pf3 groups. Apparently, in the United States, when professional people dominate a community, it is likely to be a college town.

The other professional cities tend to be medical centers of a wide variety of types. Two-thirds of the 19 non-academic centers in which professional people are present in abnormally large numbers are the sites of state hospitals for the insane. Another has a veterans' hospital, one a hospital for the deaf and dumb, etc. Only Rochester, Minnesota, and perhaps Temple, Texas, are general medical centers. However, Rochester (32.3 per cent) is the only medical center to receive a Pf3 rating.

Professional centers have a widespread distribution with at least one center in almost every state. These centers by and large are small cities, with only one, Madison, Wisconsin, over 100,000 population.

*Transportation and communication.—* Many people have characterized the United States as "an experiment in transportation." And in some 96 cities transportation and communication are carried on to a significantly above average degree (see Fig. 5). Transportation in the United States is predominantly land transportation, and fully seven-eighths of these cities are railroad centers. Altoona, Pennsylvania; Hornell, New York; North Platte, Nebraska; and Cleburne, Texas, are outstanding examples. They are usually small cities, division and junction points along main-line railways.

Exceptions to the above generalizations are made possible, in part, by the large shipments of iron ore on the Great Lakes. Of the 7 lake ports in this category, 6— Duluth, Minnesota, Ashland, Wisconsin, Marquette and Escanaba, Michigan, and Ashtabula and Conneaut, Ohio—are important ore ports. Green Bay, Wisconsin, is more of a general lake port. Five cities along the Atlantic or Gulf coasts have an unusual proportion of the labor force in this activity. They are New Orleans, Galveston, St. Augustine, Jacksonville, and Newport News.

*Personal service.—*Personal service is performed by an outstandingly large proportion of people in 92 cities in the United States. Generally these are cities that for one reason or another attract a transient, or at least a semitransient, population. Cities of sunshine in Florida, California, and Arizona account for more than one fourth of all personal service centers. Famous old resort cities like Saratoga Springs, Atlantic City, and Hot Springs, are included. Also included are the newer Nevada cities of legalized gambling, non-waiting matrimony, and easy divorce.

Other personal service centers include 14 of the smaller college towns, and a goodly number of cities that are near military posts. Rochester, Minnesota, previously mentioned as a medical center, has the largest proportion of personal service workers in its labor force—exactly one-third. Las Vegas, Nevada, is a close second, with a percentage of 30.5.

*Public administration.—*Cities supplying public administration (or governmental) services are almost exclusively of two general types. They are either political capitals or cities near large military installations. Of the 85 cities in this category, about one-fourth are political capitals. One of these is Washington, D.C., with a high of 31.6 per cent of its labor force employed in this activity. The other 23 cities are state capitals; those in the Pb3 group are Olympia, Sacramento, Harrisburg, Helena, Jefferson City, and Frankfort.

A somewhat new phenomenon in American urban activities, but common in other parts of the world, is the service performed by what are usually called garrison cities. A large number of cities receive a classification in this group because of their proximity to large army, naval, or air installations. Warrington and Key West, Florida; Newport, Rhode Island; Riverview, Virginia; and Junction City, Kansas, are examples from this group.

*Wholesale trade.*—Wholesaling, as defined for census purposes, has really two meanings: first, the sale of commodities in large quantities to retailers; and, second, the assembly and sale of commodities to jobbers. Thus, small cities serving areas of intensive agiculture producing crops requiring sorting and packing, such as citrus fruits and vegetables, are often places where wholesale trade of the second type is permitted an unusual development (see Fig. 8). Most cities in the W3 category are of this type: Corona (citrus), El Centro (vegetables), Santa Paula (lemons), Watsonville (lettuce), and Brawley (vegetables), in California; Mercedes (citrus and vegetables), and Edinburg (citrus), in Texas; Sanford (celery), and Fort Pierce (vegetables), in Florida; Moorhead (potatoes), in Minnesota; and Suffolk (peanuts), in Virginia, are examples.

Wholesaling centers in the more traditional sense, as distributing points for bulk lot goods—such as groceries, hardware, or drugs—to the retailers in the surrounding towns, are usually somewhat larger cities. New Orleans, Denver, and Portland, Oregon, are good examples.

No cities in the area of the "manufacturing belt" are classified as wholesaling cities. Aside from this exception, their distribution is generally widespread.

*Finance, insurance, and real estate.*—In 123 cities, the services of finance, insurance, and real estate are performed in outstanding proportions. These cities are widely scattered over the country, as indicated in Figure 9. Forty-two states in the Union have at least one city of this type. This is a triple-headed category, and perhaps the cities in the group are also of three general types.

Three-fourths of the 17 cities in the F3 group are insurance centers. Hartford, Connecticut, Bloomington, Illinois, Stevens Point, Wisconsin, and Des Moines, Iowa, are outstanding examples.

On the other hand, one would expect that in the F3 cities of Newport Beach, California, and Fort Lauderdale and Hollywood, Florida, many persons support themselves by selling real estate.

This is the only category that includes a large number of the very large cities (seven of the twelve urban areas with over a million people fall into the F category) and perhaps these very large cities are not specialized but are important in banking and other financial activities as well as insurance and real estate. New York, an urban unit of nearly 13 million persons, falls into the F2 category, and Dallas, with over half a million people, is an F3 city.

*Mining.*—Fewer people in urban areas provide the nation with mining service than are required for any other activity. Only 46 of the 897 cities fit into this category. Although it is quite true that much mining activity takes place in settlements of less than 10,000 persons, it is also true that this activity generally provides employment for fewer people than any of the other services listed.

"Gold" someone said, "is where you find it." Likewise, above-normal mining activity is possible only in conjunction with mineral deposits and thus is easily explained. Of the 47 cities in this category, 3—Hibbing (35.02 per cent) and Virginia City (23 per cent), Minnesota, and Ironwood (26.77 per cent), Michigan—are iron centers. One, Butte (32.1 per cent), Montana, is a copper city, and another, Carlsbad (29.46 per cent), New Mexico, is important for potash. All the above, as the percentages would indicate, are Mi3 cities. The remaining 42 centers important for mining are evenly divided between the older coal cities in Pennsylvania, West Virginia, Illinois, Kentucky, etc., and the newer petroleum cities of Texas, Oklahoma, Kansas, etc.

*Diversified cities.*—Two hundred and forty-six cities are not sufficiently high in proportion of their labor force in any single service to receive a special classification and hence remain as more or less average or diversified cities. These cities generally exhibit a high degree of concentration in the northeastern and southeastern parts of the country, with the exception of Florida (see Fig. 11).

## SUMMARY

A study of this sort is perhaps more useful as a reference tool than as an end in itself. With the use of Tables 1 and 2 and Figure 1, for example, data from the 1950 Census of Population on the economic activities of any city can be quickly placed in its proper perspective in relation to all other United States cities. Then, too, by the preceding classification, cities that are similarly outstanding in any service can be

separated, objectively and understandably, and subjected to further analysis.

It is in the further analysis of cities with similar services that a classification of this sort is primarily valuable, though little use has been made in this respect of classifications available in the past. For example, how do cities in each of the above categories compare in other significant things, such as rate of growth, per capita income, ethnic composition of the population, behavior of employment during various phases of the business cycle, ratio of basic to nonbasic employment, and so on? Is there more correlation in these and similar items among cities of the same service type or among cities in the same region?

## APPENDIX

### A SERVICE CLASSIFICATION OF AMERICAN CITIES

#### KEY

|  | Plus 1 SD | Plus 2 SD | Plus 3 SD |
|---|---|---|---|
| Manufacturing | Mf | Mf2 | Mf3 |
| Retail trade | R | R2 | R3 |
| Professional service | Pf | Pf2 | Pf3 |
| Transportation and communication | T | T2 | T3 |
| Personal service | Ps | Ps2 | Ps3 |
| Public administration | Pb | Pb2 | Pb3 |
| Wholesale trade | W | W2 | W3 |
| Finance, insurance, and real estate | F | F2 | F3 |
| Mining | Mi | Mi2 | Mi3 |
| Diversified | D | | |

#### ALABAMA

| Anniston | Pb |
| Auburn | Pf3Ps2 |
| Birmingham | D |
| Decatur | D |
| Dothan | RW |
| Florence | D |
| Gadsden | Mf |
| Huntsville | RPbF |
| Mobile | Pb |
| Montgomery | PbF |
| Opelika | D |
| Phenix City | D |
| Selma | D |
| Sheffield | T |
| Talladega | D |
| Tuscaloosa | Pf |

#### ARIZONA

| Amphitheater | R |
| Phoenix | PsWF |
| Tucson | Ps2PfF |

#### ARKANSAS

| Blytheville | R2Ps |
| Camden | D |
| El Dorado | D |
| Fayetteville | Pf2Ps |
| Fort Smith | RW |
| Helena | D |
| Hot Springs | Ps3R |
| Jonesboro | RTW |
| Little Rock–North | |
| Little Rock | TWF |
| Pine Bluff | TW |
| Texarkana | Pb |

#### CALIFORNIA

| Alisal | W3 |
| Anaheim | W |
| Antioch | Mf |
| Bakersfield | Ps |
| Brawley | W3 |
| Chico | RWF |
| Corona | W3Ps |

| Costa Mesa | Mf |
| El Centro | R3W3PsPbF |
| Eureka | D |
| Fresno | PsWF |
| Fullerton | W |
| Hanford | R3 |
| Lodi | D |
| Los Angeles | F |
| Madera | R2 |
| Merced | R2Pb |
| Modesto | RWF |
| Monterey | Ps2R |
| Napa | D |
| Newport Beach | F3R |
| Oceanside | R2PsW |
| Oildale | Mi2R |
| Ontario | D |
| Orange | Pf |
| Oxnard | Pb3W2 |
| Petaluma | W2R |
| Pittsburg | Mf |
| Pomona | W |
| Redding | R |

| | | | | | |
|---|---|---|---|---|---|
| Riverside | PbWF | Clearwater | Ps2F | Bloomington | F3 |
| Sacramento | Pb3 | Daytona Beach | Ps3F2R | Cairo | RW |
| Salinas | W2RF | Fort Lauderdale | F3Ps2R | Canton | D |
| San Bernardino | Pb | Fort Myers | R2Ps | Carbondale | PfT |
| San Buenaventura | MiPb | Fort Pierce | W3RF | Centralia | T3 |
| San Diego | Pb2PsF | Gainesville | Pf3Ps | Champaign | Pb3Ps |
| San Francisco– | | Hollywood | Ps3F3 | Chicago | F |
| Oakland | F2 | Jacksonville | TPsPbFW | Collinsville | D |
| San Jose | D | Key West | Pb3Ps | Danville | D |
| San Luis Obispo | RPfT | Lakeland | F | Decatur | D |
| Santa Ana | RPbF | Lake Worth | R2F2Ps | De Kalb | D |
| Santa Barbara | Ps2F | Miami | Ps3RF | Dixon | D |
| Santa Cruz | Ps2RF | Ocala | R2Ps | Elgin | D |
| Santa Maria | RPsW | Orlando | Ps2F2W | Freeport | F2 |
| Santa Paula | W3Pb | Panama City | Pb | Galesburg | T2 |
| Santa Rosa | R2WF | Pensacola | Pb2 | Harrisburg | Mi3 |
| Seaside | Ps2RPb | St. Augustine | Ps2T | Jacksonville | Pf3 |
| Stockton | Pb | St. Petersburg | Ps2F2R | Joliet | D |
| Tulare | R3W | Sanford | W3 | Kankakee | D |
| Visalia | R | Sarasota | Ps3RF | Kewanee | Mf |
| Watsonville | W3R | Tallahassee | Pb2Pf | La Salle | Mf |
| | | Tampa | PsW | Lincoln | Pf |
| **COLORADO** | | Warrington | Pb3 | Macomb | R |
| | | West Palm Beach | Ps3RF | Marion | Mi2 |
| Boulder | Pf3Ps2 | | | Mattoon | T2 |
| Colorado Springs | Ps2F | **GEORGIA** | | Monmouth | F3R |
| Denver | WF | | | Mount Vernon | D |
| Fort Collins | Pf2F | Augusta | D | Ottawa | D |
| Grand Junction | TW | Albany | W | Pekin | D |
| Greeley | RPfWF | Americus | D | Peoria | D |
| Pueblo | Pb | Athens | Pf | Quincy | D |
| Trinidad | RMi | Atlanta | F2 | Rockford | Mf |
| | | Brunswick | Ps2 | Springfield | PbF |
| **CONNECTICUT** | | Columbus | D | Sterling | Mf |
| | | Dalton | Mf | Streator | Mf |
| Ansonia | Mf2 | Decatur | F3W | Urbana | Pf3 |
| Bridgeport | Mf | Dublin | D | Waukegan | Pb |
| Danbury | Mf | Gainesville | W | West Frankfort | Mi3 |
| Derby | Mf2 | Griffin | D | Wood River | Mf |
| Hartford | F3 | La Grange | Mf | | |
| Meriden | Mf | Macon | Pb | **INDIANA** | |
| Middleton | D | Marietta | F | | |
| New Britain– | | Moultrie | D | Anderson | Mf |
| Bristol | Mf2 | Rome | D | Bedford | D |
| New Haven | D | Savannah | D | Bloomington | Pf3 |
| New London | Pb | Thomasville | D | Columbus | Mf |
| Norwich | D | Valdosta | D | Connersville | Mf |
| Shelton | Mf | Waycross | T3 | Crawfordsville | D |
| Stamford-Norwalk | D | | | Elkhart | Mf |
| Torrington | Mf | **IDAHO** | | Elwood | Mf |
| Wallingford | Mf2 | | | Evansville | D |
| Waterbury | Mf | Boise City | F2PbW | Fort Wayne | D |
| Willimantic | Mf | Caldwell | RW | Frankfort | T3 |
| | | Coeur d'Alene | D | Goshen | Mf |
| **DISTRICT OF COLUMBIA** | | Idaho Falls | W2R | Huntington | D |
| | | Lewiston | R | Indianapolis | F |
| Washington | Pb3F | Moscow | Pf3Ps2 | Kokomo | Mf |
| | | Nampa | T2 | Lafayette | D |
| **DELAWARE** | | Pocatello | T3 | La Porte | Mf |
| | | Twin Falls | R2W2 | Logansport | T2 |
| Wilmington | D | | | Marion | D |
| | | **ILLINOIS** | | Michigan City | D |
| **FLORIDA** | | | | Muncie | Mf |
| Bradenton | RPsF | Alton | D | | |
| Brownsville-B.-G. | Pb3 | Aurora | D | | |

### INDIANA—*Continued*

| | |
|---|---|
| New Castle | Mf |
| Peru | T3 |
| Richmond | Mf |
| Shelbyville | D |
| South Bend | Mf |
| Terre Haute | D |
| Valparaiso | D |
| Vincennes | R |
| Wabash | Mf |
| Washington | T3 |
| West Lafayette | Pf3Ps |

### IOWA

| | |
|---|---|
| Ames | Pf3Ps |
| Boone | T3 |
| Burlington | W2 |
| Cedar Rapids | R |
| Charles City | D |
| Clinton | D |
| Davenport, Ia.–<br>Rock Island–<br>Moline, Ill. | D |
| Des Moines | F3 |
| Dubuque | D |
| Fort Dodge | R |
| Fort Madison | T2 |
| Iowa City | Pf3 |
| Keokuk | D |
| Marshalltown | D |
| Mason City | D |
| Muscatine | D |
| Newton | Mf |
| Oskaloosa | R |
| Ottumwa | D |
| Sioux City | W2 |
| Waterloo | D |

### KANSAS

| | |
|---|---|
| Arkansas City | T2 |
| Atchison | D |
| Chanute | T |
| Coffeyville | D |
| Dodge City | W2R2T |
| El Dorado | Mi |
| Emporia | T2 |
| Fort Scott | F3T |
| Garden City | R2 |
| Great Bend | Mi2 |
| Hutchinson | WR |
| Independence | D |
| Junction City | Pb3R2Ps |
| Lawrence | Pf2Ps |
| Leavenworth | Pb3 |
| Manhattan | Pf3PsPbF |
| Newton | T3 |
| Ottawa | R |
| Parsons | T3 |
| Pittsburg | T |
| Salina | RWF |
| Topeka | TPbF |

| | |
|---|---|
| Wichita | F |
| Winfield | Pf |

### KENTUCKY

| | |
|---|---|
| Bowling Green | D |
| Frankfort | Pb3 |
| Henderson | D |
| Hopkinsville | RPs |
| Lexington | PfPs |
| Louisville | D |
| Madisonville | Mi3 |
| Middlesborough | Mi2R |
| Owensboro | D |
| Paducah | T2 |
| Richmond | PfPb |

### LOUISIANA

| | |
|---|---|
| Alexandria | Ps |
| Bastrop | Mf |
| Baton Rouge | D |
| Bogalusa | D |
| Crowley | D |
| Houma | Mi3 |
| Lafayette | D |
| Lake Charles | D |
| Monroe | PsW |
| New Iberia | MiW |
| New Orleans | TWF |
| Opelousas | R |
| Ruston | Pf2 |
| Shreveport | D |
| West Monroe | RW |

### MAINE

| | |
|---|---|
| Auburn | Mf |
| Augusta | Pb2 |
| Bangor | W |
| Bath | D |
| Biddeford | Mf2 |
| Lewiston | Mf |
| Portland | WF |
| Saco | Mf |
| Sanford | Mf2 |
| Waterville | D |

### MARYLAND

| | |
|---|---|
| Annapolis | Pf3Pb2 |
| Baltimore | D |
| Cambridge | D |
| Cumberland | T3 |
| Frederick | Pb |
| Hagerstown | D |
| Salisbury | D |

### MASSACHUSETTS

| | |
|---|---|
| Adams-Renfrew | Mf2 |
| Boston | F |
| Brockton | Mf |
| Clinton | Mf |

| | |
|---|---|
| Fall River | Mf |
| Fitchburg | Mf |
| Gardner | Mf |
| Gloucester | W2 |
| Greenfield | Ps |
| Haverhill | Mf |
| Leominster | Mf2 |
| Lawrence | Mf |
| Lowell | Mf |
| Marlborough | Mf |
| Milford | Mf2 |
| New Bedford | Mf |
| Newburyport | Mf |
| North Adams | Mf |
| Northampton | D |
| Plymouth | D |
| Southbridge | Mf2 |
| Springfield–<br>Holyoke | Mf |
| Taunton | Mf |
| Webster | Mf2 |
| Worcester | D |

### MICHIGAN

| | |
|---|---|
| Adrian | D |
| Albion | Mf |
| Alpena | D |
| Ann Arbor | Pf3 |
| Battle Creek | D |
| Bay City | D |
| Benton Harbor | Mf |
| Cadillac | D |
| Detroit | Mf |
| Escanaba | T2 |
| Flint | Mf |
| Grand Rapids | D |
| Holland | D |
| Ironwood | Mi3 |
| Jackson | D |
| Kalamazoo | D |
| Lansing | D |
| Marquette | T2Pb |
| Menominee | Mf |
| Midland | Mf |
| Monroe | Mf |
| Mount Pleasant | PfMi |
| Muskegon | Mf |
| Niles | MfT |
| Owosso | D |
| Pontiac | Mf |
| Port Huron | D |
| Saginaw | Mf |
| St. Joseph | Mf |
| Sault Ste Marie | D |
| Springfield Place | Mf |
| Traverse City | Pf |
| Willow Run | Pf2 |
| Ypsilanti | D |

## MINNESOTA

| | |
|---|---|
| Albert Lea | D |
| Austin | Mf |
| Bemidji | R |
| Brainerd | T3 |
| Duluth, Minn.– | |
| Superior, Wis. | T2W |
| Faribault | Pf2 |
| Fergus Falls | RPf |
| Hibbing | Mi3 |
| Mankato | W2R |
| Minneapolis– | |
| St. Paul | F2W |
| Moorhead | W3R |
| Owatonna | F3 |
| Red Wing | D |
| Rochester | Pf3Ps2 |
| St. Cloud | Pf |
| Virginia | Mi3 |
| Winona | D |

## MISSISSIPPI

| | |
|---|---|
| Biloxi | Ps2Pb |
| Clarksdale | RPs |
| Columbus | D |
| Greenville | D |
| Greenwood | W2R |
| Gulfport | Ps |
| Hattiesburg | D |
| Jackson | PsF |
| Laurel | Ps3 |
| McComb | T3R |
| Meridian | D |
| Natchez | D |
| Pascagoula | D |
| Tupelo | W2 |
| Vicksburg | D |

## MISSOURI

| | |
|---|---|
| Cape Girardeau | D |
| Carthage | D |
| Columbia | Pf3Ps |
| Fulton | Pf3 |
| Hannibal | T |
| Jefferson City | Pb3 |
| Joplin | W2R |
| Kansas City | F |
| Kirksville | RPf |
| Mexico | D |
| Moberly | T3 |
| Poplar Bluff | RT |
| St. Charles | Mf |
| St. Joseph | W |
| St. Louis | Ps |
| Sedalia | T2W |
| Sikeston | RW |
| Springfield | TW |
| Webster Groves | F3W |

## MONTANA

| | |
|---|---|
| Anaconda | Mf |
| Billings | W2RPsF |
| Bozeman | Pf2RPs |
| Butte | Mi3 |
| Great Falls | TF |
| Helena | Pb3F3 |
| Missoula | PfT |

## NEBRASKA

| | |
|---|---|
| Beatrice | D |
| Fremont | RW |
| Grand Island | TWF |
| Hastings | RW |
| Kearney | R3Pf2Ps2W |
| Lincoln | F2 |
| Norfolk | R2W2 |
| North Platte | T3 |
| Omaha | F3W |
| Scottsbluff | R2W |

## NEVADA

| | |
|---|---|
| Las Vegas | Ps3 |
| Reno | Ps2F |

## NEW HAMPSHIRE

| | |
|---|---|
| Berlin | Mf2 |
| Claremont | Mf |
| Concord | PfPbF |
| Dover | Mf |
| Keene | F |
| Laconia | D |
| Manchester | Mf |
| Nashua | Mf |
| Portsmouth | D |
| Rochester | Mf |

## NEW JERSEY

| | |
|---|---|
| Asbury Park | Ps3RPb |
| Atlantic City | Ps3R |
| Bridgeton | Mf |
| Burlington | Mf |
| Long Branch | Pb3 |
| Millville | Mf |
| Phillipsburg | Mf |
| Princeton | Pf3 |
| Red Bank | Pb2F |
| Trenton | Pb |

## NEW MEXICO

| | |
|---|---|
| Albuquerque | Pb2PsF |
| Carlsbad | Mi3 |
| Clovis | T2Ps |
| Hobbs | Mi3 |
| Las Cruces | Pb2R |
| Roswell | Ps2RPb |
| Santa Fe | R2Pb2Ps |

## NEW YORK

| | |
|---|---|
| Albany-Troy | Pb2 |
| Amsterdam | Mf2 |
| Auburn | Mf |
| Batavia | D |
| Beacon | Pf2 |
| Binghamton | R3Mf |
| Buffalo | D |
| Corning | Mf |
| Cortland | Mf |
| Dunkirk | Mf |
| Elmira | D |
| Fulton | Mf2 |
| Geneva | D |
| Glens Falls | F3 |
| Gloversville | Mf |
| Hornell | T3 |
| Hudson | D |
| Ithaca | Pf3 |
| Jamestown | Mf |
| Johnstown | Mf |
| Kingston | D |
| Lockport | Mf |
| Massena | Mf |
| Middletown | Pf |
| Newark | RPf |
| Newburgh | D |
| New York–North- | |
| eastern N.J. | F2 |
| Niagara Falls | Mf |
| Ogdensburg | Pf |
| Olean | D |
| Oneida | Mf |
| Oneonta | T3 |
| Oswego | D |
| Peekskill | T |
| Plattsburgh | Pf |
| Poughkeepsie | D |
| Rochester | Mf |
| Rome | Mf |
| Saratoga Springs | Ps2 |
| Schenectady | Mf |
| Syracuse | D |
| Utica | D |
| Watertown | F |

## NORTH CAROLINA

| | |
|---|---|
| Albemarle | Mf |
| Asheville | Ps |
| Burlington | Mf |
| Charlotte | WF |
| Concord | Mf |
| Durham | D |
| Elizabeth City | D |
| Fayetteville | Ps2R |
| Gastonia | Mf |
| Goldsboro | D |
| Greensboro | F |
| Greenville | Ps |
| Henderson | D |

NORTH CAROLINA—*Continued*

| | |
|---|---|
| Hickory | D |
| High Point | Mf |
| Kannapolis | Mf2 |
| Kingston | D |
| Lexington | Mf |
| Monroe | D |
| New Bern | Pb2 |
| Raleigh | F2PfPbPs |
| Reidsville | Mf |
| Rocky Mount | T |
| Salisbury | T |
| Sanford | D |
| Shelby | D |
| Statesville | D |
| Thomasville | Mf2 |
| Wilmington | T |
| Wilson | D |
| Winston-Salem | D |

NORTH DAKOTA

| | |
|---|---|
| Bismarck | Pb2WF |
| Fargo | W2F2R |
| Grand Forks | T |
| Jamestown | RTPf |
| Minot | RTW |

OHIO

| | |
|---|---|
| Akron | Mf |
| Alliance | Mf |
| Ashland | Mf |
| Ashtabula | T3 |
| Athens | Pf2 |
| Bellefontaine | T3 |
| Bowling Green | Pf2R |
| Bucyrus | D |
| Cambridge | D |
| Canton | Mf |
| Chillicothe | D |
| Cincinnati | D |
| Cleveland | D |
| Columbus | F |
| Conneaut | T3 |
| Coshocton | D |
| Dayton | Pb |
| Defiance | D |
| Delaware | Pf |
| East Liverpool | Mf |
| Findlay | D |
| Fostoria | Mf |
| Fremont | D |
| Hamilton | Mf |
| Kent | Pf |
| Lancaster | Mf |
| Lima | D |
| Lorain | Mf |
| Mansfield | Mf |
| Marietta | D |
| Marion | T |
| Mount Vernon | D |
| Newark | D |

| | |
|---|---|
| New Philadelphia | D |
| Painesville | Mf |
| Piqua | Mf |
| Portsmouth | T |
| Salem | Mf |
| Sandusky | Mf |
| Sidney | Mf |
| Springfield | D |
| Steubenville | Mf |
| Tiffin | D |
| Toledo | D |
| Troy | Mf |
| Van Wert | DF |
| Washington | R |
| Wooster | Pf |
| Xenia | Pb3 |
| Youngstown | Mf |
| Zanesville | D |

OKLAHOMA

| | |
|---|---|
| Ada | RPs |
| Ardmore | RF |
| Bartlesville | Mi3 |
| Chickasha | R |
| Duncan | Mi3 |
| Durant | R2 |
| El Reno | T3Pb |
| Enid | RW |
| Guthrie | Ps |
| Lawton | Ps2RPb |
| McAlester | Pb3R |
| Miami | D |
| Muskogee | D |
| Norman | Pf3Ps |
| Oklahoma City | Pb2F2 |
| Okmulgee | D |
| Ponca City | D |
| Sapulpa | D |
| Seminole | Mi3 |
| Shawnee | D |
| Stillwater | Pf3Ps |
| Tulsa | F |

OREGON

| | |
|---|---|
| Albany | R |
| Astoria | D |
| Bend | D |
| Corvallis | Pf3Ps2 |
| Eugene | PfPsF |
| Klamath Falls | RT |
| Medford | RWF |
| Pendleton | D |
| Portland | WF |
| Salem | PbF |
| Springfield | D |

PENNSYLVANIA

| | |
|---|---|
| Allentown-Bethlehem | Mf |
| Altoona | T3 |

| | |
|---|---|
| Berwick | Mf |
| Bloomsburg | D |
| Bradford | Mi |
| Bristol | Mf2 |
| Butler | D |
| Cannonsburg | D |
| Carlisle | Pb2 |
| Chambersburg | Pb3 |
| Coatesville | Mf |
| Columbia | MfPb |
| Connellsville | T2 |
| Conshohocken | Mf2 |
| Donora | Mf2 |
| Du Bois | T2 |
| Easton | Mf |
| Ellwood City | Mf2 |
| Erie | D |
| Farrell | Mf2 |
| Franklin | D |
| Greensburg | F |
| Hanover | Mf |
| Harrisburg | Pb3T |
| Hazleton | Mi2 |
| Indiana | Mi2Pf |
| Jeannette | Mf |
| Johnstown | D |
| Lancaster | Mf |
| Latrobe | Mf |
| Lebanon | Mf |
| Lewistown | D |
| Lock Haven | D |
| Mahanoy City | Mi3 |
| Meadville | D |
| Monessen | Mf2 |
| Mount Carmel | Mi3 |
| New Castle | T |
| Norristown | Mf |
| Oil City | D |
| Philadelphia | F |
| Phoenixville | Mf |
| Pittsburgh | D |
| Pottstown | Mf |
| Pottsville | Mi |
| Reading | Mf |
| Scranton | Mi2 |
| Shamokin | Mi2 |
| Sharon | Mf |
| Shenandoah | Mi3 |
| State College | Pf3Ps |
| Sunbury | T |
| Tamaqua | TMi3 |
| Uniontown | R2Mi2 |
| Warren | D |
| Washington | D |
| Waynesboro | Mf |
| West Chester | Pf |
| Williamsport | D |
| Wilkes-Barre | Mi3 |
| York | D |

### RHODE ISLAND

| | |
|---|---|
| Bristol | Mf2 |
| Central Falls | Mf2 |
| Newport | Pb3 |
| Providence | Mf |
| Woonsocket | Mf2 |

### SOUTH CAROLINA

| | |
|---|---|
| Anderson | D |
| Brandon-Judson | Mf3 |
| Charleston | D |
| Columbia | F |
| Florence | T |
| Greenwood | D |
| Greenville | F |
| Orangeburg | D |
| Rock Hill | Mf |
| Spartanburg | D |
| Sumter | F |

### SOUTH DAKOTA

| | |
|---|---|
| Aberdeen | R2WF |
| Huron | RTW |
| Mitchell | R2W2 |
| Rapid City | Ps2RPb |
| Sioux Falls | W2F |
| Watertown | R2W2 |

### TENNESSEE

| | |
|---|---|
| Bristol | D |
| Chattanooga | D |
| Clarksville | D |
| Cleveland | D |
| Columbia | D |
| Dyersburg | R |
| Elizabethton | D |
| Jackson | T |
| Johnson City | W |
| Kingsport | Mf |
| Knoxville | D |
| Memphis | W |
| Morristown | D |
| Murfreesboro | Pf |
| Nashville | F |
| Oak Ridge | MfPb |

### TEXAS

| | |
|---|---|
| Abilene | PsWF |
| Alice | Mi2 |
| Amarillo | W2TPs |
| Austin | PbF |
| Baytown | Mf |
| Beaumont | D |
| Big Spring | RT |
| Borger | Mi |
| Brownsville | D |
| Brownwood | RW |
| Bryan | Pf |

| | |
|---|---|
| Cleburne | T3 |
| Corpus Christi | PsPb |
| Corsicana | D |
| Dallas | F3W |
| Del Rio | RTPs |
| Denison | T3 |
| Denton | Pf2 |
| Edinburg | W3R |
| El Paso | T |
| Fort Worth | D |
| Gainesville | RMi |
| Galveston | T2F2 |
| Garland | WF |
| Greenville | R |
| Harlingen | RWF |
| Houston | F |
| Kingsville | T2 |
| Lamesa | MiR |
| Laredo | R |
| Longview | D |
| Lubbock | RWPsF |
| Lufkin | D |
| McAllen | RWF |
| McKinney | Pf |
| Marshall | T |
| Mercedes | W3R |
| Midland | Mi3 |
| Mission | R |
| Nacogdoches | D |
| New Braunfels | Ps |
| Odessa | Mi3 |
| Orange | D |
| Palestine | T3 |
| Pampa | Mi2 |
| Paris | R |
| Plainview | R2 |
| Port Arthur | Mf |
| San Angelo | RPs |
| San Antonio | Ps3Pb2F |
| San Benito | W3 |
| Sherman | D |
| Snyder | Mi3 |
| Sweetwater | R |
| Temple | Pf |
| Terrell | Pf |
| Texarkana | Pb2 |
| Texas City | D |
| Tyler | RF |
| Vernon | R2 |
| Victoria | D |
| Waco | W |
| Waxahachie | R |
| Wichita Falls | RMiPs |

### UTAH

| | |
|---|---|
| Logan | Pf2R |
| Ogden | Pb3T2 |
| Provo | Pf |
| Salt Lake City | F |

### VERMONT

| | |
|---|---|
| Barre | F |
| Burlington | Pf |
| Rutland | T |

### VIRGINIA

| | |
|---|---|
| Bristol | D |
| Charlottesville | Pf |
| Danville | D |
| Fredericksburg | D |
| Harrisonburg | RW |
| Hopewell | Mf |
| Lynchburg | D |
| Martinsville | Mf |
| Newport News | TPb |
| Newsome Park | D |
| Norfolk-Ports- mouth | Pb2 |
| Petersburg | D |
| Richmond | F2 |
| Riverview | Pb3Ps |
| Roanoke | T2 |
| Staunton | D |
| Suffolk | W3 |
| Waynesboro | Mf |
| Winchester | R |

### WASHINGTON

| | |
|---|---|
| Aberdeen | D |
| Bellingham | D |
| Bremerton | D |
| Everett | D |
| Hoquiam | Mf |
| Kennewick | D |
| Longview | Mf |
| Olympia | Pb3 |
| Pasco | T2 |
| Port Angeles | D |
| Pullman | Pf3Ps |
| Puyallup | D |
| Richland | Mf2 |
| Seattle | F2 |
| Spokane | F2W |
| Tacoma | PbF |
| Walla Walla | D |
| Wenatchee | RWF |
| Yakima | W2RF |

### WEST VIRGINIA

| | |
|---|---|
| Beckley | Mi3 |
| Bluefield | T2WF |
| Charleston | D |
| Clarksburg | D |
| Fairmont | Mi2 |
| Huntington, W.Va.-Ash- land, Ky. | T |
| Martinsburg | D |
| Morgantown | PfMi |

| WEST VIRGINIA—*Continued* | | Fond du Lac | D | Sheboygan | Mf |
|---|---|---|---|---|---|
| Moundsville | Mf | Green Bay | TW | Stevens Point | F3 |
| Parkersburg | D | Janesville | D | Two Rivers | Mf2 |
| South Parkersburg | Mf | Kenosha | Mf | Watertown | D |
| Weirton | Mf2 | La Crosse | D | Waukesha | D |
| Wheeling | D | Madison | Pf2PbF | Wausau | F3 |
| | | Manitowoc | Mf | Wisconsin Rapids | Mf |
| WISCONSIN | | Marinette | D | | |
| Appleton | D | Marshfield | W | WYOMING | |
| Ashland | T2 | Menasha | Mf2 | Casper | Mi |
| Beaver Dam | D | Milwaukee | D | Cheyenne | T3Pb2 |
| Beloit | Mf | Neenah | Mf | Laramie | T2Pf2Pb2 |
| Chippewa Falls | D | Oshkosh | D | Rock Springs | T2 |
| Eau Claire | D | Racine | Mf | Sheridan | D |

## URBAN POPULATION STUDIES

Geographers are turning their attention increasingly to the spatial aspects of urban populations. Analyses have been made of variations in the distribution of people within cities and in their outlying areas; of population changes resulting, in particular, from in- and out-migrations; of the clustering of people of similar racial, ethnic, religious, or occupational groups; and of spatial variations in birth and death rates from one part of the city to another. These studies have contributed significant generalizations regarding the social and economic characteristics of our urban inhabitants.

The distribution of urban populations by place of residence varies considerably according to type and size of cities. Characteristically, however, areas of highest density are near the central business district, with declining densities away from the center. The rate of decline, however, is not uniform in all parts of the city, for people tend to be more highly concentrated along or near radial transportation routes than in sections removed from major thoroughfares.

Spatial differences in the composition of urban populations are a result of segregation, either voluntary or involuntary. The former occurs when individuals or families on their own initiative seek to live with others of their own kind and apart from those who differ from them in race, nationality, creed, or level of income. Involuntary segregation occurs when families or individuals are required by law or custom, or both, to live in designated areas or are prevented from living in areas occupied by those who differ in certain respects. For example, American cities are apt to have Negro areas in which few, if any, white people live. The amount of involuntary segregation within a specific city depends on the preferences and prejudices of its inhabitants.

Robert T. Novak's article, "Distribution of Puerto Ricans on Manhattan Island," deals with the concentration of Puerto Ricans in six major areas in the Borough of Manhattan. These clusterings can be accounted for by (1) low-cost housing and (2) location near express stops or terminals on major subway or bus lines. In general, Puerto Ricans migrating to cities within continental United State find homes in areas adjacent to other racial and ethnic minorities and have many contacts with these peoples.

Howard J. Nelson, for his study, "Some Characteristics of the Population of Cities in Similar Service Classifications," investigated possible variations in the social and economic characteristics of inhabitants of cities of different functional or service classifications. He found that variations in the rate of change in population in the 1940–50 decade were strongly affected by a city's major service. He investigated such characteristics as the average proportion of persons sixty-five years and older; the average number of school years completed; the proportion of males and females in the labor force; unemployment; and average income. He also found that regional location is a factor in explaining the social and economic makeup of our modern cities.

The remaining article included in this section, Chapin and Stewart's "Population Densities around the Clock," deals with the daytime-nighttime variations in the total population distribution throughout an entire urban area and relates the patterns of home-work relationships of the work population of a city. Information of the kind presented is useful, particularly in determining principles of planning land use and in developing comprehensive city plans.

ROBERT T. NOVAK

# DISTRIBUTION OF PUERTO RICANS ON MANHATTAN ISLAND

Residents of the island of Puerto Rico can move freely between their homeland and the continental United States. The result has been a great influx of these people to the mainland. In 1950 there were in the continental United States 301,375 persons of Puerto Rican birth or parentage,[1] a number equivalent to more than 10 per cent of the total population of Puerto Rico itself.

Census of 1950 about 83 per cent of the persons of Puerto Rican birth in the continental United States were enumerated there. Concentration increased progressively from 1910, when about 37 per cent of all Puerto Ricans in the continental United States lived in New York City, to 1940, when the percentage was about 88. The

TABLE 1

PUERTO RICANS IN THE CONTINENTAL UNITED STATES AND
IN NEW YORK CITY, 1910–50*

| CENSUS YEAR AND GENERATION | CONTINENTAL UNITED STATES | | NEW YORK CITY | |
|---|---|---|---|---|
| | Number | Per Cent Increase | Number | Per Cent of Total |
| By birth: | | | | |
| 1910............ | 1,513 | .......... | 554 | 36.6 |
| 1920............ | 11,811 | 680.6 | 7,364 | 62.4 |
| 1930............ | 52,774 | 346.8 | not available | .......... |
| 1940............ | 69,967 | 32.6 | 61,463 | 87.8 |
| 1950............ | 226,110 | 223.2 | 187,420 | 82.9 |
| By parentage: | | | | |
| 1950............ | 75,265 | .......... | 58,460 | 77.7 |

\* Source: "Puerto Ricans in Continental United States," Census of Population, 1950, Special Report, P-E, No. 30 (U.S. Bureau of the Census, 1953), p. 3D-4. Statistics for 1950 are for April of that year and are based on a 20 per cent sample area. Puerto Ricans "by parentage" were born in the continental United States.

Puerto Rican immigrants have largely settled in New York City (Table 1): in the

Reprinted from *Geographical Review*, XLVI (April, 1956), 182–86, with permission of the author and the editor. (Copyright, 1956, by the American Geographical Society, New York.)

[1] In this report Puerto Ricans are persons born in Puerto Rico or persons born elsewhere with one or both parents of Puerto Rican birth; that is, migrants from Puerto Rico and their children who are presently living in the United States. No census data earlier than 1950 are available for persons of Puerto Rican parentage.

slight drop in 1950 may indicate a reversal of the trend.

The total number in New York City, however, has continued to increase rapidly. From 554 in December, 1910, the number rose to 245,880 in April, 1950, and 275,200 by the end of that year (Table 2). According to the best estimates available, there were in New York City at the end of 1954 some 514,200 Puerto Ricans.[2]

[2] The *New York Times,* April 4, 1955, p. 1, stated that the population growth of Puerto Ricans in New York City since 1950 was 239,000.

Puerto Ricans have settled in all five boroughs of New York (Table 3), but by far the greatest concentration is in Manhattan Borough, where a total of 138,507 Puerto Ricans lived in 1950, 56 per cent of the number in the entire city.

The distribution of the Puerto Ricans on Manhattan Island is by no means uniform, though all but 22 of the 284 census tracts have some Puerto Rican inhabitants. Of the 22 census tracts with no Puerto Rican

cent, eleven a percentage from 16 to 40, and five a percentage from 40 to 76. No census tract has a percentage greater than 76.

The distribution pattern (Fig. 1) shows six major areas of Puerto Rican concentration on Manhattan Island. The greatest is in the northeast, extending from East 91st Street north to West 140th Street, thence west to Lenox Avenue and east to the Harlem and East rivers; this is also the main

TABLE 2

PUERTO RICANS IN NEW YORK CITY, 1940–53*

| Year | Total | Birth | Parentage |
|---|---|---|---|
| Apr. 1940. . . . . . . . . . . . . . | not available | 61,463 | not available |
| Apr. 1950. . . . . . . . . . . . . . | 245,880 | 187,420 | 58,460 |
| Dec. 1950. . . . . . . . . . . . . . | 275,200 | 210,000 | 65,200 |
| 1951 (est.). . . . . . . . | 326,300 | 251,000 | 75,300 |
| 1952 (est.). . . . . . . . | 382,900 | 296,200 | 86,700 |
| 1953 (est.). . . . . . . . | 455,000 | 355,000 | 100,000 |

* Source: A. J. Jaffe (ed.), *Puerto Rican Population of New York City* (New York: Bureau of Applied Social Research, Columbia University, 1954), p. 6.

TABLE 3

PUERTO RICANS IN NEW YORK CITY BY BOROUGH, APRIL, 1950*

| Borough | Total | Puerto Ricans | Percentage |
|---|---|---|---|
| Bronx. . . . . . . . . . . . . . . . . . . | 1,451,277 | 61,924 | 25.1 |
| Brooklyn. . . . . . . . . . . . . . . | 2,738,175 | 40,299 | 16.4 |
| Manhattan. . . . . . . . . . . . . . | 1,960,101 | 138,507 | 56.2 |
| Queens. . . . . . . . . . . . . . . . . | 1,550,849 | 4,836 | 2.0 |
| Richmond. . . . . . . . . . . . . . | 191,555 | 740 | 0.3 |

* Source: *Population of Puerto Ricans (Birth or Parentage) for New York City* (New York:Research Bureau, Welfare and Health Council of New York City, 1952), p. 7.

population, eight are represented by major city parks with no population at all. Of the other 14, nine are contiguous in a single area between Canal Street and Liberty Street in downtown Manhattan, which is mainly a business section; three are islands devoted to institutional use; and the other two are isolated tracts in northern Manhattan along the Harlem River.[3] In 147 of the remaining 262 census tracts Puerto Ricans constitute only 2 per cent or less of the population; ninety-nine tracts have a Puerto Rican population of 3 to 15 per

Negro district of New York City. This area contains five census tracts that are 40 to 76 per cent Puerto Rican. These five contiguous tracts adjoin the northeast corner of Central Park, and surrounding them are five that are 16 to 40 per cent Puerto Rican and thirteen that are 3 to 15 per cent. The whole area of twenty-three tracts

[3] Census-tract data for this study have been taken from the New York City Welfare and Health Council's publication *Population of Puerto Ricans* (see footnote to Table 3). This report is based on the percentage of Puerto Ricans in each census tract.

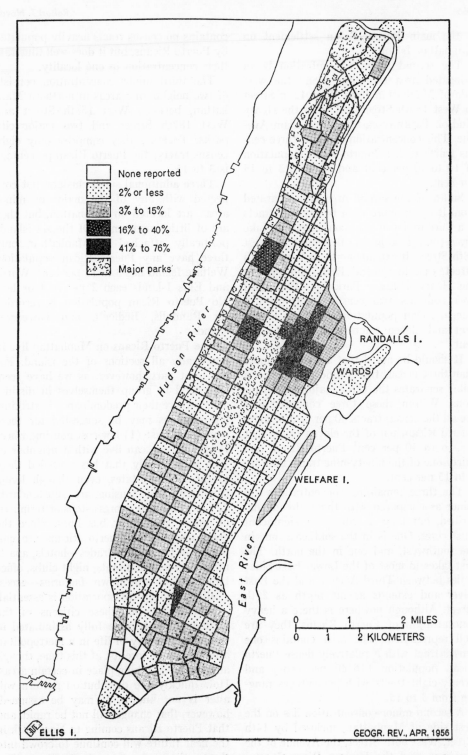

None reported

2% or less

3% to 15%

16% to 40%

41% to 76%

Major parks

RANDALLS I.

WARDS

WELFARE I.

*Hudson River*

*East River*

0         1         2 MILES

0    1        2 KILOMETERS

ELLIS I.

GEOGR. REV., APR. 1956

FIG. 1.—Distribution of Puerto Ricans on Manhattan Island, 1950, based on percentage of total population for each census tract.

is the main Puerto Rican settlement on Manhattan Island.

The second major concentration is an elongated area extending along the west side of Manhattan from West 122d Street to West 155th Street and from the Henry Hudson Parkway east to Amsterdam Avenue. This concentration contains three census tracts with a Puerto Rican population of 16 to 40 per cent and six with 3 to 15 per cent.

South of the second area and separated from it by no more than two census tracts is a third major area of concentration. Like the second, it is linear. Beginning at West 78th Street, it extends north to West 114th Street, east to Central Park, and west to the Henry Hudson Parkway. This third area contains two census tracts with a Puerto Rican population of 15 to 40 per cent and eleven tracts with 3 to 15 per cent.

It should be noted that a space no more than three census tracts wide (about half a mile) separates the three major concentrations. Within these three concentrations are all the census tracts 40 per cent or more Puerto Rican, ten of the eleven tracts that are 16 to 40 per cent Puerto Rican, and thirty-one of the ninety-nine tracts that are 3 to 15 per cent.

The three remaining concentrations are minor as compared with those already described, but they do constitute significant clusterings. One is in the southeast, one in the southwest, and one in the north. The first takes in most of the Lower East Side; it lies between Third Avenue and the East River and extends as far north as 29th Street. Although nowhere is there a heavy concentration of Puerto Ricans, they are well represented. The area contains one census tract with a relatively dense Puerto Rican population (16–40 per cent) and twenty-eight tracts with percentages ranging from 3 to 15.

A second minor concentration lies on the west side of Manhattan, inclosed by 14th Street, West 66th Street, the Avenue of the Americas, and the Hudson River. It also contains no census tracts heavily populated by Puerto Ricans, but it does well illustrate their concentration in one locality.

The third minor concentration consists of two neighboring areas in northern Manhattan, between West 158th Street and West 187th Street and two major city parks. Together they comprise only eight census tracts; the Puerto Rican percentage is 3 to 15.

Three additional small clusters, not connected with any of the major or minor areas, are located on Manhattan, but they are of little importance. Of the six islands politically attached to Manhattan, only three have any Puerto Rican population. Welfare Island has 3 to 15 per cent, Wards and Ellis Islands each 2 per cent or less. No Puerto Rican population is recorded for Randalls, Bedloe's, and Governors islands.

The Puerto Ricans on Manhattan live in practically all sections of the island. For the most part, however, as we have seen, they tend to group themselves in distinct areas, where their predominance is striking. Two reasons may be suggested for these concentrations: (1) low-cost housing, where Puerto Ricans can live with a neighbor or with some family that has preceded them to the United States, even though living conditions and housing are substandard; (2) location near express stops or terminals on major subway or bus lines. Since the great majority of Puerto Ricans are employed in the service trades—hotels, apartment houses, restaurants, night clubs, office buildings, or downtown factories—accessibility to cheap transportation is essential.

Whether or not these citizens of the United States become fully assimilated in the American way of life in a metropolitan area cannot be forecast at this time, though adjustment is taking place in certain areas. How quickly the distribution pattern will alter is not known. It may be assumed, however, that change will not be rapid, and that Puerto Ricans coming to New York in the near future will continue to crowd into the existing major centers of concentration.

# SOME CHARACTERISTICS OF THE POPULATION OF CITIES IN SIMILAR SERVICE CLASSIFICATIONS

Geographers and other students of cities on several occasions have classified the urban centers of the United States according to their major services or dominant function. The knowledge that Kannapolis, North Carolina, has manufacturing employment of unusual proportions, that Conneaut, Ohio, is high in transportation and communication service, or that Warrington, Florida, has an abnormally large proportion of its labor force working in public service has utility of itself. For example, the *Municipal Yearbook* for almost a dozen years has included an economic classification of cities as general urban reference material.

However, in the author's opinion, the major value of urban classification is not its usefulness as a reference tool. Rather it is in the utilization of a classification for further and more penetrating analyses of urban areas. For example, studies of the social and economic characteristics of the population of our cities are now susceptible to much needed refinement. Little has been attempted in the past in this direction. Analyses have been made of population change, age, educational attainment, labor force participation, and so on, of the urban population in general.[1] But slight progress has been made in investigating the possible variation of items of this sort among cities of different functions or service classifications. The aim of the first portion of this article is to investigate the possibility of such correlations.

Geographers, accustomed to thinking in terms of regional differentiation, may not be completely satisfied with the above analysis. For them a further question remains: How does *location* affect the social and economic characteristics of cities in similar service classifications? An attempt has been made in the second part of the article to find some tentative answers to this regional question.

## PROCEDURE

A classification worked out by the author and published as "A Service Classification of American Cities,"[2] forms the basis of this experiment. Space prohibits a general summary here and the reader is referred to the original article. It need only be said that from material in the 1950 Census of Population 897 urban areas of over 10,000 population were classified according to concentrations of employment into nine service groups (Table 1).

Concentrations were recognized if they were one or more standard deviations from an established national mean of employment in the various fields of service. Cities not high in any service were grouped together under a "diversified" class. A city could have recognized concentrations in more than one service.

The 1950 Census of Population has available (Vol. II, Table 35) for the same 897 urban centers, a number of items of information about the population and labor force. From the census the following seven

Reprinted from *Economic Geography*, XXXIII (April, 1957), 95–108, with permission of the author and the editor. (Copyright, 1957, by Clark University, Worcester, Mass.)

[1] For one recent example see Donald J. Bogue, "Urbanism in the United States, 1950," *American Journal of Sociology*, LX (1955), 471–86.

[2] Howard J. Nelson, "A Service Classification of American Cities," *Economic Geography*, XXXI (1955), 189–210 [see above, pp. 139–60].

categories, important in the better understanding of cities, were chosen for investigation:

1. Percentage increase in population, 1940–50
2. Proportion of the population 65 years old or over
3. Average number of school years completed, persons 25 years old or older
4. Participation in the labor force—per cent of total males, 14 years old or older, actually employed
5. Participation in the labor force—per cent of total females, 14 years old or older, actually employed
6. Per cent unemployed—census week (April, 1950)
7. Median income in 1949

TABLE 1

SERVICE GROUPS CLASSIFICATION BASED ON STANDARD DEVIATIONS

| | Plus 2SD | Plus 3SD |
|---|---|---|
| Manufacturing............. | Mf2 | Mf3 |
| Retail trade................ | R2 | R3 |
| Professional service......... | Pf2 | Pf3 |
| Transportation and communication.................. | T2 | T3 |
| Personal service............ | Ps2 | Ps3 |
| Public administration........ | Pb2 | Pb3 |
| Wholesale trade............. | W2 | W3 |
| Finance, insurance, and real estate................... | F2 | F3 |
| Mining.................... | Mi2 | Mi3 |

Statistics were compiled for each of the 897 cities under study in each of the above seven categories.[3] Two simple approaches were used in an attempt to interpret the statistics—means and extremes. First, averages were computed for each category in all of the SD3 and SD2 cities for each of the nine service classifications. Only SD3 and SD2 cities were used in the averaging, instead of all of the cities in each class, in

[3] It is difficult to secure comparable data on population change. Data on percentage change in population are non-existent for the 157 urban areas —divisions used where available in the service classification—as they are new census units, formed only in 1950. For these 157 places percentage change in population for standard metropolitan areas, a slightly larger census unit, was substituted.

an attempt to restrict consideration to urban areas where each service was heavily concentrated and thus would be most likely to affect the characteristics of the cities. The results of these computations appear as Table 2 in this article.

In the thought that extremes may also be revealing, the ten highest and the ten lowest cities (using the entire group of 897 cities) in each of the seven categories were noted and will be used, as appropriate, for illustrations. All cities that lost population and all cities that increased by 100 per cent or more in the 1940–50 decade were also recognized for illustrative purposes.

MANUFACTURING CITIES

The thirty cities classified Mf3 or Mf2, when compared to other classes of cities, have three of the highest and two of the lowest averages in the seven categories investigated, confirming the distinctiveness of the group (Table 2).

On the average, cities with an extreme concentration of manufacturing changed little in population during the 1940–50 decade, increasing an average of only 2.2 per cent, compared to the average of all cities of 27.9 per cent. In fact, not one of the manufacturing cities here considered gained as much as 20 per cent in population while eight of the group lost population. (But comparable data are available for only twenty of the thirty cities. Others include unincorporated areas such as Richland, Washington, Mf2, a creation of the decade, and cities newly incorporated since 1940, such as Weirton, West Virginia, Mf2.)

The proportion of the population over 14 years of age, both male and female, in the labor force in the Mf3 and Mf2 cities, is greater than that of the cities of any other class—almost 83 per cent of the men and about 36 per cent of the women are workers. The extreme is Richland, Washington (Mf2), which has a larger percentage of its men working than any other city in the country—91.4 per cent.

With average earnings of $3,134, Mf3

and Mf2 cities are strikingly ahead of cities in other classes. The next highest class, mining cities, runs a rather poor second with $2,822. Once again Richland, Washington (Mf2), heads the list with $4,629. In fact, five of the ten cities highest in average earnings are manufacturing cities.

In spite of their high earnings, the people of these thirty cities have the lowest average number of years of school com-

group in a similar calculation. This has been done in Table 3. Though the individual percentages are changed somewhat, all the above major generalizations are still possible, lending additional weight to their validity.

### RETAIL TRADE

Twenty-seven cities belong to either the R3 or R2 category. None of their averages is the highest or the lowest in the group,

TABLE 2

AVERAGES OF SELECTED CRITERIA FOR ALL CITIES AND FOR ALL SD3 AND SD2 CITIES*

| | All Cities | Mf3 and Mf2 | R3 and R2 | Pf3 and Pf2 | T3 and T2 | Mi3 and Mi2 | Pb3 and Pb2 | Ps3 and Ps2 | W3 and W2 | F3 and F2 |
|---|---|---|---|---|---|---|---|---|---|---|
| Percentage increase in population, 1940–50 | 27.9 | 2.2 | 39.4 | 65.0 | 17.5 | 31.1 | 40.0 | 61.0 | 30.4 | 35.6 |
| Per cent 65 years old or older | 8.6 | 7.6 | 9.0 | 7.6 | 9.7 | 7.4 | 7.3 | 9.2 | 7.7 | 10.0 |
| Average years of school completed | 10.0 | 8.9 | 10.5 | 12.3 | 10.4 | 9.7 | 10.8 | 11.0 | 9.9 | 11.1 |
| Participation in labor force, per cent of males | 77.8 | 82.8 | 77.1 | 55.8 | 78.0 | 79.2 | 77.8 | 73.2 | 80.0 | 75.6 |
| Participation in labor force, per cent of females | 32.8 | 35.9 | 30.3 | 34.1 | 29.2 | 27.1 | 33.0 | 33.3 | 33.0 | 34.6 |
| Per cent unemployed | 5.1 | 5.4 | 6.7 | 3.6 | 4.7 | 5.5 | 4.7 | 5.8 | 6.9 | 4.1 |
| Median income | $2,643 | $3,134 | $2,560 | $1,674 | $2,733 | $2,822 | $2,658 | $2,227 | $2,566 | $2,780 |
| Number of cities | 897 | 30 | 27 | 39 | 50 | 34 | 41 | 36 | 36 | 35 |

* Source: Compiled from Census of Population, 1950, Vol. II, Table 35.

pleted, 8.9—almost a year under the next lowest class—and a difference of nearly 3.5 years from the highest group, professional service cities. However, none of the manufacturing cities appears in the list of the ten lowest in educational achievement.

Manufacturing cities have generally a lower percentage of persons 65 and over than the average city and in April, 1950, had a slightly larger percentage of unemployed than the average city. The city with the lowest rate of unemployment in the country was Two Rivers, Wisconsin (Mf2), with 0.9 per cent unemployed.

Because of the large proportion of the labor force that must be employed in manufacturing (43.11 per cent), before a city receives even an Mf classification, it is valid to include all the 153 cities of the Mf

TABLE 3

AVERAGES OF SELECTED CRITERIA FOR MANUFACTURING CITIES*

| | All Cities | Mf3 and Mf2 | All Mfg. |
|---|---|---|---|
| Percentage increase in population, 1940–50 | 27.9 | 2.2 | 14.4 |
| Per cent 65 years old or older | 8.6 | 7.6 | 8.5 |
| Average years of school completed | 10.0 | 8.9 | 9.6 |
| Participation in labor force, per cent of males | 77.8 | 82.8 | 84.3 |
| Participation in labor force, per cent of females | 32.8 | 35.9 | 35.7 |
| Per cent unemployed | 5.1 | 5.4 | 5.1 |
| Median income | $2,643 | $3,134 | $3,139 |
| Number of cities | 897 | 30 | 183 |

* Source: Compiled from Census of Population, 1950, Vol. II, Table 35.

and the averages are usually not too far from the national mean. These retail cities grew an average of almost 40 per cent, one of the twenty-seven cities lost population; none gained as much as 100 per cent in the last decade.

Retail cities have slightly more than the national average of persons 65 years old or older, and the city with the largest proportion of elderly population in the United States, Lake Worth, Florida (R2F2Ps), with 21.5 per cent of the population 65 or over, belongs at least partially to this group.

In the proportion of either males or females in the labor force, retail cities are under the national average. This is also true of average earnings.

The percentage of unemployed is somewhat above the national average, 6.7 per cent as compared to 5.1 per cent. Four retail cities are among the ten cities with the highest proportion of unemployed in the nation: Madera, California (R2), with 15.9 per cent unemployed; Tulare, California (R3W), 15.3 per cent; Blytheville, Arkansas (R2Ps), 14.8 per cent; and Hanford, California (R3), 14.6 per cent.

## PROFESSIONAL SERVICE

In five out of the seven categories under discussion professional service cities register the highest and the lowest figures. They thus share with manufacturing cities the distinction of being the most "extreme." However, in the case of professional service cities considerable significance is lost in the comparison because of the difficulty of interpreting the census data. In 1950 for the first time college students were considered residents of the city in which they were attending classes. As a large number of professional service cities are the locations of colleges and universities with large enrolments, the new census procedure has a direct bearing on their reported populations. Also, as students are a specialized group, their presence imparts unique characteristics to the cities involved.

Professional service cities grew an average of 65 per cent in the last census decade—the largest proportion of any class of city. A good deal of this growth, however, may be attributed to the newly counted students. Nine out of the thirty-nine Pf3 and Pf2 cities show apparent increases of more than 100 per cent. None has registered a decline.

In average number of years of school completed, understandably, the Pf3 and Pf2 cities are the highest of the groups, averaging 12.3 years. In fact, all ten cities with the highest average schooling belong to the Pf3 and Pf2 class. State College, Pennsylvania (Pf3Ps), 14.8 years; West Lafayette, Indiana (Pf3Ps), 14.6 years; and Pullman, Washington (Pf3Ps), 14.2 years, lead the list.

The student component, too, reduces the proportion of males participating in the labor force to an unusual figure, 55.8 per cent, nearly 20 per cent lower than any other group average. The lowest nine cities in the United States in this category are professional service cities. Princeton, New Jersey (Pf3), with 39 per cent has the lowest figure and is the only city where a larger proportion of the females than the males are in the labor force.

The proportion of persons 65 and over is relatively low, but not at a record figure. Willow Run, Michigan (Pf2), however, with less than 1 per cent of its inhabitants over 65 has the lowest figure for any city in the country. (This unusual urbanized area in 1950 consisted essentially of a veterans' housing project in which a portion of its residents were students at the nearby University of Michigan.) On the other hand, Fulton, Missouri (Pf3), and Jacksonville, Illinois (Pf3), cities without large college enrolments, are in the highest ten, with 16.5 and 15.9 per cent over 65 respectively.

Professional cities have the lowest average unemployment of any of the service groups, and three cities are in the lowest group of ten.

Average earnings, also, are the lowest of any category, with an average of only

$1,674. All of the ten lowest cities belong to the professional service group, with State College, Pennsylvania (Pf3Ps), the city where professional service is the most concentrated, at the bottom, with $824. Presumably this is tied up with the many part-time and unskilled jobs available in a college community.

## TRANSPORTATION AND COMMUNICATION CITIES

Although the average percentages of the fifty cities receiving a T3 or a T2 classification are not the highest or lowest in any category, these transportation and communication cities are not without distinction.

Growth during the last census decade has been relatively small. Only manufacturing cities have grown less than the 17.5 per cent that is the average of this group. Eleven of the T3 and T2 cities actually lost population, while two increased more than 100 per cent. These are Pasco, Washington (T2) (the scene of the Northern Pacific's new classification yard and a transportation center of the Columbia River Basin), which increased 161.4 per cent; and Kingsville, Texas (T2), 117.1 per cent.

Transportation cities have a larger than average proportion of old people. The group is second only to mining in the proportion 65 and over, some 9.7 per cent as compared to a national average of 8.6 per cent. Two cities in the top ten in this respect are from the transportation and communication group: Moberly, Missouri (T3), 15.1 per cent, and Boone, Iowa (T3), 15.0 per cent.

The proportion of males in the labor force is slightly above the average city, and, as transportation is not a field offering many opportunities for female employment, the average proportion of women in the labor force is very low, 29.2 per cent, as compared to an average, 32.8 per cent; only mining is lower. Boone, Iowa (T3), is found among the lowest ten cities with only 22.2 per cent of its females in the labor force.

## MINING CITIES

Understandably, the handling of coal, oil, or ore does not offer much of an opportunity for women workers. Generally speaking, the thirty-four cities with a Mi3 or Mi2 classification have at least one common characteristic—the proportion of females in the labor force is low—only 27.1 per cent, the lowest of any of the service classes of cities. Five cities in the lowest ten are mining cities, with coal, oil and iron ore all represented.

Other characteristics, however, seem to be correlated to the mineral mined, particularly whether coal or oil is the product. When all the cities are averaged together, much of what is distinctive is canceled out. Averages were taken for the seventeen coal mining cities and the twelve oil producing centers separately. The effects of the changing use patterns of these two fuels during the last decade are clearly reflected in the results.

Eleven of the seventeen coal mining centers lost population, including all eight mining cities of the Mi3 and Mi2 group located in the anthracite region. In contrast, all twelve oil centers gained in the 1940–50 period. The average gain was 88 per cent. Four of the twelve cities more than doubled in size and two increased over 200 per cent: Snyder, Texas (Mi3), 214.8 per cent, and Odessa, Texas (Mi3), 208.1 per cent. The oil cities have only 4.8 per cent of their population 65 or over, an extremely low percentage, while the coal cities' average is 8.9, a fraction above the national mean.

The proportion of males in the labor force is below average, 74.9 per cent in the coal mining towns and very high, 84.4 per cent, in the oil centers.

On the average, it is much more profitable to work in oil centers than in coal mining towns. The seventeen oil centers have an average income of $3,216, higher than any entire class, while the coal cities average of $2,468 is below par. Unemployment also exhibits a contrast from one type of mining city to another. The coal mining cities have an average of 6.7 per cent unemployed, above an average figure; oil centers, 4.3 per cent, below the national mean.

## PUBLIC ADMINISTRATION

The forty-one public administration cities with Pb3 or Pb2 classifications can be divided into two general groups—sixteen capital cities, and twenty-five other cities, mainly urban centers near military establishments. Reflecting the increase in the complexity of government and the growth of the military establishment, both groups of cities have registered population increases in the past census decade. The capitals increased 27 per cent, but the 25 non-capital cities grew almost twice as fast with approximately a 50 per cent increase. Four public administration cities increased over 100 per cent, all belong to the non-capital group: Oxnard, California (Pb3W2), 153.2 per cent; Panama City, Florida (Pb), 122.3 per cent; Albuquerque, New Mexico (Pb2PsF), 109.9 per cent; and Key West, Florida (Pb3Ps), 104.5 per cent. (For two Pb3 cities, Warrington, Florida, and Brownsville-Brent-Goulding, no information was available in 1940, so no comparisons can be made.)

If all the Pb3 and Pb2 cities are taken together, they have the smallest proportion of persons 65 or over of any group of cities—7.3 per cent. However, the twenty-five non-capital cities, with an average figure of 6.9 per cent, are the outstanding segment in their lack of old people.

The sixteen capitals have a high average number of school years completed—11.2, second only to professional service cities. The other twenty-five Pb3 and Pb2 cities are above average but not significantly so.

The proportion of the males in the labor force is not distinctive in public administration cities. However, female file clerks and secretaries bring up the proportion of women in the labor force for the sixteen capital cities to 37.3 per cent, a higher percentage than for any other entire group, even higher than the average for manufac-

turing cities. The non-capitals, on the other hand, are slightly lower than the average city in this measure. Key West, Florida (Pb3Ps), with only 19.2 per cent of its female population in the labor force is the second lowest city in the country in this quality.

The sixteen capitals have a relatively high average income—$2,810, considerably above average, actually, second only to manufacturing cities. Non-capital cities, on the other hand, are lower than average. The capitals, too, exhibiting the stability of governmental employment, have relatively few people unemployed, being second only to professional service cities. Other public administration cities are slightly above average in this measure.

## PERSONAL SERVICE CITIES

Cities high in personal service tend to be those that attract a transient or semitransient population, and thus, in the Ps3 and Ps2 range, they consist mostly of resort and retirement towns. Personal service cities probably have had a greater actual increase in population than cities in any other category. Statistically they are second to professional service cities, but, as has been pointed out, data for the last-named class are misleading. The thirty-six cities classified Ps3 or Ps2 increased by an average of 61 per cent, or more than double the national average of 27.9 per cent. None lost population. The gain for Atlantic City (Ps3R) of only 6.7 per cent was low for the group. Five of the thirty-six cities have more than doubled their population in the last decade. Las Vegas, Nevada (Ps3), with a ten-year increase of 192.4 per cent, is high for the group.

The proportion 65 years old or over is higher than average. St. Petersburg, Florida (Ps2F2R), with 21.1 per cent 65 years old or older, and Santa Cruz, California (Ps2RF), 20.6 per cent, are the second and third "oldest" cities in the nation.

Again, if professional service cities are omitted because of comparison difficulties, the Ps3 and Ps2 cities have a lower average percentage of their men in the labor force than any other group, (73.2 per cent compared to 77.8 per cent national average), a not unexpected situation in resort and retirement towns. However, these cities provide employment for a larger than average proportion of the cities' women.

Unemployment is a bit higher than the average. Average earnings are low—it is only the professional service cities with their college student part-time workers that keep this group from recording the lowest figure by this measure.

## WHOLESALING CITIES

The thirty-six cities classified as W3 or W2 generally belong to the group of cities that assemble agricultural produce for shipment from the area. In these relatively small cities, growth has been about average, some 30.4 per cent.

Wholesale cities distinguish themselves in only one item—they have the highest average amount of unemployment of any group of cities, 6.9 per cent. (If the W3 cities are taken separately, it is even worse —9.6 per cent.) One wholesaling city, Brawley, California (W3), 14.6 per cent, is among the poorest ten cities in this respect. On the other hand, Dodge City, Kansas (W2R2T), is in the best ten cities by this measure, with only 1.4 per cent unemployed.

The average number of school years completed is not far from the national average, but four cities of these thirty-six are in the bottom ten, with San Benito, Texas (W3), the lowest in the country, having an average of only 5.0 years.

The proportion of people 65 and over is quite low, and the average wage is also. Both men and women are in the labor force in somewhat larger percentages than on the average.

## FINANCE, INSURANCE, AND REAL ESTATE

The thirty-five cities in the F3 and F2 group include mainly insurance centers and a few cities, particularly in Florida, where the real estate business is significant. But

in the list also are some very large cities with a wide variety of employment coming under this heading.

The rate of growth of these cities is not far from the average, and the proportion of men and women in the labor force shows little distinctiveness. However, this group of cities has the highest proportion of those 65 and over of any group, 10.0 per cent, and five finance, insurance, and real estate cities are in the list of the top ten.

This group is also distinct in that average number of school years completed is high, 11.1, and that the proportion of unemployed is low, the second lowest of all the groups. Decatur, Georgia (F3W), with 1.2 per cent out of work is the next to the lowest city in the nation in this quality.

## SOME GENERALIZATIONS

It is evident that variations in economic and social qualities of American cities are, in part at least, correlated with the function or service class to which a city belongs. From the seven categories investigated in the preceding sections, generalizations like the following can be made.

Variations in the rate of change in population in the 1940–50 decade were strongly affected by a city's major service. The population in personal service and professional service cities increased by more than double the average rate (though for professional service cities the increase may be more apparent than real). Generally public service cities, particularly those in the non-capital group, increased at faster than the usual rate, as did retailing cities. However, the average manufacturing city increased least of all, almost standing still, while transportation and communication cities increased at a rate significantly lower than the national mean.

The average proportion of persons 65 years old and over is relatively uniform in American cities of whatever service classification. However, financial cities and transportation centers have slightly more than the average number of persons 65 and over, whereas public service cities, especially those of the non-capital group, have the lowest average percentage. In addition, professional service cities, manufacturing cities, and even wholesaling cities have a smaller than average proportion.

The average number of school years completed varies by almost three and one-half years among cities of the various service classes. Professional service cities lead, with a high of 12.3 years, but financial and personal cities are also above average. Manufacturing cities are low, with the average a full year under the cities of any other service group—8.9 years.

The proportion of males in the labor force ranges from about 56 to 83 per cent, depending on the type of city under consideration. Professional service cities have an extremely low percentage, 55.8, compared to the average of 77.8 per cent. Other groups vary much less from the mean, though personal service cities are rather low—73.2 per cent, and manufacturing cities are the highest of all, with an average of 83 per cent of their men over 14 employed.

The average percentage of females in the labor force, 32.8, is less than half that of the males, and it also varies proportionally less from the mean. Mining cities are significantly low, 27.1, and transportation cities are also below normal. Manufacturing cities, on the other hand, are high, but only three percentage points above the average.

Unemployment, measured in the census week in April, 1950, was far from uniform in the cities of the various service classifications. Wholesaling cities, averaging 7 per cent, are high, but mining cities and retail cities are not far behind. Financial centers are low in this criterion, with an average of only 4.1 per cent unemployed.

One of the most important measures of city well-being, average income, exhibits variations second only in magnitude to change in population among the nine service classes. Manufacturing cities are way out in front, with an over-all average of $3,140, while professional service cities are

the lowest of the groups, averaging only $1,671. Personal service cities are also notably low, while the other six classes are considerably nearer the mean.

REGIONAL VARIATION

As has been seen, cities in one service class vary considerably from those of another class in numerous instances and in important ways. But still the geographic question remains unanswered: How does regional location affect the general social and economic characteristics of cities in similar service classifications? In an attempt to satisfy normal geographic curiosity a simple procedure was devised (after considerable experiment) to try to shed some light on the above question.

The same 897 urban areas of over 10,000 population (used throughout the study) were divided according to their location in one of the four major census regions: West, North Central, Northeast, and South. Averages were computed for the same seven categories as before for all the cities in each region. The results appear as column 1, Table 4. These regional averages were compared with the United States averages and the variations above or below the national mean indicated by (—) if below and (+) if above. A (0) indicates no variation.

Averages were also found for the SD3 and SD2 cities in each service classification (except for manufacturing, where all cities were used, as explained previously) in each of the four census regions. These averages appear in columns 2 to 9 in Table 4, with variations from the averages of the same service class of cities in the entire United States indicated by the symbols noted above. (Mining cities, because of the close correlation of characteristics to the type of mineral extracted, were not computed separately.)

The importance of regional location is evident from a casual inspection of Table 4. The general characteristics of a region tend to be impressed on all classes of cities within an area—without, however, obliterating variations attributable to the serv-

TABLE 4

### AVERAGES OF SELECTED CRITERIA FOR ALL CITIES, AND SD3 AND SD2 CITIES IN THE UNITED STATES AND BY CENSUS REGION*

| | All Cities | All Mfg. Cities | R3 and R2 Cities | Pf3 and Pf2 Cities | T3 and T2 Cities | Ps3 and Ps2 Cities | Pb3 and Pb2 Cities | W3 and W2 Cities | F3 and F2 Cities |
|---|---|---|---|---|---|---|---|---|---|
| | U.S.A. | | | | | | | | |
| Per cent increase in population | 27.9 | 14.4 | 39.4 | 65.0 | 17.5 | 61.0 | 40.0 | 30.4 | 35.6 |
| Per cent 65 years old or older | 8.6 | 8.5 | 9.0 | 7.6 | 9.7 | 9.2 | 7.3 | 7.7 | 10.0 |
| Years of school completed | 10.0 | 9.6 | 10.5 | 12.3 | 10.4 | 11.0 | 10.8 | 9.9 | 11.1 |
| Per cent males in labor force | 77.8 | 84.3 | 77.1 | 55.8 | 78.0 | 73.2 | 77.8 | 80.0 | 75.6 |
| Per cent females in labor force | 32.8 | 35.7 | 30.3 | 34.1 | 29.2 | 33.3 | 33.0 | 33.1 | 34.6 |
| Per cent unemployed | 5.1 | 5.1 | 6.7 | 3.6 | 4.7 | 5.8 | 4.7 | 6.9 | 4.1 |
| Average earnings | $2,643 | $3,139 | $2,560 | $1,674 | $2,733 | $2,227 | $2,658 | $2,566 | $2,780 |
| Number of cities | 897 | 183 | 27 | 39 | 50 | 36 | 41 | 36 | 35 |
| | West | | | | | | | | |
| Per cent increase in population | +50.8 | +43.9 | +57.4 | −48.8 | +56.3 | +65.9 | +60.3 | +37.7 | +60.8 |
| Per cent 65 years old or older | −8.5 | −6.0 | −7.8 | −7.5 | −6.7 | −8.8 | −6.8 | −6.6 | −9.4 |
| Years of school completed | +11.3 | +10.8 | +10.6 | +12.8 | +11.3 | +11.7 | +11.4 | +10.5 | +12.1 |
| Per cent males in labor force | −77.5 | +84.6 | −77.0 | +58.8 | +79.5 | −71.4 | −77.5 | +82.1 | +78.6 |
| Per cent females in labor force | −31.5 | −29.2 | +30.9 | −33.2 | −30.3 | −33.2 | −32.9 | +34.0 | −33.9 |
| Per cent unemployed | +7.3 | +5.9 | +10.0 | +4.8 | +6.8 | +7.7 | +6.0 | +10.2 | +5.7 |
| Average earnings | +$2,980 | +$3,579 | +$2,866 | +$1,888 | +$3,102 | +$2,422 | +$2,996 | +$2,977 | +$3,181 |
| Number of cities | 125 | 7 | 9 | 8 | 9 | 12 | 12 | 13 | 6 |
| | North Central | | | | | | | | |
| Per cent increase in population | −16.3 | +44.5 | −29.1 | +70.0 | −5.6 | −40.6 | −29.9 | −17.9 | −12.1 |
| Per cent 65 years old or older | +9.8 | +8.7 | 0 9.0 | +8.2 | +11.1 | +9.3 | +8.4 | +9.4 | +10.4 |
| Years of school completed | +10.3 | +10.0 | +11.0 | 0 12.3 | −10.1 | +11.9 | +10.9 | +10.7 | −10.7 |
| Per cent males in labor force | +78.0 | −83.3 | +79.2 | +57.2 | −77.5 | +76.4 | −72.4 | −78.3 | +77.6 |
| Per cent females in labor force | −31.5 | −31.5 | +30.9 | +34.2 | −28.3 | +35.3 | 0 33.0 | −32.0 | −34.3 |
| Per cent unemployed | −3.8 | −3.8 | −3.5 | −3.3 | −3.6 | −3.8 | −3.6 | −3.3 | −3.0 |
| Average earnings | +$2,790 | +$3,201 | +$2,654 | +$1,733 | +$2,746 | +$2,622 | −$2,503 | +$2,685 | +$2,864 |
| Number of cities | 288 | 63 | 9 | 19 | 24 | 3 | 6 | 12 | 13 |

*Source: Compiled from Census of Population, 1950, Vol. II, Table 35.

TABLE 4—*Continued*

| | All Cities | All Mfg. Cities | R3 and R2 Cities | Pf3 and Pf2 Cities | T3 and T2 Cities | Ps3 and Ps2 Cities | Pb3 and Pb2 Cities | W3 and W2 Cities | F3 and F2 Cities |
|---|---|---|---|---|---|---|---|---|---|
| | | | | | Northeast | | | | |
| Per cent increase in population | − 7.1 | − 5.4 | − 26.0 | + 73.7 | − 0.8 | − 12.1 | − 16.8 | − 4.7 | − 11.9 |
| Per cent 65 years old or older. | + 9.7 | + 9.2 | + 9.6 | − 7.4 | + 11.2 | + 11.2 | + 9.4 | + 11.0 | − 9.4 |
| Years of school completed... | − 9.7 | 9.0 | − 10.2 | 12.2 | 10.3 | 9.8 | 10.4 | 9.4 | 10.2 |
| Per cent males in labor force. | − 77.6 | − 80.1 | + 77.5 | − 47.5 | − 76.3 | + 77.0 | + 78.8 | − 77.7 | + 80.1 |
| Per cent females in labor force | + 33.6 | + 35.9 | − 31.8 | + 35.3 | − 28.5 | − 33.2 | 0 33.0 | − 26.5 | + 36.3 |
| Per cent unemployed....... | + 5.9 | + 5.8 | − 5.6 | + 4.5 | + 5.7 | + 7.1 | − 4.1 | + 9.7 | + 5.9 |
| Average earnings.......... | + $2,795 | − $2,943 | + $2,979 | − $1,646 | − $2,571 | + $2,258 | + $2,712 | + $2,711 | + $3,044 |
| Number of cities....... | 185 | 88 | 2 | 4 | 5 | 3 | 8 | 1 | 3 |
| | | | | | South | | | | |
| Per cent increase in population | + 41.9 | + 14.8 | + 39.7 | + 94.6 | + 19.7 | + 69.2 | + 43.5 | + 39.1 | + 52.6 |
| Per cent 65 years old or older. | − 6.9 | − 4.8 | + 10.4 | − 6.1 | − 8.3 | − 9.1 | − 6.2 | − 6.0 | 0 10.0 |
| Years of school completed... | − 9.6 | − 8.7 | − 10.1 | 12.2 | 9.5 | 10.7 | − 10.4 | 8.2 | 0 11.1 |
| Per cent males in labor force. | + 78.4 | − 83.4 | − 74.5 | − 53.6 | + 78.1 | + 73.3 | + 79.7 | − 79.5 | − 74.2 |
| Per cent females in labor force | + 34.5 | + 41.5 | − 31.3 | + 34.2 | + 30.2 | + 33.6 | 0 33.0 | + 34.1 | + 34.7 |
| Per cent unemployed....... | 0 5.1 | − 4.4 | − 6.0 | − 2.6 | + 4.8 | − 4.6 | − 4.6 | − 6.8 | − 4.0 |
| Average earnings.......... | − $2,260 | − $2,811 | − $1,984 | − $1,318 | − $2,418 | − $2,026 | − $2,421 | − $1,886 | − $2,449 |
| Number of cities....... | 299 | 25 | 7 | 8 | 12 | 18 | 15 | 10 | 13 |

ice class. An analysis of the four regions follows.

*West.*—The West's general regional characteristics are strongly impressed on all classes of cities within the area, although variations attributable to service do remain. For five out of the seven categories, however, population change, proportion 65 and over, number of school years completed, proportion unemployed, and average earnings, the West's characteristics—above or below the national average—are reflected in the cities of each service group within the region, almost without exception.

For example, the West's cities in general have experienced rapid growth. In all but one of the eight service classifications, the average growth of the cities in the West has been faster than the national mean for cities in the respective classification. The exception is professional service cities. The eight western representatives increased by half again over the 1940 population, but failed to reach the national rate of 65 per cent. The region's influence is well illustrated by manufacturing cities, which grew very little on a nationwide average but increased by about 44 per cent in the West. But variations among cities of different services remain—wholesale cities, for example, increased 37.7 per cent in the area while personal service cities led the regional growth with 65.9 per cent.

Not one single exception to the regional trend occurred in four categories. The region is slightly below average in the proportion of its population 65 and over, and every class of city in the West is also below the national average for its classification. The area is above average in the proportion of persons unemployed, and every group of western cities with similar services is also above the respective national average. Wholesale cities, generally, have the highest unemployment, and as would be expected from the regional trend, the twelve wholesale cities in the West have an average of 10.2 per cent unemployed, a record high. Again, the area is above the national mean in average earnings and every class of city has above-average earnings. Manufacturing cities, which have the biggest earnings of any service classification, reach, as might be expected, their peak in the West, with a seven-city average of $3,579. In the average number of years of school completed, the West is above the mean, a full year higher than any other region, and every class of city is above the national average for their respective groups.

The proportion of the West's men and women that are in the labor force is slightly under the national average. Here the cities in the various service classes follow the regional trend in five cases out of eight, in the case of the females, but vary from it in five instances in the male averages. All told, however, the West is an excellent example of strong regional character and its influence on cities of all service classifications.

*North central.*—The cities of the north central section of the United States are not characterized by quite as strong regional qualities in the seven categories under discussion as the cities of the West. Nevertheless, the increase in population of the north central cities was less than the national average, the proportion 65 years old or more was greater than the United States mean, the percentage of unemployed was less than the country's average, and the average income was above the national mean. These regional qualities were readily apparent in the cities of almost every service class.

North central cities, on the average, increased only 16.3 per cent in the 1940–50 decade, compared to a national average of 27.9 per cent, and all classes of cities in the region gained less than their respective national averages with two exceptions: professional service cities and manufacturing cities. The increase in population of the manufacturing cities in the area is really exceptional, 44.5 per cent, the highest of that class in any region, including the West and South where generally large population gains were registered.

The area has a higher than average percentage of persons 65 years old or older and this is reflected in higher than average percentages (or in one instance, the same percentage) for all of the eight classes of cities, without exception.

Unemployment is lower in the north central section than the average for the country. Again, in every class of city in this area, unemployment is lower than the national average, and it never rises above 3.8 per cent.

Similarly, earnings in the region are above average, and in seven out of eight classes of cities in the area average earnings are higher than the national mean of the group.

In the three remaining categories the regional reflection is not quite so uniform, but it is still significant. The north central area is above average in years of school completed, in five of the service classes of cities in the region the average is above the national mean, and in one class it is the same figure. The region is slightly above average in males and below average in females in the labor force. Cities of the various service classes follow the regional lead in about 50 per cent of the cases.

*Northeast.*—In the Northeast, as in the north central area, cities in similar service classes tend to be strongly influenced by regional trends but do not conform to them with quite the unanimity of those in the West. Nevertheless, in five of the seven categories under observation, only one or two service classes fail to follow the regional trend.

The growth of northeastern cities in general was considerably below the United States average, and for all classes of cities save one the average growth was far below the national average for each group. The Pf3 and Pf2 cities in the area (there are only four of them) gained an apparent 73.7 per cent, somewhat more than the national average for that group and almost three times the next highest figure.

Then, too, the cities of the area have an average below the national mean in number of school years completed. Though the various service classes vary from a low of 9.0 to a high of 12.2 years, in every instance the figure is below the average for the respective service class of city.

The cities of the Northeast are characterized by above-average figures for the proportion 65 and over, the percentages of their women in the labor force, and the number unemployed. Generally, cities in all service classes agree with the regional trend, but with two exceptions in each category. Average earnings are also slightly above average in the region, but this tendency has three exceptions among the service classes. Significantly, manufacturing cities, of which there are eighty-eight in this area, are below the national average in earnings for this class of city.

*South.*—In the South, as in the West, the region's characteristics are strongly reflected in all classes of cities within the area, though, as before, variations attributable to service class are still present. For six of the seven categories investigated, however,

the South's characteristics, above or below the national average, are carried over in the cities of each service group, almost without exception.

The South's urban growth in the 1940–50 decade was well above the national average, and this population increase was reflected in cities of every class. There were the usual variations, from a low of 14.8 per cent in manufacturing cities to an apparent high of a 94.6 per cent average increase in the professional service cities.

The average number of school years completed varies within the South by a full four years, from 8.2 years in the area's wholesaling cities (a national record low) to 12.2 years in the professional service cities of the South. Even so, the South is characterized by a lower than average number of school years completed; and no service class, in spite of the large variations illustrated above, has a regional figure higher than the national average for its class.

Average earnings in the South are generally low, and for all the eight classes of cities investigated average income in the South is lower than for the national average of the class. Professional service cities nationally have the lowest average income, and, as one would expect, the $1,318 average of the eight professional service cities in the South is the lowest average for any regional group in the country.

The South generally has a larger proportion of women in the labor force than the United States average, and all the classes of cities in the area also have a figure the same as or greater than the national average. The South's 41.5 per cent of women employed in manufacturing cities is high for the country.

The generally small proportion of people in the cities of the South that are 65 or over is apparent in that, for all classes of cities except retail trade, the South has the same as or a smaller percentage than the national average. Similarly, the proportion unemployed in the South is low, and for all classes of cities except transportation cities the figures are below the national averages.

## NEGROES

Because of the historic concentration of the American Negro in the South, consideration of this important ethnic feature of our cities was reserved for discussion here. However, the proportion of Negroes (the census term is non-whites, but for our purposes it can be considered as Negroes) were tabulated for the 897 cities previously used, and divided according to the average for census regions and service class of city. The results appear as Table 5.

The South is habitually recognized as the traditional home of the Negro, and in spite of recent migrations the South's average

The three personal service cities of the Northeast have an average of 17 per cent Negroes, a figure comparable to many classes of cities in the South. These three cities are Atlantic City, New Jersey (Ps3R); Asbury Park, New Jersey (Ps3RPb); and Saratoga Springs, New York (Ps2). Then, too, public service cities in both the Northeast and the north central region have two or three times the regional average of Negroes. Finally, perhaps contrary to general opinion, in no section of the country do manufacturing cities have anywhere near the largest proportions of Negroes, compared to other classes of cities, in their respective regions.

TABLE 5

PER CENT NON-WHITE IN ALL CITIES, ALL MANUFACTURING CITIES, AND
ALL SD3 AND SD2 CITIES*

|  | All Cities | All Mfg. Cities | R3 and R2 Cities | Pf3 and Pf2 Cities | T3 and T2 Cities | Ps3 and Ps2 Cities | Pb3 and Pb2 Cities | W3 and W2 Cities | F3 and F2 Cities |
|---|---|---|---|---|---|---|---|---|---|
| West............ | 2.8 | 1.5 | 5.1 | 0.6 | 3.2 | 4.1 | 2.8 | 3.7 | 3.1 |
| North central .... | 3.4 | 3.4 | 1.8 | 4.5 | 2.6 | 1.5 | 9.7 | 1.6 | 2.4 |
| Northeast........ | 3.0 | 1.8 | 3.0 | 5.2 | 0.9 | 17.0 | 6.2 | 0.1 | 5.0 |
| South........... | 21.5 | 15.5 | 17.3 | 16.0 | 17.6 | 21.2 | 21.6 | 21.3 | 18.7 |

* Source: Compiled from Census of Population, 1950, Vol. II, Table 35.

proportion of Negroes, 21.5 per cent, is far larger than the average proportion of cities in other regions. (There are only seven urban communities of over 10,000 persons in the nation with over 50 per cent of their population Negro, and they are all in the South.) In every service class, the southern city has retained leadership. However, variations occur from southern cities of one class to another. Personal service, public administration, and wholesale cities lead in the proportion of Negroes with about one-fifth of their population Negro, while the other classes average slightly less, from 15 to 18 per cent. It is worthy of special notice that manufacturing cities in the South, on the average, have the fewest Negroes.

Outside the South, Negroes in larger than the usual proportions of their respective regions are found in several classes of cities.

## SUMMARY

The foregoing discussion indicates the influence of both service class and regional location on the characteristics of a city, at least as far as the categories we have discussed are concerned. Generally, the characteristics of a region tend to be impressed on all classes of cities within an area, without, however, obliterating the large variations attributable to the service class. This is particularly true in six of the categories: percentage change in the population, per cent 65 years old or older, years of school completed, average income, percentage unemployed, and proportion of Negro population. Participation in the labor force, by both males and females, on the other hand, seems the least strongly affected by regional location.

F. STUART CHAPIN, JR., and PEARSON H. STEWART

# POPULATION DENSITIES AROUND THE CLOCK

Few planning agencies have the resources to carry out elaborate census surveys, much less conduct experimental trial runs into untried research areas. They look to private research groups, federal agencies, and universities for the kind of experimentation needed in opening the way for applied research.

There are two relatively new areas in population research which have been of growing interest to planning agencies in recent years. One concerns the daytime-nighttime variations in total population distribution throughout an entire urban area, and another relates to patterns of home–work relationships of the working population of a city.

The University of North Carolina's Institute for Research in Social Science, under a research contract with a defense agency, recently had an opportunity to do some exploratory work in both of these general areas. Although this work has scarcely scratched the surface, some aspects of it are here presented in the hope of assisting city planners to outline more clearly their interests and needs in these research areas.

Both investigations were made possible by the availability of data assembled by state highway commissions in co-operation with the U.S. Bureau of Public Roads. The information came from a series of Metropolitan Area Traffic Studies which have been conducted in one hundred or more cities throughout the country during the past ten years. The pilot city chosen by the University was Flint, Michigan. Home interviews of approximately 5 per cent of the population were conducted in the built-up area of Flint by the Michigan State Highway Department. To provide coverage

Reprinted from *The American City* (October, 1953), with permission of the author and the editor. (American City Magazine Corporation, New York.)

of those areas outside the central city, roadside interviews at major entrance points to the central area were made. These interviews, however, were less complete than the home interviews.

Although these surveys were primarily set up to obtain information to be used for traffic analyses, they included sufficient information on basic population characteristics, along with automobile and transit trips made by each member of a household, so that we were able to use the information effectively in determining the daytime-nighttime population distribution.

In Flint, as was expected, we found that as the number of people increased in the manufacturing and central business areas during working hours, the population in the residential areas decreased. By further analyzing the traffic-study data, we were able to measure the changes in the density, both in amount and time.

The hour of least variation in Flint was 4:00 A.M. The greatest shifts in population density occur in the work areas of Flint. For example, the density of the central business district varies from about nine persons per acre at 6:00 A.M. to about fifty-five persons per acre at 3 P.M.

There is less variation in density in residential areas than in the work areas. Variations in the rural areas are slight; variations in residential areas immediately around the central business district are small because of the spilling-over of commercial and small industrial uses into the adjoining residential areas; and variations in density in suburban residential areas are the largest of any of the residential areas of Flint.

During the daytime hours about 25 per cent to 30 per cent of the people in the Flint urban area are concentrated in the small work areas. At night about 97 per cent of the people present in the Flint area

LEGEND (PERSONS / MILLION SQUARE FEET)

| | |
|---|---|
| 0-99 | 200-299 |
| 100-199 | 300-399 |

| | |
|---|---|
| 400-499 | 600-699 |
| 500-599 | 700-799 |

| | |
|---|---|
| 800-899 | 1000-1249 |
| 900-999 | 1250-1499 |

4 AM

3 PM

6 PM

Fig. 1

are widely dispersed in the residential areas.

The data gathered in the traffic study and the home interviews provided information on where people live in relation to their place of employment. The General Motors plants in Flint comprise almost the entire economic base of the city. It was not surprising, then, to find that the residential pattern of the workers of the five major plants was the same as the residential pattern for the city as a whole. Variations in the distribution patterns of the residences of workers were apparent from plant to plant, however.

The residences of workers in the Buick plant, the oldest of the five plants, are most concentrated around the plant. On the other hand, the residences of the workers of the newest plant, the Chevrolet Assembly–Fisher Body No. 2 plant, are more widely dispersed than those of the workers of any other plant.

The importance of the studies of the relationship of worker residences to places of employment has been emphasized many times. Viewed either way—from the point of view of locating housing developments in relation to centers of employment or from the point of view of properly locating industrial plants in relation to existing housing for workers—this kind of research is sorely needed to provide guiding site-selection principles to planning agencies.

The University of North Carolina study is designed to be applied to a large number of industrial plants and industrial areas. Such factors as the following are among those to be examined:

1. Population size of urban area in which plant is located
2. Location of manufacturing areas within the urban area
3. Location and adequacy of thoroughfare and transit facilities in the urban areas
4. The length of time the plant has been in operation
5. The pattern of densities of residential development within the urban area
6. Wage-index classification of plant
7. Size of plant in terms of employment
8. Extent, adequacy, and location of housing with rental and sale ranges within reach of plant workers
9. Extent, adequacy, and location of community facilities in relation to housing areas available to workers
10. Location of other employment centers within urban area and region.

A systematic coverage of an appropriate sample of cases should throw considerable light on which of these and other factors appear to be consistently associated with particular types of settlement patterns.

This daytime-nighttime investigation was aimed at devising a way to obtain a picture of the ebb and flow of the total population of a city (normally recorded in the census only by place of residence) as it redistributes itself throughout the urban area at different hours of the day or night. The implications of such information to the research undertaken by planning agencies are many. First and foremost, of course, is its use in traffic and transportation analysis. What is added here that is not usually available in the digests of the Metropolitan Area Traffic Studies is the opportunity for analyzing traffic, parking, and transit facilities in relation to shifting population densities in different areas of a city for certain critical periods of the day when large numbers of people are congregated in a relatively small area.

Another important use of these data relates to the possibilities of developing not only much more realistic density standards in residential areas, but also of experimenting with the use of density standards in business, industrial, and other areas of high population concentration, possibly extending the present principle of density control in zoning ordinances to include "congestion limits" permitted in business, industrial, and recreation areas. Still another valuable use of the information relates to local programs for industrial dispersion and defense and disaster planning. It is this kind of research that planning agencies vitally need in determining land use planning principles, optimum densities, and zoning controls, and in developing comprehensive city plans.

## CITIES AS CENTRAL PLACES

Previous selections in this book have demonstrated that among the most important urban functions are those which cities, towns, villages, and hamlets perform for the areas most immediately contiguous: the "continuous hinterland" or "umland." The number and complexity of these functions vary with the size of the city and with other variables, including the nature of the areas which are served. Within a large region, however, some of the functions occur almost universally in urban settlements of a given size. These are known as "central-place" functions, and the settlements within which they occur are called "central places." Central places are distinguished from urban settlements whose chief functions are related to the occurrence of particular natural resources or to location along transportation routes connecting major sources of raw materials with markets.

Having determined the nature of the central-place functions, to understand urban settlements we must next determine the areas for which a given urban place serves as the center for each of the respective functions. The first article in this group, by Howard L. Green, an economic geographer, discusses the delimitation of the boundary between the respective hinterlands of two of the largest urban places: New York and Boston. Some of the specific criteria are applicable to many smaller urban central places, and the methods and techniques which are described may be used, with some modifications, in delimiting and bounding the hinterlands of urban places of any size or complexity. It is clear, from the empirical evidence accumulating from studies such as this, that there is an order or system to the arrangement and location of central places and that relationships exist between the size and diversity of functions of a center, on the one hand, and the extent of the hinterland, on the other hand. It is also clear that the locations of central places are related to their size, character, and complexity.

The second article in this group, by Edward Ullman, is a noteworthy expression of one theory that attempts to fit empirical facts relating central places and their hinterlands or service areas into a meaningful pattern that will explain the location of central places. The article is based largely upon the work of Walter Christaller, a German geographer whose studies of central places in south Germany have become classics in the literature of urban geography.

Among the major concepts of the organization and structure of urban functions and locations is that of the hierarchy of central places—a concept which has in recent years attracted the interest of a number of geographers who have conducted empirical studies in specific areas designed to test the theory. The two last articles in this group describe the methods and findings of three such studies, all involving determinations of the functions and service areas of relatively small central places in southwestern Wisconsin, southern England, and in the northwestern part of the state of Washington, respectively. Other studies, not reproduced in this book, confirm the existence of a hierarchy of central places ranging from the smallest hamlet to the largest metropolis and including a hierarchy of functional concentrations, such as shopping centers, within the larger and more complex cities. Among the relationships which have been investigated are those of the range of goods and services provided by centers of each given order within a hierarchy, the threshold or minimum population or income required to support a given type of establishment, and the relationships of establishments of various types to the sizes of central places within which they occur. Some studies are primarily concerned, as are those here reproduced except the first, with the hierarchy of small urban settlements in relation to rural areas which they serve; others, at the opposite end of the scale, are concerned with the role and hinterlands of large metropolises which have regional, continental, or world-wide significance. Studies of cities as central places and the development of empirical hypotheses relating size, functions, and location of urban settlements constitute a large and important portion of the recent and current work of the urban geographer.

HOWARD L. GREEN

# HINTERLAND BOUNDARIES OF NEW YORK CITY AND BOSTON IN SOUTHERN NEW ENGLAND

The concept of the metropolitan community upon which this study is based holds that a large city tends to organize the region surrounding it, that such cities enter into a relationship with their hinterlands.[1] The city is the focal point of regional activity, with the hinterland carrying on functions necessary to the metropolitan community as a whole. The purpose of this paper is to define and analyze the hinterland boundaries in southern New England between two such large cities, New York and Boston.

## THE NEW ENGLAND REGION

The traditional concept of New England as a homogeneous metropolitan region focusing upon Boston has been increasingly questioned during the last quarter-century. As early as 1930, Kent Hubbard, president of the Connecticut Manufacturers' Association, suggested that Connecticut should leave New England because that state was farther advanced than the rest of New

Reprinted from *Economic Geography*, XXXI (October, 1955), 283–300, by permission of the author and the editor. (Copyright, 1955, by Clark University, Worcester, Mass.)

[1] McKenzie defined the territorial differentiation of functions in the metropolitan community as follows: "Communications, finance, management and the more specialized commercial and professional services, are becoming more highly concentrated in or near the center of the dominant city; while other activities, such as manufacturing, the less specialized forms of merchandising, and institutions catering to leisure time activities, are becoming more generally dispersed throughout the region, in accordance with local conditions of topography, transportation and population pattern" (R. D. McKenzie, *The Metropolitan Community* [New York, 1933], pp. 70–71). See also, N. S. B. Gras, *Introduction to Economic History* (New York, 1922), pp. 187–269.

England.[2] A few months later, Frederick G. Fasset wrote, "If there was a New England as revealed by a common outlook, it has ceased to exist."[3]

In 1950, John H. Fenton stated that New England "appears actually to have been subdividing for the last twenty years" into three parts—Maine, New Hampshire, and Vermont forming one area; Massachusetts and Rhode Island another. Connecticut, however, "because of its geographical position relative to the metropolitan New York area, might be considered a third subdivision, possibly even embodying the best of the old New England tradition."[4] Fenton's informants based their opinions on "intangibles" and were "unsupported by statistics." Thus, despite widespread obituaries on the demise of New England, there has been little quantitative corroboration.

## PREVIOUS DELIMITATIONS

Three earlier studies of metropolitan regions are examined here as aids to defining the hinterland boundary between New York City and Boston (Fig. 1).

*Park and Newcomb.*—In "Newspaper Circulation and Metropolitan Regions," Park and Newcomb claim that the distribution of newspapers is related to the distribution of economic and social features; therefore, a map of newspaper regions measures social and economic regions.[5] To illustrate, they note a correlation between

[2] *Boston Evening Transcript*, November 12, 1930, p. 8.

[3] *Boston Evening Transcript*, January 26, 1931, p. 15.

[4] *New York Times*, July 23, 1950, p. 40.

[5] R. E. Park and C. Newcomb, chap. 8, pp. 98–110, in McKenzie, *op. cit.*

newspaper circulation and wholesale trade, and a further correlation between Chicago newspaper distribution and the sale of train passenger tickets to and from Chicago.

Park and Newcomb selected forty-one cities as metropolitan centers (Federal Reserve cities and six others), picked the dominant morning newspaper as representative

their areas of domination appears to run on a line from Williamstown, in northwestern Massachusetts, to Westfield, near the Massachusetts-Connecticut state line. From there the boundary proceeds to a point south of Providence. Then the boundary curves seaward to the vicinity of Newport.

Questions arise: How representative is a

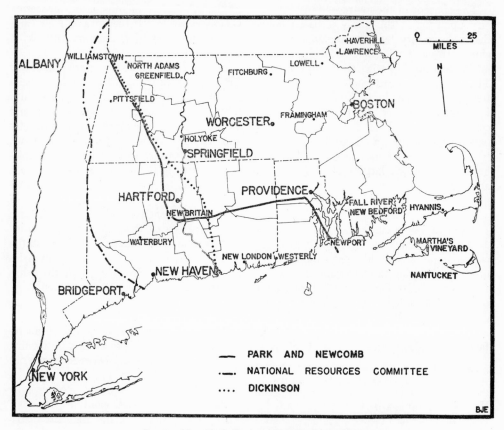

Fig. 1.—New York–Boston hinterland boundary

of the community, and mapped the newspaper's distribution. The boundary line lay at a point where one metropolitan paper replaced another as the dominant one. Audit Bureau of Circulations figures were utilized to give a common source of information.

For southern New England, the *Boston Globe* and the *New York Times* were chosen for study. The boundary between

single criterion—newspaper circulation—as a measure of the extent of a metropolitan region? Shall we assume that one function is so constituted that it can speak for the others? The author of this article believes that metropolitan newspaper circulation tells us about metropolitan newspaper circulation. It may be a clue, but only a clue, to other functions.

*National Resources Committee.*—A sec-

ond source of metropolitan regional delimitation is a study published in *Regional
Factors in National Planning and Development.*[6] This report contains a map showing
"Possible Planning Regions Based upon
Metropolitan Influence." The boundary
between the respective hinterlands of New
York City and Boston runs along the edge
of Fairfield County in southwestern Connecticut, coincides with the western Connecticut and Massachusetts borders, and
includes a small part of eastern New York
State opposite Williamstown as part of the
Boston region.

The map, according to the report, is
based upon studies of ninety-six metropolitan areas (1930 Census definition) and
forty-three areas of newspaper circulation
from metropolitan cities. However, it is
difficult to see the relation between these
criteria and the resulting regions. A study
of the location of those metropolitan areas
that lie in southern New England does not
give the facts upon which to draw such
boundaries, nor does the Park and Newcomb study of newspaper circulation yield
results congruent with the map presented.
The more important considerations, it appears, were the limits of the Federal Reserve districts and state boundaries.

*Dickinson.*—Dickinson defined hinterland boundaries by analyzing and mapping
various kinds of service areas.[7] The resulting boundary in New England places eastern Connecticut—Tolland, Windham, and
New London counties—in Boston's zone of
influence, and continues toward the northwest, running between Hartford and Springfield and on across Berkshire County to
the corner of Massachusetts.

That these three studies do not agree on
the location of the boundary zone between
New York City and Boston is obvious. In
Massachusetts, the boundary may fall either east or west of Berkshire County; in

[6] (Washington: National Resources Committee,
1935), pp. 158–59.

[7] R. E. Dickinson, "The Metropolitan Regions of
the United States," *Geographical Review,* XXIV
(1934), 278–91.

Connecticut, boundary variations cover
most of the state. One study includes part
of Rhode Island in the New York area; the
others do not. There is need, therefore, to
define a usable boundary girdle.

## The Approach

In this paper, the boundary between the
New York City and the Boston metropolitan hinterlands is determined from a study
of the respective metropolitan functions of
the two cities. Ideally, the most important
metropolitan functions should be chosen as
measures. In practice, however, this is impossible because of lack of data. Nevertheless, a variety of functional indicators can
be measured that will provide a sample
wide enough to establish the extent and
importance of the two hinterlands. Measures of each of the following functions will
be presented: transportation (truck, railroad, ship); communications (newspaper
circulation, telephone calls); agriculture;
recreation; manufacturing; and finance.

## Transportation

The revolution in transportation during
the past century has altered both the size
and shape of metropolitan regions. Formerly, ships from numerous coastal cities
distributed products from small, circumscribed hinterlands to other coastal centers
and to foreign ports. Then railroads, focusing upon any given center, spread the axial
range of its metropolitan influence. Finally,
motor transport, free from the confines of
either a waterfront location or rails, diffused metropolitan influence into every
hamlet.

To define the boundary of transportation
flow, available data for three prime movers
of persons and goods—railroads, ships, and
motor trucks—are examined here.

*Rail freight.*—Because trucking is cheaper than rail transport for short-haul freight,
little rail tonnage is carried between either
New York City or Boston and intermediate
points. Of almost two million tons of freight
analyzed by the New Haven Railroad in
one sample period, only 2.5 per cent of the

total was conveyed between New York City
and southern New England points and
about the same percentage between Boston
and towns in this same three-state region.
Since more than half of this small percentage of traffic is between New York and
Boston themselves, rail freight movements
between hinterland cities and either metropolis are of little importance.[8]

Two factors limit the utility of the information. First, rail routes cover only specific points along the tracks. Isopleths of
passenger traffic, therefore, are interpola-
tions connecting known stations and passing through many points set at some distance from the tracks. A second limiting
characteristic is the lack of direct connection at every station with both New York

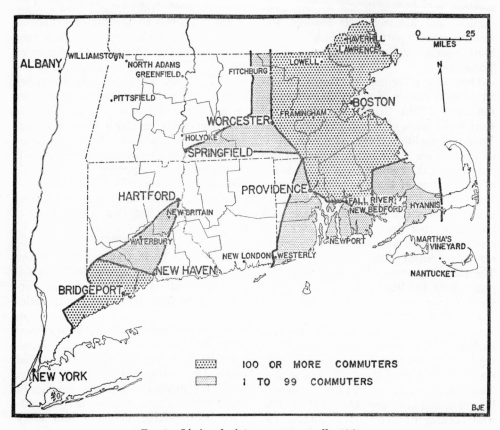

FIG. 2.—Limits of winter commuter traffic, 1951

*Rail passengers.*—Passenger traffic, however, is more important. Data on point-to-
point ticket sales have been compiled by
the railroads of the region, although not all
this information is gathered for the same
period. In those places where information
is recorded by different years, however,
there appear to be few discrepancies.

[8] Conversation with Mr. John Ramsey, Research
Department, New Haven Railroad.

and Boston. Stockbridge, Massachusetts,
for example, enjoys direct connections with
New York City via the New Haven Railroad; in order to reach Boston, it is necessary to change at Pittsfield to a Boston
and Albany train. Despite these limitations,
the data offer a realistic picture of rail passenger traffic flow.

Both metropolises have well-developed
zones beyond their built-up areas from

which people commute daily. Major commuter zones are, of course, areas with which a metropolis has a tightly knit community of interest. Places with 100 or more daily commuters lie largely within one-and-a-half hours' travel time from each city (Fig. 2). From New York City, places with 100 or more commuters reach as far north as Danbury and New Haven, including the the Connecticut Valley to Hartford, a trip of over 100 miles each way; the extremes to Boston are almost as great. On the three rail lines leading into Boston from southern New England, the following are absolute points: Gardner, Massachusetts, on the Boston and Maine route (65 miles); Springfield, Massachusetts, on the Boston and Albany line (98 miles); and Westerly,

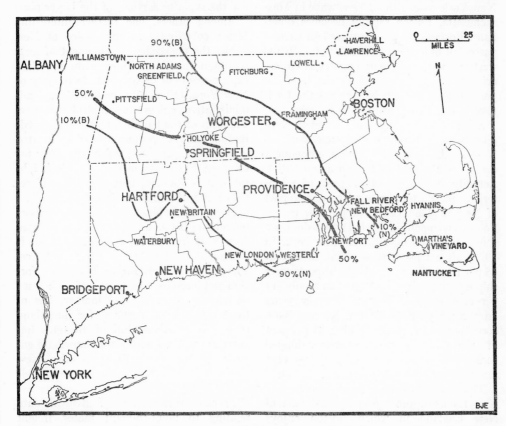

FIG. 3.—Percentage of railroad coach passenger flow between New York, Boston, and hinterland points

entire Connecticut panhandle. For commuters to Boston, the zone extends in an arc with a 40-mile radius including Fitchburg, Worcester, Providence, Fall River, New Bedford, and Plymouth. During the summer the belt is extended south of Plymouth to nearer portions of Cape Cod.

Beyond these limits are extremes set by a few hardy commuters: the extreme distance to New York extends northward in Rhode Island, on the New Haven road (88 miles). Because time-distance accessibility is a prime consideration, it is not surprising that commuter traffic actually crosses the hinterland boundaries as determined by other measures.

For rail coach passengers, the boundary nearly bisects southern New England (Fig. 3). However, along the coastal route of the New Haven Railroad, the New York 90 per cent isopleth (of the total movement to New York and Boston combined) extends to New London, half the total distance to Boston, whereas the 50 per cent isopleth reaches almost to Providence. Along the inland route, via the Connecticut Valley, the 90 per cent isopleth for New York extends to Hartford, again half the total distance to Boston. Springfield lies within the New York zone, although eastward in Massachusetts, Boston rapidly becomes dominant. Boston's 90 per cent isopleth encompasses all of eastern Massachusetts. In the western interior the hilly country is largely oriented to New York with the breaking point near Pittsfield. Northward the territory is linked primarily with Boston.

*Shipping.*—The dominant trend in shipping is an increased use of New York by New England shippers and a consequent decline of the port of Boston as an outlet. Actually, it is incorrect to speak of a hinterland for Boston, because there is no part of New England (with the possible exception of metropolitan Boston) that does not ship most of its exports via New York. In 1928, an extensive survey indicated that 65 per cent of New England's exports were shipped through New York and only 14 per cent through Boston.[9] Twenty years later, a study by the Federal Reserve Bank corroborated the earlier results: 81 per cent of the manufacturers queried shipped through New York, and only 12 per cent said that they shipped by way of Boston.[10]

The decline of Boston as exporter for New England, and especially that part of New England in which Boston enjoys freight-rate advantages, is well known. The reason: a lack of bulk exports available for shipment through Boston. Most northeastern overseas shipments are composed of high-value manufactured goods, usually shipped in small amounts to any one specific destination. The Boston area is particularly deficient in bulk cargo; hence infrequent sailings are made from the port of Boston. Shippers, seeking full cargoes, use ports offering sufficient heavy cargo to fill out the load. This need is satisfied by New York, and New England manufacturers use the superior services of the larger port.

Among others, one further interesting factor contributes to the choice of New York: the unexcelled development of metropolitan functions. Many firms maintain export agents or departments in the city of New York. Often, also, marketing and administrative offices are centralized here. The sum of the banking, marketing, distribution, and transportation facilities located in New York City is a major attraction for shippers. Even with more favorable freight rates, it is doubtful that Boston could regain much of its lost tonnage.

It is impossible to delimit the import boundaries between New York and Boston. New York imports for the entire nation; it is the national terminal port par excellence. Though the port of Boston is a major foreign and intercoastal importer of such items as petroleum, sugar, and lumber, few of these supplies are destined for hinterland communities. Almost all of Boston's imports are utilized within the immediate environs of the city.[11] Eighteen other New England ports receive cargo for use in their local areas.

*Truck transportation.*—Statistical data relating to point-to-point motor freight movement are scant. Gathering accurate information is difficult, since over 300 independent motor carriers operate in southern New England and few operate between all points in the three-state region. These findings, therefore, gathered from trucking industry spokesmen, are informed esti-

[9] C. E. Artman and S. H. Reed, *Foreign Trade Survey of New England* (Bureau of Foreign and Domestic Commerce, "Domestic Commerce Series," No. 40 [Washington, 1931]).

[10] A. P. Sullivan, "The Port of Boston," *Monthly Review* (Federal Reserve Bank of Boston), XXXII (February, 1950), 1–7.

[11] War Department and U.S. Maritime Commission, *The Port of Boston, Mass.* ("Port Series," No. 3 [rev. ed.; Washington, D.C., 1946]), pp. 301–6.

mates.[12] The resulting pattern gives Boston dominance within 35 miles. The remainder of the southern New England area has greater interchange with New York City. Providence, though near the boundary line, moves more tonnage to and from New York. Worcester and Fitchburg are the western limits of Boston's dominance of metropolitan freight interchange.

## COMMUNICATIONS

Rapid and efficient communications have spread the influence of the metropolis over wide areas. The daily metropolitan press has become a powerful force in the acceptance of urban ideals and ideas throughout the larger community. The ability to talk person-to-person, provided by the telephone, has further extended commercial and social links with the central city.

*Newspapers.*—Metropolitan newspaper circulation frequently is used to measure metropolitan influence. The choice of one or two newspapers from each of the two cities as a basis for measuring the extent of metropolitan influence would merely repeat the incompleteness of earlier studies. However, Audit Bureau of Circulations figures, published annually, afford a comparable measure of New York and Boston distribution. Such figures are tallied for each hinterland community for all newspapers.[13]

The information available in A.B.C. statements offers several problems of tabulation. First, Boston and New York papers are audited at different seasons of the year. Boston figures used are for the twelve months ending March 31, 1949, whereas the New York figures represent the year ending September 30, 1949. The variation introduced by this difference appears mi-

[12] From discussions with Mr. R. Woodbury of the New England Motor Rate Bureau, Inc., Boston, and Mr. H. Wagner of Malkin Motor Freight Co., Cambridge.

[13] Included are, for Boston, *Herald-Traveler, Globe, Post,* and *Record-American;* for New York, *New York Times, Herald-Tribune, Journal-American World-Telegram, Post, Sun, Daily News,* and *Mirror.*

nor. A second difficulty of tabulation arises from the lack of uniformity of community names; the destination of New York papers in New England is listed by post office address, the destination of Boston papers in New England, by town names. For purposes of clarity, the data were reclassified by town names.

A final problem is posed by towns that are an integral part of a larger metropolitan area, such as bedroom communities. To eliminate variations, data for each metropolitan area (as defined by the census) are gathered into a composite figure for the entire area.[14]

The resulting map indicates that the spatial transition between areas that lie distinctly within the New York readership zone and those that lie in Boston's are narrow and clearly marked (Fig. 4). At some points, the New York circulation drops from 90 per cent of the combined New York and Boston circulation to less than 10 per cent within the short space of 30 miles. The 50 per cent boundary lies slightly east of Williamstown in northwestern Massachusetts, veers westward to the New York border and recurves eastward to the Massachusetts-Connecticut boundary south of Springfield, continues across eastern Connecticut to the Rhode Island border and arches northward some ten miles along the immediate coastal fringe.

Areas of almost complete dominance by one metropolis or the other are large. New York circulation is over 90 per cent of the combined New York City and Boston circulation in all of western Connecticut and even the southwestern corner of Massachusetts. The Boston 90 per cent isopleth of metropolitan circulation also encompasses a wide area. It extends south from Greenfield in northwestern Massachusetts, runs along the eastern border of the Connecticut Valley in Massachusetts, and finally curves southeastward to the Providence area. Cape

[14] For instance, the Brockton, Massachusetts, metropolitan area includes 11 towns, whose circulations have been totaled into one area figure.

Cod, a popular New York vacation area, is not within the 90 per cent Boston influence zone.

The extent of intermixture of metropolitan papers in the Connecticut Valley is noteworthy. From Middletown and Meriden on the south to Greenfield on the north —a distance of more than 70 miles—neither

causes a less sharp transition on the northern side of the boundary. The national character of New York's papers, transcending regional bounds, may be one cause of this feature; the higher editorial quality of New York papers in comparison with the Boston dailies is another.

*Telephone calls.*—Though newspapers

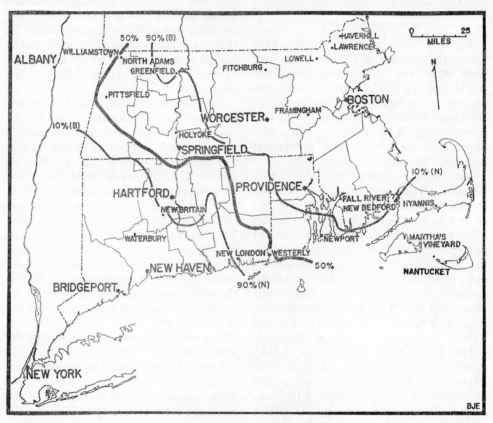

Fig. 4.—Percentage of southern New England circulation for all New York and Boston daily newspapers.

New York nor Boston has 90 per cent of the metropolitan readership. Perhaps because of the large hinterland cities of Hartford and Springfield, roughly equidistant from New York City and Boston, the region looks to both of the larger cities with some degree of interest yet maintains a semi-independent attitude.

The comparatively large circulation of New York papers in Boston's territory

have been widely used as a measure of metropolitan influence, long-distance telephone calls are an equally valid measure.[15] The excellence of telephone data lies in their comprehensive nature; they record

[15] Use of telephone calls as measures of the centrality of specific communities was suggested by E. Ullman, "A Theory of Location for Cities," *American Journal of Sociology*, XLVI (1941), 858 [see below, pp. 202–9].

both the economic and the social links of people separated by distance. In addition, they have three specific advantages over newspaper circulation: (1) Most newspapers make little attempt to push circulation beyond the trading area of their advertisers, whereas people make necessary telephone calls without consideration of trading area boundaries; (2) The telephone time-distance factor is reduced because telephone calls cover great distance with little elapsed time; (3) There is no problem of differences in quality (as with newspapers) affecting comparability. There is, however, one weakness in telephone call data: costs rise with increased call distances.

Two characteristics of the data affect the results. First, telephone call surveys are normally made during the summer, when long-distance calls are at a peak. The influx of New York City residents into southern New England during this vacation period increases New York City's proportion of the total in vacation areas, particularly in western Massachusetts, southern Rhode Island, and Cape Cod. Second, the two Bell Telephone Companies operating in New England gather data differently.[16] For all states except Connecticut, the sample includes day and night messages; in Connecticut, day toll message data only are available. Though this introduces a variation, the difference appears minor.

The 50 per cent telephone isopleth describes an arc from western Massachusetts along the Connecticut boundary to eastern Connecticut and then coastwise, bisecting Nantucket and Martha's Vineyard (Fig. 5). This line is similar to the newspaper boundary, although the distance between isopleths is greater than that described by newspaper circulation. The New York City 90 per cent isopleth encloses Connecticut west of Bridgeport, whereas Boston's 90 per cent isopleth pre-empts eastern Massachusetts.

Calls between Boston and Connecticut River Valley communities are greater than anticipated. One possible explanation: calls

between Connecticut subsidiaries and Boston administrative offices. A number of government agencies, for instance, with regional headquarters in Boston, have branch offices in Hartford and Springfield with which frequent contact is necessary.

## AGRICULTURE

In less mobile eras, urban centers developed because of the ability of the agricultural hinterland to produce surpluses. Southern New England reverses this theme; agriculture exists only in response to the demands of the great urban population.[17] The result is that the largest agricultural production in the area—dairy products, poultry, and eggs—fills immediate needs of the nearby communities and is not of significance for comparing the hinterland boundary between New York City and Boston.

In the economy of southern New England, agriculture utilizes only a small proportion of the total number of wage earners. For all of New England, including the more rural northern states, agriculture, forestry, and fishing combined, accounted for only 6 per cent of the employed workers in 1940.[18] In the main, New England is dependent upon other parts of the country for the greater part of its food.

Despite the attention given to milk production, southern New England is a deficit area which must import dairy products in order to satisfy its demands.[19] Practically

16 The New England Telephone and Telegraph Company serves all New England except Connecticut. The latter is served by the Southern New England Telephone Company.

17 "If the agriculture of New England had to be described in one sentence, that sentence would be that New England has the kind of agriculture that is commonly found near metropolitan centers" (J. D. Black, *The Rural Economy of New England* [Cambridge, 1950], p. 228).

18 Black, *op. cit.*, p. 87.

19 For complete discussions of the dairy industry see P. McComas, "The New England Dairy Industry" (Ph.D. diss., Harvard University, 1947); W. H. Brown, "The Economics of Dairy Farming in Southern New England (Ph.D. diss., Harvard University, 1949); and Black, *op. cit.*, pp. 292–382.

the total production is consumed in local centers, almost none of it going either to New York City or Boston. Connecticut and Massachusetts combined provide less than 1 per cent of the milk received in New York City.[20] Most of this originates on farms in the extreme western portions of these states. Nearly all of Boston's milk is a major source of income for farmers. The Connecticut supply of eggs and broilers finds its terminus largely in New York City. The rising production in New Hampshire and eastern Massachusetts is destined for the metropolitan Boston market.

Other crop and livestock production in southern New England represents only a

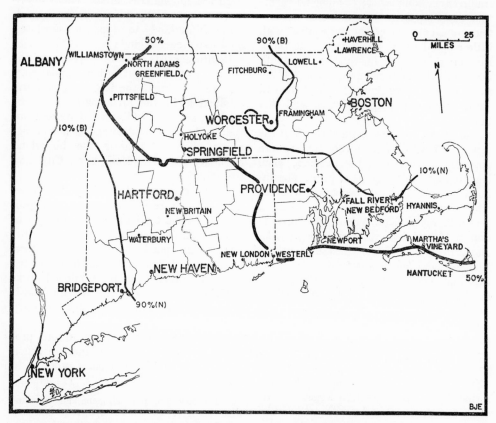

Fig. 5.—Percentage of all southern New England telephone calls from hinterland points to New York and Boston

produced in northern New England, with just a small amount coming from the Massachusetts area northwest of Boston.

Poultry and egg production in New England has recently shown a notable increase, so that today it competes with dairying as

[20] "Report of the New York Milkshed Price Committee," transmitted to the Market Administrator, New York Metropolitan Milk Marketing Area, February, 1949, p. 166.

small proportion of farm income, and supplies the metropolitan New York and Boston markets with a negligible amount of their total food supply. There is no sharp line of demarcation between the agricultural marketing areas of New York City and Boston. The intermediate urban centers consume a major portion of the agricultural supply within their own immediate vicinities.

## RECREATION

Both New York City and Boston experience a summer exodus of vacationers into the hinterland. Not all metropolitan inhabitants spend their vacations within the hinterland; in an era of automobiles and airplanes, many travel farther for recreation. Nevertheless, many inhabitants take vacations within their metropolitan regions. A statistical study by the New England Council makes it possible to map the home state of vacationers.[21]

The home states data do not yield specific facts about the resorts patronized by New York City and Boston residents. The total population of New York and New Jersey, however, is about twice that of the New York City Standard Metropolitan Area; likewise, the Boston Standard Metropolitan Area contains about one-half the inhabitants of Massachusetts. We assume in comparing home states that half of the Massachusetts vacationers are Bostonians and half those from New York and New Jersey are New Yorkers. This measure is rough but does suggest an answer.

The results depict a two-pronged movement of New York–New Jersey residents during vacation seasons: one advance is made northward into the interior hill-country of Connecticut and Massachusetts; the other (probably representing more people) along the Atlantic shoreline toward Cape Cod (Fig. 6).

Massachusetts residents exhibit a similar type of movement although in a different region. The coastal movements extend southward along the Massachusetts coast to Cape Cod and northward to the Maine–New Hampshire shoreline. A second thrust runs inland toward the hill and lake country of New Hampshire. In Massachusetts, the one exception, Hampden County, is probably due to the inclusion of urban hotels in Springfield.

## MANUFACTURING

Southern New England is primarily an industrial community; manufacturing provided 47 per cent of all employment in 1947, a resultant income of 726 dollars for each person in New England. The region's metropolitan orientation is analyzed in two ways—in the relocation of new plants in southern New England and in the directorship of large plants already located in the area.

Twenty plant relocations in New England recently were studied in detail by Ellis; eleven represented shifts into New England from other regions.[22] Nine of the eleven shifts were from the New York City area, whereas the other two, from greater distances, represented movements into New England to be closer to the New York City market. Though this sample is small, it indicates that a considerable proportion of the relocations in southern New England is the overflow of New York–oriented firms into the hinterland. Much of Connecticut's new industry—62 per cent of the firms established during the five years 1945–50 —are located in Fairfield and New Haven counties, both within commuting distance of New York City.[23]

The geographic ties of members of industrial boards of directors is a second way of determining metropolitan orientation. If the business addresses of directors (of all manufacturing firms employing more than 500 persons in southern New England) is

[21] By interviews and questionnaires, a large sample of resort proprietors were asked from what state the greatest number of their patrons come. For resorts located in Connecticut and Rhode Island, the proprietors' answers were tallied for the state as a whole, whereas, in Massachusetts, the results were recorded by county in which the resort is located. See New England Council, *New England Vacation Business Inventory,* Part 1, *Overnight Accommodations for New England Vacation Visitors: A Statistical Summary* (Boston, 1947).

[22] G. H. Ellis, "Postwar Industrial Location in New England" (Ph.D. diss., Harvard University, 1949), pp. 160–75; see also his article, "Why New Manufacturing Establishments Located in New England: August 1945 to June 1948," *Monthly Review* (Federal Reserve Bank of Boston), XXXI (April, 1949), 1–12.

[23] *Connecticut Business Review* (Connecticut Development Commission, Hartford, 1950), p. 13.

either in New York City or Boston, we assume that the metropolis has a hand in directing the management of the firm.[24]

On the basis of this measure, nearly all of the three-state area is more closely linked to New York City than to Boston (Fig. 7). The limits of Boston's dominance are Fall River–New Bedford on the south

forty-four are there more Boston directors; forty-two firms have more New York directors. In one, there is an equal number from New York and Boston. The Providence area in Rhode Island, though but 40 miles from Boston, has three firms with more New York directors to every one for Boston. In Massachusetts centers, Spring-

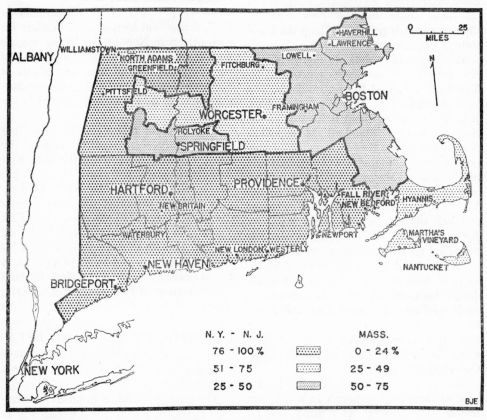

FIG. 6.—Vacationists' state of origin—all vacation places

and Worcester on the west. To the north, there is a minor extension of Boston influence westward along the northern border of the state—an area with few industrial firms.

In Connecticut, major industrial hinterland centers have practically no ties to Boston (Table 1). In only one firm out of

[24] The basic source of information is *Poor's Register of Directors and Executives, United States and Canada* (New York, 1951).

field maintains the three-to-one New York ratio seen in Providence, whereas the Worcester, Fall River–New Bedford, and Lawrence-Lowell areas are evenly divided between New York and Boston.

### FINANCE

The development of financial dominance is a characteristic feature of the fully developed metropolitan center. Regional financial functions today are largely em-

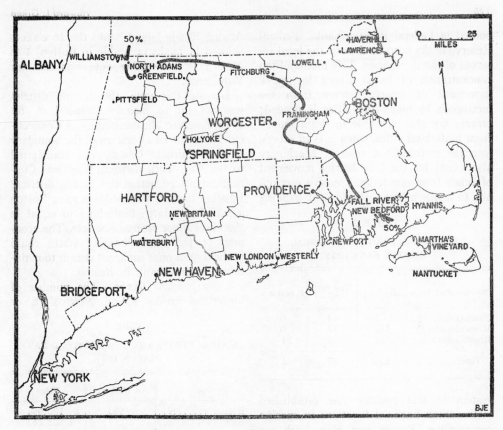

Fig. 7.—Percentage of directors' business address—major hinterland manufacturing firms

TABLE 1

HINTERLAND FIRMS

(500 or More Employees)

| Metropolitan Area* | Number | New York or Boston Directors | More New York Directors | More Boston Directors |
|---|---|---|---|---|
| Connecticut: | | | | |
| Bridgeport................. | 25 | 18 | 17 | 0 |
| New Haven................. | 14 | 10 | 10 | 0 |
| Waterbury.................. | 14 | 9 | 9 | 0 |
| New Britain–Bristol ........ | 16 | 3 | 2 | 1 |
| Hartford.................. | 14 | 4 | 4 | 0 |
| Rhode Island: | | | | |
| Providence................ | 46 | 32 | 24 | 8 |
| Massachusetts: | | | | |
| Springfield................ | 28 | 22 | 16 | 5 |
| Worcester................. | 9 | 6 | 3 | 3 |
| Fall River–New Bedford..... | 25 | 14 | 6 | 7 |
| Lawrence-Lowell† .......... | 17 | 15 | 6 | 8 |

* Standard Metropolitan Area as defined in 1947 Census of Manufacturers.
† Standard Metropolitan Area as defined in 1950 Census of Population.

bodied in Federal Reserve banks. Federal Reserve banks keep on deposit the legal reserves of member banks. This metropolitan concentration of funds allows for quick movement of reserve money from the metropolis to hinterland cities if needed; powers are also available to drain money from hinterland cities, when it is in excess, into the metropolitan reserve. Machinery also exists for the interdistrict movement of funds from one federal reserve metropolis to another. Thus, the present banking

TABLE 2

First-Choice Vote for Federal Reserve Bank City

| Member Bank State | Boston | New York City | Providence |
|---|---|---|---|
| Connecticut...... | 7 | 64 | 0 |
| Massachusetts.... | 137 | 17 | 0 |
| Rhode Island..... | 11 | 4 | 1 |
| Total.......... | 155 | 85 | 1 |

system in this country has established metropolitan financial functions in specific communities. Boston and New York are two such centers.

Two indicators shed light on this situation: (1) the votes by banks for choice of Federal Reserve City and subsequent adjustments, and (2) New York and Boston banks listed as correspondents of hinterland banks.

*Federal Reserve districts.*—In choosing sites for metropolitan regional Federal Reserve Banks in 1914, the Senate committee charged with the responsibility polled future member banks on their three preferences of cities as Federal Reserve headquarters[25] (Table 2). The results of the first-place votes are particularly revealing: as early as 1914, only 7 of 71 banks in Connecticut listed Boston as first choice. Even in Massachusetts, 17 of 154 banks thought New York a superior location.

[25] *Location of the Reserve Districts in the United States,* Senate Document 485, 63d Congress, 2d session, 1914, pp. 352–55.

Among Rhode Island banks the 16 choices showed 11 banks favorable to Boston, 4 to New York; the other vote was cast for Providence.

Despite this vote, the Boston district was set up to include Connecticut. By 1915, however, the complaints of Connecticut banks forced alteration of the boundary so that Fairfield County was transferred to the New York district. Why was Connecticut placed within the Boston district? Possibly because this addition gave Boston a sufficiently large hinterland to equal in size most other reserve districts. The economy of the five remaining states could probably not offer sufficient reason to maintain a reserve bank in Boston.

*Correspondent banks.*—The number of hinterland banks listing New York or

TABLE 3

Checks Cleared by One Hartford Bank March, 1943

| Origin | No. of Checks | Value |
|---|---|---|
| Boston.......... | 993 | $ 180,994 |
| New York City... | 7,074 | 2,805,162 |

Boston houses as correspondents is another measure of metropolitan orientation, although a rough gauge. The difficulty with this criterion is that a New York correspondent may get 99 per cent of the business and a Boston bank but 1 per cent, yet both would be listed as correspondents. As an example, Hartford banks listed more than twice as many New York as Boston correspondents; yet one bank shows more than seven times as many checks from New York at a total value fourteen times greater than checks originating in Boston[26] (Table 3).

Nearly all Connecticut banks list a majority of New York correspondents (Fig. 8). The sparsely settled eastern and northeastern parts of the state, closer to

[26] Brief prepared by Hartford Chamber of Commerce for Civil Aeronautics Board: "Statement of Facts concerning Hartford, Conn., 1943," p. 10.

Boston, are less completely oriented to New York houses. In Massachusetts, the state borders are the boundary except for Williamstown in the extreme northwest and Springfield (where correspondents are equally divided between the metropolitan centers). Boston banks are dominant by at least two to one throughout the state, with

There is a marked tendency for large hinterland cities to show stronger links with New York City than smaller communities in the same general area. Springfield is evenly divided, although Holyoke is definitely oriented to Boston. Worcester is less strongly linked with Boston than its location would indicate; similarly New

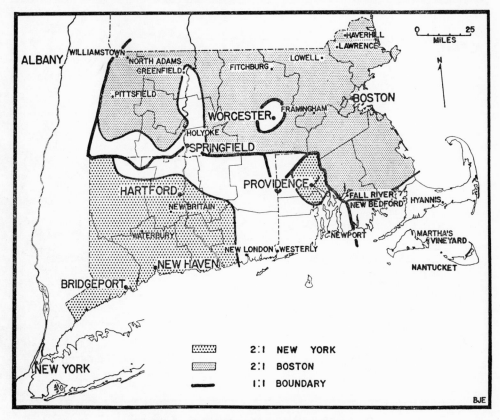

FIG. 8.—Orientation of correspondent banks

several exceptions: Greenfield and Northampton in the Connecticut River Valley; Worcester; New Bedford; and possibly Cape Cod and southern Berkshire County (these two areas have few banks).

Rhode Island offers an interesting contrast. Whereas the southern half of the state appears in the boundary zone, and but slightly weighted on the New York side, Providence is strongly linked with New York City.

Bedford. Providence, but 40 miles from Boston, is most completely tied to New York City. These facts, and discussions with bankers, indicate that major cities in the area look toward the financial capital of the country rather than to the regional center at Boston.

A second major factor in delimiting correspondent bank boundaries appears to be the importance of state borders. With few exceptions, Connecticut and Rhode Island could be placed within the New York sphere, and Massachusets within the Boston zone.

## COMPOSITE BOUNDARY

Seven functional indicators presented in this paper can be synthesized to give a

the seven functional indicators measured stretches southwestward from the vicinity of North Adams to Pittsfield, then recurves in an arc, passing near Holyoke (Fig. 9). It arches northward from its southeasterly path to include Providence in the New York hinterland. Finally, this

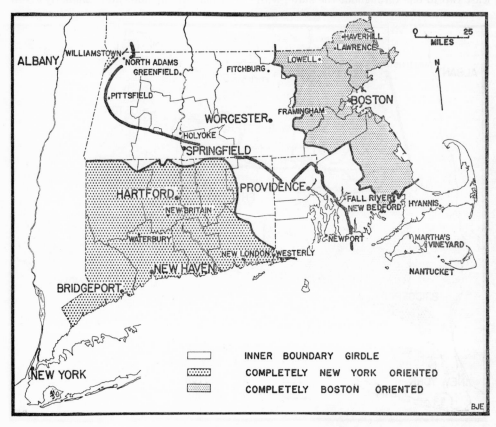

FIG. 9.—Median boundary, seven hinterland measures

composite boundary. The indicators are: (1) railroad coach ticket purchases, (2) an estimate of truck freight movement to New York and Boston, (3) metropolitan newspaper circulation, (4) long-distance telephone calls, (5) metropolitan origin of vacationers, (6) business addresses of directors for major industrial firms, and (7) metropolitan correspondents for hinterland banks.

The median or middle boundary of

median boundary follows the Rhode Island–Massachusetts border to the sea.

Connecticut, with the minor exception of the extreme eastern section, is linked with New York by every measure. The northwestern tip of Berkshire County, Massachusetts, also shows a strong affinity for New York, as do southern coastal fringes of Rhode Island.

Of the three-state area, eastern Massachusetts alone is tied closely to Boston.

This strongly Boston-oriented section is bounded on the west by the eastern border of Worcester County and on the south by the farther limits of Plymouth County.

## CONCLUSION

These results in part bear out the contention that Connecticut does not belong to the same region as Massachusetts. However, it is not just the proximity of Connecticut to New York City that is the reason for this realignment, as has been contended, but rather the close functional community of interest between the two. If the realignment of regions is to be based upon functional ties with metropolitan centers—nodal rather than homogeneous regions—then most of Rhode Island and southwestern Massachusetts must also be included within the New York City region.

New England remains a regional name, perhaps connoting an area with a uniform historical development pattern prior to the era of suburban expansion, of the telephone, the automobile, the airplane, and the metropolitan centralization of management and finance.

EDWARD ULLMAN

# A THEORY OF LOCATION FOR CITIES

## I

Periodically in the past century the location and distribution of cities and settlements have been studied. Important contributions have been made by individuals in many disciplines. Partly because of the diversity and unco-ordinated nature of the attack and partly because of the complexities and variables involved, a systematic theory has been slow to evolve, in contrast to the advances in the field of industrial location.[1]

The first theoretical statement of modern importance was von Thünen's *Der isolierte Staat,* initially published in 1826, wherein he postulated an entirely uniform land surface and showed that under ideal conditions a city would develop in the center of this land area and concentric rings of land use would develop around the central city. In 1841 Kohl investigated the relation between cities and the natural and cultural environment, paying particular attention to the effect of transport routes on the location of urban centers.[2] In 1894 Cooley admirably demonstrated the channelizing influence that transportation routes, particularly rail, would have on the location and development of trade centers.[3] He also called attention to break in transportation

Reprinted from *American Journal of Sociology,* XLVI (May, 1941), 835–64, by permission of the author and editor. (Copyright, 1941, by the University of Chicago.)

[1] Cf. Tord Palander, *Beiträge zur Standortstheorie* (Uppsala, Sweden, 1935), or E. M. Hoover, Jr., *Location Theory and the Shoe and Leather Industries* (Cambridge, Mass., 1937).

[2] J. G. Kohl, *Der Verkehr und die Ansiedlungen der Menschen in ihrer Abhängikeit von der Gestaltung der Erdoberfläche* (2d ed.; Leipzig, 1850).

[3] C. H. Cooley, "The Theory of Transportation," *Publications of the American Economic Association,* IX (May, 1894), 1–148.

as a city-builder just as Ratzel had earlier. In 1927 Haig sought to determine why there was such a large concentration of population and manufacturing in the largest cities.[4] Since concentration occurs where assembly of material is cheapest, all business functions, except extraction and transportation, ideally should be located in cities where transportation is least costly. Exceptions are provided by the processing of perishable goods, as in sugar centrals, and of large weight-losing commodities, as in smelters. Haig's theoretical treatment is of a different type from those just cited but should be included as an excellent example of a "concentration" study.

In 1927 Bobeck[5] showed that German geographers since 1899, following Schlüter and others, had concerned themselves largely with the internal geography of cities, with the pattern of land use and forms within the urban limits, in contrast to the problem of location and support of cities. Such preoccupation with internal urban structure has also characterized the recent work of geographers in America and other countries. Bobeck insisted with reason that such studies, valuable though they were, constituted only half the field of urban geography and that there remained unanswered the fundamental geographical question: "What are the causes for the existence, present size, and character of a city?" Since the publication of this article, a number of urban studies in Germany and some in other countries have dealt with

[4] R. M. Haig, "Toward an Understanding of the Metropolis: Some Speculations Regarding the Economic Basis of Urban Concentration," *Quarterly Journal of Economics,* XL (1926), 179–208.

[5] Hans Bobeck, "Grundfragen der Stadt Geographie," *Geographischer Anzeiger,* XXVIII (1927), 213–24.

such questions as the relations between city and country.[6]

## II

A theoretical framework for study of the distribution of settlements is provided by the work of Walter Christaller.[7] The essence of the theory is that a certain amount of productive land supports an urban center. The center exists because essential services must be performed for the surrounding land. Thus the primary factor explaining Chicago is the productivity of the Middle West; location at the southern end of Lake Michigan is a secondary factor. If there were no Lake Michigan, the urban population of the Middle West would in all probability be just as large as it is now. Ideally, the city should be in the center of a productive area.[8] The similarity of this concept to von Thünen's original proposition is evident.

Apparently many scholars have approached the scheme in their thinking.[9] Bobeck claims he presented the rudiments of such an explanation in 1927. The work of a number of American rural sociologists shows appreciation for some of Christaller's preliminary assumptions, even though done before or without knowledge of Christaller's work and performed with a different

end in view. Galpin's epochal study of trade areas in Walworth County, Wisconsin, published in 1915, was the first contribution. Since then important studies bearing on the problem have been made by others.[10] These studies are confined primarily to smaller trade centers but give a wealth of information on distribution of settlements which independently substantiates many of Christaller's basic premises.

As a working hypothesis one assumes that normally the larger city, the larger its tributary area. Thus there should be

[6] A section of the International Geographical Congress at Amsterdam in 1938 dealt with "Functional Relations between City and Country." The papers are published in Vol. II of the *Comptes rendus* (Leiden: E. J. Brill, 1938). A recent American study is C. D. Harris, "Salt Lake City: A Regional Capital" (Ph.D. diss., University of Chicago, 1940). Pertinent also is R. E. Dickinson, "The Metropolitan Regions of the United States," *Geographical Review*, XXIV (1934), 278–91.

[7] *Die zentralen Orte in Süddeutschland* (Jena, 1935); also a paper (no title) in *Comptes rendus du Congrès internationale de géographie Amsterdam* (1938), II, 123–37.

[8] This does not deny the importance of "gateway" centers such as Omaha and Kansas City, cities located between contrasting areas in order to secure exchange benefits. The logical growth of cities at such locations does not destroy the theory to be presented (cf. R. D. McKenzie's excellent discussion in *The Metropolitan Community* [New York, 1933], pp. 4 ff.).

[9] Cf. Petrie's statement about ancient Egypt and Mesopotamia: "It has been noticed before how remarkably similar the distances are between the early nome capitals of the Delta (twenty-one miles on an average) and the early cities of Mesopotamia (averaging twenty miles apart). Some physical cause seems to limit the primitive rule in this way. Is it not the limit of central storage of grain, which is the essential form of early capital? Supplies could be centralised up to ten miles away; beyond that the cost of transport made it better worth while to have a nearer centre" (W. M. Flinders Petrie, *Social Life in Ancient Egypt* [London, 1923; reissued, 1932], pp. 3–4).

[10] C. J. Galpin, *Social Anatomy of an Agricultural Community* (University of Wisconsin Agricultural Experiment Station Research Bull. 34 [1915]), and the restudy by J. H. Kolb and R. A. Polson, *Trends in Town-Country Relations* (University of Wisconsin Agricultural Experiment Station Research Bull. 117 [1933]); B. L. Melvin, *Village Service Agencies of New York State, 1925* (Cornell University Agricultural Experiment Station Bull. 493 [1929]), and *Rural Population of New York, 1855–1925* (Cornell University Agricultural Experiment Station Memoir 116 [1928]); Dwight Sanderson, *The Rural Community* (New York, 1932), esp. pp. 488–514, which contains references to many studies by Sanderson and his associates; Carle C. Zimmerman, *Farm Trade Centers in Minnesota, 1905–29* (University of Minnesota Agricultural Experiment Station Bull. 269 [1930]); T. Lynn Smith, *Farm Trade Centers in Louisiana 1905 to 1931* (Louisiana State University Bull. 234 [1933]); Paul H. Landis, *South Dakota Town-Country Trade Relations, 1901–1931* (South Dakota Agricultural Experiment Station Bull. 274 [1932]), and *The Growth and Decline of South Dakota Trade Centers, 1901–1933* (Bull. 279 [1938]), and *Washington Farm Trade Centers, 1900–1935* (State College of Washington Agricultural Experiment Station Bull. 360 [1938]). Other studies are listed in subsequent footnotes.

cities of varying size ranging from a small hamlet performing a few simple functions, such as providing a limited shopping and market center for a small contiguous area, up to a large city with a large tributary area composed of the service areas of many smaller towns and providing more complex services, such as wholesaling, large-scale

proposition, and the city would be in the center. However, if three or more tangent circles are inscribed in an area, unserved spaces will exist; the best theoretical shapes are hexagons, the closest geometrical figures to circles which will completely fill an area (Fig. 1).[11]

Christaller has recognized typical-size

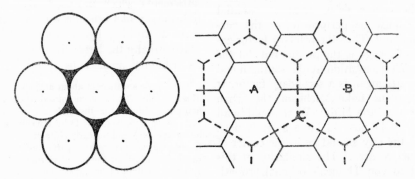

Fig. 1.—Theoretical shapes of tributary areas. Circles leave unserved spaces, hexagons do not. Small hexagons are service areas for smaller places, large hexagons (*dotted lines*) represent service areas for next higher-rank central places.

TABLE 1

| CENTRAL PLACE | TOWNS | | TRIBUTARY AREAS | |
| --- | --- | --- | --- | --- |
| | Distance Apart (Km.) | Population | Size (Sq. Km.) | Population |
| Market hamlet (*Marktort*).......... | 7 | 800 | 45 | 2,700 |
| Township center (*Amtsort*)......... | 12 | 1,500 | 135 | 8,100 |
| County seat (*Kreistadt*)............. | 21 | 3,500 | 400 | 24,000 |
| District city (*Bezirksstadt*).......... | 36 | 9,000 | 1,200 | 75,000 |
| Small state capital (*Gaustadt*)....... | 62 | 27,000 | 3,600 | 225,000 |
| Provincial head city (*Provinzhauptstadt*) | 108 | 90,000 | 10,800 | 675,000 |
| Regional capital city (*Landeshauptstadt*) | 186 | 300,000 | 32,400 | 2,025,000 |

banking, specialized retailing, and the like. Services performed purely for a surrounding area are termed "central" functions by Christaller, and the settlements performing them "central" places. An industry using raw materials imported from outside the local region and shipping its products out of the local area would not constitute a central service.

Ideally, each central place would have a circular tributary area, as in von Thünen's

settlements, computed their average population, their distance apart, and the size and population of their tributary areas in accordance with his hexagonal theory as Table 1 shows. He also states that the number of central places follows a norm

[11] See August Lösch, "The Nature of the Economic Regions," *Southern Economic Journal*, V (1938), 73. Galpin (*op. cit.*) thought in terms of six tributary-area circles around each center. See also Kolb and Polson, *op. cit.*, pp. 30–41.

from largest to smallest in the following order: 1:2:6:18:54, etc.[12]

All these figures are computed on the basis of South Germany, but Christaller claims them to be typical for most of Germany and western Europe. The settlements are classified on the basis of spacing each larger unit in a hexagon of next-order size, so that the distance between similar centers in the table above increases by the $\sqrt{3}$ over the preceding smaller category (in Fig. 1, e.g., the distance from $A$ to $B$ is $\sqrt{3}$ times the distance from $A$ to $C$). The initial distance figure of 7 km. between the smallest centers is chosen because 4–5 km., approximately the distance one can walk in one hour, appears to be a normal service-area limit for the smallest centers. Thus, in a hexagonal scheme, these centers are about 7 km. apart. Cristaller's maps indicate that such centers are spaced close to this norm in South Germany. In the larger categories the norms for distance apart and size of centers appear to be true averages; but variations from the norm are the rule, although wide discrepancies are not common in the eastern portion of South Germany, which is less highly industrialized than the Rhine-Ruhr areas in the west. The number of central places of each rank varies rather widely from the normal order of expectancy.

The theoretical ideal appears to be most nearly approached in poor, thinly settled farm districts—areas which are most nearly self-contained. In some other sections of Germany industrial concentration seems to be a more important explanation, although elements of the central-place type of distribution are present. Christaller points out that Cologne is really the commercial cen-

[12] Barnes and Robinson present some interesting maps showing the average distance apart of farmhouses in the driftless area of the Middle West and in southern Ontario. Farmhouses might well be regarded as the smallest settlement units in a central-place scheme, although they might not be in the same numbered sequence (James A. Barnes and Arthur H. Robinson, "A New Method for the Representation of Dispersed Rural Population," *Geographical Review*, XXX [1940], 134–37).

ter for the Ruhr industrial district even though it is outside the Ruhr area. Even in mountain areas centrality is a more important factor than topography in fixing the distribution of settlements. Christaller states that one cannot claim that a certain city is where it is because of a certain river —that would be tantamount to saying that if there were no rivers there would be no cities.

## III

Population alone is not a true measure of the central importance of a city; a large mining, industrial, or other specialized-function town might have a small tributary area and exercise few central functions. In addition to population, therefore, Christaller uses an index based on number of telephones in proportion to the average number per thousand inhabitants in South Germany, weighted further by the telephone density of the local subregion. A rich area such as the Palatinate supports more telephones in proportion to population than a poor area in the Bavarian Alps; therefore, the same number of telephones in a Palatinate town would not give it the same central significance as in the Alps. He claims that telephones, since they are used for business, are a reliable index of centrality. Such a thesis would not be valid for most of the United States, where telephones are as common in homes as in commercial and professional quarters.

Some better measures of centrality could be devised, even if only the number of out-of-town telephone calls per town. Better still would be some measure of actual central services performed. It would be tedious and difficult to compute the amount, or percentage, of business in each town drawn from outside the city, but some short cuts might be devised. If one knew the average number of customers required to support certain specialized functions in various regions, then the excess of these functions over the normal required for the urban population would be an index of centrality.[13] In several states rural sociologists and others have computed the average number of certain functions for towns of a given size. With one or two exceptions only small towns have been analyzed. Retail trade has received most attention, but professional and other services have also been examined. These studies do not tell us actually what population supports each service, since the services are supported both by town and by surrounding rural population, but they do provide norms of function expectancy which would be just as useful.[14]

A suggestive indicator of centrality is provided by the maps which Dickinson has made for per capita wholesale sales of cities in the United States.[15] On this basis centers are distributed rather evenly in accordance with regional population density. Schlier has computed the centrality of cities in Germany on the basis of census returns for "central" occupations.[16] Refinement of some of our census returns is desirable before this can be done entirely satisfactorily in the United States, but the method is probably the most promising in prospect.

[13] In Iowa, e.g., almost all towns of more than 450 inhabitants have banks, half of the towns of 250–300, and 20 per cent of the towns of 100–150 (according to calculations made by the author from population estimates in *Rand McNally's Commercial Atlas* for 1937).

[14] See particularly the thorough study by B. L. Melvin, *Village Service Agencies, New York State 1925;* C. R. Hoffer, *A Study of Town-Country Relationships* (Michigan Agricultural Experiment Station Special Bull. 181 [1928]) (data on number of retail stores and professions per town) ; H. B. Price and C. R. Hoffer, *Services of Rural Trade Centers in Distribution of Farm Supplies* (Minnesota Agricultural Experiment Station Bull. 249 [1938]); William J. Reilly, *Methods for the Study of Retail Relationships* ("Bureau of Business Research Monographs," No. 4, University of Texas Bull. 2944 [1929]), p. 26; J. H. Kolb, *Service Institutions of Town and Country* (Wisconsin Agricultural Experiment Station Research Bull. 66 [1925]) (town size in relation to support of institutions) ; Smith, *op. cit.,* pp. 32–40; Paul H. Landis, *South Dakota Town-Country Trade Relations, 1901–1931,* p. 20 (population per business enterprise), and pp. 24–25 (functions per town size) ; Zimmerman, *op. cit.,* pp. 16 and 51 ff.

[15] *Op. cit.,* pp. 280–81.

Another measure of centrality would be the number of automobiles entering a town, making sure that suburban movements were not included. Figures could be secured if the state-wide highway planning surveys in forty-six states were extended to gather such statistics.

## IV

The central-place scheme may be distorted by local factors, primarily industrial concentration or main transport routes. Christaller notes that transportation is not an areally operating principle, as the supplying of central goods implies, but is a linearly working factor. In many cases central places are strung at short intervals along an important transport route, and their tributary areas do not approximate the ideal circular or hexagonal shape but are elongated at right angles to the main transport line.[17] In some areas the reverse of this normal expectancy is true. In most of Illinois, maps depicting tributary areas show them to be elongated parallel to the main transport routes, not at right angles to them.[18] The combination of nearly uniform land and competitive railways peculiar to the state results in main railways running nearly parallel and close to one another between major centers.

In highly industrialized areas the central-place scheme is generally so distorted by industrial concentration in response to

[16] Otto Schlier, "Die zentralen Orte des Deutschen Reichs," *Zeitschrift der Gesellschaft für Erdkunde zu Berlin* (1937), pp. 161–70. See also map constructed from Schlier's figures in R. E. Dickinson's valuable article, "The Economic Regions of Germany," *Geographical Review,* XXVIII (1938), 619. For use of census figures in the United States see Harris, *op. cit.,* pp. 3–12.

[17] For an illustration of this type of tributary area in the ridge and valley section of east Tennessee see H. V. Miller, "Effects of Reservoir Construction on Local Economic Units," *Economic Geography,* XV (1939), 242–49.

[18] See, e.g., *Marketing Atlas of the United States* (New York: International Magazine Co., Inc.) or *A Study of Natural Areas of Trade in the United States* (Washington, D.C.: U.S. National Recovery Administration, 1935).

resources and transportation that it may be said to have little significance as an explanation for urban location and distribution, although some features of a central-place scheme may be present, as in the case of Cologne and the Ruhr (p. 858).

In addition to distortion, the type of scheme prevailing in various regions is susceptible to many influences. Productivity of the soil,[19] type of agriculture and intensity of cultivation, topography, governmental organization, are all obvious modifiers. In the United States, for example, what is the effect on distribution of settlements caused by the sectional layout of the land and the regular size of counties in many states? In parts of Latin America many centers are known as "Sunday towns"; their chief functions appear to be purely social, to act as religious and recreational centers for holidays—hence the name "Sunday town."[20] Here social rather than economic services are the primary support of towns, and we should accordingly expect a system of central places with fewer and smaller centers, because fewer functions are performed and people can travel farther more readily than commodities. These underlying differences do not destroy the value of the theory; rather they provide variations of interest to study for themselves and for purposes of comparison with other regions.

The system of central places is not static or fixed; rather it is subject to change and

[19] Cf. the emphasis of Sombart, Adam Smith, and other economists on the necessity of surplus produce of land in order to support cities. Fertile land ordinarily produces more surplus and consequently more urban population, although "the town . . . may not always derive its whole subsistence from the country in its neighborhood . . ." (Adam Smith, *The Wealth of Nations* ["Modern Library" edition; New York, 1937], p. 357; Werner Sombart, *Der moderne Kapitalismus* [2d rev. ed.; Munich and Leipzig, 1916], I, 130–31).

[20] For an account of such settlements in Brazil see Pierre Deffontaines, "Rapports fonctionnels entre les agglomérations urbaines et rurales: un exemple en pays de colonisation, le Brésil," *Comptes rendus du Congrès internationale de géographie Amsterdam* (1938), II, 139–44.

development with changing conditions.[21] Improvements in transportation have had noticeable effects. The provision of good automobile roads alters buying and marketing practices, appears to make the smallest centers smaller and the larger centers larger, and generally alters trade areas.[22] Since good roads are spread more uniformly over the land than railways, their provision seems to make the distribution of centers correspond more closely to the normal scheme.[23]

Christaller may be guilty of claiming too great an application of his scheme. His criteria for determining typical-size settle-

[21] The effects of booms, droughts, and other factors on trade-center distribution by decades are brought out in Landis' studies for South Dakota and Washington. Zimmerman and Smith also show the changing character of trade-center distribution (see n. 10 of this paper for references). Melvin calls attention to a "village population shift lag"; in periods of depressed agriculture villages in New York declined in population approximately a decade after the surrounding rural population had decreased (B. L. Melvin, *Rural Population of New York, 1855–1925*, p. 120).

[22] Most studies indicate that only the very smallest hamlets (under 250 population) and crossroads stores have declined in size or number. The larger small places have held their own (see Landis for Washington, *op. cit.*, p. 37, and his *South Dakota Town-Country Trade Relations 1901–1931*, pp. 34–36). Zimmerman in 1930 (*op. cit.*, p. 41) notes that crossroads stores are disappearing and are being replaced by small villages. He states further: "It is evident that claims of substantial correlation between the appearance and growth of the larger trading center and the disappearance of the primary center are more or less unfounded. Although there are minor relationships, the main change has been a division of labor between the two types of centers rather than the complete obliteration of the smaller in favor of the larger" (p. 32).

For further evidences of effect of automobile on small centers see R. V. Mitchell, *Trends in Rural Retailing in Illinois 1926 to 1938* (University of Illinois Bureau of Business Research Bull., Ser. 59 [1939]), pp. 31 ff., and Sanderson, *op. cit.*, p. 564, as well as other studies cited above.

[23] Smith (*op. cit.*, p. 54) states: "There has been a tendency for centers of various sizes to distribute themselves more uniformly with regard to the area, population, and resources of the state. Or the changes seem to be in the direction of a more efficient pattern of rural organization. This redistri-

ments and their normal number apparently do not fit actual frequency counts of settlements in many almost uniform regions as well as some less rigidly deductive norms.[24]

Bobeck in a later article claims that Christaller's proof is unsatisfactory.[25] He states that two-thirds of the population of Germany and England live in cities and that only one-third of these cities in Germany are real central places. The bulk are primarily industrial towns or villages inhabited solely by farmers. He also declares that exceptions in the rest of the world are common, such as the purely rural districts of the Tonkin Delta of Indochina, cities based on energetic entrepreneurial activity, as some Italian cities, and world commercial ports such as London, Rotterdam, and Singapore. Many of these objections are valid; one wishes that Christaller had better quantitative data and were less vague in places. Bobeck admits, however, that the central-place theory has value and applies in some areas.

The central-place theory probably provides as valid an interpretation of settlement distribution over the land as the concentric-zone theory does for land use within cities. Neither theory is to be thought of as a rigid framework fitting all location facts at a given moment. Some, expecting too

much, would jettison the concentric-zone theory; others, realizing that it is an investigative hypothesis of merit, regard it as a useful tool for comparative analysis.

## V

Even in the closely articulated national economy of the United States there are strong forces at work to produce a central-place distribution of settlements. It is true that products under our national economy are characteristically shipped from producing areas through local shipping points directly to consuming centers which are often remote. However, the distribution of goods or imports brought into an area is characteristically carried on through brokerage, wholesale, and retail channels in central cities.[26] This graduated division of functions supports a central-place framework of settlements. Many non-industrial regions of relatively uniform land surface have cities distributed so evenly over the land that some sort of central-place theory appears to be the prime explanation.[27] It should be worth while to study this distribution and compare it with other areas.[28]

[26] Harris, *op. cit.*, p. 87.

[27] For a confirmation of this see the column diagram on p. 73 of Lösch (*op. cit.*), which shows the minimum distances between towns in Iowa of three different size classes. The maps of trade-center distribution in the works of Zimmerman, Smith, and Landis (cited earlier) also show an even spacing of centers.

[28] The following table gives the average community area for 140 villages in the United States in 1930. In the table notice throughout that (1) the larger the village, the larger its tributary area in each region and (2) the sparser the rural population density, the larger the village tributary area for each size class (contrast mid-Atlantic with Far West, etc.).

bution of centers in conjunction with improved methods of communication and transportation has placed each family in frequent contact with several trade centers. . . ."

In contrast, Melvin (*Rural Population of New York, 1855–1925*, p. 90), writing about New York State before the automobile had had much effect, states: "In 1870 the villages . . . were rather evenly scattered over the entire state where they had been located earlier in response to particular local needs. By 1920, however, the villages had become distributed more along routes of travel and transportation and in the vicinity of cities."

[24] This statement is made on the basis of frequency counts by the author for several midwestern states (cf. also Schlier, *op. cit.*, pp. 165–69, for Germany).

[25] Hans Bobeck, "Über einige functionelle Stadttypen und ihre Beziehungen zum Lande," *Comptes rendus du Congrès internationale de géographie Amsterdam* (1938), II, 88.

|  | COMMUNITY AREA IN SQUARE MILES | | |
|---|---|---|---|
| REGION | Small Villages (250–1,000 Pop.) | Medium Villages (1,000–1,750 Pop.) | Large Villages (1,750–2,500 Pop.) |
| Mid-Atlantic | 43 | 46 | 87 |
| South | 77 | 111 | 146 |
| Middle West | 81 | 113 | 148 |
| Far West | | 365 | 223 |

[Footnote 28 continued on p. 209]

In New England, on the other hand, where cities are primarily industrial centers based on distant raw materials and extraregional markets, instead of the land's supporting the city the reverse is more nearly true: the city supports the countryside by providing

[Footnote 28 continued from p. 208]

Although 140 is only a sample of the number of villages in the country, the figures are significant because the service areas were carefully and uniformly delimited in the field for all villages (E. deS. Brunner and J. D. Kolb, *Rural Social Trends* [New York, 1933], p. 95; see also E. deS. Brunner, G. S. Hughes, and M. Patten, *American Agricultural Villages* [New York, 1927], chap. ii).

In New York 26 sq. mi. was found to be the average area per village in 1920. "Village" refers to any settlement under 2,500 population. Nearness to cities, type of agriculture, and routes of travel are cited as the three most important factors influencing density of villages. Since areas near cities are suburbanized in some cases, as around New York City, the village-density in these districts is correspondingly high. Some urban counties with smaller cities (Rochester, Syracuse, and Niagara Falls) have few suburbs, and consequently the villages are farther apart than in many agricultural counties (B. L. Melvin, *Rural Population of New York, 1925–1955*, pp. 88–89; table on p. 89 shows number of square miles per village in each New York county).

In sample areas of New York State the average distance from a village of 250 or under to another of the same size or larger is about 3 miles; for the 250–749 class it is 3–5 miles; for the 750–1,249 class, 5–7 miles (B. L. Melvin, *Village Service Agencies, New York, 1925*, p. 102; in the table on p. 103 the distance averages cited above are shown to be very near the modes).

Kolb makes some interesting suggestions as to the distances between centers. He shows that spacing is closer in central Wisconsin than in Kansas, which is more sparsely settled (J. H. Kolb, *Service Relations of Town and Country* [Wisconsin Agricultural Experimental Station Research Bull. 58 (1923)]; see pp. 7–8 for theoretical graphs).

In Iowa, "the dominant factor determining the *size* of convenience-goods areas is distance" (*Second State Iowa Planning Board Report* [Des Moines, April, 1935], p. 198). This report contains fertile suggestions on trade areas for Iowa towns. Valuable detailed reports on retail trade areas for some Iowa counties have also been made by the same agency.

a market for farm products, and thus infertile rural areas are kept from being even more deserted than they are now.

The forces making for concentration at certain places and the inevitable rise of cities at these favored places have been emphasized by geographers and other scholars. The phenomenal growth of industry and world trade in the last hundred years and the concomitant growth of cities justify this emphasis but have perhaps unintentionally caused the intimate connection between a city and its surrounding area partially to be overlooked. Explanation in terms of concentration is most important for industrial districts but does not provide a complete areal theory for distribution of settlements. Furthermore, there is evidence that "of late . . . the rapid growth of the larger cities has reflected their increasing importance as commercial and service centers rather than as industrial centers."[29] Some form of the central-place theory should provide the most realistic key to the distribution of settlements where there is no marked concentration—in agricultural areas where explanation has been most difficult in the past. For all areas the system may well furnish a theoretical norm from which deviations may be measured.[30] It might also be an aid in planning the development of new areas. If the theory is kept in mind by workers in academic and planning fields as more studies are made, its validity may be tested and its structure refined in accordance with regional differences.

[29] U.S. National Resources Committee, *Our Cities —Their Role in the National Economy: Report of the Urbanism Committee* (Washington: Government Printing Office, 1937), p. 37.

[30] Some form of the central-place concept might well be used to advantage in interpreting the distribution of outlying business districts in cities (cf. Malcolm J. Proudfoot, "The Selection of a Business Site," *Journal of Land and Public Utility Economics*, XIV [1938], esp. 373 ff.).

JOHN E. BRUSH and HOWARD E. BRACEY

# RURAL SERVICE CENTERS IN SOUTHWESTERN WISCONSIN AND SOUTHERN ENGLAND

Comparative analysis of the distribution of rural service centers in southwestern Wisconsin[1] and southern England[2] shows that the spatial patterns are alike. Though the two areas are unlike in population density, urbanization, and transportation and though there are profound differences in settlement history, two orders of service centers exist in both, spaced at about 21-mile and 8- or 10-mile intervals. A third, and still lower, order, spaced at 4- to 6-mile intervals, also appears in both areas. It is impossible to equate the functional importance of rural service centers in Wisconsin and England because of economic and cultural differences. Indeed, distinctive functional types of centers should exist in every major economic or cultural realm on the earth. But the similarities in distribution pattern in Wisconsin and England suggest that there are certain common spatial relationships in the hierarchy of rural service centers.

## POPULATION DISTRIBUTION

The nine southwestern counties of Wisconsin (Fig. 1) and the six southern counties of England (Fig. 2) that make up the two areas are situated in regions of moderate relief and fairly uniform rural population distribution. The Wisconsin area, to-taling 7,170 square miles, is a rolling plain or hill land, generally more than a thousand feet above sea level. The surface is formed by dissection of nearly horizontal strata of limestone, shale, and sandstone but has local relief of less than 200 or 300 feet, except for the rugged bluffs near the Mississippi and Wisconsin rivers. Average rural population density is 30 persons to a square mile, ranging from as low as 20 to as high as 40 or 50, especially near the city of Madison. The English area is almost the same size, 6,969 square miles. There are stretches of highland more than 600 feet above sea level, but the predominant lowlands have local relief of less than 300 feet. The highest parts are in the chalk uplands of Wiltshire, Hampshire, and Berkshire, and in the hill country of the Brendons and Exmoor in western Somerset, where abrupt slopes and altitudes of somewhat more than a thousand feet are common. The average rural population density in the six English counties is 182 to a square mile. Villages of several hundred residents and country towns of 2,000–15,000 are the rule, in contrast with the single farmsteads and hamlets, villages, or small towns of fewer than 5,000 in rural Wisconsin.[3] Rural

[3] The *rural* population in the Wisconsin counties, according to the official definition of *rural* adhered to by the United States Bureau of the Census, includes the inhabitants of small towns and villages where the number is less than 2,500 persons as well as the open-country population. In England the meaning of *rural* is not strictly defined by the official census in terms of the number of residents in any closely built-up settlement. Municipal administrative areas such as cities and boroughs are considered urban, though in certain of them the number of inhabitants is only 1,000. Civil parishes, some of which comprise more than one village, and some scattered dwellings are considered *rural* if ad-

Reprinted from *Geographical Review*, XLV (October, 1955), 559–69, by permission of the authors and the editor. (Copyright, 1955, by the American Geographical Society, New York.)

[1] J. E. Brush, "The Hierarchy of Central Places in Southwestern Wisconsin," *Geographical Review,* XLIII (1953), 380–402.

[2] H. E. Bracey, *Social Provision in Rural Wiltshire* (London, 1952) ; *idem, Towns as Rural Service Centres* (Institute of British Geographers Publication No. 19 [1954]), pp. 95–105.

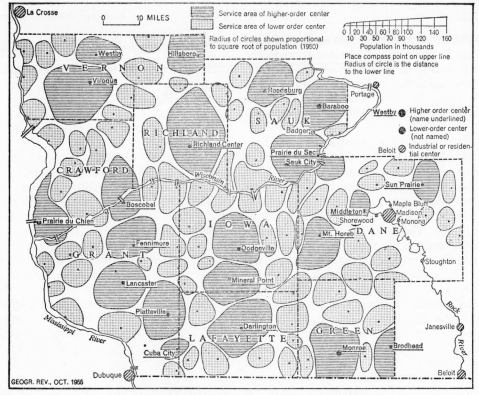

FIG. 1.—Rural service centers in southwestern Wisconsin

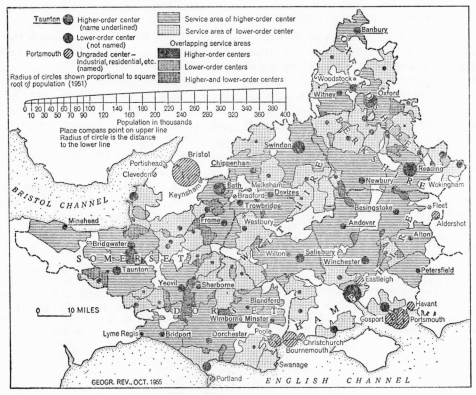

FIG. 2.—Rural service centers in southern England

densities as low as 50 to a square mile are found only over considerable areas in the hill country of western Somerset. The total rural population in the six English counties[4] is nearly five times that in the nine Wisconsin counties[5]—998,000, as compared with 217,000.

The total urban population of the English area, 1,930,000, is more than 12 times that of the Wisconsin area, 158,000. More than two-thirds of the urban residents in the Wisconsin area are in one county, about 100,000 concentrated in Madison and its suburbs. The large cities of the English area, such as Portsmouth, Southampton, and Bournemouth on the south coast and Reading and Oxford inland, have each between 100,000 and 300,000 inhabitants and account for about half the urban residents in the six counties. English country towns are generally much larger than Wisconsin towns, but in regard to rural services the dispersion of towns throughout both areas is more significant than the difference in the sizes of rural service centers or the presence of cities in the peripheral areas.

## TRANSPORTATION AND ECONOMY

Land occupance is continuous and accessibility good throughout the two areas. Both are covered with farms and are served by close networks of improved highways and secondary roads and by numerous rail lines. The rivers of the English area are small, easily bridged, and unnavigable except in their estuaries. In the Wisconsin area, only two rivers form barriers to land transportation. The Wisconsin River, no longer used for navigation, is bridged in

many places. But the Mississippi, across which few bridges or ferries exist, is a navigable waterway and has had somewhat the same role in transportation as the coasts of the English area. In both areas water transportation is not now important to the development of towns and villages as local trade centers.

The functions of the land transportation system in the two areas differ markedly. In southwestern Wisconsin little local use is made of the railways because of competitive services offered by trucking firms and because of the prevalence of private passenger cars and farm trucks. Although the rail lines are neglected and some have been abandoned entirely, the vehicular traffic density on the roads may well be heavier in the Wisconsin area than in the English area. Yet bus services are much better developed in southern England. English towns are served by several scheduled routes on which buses run several times a day.[6] The residents of all except the most out-of-the-way villages can ordinarily get to one or more towns by bus. In England agricultural produce or freight is carried between farm and local market by road transport, but for longer hauls rail is more often used, though long-distance road haulage is increasing.

In both areas the economic base of the rural population is agriculture, but there are large numbers of rural non-farm people and certain urban-industrial concentrations. Southwestern Wisconsin farms are predominantly of the dairy type, producing milk for cheese-making and, secondarily, livestock for slaughter. On the heavy clay lands of southern England dairying, with concentration on fresh milk supplies for London and other large cities, is also important. Large acreages, however, are de-

---

ministered by rural district councils, though the aggregate parish population may be as large as 3,000 or 4,000. One rural parish has as many as 20,000.

[4] All population figures cited are taken from *Census* [of] *1951, England and Wales, Preliminary Report* (London: General Register Office, 1951).

[5] All population figures cited are taken from U.S. Census of Population, 1950, Vol. I, *Number of Inhabitants* (Washington, D.C.: U.S. Bureau of the Census, 1952), chap. 49, "Wisconsin."

[6] F. H. W. Green, *Motor-Bus Centres in South-West England Considered in Relation to Population and Shopping Facilities* (Institute of British Geographers Publication No. 14 [1949]), pp. 57–68; idem, "Urban Hinterlands in England and Wales: An Analysis of Bus Services," *Geographical Journal*, CXVI (1950), 64–88.

voted to the cultivation of grain and feed-stuffs, stock-raising, and fruit-growing.

In the Wisconsin area, Madison with its suburbs forms the only major concentration of manufacturing and other non-agricultural activities. Madison and the minor manufacturing town of Stoughton, in Dane County, mark the westernmost extension of the Rock River manufacturing region.[7] One-half to two-thirds of the working population in the eight other counties are employed directly in agriculture and the remainder in trade, services, and professions.

In southern England more persons are employed in agriculture, but they represent a smaller proportion of the total occupied population. As much as 30 per cent of the total working population is employed in manufacturing in Somerset and Wiltshire, as compared with 12 per cent in agriculture. Yet this has not destroyed the close relationships existing between most of the towns and the adjacent rural population. The naval shipyards of Portsmouth, the shipping services and industries of South-ampton, and the resort trade of Bourne-mouth, Clevedon, and other coastal places far outweigh their rural service functions. Bristol, with some 440,000 inhabitants, is a still larger urban-industrial concentration, but it lies just outside the limit of the study area and is excluded from consideration, though its suburbs push into Somerset and its influence as a rural service center is felt over much of the northern part of that county. Reading, Oxford, Bath, and Swindon are the only large towns in the area that function as rural service centers and also exhibit significant concentrations of manufacturing or commerce not related to rural service. All towns and villages were included in the survey, but those with slight rural service function were ignored in the subsequent detailed analysis, which embraced the seventy most important rural centers. The six counties are situated well away from the major English manufactur-ing districts, and the survey area is one of the largest tracts of mixed farming in England. In this respect, therefore, it is comparable with the southwestern part of Wisconsin, which lies outside the main manufacturing belt of the United States.

## CRITERIA OF CENTRALITY

The role of a place as a trade center, or its centrality, may be ascertained by either of two methods: (*a*) assessment of the business and services existing in the center; or (*b*) measurement of the area dependent on the center for goods and services. In other words, one may ask: Is there a given kind of retail store or service in the center? Or, alternatively: Where do the people live who go to the center to obtain a certain commodity or service?

The first method, followed by Dickinson[8] and Smailes[9] in their work in the United Kingdom, is the one applied in southwestern Wisconsin. All retail and wholesale trading establishments, banking and financial agencies, trades and personal services, amusements and various other services, including professions and government administration, are considered in the determination of each center's status. The present-day functional development of service centers in southwestern Wisconsin can be assumed to be in accord with the requirements of farmers and other rural people because of the almost complete absence of other urbanizing influences. The limits of the area served by a center are determined by the existence of traffic divides, as shown in the pattern of daily traffic movement toward the center and toward other centers.

The second method, in which the criterion is use of the center by rural residents, is the one applied in southern England. This is the method commonly followed by sociological investigators in the United States in their studies of rural community

[7] J. W. Alexander, *Geography of Manufacturing in the Rock River Valley* ("Wisconsin Commerce Papers," Vol. I, No. 2 [1949]).

[8] R. E. Dickinson, "The Distribution and Functions of the Smaller Urban Settlements of East Anglia," *Geography*, VII (1932), 19–31.

[9] A. E. Smailes, "The Urban Hierarchy in England and Wales," *Geography*, XXIX (1944), 41–51.

relationships.[10] In the analysis of the six English counties the centers visited by village residents for medical supplies and services, clothing and household goods, and banking and entertainment are determined by means of questionnaires. The importance of each service center is measured by the number of villages partly or wholly dependent on it, and the extent of the service area is taken to include all villages using the center for three out of the four broad groups of services. The existence of other facilities and service establishments of the kinds used is implicit in the findings, but no attempt is made to assess them directly.

The advantage of the criterion of use by rural people is not only that it results in a more accurate map of service areas but also that it separates the rural component of centrality from the urban component. This is especially important in assessing the centrality of English cities and towns, some of which have large components of centrality based on urban activities unrelated to the surrounding rural villages. However, development of a majority of the centers in the six English counties—as of those in the nine Wisconsin counties—is closely linked with satisfaction of the needs of rural people.

Working independently, the writers of this paper arranged the centers of their respective survey areas in order of importance. Each identified a group of higher-order centers, though no abrupt break in functions or facilities was recognizable. One out of every five centers in Wisconsin, and one out of three centers in the English

10 For a summary of sociological methodology see C. P. Loomis and J. A. Beegle, *Rural Social Systems* (New York, 1950). For other approaches to the problems of centrality see J. H. Kolb and LeR. J. Day, *Interdependence in Town and Country Relations* (University of Wisconsin Agricultural Experiment Station Research Bull. 172 [1950]); and Rutledge Vining, "Delimitation of Economic Areas: Statistical Conceptions in the Study of the Spatial Structure of an Economic System," *Journal of the American Statistical Association,* XLVIII (1953), 44–64.

area, appeared to belong to a higher order of centrality.

It is clear that significant differences of function exist and that a given type of retail store or specialized service may develop in one country and not in the other. Certain aspects of service function may pertain to higher-order centers in one country and to lower-order centers in the other. A differentiating feature of the higher-order centers in England is their development as shopping centers. More villages depend on the higher-order centers for shopping (retailing of clothing, household goods, and various specialized types of consumers' goods) than for professions (medical services and supplies and banking). The second group appears to be fairly well represented in the towns of the lower order. Although Wisconsin towns are also well developed as retail shopping centers, medical and other professional services, except schools, and entertainment are infrequently found in villages. As a result, rural residents in southwestern Wisconsin must go to town for specialized commodities except automotive equipment, lumber, and hardware and farm equipment, and for all services except banking and secondary schooling.

## THE SPATIAL PATTERN OF THE HIERARCHY

In order to demonstrate clearly the existence of higher and lower orders, it is necessary to analyze the distribution of rural centers and their areas. Figures 1 and 2 reveal for Wisconsin and England parallel patterns in spacing, service areas, and arrangement of higher- and lower-order centers (Table 1). Similarities in the distribution patterns can be summarized as follows:

1. Higher-order centers occur at a mean distance of 21 miles from one another in both areas.

2. Lower-order centers occur at a mean distance of 10 mlies from one another or from centers of a higher order in Wisconsin and a mean of 8 miles in England.

3. Higher-order centers have service areas of 129 and 128 square miles in Wisconsin and England respectively; lower-order centers have service areas of 32 and 48 square miles respectively.

4. Higher-order centers tend to form clusters or tiers with few or no centers of lower order close to them.

5. Lower-order centers tend to form rows or

served by towns or cities whose rural service functions are too unimportant for them to be ranked with the seventy towns studied. Some of this unassigned territory is served by centers of a third and lower order, which in Wisconsin corresponds to hamlets and in England can be described as service villages. Centers of this third or-

TABLE 1

AVERAGE POPULATION, SERVICE AREAS, AND INTERCENTER DISTANCES
SOUTHWESTERN WISCONSIN AND SOUTHERN ENGLAND*

| | HIGHER-ORDER CENTERS | | LOWER-ORDER CENTERS | |
| --- | --- | --- | --- | --- |
| | 19 Towns, SW. Wisconsin | 26 Higher Dist. Centers, S. England | 73 Villages, SW. Wisconsin | 44 Lower Dist. Centers, S. England |
| Median population† | 2,515 | 13,850 | 400 | 5,080 |
| Mean population | 3,330 | 25,950 | 480 | 12,425 |
| Mean size of service areas (sq. mi.) | 129 | 128 | 32 | 48 |
| Mean population of service areas | 2,440 | 21,080 | 610 | 7,180 |
| Mean intercenter distance (mi.) | 21 | 21 | 10 | 8 |

* The data for southwestern Wisconsin apply only to the area west of Madison, excluding eastern Dane County and part of eastern Green County (see map, *Geographical Review*, XLIII [1953], 381, Fig. 1). The service area of a center is the territory clearly demonstrated by analysis of traffic flow to be dependent for services on that town or village; the ill-defined borders of transition from one service area to another are not included. The service area of a center in southern England is the territory that includes all villages using the center for at least three out of four of the following groups of services: shopping, medical supplies and services, business professions, and entertainment. There is overlapping of certain adjacent service areas; there is also territory unassigned because the villages are served by very small or very large centers, not belonging in either of the two orders considered here.

† The medians of population provide a better basis for comparison than the means because of the existence of a few large centers in southern England, which unduly weight the means.

belts hemmed in by the service areas of higher-order centers and crowded close to one another with their smaller service areas.

Intercenter distances would be similar in both areas if the centers were spaced hexagonally,[11] but the parallels in actual geographic patterns are more significant than this theoretical similarity. The significant features of the spatial patterns which appear in both countries are that the higher-order centers have larger service areas and that the lower-order centers exist only in the regions beyond 8–10 miles from the higher-order centers and not even there if the higher-order centers are as close to one another as 10–12 miles. The map of southern England (Fig. 2) shows overlapping of areas served by competing centers. It also shows certain territories not clearly under the influence of centers of either order but

[11] If the seventy rural service centers in the six English counties were spaced at equal distances in a perfect hexagonal pattern, they would be 10.7 miles apart. In the part of southwestern Wisconsin west of Madison (see the *Geographical Review*, XLIII [1953], 381, Fig. 1), the ninety-two centers of village or town rank would be 10.0 miles apart if spaced in a perfect hexagonal pattern. The formula used in these computations, given in the *Geographical Review*, XLIII (1953), 393, Table II, footnote *a*, should read as follows:

$$D = 1.07\sqrt{\frac{A}{n}}$$

where $D$ is the distance between the centers, $A$ is the total area within which the centers are dispersed, and $n$ is the number of centers. The formula calls for nothing more than the square root of the density of centers within the area multiplied by a constant factor and should not be considered as giving a true measurement of scattering or dispersion. Certain errors in the expression of this formula in the citation above were kindly pointed out by Dr. Clyde P. Patton of the Department of Geography, Syracuse University, Syracuse, New York.

der occur in Somerset at intervals of 4–6 miles from one another or from a center of a higher order.[12] In Wisconsin they occur at intervals of 5–6 miles. The hamlets in Wisconsin are found chiefly in the transitional territories, left blank on the map (Fig. 1), between the well-defined service areas dominated by higher-order centers. The people residing in these transitional territories are dependent on the nearest villages or towns for all except the rudimentary services provided by the hamlets. Service relationships are much more complex in the suburban fringe surrounding Madison and in the lake region extending southward in Dane County toward Stoughton.

## POPULATION AND CENTRALITY

These parallels in spatial hierarchy are clear, though the resident population of centers in both orders is much larger in England (Table 1). Towns in southwestern Wisconsin have a median population only one-fifth that of the higher-order centers in southern England. The latter show a ratio of about six persons in the center to five persons in the service area, as compared with seven to five in southwestern Wisconsin. Thus it would seem that the larger town population in England correlates with the higher density of rural population. The median population of villages in southwestern Wisconsin is less than one-tenth as large as that of their English counterparts. Again, this is in accord with the higher density of population in the service areas in England.

Terms denoting size and rank in the hierarchy in the two countries cannot be used interchangeably. A village of 370 in southwestern Wisconsin, such as Barneveld, is a service center for some 600 persons living on farms within a radius of 4–6 miles. This village is analogous in the hierarchy

to a small country town in England, such as Castle Cary, with 2,180 inhabitants, which serves the needs of ten or a dozen villages within a radius of 4–6 miles, each with several hundred inhabitants. A well-developed town of about 4,600 in southwestern Wisconsin, such as Richland Center, serving some 4,000 people in the rural territory as far as 10–15 miles around is a small town by English standards. Although the English center of Salisbury in Wiltshire, with 32,900 inhabitants, does not serve a larger rural territory, fifty-four villages, with an aggregate rural population of more than 24,000 persons, depend on it for a majority of their ordinary goods and services.

## EVOLUTION OF SERVICE CENTERS

The fact that close agricultural settlement has existed in southern England for 1,500 years does not seem to have led to any significant difference in the spacing of service centers as they appear today in the two countries, though only 100–125 years have elapsed since the time of agricultural settlement in Wisconsin. Indeed, in certain respects there has been a parallel evolution of centers. During medieval times there were market towns in southern England, spaced at intervals of 4–6 miles, that served as rudimentary trade centers, accessible by cart roads from the rural villages within an hour's journey.[13] Many English villages are vestigial service centers once of a higher order. In the early nineteenth century, before the coming of railways and automotive vehicles, hamlets also developed in Wisconsin at intervals of 5–6 miles and served as rudimentary trade centers for the farmers living a journey-hour away by wagon roads.

Railway construction in the late nineteenth century had a marked effect in stimulating the growth of trade centers in Wisconsin. The effect of railways was less noticeable in England, but the improvement of roads and the spread of bus services since 1920 appear to have had much

---

[12] Dickinson found that there are "small towns" with 1,000–2,000 population in East Anglia, spaced at about four-mile intervals (R. E. Dickinson, *City Region and Regionalism* [London, 1947], pp. 87–89).

[13] A journey-hour on foot or by cart, traveling at the rate of 3 miles an hour.

the same effect in the growth of large towns as the improvement of roads and the spread of private automobile transportation have had in Wisconsin. Development of professional services, banking, and entertainment in Wisconsin has been concentrated in the centers of higher order more than in southern England. This may reflect differences in the relative ease of movement in the two countries. Few English workingmen own private cars. Travel by bus increases the journey time and adds to the general inconvenience of a trip to town; this tends to reduce the length and frequency of journey. On the other hand, the persistence of services in lower-order centers may indicate a conservatism on the part of the English— a reluctance to withdraw their patronage from the business people who have served their fathers and grandfathers in satisfying their more personal needs. Some medieval market towns in England continue as service villages just as in Wisconsin the hamlets survive as relict trade centers.

## SOME CONCLUSIONS

The fact that analogous geographic patterns have developed in these two widely separated rural territories suggests that the spatial hierarchy of central places is related to distance factors that have a dominant influence in areas of low relief and fairly uniform rural population distribution, despite differences in population density, economic functions, and social or political institutions. The fact that rudimentary centers developed at about six-mile intervals in both areas during the time of primitive transportation leads to the conclusion that the basic distance factor was the time and effort required to get to any trade center by cart or on foot. The effect of railways was much more significant in Wisconsin than in England because rural settlement and agriculture were still undergoing rapid evolution in the last half of the nineteenth century. The similar effects of automotive vehicles and improved roads in the twentieth century are perhaps unexpected. Although the functional hierarchy is certainly much more variable from place to place and year to year than the rigid system first described by Christaller,[14] it is probable that the spatial relationships observed in Wisconsin and England hold true throughout most of the closely settled parts of northwestern Europe.[15] There is need for further comparative analysis of the hierarchy in the countries of eastern and southern Europe and in various parts of the United States in order to determine the limits of variability. There is need also to extend the testing of the principles tentatively presented here to other regions of European settlement such as the British Dominions and Latin America and to regions of non-European settlement in Africa and Asia.

[14] Walter Christaller, *Die zentralen Orte in Süddeutschland* (Jena, 1933).

[15] See the studies reviewed by J. E. Brush, "The Urban Hierarchy in Europe," *Geographical Review*, XLIII (1953), 414–16. Other recent work along these lines in Europe has been published by Hans Carol ("Industrie und Siedlungsplanung," *Plan: Schweizerische Zeitschrift für Landes-, Regional- und Ortsplanung*, VIII [1951], 191–206) ; "Die Entwicklung der Stadt Zürich zur Metropole der Schweiz," *Geographische Rundschau*, V [1953], 304–7), by Karlheinz Hottes ("Die zentralen Orte im oberbergischen Lande," *Forschungen zur Deutschen Landeskunde*, LXIX [1954]), and by Rudolf Klöpper ("Entstehung, Lage und Verteilung der zentralen Siedlungen in Niedersachsen," *Forschungen zur Deutschen Landeskunde*, LXXI [1952]; "Der Einzugsbereich einer Kreisstadt," *Raumforschung und Raumordnung*, XI [1953], 73–81).

BRIAN J. L. BERRY and WILLIAM L. GARRISON

# THE FUNCTIONAL BASES OF THE CENTRAL-PLACE HIERARCHY

It is obvious that urban centers differ, each from others. On the intuitive level one notion of difference is that of classes of urban centers. The wealth of descriptive terms available illustrates this notion: hamlet, village, town, city, metropolis, and the like. The present study is concerned with this problem of the differentiation of centers into broad classes. In particular it provides original and urgent evidence that a system of urban center classes exists of the type identified on an intuitive level above.

There are several reasons for producing evidence of a system of classes (hereafter termed the hierarchical class-system) at this time. A considerable body of theory relating to city size, function, and arrangement has accumulated. One of the implications of this theory is that there exists a hierarchical class-system.[1] Ample evidence is available that other implications of this theory are valid, namely, that larger centers are functionally more complex than smaller centers, with this increasing functional complexity being accompanied by increasing size of the urban complementary region,[2] and that by virtue of the differen-

Reprinted from *Economic Geography*, XXXIV (April, 1958), 145–54, by permission of the authors and the editor. (Copyright, 1958, by Clark University, Worcester, Mass.)

[1] Walter Christaller, *Die zentralen Orte in Süddeutschland* (Jena, 1933), trans. C. Baskin at the Bureau of Population and Urban Research, University of Virginia, 1954; and August Lösch, *Die räumliche Ordnung der Wirtschaft* (Jena, 1944), trans. W. H. Woglom and W. F. Stolper as *The Economics of Location* (New Haven, 1954). The works of Christaller and Lösch are related in Brian J. L. Berry, "Geographic Aspects of the Size and Arrangement of Urban Centers" (M.A. thesis, Department of Geography, University of Washington, 1956). See also Walter Isard, *Location and Space Economy* (New York, 1956).

tial provision of central functions there is interdependence between urban centers in the provision of central goods and services.[3] On the other hand, there has been no satisfactory evidence provided that would suggest that a hierarchical class-system of centers does indeed exist.

Despite many attempts at the assignment of towns to classes or grades[4] the converse has seemed to be more likely. The a priori methods used by most of the studies have led to serious doubts as to

[2] W. J. Reilly, *Methods of the Study of Retail Relationships* (University of Texas Bull. 2944 [1929]); *idem, The Law of Retail Gravitation* (New York, 1931).

[3] C. J. Galpin, *Social Anatomy of an Agricultural Community* (University of Wisconsin Agricultural Experiment Station Research Bull. 34 [1915]); see also A. E. Smailes, "The Urban Hierarchy in England and Wales," *Geography*, XXIX and XXX (1944), 41–51; *idem,* "The Urban Mesh of England and Wales," *Institute of British Geographers, Transactions and Papers*, 1946, pp. 85–101.

[4] An extensive bibliography appears in Berry, *op. cit.* Some of the better-known works are John E. Brush, "The Hierarchy of Central Places in Southwestern Wisconsin," *Geographical Review*, XLIII (1953), 380–402; H. E. Bracey, "Towns as Rural Service Centres," *Institute of British Geographers, Transactions and Papers*, XIX (1953), 95–105; *idem,* "A Rural Component of Centrality Applied to Six Southern Counties of the United Kingdom," *Economic Geography*, XXXII (1956), 38–50; Galpin, *op. cit.;* Sven Godlund, *Bus Services, Hinterlands and the Location of Urban Settlements in Scania.* ("Lund Studies in Geography," Series B, "Human Geography," Vol. III, 1951); H. Carter, "Urban Grades and Spheres of Influence in South West Wales," *Scottish Geographical Magazine*, LXXI (1955), 43–56; R. E. Dickinson, "The Distribution and Functions of the Smaller Urban Settlements of East Anglia," *Geography*, XVII (1932), 19–31. Also see the very appropriate comments of H. C. Carter, "The Urban Hierarchy and Historical Geography: A Consideration with Reference to North-East Wales," *Geographic Studies*, III (1956), 85–101.

whether a class-system is present in other than arbitrary form, and to the alternate idea that perhaps instead of a class-system there only exists differentiation along a continuum.[5] Vining, for example, has written about the single best-known empirical study of the central-place hierarchy, that of John E. Brush:[6]

> There is no evidence . . . that exactly three natural partitions may be observed in this array of numbers of establishments. . . . The terms hamlet, village, and town are convenient modes of expression; but they do not refer to structurally distinct natural entities. . . . Clearly, it is arbitrary to divide the array into three partitions rather than into a greater or lesser number; and similarly arbitrary is the determination of where to put the dividing points separating the different classes or types. Having drawn the lines, one may list certain kinds of activities which are typically found within each of the designated classes of center, . . . not all members of a class will contain all the activities listed and most of the communities within a class will contain activities not listed. [This] . . . is not an independently derived basis for a classification of communities by type. Rather it is itself derived from a previous partitioning of an array which appears as something similar to an arrangement of observations that have been made upon a continuous variable.[7]

These criticisms of Brush's study may well be valid. That he used an arbitrary division and then proved what he had in fact assumed is without question (this criticism applies to more studies of central places than is generally realized).[8] The ensuing discussion serves to disprove the implication which Vining drew from this fact, that central places are differentiated along a continuum rather than in a class-system.

The finding of a hierarchical class-system verifies implications of theory and thus performs one classic function of empirical research in the accretion of knowledge. In the present case the need for the performance of this classic function is quite pressing because alternate theories are available to explain characteristics of systems of cities.[9] To the extent that verification is provided for previously unverified schemes, the present study increases the attractiveness of these schemes versus more recent schemes which do not include hierarchical concepts. It might be added that the present study provides examples of taxonomic methods for the empirical study of the hierarchical class-system and these methods may be found useful in ensuing studies; it was designed as a *critical study* which may be checked in the study area (Snohomish County, Washington) and which is capable of being reproduced by the methods provided in other areas and at levels of the central-place hierarchy other than the universe of small centers considered in the present case.

## THE HIERARCHICAL CONCEPT

The hierarchical class-system implication is an integral part of the spatial model of central places developed by Walter Christaller,[10] the generic base and single most important statement of central place theory. The model states that central places belong to one or another of class subsets. Each class possesses specific groups of central functions and is characterized by a discrete population level of its centers. Note that (1) classes are arranged one to another in a hierarchy such that the central places of functionally more complex classes possess all the groups of functions of less complex classes plus a group of function differentiating them from the central

[5] Rutledge Vining, "A Description of Certain Spatial Aspects of an Economic System," *Econimic Development and Cultural Change*, III (1955), 147–95.

[6] Brush, *op. cit.*

[7] Vining, *op. cit.*, pp. 167–69.

[8] See, for example, Carter, *op. cit.*; Smailes, *op. cit.*

[9] Brian J. L. Berry and William L. Garrison, "Alternate Explanations of Urban Rank-Size Relationships," *Annals of the Association of American Geographers*, XLVIII (March, 1958), 83–91; N. Rashevsky, *Mathematical Theory of Human Relations* (Bloomington, 1947); and H. A. Simon, "On a Class of Skew Distribution Functions," *Biometrika*, XLII (1955), 425–40.

[10] Christaller, *op. cit.*

places of less complex classes, and (2) discrete population levels of the central places of each class are thought to arise because the income which supports the population of a central place is brought into the center by the activities which provide goods and services for surrounding consumers. Since the central places of each class possess discrete groups of activities, they also tend to have discrete population levels.

TABLE 1

CLASSES OF CENTRAL PLACES AND ASSOCIATED GROUPINGS OF CENTRAL FUNCTIONS IN SNOHOMISH COUNTY, WASHINGTON

| CENTRAL FUNCTIONS | CLASSES OF CENTRAL PLACES | | |
|---|---|---|---|
| | A* | B | C |
| *Variates:* | | | |
| Group $1_1$....... | $p$† | $f$ | $f$ |
| Group $2_1$....... | ......... | $p$ | $f$ |
| Group $3_1$....... | ......... | $s$ | $f$ |
| *Attributes:* | | | |
| General store.... | $p$ | ............... | ............... |
| Group $1_2$....... | $s$ | $p$ | $f$ |
| Group $2_2$....... | ......... | $p$ | $f$ |
| Group $3_2$....... | ......... | $s$ | $p$ |

\* A Class A center, for example, provides a partial range of functions of group $1_1$, a few of the functions of group $1_2$, and most, although not all, of the centers will have general stores.

† $p$—partial range; $f$—full range; $s$—some.

## AN OBSERVED HIERARCHY OF CENTRAL PLACES

Evidence is provided here that a hierarchy of central places does exist. In Snohomish County, Washington, the area in which the present study was undertaken, it was found that centers could be arranged into three types, called A, B, and C (Table 1). These three types were defined on the basis of the presence of urban functions $1_1$, $1_2$, . . . , etc., in varying degrees. In other words, in Snohomish County it was found to be possible to treat central places taxonomically and derive center types A, B, and C (say, hamlets, villages and towns, respectively) on a functional basis. It was shown that these center types differ more

one type from another than they differ within types.

The data utilized involved thirty-three of the smaller central places of the county (Fig. 1). Since the present study was in the interest of expediency limited to small central places, excluded from the field survey was the largest center in the county, Everett. Several of the smaller communities on the northern and southern margins of the county were also excluded. Reasons for the exclusion of these centers, an elaboration of the data used in the study, and relevant maps of the travel patterns of the rural residents to the central places are available elsewhere.[11]

Of the thirty-three centers studied, twenty were of Class A, which contains the lowest complex of central functions; nine were of Class B; and four were of Class C, which contains the most complex grouping of functions. In these centers considered in toto it was possible to recognize sixty-three kinds of central functions (in addition four non-central functions and other characteristics of the centers were included within the study).[12] These could be differentiated into seven classes of functions (three and four classes in each of the broad groups, respectively), distinguished in terms of the hierarchical concept.

This preliminary summary of the data is at best quite gross. Any discussion of the exact nature of the hierarchy requires an elaboration of the functional classes and the classes of centers, and a clarification of what is meant by "some," a "partial range," and a "full range" of central func-

[11] William L. Garrison, *The Benefits of Rural Roads to Rural Property* (Seattle, 1956), pp. 35–36; and R. G. Hennes, B. O. Wheeler, and W. L. Garrison, "Washington State Highway Impact Studies," *Highway Research Board Proceedings,* 1957.

[12] These four non-central functions or other characteristics of the centers are whether the settlement is an incorporated city and whether it possesses a water supply system, a sewage disposal system, or an office of an electricity distribution system.

tions. Too, it is necessary to detail the evidence on which the study is based, both to verify the viability of the classes and, because the classes evolve directly from the evidence, to establish the characteristics of the classification. The ensuing discussion provides this elaboration.

It will be noted that in the above paragraphs the hierarchical class-system of centers was assumed to follow from the class-system of functions. The assumption is derived from the implications of theory. A further note on this notion is included in the ensuing parts of the study.

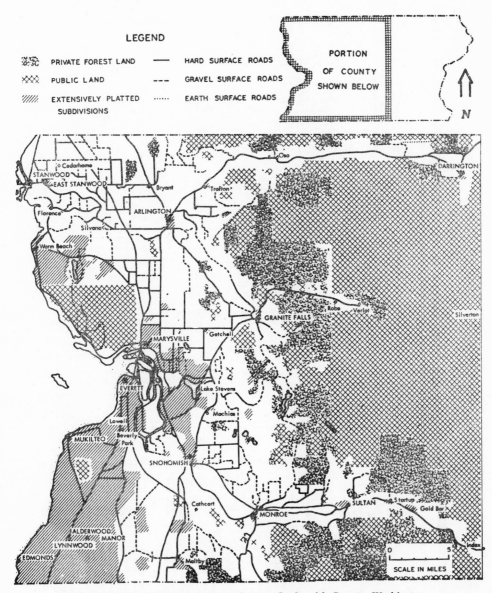

LEGEND

🎯 PRIVATE FOREST LAND    —— HARD SURFACE ROADS

✕✕✕ PUBLIC LAND    --- GRAVEL SURFACE ROADS

▨ EXTENSIVELY PLATTED    ······ EARTH SURFACE ROADS
       SUBDIVISIONS

PORTION OF COUNTY SHOWN BELOW

N

Fig. 1.—Locational features of the study area, Snohomish County, Washington

TABLE 2

## The Functional Bases of Classes of Central Places in Snohomish County: Variates

Columns are grouped by class: **A** (Verlot through Lake Stevens), **B** (Alderwood Manor through Edmonds), **C** (Monroe, Arlington, Snohomish, Marysville).

| Central Functions | Threshold Population | B-Value | Verlot | Silverton | Trafton | Florence | Getchell | Robe | Bryant | Cedarhome | Oso | Maltby | Cathcart | Machias | Index | Warm Beach | Startup | Gold Bar | Silvana | Lowell | Beverly Park | Lake Stevens | Alderwood Manor | Granite Falls | Darrington | Mukilteo | Sultan | Lynnwood | East Stanwood | Stanwood | Edmonds | Monroe | Arlington | Snohomish | Marysville |
|---|---|---|---|---|---|---|---|---|---|---|---|---|---|---|---|---|---|---|---|---|---|---|---|---|---|---|---|---|---|---|---|---|---|---|---|
| Population | | | 20 | 15 | 25 | 300 | 25 | 50 | 150 | 100 | 200 | 700 | 175 | 200 | 220 | 314 | 300 | 325 | 300 | 1600 | 725 | 2586 | 600 | 600 | 974 | 900 | 850 | 500 | 390 | 720 | 2996 | 1684 | 1915 | 3494 | 2460 |
| Number of Activities | | | 1 | 2 | 2 | 2 | 3 | 3 | 3 | 4 | 4 | 4 | 5 | 5 | 6 | 6 | 8 | 9 | 10 | 12 | 13 | 16 | 22 | 25 | 25 | 28 | 34 | 36 | 38 | 42 | 42 | 56 | 59 | 62 | 64 |
| 1 { Filling stations | 196 | 1.35 | 1 | 1 | | 1 | 1 | 1 | 1 | 1 | 2 | 2 | 1 | 2 | | 1 | 2 | 1 | 1 | 1 | 1 | 3 | 4 | 4 | 3 | 3 | 6 | 9 | 3 | 4 | 7 | 8 | 6 | 3 | 9 |
| Food stores | 254 | 1.74 | | | | | | | 1 | | | 1 | | | | | 2 | 2 | 2 | 1 | | 2 | 3 | 3 | 2 | 1 | 3 | 3 | 3 | 2 | 6 | 6 | 4 | 6 | 5 |
| Churches | 265 | 1.29 | | 1 | | | | 1 | | | | | 1 | | | 1 | 2 | | 1 | 1 | 1 | 2 | 3 | 3 | 2 | 1 | 3 | 3 | 2 | 2 | 8 | 8 | 9 | 17 | 5 |
| Restaurants | 276 | 1.33 | | | 1 | | | 1 | | 1 | 1 | 1 | 1 | | | | 2 | 4 | | 1 | | 1 | 2 | 2 | 2 | 1 | 4 | 3 | 2 | 2 | 8 | 6 | 9 | 7 | 14 |
| Taverns | 282 | 1.65 | | | | 1 | | | 1 | 1 | | 1 | | | | 1 | 1 | 1 | 1 | 2 | 1 | 2 | 2 | 2 | 3 | 1 | 3 | 3 | 3 | 2 | 5 | 5 | 3 | 7 | 2 |
| Elementary schools | 322 | 1.67 | | | 1 | | 1 | | | 1 | 1 | 1 | 1 | 1 | | 1 | 1 | 1 | 1 | 1 | 1 | 1 | 1 | 1 | 1 | 1 | 1 | 1 | 1 | 3 | 1 | 2 | 4 | 6 | 6 |
| Physicians | 380 | 1.42 | | | | | | | | | | | | | | | | | | | | 3 | | 1 | 1 | | 1 | 1 | 1 | | 5 | 3 | | 5 | 3 |
| Real estate agencies | 384 | 1.40 | | | | | | | | | | | | | | | | | | | | | 2 | | | 1 | | 1 | 1 | 2 | | 2 | 3 | 7 | 6 |
| Appliance stores | 385 | 1.46 | | | | | | | | 1 | | | | | | 1 | | 1 | 2 | 1 | 1 | 2 | 1 | 1 | 2 | 2 | 1 | 6 | 1 | 2 | 4 | 2 | 4 | 10 | 2 |
| Barber shops | 386 | 2.39 | | | | | | | | | | | | | | | | | | | | 1 | | | 1 | | 1 | 1 | 1 | 1 | 2 | 1 | 1 | 4 | 4 |
| Auto dealers | 398 | 1.35 | | | | | | | | | | | | | | | 1 | 4 | 1 | 1 | | 2 | 2 | 1 | 1 | 1 | 1 | 1 | 1 | 2 | 4 | 3 | 2 | 3 | 2 |
| Insurance agencies | 409 | 1.32 | | | | | | | | | | | | | | | | | | 1 | | | | 1 | | 1 | 1 | 1 | 2 | 1 | 4 | 4 | 10 | 10 | |
| Bulk oil distributors | 419 | 1.56 | | | | | | | | | | | | | | | 1 | 1 | | | 1 | 1 | 1 | 1 | 3 | 1 | 2 | 2 | 4 | 2 | 4 | 4 | 1 | 5 | 6 |
| Dentists | 426 | 1.57 | | | | | | | | | | | | | | | | | | | | | | | 1 | | | 1 | 3 | 1 | 3 | 3 | 1 | 5 | 1 |
| Motels | 430 | 1.56 | | | | | | | | | | | | | 1 | | | | | | | | | 1 | 3 | | | 1 | 1 | | 5 | 2 | 5 | 3 | 6 |
| Hardware stores | 431 | 1.90 | | | | | | | | | | | 1 | | 1 | 1 | | 1 | | 1 | 1 | | 2 | 1 | 1 | 1 | 1 | 1 | 1 | 1 | 1 | 4 | 4 | 6 | 2 |
| Auto repair shops | 435 | 1.72 | | | | | | | | | | | | | 1 | | | | | | | 1 | 1 | 1 | 3 | 1 | 2 | 3 | 1 | 1 | 5 | 4 | 2 | 6 | 6 |
| 2 { Fuel dealers (coal, etc.) | 453 | 1.78 | | | | | | | | | | | | | 1 | | | | | | | | 2 | 1 | 1 | 1 | 2 | 1 | 2 | 1 | 3 | 1 | 4 | 2 | 2 |
| Drug stores | 458 | 2.23 | | | | | | | | | | | | | | | | | | 1 | | 1 | 1 | 1 | | 1 | 1 | 1 | 1 | 2 | 4 | 1 | 1 | 3 | 4 |
| Beauticians | 480 | 1.89 | | | | | | | | | | | | | | | | | | | | 1 | 1 | 1 | | 1 | 1 | 3 | 1 | 1 | 3 | 4 | 4 | 3 | 1 |
| Auto parts dealers | 488 | 1.94 | | | | | | | | | | | | | | | | 1 | | | 1 | | 2 | 1 | 1 | 1 | 1 | 1 | 1 | 2 | 4 | 4 | 1 | 3 | 1 |
| Meeting halls | 525 | 2.01 | | | | 1 | 1 | | | 1 | | 1 | | | 1 | 1 | | | | | | | | | | | | 4 | | | 2 | 4 | 2 | 2 | 1 |
| Animal feed stores | 526 | 1.79 | | | | | | | | | | | | | | | | | | | | | 1 | | 3 | | 2 | 4 | 2 | | 4 | 1 | 1 | 2 | 1 |
| Lawyers | 528 | 2.12 | | | | | | | | | | | | | | | | | | | | | | | | | 1 | 1 | | | 2 | 4 | 2 | 3 | 1 |
| Furniture stores, etc. | 546 | 1.85 | | | | | 1 | | | | | | 1 | | | 1 | | 1 | | | 1 | 1 | 1 | | 1 | | 1 | 4 | 1 | 1 | 2 | 2 | 1 | 3 | 2 |
| Variety stores: 5 & 10 | 549 | 2.30 | | | | | | | | | | | | | | | | | | | | | 1 | 1 | 1 | | 1 | 4 | 2 | 1 | 4 | 1 | 2 | 3 | 4 |
| Freight lines & storage | 567 | 2.04 | | | | | | | | | | | | | | | | | | | | 1 | | 1 | 2 | | 1 | 1 | 1 | 1 | 4 | 3 | 2 | 3 | 4 |

TABLE 2—Continued

CENTRAL PLACES

| | | | A | | | | | | | | | | | | | | | | | | | | | B | | | | | | | | | C | | | |
|---|---|---|---|---|---|---|---|---|---|---|---|---|---|---|---|---|---|---|---|---|---|---|---|---|---|---|---|---|---|---|---|---|---|---|---|---|
| CENTRAL FUNCTIONS | B-VALUE | THRESHOLD POPULATION | Verlot | Silverton | Trafton | Florence | Getchell | Robe | Bryant | Cedarhome | Oso | Maltby | Cathcart | Machias | Index | Warm Beach | Startup | Gold Bar | Silvana | Lowell | Beverly Park | Lake Stevens | Alderwood Manor | Granite Falls | Darrington | Mukilteo | Sultan | Lynnwood | East Stanwood | Stanwood | Edmonds | Monroe | Arlington | Snohomish | Marysville |
| Population | | | 20 | 15 | 25 | 300 | 25 | 50 | 150 | 100 | 200 | 700 | 175 | 200 | 220 | 314 | 300 | 325 | 300 | 1600 | 725 | 2586 | 600 | 600 | 974 | 900 | 850 | 500 | 390 | 720 | 2996 | 1684 | 1915 | 3494 | 2460 |
| Number of Activities | | | 1 | 2 | 2 | 2 | 3 | 3 | 3 | 4 | 4 | 4 | 5 | 5 | 6 | 6 | 8 | 9 | 10 | 12 | 13 | 16 | 22 | 25 | 25 | 28 | 34 | 36 | 38 | 42 | 42 | 56 | 59 | 62 | 64 |
| Veterinaries | 1.97 | 579 | | | | | | | | 1 | | | | | | | | | | | | | 1 | | 1 | 1 | 1 | | 2 | 1 | | 1 | 3 | 1 | 1 |
| Apparel stores | 2.53 | 590 | | | | | | | | | | | | | | | | | | | | | | | | | | | 2 | 1 | 2 | 2 | 1 | 3 | 3 |
| Lumber yards & woodworking | 2.49 | 598 | | | | | | | | | | | | | | 1 | 1 | | | 1 | | 1 | 1 | 1 | 1 | 1 | 1 | 3 | 1 | 1 | 1 | 1 | 1 | 1 | 1 |
| Banks | 2.05 | 610 | | | | | | | | | | | | | | | | | | | | 1 | | 1 | 1 | | 1 | 1 | 1 | 2 | 2 | 1 | 2 | 1 | 1 |
| Farm implement dealers | 1.95 | 650 | | | | | | | | | | | | | | | | | | | | | | | | | | 3 | | 2 | 1 | 1 | 2 | 1 | 1 |
| Electric repair shops | 2.62 | 693 | | | | | | | | | | | | | | | | | | | 1 | 1 | | | | 1 | 1 | 1 | 1 | 1 | 2 | 3 | 2 | 1 | 1 |
| Florists | 2.40 | 729 | | | | | | | | | | | | | | | | | | | | | | 1 | | 2 | | 1 | 1 | 1 | 3 | 2 | 2 | 2 | 2 |
| High schools | 3.64 | 732 | | | | | | | | | | | | | | | | | | | | | 1 | 1 | 1 | 1 | 1 | 2 | | 1 | 2 | 1 | 1 | 1 | 1 |
| Dry cleaners | 3.56 | 754 | | | | | | | | | | | | | | | | | | | | 1 | | | | | | | | | | 2 | 2 | 1 | 2 |
| Local taxi services | 2.89 | 762 | | | | | | | | | | | | | | | | | | | | | 1 | 1 | | | 1 | | 1 | 1 | 1 | 2 | 1 | 1 | 1 |
| Billiard hall & bowling alleys | 2.56 | 789 | | | | | | | | | | | | | | | | | | | | | 1 | | | 1 | 1 | 1 | | 1 | 3 | 1 | 1 | 2 | 1 |
| Jewelry stores | 3.26 | 827 | | | | | | | | | | | | | | | | | | | | | | | | | | | | | | | | | 1 |
| Hotels | 2.92 | 846 | | | | | | | | | | | | | | | | | | | | 1 | | | | 1 | | 1 | | | | 1 | 1 | 1 | 1 |
| Shoe repair shops | 2.45 | 896 | | | | | | | | | | | | | | | | | | | | | 1 | 1 | | 1 | 1 | | | 1 | 1 | 1 | 2 | 1 | 1 |
| Sporting goods stores | 3.30 | 928 | | | | | | | | | | | | | | | | | | | | | | | | | | | | | | 2 | | | 1 |
| Frozen food lockers | 2.99 | 938 | | | | | | | | | | | | | | | | | | | | | | | | 1 | | 1 | 1 | 1 | | 1 | 2 | 1 | 2 |
| Sheet metal works | 3.80 | 1076 | | | | | | | | | | | | | | | | | | | | | | | | | | | | | | 1 | 2 | 1 | 1 |
| Department stores | 4.50 | 1083 | | | | | | | | | | | | | | | | | | | | | | | | 1 | | 1 | 1 | | 1 | 1 | 2 | 1 | 1 |
| Optometrists | 3.88 | 1140 | | | | | | | | | | | | | | | | | | | | | | | | 1 | 1 | 1 | | 1 | | | 1 | 1 | 1 |
| Hospital and clinics | 3.77 | 1159 | | | | | | | | | | | | | | | | | | | | | | | | | | | | | | | 2 | 1 | 1 |
| Undertakers | 4.19 | 1214 | | | | | | | | | | | | | | | | | | | | | | | | 1 | | 1 | | | 2 | 2 | 2 | 1 | 1 |
| Photographers | 4.56 | 1243 | | | | | | | | | | | | | | | | | | | | | | | | | | | | | | 1 | 1 | 1 | 1 |
| Public accountants | 4.11 | 1300 | | | | | | | | | | | | | | | | | | | | | | | | | | | | 1 | | | 1 | 1 | 1 |
| Laundries and laundromats | 4.66 | 1307 | | | | | | | | | | | | | | | | | | | 1 | | | | | 1 | | 1 | | 1 | | | 2 | 2 | 1 |
| Health practitioners | 4.55 | 1424 | | | | | | | | | | | | | | | | | | | | | | | | 1 | | 1 | | 1 | 1 | | | 2 | 1 |

223

## The Analysis

The problem before us was to determine whether central functions fall into groups of classes and, if so, whether these classes were associated with classes of central places, as theory suggests they ought to be. Therefore, the initial step in the research was to rank both central functions and central places. The second step was to apply tests to determine whether groupings occurred and, if so, to discover whether there were significant differences between the groupings isolated.

### Ranking the Central Functions

Fifty-two of the central functions were variates—that is, numbers of stores performing these functions varied from place to place. The remaining functions and other characteristics considered in the study were attributes—that is, central places either possessed a unit performing this function or did not possess such a unit. The method of ranking varied between these two sets.

*Variates.*—Previous empirical studies indicated that relationships exist between the population of a central place and the number of units of any function which that place possesses and this is, of course, clear from common knowledge.[13] Christaller suggested that through the working of the income mechanism the population of a center was a function of the number of types of central goods and services the central place provided.[14] Hence it was specified that the population of a center is a function of the number of stores of each type. Fifty-two scatter diagrams were prepared with population, $P$, and number of stores, $N$, as parameters to determine the relationships between $P$ and $N$ for each function. Each of the diagrams had thirty-three points, one for each of the thirty-three central places. Best-fitting curves of the exponential growth series $P = A (B^N)$, where $A$ and $B$

are the parameters to be estimated, were fitted to each of the scatters using standard least squares techniques, after logarithmic conversion.

Given these 52 best relationships it was then possible to rank the central functions on the basis of the threshold population of the center which was necessary for the first complete store to appear, that is, by the value of $P$ where $N = 1$ (Table 2).

*Attributes.*—Relationships between the fifteen attributes and the populations of the centers in which they appear were determined by calculating the point biserial coefficient of correlation between each of the activities and the population of the centers. Activities were then ranked in ascending order of these coefficients, $r_{pb}$, since it was observed that higher correlations were associated with occurrence in larger centers (Table 3).[15]

### The Measurement of Groupings between Ranked Activities

Given the ranks of central functions it was then possible to employ tests to determine whether there were associated groups among them. The tests used again varied between the two sets of central functions.

*Variates.*—Threshold sizes were treated as points upon the population-size continuum. Using the techniques developed by P. J. Clark, this distribution of points was tested for randomness by using a $\chi^2$ (chisquare) test for significant differences between expected and observed reflexive relationships.[16] The tests showed that the ob-

[13] Reilly, *op. cit.*; C. R. Hoffer, *The Study of Town-Country Relations* (Michigan Agricultural Experiment Station Bull. 181 [1928]).

[14] Christaller, *op. cit.*

[15] It is a characteristic of the point biserial coefficient of correlation, a statistic designed for the correlation of attributes and variates, that as fewer attributes occur, and as they occur in conjunction with the higher values of the variates, the correlation coefficient increases positively (compare post offices and state liquor stores) ; conversely, as fewer attributes occur, and in conjunction with the lower values of the variates, the correlation coefficient assures decreasing values (increasing negative values: compare post offices and general stores).

[16] These techniques consist of the examination of the reflexive relationships which exist between points on a line and the testing of these for significant differences with the expected random re-

served distribution of points was non-random at the 0.05 level of significance, and this observed distribution was non-random in a grouped rather than a "more even than random" manner.

Given this tendency for there to be grouping, and using Clark's criterion of a group—that every member of the group should be closer to some other member of the group than to any other point—three

flexive relationships calculated by Clark and Evans. See P. J. Clark and F. C. Evans, "Distance to Nearest Neighbor as a Measure of Spatial Relations," *Ecology*, XXXV (1954), 445–53.

TABLE 3

THE FUNCTIONAL BASES OF CLASSES OF CENTRAL PLACES IN SNOHOMISH COUNTY: ATTRIBUTES

| Group | Central Places | General Store | Feed Mill | Post Office | Weekly Newspaper | Telephone Exchange | Incorporated City | Movie Theater | Bakery | Electricity Distribution | Water Supply System | Sewage System | State Liquor Store | Public Library | Printing Press | Used Furniture Dealer |
|---|---|---|---|---|---|---|---|---|---|---|---|---|---|---|---|---|
| | | $1_2$ | | | | $2_2$ | | | | | | | | $3_2$ | | |
| | $r_{pb}$ | −.347 | .265 | .29 | .458 | .584 | 615 | 616 | 619 | .646 | .646 | .691 | .691 | .758 | .759 | .... |
| C | Marysville | | 1 | 1 | 1 | 1 | 1 | 1 | 1 | 1 | 1 | 1 | 1 | 1 | 1 | |
| C | Snohomish | | 1 | 1 | 1 | 1 | 1 | 1 | 1 | 1 | 1 | 1 | 1 | 1 | 1 | 1 |
| C | Arlington | | 1 | 1 | 1 | 1 | 1 | 1 | 1 | 1 | 1 | 1 | 1 | 1 | 1 | |
| C | Monroe | | 1 | 1 | 1 | 1 | 1 | 1 | 1 | 1 | 1 | 1 | 1 | 1 | | |
| B | Edmonds | | | | | | 1 | | | 1 | 1 | 1 | 1 | 1 | 1 | |
| B | Stanwood | | | | 1 | 1 | 1 | 1 | | | 1 | 1 | 1 | | 1 | |
| B | East Stanwood | | | 1 | | | 1 | | | 1 | | | 1 | | | |
| B | Lynnwood | | | 1 | | | | | | 1 | 1 | 1 | | | | |
| B | Sultan | | 1 | 1 | 1 | 1 | 1 | | | | 1 | 1 | | 1 | 1 | |
| B | Mukilteo | 1 | | 1 | | | 1 | | | 1 | 1 | 1 | 1 | | | |
| B | Darrington | | | 1 | | | 1 | 1 | 1 | | 1 | 1 | | | | |
| B | Granite Falls | | | | 1 | | 1 | | | | 1 | 1 | | | | |
| B | Alderwood Manor | | 1 | 1 | | | | | | 1 | | | | 1 | | |
| A | Lake Stevens | 1 | | | | | | | | | | | | 1 | | |
| A | Beverly Park | | | | | | | | | | 1 | 1 | 1 | | | |
| A | Lowell | | | | | | | | | | 1 | 1 | 1 | | | |
| A | Silvana | 1 | 1 | 1 | | | | | | | | | | | | |
| A | Gold Bar | | | 1 | | | | | | | | | | | | |
| A | Startup | | | 1 | | | | | | | | | | | | |
| A | Warm Beach | 1 | | 1 | | | | | | | | | | | | |
| A | Index | 1 | | 1 | | | | | | | | | | | | |
| A | Machias | 1 | | | | | | | | | | | | | | |
| A | Cathcart | 1 | | | | | | | | | | | | | | |
| A | Maltby | 1 | | | | | | | | | | | | | | |
| A | Oso | 1 | | | | | | | | | | | | | | |
| A | Cedarhome | 1 | | | | | | | | | | | | | | |
| A | Bryant | 1 | | | | | | | | | | | | | | |
| A | Robe | | | | | | | | | | | | | | | |
| A | Getchell | | | | | | | | | | | | | | | |
| A | Florence | 1 | | | | | | | | | | | | | | |
| A | Trafton | 1 | | | | | | | | | | | | | | |
| A | Silverton | 1 | | | | | | | | | | | | | | |
| A | Verlot | 1 | | | | | | | | | | | | | | |

groups of central functions, $1_1$, $2_1$, and $3_1$ were found to be present (Table 2).

*Attributes.*—Tests of significant differences between the $r_{pb}$'s were made at the 0.05 level of significance using standard techniques, and twelve of the attributes were found to fall into three groupings, $1_2$ and $2_2$ and $3_2$, with general stores existing as a class apart (Table 3).

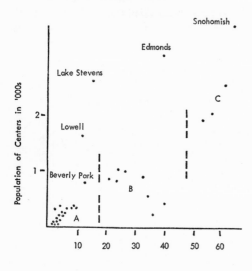

Fig. 2.—Classes of central places in Snohomish County.

## RANKING AND GROUPING THE CENTERS

The central places were represented as points on the continuum of functional complexity by the number of functions each possessed. Clark's test of randomness was then applied to this distribution of points and the chi-square test showed that the distribution of points was non-random and grouped. Using Clark's concept of a group, three groups of central places, here termed A, B, and C, could be distinguished (Fig. 2 and Tables 2 and 3).

## THE CLASSES OF CENTRAL PLACES

Given groups of central places defined on the basis of numbers of functions performed, and groups of functions, it re-

mained to be determined whether the latter could be said to be significantly associated with the former. Tables 2 and 3 were constructed and, utilizing the groupings, Table 4 derived. This table records the number of stores per function per central place.

Analysis of variance between the cells in Table 4 demonstrated significant differences to exist both between groups and between centers at the 0.95 level of confidence. Therefore, variations between groups are greater than variations within groups. This confirms the differential nature of the groupings derived utilizing the

### TABLE 4

NUMBER OF STORES PER FUNCTION PER CENTRAL PLACE IN THE CLASSES OF FUNCTIONS AND OF CENTRAL PLACES IN SNOHOMISH COUNTY, WASHINGTON

| CENTRAL FUNCTIONS | CLASSES OF CENTRAL PLACES | | |
|---|---|---|---|
| | A | B | C |
| *Variates:* | | | |
| Group $1_1$....... | 0.65* | 2.91 | 6.29 |
| Group $2_1$....... | 0.04 | 0.77 | 2.65 |
| Group $3_1$....... | 0.01 | 0.21 | 1.00 |
| *Attributes:* | | | |
| General store... | 0.70 | 0.11 | 0.00 |
| Group $1_2$....... | 0.20 | 0.45 | 1.00 |
| Group $2_2$....... | 0.04 | 0.50 | 1.00 |
| Group $3_2$....... | 0.03 | 0.28 | 0.88 |

* A value of 1.0 means that every center of the particular class in question will tend to have one store providing each function of the group of functions in question (for example, Class C centers with functions of group $2_2$).

Clark techniques and reveals the nature of the hierarchy of central places. As an extra step, it was found that general stores, the attribute existing as a group apart, were complementary with food stores (part of group $1_1$), the coefficient of correlation being —.634.

## FINDINGS

The data developed in constructing Tables 2, 3, and 4 can be generalized into the gross findings which were presented earlier in Table 1. It is apparent how the notion of classes of central places is defined with respect to the notion of functions. What is more, a technique has been provided whereby the hierarchical system may be isolated and identified, and the exact identification of an hierarchical system has been completed for Snohomish County. This is readily comprehended upon close examination of Tables 2 and 3.

It may also be shown that the three classes of towns tend toward discrete levels of population, as suggested by Christaller (Fig. 2). There are only four exceptions to the generalization of levels in terms of population—Beverly Park, Lowell, Lake Stevens, and Edmonds. It is significant that these are centers which have experienced very rapid increases in population in recent years, becoming dormitories for the Seattle area. Their functional paucity may be attributed (*a*) to the time-lag existing between population growth and the development of service industries, and (*b*) to the fact that, compared to other centers of their size, they serve relatively few people residing in immediately surrounding areas. As the time-lag diminishes, the centers can be expected to experience increasing functional complexity and possibly a rise in class status. But the dominant dormitory function suggests that some differential will persist vis-à-vis centers of comparable size in the county.

# SIZE AND SPACING OF CITIES

Although most studies in urban geography show a preoccupation with internal urban structure, many geographers are turning their attention to the number, spacing, and size of cities.

Von Thünen's scheme, postulated more than a century ago, of a single city in a large uniform hinterland of an agricultural economy is, of course, highly theoretical. More realistic is the scheme advanced a quarter of a century ago by Walter Christaller, who conceived of a hierarchy of urban centers. His ideas are outlined in the article by Ullman reproduced in the preceding section of this book.

Since the appearance of Christaller's work, several other theories relating to the number, size, and spacing of urban settlements have been formulated. H. W. Singer investigated the application of Pareto's law of distribution and found that for a whole series of countries the formula expresses very well the classification of towns according to size. G. K. Zipf put Singer's discovery in a simpler form by stating that the towns of a country are arranged according to size, the $n$th town having $1/n$th the population of the first.

Two recent articles related to the rank-size and spacing of cities are included in this section. Berry and Garrison in their recent article "Alternate Explanations of Urban Rank-Size Relationships," compare the schemes of Zipf, Christaller, Rashevsky, and Simon, and arrive at several implications of our present level of knowledge regarding city sizes.

Charles T. Stewart, Jr., in his article "The Size and Spacing of Cities," reviews the rank-size rule and examines some determinations of town spacing. He concludes that the rank-size rule has no logical basis but breaks down in many areas at both extremes. He also finds that there is nothing natural about the shape of the town-size pyramid but that relative sizes of towns in different function classes and their relative numbers vary with the stage of economic development, with a rise best indicated by the standard of living.

Much thought has also been given to the optimum size of cities, particularly in terms of optimum population density for good living conditions. B. Shindman investigates the problem in his study, "An Optimum Size for Cities," and concludes that there appears to be an optimum range in population based on the efficient operation of its particular functions, subject to the changing values and felt needs of the occupants.

BRIAN J. L. BERRY and WILLIAM L. GARRISON

# ALTERNATE EXPLANATIONS OF URBAN RANK-SIZE RELATIONSHIPS

Pick any large area. It will likely contain many small cities, a lesser number of medium-size cities, and but few large cities. This pattern of city sizes has been observed to be quite regular from one area to an-

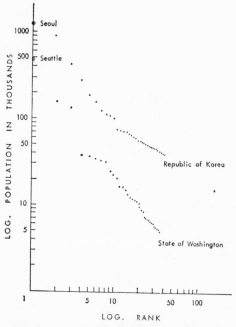

FIG. 1.—City rank-size relationships: Republic of Korea and State of Washington. Sources: *Census of the Republic of Korea, Section 1, 1955* (Seoul, 1956), and *Population of Towns and Cities in the State of Washington* (Seattle: Washington State Census Board, 1954).

other. That is, when the frequency of occurrence of city sizes in any area is compared with the frequency of occurrence of sizes in another area, the two frequencies are

Reprinted from *Annals of the Association of American Geographers*, XLVIII (March, 1958), 83–91, with permission of the authors and the editor.

very much alike. An example is furnished by a comparison of city sizes and ranks in the Republic of Korea and the state of Washington (Fig. 1). Frequencies for the two areas are quite similar. Such empirical regularities of city size have been noted many times and have long posed a challenge to those who would explain or interpret them.[1]

Several explanatory schemes directly or indirectly related to the problem of repeated regularities of patterns of occurrence of city sizes have been proposed. The present discussion brings these schemes together for comparison,[2] namely, the schemes or theories of G. K. Zipf, W. Christaller, N. Rashevsky, and H. A. Simon.[3] In the

[1] Edgar M. Hoover has pointed out the need for an adequate explanation in "The Concept of a System of Cities: A Comment on Rutledge Vining's Paper," *Economic Development and Cultural Change*, III (1955), 196–98.

[2] This article is entirely expository. It elaborates diverse ideas that the authors have found difficult to resolve and it is hoped that it will stimulate more detailed explanations. For such explanations we are already indebted to Messrs. Vir Bhatia, Harvard University, Richard Quandt, Princeton University, and Duane Marble, University of Washington.

[3] George K. Zipf, *Human Behavior and the Principle of Least Effort* (Cambridge: Addison-Wesley Press, Inc., 1949); W. Christaller, *Die zentralen Orte in Süddeutschland* (Jena: Gustav Fischer, 1933), trans. C. Baskin, at the Bureau of Population and Urban Research, University of Virginia, 1954; N. Rashevsky, *Mathematical Theory of Human Relations* ("Mathematical Biophysics Monograph Series," No. 2) (Bloomington: Principia Press, 1947); Herbert A. Simon, "On a Class of Skew Distribution Functions," *Biometrika*, XLII (1955), 425–40, reprinted as chap. 9 of *Models of Man* (New York: Wiley, 1957). Note that when practicable in our ensuing discussion of these studies the terminology of original authors is maintained.

ensuing discussion it will be noted that city-size regularities associated with Zipf have been explained by Simon, using very simple probability notions. Too, it will be noted that the city-size rule of Zipf is consistent in special cases with the theories of Rashevsky and Christaller. Since Rashevsky's scheme is a contribution to the general theory of urbanization and economic opportunity, and since Christaller's theory is the generic base of theories of urban size, function, and arrangement (subsequently generalized in several respects by August Lösch[4]), city-size relations are consistent with more general theory. The alternates and issues involved in the researchers' choice between the simple explanation offered by Simon and the less simple alternates of others pose the concluding problem of the discussion.

## CITY SIZES

The problem before us is posed by a comparison of city populations and ranks. In any area, say, a nation, cities may be ranked from the largest to the smallest according to population. The largest city would rank number 1, the second largest number 2, etc. When these ranks are then plotted against city population size, a regular relationship emerges. There are few large cities and many small ones, and there is an apparent empirical relationship between the rank of a city and its population. The size relationship takes the form $r_i (p_i{}^q)$ $=K$, when $q$ and $K$ are constants, $r_i$ is the rank of the $i$th city and $p_i$ is the population of that city. Observed distributions are concave upward and are linear or nearly so when plotted using logarithmic axes.

These city-size relations, termed the rank-size rule, have been noted by a number of persons.[5] Valuable empirical studies are due to Zipf, who has compiled and published data for several countries.[6] As W.

Isard has pointed out, however, a number of persons had noted the empirical relationships earlier.[7] The empirical evidence is formidable and has recently been reviewed by Vining[8] and Isard,[9] and augmented by G. R. Allen[10] and C. H. Madden.[11] For these reasons it will not be reviewed here.

Any empirical regularity poses problems for theory. Observations of city rank-size relationships have served both to initiate and to verify theory, the two classic func-

---

[4] August Lösch, *Die räumliche Ordnung der Wirtschaft* (Jena: Gustav Fischer, 1939), trans. W. H. Woglom and W. F. Stolper as *The Economics of Location* (New Haven: Yale University Press, 1954).

[5] Well-known references to city-size relationships in the geographical literature are those of Mark Jefferson, e.g., "The Law of the Primate City," *Geographical Review*, XXIX (1939), 226–32, and J. Q. Stewart, "Empirical Mathematical Rules concerning the Distribution and Equilibrium of Population," *Geographical Review*, XXXVII (1947), 461–85, especially pp. 462–67. A recent reference to expected city-size relationships is in P. E. James and Speridiav Faissol, "The Problem of Brazil's Capital City," *Geographical Review*, XLVI (1956), 301–17. One of the very early studies was that by Felix Auerbach, "Das Gesetz der Bevolkungskonzentration," *Petermann's geographische Mitteilungen*, LIX (1913).

[6] *Op. cit.*, and *National Unity and Disunity* (Bloomington: Principia Press, 1941).

[7] Walter Isard, *Location and Space Economy* (New York: John Wiley & Sons, 1956), pp. 55–60.

[8] "A Description of Certain Spatial Aspects of an Economic System," *Economic Development and Cultural Change*, III (1955), 147–95.

[9] *Op. cit.*

[10] "The 'Courbe des Populations': A Further Analysis," *Bulletin of the Oxford University Institute of Statistics*, XVI (1954), 179–89. Allen fitted the Pareto formula to 44 countries and finds: "The main conclusion is, therefore, that the Pareto Law can be used with much success to summarize the relationships between size of towns and number of towns above a specified size" (p. 184). The Pareto formula is similar to what Zipf has termed the rank-size rule. Explanations of it are to be found in R. G. D. Allen, *Mathematical Analysis for Economists* (London: Macmillan & Co., 1950), pp. 407–8, and D. G. Champernowne, "A Model of Income Distribution," *Economic Journal*, LXIII (1953), 318 ff. The earlier empirical application of Pareto's law to city sizes was by H. W. Singer, "The 'Courbe des Populations': A Parallel to Pareto's Law," *Economic Journal*, XLVI (1936), 254–63.

[11] "The Growth of Cities in the United States: An Aspect of the Development of an Economic System" (Ph.D. diss., University of Virginia, 1954).

tions of empirical work. Zipf has attempted
to erect a scheme to explain rank regularities and Rashevsky has turned to Zipf's
observations for partial verification of his
theoretical scheme. Like Zipf, Simon has
attempted a theoretical scheme to explain
empirical regularities, and as with Rashevsky, observations of rank-size relationships
are consistent with the scheme of Christaller.
Empirical regularities, then, are a common
element in a variety of undertakings and
they serve as a link among divergent approaches to a common problem.

In connection with rank-size relationships
the question has been asked, Is there in
fact a regularity?[12] A scatter of dots formed
by plotting the sizes of cities versus their
rank never presents a perfect alignment of
dots along a mean line. One dot will fall
above the line, another below, and so on.
Some misfit is expected, of course, owing to
different definitions of the area of the city
and other data liabilities.[13] The problem is
whether regularity occurs, leaving these
sources of error in the data aside.

It is sufficient for the present problem
that regularities may exist. One point about
the problem of empirical validation should
be made, however. There is never perfect
agreement of data with theory. Thus a
number of statistical tools have been developed to test hypotheses of agreement.
Paralleling these tests but apart from the
statistical problems are problems of interpreting degrees of agreement. Plausibility
plays a part here. To the extent that regularity is plausible, it is easy to see regularity. If no plausible basis for regularity
is known, regularity is difficult to see.

The present discussion reviews plausible
bases for empirical regularities between city
sizes and ranks, and to the extent that
plausibility is provided, the present discussion serves to verify asserted regularities.

## ZIPF AND THE RANK-SIZE RULE

Perhaps the best-known elaboration of
rank-size regularities was developed by G.

K. Zipf.[14] Zipf's discussion was set within
a broad context—a general theory of human behavior—in which rank-frequency
relationships are noted for many expressions of human behavior (e.g., number of
times words were used in a novel). The
general theory was presented to explain
these regularities.

The discussion as a whole has been reviewed elsewhere.[15] Too, the portion of the
discussion treating the sizes of cities may
be extracted from the larger work without
distorting Zipf's analysis. Thus the general
works will not be reviewed at the present
time. Zipf presented evidence of strong
rank-size relationships. As a case in point,
a study of the 100 largest metropolitan districts in the United States in 1940 yielded
the best-fitting equation $r = (P^{-1})$ 10,-
000,000.[16] This equation, Zipf noted, indicated that $K = 10,000,000$ and was approximately equal to the population of the
largest metropolitan district. Since the exponent $q$ equals 1, it indicated the equality
of the forces of diversification and unification.[17] The latter requires elaboration.

*Diversification versus unification.*—Zipf's
explanation of rank-size relationships is in
broad outline quite simple. On the one
hand, it is postulated that there is a tendency for the population to be split into
many small autarchic communities. This
process, labeled "the force of diversification," is that of economical location relative to raw materials. Persons are located
to minimize the transfer cost of obtaining
raw materials. A society using many scattered raw materials would be highly disaggregated in location; a society using few
strongly localized raw materials would be
highly aggregated in location.

On the other hand, there is a reverse

[13] These problems are noted by Allen, *op. cit.*,
who also provides a measure of error or lack of fit.

[14] *Human Behavior.*

[15] See, for example, the review by Read Bain in
*Social Forces*, XXVIII (1950), 340–41.

[16] Zipf, *Human Behavior*, p. 375.

[17] *Ibid.*, p. 376.

[12] Isard, *op. cit.*, p. 57.

tendency, the force of unification. Diversification tends to minimize the difficulty of moving raw materials to the places where they are to be processed; unification tends to minimize the difficulty of moving processed materials to the ultimate consuming populace. If all persons in the society were located at the same point, then maximum unification would be achieved. When both the forces of diversification and unification are at work a distribution of population is presumed to occur that is at optimum with reference to both forces.

*The domains of goods.*—An additional concept of Zipf's theory is the notion of the domain in which goods may be economically traded. Zipf notes that different goods have different cost relationships. Some are marketed in many small domains, others in large domains, and so on. Each good is made from a unique mix of raw materials, but groups of goods may be produced in the same community.

*Formulation of the rank-size rule.*—Thus far the Zipf scheme is simple and straightforward. However, the manner by which one moves from these simple notions to the rank-size rule is less clear, namely,[18]

Since the Force of Diversification makes for a larger *n* number of small *P* communities, whereas the Force of Unification makes for a smaller *n* number of larger *P* communities, then, if we interpret the relationship as a best straight line on doubly logarithmic co-ordinates, the result will be that the *n* number of different communities, when ranked *r*, in the order of their decreasing *P* size will follow the equation (approximately):

$$r = P^{-q}K .$$

*Contributions of Zipf.*—It is certainly not clear just what are the logical links between the scheme proposed by Zipf to explain rank-size regularity and observed rank-size regularities. Thus it would not be proper to credit Zipf with an articulated empirical and theoretical analysis of the rank-size problem. On the other hand, in several important ways Zipf deserves great credit.

[18] *Ibid.*, p. 359.

Zipf's works have called emphatic attention to the rank-size problem. The number of students who have been attracted to the problem as stated by Zipf is, of course, unknown. But two of the contributions to the rank-size problem (both to be reviewed), those of Rashevsky and Simon, give direct credit to Zipf for calling attention to the problem. Both of these give credit to the empirical substantiation of rank-size regularities, rather than to Zipf's theoretical formulation of the problem.

Too, Zipf has proposed, or at least restated, components of the emerging general theory of location. His discussion of unification and diversification is related to Weberian localization schemes and the notion of the range of a good is similar to that of Christaller.[19] In this latter sense, Zipf's statements are not original, but they do have the virtue of consistency with other literature.

## CHRISTALLER AND SIZE CLASSES OF CITIES

A well-known alternate scheme to that of Zipf, both regarding the size of cities and the processes causing size regularities, is that of W. Christaller.[20] It is quite surprising that the scheme of Christaller has never (to the writers' knowledge) been compared with the scheme or the empirical observations of Zipf in terms of city sizes. The two schemes are quite similar. Both utilize notions of the domains of cities (domains of goods) for the performance of various economic activities.[21] Too, the rules of behavior leading to the spatial system of central places and associated arrangements of city sizes (diversification and unification) are quite similar.[22] In both schemes as the population of cities increases, the number of centers of this population diminishes.

[19] Zipf was cognizant of these works and used them as references.

[20] Christaller, *op. cit.*, especially pp. 63–64.

[21] *Ibid.*, pp. 20, 31, 54. Both Hoover and Vining link the schemes of Zipf and Christaller through the notion of domain.

[22] *Ibid.*, pp. 63–74.

It should be recalled that Christaller's work was somewhat broader than that of Zipf; Christaller was concerned with the spatial arrangement, function, and size of urban centers. Too, it should be recalled that Christaller did not provide a general theory in formal terms.[23] So far as general theory is concerned, there is no explicit way the scheme of Christaller may be compared with that of Zipf, despite the fact that the notions of the two schemes are, as already noted, quite similar.

*Special cases.*—Turning to special cases, however, it is practicable directly to compare the scheme of Christaller with that of Zipf. Christaller did provide a formal statement of one network of cities in homogeneous space. This is the well-known $k = 3$ network, with one "primate city" of population $K$, and $r = 1$; three cities of population $K/3$, and $r = 2$; nine cities of population $K/9$ and $r = 3$; twenty-seven of population $K/27$; etc.[24] This arrangement of city sizes may be compared directly with the rank-size rule provided by Zipf.

In order to make the comparison the steps of the hierarchy of centers in the $k = 3$ scheme are taken as ranks, $r = 1, 2, 3$, etc., and $P_i = K, K/3, K/9$, etc. A rank-size distribution in the manner of Zipf is formed if the exponent

$$q = \frac{\log (K / r)}{\log (K / 3^{r-1})}.$$

[23] Christaller addressed the general problem of city size and arrangement on an informal and intuitive level. His discussion is formal only with his example case of the $k = 3$ network. It is not clear why Christaller has been criticized for lack of generality. See the comments upon this common criticism in Brian J. L. Berry, "Geographic Aspects of the Size and Arrangement of Urban Centers" (M.A. thesis, University of Washington, 1956), pp. 7–30. Our attention has been called to C. W. Baskin's "A Critique and Translation of Walter Christaller's *Die zentralen Orte in Süddeutschland*" (Ph.D. diss., Department of Economics, University of Virginia, 1957), but we have not had the opportunity of examining this study.

[24] A discussion of this network as well as other networks is available in Lösch, *op. cit.*, p. 131.

Thus, where $r = 2$,

$$q = \frac{\log (K / 2)}{\log (K / 3^{2-1})},$$

and if

$$q \cdot \log P = \log (K / r),$$

then

$$\log P = \log (K / 2) \cdot \frac{\log (K / 3)}{\log (K / 2)},$$

and

$$P = K / 3$$

as required by Christaller's theory.

*Implications.*—In fact no great difference exists between Zipf and Christaller; on the level of the intuitive statement of basic notions the two schemes seem very much alike. Even when one turns to special cases generated by the schemes certain relationships are evident.[25] By the proper choice of relationships, the class hierarchical scheme of Christaller may take on the rank-size character of Zipf's observations. The Christaller scheme is consistent with Zipf's empirical observations, but consistency requires a rigorous choice of relationships.

## RASHEVSKY, URBANIZATION, AND ECONOMIC OPPORTUNITY

As was true of both Christaller and Zipf, N. Rashevsky's deductions bearing on city size were set within a larger context.[26] Rashevsky set out a general theory of human relations in mathematical form. In this general theory the spatial distribution of individuals and the size of cities were core topics.[27] Observed empirical regularities in the distribution of city sizes were approached differently from the two topics just mentioned.[28]

*Rural versus urban opportunities.*—Rashevsky's approach to the urbanization problem was via an evaluation of alternate

[25] It is to be noted, of course, that our Christaller formulation refers to a rank-size regularity of hierarchical classes of city sizes.

[26] Rashevsky, *op. cit.*

[27] *Ibid.*, chaps. 10 and 11.

[28] *Ibid.*, chap. 12.

economic opportunities.[29] The rural-urban division of population was seen directly related to the level of opportunities in each area. There are $N_r$ rural persons and $N_u$ urban $(N_r + N_u = N)$ and $p_r$ and $p_u$ indicate the corresponding production per person. In general,

$$p_u = f_u (N_u, N_r) ; \quad p_r = f_r (N_u, N_r) ,$$

and the condition $p_u = p_r$ is assumed. This is an extremely interesting system that leads to some interesting results bearing on relations between urbanization and population changes.[30]

While the simple system just mentioned offers a first approximation to the urbanization problem, it throws no light on the city-size problem, which is approached by enlarging the scheme to identify the number and sizes of cities. If the productivity, $p_i$, per person in cities of population size $n_i$ is

$$p_i = f (n_i, N_i)$$

(where $N_i$ is the total number of persons in all cities of size $n_i$) and $p_1 = p_2 = , \dots ,$ $= p_n$ (where $i = 1, 2, \dots , n$), then

$$p = f (n_i, N_i) ,$$

and all city sizes are presumed determined.

Now, like many schemes, once presented, these notions of Rashevsky's seem utterly elementary and obvious, and this is to Rashevsky's credit. An equilibrium in city size is presumed to be reached when the production per person in each city is the same. There is no allowance for lag, and it is not completely explicit how equilibrium processes work. But the system seems a reasonable first approximation of reality.

Is it consistent with observed rank-size regularities of the present problem? The answer to this is a qualified no; this production-opportunity view of equilibrium is not one which generates rank-size regularities directly.[31]

*Types of activities.*—On the other hand, the evidence offered by Zipf's rank-size observations was so strong that Rashevsky attempted to reformulate his city-size system in a manner that would tailor directly to rank-size observations. To do this the distribution function of the gradation of numbers of persons performing different types of activities in urban centers was considered. (For example, one could consider the distribution in urban centers of groups of persons associated with government activities.) After considerable manipulation of this idea, it was shown that city size as a function of the distribution of activities can in a special case approximate the observed rank-size distributions.

*Implications.*—As was the case with Christaller's scheme, observed rank-size regularities would seem neither to contradict nor to support the scheme of Rashevsky, which will produce rank-size relationships as a special case. As with Christaller, Rashevsky's scheme is consistent with Zipf's empirical observations, but consistency requires a set choice of relationships.

### SIMON AND A PROBABILITY EXPLANATION

Like Rashevsky, H. A. Simon attempted an explanation of observed rank-size regularities.[32] Simon's explanation formed an integral part of an approach to a general systems theory based on broad analogies between the frequency distribution of a wide variety of biological, social, and economic phenomena observed by Zipf and

---

[29] Rashevsky's discussion is entirely in economic terms, i.e., he speaks of the opportunities for the production of economic goods. As he points out (*ibid.*, p. ix), however, the discussion could have been cast around satisfaction functions. This practicability removes the argument that Rashevsky's discussion is overly restricted.

[30] *Ibid.*, pp. 85–87, and Rashevsky, "Contribution to the Theory of Human Relations: Outline of a Mathematical Theory of the Size of Cities, VII," *Psychometrica*, VIII (1943), 87–90.

[31] This conclusion is reached by Rashevsky, *ibid.*, pp. 94–95. For some interesting empirical observations relating to population distribution and city sizes see A. H. Hawley, *The Changing Shape of Metropolitan America* (Glencoe, Ill.: Free Press, 1956), pp. 34 ff.

[32] *Op. cit.*

others.[33] Such phenomena include distributions of words in prose samples by frequency of occurrence, distributions of numbers of scientists by numbers of papers published, distributions of incomes by size (Pareto distributions), and distributions of biological genera by numbers of species, in addition to the distributions of city sizes. Simon was unwilling to suppose initially that there was any connection between these phenomena other than that known probability mechanisms might provide satisfactory abstract models of each and provide the bases of analogies.

*The distributions.*—Simon argued that the distribution of city sizes was one of a family of distributions which have the following general characteristics in common:

1. They are J-shaped, or at least highly skewed, with very long upper tails which can be approximated closely by a function of the form

$$f(i) = (a/i^k) \, b^i \, ,$$

where $a$, $b$, and $k$ are constants, and the convergence factor $b$ is so close to 1 that it often may be disregarded. Thus, for example, the number of cities that have a population $i$ is approximately $a/i^k$.

2. The exponent $k$ is of the form $1 < k < 2$.

3. The function describes the distribution not merely in the tail but also for small values of $i$. In this case it may be shown, for example, that $f(2)/f(1) = \frac{1}{3}$ and $f(2)/f(n) = \frac{1}{2}$, where

$$n = \sum_{i=1}^{\infty} f(i) \, .$$

These three properties just identified define the class of functions which Simon terms the Yule distribution. The term is used because G. Udny Yule used the distribution some years ago to explain the distribution of biological genera.[34] Simon reconstructed Yule's probability model, using only a weak set of assumptions and modern theory,[35] and made the initial steps in applying it to city sizes.

*Underlying mechanism.*—Stated in terms of the city-size problem, the distribution derived by Simon is evolved under roughly the following notions. Consider a total population $k$ distributed in cities, with a city considered to be an aggregate of population larger than some threshold size. The probability that the $(k + 1)$st person being found in cities of size $i$ is assumed to be proportional to $i[f(i, k)]$. It is also assumed that there is a constant probability $\alpha$ that the $(k + 1)$st person will be in cities not previously of threshold size when the total population was $k$.[36]

It must be emphasized that these are extremely weak assumptions. They would hold roughly, for example, if population change were simply proportional to present population.

*The model.*—It is not practicable to reproduce Simon's derivation of the probability model here.[37] The derived set of equa-

[33] For a development of this notion of a general systems theory see H. A. Simon and A. Newell, "Models: Their Uses and Limitations," in L. D. White (ed.), *The State of the Social Sciences* (Chicago: University of Chicago Press, 1956), pp. 78–79.

[34] "A Mathematical Theory of Evolution Based on the Conclusions of Dr. J. C. Willis, F.R.S.," *Philosophical Transactions*, CCXIII (1924), 21–84. Vining, *op. cit.*, recognized the contribution of Yule.

[35] But in several alternate formulations Simon was able to show that a variety of different assumptions did not materially alter the shape of the derived distribution. This he took to indicate the value of the probabilistic explanation.

[36] Whereas the second assumption is very weak, Simon states that the first assumption will be satisfied if the growth rates of cities are stable, not for each city, but for aggregates of cities in each population band. There seems ample evidence of this stability in the pattern of urban growth. See, for example, C. H. Madden, "On Some Indications of Stability in the Growth of Cities in the United States," *Economic Development and Cultural Change*, IV (1956), 236–53.

[37] Simon, "On a Class of Skew Distribution Functions." The use of the derived equations does not follow the precise form prescribed by Simon for city sizes, in which $f(i)$ is the number of cities equal to or greater than size $i$, but the form out-

tions from which expected distributions of cities may be calculated is as follows:

$$a = n_k/k , \qquad (a)$$

$$f(1) = \frac{n_k}{2-a}, \qquad (b)$$

$$\frac{f(i)}{f(i-1)} = \frac{(1-a) \cdot (i-1)}{1+(1-a)i} \qquad (c)$$

where $k$ is the total urban population in the $n_k$ cities of greater than threshold size, and $f(i)$ is the number of cities of population $i$. From equations $(a)$ and $(b)$ and by successive application of equation $(c)$ the expected distribution of city sizes can be constructed. Since the situation will scarcely, if ever, be found in which $\alpha > \varepsilon$ (where $\varepsilon$ is an extremely small number), we may write this system in the more simplified form:

$$f(1) = \frac{n_k}{2} \qquad (b^*)$$

$$\frac{f(i)}{f(i-1)} = \frac{i-1}{1+i}. \qquad (c^*)$$

From $(b^*)$ and by successive application of $(c^*)$ the expected distribution of city sizes may then be constructed.

*An example.*—The accuracy with which the stochastic model developed by Simon represents the distribution of city sizes may be illustrated by data from the state of Washington. Five thousand urban residents were taken to constitute the threshold at which a nucleated settlement became a city (this figure is entirely arbitrary). Hence $f(1)$ was interpreted as the number of cities with populations of 5,000–10,000; $f(2)$ is the number of cities with between 10,000 and 15,000 population; $f(3)$, 15,000–20,000, etc.

The number of cities with populations of 5,000 or greater, $n_k$, was 36. Hence, as expected in equation $(a)$, $\alpha$ was extremely small, for $k$ was, relatively speaking, very

lined in Brian J. L. Berry and William L. Garrison, "A Probability Model of the Distribution of City Sizes" (mimeographed manuscript, Department of Geography, University of Washington, 1957).

large. From the simplified form of the model, therefore:

$$f(1) = 36/2 = 18 \qquad (b^*)$$

$$\frac{f(i)}{f(i-1)} = \frac{f(2)}{f(1)} \qquad (i=2) ,$$

$$\frac{f(2)}{18} = \frac{2-1}{1+2} \qquad (c^*)$$

$$f(2) = 18 \cdot 1/3 = 6 .$$

By successive application of equation $(c^*)$ where $i = 3$, $i = 4$, etc., the a priori distribution of cities in the various size classes

TABLE 1

City Sizes in the State of Washington

| Population of Cities (in 1,000's) | Number of Cities of This Population $f(i)$ | | Number of Cities Equal to or Greater than This Population $(r_i)$ | |
|---|---|---|---|---|
| | Expected | Observed | Expected | Observed |
| 5–10 | 18 | 16 | 36 | 36 |
| 10–15 | 6 | 6 | 18 | 20 |
| 15–20 | 3 | 3 | 12 | 14 |
| 20–25 | 2 | 2 | 9 | 11 |
| 25–30 | 1 | 1 | 7 | 9 |
| 30–35 | 1 | 2 | 6 | 8 |
| 35+ | 5 | 6 | 5 | 6 |

has been calculated for the state in Table 1. Note the close resemblance of actual and a priori distributions.

The distribution of $f(i)$, the number of cities of size $i$, may be readily converted into the rank-size distribution, where $r_i$ is the number of cities of size equal to or greater than size $i$, by the use of the following transformation

$$r_i = n_k - f(i_j)$$

where $r_i$ is the number of centers of population equal to or greater than $i$, $n_k$ is as before, and $f(i_j)$ is the total number of centers of population less than $i$. Again, the close resemblance between expected and observed frequencies of city sizes by ranks may be seen in Table 1.

## STATUS OF THE PROBLEM

There seems to be no doubt that the empirical regularity with which we are concerned exists. The weight of empirical evidence for regularities has been given substance by Simon's derivation of accurate expected distributions utilizing stochastic processes and probability concepts. Plausibility does not require real understanding of causal processes, however, and it is not immediately clear where one should look for causal explanations.

*The simplest alternate.*—Walter Isard has noted that "Zipf . . . has intuitively associated city size with the market area complex . . . although the logic connecting his statistical findings on the one hand and his Forces of Unification and Diversification and the principle of least effort on the other hand is not at all clear."[38] The notions of Christaller and Rashevsky are tenuously linked to the problem of rank-size, relating only in special cases. These theories may be suggested to explain city-size regularities, but they seem both divergent and generally inadequate.

If we were to use the dictum of the simplest of alternate hypotheses, the selection of explanations would be clear. Instead of the troublesome theories of Zipf, Rashevsky, and Christaller, one would rely for explanation of city-size regularities on the implications of the work of Simon. Simon's scheme is simple and it works (in Washington state, for example, the expected frequency was very much like the observed distribution of city sizes). The alternatives are to derive explanations of the observed distributions of city sizes from underlying distributions of occupations (Rashevsky), or of agglomeration and dispersion tendencies (Zipf and Christaller). These require very specific and not very plausible assumptions about the distribution of occupations and dispersion and agglomeration tendencies, and such assumptions simply serve to transfer the mystery from the frequency distribution of city sizes to other frequency distributions.[39]

But on the other hand, the city-size problem seems to be a case where the available simple explanation is unsatisfactory. For one thing, a probabilistic explanation in some sense refers to the presence of an infinite number of causes and the ability to predict in these terms is not enough; we wish explanations viable in explicit ways within a broad theoretical context. As John Somerville has pointed out, "no problem is worth working on that does not involve a deliberately formulated hypothesis which has scientific implications beyond the original problem."[40] Some would argue that the probabilistic explanation is meaningful in a theoretical context and has scientific implications, as noted in the discussion of average conditions in paragraphs below. The theory still leaves a central question unanswered, namely: Why is the arrangement of city sizes the outcome of simple probabilistic processes?

*What is needed.*—What are the implications from noting our present level of knowledge regarding city sizes? One answer to this question seems clear. Present knowledge of processes of urbanization is skimpy. From the standpoint of numbers of available studies, there has been little concern with a general theory of city size, function, and arrangement. What is more amazing, this is true in spite of our great concern with studies of urban areas. It is obvious that here is a place where there is great need for *articulated* empirical and theoretical research. We also need a point of view; it has to be decided what is important to explain.

*Average conditions.*—To elaborate the point of the preceding sentence, one may note that work may be done without explicitly stating the causes of rank-size distributions of city sizes. Madden has noted that the rank-size formulation exhibits sta-

---

[38] Isard, *op. cit.*, p. 60.

[39] These sentences follow remarks made by Simon in a similar context: "Productivity among American Psychologists: An Explanation," *American Psychologist*, IX (1954), 805.

[40] John Somerville, "Umbrellaology, or Methodology in Social Science," *Philosophy of Science*, VIII (1941), 564.

bility over time.[41] Others have noted stability from nation to nation, and Simon gives us a simple explanation for this stability. This, then, is an average condition, both from empirical and theoretical points of view. We have already mentioned the notion of a general systems theory.[42] One point emphasized in this theory is that living systems tend to maintain steady states of many variables which keep all subsystems in order of balance both with one another and with their environments. These steady states are described in terms of entropy, in accordance with the second law of thermodynamics, in which entropy is a state of randomly distributed energy and, essentially, a "normal or average state" of equilibrium. That the rank-size distribution is a random state is borne out by Simon. As such it is a condition of entropy or equilibrium and is a proper subject of systems theory. Thus city-size problems may be treated as average conditions, *and* in the more general context of the development of systems theory.

*Variations.*—On the other hand, one may argue that it is variations from and between average conditions which pose the problems for theory.[43] A region containing cities all approximately the same size would pose many interesting questions. A region with a rank-size arrangement of cities merely represents the occurrence of average conditions. Too, many interesting problems would result from comparisons of city-size frequencies in different regions.[44] Absence of significant differences between frequencies would indicate that similar processes of urbanization were operating in both regions; presence of significant differences would indicate the operation of differential forces of urbanization.

Average conditions can also contain within them important problems. Madden maintains that if the empirical distributions are plotted for a series of years, it is possible to trace the fortunes of cities or groups of cities within these average conditions and relative both to other cities and to the general tendency for growth in the economy. These variable fortunes may then be taken and explained as the first step in the explanation of the general processes of economic growth in the economy.[45]

What is apparent from the foregoing is that a variety of points of view of the problem are permissive, but that search for important causes can also take one *away* from factors generating average conditions (the normal state, or entropy), even though, as Madden has pointed out, one may still perform valuable work within the context of average conditions. It is clear that, in any case, the available explanation for city-size relationships is a base on which to build or to relate city-size relationships to other relationships. It is certainly not the answer to all city-size problems.

[41] Madden, *op. cit.*

[42] A lucid development of this idea has been provided by J. G. Miller in "Toward a General Theory for the Behavioral Sciences," *American Psychologist*, X (1955), 513–32.

[43] James and Faissol (*op. cit.*) provide an example of this point of view. It should also be remembered that Mark Jefferson thought in terms of a "law" of the primate city (*op. cit.*).

[44] It would be interesting to treat the rank-size distribution as a lognormal distribution, for as Aitchison and Brown have noted, ". . . many of these distributions [of Zipf] may be regarded as lognormal, or truncated lognormal, with more prosaic foundations in normal probability theory" (J. Aitchison and J. A. C. Brown, *The Lognormal Distribution* [Cambridge, 1957], p. 102). It would then be possible to test for significant differences from lognormalcy for any one distribution, and for significant differences between lognormal distributions, using the tests outlined by Aitchison and Brown. W. C. Krumbein is one of the several geologists who have used lognormal distributions to characterize distributions ("Application of Statistical Methods to Sedimentary Rocks," *Journal of the American Statistical Association*, XLIX [1954], 5).

[45] Madden, *op. cit.*, and "Some Spatial Aspects of Urban Growth in the United States," *Economic Development and Cultural Change*, IV (1956), 371–87; J. R. P. Friedmann, "Locational Aspects of Economic Development," *Land Economics*, XXXII (1956), 213–27.

CHARLES T. STEWART, JR.

# THE SIZE AND SPACING OF CITIES

The regular spacing of towns has often been noted. The distance between any two adjacent towns in the same size class fits fairly well the formula $(P1P2)/D=A$, in which $P1$ and $P2$ stand for the populations of the two towns and $D$ for the distance between them and $A$ is a constant for any given region. The distribution of towns by size has also been shown to follow an empirical rule, the so-called rank-size rule. In Zipf's version,[1] the rule states that if all towns in a region are arranged in descending order by population, the size of the $r$th town is $1/r$ the size of the largest town, according to the series 1, 1/2, 1/3, 1/4, . . . , $1/r$. More analytical work, notably that of Christaller and Lösch,[2] based on function rather than on population, seeks to demonstrate a regularity in the town hierarchy, both in the relative numbers of towns serving as local, regional, and interregional centers and in the consequent ratios of the distance between towns in the several stages of subordination and superordination of function.

The rank-size rule is an empirical finding, not a logical structure. Nevertheless, its partial verification suggests an underlying logical basis.[3] On the other hand, the doctrine that there is a typical town-size pyramid is principally an analytical scheme. Christaller purports to find verification, but his data have been challenged; Lösch is

satisfied with Christaller's evidence for only one of the seven functional classes that Christaller distinguishes and in his own research fails to find convincing evidence of clustering of town sizes to correspond to a limited number of discrete functional constellations. There is no coincidence, even theoretically, between the rank-size rule for cities and a functional size-class hierarchy of the type postulated by Christaller and Lösch. The former yields a smooth descending curve of town sizes; the latter a ladder of successively lower size classes of towns, grouped around a limited number of discrete normal values corresponding to discrete functional constellations. Even a gross coincidence of the two distributions of towns by size is possible only for specific combinations of values for $k$—the number of towns in one functional category subordinate to a town in the next higher category—and ratios of populations of typical towns in different functional size classes.

The conditions under which the rank-size rule holds good are not the same as those required for development of a clearcut town size-class hierarchy. A study of divergences from the rule and their causes may provide clues to a logical basis, if any, for the rule itself. In this manner it is hoped that a step can be taken toward reconciling the apparently conflicting results of the empirical curve-fitting approach of Zipf and the analytical model-building approach of Lösch.

Reprinted from *Geographical Review*, XLVIII (April, 1958), 222–45, with permission of the author and the editor. (Copyright, 1958, by the American Geographical Society, New York.)

[1] G. K. Zipf, *National Unity and Disunity* (Bloomington, Ind., 1941).

[2] August Lösch, *The Economics of Location*, trans., from 2d ed., W. H. Woglom with the assistance of W. F. Stolper (New Haven, 1954), particularly chap. 24. Christaller's work is summarized by Edward Ullman in "A Theory of Location for Cities," *American Journal of Sociology*, XLVI (1941), 853–64 [see above, pp. 202–9].

## THE RANK-SIZE RULE

Examples given by Zipf of divergences of rule from reality point to one condition for

[3] Zipf (*op. cit.*, pp. 43–46 and 192–96), in examples of the use of divergences from the rule as clues for the diagnosis of social disequilibrium, clearly regards the rule as more than an empirical generalization.

the approximation of the rule in fact: the region to which it applies must be complete, that is, not part of a larger region or greatly overlapping another region. Areas to which the rank-size rule may be applied can be defined in terms of their self-sufficiency as measured by the ratio of their external trade to their total trade. If this ratio is less than 10 per cent, as it is for the United States and the Soviet Union, there is no doubt that application of the rule is legitimate.

A high "foreign"-trade ratio does not completely invalidate the rank-size rule; the rule remains relevant for towns and small cities whose functions and hinterlands are limited, but it breaks down for the larger cities whose economic functions and influence transcend the boundaries of the country. Thus London is much too large in terms of the population of other large British cities. Other Commonwealth countries tend to have leading cities smaller than postulated by the rank-size rule. This fact suggests that possibly a low foreign-trade ratio is not enough to make a region or nation a logical illustration of the rank-size rule. A country that provides administration, capital, and security for an area much larger than itself will have an excessive number of people in its largest city; a country in a colonial or dependent position in these respects will have, according to the rank-size rule, an

large area of the country; this distribution emphasizes New York's peripheral coastal site and the two-ocean nature of United States sea transport. Principal cities of other maritime countries may not be seaports at all, and countries that carry on considerable trade by sea may have no seacoast or seaport. Such trade patterns simply mean that often regions to which the rank-size rule logically applies fail to coincide with national boundaries. Varying degrees of concentration of government functions and activities, and varying political decisions on the location of government seats, represent another diversifying factor, one that cannot be eliminated by juggling boundaries of the area within which the rank-size rule is tested.

The populations of the five largest cities in every country in the world were examined to determine the applicability of the rank-size rule. A few countries were eliminated—those which have recently experienced great changes in territory and population; divided countries (for example, Germany and Pakistan); and countries whose area or urban population is so small that they have only one true city (for example, Iceland). The ratio of the population of the largest city to that of the second-largest city in each of the remaining seventy-two countries is summarized as follows:

| Ratio | 1–1.5 | 1.5–2 | 2–2.5 | 2.5–3 | 3–4 | 4–5 | 5–10 | 10– |
|---|---|---|---|---|---|---|---|---|
| No. of countries.. | 14 | 6 | 9 | 2 | 20 | 3 | 16 | 2 |

insufficient number of people in its largest city.

Indeed, the largest cities are poor points of reference in fitting theoretical and actual city-size distribution curves. The large hinterlands of these few cities are unique; so to some extent are the determinants of the growth of the cities and the function constellations they perform. For example, functions that in the United Kingdom are monopolized by London are divided in the United States among New York and various other cities: government functions are centered in Washington, D.C., transportation functions partly in Chicago and West Coast ports and partly in New York because of the

These figures show clearly that the ratios do not tend to cluster around 2, as the rank-size rule postulates. The range of values is large (highest value is 17.0, for Uruguay), and the median is 3.25. A significant feature is the large number of countries with very low values and the small number with values between 1.5 and 2. The gap in this range is greater than it seems in the summary data above: five of the six countries have ratios between 1.51 and 1.62. Also of possible significance is the fact that of the world's seven giant countries, four—Brazil, India, Australia, and the U.S.S.R.—have ratios less than 1.5; Canada has a ratio of 1.51; and only the United States and China have ratios exceeding 2 (2.18 and 2.24, respectively).

Data from countries diverse in so many ways do not test the validity of the concept of a functional hierarchy of towns. The spacing of towns that are comparable in function is regular only in homogeneous areas. In such areas towns of comparable function tend to be of comparable size, so that, specialized towns excepted, the two measures should be interchangeable. A homogeneous area is requisite also for realization of the theoretical distribution of towns by functional class. Differences in soil fertility, in concentration of mineral deposits, in cultural endowment, in transpor-

and function classes, it may be sufficiently uniform to diverge noticeably from the urban ecology postulated by the rank-size rule.

It was noted above that of the world's seven giant countries, five have very low ratios of largest to second-largest city, and the other two have only moderate ratios, well below the world median. Zipf has used several of these countries as illustrations of the rank-size rule, and one of them, the United States, seems to provide the best fit of all. It is likely that their low ratios are attributable to their large areas and that no such low ratios will be found in their subdivisions. To test this hypothesis, the popu-

TABLE 1

RATIO OF POPULATION OF LARGEST CITY TO POPULATION OF SECOND LARGEST CITY

| Country | 1–1.5 | 1.5–2 | 2–2.5 | 2.5–3 | 3–4 | 4–5 | 5–10 | 10 and over | Median Ratio |
|---------|-------|-------|-------|-------|-----|-----|------|-------------|--------------|
| Australia (states).. | 0 | 1 | 0 | 0 | 0 | 0 | 0 | 5 | 14.24 |
| Brazil (states)..... | 2 | 1 | 3 | 0 | 2 | 4 | 2 | 6 | 4.82 |
| Canada (provinces) | 2 | 1 | 2 | 0 | 1 | 0 | 4 | 0 | 2.84 |
| India (states)..... | 6 | 4 | 0 | 1 | 5 | 2 | 2 | 0 | 2.37 |
| United States (states)........ | 14 | 6 | 7 | 5 | 6 | 1 | 4 | 5 | 2.31 |
| U.S.S.R. (republics).......... | 3 | 2 | 1 | 2 | 2 | 2 | 3 | 0 | 2.67 |

tation channels (including coast lines), will distort the spatial ordering of towns and the ratio of numbers of towns in the several town-size (or function) classes. By contrast, the rank-size rule purports to hold good in areas of great internal diversity and seems to apply equally well to very unalike areas. One is even tempted to ask whether it fits reality as well in homogeneous areas as in variegated areas; whether its good fit for some large conglomerate areas may not be the result of a sort of normal distribution of diversity in the area that blurs the theoretically sharp segregation of towns into distinct size and function classes and results in a more nearly contiguous gradation of towns by size if not by function. Although no large area may be uniform enough to reveal clearly the theoretical pyramid of town size

lations of the five largest cities were obtained for each of the major political divisions in the United States, Canada, Australia, and Brazil, and, where available, for India and the U.S.S.R. Most of these states and provinces exhibit less internal diversity than the country as a whole. Their ratios can serve to test the hypothesis that the rank-size rule properly applies only to diverse regions and is necessarily a random distribution; that, at least for the largest cities, the rule breaks down in fairly small and homogenous areas. The results for the two largest cities are summarized in Table 1.

For the United States the ratios show wide dispersion, from 1.08 (Virginia and Connecticut) to 32.37 (Illinois). Perhaps the most remarkable result is the large number of states, fourteen in all, clustered in the small range between 1 and 1.5. A closer examination of these fourteen states shows that most of them fall in one of three categories: states whose central cities lie beyond the state borders (Connecticut, New Jersey); states too sparsely populated to support any sizable cities (Montana, Idaho, Nevada, Wyoming, North Dakota); and states too large for a single central city and containing two such cities or more (Kansas, Oklahoma, Texas). Not large area alone but a combination of large area and moderate to low population density makes a state too large for a single center; in Florida, with centers at Miami and Jacksonville (and a subcenter at Tampa), it is length rather than area that requires two central cities. Elimination of states without centers, grouping of two or more states that share a single center, and division of large states with multiple centers into substates would greatly reduce the number of territorial divisions with low ratios (and somewhat reduce the number with very high ratios).

Brazil, with an area larger than that of the United States but with less than half as many states and a much lower degree of interdependence between states, shows less dispersion and a more pronounced tendency toward high ratios of largest to second-largest city. Paraíba, with 1.24, has the lowest ratio, and Pará, with 16.02, the highest. Only three of the twenty states have ratios under 2; of these, one is too large and too sparsely populated to have a central city, and another has a central city outside its borders. No fewer than six states exceed a ratio of 10. The two with the highest ratios, Amazonas and Pará, are large states with sparse populations, which would be unable to support cities at all were it not that their populations are concentrated in a very small proportion of their total area, and that their capital cities are the two largest Amazon River ports.

Of Canada's ten provinces, only two have low ratios, and both of them, Alberta with 1.24 and Saskatchewan with 1.35, are large agricultural provinces with two or more central cities of comparable size and function.

If each of the two provinces with low ratios is divided between its two principal cities, the resulting ratios are about 3, 3, 6, and 16 (the last for the oil center of Edmonton, the only real city in its part of Alberta).

In India, most of the Part C states (states administered by the central government) have been excluded because of small size and lack of urban development. Low ratios in this country can be explained by the same reasons as in the other countries, but an additional factor is important. It is notable that every state with a low ratio has a smaller proportion of urban to rural population than India as a whole, whose proportion is itself low. These states lack a true urban hierarchy because of the lack of integration of the large rural population within an urban network. Low income and, therefore, small demand for urban products and services, combined with the slight commercialization of agriculture, preclude close interdependence of the rural population and the urban centers.

Division of the Soviet Union into economic regions might be more meaningful than use of existing republics (whose boundaries are largely based on ethnic criteria), particularly the huge R.S.F.S.R., which extends from Leningrad to Vladivostok. The same is true to a smaller extent of the other countries studied. A division into economic regions, however, would weigh the data in favor of Lösch's model, which is not the purpose of this survey. The three republics with very low ratios are the R.S.F.S.R. and the large Ukrainian and Kazakh S.S.R.'s.

Most remarkable of all are the ratios for Australia. Five of its six states have ratios in excess of 10, and the sixth, Tasmania, with a ratio of 1.93, has only meager urban development. About 54 per cent of Australia's population lives in the five largest cities, one in each state except Tasmania. The concentration of the population near the seacoast and other favorable factors such as high income make it possible for each state, in spite of its large size, to have a central city.

The reasons regarded as explaining the low ratios of some states and provinces apply, with modifications, to many of the countries with low ratios. Size, exaggerated by poor transportation and low incomes, can account for a low ratio and the existence of multiple centers in South Africa, Spain, and Yugoslavia; in Yugoslavia topography and history also have major influence. An elongated shape explains the lack of a central city much larger than any other in Italy, Indonesia (actually Java), and New Zealand. Perhaps no country can be said to have its central city in another country, but the Netherlands has great ports whose size is due to transit trade with western and central Europe. There are a number of countries whose populations are too self-sufficient

ly well populated, mainly agricultural countries whose agriculture is commercialized, not by virtue of the large size of the central city so much as by virtue of the small size of other cities. It tends to be low or moderate for highly industrialized countries, principally because of the large size of some industrial and commercial centers. Countries and states with high rural population densities have low or moderate ratios; countries and states with very large populated areas also have low ratios.

The relative sizes of the five largest cities in each country, and in the major political divisions of most of the giant countries, are given in Table 2. The results diverge con-

TABLE 2

MEDIAN SIZE OF FIVE LARGEST CITIES AS A FRACTION ON THE LARGEST CITY

|  | Largest | Second | Third | Fourth | Fifth |
|---|---|---|---|---|---|
| 72 countries.............. | 1 | 0.315 | 0.200 | 0.140 | 0.120 |
| Australia (states).......... | 1 | 0.076 | 0.0405 | 0.024 | 0.019 |
| Brazil (states)............. | 1 | 0.210 | 0.135 | 0.105 | 0.0785 |
| Canada (provinces)........ | 1 | 0.340 | 0.220 | 0.140 | 0.078 |
| India (states)............. | 1 | 0.440 | 0.365 | 0.280 | .......... |
| United States (states)....... | 1 | 0.435 | 0.310 | 0.200 | 0.165 |
| U.S.S.R. (republics)........ | 1 | 0.375 | .......... | .......... | .......... |
| Rank-size rule............. | 1 | 0.500 | 0.333 | 0.250 | 0.200 |

and/or too small and scattered to provide an economic base for a town hierarchy, or even for a spatially continuous network of towns. Such countries, however, do not have very low ratios because they have an administrative and fiscal capital. They are not comparable with countries that have a centralized economic structure and an area under uninterrupted urban influence.

Because of the great diversity of countries and even of states and provinces, the data on relative size of the largest city in each country and in the major divisions of six giant nations do not cluster neatly around a single value. Only tentative conclusions can be drawn from the data. The majority of ratios are much higher than the rule postulates; divergence from the rule is greater for homogeneous, and smaller for heterogeneous, areas. The ratio is highest for fair-

siderably from the rank-size rule. For most countries not only is the second city much less than half the size of the largest but other ratios also differ somewhat from the rule. The size difference between second and third cities, and between third and fourth cities, is larger than the rule postulates. The fourth and fifth cities are close together in size. The divergences between fact and rule are small except for the gap between the first and second cities and are not reproduced in every giant country. They mask a confusing variety of ratios. The range of values obtained for the ratios between any two successive cities is large and fails completely to cluster around a central value. This extraordinary range is more conclusive than any arbitrary measure of central tendency, and more significant than the divergences between the empirical ratios and the rank-size rule.

The data are not sufficiently refined to suggest an incipient stratification of cities by size such as Lösch postulates. Examination of most countries showing any degree of urban development reveals more than one type of urban arrangement by size in the upper part of the town-size pyramid. By proper selection of countries—placing in one group those with a clear-cut central city and in another those with two central cities or more—and by considering a larger number of cities, stratification may or may not become evident. It may be useful to group only countries with considerable urban development and exclude those whose urban sphere blankets only a small part of the total area. It may further be suggested that in advanced countries the urban-rural dichotomy as measured by residence has lost much of its meaning; other concepts of relevant population, such as employment or trading population, should be considered.

An empirical rule derived from world-wide data on the relative size of cities near the apex of the town-size pyramid has no logical foundation. Its condition is a particular, impermanent, world-wide historical context. The rule does not hold for any grouping of similar countries. At the base of the pyramid the rule also tends to break down. It may be more accurate to say that population statistics on small towns should not be used to test the rank-size rule without considerable refinement. In many countries numerous settlements can be found in the same size range as towns of the lowest order (that is, providing the minimum services regularly found in the area) but lacking the functional attributes of the lowest-order towns. A group of houses huddled together for company or for safety may have an orderly pattern of distribution in space and a normal curve of distribution by size, but the principles which determine spacing and size are not those which guide other settlements and cities with standard economic functions. Settlements that do not belong at the base of the town-size pyramid are mainly colo-

nies of peasant cottages but include also villages with an economic rationale, albeit a narrow one, such as fishing villages or mining towns comprising households, the single industry, and no more. Such single-purpose economic settlements show much less regularity than peasant villages in spacing and probably also in size.

Population statistics on towns terminate abruptly at arbitrary lower limits, usually 2,000 to 3,000. Many centers of less than the minimum population do fulfil urban functions and therefore belong in the functional hierarchy of towns. On the other hand, many towns that are included in urban statistics because their populations exceed the arbitrary minimum are not towns at all in function. Small towns with rudimentary urban functions may include widely varying agricultural components, so that their populations are poorly correlated with their urban functions. Lack of comprehensive data on functions of small towns both smaller and larger than the minimum required for inclusion in urban statistics precludes any attempt to measure the shape of the town-size pyramid near its base. There are reasons to believe, however, that statistical towns which lack urban functions are fairly common in countries with intensive subsistence agriculture, such as India and China, though they are rare in the United States. The joint result of allowing for the large relative size of principal cities and of eliminating statistical towns without urban functions would be a slightly S-shaped logarithmic distribution of towns by size. Many of Zipf's graphs conform more closely to a theoretical S shape than to the straight-line distribution he proposes.

### SOME DETERMINANTS OF TOWN SPACING

*Rural population density.*—Lösch finds the distance between towns in a given size class to be greater in Iowa than in the United Kingdom, and greater in Nebraska than in Iowa. The density of rural (or, better, agricultural) population, which clearly varies inversely with the distance between

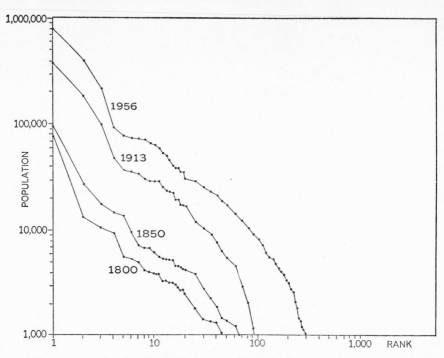

FIG. 1.—The S-curve in Sweden. The small size of Stockholm relative to the size of the next two largest cities, Göteborg and Malmö, is attributable to Stockholm's peripheral and somewhat remote location on the north Baltic, and to the role of Göteborg and Malmö as regional centers and as seaports close to the North Sea and to Denmark, respectively.

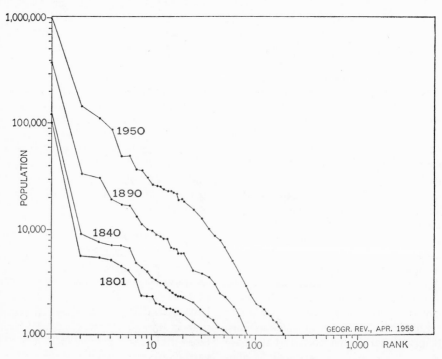

GEOGR. REV., APR. 1958

FIG. 2.—Development of an S-shaped distribution of cities by size: Denmark

sizable towns, must be considered in order to determine theoretically, or to explain empirically, the distance between towns of a given size. However, the distance between towns of the lowest order seems to be a constant for a wide range of rural population densities. For example, nearly the same typical distance has been found to obtain between equivalent types of trading centers in England and in Wisconsin despite the great difference in population density, both total and rural.[4] In deference to the greater density, the British trading center is much larger than its Wisconsin counterpart.[5] Roughly similar local transport facilities seem to dictate similar spacing of lowest-order towns performing equivalent functions in both areas, whereas large differences in rural population density are reflected in large differences in the populations of towns performing the same functions in the two areas.

The exact nature of the relation of population density, on the one hand, to spacing of towns of a given function type and, on the other, to population of towns with a given spacing has not been determined. Correlations are misleading without consideration of the historical process that brought them about and of the causal relations that result. In one case high rural population density may explain the close spacing and large size of towns, but in another case low or declining rural density is the result of urban growth. The relationship applies only to towns and cities that are closely integrated with their surrounding countrysides.

The integration between towns and country can be measured by the degree of their interdependence. The country is dependent on the city in proportion as its agricultural produce is raised for the city, and particularly in proportion as the country specializes its production and relies on the city as a service center and a source of goods. The city's needs are much more diverse than the possible products of its agricultural hinterland. A better measure of integration is the city's dependence on its rural hinterland as a source of external income, earned by the sale of goods and services.[6] There are cases of one-sided dependence and even of town and surrounding countryside wholly untouched by each other—some mining towns, for instance, or military installations—but the normal relation is symbiotic. Only when both dependent relations are fairly strong is there a close connection between town size or spacing and rural population density.

*The urban-rural ratio.*—The existence of large cities in any number is based on a sizable urban population. The hinterland of the large city consists of other cities and towns. Rural population density is an explanation of spacing (or of size) only for towns and small cities oriented toward their rural hinterlands. The larger the urban share of total population, the larger is the proportion of urban population living in cities that serve other cities, and the smaller the proportion in towns that cater to their rural peripheries. The higher the urban ratio, then, the greater is the concentration of urban population in large cities, and the closer their spacing relative to the spacing of towns and small cities. Since the size and spacing of large cities depend both on the urban ratio and on urban population density (that is, on total urban population divided by the total space in which towns and cities are scattered), empirical determination of the relation between the urban ratio and urban spacing seems unlikely. To measure the effects of the urban ratio on absolute

[4] J. E. Brush and H. E. Bracey, "Rural Service Centers in Southwestern Wisconsin and Southern England," *Geographical Review*, XLV (1955), 559–69 [see above, pp. 210–17].

[5] The two are not strictly comparable, however, since stores and services are found in the British town that could not be supported in its nearest Wisconsin equivalent because the tributary population is too small.

[6] Since a large part of the city's income is derived from the spending of its residents, it is not the total income but that sizable part of it earned by providing goods and services purchased by nonresidents which is relevant for determining the extent of the city's dependence on its immediate hinterland.

distances between towns in different size classes, it would be necessary to compare countries with almost the same total populations and total areas but different urban ratios.[7]

*Commercialization of agriculture.*—Even with a given rural population density and a given urban-rural ratio, the size of a town is only an indirect index of its distance from similar towns and of its place in the hierarchy of towns. For size is incidental to function. Both the functions of towns and the efficiency with which these functions are performed vary considerably from country to country; on both counts, therefore, the spacing of towns of given size and the shape of the town-size pyramid (the relative numbers of towns of different size classes) should also vary somewhat from country to country.

Let us consider the division of functions between town and country and between large and small towns. In most backward countries the rural population is nearly self-sufficient. It provides all its own food locally without intermediation of middlemen except at the village level, and it manufactures most of its other household requirements from local raw materials. The main service purchased is agricultural labor; the only services required from the towns to any extent are credit and transportation. In such preindustrial subsistence economies the few towns are located not in relation to the distribution of the rural population and of rural villages but in relation to the thin network of trade routes for high-value goods and to administrative or military districts. The villages are oriented to the countryside

and the agricultural population, being much more numerous relative to towns than they are in countries with commercialized agriculture and industrial development; the towns face one another only.

In regions where agriculture is commercialized, farm and urban populations cannot live in separate worlds. Agricultural specialization means a transfer of processing and manufacturing from the household and small village to the town and city. The farm household has to purchase a widening range of agricultural products; the towns become middlemen between farm and farm, farm region and farm region. Economic society, and with it all society, becomes less loosely knit; division of functions between farms, small towns, and larger towns becomes more clear-cut, and their interrelationship in space and in numbers and population more definite. The greater the specialization, the greater is the tendency to transfer functions from the small towns to the larger ones, and the larger the area that can be regarded as self-sufficient in any respect.

*Standard of living.*—The ratio of agricultural to non-agricultural population, when due allowance has been made for the region's external-trade position in farm products, is an indirect measure of another determinant of the distribution of urban population—the standard of living. The urban ratio in predominantly wheat-growing regions of the United States is much higher than in comparable regions of the Ukraine. Furthermore, in areas of comparable urban population density, the larger towns seem more closely spaced in the United States and the very small towns in the U.S.S.R.[8]

High income of American wheat farmers means that nearly all have cars; high income of American society at large means that the road network in rural areas is denser than in the Soviet Union and roads

[7] Moreover, the size and spacing of the larger cities are highly sensitive to income levels, the pattern of government employment, the trade matrix, and industrial localization—influences that either little affect the small towns or average out over large numbers of them. The fact that in India, with an urban population not much smaller than that of the United States but with a much lower urban ratio, only 39 per cent of the urban population lives in cities of more than 100,000, in contrast with 50 per cent in the United States, is, of course, not useful as evidence. The countries and their standards of living differ greatly.

[8] Many sovkhozy and kolkhozy in the U.S.S.R. must be regarded as small towns in respect to their functions; since the full range of their services may be available only for residents, they are more like the "private" towns of the past than the "public" towns of our day.

are better. High income of both farmers and urban residents in the United States means that a much larger part of income is spent for manufactured goods and for services, that is, for the products of urban industry. This statement is nothing but a rewording of Engel's law that with increasing income a decreasing proportion is spent on food. Even for income at levels where an increment results mainly in diversification of the diet and consumption of luxuries, the statement holds good, since relief from a monotonous diet requires increased trade conducted largely through cities as well as increased agricultural processing. The high American farm productivity has two effects, both raising the ratio of urban to farm population and, therefore, tending to crowd sizable cities more closely together: a single American farmer can provide enough food and other agricultural products to support more people in towns than a Ukrainian farmer can; and he can, because of his productivity, spend a larger proportion of his higher income on urban goods and services. The larger urban population, itself having a high income relative to urban populations in the Ukrainian wheat belt, can in turn spend a larger proportion of its income on urban products.

## THE TOWN-SIZE PYRAMID

Mention has been made of the fact that the ratio of small to large cities is much higher in India than in the United States. Although higher income alone explains why the urban ratio in the United States wheat belt is higher than in the Ukraine or other low-income agricultural regions, it provides no obvious explanation for the greater concentration in large cities—that is, for the closer spacing of large cities and the wider spacing of small towns—in the United States than in countries with about the same urban population density. Low urban ratio and low standard of living are in all probability the cause for the large proportion of towns and town population in the lower levels of the town-size pyramid in India.

They are closely related, at least within a single country over time, and both are positively correlated with a third factor, low specialization, which has also been mentioned as resulting in the same type of distribution of towns by size. Some reasons will be offered why these associations hold good, and consideration will be given to their implications for $k$, the ratio of numbers of towns in succesive functional classes. The fact that urban population is more highly concentrated in the larger cities in the United States than in India suggests that $k$ is smaller in the United States but does not imply it; for towns of the same size in the two countries do not necessarily fall in the same functional category, nor need the population ratios of towns in different functional categories be the same in all countries.

*Some distorting influences.*—First we need some assurance that $k$ (and the functional categories of towns to which it has reference) is more than a convenient but arbitrary division of a spectrum of town sizes and functions. This is the belief of Christaller, who distinguished seven classes of towns in South Germany.[9] It seems also to be the conclusion of Green,[10] who found five classes in England and Wales, and of Smailes,[11] whose study of the same areas also distinguished five classes. When allow-

[9] Ullman, *op. cit.* [see n. 2 above], p. 857.

[10] F. H. W. Green, "Urban Hinterlands in England and Wales: An Analysis of Bus Services," *Geographical Journal,* CXVI (1950), 64–88.

[11] A. E. Smailes, "The Urban Hierarchy in England and Wales," *Geography,* XXIX (1944), 41–51. Below the level of full-fledged towns Smailes mentions two classes: subtowns and urban villages. Among cities and towns (whose minimum population he puts at 10,000) Smailes distinguishes in some places three classes (for example, p. 50): city, major town (or minor city), and town. Elsewhere (see map on p. 43) he breaks down the first class into cities and major cities. On page 46, note 5, he distinguishes London and Manchester from other major cities. His conclusions that $k = 3$ refer to three, not four or five, classes of towns and cities. It may well be argued that Scotland, at least, should also be counted in calculating the value of $k$ for major cities.

ance is made for the fact that Christaller's classes are differentiated according to the administrative principle as well as according to the trade and service principle, which is used exclusively in the English studies, the coincidence in the number of classes and their correspondence in function are striking. The values of $k$ in the studies referred to all lie between 3 and 4.[12] No one has challenged the logic of such an arrangement of towns; yet attempts to find a corresponding grouping of towns and cities in a limited number of size classes instead of their dispersion in a nearly continuous curve have proved at best only partly successful. Lösch's contention that the uneven distribution of minerals and their related industries, differences in fertility, ability, and so on, are always sufficient to distort the size pattern[13] is only part of the story. The hierarchy of economic function, although by far the most important, is not the only one. The administrative hierarchy, for example, is largely unrelated to the economic and has its own values for $k$. In the United States the value for $k$ for each of the three branches of government is 48 at the national level and varies widely at state levels but is never as low as 3. The federal courts have their own value for $k$; the Federal Reserve System has twelve districts; the executive branch has ten departments—these are only a few among the many orderings of government functions that affect the shape of the town-size pyramid. The common practice of locating government centers away from the largest cities, except at the county level, sets the administrative principle in opposition to the trade and service principle in shaping the pattern of town sizes. Nor is the working of the administrative principle limited to government functions. Private organizations have their own bureaucracies and administrative hierarchies; these tend, however, to coincide with the hierarchies of economic function.

Government activities, unlike mining or fishing, show no great spatial preferences. The distribution over space of government functions and of the required personnel and its associated population can be expected to follow an orderly pattern in any one region. Employment in one of the main government functions, public schools, shows little bias for city size in cities large enough to support their own high schools. The distorting effect of the government functions on the trade and service hierarchy of towns is the result of a different locational principle and of a different value for $k$; the effect should be felt equally throughout any one region. The distorting effect of mining activities and their associated population, located on the basis of unequally distributed resources, will show marked regional bias and is entirely absent in some areas. The fact that government and mining employment and its dependent population are small does not mean that the distorting effect is small. It is a big part of employment in activities whose location is largely independent of existing or expected distributions of population. Particularly in countries with high standards of living, large satellite populations employed in service industries or in market-oriented manufactures cluster around relatively small nuclei of autonomous employment, such as government, mining, and mineral-oriented manufactures, and greatly distort the spatial uniformity and hierarchical gradation of the town ecology.

*Limitations on the number of town classes.*—The conclusion of the few studies mentioned on the United States and on parts of western Europe, that most towns can be placed clearly within one of a very few functional types arranged in hierarchical order, can be supplemented by some comments on the logic of the location of economic activities. The countries studied are all in a fairly rapid process of evolution, with towns advancing and retrogressing in the functional scale and with towns changing greatly in population both as a result of general population increase and technological progress and as a correlate of their changed functional status. Thus it is not

[12] See also Lösch, *op. cit.*, pp. 434–35.

[13] *Ibid.*, pp. 437, 438.

surprising that the functional gradations of town classes are not everywhere clear-cut and that some towns do not fall clearly in one functional grouping rather than another.

That town classes are few, not many, and that the functional gradations between them are large, not almost imperceptible, can be attributed to two general facts: indivisibility in the unit of production—factory, service establishment, transport route, or individual specialist—and complementarity in space between different products and services requiring their joint location. Complementarity is a form of indivisibility; in effect it reduces the number of independent units and therefore the number of possible increments of goods and services provided by successively larger towns. Complementarity in demand includes both joint use, which reduces the number of independent commodities and services, and complementarity in shopping convenience (largely between stores selling goods unrelated in use), which reduces the number of types of shopping districts. An excellent example of complementarity in space is the shopping center. Its component stores, which are usually pretty much the same throughout the country, were once selected by trial and error. But the lesson has been learned, so that the equilibrium composition of the shopping center is now often planned for. The department store, a higher-order shopping center under one roof, illustrates the identity of the principles of complementarity and indivisibility.

Similar complementarities exist in supply: firms relying on the same supply sources tend to be located close together; many firms are located close to the suppliers of their major inputs. One restriction on the size of an undertaking, and hence on the total number of its type, has no counterpart in demand at the retail level, though it does at the wholesale. This is the minimum scale of operation, expressed as the minimum sales volume necessary to support a store or factory, which may be set by purely physical indivisibilities. The interplay of these

often conflicting forces—consumer convenience on the one hand, and economies of scale, on the other—determines spacing and size not only of firms but of shopping districts and manufacturing centers. Consumer convenience alone leads to dispersed location and a large number of establishments of the same kind; for example, it would dictate a department store in every village. Economies of scale (of firm) or of concentration (of industry) might create monopoly or restrict establishments of the same kind to a single city. Examples of consumer convenience are found in some services, such as utilities in every house and mailboxes at every corner. Examples of spatial concentration and scale include the motion-picture and diamond-cutting industries as examples of localization and the Post Office Department as an example of monopoly.

Complementarity and the advantages of scale and concentration reduce the number of size classes of towns, both as trading centers and as industrial complexes, and widen the gap between different classes of towns in function and population. Information does not exist suitable for deciding whether or not these factors alone are enough to reduce the classes of towns to the order of 6–7. The nature of modern transportation networks is a further factor tending strongly to reduce the number of town classes. Economic limitations on the number of high-speed, heavy-duty transport routes are a result of their indivisibility and the consequent high minimum scale of operation (volume of traffic) required for their economic provision. The existence and scarcity of heavy-duty transport routes are assurance that gradations in goods and services available must be sufficient to draw customers in large numbers to the town offering the wider range of goods and services from the tributary areas of towns offering a narrower range. Some towns, centrally located, are easily accessible on all sides; others are not. Inhabitants of any one town have a limited number of indifferently located alternative shopping and service centers; complementarities of shopping time and effort dictate that their purchases will be concentrated in one or two other towns (if not in their own town), not diffused in many directions.

## "K" AS A FUNCTION OF ECONOMIC WELFARE

Per capita income seems to be the best rough index of the spacing of towns with comparable functions and the composition of town functions in regions with about the same density of farm population and the same degree of agricultural commercialization. In wealthy countries the disparity in cost and convenience between rural transport and interurban transport is smaller than in poor countries. On this ground wealthy countries should have a lower ratio of small to medium and large towns than poor countries. The effective trade and service areas of the sizable towns and the cities are sufficiently large, because of good transportation, to absorb the functions of many peripheral villages and small towns that in poorer countries would fall outside their sphere of influence because of the low mobility and simpler needs of rural residents.

A high standard of living, itself a product of specialization, tends to increase specialization further both in farm and in town. As towns grow in size, and as their populations grow in per capita income, many functions are shifted from the household to the market—for example, kitchen gardening, laundering, food preservation and preparation, tailoring and dressmaking, and household repairs. With this increase in range of services demanded of the market, and with more general use of these services, the size of the viable community increases, and therefore the number of viable communities decreases (unless a growing population is assumed).

The transfer of functions from the household, where they are performed intermittently by individuals often without special skill, usually without proper equipment and training, and always without the economies of specialization and scale, greatly increases efficiency in every function. One might expect, therefore, that the size of town required to perform a given function would

tend to fall. In fact this does not happen; revolutions in the organization of production and distribution and in services create the need for new services and manufactures; the functions of every town are revised. Furthermore, the accompanying increase in per capita income widens the consumption horizons of the town population and opens up opportunities for new products and services.

Town functions and the hierarchy of functional town classes reflect the pattern of demand, which is dependent on the level of income and its distribution, on the role of government, and on prevailing tastes. The hierarchy of town-size groups corresponding to the hierarchy of function constellations that is characteristic of the United States does not exist in the U.S.S.R. or India; the same size groups in the three countries have different function constellations; the same function constellations probably cannot be found at all or, if found, will not occur in towns either in the same size bracket or in the same stage in the hierarchy.

The conclusion that per capita income materially affects the shape of the town-size pyramid need not be based on correlations between income and some index of concentration of urban population in the larger cities. More specific evidence is available that, for the United States, leads to the same conclusion. This evidence relates to the economic functions of towns, which are defined to include all goods and services bought and sold. The important role of these functions and the strong gravitational pull they exert on the location of non-economic functions assure us that the restricted range of the evidence need not qualify the conclusion. Reference has already been made to Engel's law. A second empirical generalization on the progress of economic welfare has been made by Clark,[14] who observes in advanced countries a relative growth in the share of services, or tertiary industry, at the expense of manufacturing or other second-

[14] Colin Clark, *The Conditions of Economic Progress* (2d ed.; London, 1951), chap. 9, esp. pp. 395–401.

ary industry. This generalization has recently been subjected to criticisms that limit the scope of its application to a particular historical context. It still holds for countries with well-developed and progressive economies.[15] Since the bulk of both manufacturing and service industry is located in urban areas, a shift to services affects the town-size pyramid if they show a higher degree of concentration in larger cities than manufactures do. Higher incomes also alter the composition of demand for both goods and services; there is no doubt that the shift is to services which show a strong preference for larger cities, and it seems probable that the net effect is in the same direction for manufactures. Reilly,[16] among others, has shown that the higher an individual's income, the larger is the minimum size of the city which can retain his custom, and the farther he is willing to travel for his shopping. Furthermore, it is precisely the categories of expenditure that bulk largest in high-income groups—luxuries, fashion goods, personalized products and services— that require the largest minimum town size to retain resident trade. Indeed, only the larger towns can support a wide range of the luxury products and services that are prominent in the budgets of wealthy countries. Studies have been made of the minimum tributary populations, with allowance for their incomes, required to support given types of stores and services; studies also exist on minimum population densities required to support stores and services of different types.[17] These studies show that stores and services whose importance grows with income tend to have high minimum tributary populations and population densities, whereas stores and services whose importance declines with income have low minimums. Purely as a double check on the

other types of evidence suggested may be mentioned the residence distribution of the well-to-do. There is some tendency for average per capita income to vary directly with town size, particularly if the wealthy suburbs of large cities are included in computing their per capita incomes. More significant than slight differences in per capita income is the proportionately greater concentration in larger cities of families in the upper income brackets—the upper 20 per cent of families by income, say, in whose budgets agricultural products and the services available, and goods manufactured, in small towns are decidedly less important than in budgets of the urban population as a whole.

## DEVELOPMENT OF "K"

In the natural course of autonomous regional development new towns arise and a few of the old ones grow to perform functions that were neither necessary nor feasible in the stage of subsistence agriculture; the number of town classes increases. The lower-order towns develop first, then the higher order.[18] The relation $k$ between any two successive town classes starts from a high value and declines, and/or the size differences between various classes of towns, expressed as the ratio of typical town populations, $Pa/Pb$, are small at first and then increase. It seems likely that $Pa/Pb$ increases, whereas $k$ remains relatively constant, since $k$ depends largely on relative distances, whereas $Pa/Pb$ to a significant degree is a function of income. Large decreases in $k$ occur only with the development of new, higher-order town classes. At

[15] See P. T. Bauer and B. S. Yamey, "Economic Progress and Occupational Distribution," *Economic Journal*, LXI (1951), 741–55.

[16] W. J. Reilly, *Methods for the Study of Retail Relationships* (*University of Texas, Bureau of Business Research, Research Monograph No. 4* [1929]), pp. 7, 9, 40.

[17] On minimum populations see H. G. Canoyer, *Selecting a Store Location* ("*U.S. Bureau of Foreign and Domestic Commerce Economics Series*," *No. 56* [1946]); *Reilly, op. cit.*; R. S. Vaile (ed.), *The Small City and Town* (Minneapolis, 1930), pp. 12–16. See also R. D. McKenzie, *The Metropolitan Community* (New York and London, 1933), chap. 19.

[18] The theoretical shape of the logarithmic distribution of towns by size would be an inverted *S*, which would gradually straighten out and eventually become a normal *S*.

first there are few towns in the new class, but in time their numbers reach the full complement for the class. After introduction of a large foreign-trade factor based on mineral exploitation and foreign capital movements or on plantation agriculture, an inverse process can occur: the rise of a metropolis based on foreign trade and on administration and catering to the wants of resident foreigners and of a small indigenous wealthy class. This may happen long before the intermediate town classes are fully developed, and before the income and way of life of most of the population become modeled on the metropolitan example. As the intermediate classes of towns develop, the differences in function and in population of the several town classes increase, but their hierarchical grouping by function persists. The higher-order towns, whose number increases, at first have small hinterlands because of poor transportation; eventually the hinterlands expand until they blanket the countryside and overlap one another, and the hinterland, both in numbers and in income, gains a larger share in urban life. Stability of three variables—the number of classes in the functional hierarchy of towns and the two ratios $k$ and $Pa/Pb$ (respectively, the ratios of number of towns and of typical town populations in successive classes)—characterizes a society that has reached an equilibrium of centrifugal and centripetal forces for current technology and residential preferences.

The earlier stages of autonomous commercial and industrial development are marked by an increase in the number and size of higher-order towns—the higher the order, the later the appearance of towns—and an increase in the number of town-function classes. The later stages, although showing greater increase in the number and size of higher-order towns (which are hard to separate from increases in population and in urban-rural ratio), are characterized more by a decrease in the number of towns in the lowest order or two. Eventually the lowest order practically disappears, and its

place in the town-function pyramid is taken by the next-lowest order, which loses some of its functions but manages to survive. This at least is the picture in the United States and Britain, where many service villages and small towns have lost their economic functions and survive, if at all, only as a cluster of houses. The towns gobbled up the service villages for two reasons: the revolution in local transportation, and higher cash incomes. The service villages were spaced closely enough that all inhabitants of the countryside could reach them on foot or by horse-drawn vehicles on poor roads in about an hour. Better roads, buses, and automobiles greatly increased the distance customers could travel in an hour. However, ease of travel alone cannot explain the decline of service villages, for the short trip is preferred to the long. Increased cash income and consequent greater diversity of individual purchases required a size and variety of stocks and shops that the service village, with its small tributary population and sales, could not hope to maintain profitably. In Britain the high population density, both rural and urban, and the compact spacing of towns also contributed to the obsolescence of the service village and the consolidation of its functions in the next-higher town class. One may speculate that with the continuously growing consumers' range of travel, workers' range of commutation, and per capita income the same fate may overtake the small towns that retain their trade in staples. As the proportion of staples in the budget of most consumers drops further, the purchase of staples becomes more and more subsidiary to the purchase of goods and services that can be provided in adequate quantity and variety by only a large town or city. On the other hand, the mobility of the individual and the large and widening range of his daily travel mean that residence in or near an urban center is no longer requisite for access to urban amenities, and the choice of residence acquires a degree of independence it has never had before in the history of cities.

## Determinants of "K"

A few general conclusions can be reached on the determinants of $k$ and its consequent values. The determinants of $k$ between the two lowest orders of town are unique because of the nature of the spacing of towns of the lowest order. The minimum distance between such towns is the distance required to provide the tributary population needed to support the staple services and products the towns supply; the actual distance will be such that all inhabitants live within about an hour of a trading center if such spacing provides the necesary minimum tributary population. In sparsely settled areas lowest-order towns will be widely spaced; but they will be just as closely spaced in areas ranging from moderately to densely settled, if local transportation facilities are equally developed, though their populations will vary with rural population density. The determinants of spacing for lowest-order towns are local transportation and rural population density. The value of $k$ will be high in areas with poor local transportation, and low in areas with high rural population density. The explanation for the second statement is as follows. Since the population of lowest-order towns varies with rural population density, fewer such towns are required to support a single town of the next-higher order, and therefore—for a given level of per capita income—$k$ can be smaller than in a less densely settled area. The determinants of $k$ for all other town classes except the highest are the relative availability of transport facilities and the relative importance, in terms of income and employment, of the functions characteristic of the different functional town classes. Except in the lowest town classes, substantial interregional differences in relative availability of transport betwen different town classes are exceptional, and this determinant of $k$ should be the same in all countries for the town classes of higher order. Greater relative importance of the functions performed exclusively or preponderantly in the progressively higher orders of towns is close-

ly related to high incomes and the diversification of demand and expenditure that results from high incomes. Therefore $k$ should be lower in wealthy countries than in poor countries. Finally, the value of $k$ between the two highest orders of cities may be affected by another extraneous determinant. The largest cities in a number of countries have natural hinterlands that transcend national boundaries. Their tributary areas, and therefore the value of $k$, may fluctuate with the ebb and flow of empire. Or national trade blocks may be erected, so that two truncated metropolitan cities exist where there was room for only one, and the value of $k$ is lowered.

## Tentative Conclusions

Many statements have been made that must be verified by extensive statistical work. Until the evidence is complete, the following conclusions must be regarded as tentative.

The rank-size rule, although in many cases a reasonable approximation to the actual distribution of towns by size, has no logical basis. It breaks down in many areas at both extremes—the largest and the smallest towns. Its applicability in the middle range in large areas is due partly to diversity within the area in the value of the determinants of town size and spacing and partly to the gross coincidence of the rank-size curve and the town-function pyramid. The rule is a better description of reality for large heterogeneous areas than for small homogeneous areas, where town size, spacing, and functions are most closely interconnected.

Reasons have been given, in terms of complementarities in demand and in supply and in terms of the limited number of transport routes, why towns must fall within a limited number of functional groups and why the gradations in function between these groups must be substantial. The failure of towns to fall within clear-cut size groups to correspond with their function groups is the result, first, of the variations in the values of the determinants of town size and spacing (including uneven distribution of natural resources), which smooth the stepladder distribution into an approximation of the rank-size rule; and, second, of the existence of conflicting hierarchical principles, mainly the hierarchy of government administration, which distort the theoretically steplike distribution of town sizes according to economic functions.

There is nothing "natural" about the shape of the town-size pyramid. The relative sizes of towns in different function classes and their relative numbers (or the value of $k$) vary with the stage of economic development. Several determinants of $k$ have been mentioned, of which the standard of living is the most nearly complete index. A rise in the standard of living tends to reduce the value of $k$ and to increase the difference in population of towns in different function classes. It also shifts many functions from lower-order to higher-order towns, with resultant loss of function by lowest-order towns and growth of new, higher functional orders of towns, the metropolitan centers. Well-structured areas of urban dominance tend to have an S-shaped, rather than a linear logarithmic, distribution of towns by size.

# AN OPTIMUM SIZE FOR CITIES

In recent years, faced with the trend within Western culture toward increasing urbanization, planners and other social scientists have begun to think about the problem of how far urbanization will go. Should the larger centers be allowed to grow indefinitely in population and area or should the development be arbitrarily stopped? If the development is to be halted, at which stage should it occur with respect to a city's population and area? This question immediately raises the basic problem of what should be the optimum size for large urban centers, known generally as cities.

This problem has been examined by a number of town planners and sociologists. For the most part their investigations have been brief and in many cases quite limited in scope. The criteria used for determining an optimum size for cities have varied greatly. Duncan[1] and Ogburn[2] indicate a selected optimum of 50,000–100,000 people, based on the per capita cost of muncipal services in urban centers in the United States with a population greater than 25,000, i.e., on a selected quantitative statistical basis without considering, as both Duncan and Thomas Sharp[3] point out, the quality and the scope of these services as well as the length and continuity of their operation. Ebenezer Howard,[4] whose optimum is 30,-000 people[5] and Le Corbusier,[6] who considers a city of 3,000,000 as ideal, based their estimates on what they personally believed to be the best size, i.e., their estimates were entirely subjective. Still others like Brennan,[7] whose optimum is 10,000–20,000, based their findings on a desirable social life for the inhabitants.

None of these observers, however, mentioned the problems raised by the very meanings of the words "optimum size for cities." The *Shorter Oxford English Dictionary* defines "optimum" as the "best" or "most desirable"; "size" as the "magnitude," "bulk," "bigness," or "dimensions" of anything; and "city" as a name for any urban center greater in size than a town. The application of these terms to urbanism and to town planning has the following implications:

If one considers an optimum size for cities, the question immediately raised is, The optimum for what?—for internal ease of movement, for economic provision of services, for a desirable social life, for "urban life," or for defense in time of war? When one considers the word "size," its several aspects in this case become rapidly apparent. Urban centers cover a horizontal area and also have a vertical extent. Size

Reprinted from *Canadian Geographer*, No. 5 (1955), pp. 85–88, with permission of the author and the editor. (Published by the Canadian Association of Geographers, Ottawa, Canada.)

[1] O. T. Duncan, "The Optimum Size of Cities," *Reader in Urban Sociology*, ed. P. K. Hatt and A. J. Reiss (Glencoe, Ill.: Free Press, 1951), pp. 632–45.

[2] W. F. Ogburn, *Social Characteristics of Cities*, (Chicago: International Managers' Association, 1937).

[3] T. Sharp, *Town Planning* (London: Pelican Books, 1940), p. 69.

[4] M. S. Briggs, *Town and Country Planning* (London: Allen & Unwin, 1948), p. 24.

[5] Many followers of the English school of town and regional planners which developed following Howard's Garden City principle believe the optimum size for cities to be 30,000–50,000 people.

[6] Charles E. Jeanneret-Gris (Le Corbusier, pseud.), *City of Tomorrow and Its Planning*, trans. from the 8th French ed. of *Urbanisme* by Frederick Etchells (London: Architectural Press, 1947), p. 172.

[7] T. Brennan, *Midland City* (London: Dennis Dobson, Ltd., 1949), p. 47.

here also means total population, a population which can be concentrated by vertical accumulation or dispersed thinly over a broad horizontal area. The word "city," according to the above, means an urban center greater in population than a town. Within our culture the population size for cities has been defined legally. In Ontario, for example, it is an agglomeration of 15,000 people; in Saskatchewan it is a population of 5,000 people concentrated on 640 acres or less; in Wisconsin it is a population of 1,000 on 320 acres or less. It is quite obvious, then, considering all the implications of the above, that an answer to the question, What is the optimum size for cities? can be given only after a very great number of complex criteria have been examined, analyzed, weighed, and a synthesis attempted in order to resolve the contradictory nature of many of the various factors. Any estimates such as those submitted by the sociologists and planners mentioned would be wholly inadequate unless they were closely linked to the geographic character, distributions, and functional patterns of the regions within which the centers were to be found.

Despite this, however, there are several general considerations which do apply to the resolving of the problem. First, size may be taken to refer almost completely to the total population of the urban center, for the distribution of this population over a horizontal and/or a vertical area will depend on the physical nature of the site and the general cultural levels of all the people occupying the site, that is, their felt needs and desires for social living and the technical skills they have to translate these feelings into actuality. Second, in each major geographic region there seems to be a hierarchy of interrelated urban centers. This hierarchy is based on the services and functions of the individual centers. The interrelationships are not permanent but change with time, as the culture of the region changes. In an open economy based on competition such as one finds in those regions occupied by western European culture, not only can func-

tions change in the long period of time when the entire culture changes, but they can also change within a short period of time, within the same cultural period. In a closed economy, in a region dominated by a single, strong central authority, it is possible for the functions and therefore the hierarchy to remain static or rigid within any one cultural period. Changes in function in the latter are also subject to very tight control by the central authority.

If one assumes that the hierarchy of interrelated functions of urban centers is a valid concept, then one can arrive at an optimum size for each of the centers on the hierarchy. This optimum size cannot have an absolute value but will be a range in population. It will have a maximum and a minimum figure based on the greatest efficiency of operation of all the functions of the individual urban centers. The greater the number of functions for any one center, the greater this range will be. Whether the efficiency or the degree of efficiency is translated in terms of production or money or social living or some other criterion, will depend on the general culture of the geographic region.

There are, however, a number of cases which tend to qualify this approach to determining an optimum size. These are the urban centers whose functions do not readily seem to fit into any hierarchy, such as resort towns, military towns, university towns, or isolated mining and pulp mill towns. The optimum, or rather the maximum-minimum range in population for these will vary in a manner similar to those urban centers which find themselves at the bottom of a hierarchy, that is, those concerned with the production of primary products. The population will vary as the rate of exploitation of the available resources, be they minerals, timber, fish, university lecturers, or a sandy stretch of coast line in a semitropical climate. For the former and for other centers of primary production in a geographic area which has had a relatively long period of settlement, knowing the rate of exploitation of the available resources, the planner can predict quite safely the optimum size for the community whose function it is to exploit or directly service the exploiters of each particular resource, subject, of course, to the vagaries of "market prices." This can be illustrated by a number of Ontario examples. According to the 1951 (9th) Census of Canada, the population of the nation has been growing over the past four decades at an average rate of 2.1 per cent per annum (except for the depression decade 1931–41). During the past decade the increase in population has taken place in the urban centers, while the rural population of Canada was

and the resulting density of population. A number of centers in Lambton County illustrate this point. Although Arkona, Thedford, and Watford fulfil similar functions, the population of each is quite different, although each is stabilized. Oil Springs is an example of what can happen with a change in function. An oil-producing center from 1861 to 1866, it had reverted to a farming market and service center by 1871. A boom in the oil industry saw a rapid climb in population in answer to the added function of oil production. The rapid decline of the Oil Springs field shortly after 1901 resulted

TABLE 1

THE FUNCTIONS AND POPULATION GROWTH OF CERTAIN URBAN CENTERS IN ONTARIO

| URBAN CENTER | FUNCTIONS | POPULATION | | | | | | |
|---|---|---|---|---|---|---|---|---|
| | | 1891 | 1901 | 1911 | 1921 | 1931 | 1941 | 1951 |
| Arkona........ | Farm service center | 463 | 468 | 424 | 420 | 420 | 406 | 370 |
| Thedford...... | Farm service center | 616 | 633 | 559 | 524 | 559 | 623 | 616 |
| Watford....... | Farm service center | 1,299 | 1,279 | 1,092 | 1,059 | 979 | 1,076 | 1,201 |
| Oil Springs..... | Farm service center and oil production | 1,138 | 1,018 | 646 | 490 | 394 | 458 | 433 |
| Sarnia......... | Multifunctional regional capital | 6,692 | 8,176 | 9,947 | 14,877 | 18,191 | 18,734 | 34,697 |
| Iroquois Falls... | Pulp and paper manufacturing | ........ | ........ | ........ | 1,178 | 1,476 | 1,302 | 1,342 |

reduced 6 per cent in relation to the total population. Centers with more or less stabilized single functions showed a general population increase of 0 to 1.75 per cent per annum, whereas centers with a number of functions increased at a general rate of 2 to 3.5 per cent per annum. Small farm service and market centers (some with light manufacturing), mining towns and pulp and paper towns illustrate the former. Regional capitals and distribution centers, which are to be found near the top of the hierarchy, illustrate the latter. Table 1 indicates the stability of population in the former. They are, however, dependent in their size on the population of the hinterland they service. This population is dependent, in turn, on the length of the period of settlement, the patterns of occupation (e.g., farming types)

in the center again becoming unifunctional, with a stable population unable to maintain many of the former services, such as specialized shops. Sarnia, also in Lambton County, is an example of a regional capital performing a number of functions. It provides a number of services for a large hinterland, but this hinterland is limited in extent to the south and east by the service areas of Chatham and London. Sarnia, however, because of its manufactures serves the nation as a whole and southern Ontario in particular. Its population thus has continued to grow almost directly proportionally to the increase in the manufacturing function, for its other functions, such as administration, provision of services, recreation, and transportation, have remained more or less the same. In this respect one can place it in the rank of small multifunctional regional capitals such as Sault Ste Marie, Guelph, Brantford, and Kingston.

New techniques of production may, in time, alter the validity of the production of an optimum in the case of unifunctional centers of the type noted above. With respect to resort centers, as an example of an unstable unifunctional center, there is less possibility of adequately predicting an optimum size, since the frequenting of such places is usually subject to the general felt needs and desires of a great number of people in many regions. The popularity of a particular resort is thus subject to the public whim. When one considers Atlantic City, Blackpool, Miami, and even Grand Bend in Ontario, it seems that there is almost no maximum in size to be set. However, the maximum in this case is the one which can efficiently bear the cost of the municipal services for the seasonal maximum, that is, the least number of visitors necessary during the season to maintain the "plant" established.

In summation, for a planner or a sociologist or a geographer, or anyone else to predict the optimum size for cities and other urban centers, he must recognize a number of factors. The first of these is that the trend toward urbanization of the world's population is part of general culture change and to attempt to predict where or when it will stop is practically impossible, since no man knows for certain what the future holds in store. But one factor that can be recognized and predicted more or less definitely is that each urban center performs certain functions in relation to all other urban centers and to the area about it. These functional relationships vary from region to region throughout the world and are inexorably linked to the cultural levels of the peoples occupying the different regions. It must be recognized that these functional relationships are not static, particularly in an economy dominated by competition, but change with time within each region and from region to region as the processes of diffusion and acculturation take place.

For each urban center there appears to be an optimum range in population based on the efficient operation of its particular functions, subject to the changing values and felt needs of its occupants. Thus it is evident that the optimum size for any urban center can be determined only after a comprehensive understanding has been obtained of the character and interrelationships of the region within which it is located.

# URBAN LAND-USE SURVEY AND MAPPING TECHNIQUES

The previous sections of this book have been concerned with the nature of cities, their functions, and the relations of cities to each other and to the regions which they serve.

Of equal importance to the urban geographer are the internal patterns of land uses and functions within cities and metropolitan areas: the nature, extent, location, and interrelations of the various types of establishments which together form the physical and functional patterns of cities. Geographers are concerned with past, present, and future urban patterns and with the operation of forces which affect the development of these patterns.

Until relatively recently, much of the research on the internal structure and organization of cities and metropolitan areas consisted of studies of individual cities or of specific types of land uses and functions within individual cities. An increasing proportion of the literature of urban geography now is concerned with the formulation and testing of general principles of urban growth and structure, involving comparative studies of many cities. A few such principles have tentatively been stated as the result of such empirical studies, but the field is relatively new and there is a need for many more comparative studies. With an understanding of the principles of urban land-use location, development, and evolution, the geographer will be able to apply his knowledge more and more to the solution of practical problems relating to comprehensive city and metro-politan planning, as well as those concerned with the location and development of specific tracts and portions of cities. In these fields the geographer works closely with other disciplines, especially land economics, urban sociology, politi-cal science, and the design fields of architecture, landscape architecture, and engineering. Planning agencies and business organizations look increasingly toward the geographer for guidance in decisions about the utilization of urban land.

Most of the material in the following sections of this book is concerned with the internal structure and organization of urban land and with the institutional framework within which decisions about the use of urban land are made. Individual categories of urban land use are discussed in some detail.

This section is especially concerned with techniques of studying and mapping the associations of land uses and functional areas within cities. It contains three articles describing studies and maps of urban land uses, for the preparation of which geographers are especially well equipped.

The first article, by a well-known urban land economist and real estate consultant, describes a series of maps prepared during the 1930's for a large number of American cities using comparable criteria and categories. These maps were major products of comprehensive land-use surveys and real property inventories carried on during the Great Depression, primarily as work-relief programs, and employing extensive forces of "white collar" workers. The surveys produced material which has been the basis of much of the city planning in many cities during subsequent years. The book from which the excerpt was taken is the one which first stated the now well-known wedge or sector theory of urban growth and structure—a theory resulting from analysis of the materials described in this excerpt.

The second article, by a prominent planning consultant, discusses one classification of urban land uses and the type of survey which is commonly made as an early stage in the process of comprehensive city planning. The book in which the excerpt appeared is a revision of an earlier work by the same author. In both books, comparisons are made, using identical criteria and categories, of the quantities and locations of urban land uses in a large number of American cities.

The third article is by a geographer who has devoted his career to the field of marketing and who has become one of the most frequently consulted experts on problems of retail location in cities, especially of supermarkets. In this article he describes his process of constructing basic maps of population distribution within cities and of urban land uses, maps which form the bases of many locational decisions.

# TYPES OF MAPS USEFUL IN THE ANALYSIS OF CITY STRUCTURE AND GROWTH

Several types of maps have been used in this study as illustrative of the suggested techniques. Scattered throughout the text have been references to their method of construction. Here the several kinds of maps used in analysis are described.

*Land survey maps.*—The United States Geological Survey has made maps of a large number of urban areas which show the framework of blocks in a city and the watercourses, elevations, valleys, and other natural topographical features. These maps also show proportions of the land area which have been built upon. This type of map is available for some areas for periods as far back as the early nineties. They are useful in revealing the boundaries of the settled areas of cities, as well as the interstices within the inner structure.

*Land coverage maps.*—These maps are now made as a regular part of all real property surveys. They do not indicate the specific location of buildings within the block, but they do show the proportion of land in each block in permanent use and the portion that is occupied by structures. They do not indicate topographical features, but they have the advantage of being of more recent date.

*Settled area maps.*—These are maps on which all areas have been filled in solidly where the buildings are close enough together to be classed as urban—i.e., where there is at least one house to the acre. Such maps are useful in showing the boundaries of urban development in a comprehensive view in which the detail of single structures

Reprinted from Federal Housing Administration, *The Structure and Growth of Residential Neighborhoods in American Cities* (Washington, D.C.: Government Printing Office, 1939), pp. 129–30.

is subordinated to the outline of the entire urban body.

*Land-use maps.*—These maps show the type of use made of each parcel of land in the city. They may take one of two forms. Either each type of use in the city may be shown on a separate map or all the different types of land use are shown on a single map. Usually, the intensity of land use is indicated by the amount of street frontage occupied. Different types of cross-hatching are used to represent different uses, and no attempt is made to show separate structures in case adjacent buildings are devoted to the same type of use. This type of map is now made as a regular part of all real property surveys.

*Block data maps.*—This is a device that overcomes some of the disadvantages of other types of maps purporting to show data which have been gathered in real property surveys. Written in the blank space in each block on a map of a city are a number of different figures arranged in a definite order. Each figure represents a given characteristic for that block expressed either as an average of all dwelling units within the block or as a percentage of the total number of dwelling units or structures in the block. It is thus possible to make comparisons between numerous different factors in every block. The Division of Economics and Statistics of the Federal Housing Administration has block data maps for 142 cities. This type of map is now made as a regular part of all real property surveys.

*Special factor maps.*—Individual block characteristics are colored or cross-hatched on single maps to portray keyed gradations of such characteristics. Thus the relative condition of the several types of residential neighborhoods in a city may be seen at a glance when mapped according to gradations of individual characteristics. A series of such special-factor maps superimposed upon one another may serve to delineate an area in which the quality of housing is within definite limits. This type of map is now also prepared as a regular part of all real property surveys. For each survey, special factor maps are drawn for (1) average block rents, (2) age of structures, (3) condition of structures, (4) owner occupancy, (5) overcrowding, (6) race, (7) sanitary facilities, (8) length of occupancy for both owners and tenants, and (9) mortgage status.

*Rental area maps.*—These maps show the rough pattern of distribution of rental neighborhoods in any city. The blocks of similar rent are grouped together in relatively homogeneous areas. Usually some blocks are included that do not fall in exactly the same rental group, but rental area maps thus smooth out to a certain extent the scattered appearance of the array of individual blocks. While such rental area maps do not show the intermingling of the blocks of different rental groups in the transition zones between the clusters of the highest rental blocks and those lower in the rental scale, they do bring out in sharp relief the location of different types of residential rental areas.

*Dynamic factor maps.*—Most of the maps listed above are primarily of use in the analysis of the structure of cities. However, a time series of settled area maps, land-use maps, and rental area maps are useful in studying the growth of cities. Such series, spaced at appropriate time intervals, are termed "dynamic factor" maps. The data for maps based on time intervals are difficult to obtain.

## THE LAND-USE SURVEY

Cities have grown largely as a result of industrial activities that require a concentrated population. It follows that urban land is required for these activities and for housing. Knowledge of the composition of the urban area is a prerequisite to rational planning and zoning. This planning requires both knowledge of the broad characteristics of the urban pattern and quantitative analysis of the space devoted to each type of land use.

### THE EVOLUTION OF LAND USES

Urban communities have developed as a part of our social and economic system. The amount of land utilized by specific activities and their spatial distribution reflect the requirements of this system. In our communities, however, the existing arrangement of land uses, though essentially functional, is not a criterion of modern community design. The pattern is, to a large extent, a product of past growth and activities; it does not necessarily represent the most efficient pattern. This is understandable, for urban areas have grown under varying pressures and have been subjected to a multitude of personal whims and desires. Yet, despite the lack of formal planning in early cities, the land-use pattern that has evolved is essentially functional.

The community is a dynamic organism constantly changing in a variety of ways to meet new needs and conditions. The change that has occurred in one community is illustrated in Figure 1. As the community grows older its physical parts become obsolete and should be rebuilt. With each technical im-

Reprinted from *Land Uses in American Cities* (Cambridge, Mass.: Harvard University Press, 1955), pp. 11–19, by permission of the author and the publisher. (Copyright, 1955, by the President and Fellows of Harvard College.)

provement they become less efficient and a change in the utilization of land inevitably occurs. Moreover, as the community ages, there are progressive changes in the social and economic structure, in the characteristics of the population, in the size of families, in age composition, and in the nature of occupations. These tend to produce new and different demands on the service of land.

But the greatest change in the urban community is perhaps a result of growth itself. With the increase in population through natural accrual or by migration, new living and working space must be added to the community. This demand may be satisfied by peripheral expansion, by the internal rearrangement of land uses—either through the displacement of one use by another or by the infilling of vacant property—or by the more intensive use of land and existing buildings. These growth processes are relatively slow and are more characteristic of high-value areas, such as central commercial or industrial districts commanding good market prices. More often, community growth flows into areas offering the least physical or economic resistance to expansion. Thus the predominant type of growth occurs in the form of lateral expansion into surrounding agricultural areas where raw land is converted to urban purposes.

Whatever the nature of the growth, it is apparent that the land-use pattern, as well as the amount of land utilized for a particular purpose, and often the density of development are constantly undergoing change. Part of this change may be superficial but most is a direct response to the changing needs of the community.

### TYPES OF LAND USE

In the study of urban land use, we are concerned with surface utilization; there-

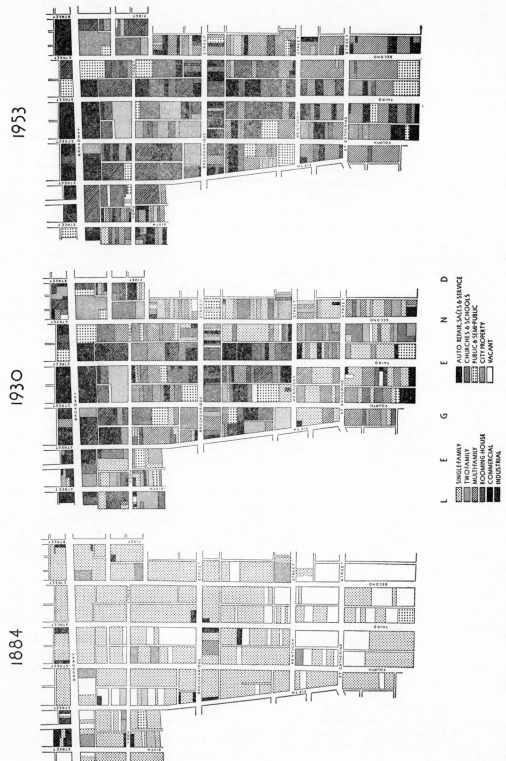

1884      1930      1953

L   E   G   E   N   D

SINGLE-FAMILY      AUTO REPAIR, SALES & SERVICE
TWO-FAMILY      CHURCHES & SCHOOLS
MULTI-FAMILY      PUBLIC & SEMI-PUBLIC
ROOMING HOUSE      CITY PROPERTY
COMMERCIAL      VACANT
INDUSTRIAL

Fig. 1.—Louisville, Kentucky. Changing use of land during a seventy-year period. (Courtesy of Louisville and Jefferson County Planning and Zoning Commission, Louisville, Kentucky.)

fore we consider all land in the urban area to be either developed or vacant or water area. The term "developed" includes all land that is used for purposes that are recognized as urban in character, whether public or private in nature, and whether devoted to an open use such as parks or playgrounds, or to a site use such as residence, industry, or commerce. Vacant land is that not given over to any urban use even though it may be potentially available for development. Thus

Broadly speaking, about one-half of all land in urban use is privately developed; and the other half is in public use. In the preparation of the city plan the designer is concerned largely with the public land: streets, parks, schools, public buildings, and utilities (both public and private). In zoning it is important that the "load on the land" imposed by private development be in scale and in harmony with the usage of the public land and facilities. It is in this

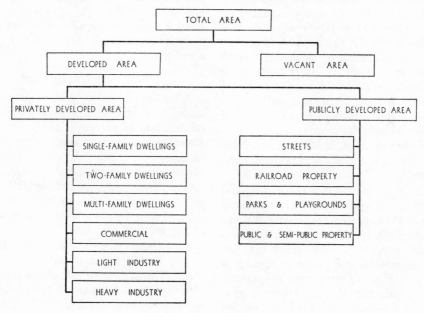

Fig. 2.—Uses of urban land

for our purposes, agricultural land is considered vacant land. Water areas include natural and artificial bodies of water and represent no urban use except when embraced within a park or recreational area. Broadly, then, the land we are concerned with can be described as land now used for purposes that are characteristically urban.

All urban land may be classified according to its use. These uses, as illustrated graphically on Figure 2, include residence, commerce, industry, streets, railroads, recreation centers, and public or semipublic facilities. All land may be placed for planning purposes in one or another of these groups.

context that the several functional uses of land will be reviewed.

### Privately Developed Areas

These areas include land developed by private interests or by the public if operated in a private or proprietary capacity (for example, public housing, the use of which is essentially private in nature). Functional uses in this group include the following: single-family dwellings, two-family dwellings, multifamily dwellings, commercial areas, light industry, and heavy industry.

The titles of these uses are largely self-explanatory; however, some exceptions should be noted. A single-family dwelling is a detached structure used for residence by one family or household alone. Two-family dwellings include various forms of structures such as the "duplex" or the "semi-detached," but essentially any structure designed for or occupied by two households. Multifamily dwellings include tenements, apartments, and apartment hotels for non-transients, dwellings which house three or more families or households. Rooming and lodging houses are also included in this classification. It should be noted here that practical considerations in survey practices require a certain latitude. For example, it is not always possible to detect by inspection the incidental housing of one or two roomers in seemingly private dwellings. Thus single or two-family dwellings having two roomers or less are not altered in classification.

Commercial uses include all land and building wherein trade or business is conducted, for example, merchandising, business offices, amusement, and personal service uses.

Industry is divided into two types, light and heavy. Although these are not precisely appropriate terms, they are in common usage to distinguish unobjectionable industrial processes from those that are, or may become, objectionable in close proximity to other types of uses where people live or work. Thus, all industries that are known to emit smoke, dust, odor, or undue noise are classed as heavy industry. Conversely, other forms of manufacturing, storage, processing, or the like without these objectionable characteristics are classified as light industry.[1]

## PUBLICLY DEVELOPED AREAS

Urban land in this group falls within the following broad classifications: streets, railroad property, parks and playgrounds, and public and semipublic property.

Public and semipublic property includes city property, airports, public and private schools, churches and cemeteries, and other institutional property. This general category includes uses, developed by either public or private capital, which may in fact be public facilities or may be restricted, as in the case of private clubs, to a select group. However, in both cases a large number of people use the facility and the use is essentially public in nature.

The remaining portion of land within the urban area not included in the above groups of privately and publicly developed areas is unimproved vacant land and water areas. The meaning of these terms is evident; they are included in this study to give a comprehensive accounting of all acreage within the community, although as quantities they lack significance.

## THE LAND-USE SURVEY

A land-use inventory and its analysis are essential tools in the preparation and administration of a comprehensive city plan. Knowledge of land use is more than a planning precept; it has legal significance. The community in exercising its planning and zoning powers must, as enabling acts put it, give "reasonable consideration to the character of each district and its particular suitability for particular uses."

As with all research, the land-use survey should be planned and programed in advance. The purpose of the survey should be identified and the amount of information and the degree of detail should be balanced against their ultimate use. Further, the survey technique should be standardized and the statistical and graphic form of data presentation determined.[2]

There are, of course, variations in the scope and techniques of land-use surveys. The technique employed will depend on such factors as conditions peculiar to the community, the detail of information de-

[1] The use of control devices such as smoke abatement units, air conditioning, etc., may permit the upgrading of some industries.

[2] The land-use survey is often employed as a means of collecting other basic data. For example, some cities have expanded the land-use survey to include information on age and condition of structures and housing characteristics; such surveys would be more properly termed "housing surveys" or "real property inventories." These are separate and distinct from the analysis of the use of land, with which this study is concerned.

sired, and to some degree on personal preferences. However, the following method is in most common use and is suitable for the majority of purposes.

The land-use survey requires a field investigation. Prior to this field investigation, however, preliminary work should be done to obtain information as to street and lot lines, and such land-use data as may be secured from assessors' files, insurance atlases, real estate atlases, and aerial photographs. It is customary to record the desired information on a set of sectional maps usually having a scale of from one hundred to two hundred feet to the inch. In general, the field sheet must be of an adequate size to permit showing established property lines and dimensions as well as existing information and penciled notations.

The field investigation is a lot-by-lot inspection to determine specific land utilization. In older central city areas of mixed use greater care is required in determining uses than in newly developed sections of single-family detached dwellings. After the inspection of a parcel, its use is marked on the field sheet along with any necessary explanatory facts or comments. After completion of the field investigation, the land-use data on the field sheets is transferred to a final map. Usually this final "use map" is prepared in vivid colors to emphasize each of the separate types of use as well as the over-all pattern. The field sheets are retained for reference and record purposes.

The final land-use map depicts each classification or type of use of land in color or by an appropriate symbol representing a particular use classification. This map may be of sectional sheets, or it may be an over-all map covering the entire area, or both. Since the draftsmanship of this map will be of high quality, the scale can be larger, up to, say, five hundred feet to the inch.

## LAND-USE ANALYSES

The applications of land-use data for planning purposes are manifold. For ex-

ample, they can be used to determine commercial markets, to locate institutions such as churches and schools, or for zoning purposes. Therefore, the type of statistical analysis in any given situation will be determined by the problems under study. In zoning studies, with which we are concerned here, it is essential to know the amount of land used for various purposes. Computations of lot and parcel areas, arranged according to each major type of use, should be made for individual blocks, then summarized for permanent unit areas or neighborhoods, and finally for the entire community. The result of these summaries is generally expressed as an area in acres, in percentages of total areas, and as a ratio of land used to given units of population. Zoning that is based on the facts of actual use of land will have far greater validity than that based upon opinions unsupported by such facts.

The land-use map represents the conditions on a given date, and its validity becomes progressively less with each change in use of property. Thus, it is important to keep this graphic and statistical information current. In the interim, changes in land use can be recorded from building permits issued or from insurance atlas records; however, these are never fully effective. Periodic revisions, yearly if possible, should be made.

In conclusion, the value of land-use surveys tabulated in the manner described lies in comparative statistics. But, as with all comparisons of this nature there are definite limits of applicability. A community's future land-use requirements cannot be projected with complete accuracy on a basis of current ratios. Likewise, a comparison of land uses between two or more communities will disclose differences due to character and physiography. However, in both cases such comparisons can be instructive. In combination with other basic studies, and with good judgment, current land-use data offer a factual base for improved planning and zoning practices.

WILLIAM APPLEBAUM

# A TECHNIQUE FOR CONSTRUCTING A POPULATION
# AND URBAN LAND-USE MAP

Population data alone are not sufficient for the construction of an accurate population map of a city. Even if such data were available by city blocks, which is rarely so, information on the use of land is essential for an accurate allocation of population *within* each block. Furthermore, the land-use data can be employed to chart non-residential uses on the same map.

This paper has a twofold purpose: first, it deals with the sources and nature of the available urban land-use and population data; second, it describes a technique which the author has used since 1931 in constructing over a hundred urban population and land-use maps.[1]

This technique is a useful tool to marketing research and city planning.[2]

## URBAN LAND-USE DATA

The land use of the urban areas in the United States is fairly completely mapped, thanks to the service of the Sanborn Map Company, which has constructed maps and atlases for practically every city, town, and village, and many unincorporated communities in the United States.

The Sanborn maps are plotted on uniform-size sheets to a scale of 1 inch to either

50 or 100 feet. These maps show streets, blocks, lot lines, structures, railroad tracks, and other features of the cultural landscape; the material of construction, use, height, shape, and other characteristics of each structure are designated by various conventions. The Sanborn Company maintains a nationwide service which enters corrections on the maps at frequent intervals.[3]

Sanborn maps are available in every substantial urban community, in the city hall, the county courthouse, or a realtor's office. All fire insurance rating bureaus have Sanborn maps. Frequently, such a bureau may have atlases for practically every city, town, and village for an entire state. Some of these bureaus supplement the Sanborn maps with charts of their own construction.

In addition to the Sanborn maps, urban land-use data are available in many city-planning offices.[4] The scale and technique employed in plotting land-use data varies somewhat with each city-planning office. These maps do not depict the characteristics of buildings as completely as do the Sanborn maps.

## POPULATION DATA

The population of all incorporated places regardless of size was enumerated in 1930, 1940, and 1950 by enumeration districts. For each smaller place there may have been only one enumeration district. These enumeration districts vary in size of area and

Reprinted from *Economic Geography*, XXVIII (July, 1952), 240–43, by permission of the author and the editor. (Copyright, 1952, by Clark University, Worcester, Mass.)

[1] The author developed this technique in 1931 in the course of his work on the secondary commercial centers of Cincinnati. Subsequently, he and others have used this technique in the study of urban markets.

[2] See "Population Analysis of Small Areas," Business Information Service, Office of Domestic Commerce, U.S. Department of Commerce, Washington, D.C., May, 1950.

[3] For a full discussion of Sanborn maps see the excellent article by Robert L. Wrigley, Jr., "The Sanborn Map as a Source of Land Use Information for City Planning," *Land Economics*, May, 1949, pp. 216–19.

[4] The Housing Act of 1949 requires a community to prepare a land-use plan to qualify for federal aid for slum clearance and urban development.

number of population. Most enumeration districts in 1950 had between 900 and 1,000 people, although the range was from 0 to over 2,000, and the over-all average was somewhat under 700.[5]

Population figures by enumeration districts can be procured from the Bureau of the Census at a nominal cost for photostatic reproduction. Maps showing boundaries of enumeration districts are more expensive (but reasonable) because the boundaries must be drawn by hand. Photostats of typed verbal descriptions of enumeration district boundaries can be secured at less expense.[6]

## TECHNIQUE FOR CONSTRUCTING THE MAP

With an adequate base map, population and land-use data, and a city directory, the construction of a map showing the distribution of population and urban land use is not difficult. First the boundaries of all enumeration districts are laid off on the base map; then the various land uses in each block are transferred from a Sanborn atlas to the same base map. Different colors or conventions are used to designate the various types of non-residential use.

Block data on dwelling units were published by the Bureau of the Census for 1940 (not available for previous censuses) and are being published for 1950, for cities with a population of 50,000 and over. Hence, it is a very simple matter to enter on the base map the number of dwelling units in each block. However, for cities with populations of less than 50,000 the number of dwelling units in each block is ascertained, within a tolerable margin of error, by counting the

"family" dwelling units on the Sanborn maps. A city directory is consulted to determine the number of apartments in each multiple-family building, as the Sanborn maps do not show this information. Since these maps do show the address of each building, comparatively little time is consumed in consulting the city directory.

The Sanborn maps usually do not cover the very sparsely populated areas along the fringe of a city. Hence a small amount of supplementary field work is necessary to complete the information.

The next stage in the procedure involves the allocation of population within each block in every enumeration district. The number of dwelling units is computed for each enumeration district and divided into the total of the non-institutional[7] population within the district; the quotient obtained represents the population index per dwelling unit for the district. Population for each block is computed by multiplying the number of dwelling units in the block by the population index per dwelling unit. The number of people computed for each block is recorded inside the block on the base map.

The final stage of the work is chiefly a matter of drafting. A cloth tracing is made of the city base map and upon it are plotted the population data by dots—for smaller cities 10 or 20 people to the dot, for larger cities as high as 50 people may be represented by a dot. Care should be exercised in allocating the dots within each block to conform with the residentially used land.[8] Circles instead of dots may be used to designate institutional population. When the dots have been plotted, the product represents a population map. The addition of the non-residential uses to the same tracing com-

[5] The low average is due to two factors: (1) most institutions were made separate enumeration districts and (2) the need for observing the boundaries of local political divisions of areas resulted in many cases in enumeration districts with little or no population.

[6] See also the valuable index to the 1950 Census data on population and housing for areas smaller than states, U.S. Census of Population and Housing, 1950, *Key to Published and Tabulated Data for Small Areas* (Washington, D.C.: Government Printing Office, 1951).

[7] Where enumeration districts still contain institutional as well as non-institutional population, it is necessary to subtract the institutional population from the total population in the enumeration district and to locate the institutional population where it belongs on the map.

[8] In the preparation of a black-and-white map, difficulties arise in showing residential and other uses where the buildings are multifunctional, hence some compromise in drafting is unavoidable.

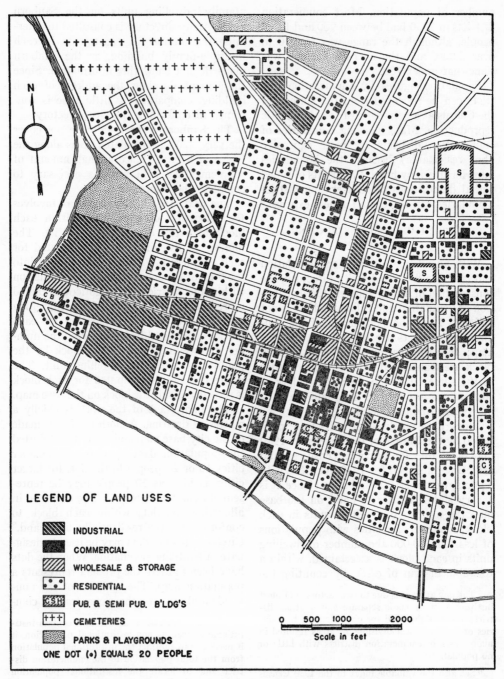

## LEGEND OF LAND USES

- INDUSTRIAL
- COMMERCIAL
- WHOLESALE & STORAGE
- RESIDENTIAL
- PUB. & SEMI PUB. B'LDG'S
- CEMETERIES
- PARKS & PLAYGROUNDS

ONE DOT (•) EQUALS 20 PEOPLE

Scale in feet
0    500    1000         2000

FIG. 1.—A population and urban land-use map such as this is the end product of the method described

pletes the map. Obviously the dots designate residential land use and at the same time present a graphic as well as a quantitative measure of the distribution of urban population.

## APPRAISAL OF THE TECHNIQUE

Slight inaccuracies are inherent in this method of procedure, as it ignores home vacancies, demolition or construction of dwellings since the last census enumeration, "doubling-up" of families, and residential occupancy of normally non-residential structures; some error arises also from the use of dots having a round value of population. However, these inaccuracies are within a tolerable error.

From the standpoint of time and cost involved, this technique is believed to be the most satisfactory developed to date and has been employed successfully in the study of many urban markets. The author has been able to construct such a map for a city of 100,000 population in one week, and for a city of 500,000 population in about three weeks—including the supplementary field work done by automobile but excluding the final ink drafting.

# GENERAL NATURE OF CITY STRUCTURE

With knowledge of the land-use patterns of cities and of the locations of the various functional associations of land uses within cities and metropolitan areas, as described in the articles in the previous section of this book, the geographer can present general descriptive hypotheses concerning the patterns of cities and the ways in which such patterns develop. During the past two or three decades, the formulation of such general hypotheses has increasingly involved the application of relatively sophisticated quantitative and mathematical techniques. The three articles in this section have been selected as inherently important because they represent landmarks in the development of geographic thinking on this subject. Each has become a classic in this field.

The first article, on the nature of cities, is perhaps the best known and most widely quoted single article in the entire literature of urban geography. It has been extensively reprinted, not only in geographic anthologies, but also in readers in urban sociology and other related fields. The article summarizes very briefly the major aspects of cities with which the urban geographer has been concerned. It discusses the economic base of cities and proposes a three-category classification of cities in terms of their functions, following which it summarizes the three best-known descriptive hypotheses of urban growth and structure: the concentric zonal hypothesis, the wedge or sector hypothesis, and the multiple-nuclei hypothesis.

The second article, although older, represents an important statement of the operation of basic forces, the resultant of which is the evolution of the city's functional and physical form. Although the principles had previously been known to land economists, Colby's contribution consisted of a formulation of the principles in geographic terms and in the presentation of numerous examples.

The third article, by an urban land economist, presents a statement of essentially the same principles in terms of the operation of the market for urban land and indicates some of the applications of the principles of urban land economics to the process of making decisions about the location of urban land uses.

It is clear that the principles of urban land economics are basic to the evolution of the patterns of urban land uses and the physical structures of cities in any society in which the land market operates freely. One of the major concerns of the urban geographer is with the demand and cost elements which affect land use. The relative demand for various uses of land in various locations, however, is not the sole determinant of the ultimate use, for social considerations transcending the operation of purely economic forces in the land market are important. The normal operation of the real estate market, for example, cannot provide for parks, highways, and other public land uses, and therefore intervention in the market is frequently necessary. The geographer, of course, is concerned with the total land-use patterns of cities, including both public and private uses of land. Indispensable to an understanding of such patterns is knowledge of the land market, of the decision-making processes of both public agencies and private firms and individuals, and of the broader requirements of society for the various activities and functions which take place on urban land.

CHAUNCY D. HARRIS and EDWARD L. ULLMAN

## THE NATURE OF CITIES

Cities are the focal points in the occupation and utilization of the earth by man. Both a product of and an influence on surrounding regions, they develop in definite patterns in response to economic and social needs.

Cities are also paradoxes. Their rapid growth and large size testify to their superiority as a technique for the exploitation of the earth; yet by their very success and consequent large size they often provide a poor local environment for man. The problem is to build the future city in such a manner that the advantages of urban concentration can be preserved for the benefit of man and the disadvantages minimized.

Each city is unique in detail but resembles others in function and pattern. What is learned about one helps in studying another. Location types and internal structure are repeated so often that broad and suggestive generalizations are valid, especially if limited to cities of similar size, function, and regional setting. This paper will be limited to a discussion of two basic aspects of the nature of cities—their support and their internal structure. Such important topics as the rise and extent of urbanism, urban sites, culture of cities, social and economic characteristics of the urban population, and critical problems will receive only passing mention.

### THE SUPPORT OF CITIES

As one approaches a city and notices its tall buildings rising above the surrounding land and as one continues into the city and observes the crowds of people hurrying to

Reprinted from *Annals of the American Academy of Political and Social Science*, CCXLII (November, 1945), 7–17, by permission of the authors and the editor. (Copyright, 1945, by the American Academy of Political and Social Science, Philadelphia.)

and fro past stores, theaters, banks, and other establishments, one naturally is struck by the contrast with the rural countryside. What supports this phenomenon? What do the people of the city do for a living?

The support of a city depends on the services it performs not for itself but for a tributary area. Many activities serve merely the population of the city itself. Barbers, dry cleaners, shoe repairers, grocerymen, bakers, and movie operators serve others who are engaged in the principal activity of the city, which may be mining, manufacturing, trade, or some other activity.

The service by which the city earns its livelihood depends on the nature of the economy and of the hinterland. Cities are small or rare in areas either of primitive, self-sufficient economy or of meager resources. As Adam Smith stated, the land must produce a surplus in order to support cities. This does not mean that all cities must be surrounded by productive land, since strategic location with reference to cheap ocean highways may enable a city to support itself on the specialized surplus of distant lands. Nor does it mean that cities are parasites living off the land. Modern mechanization, transport, and a complex interdependent economy enable much of the economic activity of mankind to be centered in cities. Many of the people engaged even in food production are actually in cities in the manufacture of agricultural machinery.

The support of cities as suppliers of urban services for the earth can be summarized in three categories, each of which presents a factor of urban causation:[1]

1. Cities as central places performing

[1] For references see Edward Ullman, "A Theory of Location for Cities," *American Journal of Sociology*, XLVI (May, 1941), 853–64 [see above, pp. 202–9].

comprehensive services for a surrounding area. Such cities tend to be evenly spaced throughout productive territory (Fig. 1). For the moment this may be considered the "norm" subject to variation primarily in response to the ensuing factors.

2. Transport cities performing break-of-bulk and allied services along transport routes, supported by areas which may be remote in distance but close in connection because of the city's strategic location on

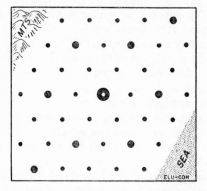

FIG. 1.—Theoretical distribution of central places. In a homogeneous land, settlements are evenly spaced; largest city in center surrounded by 6 medium-size centers which in turn are surrounded by 6 small centers. Tributary areas are hexagons, the closest geometrical shapes to circles which completely fill area with no unserved spaces.

transport channels. Such cities tend to be arranged in linear patterns along rail lines or at coasts (Fig. 2).

3. Specialized-function cities performing one service such as mining, manufacturing, or recreation for large areas, including the general tributary areas of hosts of other cities. Since the principal localizing factor is often a particular resource such as coal, water power, or a beach, such cities may occur singly or in clusters (Fig. 3).

Most cities represent a combination of the three factors, the relative importance of each varying from city to city (Fig. 4).

## CITIES AS CENTRAL PLACES

Cities as central places serve as trade and social centers for a tributary area. If the

land base is homogeneous these centers are uniformly spaced, as in many parts of the agricultural Middle West (Fig. 1). In areas of uneven resource distribution, the distribution of cities is uneven. The centers are of varying sizes, ranging from small hamlets closely spaced with one or two stores serving a local tributary area, through larger villages, towns, and cities more widely spaced with more special services for larger tributary areas, up to the great metropolis such as New York or Chicago offering many specialized services for a large tributary area composed of a whole hierarchy of tributary areas of smaller places. Such a net of tributary areas and centers forms a pattern somewhat like a fish net spread over a beach, the

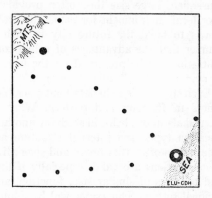

FIG. 2.—Transport centers, aligned along railroads or at coast. Large center is port; next largest is railroad junction and engine-changing point where mountain and plain meet. Small centers perform break of bulk principally between rail and roads.

network regular and symmetrical where the sand is smooth but warped and distorted where the net is caught in rocks.

The central-place type of city or town is widespread throughout the world, particularly in non-industrial regions. In the United States it is best represented by the numerous retail and wholesale trade centers of the agricultural Middle West, Southwest, and West. Such cities have imposing shopping centers or wholesale districts in proportion to their size; the stores are supported by the trade of the surrounding area. This contrasts with many cities of the industrial East, where the centers are so close together that each has little trade support beyond its own population.

Not only trade but social and religious functions may support central places. In some instances these other functions may be the main support of the town. In parts of Latin America, for example, where there is little trade, settlements are scattered at relatively uniform intervals through the land as social and religious centers. In contrast to most cities, their busiest day is Sunday, when the surrounding populace attend church and engage in holiday recreation, thus giving rise to the name "Sunday town."

Most large central cities and towns are

FIG. 3.—Specialized-function settlements. Large city is manufacturing and mining center surrounded by a cluster of smaller settlements located on a mineral deposit. Small centers on ocean and at edge of mountains are resorts.

also political centers. The county seat is an example. London and Paris are the political as well as trade centers of their countries. In the United States, however, Washington and many state capitals are specialized political centers. In many of these cases the political capital was initially chosen as a centrally located point in the political area and was deliberately separated from the major urban center.

### CITIES AS TRANSPORT FOCI AND BREAK-OF-BULK POINTS

All cities are dependent on transportation in order to utilize the surplus of the land for

their support. This dependence on transportation destroys the symmetry of the central-place arrangement, inasmuch as cities develop at foci or breaks of transportation, and transport routes are distributed unevenly over the land because of relief or other limitations (Fig. 2). City organizations recognize the importance of efficient transportation, as witness their constant concern with freight-rate regulation and with the construction of new highways, port facilities, airfields, and the like.

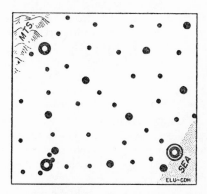

FIG. 4.—Theoretical composite grouping. Port becomes the metropolis and, although off center, serves as central place for whole area. Manufacturing-mining and junction centers are next largest. Railroad alignment of many towns evident. Railroad route in upper left of Fig. 2 has been diverted to pass through manufacturing and mining cluster. Distribution of settlements in upper right follows central-place arrangement.

Mere focusing of transport routes does not produce a city, but according to Cooley, if break of bulk occurs, the focus becomes a good place to process goods. Where the form of transport changes, as transferring from water to rail, break of bulk is inevitable. Ports originating merely to transship cargo tend to develop auxiliary services such as repackaging, storing, and sorting. An example of simple break-of-bulk and storage ports is Port Arthur–Fort William, the twin port and wheat-storage cities at the head of Lake Superior; surrounded by unproductive land, they have arisen at the break-of-bulk points on the cheapest route from the wheat-producing Prairie Provinces to the markets of the East. Some ports develop as entrepôts, such as Hong Kong and Copenhagen, supported by transshipment of goods from small to large boats or vice versa. Servicing points or minor changes in transport tend to encourage growth of cities as establishment of division points for changing locomotives on American railroads.

Transport centers can be centrally located places or can serve as gateways between contrasting regions with contrasting needs. Kansas City, Omaha, and Minneapolis–St. Paul serve as gateways to the West, as well as central places for productive agricultural regions, and are important wholesale centers. The ports of New Orleans, Mobile, Savannah, Charleston, Norfolk, and others served as traditional gateways to the Cotton Belt with its specialized production. Likewise, northern border metropolises such as Baltimore, Washington, Cincinnati, and Louisville served as gateways to the South, with St. Louis a gateway to the Southwest. In recent years the South has been developing its own central places, supplanting some of the monopoly once held by the border gateways. Atlanta, Memphis, and Dallas are examples of the new southern central places and transport foci.

Changes in transportation are reflected in the pattern of city distribution. Thus the development of railroads resulted in a railroad alignment of cities which still persists. The rapid growth of automobiles and widespread development of highways in recent decades, however, has changed the trend toward a more even distribution of towns. Studies in such diverse localities as New York and Louisiana have shown a shift of centers away from exclusive alignment along rail routes. Airways may reinforce this trend or stimulate still different patterns of distribution for the future city.

CITIES AS CONCENTRATION POINTS FOR
SPECIALIZED SERVICES

A specialized city or cluster of cities performing a specialized function for a large area may develop at a highly localized resource (Fig. 3). The resort city of Miami,

for example, developed in response to a favorable climate and beach. Scranton, Wilkes-Barre, and dozens of nearby towns are specialized coal-mining centers developed on anthracite coal deposits to serve a large segment of the northeastern United States. Pittsburgh and its suburbs and satellites form a nationally significant iron-and-steel manufacturing cluster favored by good location for the assembly of coal and iron ore and for the sale of steel to industries on the coal fields.

Equally important with physical resources in many cities are the advantages of mass production and ancillary services. Once started, a specialized city acts as a nucleus for similar or related activities, and functions tend to pyramid, whether the city is a seaside resort such as Miami or Atlantic City or, more important, a manufacturing center such as Pittsburgh or Detroit. Concentration of industry in a city means that there will be a concentration of satellite services and industries—supply houses, machine shops, expert consultants, other industries using local industrial by-products or waste, still other industries making specialized parts for other plants in the city, marketing channels, specialized transport facilities, skilled labor, and a host of other facilities; either directly or indirectly, these benefit industry and cause it to expand in size and numbers in a concentrated place or district. Local personnel with the know-how in a given industry also may decide to start a new plant producing similar or like products in the same city. Furthermore, the advantages of mass production itself often tend to concentrate production in a few large factories and cities. Examples of localization of specific manufacturing industries are clothing in New York City, furniture in Grand Rapids, automobiles in the Detroit area, pottery in Stoke-on-Trent in England, and even such a specialty as tennis rackets in Pawtucket, Rhode Island.

Such concentration continues until opposing forces of high labor costs and congestion balance the concentrating forces. Labor costs may be lower in small towns and in industrially new districts; thus some factories are moving from the great metropolises to small towns; much of the cotton textile industry has moved from the old industrial areas of New England to the newer areas of the Carolinas in the South. The tremendous concentration of population and structures in large cities exacts a high cost in the form of congestion, high land costs, high taxes, and restrictive legislation.

Not all industries tend to concentrate in specialized industrial cities; many types of manufacturing partake more of central-place characteristics. These types are those that are tied to the market because the manufacturing process results in an increase in bulk or perishability. Bakeries, ice cream establishments, icehouses, breweries, soft-

drink plants, and various types of assembly plants are examples. Even such industries, however, tend to be more developed in the manufacturing belt because the density of population and hence the market is greater there.

The greatest concentration of industrial cities in America is in the manufacturing belt of northeastern United States and contiguous Canada, north of the Ohio and east of the Mississippi. Some factors in this concentration are large reserves of fuel and power (particularly coal), raw materials such as iron ore via the Great Lakes, cheap ocean transportation on the eastern seaboard, productive agriculture (particularly in the West), early settlement, later immigration concentrated in its cities, and an

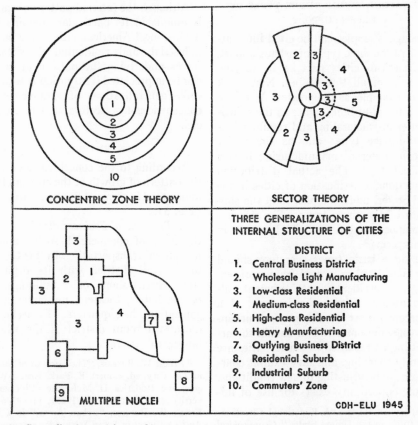

CONCENTRIC ZONE THEORY

SECTOR THEORY

MULTIPLE NUCLEI

THREE GENERALIZATIONS OF THE INTERNAL STRUCTURE OF CITIES

DISTRICT
1. Central Business District
2. Wholesale Light Manufacturing
3. Low-class Residential
4. Medium-class Residential
5. High-class Residential
6. Heavy Manufacturing
7. Outlying Business District
8. Residential Suburb
9. Industrial Suburb
10. Commuters' Zone

CDH–ELU 1945

Fig. 5.—Generalizations of internal structure of cities. The concentric-zone theory is a generalization for all cities. The arrangement of the sectors in the sector theory varies from city to city. The diagram for multiple nuclei represents one possible pattern among innumerable variations.

early start with consequent development of skilled labor, industrial know-how, transportation facilities, and prestige.

The interdependent nature of most of the industries acts as a powerful force to maintain this area as the primary home of industrial cities in the United States. Before the war, the typical industrial city outside the main manufacturing belt had only a single industry of the raw-material type, such as lumber mills, food canneries, or smelters (Longview, Washington; San Jose, California; Anaconda, Montana). Because of the need for producing huge quantities of ships and airplanes for a two-ocean war, however, many cities along the Gulf and Pacific coasts have grown rapidly during recent years as centers of industry.

### APPLICATION OF THE THREE TYPES OF URBAN SUPPORT

Although examples can be cited illustrating each of the three types of urban support, most American cities partake in varying proportions of all three types. New York City, for example, as the greatest American port is a break-of-bulk point; as the principal center of wholesaling and retailing it is a central-place type; and as the major American center of manufacturing it is a specialized type. The actual distribution and functional classification of cities in the United States, more complex than the simple sum of the three types (Fig. 4), has been mapped and described elsewhere in different terms.[2]

The three basic types therefore should not be considered as a rigid framework excluding all accidental establishment, although even fortuitous development of a city becomes part of the general urban-supporting environment. Nor should the urban setting be regarded as static; cities are constantly changing, and they exhibit characteristic lag in adjusting to new conditions.

Ample opportunity exists for use of ini-

tiative in strengthening the supporting base of the future city, particularly if account is taken of the basic factors of urban support. Thus a city should examine: (1) its surrounding area to take advantage of changes such as newly discovered resources or crops, (2) its transport in order to adjust properly to new or changed facilities, and (3) its industries in order to benefit from technological advances.

### INTERNAL STRUCTURE OF CITIES

Any effective plans for the improvement or rearrangement of the future city must take account of the present pattern of land use within the city, of the factors which have produced this pattern, and of the facilities required by activities localized within particular districts.

Although the internal pattern of each city is unique in its particular combination of details, most American cities have business, industrial, and residential districts. The forces underlying the pattern of land use can be appreciated if attention is focused on three generalizations of arrangement—by concentric zones, sectors, and multiple nuclei.

#### CONCENTRIC ZONES

According to the concentric-zone theory, the pattern of growth of the city can best be understood in terms of five concentric zones[3] (Fig. 5).

1. *The central business district.*—This is the focus of commercial, social, and civic life, and of transportation. In it is the downtown retail district with its department stores, smart shops, office buildings, clubs, banks, hotels, theaters, museums, and organization headquarters. Encircling the downtown retail district is the wholesale business district.

[2] Chauncy D. Harris, "A Functional Classification of Cities in the United States," *Geographical Review*, XXXIII (January, 1943), 85–99 [see above, pp. 129–38].

[3] Ernest W. Burgess, "The Growth of the City," in *The City*, ed. Robert E. Park, Ernest W. Burgess, and Roderick D. McKenzie (Chicago: University of Chicago Press, 1925), pp. 47–62; and Ernest W. Burgess, "Urban Areas," in *Chicago: An Experiment in Social Science Research*, ed. T. V. Smith and Leonard D. White (Chicago: University of Chicago Press, 1929), pp. 113–38.

2. *The zone in transition.*—Encircling the downtown area is a zone of residential deterioration. Business and light manufacturing encroach on residential areas characterized particularly by rooming houses. In this zone are the principal slums, with their submerged regions of poverty, degradation, and disease, and their underworlds of vice. In many American cities it has been inhabited largely by colonies of recent immigrants.

3. *The zone of independent working-men's homes.*—This is inhabited by industrial workers who have escaped from the zone in transition but who desire to live within easy access of their work. In many American cities second-generation immigrants are important segments of the population in this area.

4. *The zone of better residences.*—This is made up of single-family dwellings, of exclusive "restricted districts," and of high-class apartment buildings.

5. *The commuters' zone.*—Often beyond the city limits in suburban areas or in satellite cities, this is a zone of spotty development of high-class residences along lines of rapid travel.

SECTORS

The theory of axial development, according to which growth takes place along main transportation routes or along lines of least resistance to form a star-shaped city, is refined by Homer Hoyt in his sector theory, which states that growth along a particular axis of transportation usually consists of similar types of land use[4] (Fig. 5). The entire city is considered as a circle and the various areas as sectors radiating out from the center of that circle; similar types of land use originate near the center of the circle and migrate outward toward the periphery. Thus a high-rent residential area in the

[4] Homer Hoyt, "City Growth and Mortgage Risk," *Insured Mortgage Portfolio*, Vol. I, Nos. 6–10 (December, 1936–April, 1937), *passim;* and *idem* (U.S. Federal Housing Administration), *The Structure and Growth of Residential Neighborhoods in American Cities* (Washington: Government Printing Office, 1939), *passim.*

eastern quadrant of the city would tend to migrate outward, keeping always in the eastern quadrant. A low-quality housing area, if located in the southern quadrant, would tend to extend outward to the very margin of the city in that sector. The migration of high-class residential areas outward along established lines of travel is particularly pronounced on high ground, toward open country, to homes of community leaders, along lines of fastest transportation, and to existing nuclei of buildings or trading centers.

MULTIPLE NUCLEI

In many cities the land-use pattern is built not around a single center but around several discrete nuclei (Fig. 5). In some cities these nuclei have existed from the very origins of the city; in others they have developed as the growth of the city stimulated migration and specialization. An example of the first type is Metropolitan London, in which "The City" and Westminster originated as separate points separated by open country, one as the center of finance and commerce, the other as the center of political life. An example of the second type is Chicago, in which heavy industry, at first localized along the Chicago River in the heart of the city, migrated to the Calumet District, where it acted as a nucleus for extensive new urban development.

The initial nucleus of the city may be the retail district in a central-place city, the port or rail facilities in a break-of-bulk city, or the factory, mine, or beach in a specialized-function city.

The rise of separate nuclei and differentiated districts reflects a combination of the following four factors:

1. Certain activities require specialized facilities. The retail district, for example, is attached to the point of greatest intracity accessibility, the port district to suitable water front, manufacturing districts to large blocks of land and water or rail connection, and so on.

2. Certain like activities group together

because they profit from cohesion.[5] The clustering of industrial cities has already been noted above under "Cities as concentration points for specialized services." Retail districts benefit from grouping which increases the concentration of potential customers and makes possible comparison shopping. Financial and office-building districts depend upon facility of communication among offices within the district. The Merchandise Mart of Chicago is an example of wholesale clustering.

3. Certain unlike activities are detrimental to each other. The antagonism between factory development and high-class residential development is well known. The heavy concentrations of pedestrians, automobiles, and streetcars in the retail district are antagonistic both to the railroad facilities and the street loading required in the wholesale district and to the rail facilities and space needed by large industrial districts, and vice versa.

4. Certain activities are unable to afford the high rents of the most desirable sites. This factor works in conjunction with the foregoing. Examples are bulk wholesaling and storage activities requiring much room, or low-class housing unable to afford the luxury of high land with a view.

The number of nuclei which result from historical development and the operation of localization forces varies greatly from city to city. The larger the city, the more numerous and specialized are the nuclei. The following districts, however, have developed around nuclei in most large American cities.

*The central business district.*—This district is at the focus of intracity transportation facilities by sidewalk, private car, bus, streetcar, subway, and elevated. Because of asymmetrical growth of most large cities, it is generally not now in the areal center of the city but actually near one edge, as in the case of lake-front, riverside, or even inland cities; examples are Chicago, St. Louis, and Salt Lake City. Because established internal transportation lines converge on it, however, it is the point of most convenient access from all parts of the city, and the point of highest land values. The retail district, at the point of maximum accessibility, is attached to the sidewalk; only pedestrian or mass-transportation movement can concentrate the large numbers of customers necessary to support department stores, variety stores, and clothing shops, which are characteristic of the district. In small cities financial institutions and office buildings are intermingled with retail shops, but in large cities the financial district is separate, near but not at the point of greatest intracity facility. Its point of attachment is the elevator, which permits three-dimensional access among offices, whose most important locational factor is accessibility to other offices rather than to the city as a whole. Government buildings also are commonly near but not in the center of the retail district. In most cities a separate "automobile row" has arisen on the edge of the central business district, in cheaper rent areas along one or more major highways; its attachment is to the highway itself.

*The wholesale and light-manufacturing district.*—This district is conveniently within the city but near the focus of extracity transportation facilities. Wholesale houses, while deriving some support from the city itself, serve principally a tributary region reached by railroad and motor truck. They are, therefore, concentrated along railroad lines, usually adjacent to (but not surrounding) the central business district. Many types of light manufacturing which do not require specialized buildings are attracted by the facilities of this district or similar districts: good rail and road transportation, available loft buildings, and proximity to the markets and labor of the city itself.

*The heavy industrial district.*—This is near the present or former outer edge of the city. Heavy industries require large tracts of space, often beyond any available

---

[5] Exceptions are service-type establishments such as some grocery stores, dry cleaners, and gasoline stations.

in sections already subdivided into blocks and streets. They also require good transportation, either rail or water. With the development of belt lines and switching yards, sites on the edge of the city may have better transportation service than those near the center. In Chicago about a hundred industries are in a belt three miles long, adjacent to the Clearing freight yards on the southwestern edge of the city. Furthermore, the noise of boiler works, the odors of stockyards, the waste disposal problems of smelters and iron and steel mills, the fire hazards of petroleum refineries, and the space and transportation needs which interrupt streets and accessibility—all these favor the growth of heavy industry away from the main center of the large city. The Calumet District of Chicago, the New Jersey marshes near New York City, the Lea marshes near London, and the St. Denis district of Paris are examples of such districts. The stockyards of Chicago, in spite of their odors and size, have been engulfed by urban growth and are now far from the edge of the city. They form a nucleus of heavy industry within the city but not near the center, which has blighted the adjacent residential area, the "Back-of-the-Yards" district.

*The residential district.*—In general, high-class districts are likely to be on well-drained, high land and away from nuisances such as noise, odors, smoke, and railroad lines. Low-class districts are likely to arise near factories and railroad districts, wherever located in the city. Because of the obsolescence of structures, the older inner margins of residential districts are fertile fields for invasion by groups unable to pay high rents. Residential neighborhoods have some measure of cohesiveness. Extreme cases are the ethnically segregated groups, which cluster together although including members in many economic groups; Harlem is an example.

*Minor nuclei.*—These include cultural centers, parks, outlying business districts, and small industrial centers. A university may form a nucleus for a quasi-independent community; examples are the University of Chicago, the University of California, and Harvard University. Parks and recreation areas occupying former wasteland too rugged or wet for housing may form nuclei for high-class residential areas; examples are Rock Creek Park in Washington and Hyde Park in London. Outlying business districts may in time become major centers. Many small institutions and individual light manufacturing plants, such as bakeries, dispersed throughout the city may never become nuclei of differentiated districts.

*Suburb and satellite.*—Suburbs, either residential or industrial, are characteristic of most of the larger American cities.[6] The rise of the automobile and the improvement of certain suburban commuter rail lines in a few of the largest cities have stimulated suburbanization. Satellites differ from suburbs in that they are separated from the central city by many miles and in general have little daily commuting to or from the central city; although economic activities of the satellite are closely geared to those of the central city. Thus Gary may be considered a suburb but Elgin and Joliet are satellites of Chicago.

APPRAISAL OF LAND-USE PATTERNS

Most cities exhibit not only a combination of the three types of urban support, but also aspects of the three generalizations of the land-use pattern. An understanding of both is useful in appraising the future prospects of the whole city and the arrangement of its parts.

As a general picture subject to modification because of topography, transportation, and previous land use, the concentric-zone aspect has merit. It is not a rigid pattern, inasmuch as growth or arrangement often reflects expansion within sectors or development around separate nuclei.

The sector aspect has been applied particularly to the outward movement of residential districts. Both the concentric-theory

[6] Chauncy D. Harris, "Suburbs," *American Journal of Sociology,* XLIX (July, 1943), p. 6 [see below, pp. 544–55].

and the sector theory emphasize the general tendency of central residential areas to decline in value as new construction takes place on the outer edges; the sector theory is, however, more discriminating in its analysis of that movement.

Both the concentric zone, as a general pattern, and the sector aspect, as applied primarily to residential patterns, assume (although not explicitly) that there is but a single urban core around which land use is arranged symmetrically in either concentric or radial patterns. In broad theoretical terms such an assumption may be valid, inasmuch as the handicap of distance alone would favor as much concentration as possible in a small central core. Because of the actual physical impossibility of such concentration and the existence of separating factors, however, separate nuclei arise. The specific separating factors are not only high rent in the core, which can be afforded by few activities, but also the natural attachment of certain activities to extra-urban transport, space, or other facilities, and the advantages of the separation of unlike activities and the concentration of like functions.

The constantly changing pattern of land use poses many problems. Near the core, land is kept vacant or retained in antisocial slum structures in anticipation of expansion of higher-rent activities. The hidden costs of slums to the city in poor environment for future citizens and excessive police, fire, and sanitary protection underlie the argument for a subsidy to remove the blight. The transition zone is not everywhere a zone of deterioration with slums, however, as witness the rise of high-class apartment development near the urban core in the Gold Coast of Chicago or Park Avenue in New York City. On the fringe of the city, overambitious subdividing results in unused land to be crossed by urban services such as sewers and transportation. Separate political status of many suburbs results in a lack of civic responsibility for the problems and expenses of the city in which the suburbanites work.

CHARLES C. COLBY

# CENTRIFUGAL AND CENTRIPETAL FORCES
# IN URBAN GEOGRAPHY

The modern city is a dynamic organism constantly in process of evolution. This evolution involves both a modification of long-established functions and the addition of new functions. Such functional developments call for new functional forms, for modification of forms previously established, and for extensions of, and realignments of, the urban pattern. Apparently these developments of function, form, and pattern are governed by a definite although as yet imperfectly recognized set of forces. Among these forces, two groups stand out prominently. The first group is made up of the centrifugal forces which impel functions to migrate from the central zone of a city toward, or actually to or beyond, its periphery, while the second includes powerful centripetal forces which hold certain functions in the central zone and attract others to it. For some years the writer has compiled and tabulated examples of these movements for the purpose of recognizing and classifying the forces responsible for them. This study led to the conclusion that the centrifugal forces are made up of a combination of uprooting impulses in the central zone and attractive qualities of the periphery, while the centripetal forces focus on the central zone and make that zone the center of gravity for the entire urbanized area.

In large measure, the evidence which underlies the conclusion just stated is drawn from three sources: (1) the theses, dissertations, and other studies in urban geography which have been made at the University of Chicago, (2) the monographs issued by the Committee on Re-

Reprinted from *Annals of the Association of American Geographers*, XXIII (March, 1933), 1–20, by permission of the author and the editor.

gional Plan of New York and Environs, and (3) the field notes of the writer, particularly those for the season of 1924 when he was working on urban problems under a grant from the university. The survey involves studies of twenty-two cities; fifteen in the United States, four in Canada, and three in Great Britain. The method employed is distinctly that of reconnaissance, for an attempt is made to think through the problem before all of the available evidence has been examined. The conclusions, therefore, are extremely tentative, and, like the old railway time tables, subject to change without notice.

In compiling and classifying the evidence, it was found advisable to recognize three divisions of an urban area, namely, an inner or nuclear zone, a second or middle zone, and an outer or peripheral zone. Such zonal divisions are recognized by many geographers and are employed in such notable urban studies as the recent economic and industrial survey of metropolitan New York. In the present study the recognition of zones not only aided the discovery of the individual impulses at work but facilitated the classification of these impulses into the centrifugal and centripetal forces.

That urban functions migrate from one zone of a city to another and from one part to another part of the same zone is attested by nearly all the urban studies consulted. In the present study, however, intrazonal movements were ruled out in order to eliminate certain variables and to reduce the dimensions of the investigation. Nearly all the urban areas investigated show striking illustrations of both centrifugal and centripetal migrations. Outward migration of residential and manufacturing functions, for example, has featured the recent growth of most American cities, and rail classification yards and warehouse facilities likewise have moved outward in many places. In Los Angeles a striking example of outward migration is furnished by the movement of the Los Angeles division of the state university first from the inner to the middle zone and more recently to the outer zone. The motion picture studios likewise have moved outward. Inward movements in our cities are evidenced by the erection of multistoried apartment houses in or near the central zone, by the localization of "head offices" of many companies in that zone and by trends in certain lines of retailing. A classical illustration of centripetal movement is offered by the gradual concentration of the commercial phases of the Lancaster cotton manufacturing industry in the inner zone of the Manchester area.[1]

### Centrifugal Movements and Forces

*Movements by zones.*—The centrifugal movements are in evidence in all parts of an urban area. The central zone of a rapidly growing city always or nearly always shows evidences of expansion. The Loop district of Chicago, for example, is expanding eastward into the lake, northward across the river, westward across the South Branch, and by a realignment of the railway terminals which now bound it on the south it promises to expand in that direction. It also is expanding upward with its towers and promises to expand downward with a subway. This expansion is occasioned both by the overflow of certain functions from the inner zone and by the concentration of other functions in the inner zone. Both centrifugal and centripetal forces, therefore, are at work, but at the outset our concern is with the former.

In the second or middle zone of a city the centrifugal activities may be of two types. In many cases a movement may

[1] Manchester Civic Week Committee, *Manchester at Work* (Manchester, 1929), pp. 13–14, 20–21.

originate in zone two and carry outward to the periphery. In other cases, a migratory tendency in the second zone may further an outward movement which originated in the central zone.[2] In such cases, the impulse given in the second zone resembles that of a pumping station of a pipeline, giving fresh impetus to a flow already under way. There is abundant evidence, for example, to show that functions displaced on Manhattan Island because of congestion, rising land values, or other causes have moved to Brooklyn or Jersey City, only to be removed at some later date to Elizabeth, Newark, or even a more distant part of the metropolitan area.

The outer zones of many American cities have been characterized by rapid growth in the last two or three decades. Such growth has involved many types of activity but has been conspicuous in connection with the manufactural, residential, and recreational functions. In some cases the growth represents functional expansion or migration from the inner zones of the urban area, in other cases it represents migration to the outer zone of a city of functions previously localized in some section of the region immediately tributary to the city, while in still others it represents the establishment in the outer zone of a function entirely new to the city and to the region. Only the first-named type falls within the scope of this study. Material dealing with migrations to the peripheral zone is larger in quantity and more satisfactory in quality than for the other types of urban movement which fall within the scope of this investigation. This probably is due to (1) the recency of occurrence of many migrations to the peripheral zone, (2) the size of the resultant forms, and (3) the conspicuous developments in the urban pattern when such invasions occur.

As has been stated earlier, the evidence

[2] Similar types of centripetal activity also occur in the second zone, i.e., movements originating in the second zone and continuing to the inner zone, and tendencies in the second zone which give fresh impetus to inward movements originating in the outer zone.

in hand leads to the conclusion that the centrifugal forces which actually result in functional migration are the resultant of two components, namely, an urge to leave and an invitation to come. These forces, therefore, involve both uprooting tendencies in the central zone and attractive qualities in the outer zones. A confusing element in the study grows out of the fact that an outer zone with attractive qualities soon becomes urbanized—the periphery seems to be constantly or at least aperiodically in retreat. In dealing with such dynamic conditions the time element therefore always should be kept in mind.

*Uprooting conditions in the central zone.* —Many conditions within the central zone encourage the migration of functions from the center to the outlying parts of the urban area. In the cases thus far examined six of these conditions stand out prominently. The first is the ever increasing land and property values and the high tax rates in the central zone. Such values and rates add materially to the cost of operation and constitute ever recurring reasons for migration unless overbalanced by other conditions. The second is the traffic congestion and high cost of transportation in the central zone. The former hampers deliveries of merchandise and the movements of people, while the latter adds to cost of operation. As a result an impulse toward migration is created for all functions except those making effective use of the costly transportation facilities and services of the central zone. The third migratory condition is the difficulty of securing space, not only to permit expansion of facilities and rearrangement of activities, but to secure light and air. The fourth is the desire of many manufacturing concerns to avoid nuisance complaints or other controversies with city interests. The fifth is the difficulty, or perhaps impossibility, of acquiring in the congested central zone a special type of site such as water frontage, or of modifying a site to meet present-day needs. The sixth of the conditions promoting migration includes such items as irksome legal restrictions, outgrown laws, inherited customs, decline of the social importance of certain areas, and the like.

The conditions promoting migration from the central urban zone are illustrated concretely by the trend of the metal manufacturing industries in metropolitan New York. In recent decades, the heavy and bulky branches of the metal industries have been in process of migration from Manhattan in the central section of the metropolitan area to sites in Queens, New Jersey, and Connecticut in the outlying sections.[3] The southern half of Manhattan, for example, now has less than half the number of heavy metal workers that it had in 1900, and only five remain of the sixty-five foundries in operation on Manhattan Island in 1900. The migration of these heavy metal industries grows out of their need of space, on the one hand, and out of rising land values, on the other. Such plants cannot use high-priced land effectively, for in many cases their type of operation calls for horizontal rather than vertical space, and the vibration and weight of their machinery discourages the use of high buildings. Their noise and dirt encourages complaints from nearby property owners, and in many cases they need dumpage space in which to dispose of their refuse and dirt. These industries, moreover, do not take much profit out of contact with the types of transportation available in the central zone, while they do find in the outer zone the types of rail, truck, and in some cases the water transportation suited to their needs. The same centrifugal tendency is at work in both the chemical and woodworking industries in metropolitan New York,[4] and Frank Williams finds it in Philadelphia.[5]

[3] V. W. Lanfear, "The Metal Industry in New York and Its Environs," *Regional Plan of New York and Its Environs, Economic Series, No. 2* (New York, 1924), pp. 24–26.

[4] *Regional Plan of New York and Its Environs, Economic Series, No. 1*, pp. 21–23; *No. 4*, pp. 30–31.

[5] F. E. Williams, "Suburban Industrial Development of Philadelphia: Delaware County," *Bulletin of the Geographical Society of Philadelphia*, Vol. XXV, No. 3, p. 37.

He shows how the Baldwin Locomotive Works, formerly in the heart of Philadelphia, moved out to Eddystone in the outer zone. The move was based on the uprooting conditions of expensive land, high taxes, congestion, and ineffective transportation of the old site, and the attraction of cheaper land, lower taxes, freedom from congestion and effective transportation of the new.

Rapidly increasing congestion and other uprooting conditions in the inner zones of cities affect the residential as well as the manufactural and commercial functions. Well-known examples are Woodward Avenue in Detroit and Euclid Avenue in Cleveland—streets long famous for their beauty. Both these streets have been transformed since the turn of the century. The transformation began by the invasion of the central-zone end of the avenues by smart shops and professional offices. Later other shops and many automobile salesrooms entered the districts, the residential value of the streets rapidly declined, and the residents moved to the outer zones of the area.

In some cities, the outward movement has been progressive, one wave following another. Chicago offers many illustrations of such mobility in its residential sections. In the old days, for example, the Park Row area now occupied by the Illinois Central Station was the exclusive residential district of the south side. Later this district expanded outward along Michigan, Prairie, and contiguous streets, and still later expanded outward to the Grand Boulevard area. In time an outward migration of light manufacturing and ancillary business infringed on the inner part of the area and thereby put the wealthy people into a receptive mood for migration. This condition, combined with other conditions such as the attractive terrain and fashionable qualities of the "Gold Coast" on the north side, resulted in a considerable migration from the south side to that district. For a time the outer parts of the Michigan and Prairie avenue sections and the Grand Boulevard area were occupied by less fashionable elements, but eventually they were engulfed by an intrazonal movement, namely, an eastward expansion of the colored district. A determined but losing fight has been waged against this invasion—the momentum of colored expansion, however, overcoming without much difficulty the resistance of an area depleted of many of its leading citizens. Those who remained did so largely because of sentiment and inertia, and in a conflict of momentum versus inertia the odds favor the former.[6]

*Attractive qualities of the peripheral zone.*—The centrifugal tendencies growing out of the uprooting factors in the central zone are intensified by the attractive qualities of the outer zones. In fact, as the previous paragraph demonstrates, it is difficult to think of the one without thinking of the other.

The conditions which attract functions to the periphery of urban areas are numerous and varied. Making allowance for differences in terminology and disregarding the doubtful cases in the materials in hand, the attractive qualities of the peripheral zone may be grouped into four classes. The first is the presence of large parcels of unoccupied land which can be obtained at relatively low cost. Here space, low evaluation, and low tax rates stand in direct opposition to congestion, high evaluation, and high taxes in the central zone. The second is the presence of transportation services suited to the migrating function. In some cases, these services may be circumferential; in others they may be axial, thus giving certain parts of the outer zone direct transportation to the inner zone. A position on a belt line, for example, attracts manu-

[6] The expansion of the colored district may extend eastward clear to the lake shore. At present (1932) this appears less likely than formerly, for the electrification of the Illinois Central, the construction of the Outer Drive, and a protective organization of property owners have greatly enhanced the residential desirability of the shore district. Thus the forces of occupance wage war for desirable territory.

facturing concerns because it puts them into effective contact with all the railways entering a city, while ample space and facilities in the plants and yards reduce the cost of loading and unloading. A position in the outer zone where streets and highways are less congested, moreover, may facilitate the use of trucks. A residential development, in contrast, finds little or no interest in circumferential transportation but is vitally dependent upon rapid axial transportation of the type well illustrated by the electrified Illinois Central in Metropolitan Chicago. The third group of peripheral attractions includes the attractive site qualities possessed by particular areas in the outer zone, such as level land, good drainage, wooded slopes, or water frontage. The fourth is control or relative control of a sizable area. Such control, in the case of the residential function, makes it possible to have freedom from smoke, noise, or other nuisances, and the privilege of imposing regulations as to the type of occupance. For the manufactural function, it means freedom to lay out and to operate the plant, to dispose of waste, to develop a particular type of community, and, in short, to proceed in a manner conducive to the success of the enterprise.

The attractive qualities of the peripheral zone, particularly of large areas of cheap land and adequate transportation, are well illustrated in the development of the East St. Louis sector of metropolitan St. Louis. Development of this sector was delayed because it was subject to the floods of the Mississippi. When once a levee was built and part of the area drained, the drained areas became attractive to large-scale manufacturing industries of the basic or heavy type, and in large measure the land has been occupied by establishments of this type. Some of these establishments formerly were in St. Louis proper, some are branches of earlier developments in St. Louis, while still others chose a site in East St. Louis in preference to a site nearer the center of the metropolitan area. Thomas

points out that of the eighty heavy manufacturing establishments in the metropolitan area in 1924, sixty-five are in East St. Louis.[7] Twenty lines of railway enter the city from the east and these are connected by three transfer lines. As might be inferred, a large number of sites, combining cheap land and efficient rail transport, are available. These east side sites offer the further advantages of dumpage space in the sloughs and ponds which dot the plain and a supply of water derived either from the river or from wells "sunk at relatively low cost in the alluvium of the American Bottoms." The east side sites also offer manufacturers the advantage of receiving coal from the Illinois coal fields without having to pay toll charges across the Mississippi as they would if their plants were on the west side. The east side concerns, moreover, are able to ship their output to eastern markets without paying bridge charges.

The attraction of a particular site quality is well illustrated by the evolution of sugar-refining in metropolitan New York. Sugar-refining in the city began as early as 1730. The early refineries were located on Manhattan Island but were not on the waterfront. In 1858 a plant was located on the waterfront in Brooklyn in order that it might receive raw sugar directly from the vessels. The advantage of a waterfront site soon was demonstrated, and sugar-refining on sites back from the waterfront became a thing of the past. By 1900 decentralization had gone to the point where the plants on Manhattan had been replaced by three plants in Brooklyn, one in Queens, and one in Jersey City. By 1922, there were two in Brooklyn and one in Queens, while at a considerable distance up the Hudson a plant had been built at Edgewater and two

[7] Lewis F. Thomas, *The Localization of Business Activities in Metropolitan St. Louis* ("Washington University Studies—New Series, Social and Philosophical Sciences," No. 1 [St. Louis, 1927]), pp. 79–82. (Dissertation in geography at the University of Chicago.)

in Yonkers. This suggests that the tendency to move farther from the central zone is still in operation.[8]

The development of the iron and steel industry in the Chicago area strikingly illustrates both the uprooting tendencies of the inner zone and the attractive qualities of the outer zone, or, in reality, of the components of the centrifugal forces. In the Chicago area iron manufacture first developed along the Chicago River near the center of the city. The industry appeared as early as 1839, a blast furnace was built in 1868, and by 1876 Chicago produced almost a third of the steel rails of the country. In 1880 a new mill was built in South Chicago. The erection of this mill was concrete evidence of the operation of centrifugal forces. After 1880 production declined on the Chicago River and at present no steel is smelted in that section of the city. Production in South Chicago, however, increased rapidly, and later came the great development in Indiana Harbor and Gary. In an analysis of the migration of this industry, John Appleton emphasizes the attractive qualities of the outlying areas, his list including (1) large parcels of unoccupied land available at low prices not only for steel mills but for the auxiliary fabricating plants which utilize much of the output of the steel mills, (2) lake front or river locations, (3) the sandy character of the lake plain which made dredging and excavation for slips a simple engineering task, (4) an abundance of water, (5) marsh or lake areas for dumpage of waste materials, (6) freedom of use, in that control of the land made it practicable to perfect economies of plant layout and operation and to organize, or to permit others to organize, the contiguous areas for residential and other purposes, (7) adequate transportation facilities for assembling raw materials and distributing the output, these facilities resulting from a combination of

lake transportation and belt-line contact with all railroads entering Chicago, and (8) proximity to the Chicago reservoir of labor.[9]

Appleton, being concerned primarily with the Calumet area, did not emphasize the uprooting conditions along the Chicago River. In all probability, these included the rising value of land in the central zone, the need of room for plant expansion, the numerous bridges and other features which hinder navigation on the Chicago River, and the absence of ready contact with all the railways entering the city. Probably the fact that the steel companies could dispose advantageously of their sites along the Chicago River was another factor.

*Centrifugal forces.*—As has been stated previously, the evidence in hand leads to the conclusion that the centrifugal forces are made up of a merging of impulses, namely, a desire to leave one part of the urban area and an urge to go to another. If this is sound it appears logical to assume that the forces are made up of impulses promoting migration and that these impulses reflect the cultural-natural complex in one or more of the urban zones. It also may be assumed that the forces, to a degree, have a beginning and an end and that in logical classification the beginning and the end should be of the same kind or quality. Certainly, the material thus far surveyed substantiates the last contention, for the uprooting impulses on the one hand and the locative attractions on the other fall into satisfactory alignments. Without undue manipulation of variables, therefore, the following six forces are recognized: (1) the *spatial force,* under which congestion in the central zone uproots and the vacant spaces of the outer zones attract; (2) the *site force,* under which the greatly modified and intensively utilized natural landscape of the central zone is balanced against the

[8] Faith M. Williams, "The Food Manufacturing Industries in New York and Its Environs," *Regional Plan of New York and Its Environs, Economic Series, No. 3,* pp. 15–20.

[9] John B. Appleton, *The Iron and Steel Industry of the Calumet District* ("University of Illinois Studies in the Social Sciences," Vol. XIII, No. 2 [Urbana, 1927]), pp. 15–16, 27–28, 81–91. (Dissertation in geography at the University of Chicago.)

relatively unchanged and but little used natural landscape of the periphery; (3) the *situational force* which arises from unsatisfactory functional spacing and alignments in the central zone and the promise of more satisfactory functional spacing and alignments in the periphery; (4) the *force of social evaluation,* under which such conditions as high land values, high taxes, and inhibitions growing out of the tyranny of the past in the long-established central zone create the urge to move, and low values, low taxes, and freedom from restrictions imposed by previous occupance in the newly developing periphery represent the invitation to come; (5) the *status and organization of occupance* in which such things as the obsolete functional-forms, the crystallized pattern, the traffic congestion, and the unsatisfactory transportational facilities of the central zone in many instances stand in opposition to the modern forms, the dynamic pattern, the freedom from traffic congestion, and the highly satisfactory transportation facilities in the outer zone; and (6) the *human equation,* which includes such potent migratory impulses as arise from religious tenets, personal whims, real estate booms, manipulated politics and the like. It is thought that this last category is sufficiently vague and sufficiently comprehensive to care for all items which elude classification under other heads.

## CENTRIPETAL FORCES

The centripetal forces in urban development focus on the central zone of the city and, as previously stated, the central zone is the center of gravity of the entire metropolitan area. In this zone the number and complexity of urban functions increases greatly. Functional congestion necessitates complex functional forms and frequent adjustments in the zonal pattern. The urban cross-section in the central zone of our larger cities, moreover, is made up of multiple levels extending from the bottom of the lowest basements to the top of the tallest towers. Land values in such areas are high, in harmony with the intensive use of the land. Such intensive use indicates that the central zone possesses assets or qualities which make it highly attractive to many functions. The data already compiled include more than forty different types of these gravitative qualities. Differences in terminology, however, account for many of the types and thus, if certain cases which at present elude classification are disregarded, the attractive qualities may be classified into the following five groups: (1) site attraction, (2) functional convenience, (3) functional magnetism, (4) functional prestige, and (5) the human equation. These five groups comprise the gravitative attributes of the central zone and are per se the centripetal forces of the urban area.

*Site attraction.*—In each of the cities under study some feature of the natural landscape, inconspicuous as it may be in the present urban complex, invited occupance. In London it was a crossing of the Thames, in New York it was the accessible waterfront of the lower end of Manhattan Island, in Montreal it was a short stretch of quiet water protected by a tiny peninsula, and in St. Louis it was "the river end of a long, narrow upland spur" which Thomas calls "Downtown Upland." In many cases the attractive quality of such features has continued unabated to the present. Thus, for example, while the commercial functions established on the lower end of Manhattan have developed enormously, they never have been dislodged from the site selected by the Dutch for their trading activities. Much the same has been true of the other cities studied.

*Functional convenience.*—Many functions remain in or gravitate to the central zone of the urban area, because in that zone they can be carried on more conveniently than elsewhere. In many cases this functional convenience endows the central zone with such active qualities that it takes on a more diverse character and a more rapid tempo than the outer zones. For purposes of classification this all-important quality of convenience may be divided into three types or classes.

The first type of functional convenience possessed by the central zone is *metropolitan* (i.e., local) *convenience* and results from the fact that the central zone is the focal point, not only for the main thoroughfares in the urban pattern, but for all systems of rapid transit. Thus the fact that the central zone is the major focus of city transportation makes it the one place where the retail business, for example, conveniently can reach customers in all parts of the metropolitan area and, conversely, where all the potential customers conveniently can reach the stores and shops. In order, therefore, for a retail establishment to be convenient to patrons in all parts of the city, it must be within the focal area. In retailing, the world will beat a path to your door only if and when your door lies conveniently near the world's daily runway.

The second type of functional convenience possessed by the central zone is the *regional convenience* arising from the fact that the railways of the region dominated by the city converge on the central zone and have concentrated their passenger, mail, and express terminals in that zone. In recent years this type of convenience has been accentuated greatly by the convergence of arterial highways on the central zone. These railways and highways make the central zone accessible to the region which the city dominates and to a marked degree make that zone the point of convergence and the point of convenience for the whole area. Indianapolis, with its marked regional dominance and with many railways and highways focusing on its central zone, well illustrates this type of convenience. Furthermore, one needs only to recall the railway terminals which cluster about the central zones of London, Berlin, Paris, and Chicago, and the highway patterns about those cities, to realize the validity of the generalization.

The third type of functional convenience

possessed by the central zone is *interregional convenience* and grows out of the fact that many cities are focal points for two or more regions. This type of convenience is highly developed in the great commercial centers; in fact, they could not be great commercial centers if they did not possess it. In New York, London, and Liverpool, for example, most of the commercial port[10] is included in the central zone. In Liverpool, in fact, the landing stage where the ocean liners load and discharge passengers, mail, and express is oriented so effectively into the local transportation services that an arriving passenger can go promptly to any point in the central zone, to most points in the metropolitan area, and to most parts of Great Britain. The presence of the commercial port acts as a centripetal force attracting shipping offices, importing and exporting houses, and the like into the central zone. Such establishments add to the complexity of the central zone and emphasize its focal quality. In the central zone of any of these cities one sees evidences of contact with many countries and finds available transportation services to practically all parts of the commercial world.

All three types of functional convenience are well illustrated by the clothing industry of New York City. This city has attained national leadership in the industry and commonly produces more than 70 per cent of the women's clothing and more than 40 per cent of the men's clothing manufactured in the United States.[11] The industry, however, is highly localized in the metropolitan area, for most of it is carried on in the central zone, that is, in Manhattan south of 59th Street. The retail phase of the industry is localized in the central retail district, a district emphasized in the city's profile by the number and height of its skyscrapers.

[10] As used here the commercial port is distinguished from the industrial port.

[11] B. M. Selekman, H. R. Walter, and W. J. Couper, "The Clothing and Textile Industries in New York and Environs," *Regional Plan of New York and Its Environs, Economic Series, Nos. 7, 8, and 9*, pp. 16–17, 50, 65–77.

This district extends from about 34th Street to 58th Street and possesses great metropolitan convenience, for it is the area on which the transportation of the metropolitan area converges. On the south, the retail district is bordered by wholesale clothing, haberdashery, jewelry, and fur houses. The turnover of modern retailing is so rapid that the jobbers must be near the retailers in order to make frequent deliveries to the stores and shops. From the same sites, moreover, the jobbers can make rapid deliveries via the rapid transit lines to retailers in Newark, Brooklyn, and other subcenters within the metropolitan area and thus, like the clothing retailers, enjoy metropolitan convenience. From these same sites in the central zone the jobbers also take the benefit of regional and interregional convenience by frequent shipments by rail to their customers in other parts of the eastern seaboard region[12] and to practically all sections of the country. Conversely, buyers from all parts of the country find satisfactory railway service to New York; and arriving at the Manhattan passenger terminals they find it only a short walk from their hotels, placed conveniently near the terminals, to the streets which contain the small retail shops and to the display rooms of the jobbers.

*Functional magnetism.*—The concentration of one function in the central zone operates as a powerful magnet attracting other functions. Thus on Manhattan the wholesale phases of the clothing industry attract the manufacturing phases. The jobbers are the dictators and designers of fashion, and for convenience of performance the wholesale areas are fringed by factories and shops where the clothing and allied lines are manufactured.[13] In many cases, a profile of a building in the wholesale area shows display rooms on the street floor, offices of jobbers on the lower floors, and the manufacturing phase of the industry on the upper floors.

These lines of industry require an enormous labor force, a force up to now recruited, in large measure, from European immigrants landed conveniently near in the commercial port.[14] Convenience to the shops and factories encourages these people to live in the congested east side of lower Manhattan. Thus the residence function also is held in the congested central zone.

The attraction exerted by a cluster of functional units on other units of the same type represents another type of functional magnetism. Hurd, writing in 1902, advanced the theory that within the retail district there is a tendency for shops of the same type to cluster together, in spite of the fact that they do little or no business with each other.[15] He argued that the force which invites such clustering of functional units is the desire to insure customers against failure to find what they want. Although Hurd himself offers no evidence in support of his theory, recent urban studies do much to substantiate it. The Fifth Avenue section in New York City[16] and the central zone of Paris both show remarkable clustering of art, jewelry, and other high-class shops, and most large cities show examples in kind. The same magnetic quality betrays itself in the distribution of theaters and motion picture houses in New York and Chicago, and it appears in the distribution of parking spaces, garages, professional offices, and many other functional forms. In many cases the clustered functional units gain a momentum which distinguishes them from competitors outside of the cluster.

The central zone of the metropolitan St. Louis or "Downtown St. Louis" offers a remarkable illustration of the three centripetal forces thus far discussed, namely, site attraction, functional convenience, and

---

[12] As used here, eastern seaboard applies to the area from Boston to Washington, inclusive. This is the sea frontage of the trunk-line territory.

[13] Selekman *et al., op. cit.*, pp. 52, 65.

[14] *Ibid.*, p. 57.

[15] R. M. Hurd, *Principles of City Land Values* (3d ed.; New York, Record and Guide, 1911).

[16] D. H. Davenport, L. M. Orton, and R. W. Roby, "The Retail, Shopping and Financial Districts in New York and Its Environs," *Regional Plan of New York and Its Environs, Economic Series, Nos. 10 and 12*, pp. 20–21.

functional magnetism. This zone contains the principal wholesale, light manufacturing, and retail industries of St. Louis. The wholesale and jobbing section of the zone fronts the Mississippi River and extends westward up a small tributary valley.[17] This section served as a fur-trading post as early as 1764, and through all the vicissitudes of changing transportation the site attraction of the section has been so great that it has remained the principal commercial section of the city. During steamboat days it was the most accessible part of the waterfront. When railway transportation developed, no other section of the city was as convenient to the bridges and terminals, while with the advent of the motor truck this section found itself at the intersection of the principal arterial thoroughfares. Such allegiance to site grows out of the power of central position, accentuated by a remarkable development of the transportational functions.

From time to time during the progress of the nineteenth century, St. Louis developed additional manufacturing activities. In this development the lighter types of manufacturing became localized in or contiguous to the wholesale and jobbing section. In fact, many of the manufactural enterprises were started by firms already engaged in some phase of the wholesale trade. Thomas names boots and shoes, clothing, tobacco, and fourteen other industries as developing out of wholesale activities in the same lines. In many cases the jobbing and manufacturing activities of a firm are in the same building. Here then is functional convenience and magnetism carried to the extreme. Interestingly enough, rising land values in the wholesale section and attractive manufactural sites in the northwestern section of the city have led to the location of some of the newer light manufacturing plants in the metropolitan periphery. Such developments represent a conflict between centripetal and centrifugal forces in which the former, in this case at least, are more powerful than the latter.

*Functional prestige.*—Functional prestige

17 Thomas, *op. cit.*, pp. 44–48.

is a centripetal force of no mean importance, although the literature thus far examined contains but scant evidence bearing on the point. The Rue de la Paix in Paris furnishes an excellent example. That short street is the center of the fashion world, and a position on it along with such world-renowned firms as Worth, Paquin, and Armand in itself does much to raise a firm to a rank of importance. Savile Row in London bears much the same relation in men's fashions, while certain sections of Fifth Avenue in New York, Michigan Avenue in Chicago, and, in fact, certain blocks in almost every city carry a greater or less degree of prestige. Commonly, the origin and continuance of prestige rests on the momentum gained from a combination of functional convenience and functional magnetism.

The inner zone of many cities contains a section in which the offices of professional men such as physicians and dentists are grouped. Their presence in the central area in large measure is a matter of transportation convenience to their patrons. Their grouping in a small area, or in a special building as in San Diego and Spokane, however, is a matter of organization in order to encourage the development of functional prestige. When once the leading professional men in a particular line are localized, that locality gains functional prestige. In time the group may rest too heavily on its prestige in which case prestige breeds inertia. In that case, the grouping may be dislodged or disintegrate, if the area is in demand by a function in the process of expansion. The same principle probably applies to all types of clustering due to functional prestige.

*The human equation.*—The human equation acts both as a centripetal and as a centrifugal force. Choice, for example, leads some people to commute from outlying residential districts, while it leads others in similar financial circumstances to occupy apartments near the central business district. The human desire to be in the center of things probably leads to an overestimation of the value of a location in the central zone. Sentiment and perhaps stubbornness leads some wealthy families to cling to sites in the central zone long after the residential function as a whole has moved out of the area. Civic pride and personal vanity have led to the erection of "sky-scraper" office buildings and hotels in small cities on the Texas plains. The folly of many real estate booms and of much financial promotion is attested by many unprofitable buildings in the central zones of our cities and by decadent subdivisions on the outskirts.

Faith Williams, in a remarkable study of the food manufacturing industries of metropolitan New York, shows how a social condition affects the localization of stockyards and slaughterhouses on Manhattan Island at 60th Street.[18] The stockyards and slaughterhouses employ adult male workers and the seasonal factor is unimportant. This naturally suggests an outlying location. They cling tenaciously to their Manhattan site, however, because of their interest in the kosher trade, which must have freshly slaughtered meat. Here, then, is a religious custom acting as a centripetal force.

### BALANCE OF FORCES

In order to recognize and describe the centrifugal and centripetal forces as sharply as possible, the method thus far has been to focus attention first on one set of forces and then on the other. In reality these forces are continually in conflict. In some cases one set of forces is so strong that there is little or no question about the position which a function occupies or should occupy in the urban pattern. In other cases, the matter is uncertain. In still others, the forces have divided the function into two parts, one remaining in the central zone, the other seeking a location in the periphery. The arrangement of Northern Pacific Railway yards and shops in Spokane is an example.[19] Under the principle of local con-

[18] Faith M. Williams, *op. cit.*, pp. 20–25.

[19] Elizabeth Martin, "The Railway Pattern and Facilities of Spokane, Washington" (M.A. thesis in geography, University of Chicago, 1926).

venience the original yards of this railway were built near the center of the city. As business grew, the yards have been expanded as much as practicable, considering the complex city pattern and the associated high land values. The yards, moreover, were brought to high efficiency through improved equipment and effective organization. They were not adequate for the growing business, however, and the company in response to the centrifugal forces of space and site opened new yards on a large block of vacant land at Yardley on the eastern periphery of the city. Yardley lies outside of the zones in which the city requires grade elevation, in a section where the land is cheap. The valley floor is wide and less rough than in the heart of the city, and excellent gravel for roadbed construction is available. These qualities made it possible for the company to develop large and highly efficient yards in the new area. The balance of centrifugal and centripetal forces also is illustrated by the division of the railway shops into an emergency shop near the passenger and freight terminals in the central zone and large shops equipped to give complete service at Yardley in the peripheral zone.

The baking industry in metropolitan New York is another example of an industry in which a part is attracted to the central zone by centripetal forces, while centrifugal forces tend to spread the other parts into various sections of the metropolitan area. The former is illustrated by the biscuit- and cracker-manufacturing division of the industry, carried on in large plants in the central zone in order to be in the focal area of the transportation services both for the city and the region. The bread, cake, and pie bakeries divisions, however, are scattered through the residential districts. They need to be near their customers in order to give frequent deliveries and because their bread, cake, and other finished products are more bulky and perishable than their flour, sugar, and other raw materials. In the better residential districts they have to build and conduct their plants so that they will not be regarded as nuisances.[20]

## STATUS OF INVESTIGATION

The conclusion of the present investigation is stated in the opening paragraph of this paper. This conclusion was reached in 1930[21] and subsequent work tends to support it. This recent work, moreover, has strengthened the conviction that the conclusion must remain tentative until closely related problems have been investigated. Functional movements within individual urban zones must be studied, for they are so closely interwoven with the interzonal movements that a study of the former should throw new light on the latter. Studies of functional migration from city to country and vice versa are called for, as well as studies of the initial appearance of functions in a region and perhaps the total disappearance of other functions from the region. Each of these, and probably other studies, is inherently a part of the challenge which urban areas present to geographical investigation.

Conclusions of the type stated in this paper need to be tested by a further examination of the literature bearing on urban problems. A systematic examination now under way, for example, of English, French, and German sources may reveal data which will lead to modifications of the present viewpoint. It is thought that the results of field investigations will prove even more important. No doubt a considerable amount of valuable material is contained in reports of city-planning organizations. Unfortunately, although these reports are based on local study, the material in many of them is relatively sterile from the geographic viewpoint. In many cases such studies deal with plans for ephemeral remodeling of the urban pattern in conformity with some betterment program. No doubt they have social value, but they do not deal with the fundamentals of urban development as the geographer sees it. Systematic analysis and logical synthesis are required instead of emotion. Even the superlative work revealed in the Regional Plan of New York and Its Environs leaves much to be desired in its locative and distributive aspects.

Although the geographical contribution to the study of urban problems promises to be important, it cannot be made without numerous field studies in the geographical manner. Happily, there is a rising tide of interest in urban geography, and important field studies are under way in nearly all parts of the country. Recent advances in field technique and method should insure the quantitative data needed in testing the validity of current theory and hypotheses.

[20] Faith M. Williams, *op. cit.*, pp. 25–31.

[21] This paper was presented at the Worcester meeting of the Association of American Geographers, December, 1930.

RICHARD U. RATCLIFF

## THE DYNAMICS OF EFFICIENCY IN THE LOCATIONAL
## DISTRIBUTION OF URBAN ACTIVITIES

At this first Bicentennial Conference at Columbia University, the metropolis is to be viewed from many vantage points and to be dissected by learned men from many disciplines. It is our general assignment to consider the economic advantages and disadvantages of metropolitan concentration; it is my special task to deal with efficiency and inefficiency in the locational distribution of urban activities, that is, in the structure and arrangement of land uses. The assumption inherent in the assigned topic is that there exist locational maladjustments in the metropolis which impair its efficiency—a presumption which is amply validated by evidence all about us.

To consider the problems of locational maldistribution only in the metropolitan context is to encourage the popular but false assumption that these are the problems of size. We shall see that the problems to be viewed crop up in varying degrees of intensity in villages, towns, cities, and metropolises, for the dynamic forces of urbanism are vital wherever men and things are found compacted and the urban organism is subject to the same natural and social laws regardless of size. To ascribe the problems of the city to size is to imply that solutions lie in reversing the growth process, that is, in deconcentration; both the assumption and the implication are questionable.

We shall see that locational maldistributions are the results of a complex of forces of which growth is but one and that size

Reprinted, with changes, from *The Metropolis in Modern Life*, ed. Robert Moore Fisher (New York: Doubleday & Co., 1955), pp. 125–48, by permission of the author and the publisher. (Copyright, 1955, by the Trustees of Columbia University in the City of New York.)

as such is likely to be more advantageous than otherwise when the proper adaptations have finally been made.

Efficiency in land utilization, as in other forms of human endeavor, is measured in terms of productivity. We measure the efficiency of a factory in terms of physical output in relation to costs. Thus, for factories or for the complex of land uses which we call a city, we can improve efficiency either by increasing output without increasing costs or by maintaining the same level of output at reduced costs.

One of the basic costs in all human activity is the cost of overcoming space. Our cities exist because of the presumed advantages of proximity of man to man, man to thing, and thing to thing. People and buildings crowd the urban landscape in search of convenience of contact and communication. If everybody and everything were at the same place at the same time, there would be no costs of overcoming space; the efficiency of the locational distribution of urban activities would be at maximum. But space-costs are inherent in our physical world. There is a positive disutility of distance, a disutility which is the joint product of the functions involved, the distance, the available means of overcoming the distance, and the importance of the contact to the persons or activity involved. No matter why people want to be near something or somebody, this preference is given a value expression and becomes an economic fact and force.

Economists have long recognized the economic value of space relationships; there is the classic statement of von Thünen on the relationship between the value of agricultural land and the distance to the market.

**299**

The physical facts of our universe make space relationships as fundamental as the chemical elements which make up man and materials or the energy which is the source of light, heat, and motion. The three dimensions are as basic as life itself.

In the costs of distance we have the test for the efficiency of locational distribution of urban activities. Note that cost is an economic not a physical thing—in this context it is inconvenience with a dollar sign; it is space relationship evaluated in view of its importance to those concerned. But the city planner cannot deal with efficiency on a microscopic basis. His is the social viewpoint, and his plans and projects must be tested by aggregative criteria. Thus the space arrangements of the city are most productive, or efficient, when, in total, costs of distance are minimized. As we explore this point more fully in succeeding pages, we shall have to define costs more rigorously than would be appropriate in this introductory statement. To be consistent, we must define costs in the same terms as the benefits to be derived from minimizing costs—if our objective is social efficiency, then the costs with which we are concerned are social costs. Social costs are the sum of individual costs plus the costs to the community acting as a unit through government.

A second measure of urban efficiency, a companion to the test in terms of the frictional costs of distance, is the equitable distribution of the burden of locational costs in accordance with benefits received and in proportion to the responsibility for their creation. This is a basic economic criterion inherent in the operation of the market mechanism.

In a manner intended to be seductively sketchy, we have outlined the goals of urban productivity: to minimize the social costs of distance or space and to distribute locational costs equitably in accordance with benefits received. These are economic tests in the sense that they are made on a scale of costs, costs which are the basis of market transactions. These tests are social

tests in the sense that the underlying criterion is the welfare of the community. The balance of this paper will be devoted to an examination of the manifestations of urban inefficiency and an evaluation of them in the light of our stated objectives. First, we shall need to establish a common ground for perspective and understanding through a restatement of the principles of urban growth in an economic context.

## LOCATION THEORY

The following theoretical discussion is not a mere academic exercise; it is to be the basis for an analysis of a set of pressing urban problems and the foundation for recommendations toward a rational approach to their solution. Nor will the following material constitute a full statement of urban land theory, for there is space for only a sketch with a filling-in where there is a close connection with problems to be discussed later. More than coincidentally, the very existence of a body of theory is a tribute to a distinguished and long-time member of the faculty of the university which is sponsoring this Bicentennial Conference on "The Metropolis in Modern Life."

Robert Murray Haig of Columbia University was not trained as a land economist, nor were his contributions to this field numerous. For the most part, his distinguished career has been in the field of public finance. But when, for a time in the 1920's, he devoted his considerable talents to the fundamental problem of land-use control, he found in the tools of economic analysis a key which opened the door to an understanding of the forces which determine the urban structure. In a study made for the Regional Plan of New York, *Major Factors in Metropolitan Growth and Arrangement,* Haig set forth concepts which are the very cornerstone of modern urban land economics. His statement appeared first in the February and May, 1926, issues of the *Quarterly Journal of Economics* and later as chapters 1 and 2 of Volume I of *Re-*

*gional Survey of New York and Its Environs,* published in 1927.[1] The chapter headings suggest the basic and encompassing nature of the analysis—"The Economic Basis of Urban Concentration," "The Assignment of Activities to Areas in Urban Regions," etc. The first is an explanation of why we have cities, and the second is the rationale of their internal functional arrangement. Later workers in the field of land economics have contributed little additional of theoretical value on these subjects. The human ecologists, at the dawn of their day, enriched our understanding of cities by applying concepts from the natural sciences to human behavior in urban areas. Economists have done much to fill out the descriptive material and to develop practical applications of theory to business and planning problems. And on the theory front, there has been a reconciliation of neoclassical market concepts with Haig's fundamental explanation of human behavior. But here, we have not gone much further than the point to which Haig advanced in 1926.

It is proposed that we now summarize relevant theory in urban growth and structure—theory relevant to the problems of the day, which are the subject of later discussion.

The explanation of the urban organization of society is found in the socioeconomic activities which call for the concentration of people, buildings, and machines within a relatively small area. Cities are functional, then, and are a physical adaptation to man's requirements, primarily but not exclusively for production and consumption. Haig points out the importance of transportation in the location of cities: "The most favored spots are those from which the richest resources can be tapped with the lowest transportation costs."[2] Since the greater share of the total available labor

force is not required to perform the work of primary extraction or to man the transportation system, it is "economically 'foot free' in the sense that it is under no economic compulsion to live 'on the land.' " For the most part, the "foot free" population must carry on the processes of production and consumption at the same place. It follows, then, that the most advantageous location for both of these activities is in the cities located most favorably with respect to raw materials. It is at these "convenient assembly points" that employment opportunities are available in processing, manufacturing, distribution, and related business functions and where there is available the richest assortment of consumption goods supplied at the lowest cost. "Instead of explaining why so large a portion of the population is found in urban areas, one must give reasons why that portion is not even greater. The question is changed from 'Why live in the city?' to 'Why not live in the city?' "[3]

Haig was quite aware of the qualifications to this theoretical explanation of urban concentration, of the "consumption advantages of non-urban locations," and of "the effects upon location of perishability and variation in weight and bulk of goods." He discusses the general factors which retard or distort the pattern of industrial location and the dynamics of the forces which determine population distribution. But the fundamental principle, with all its qualifications, is that cities are a part of the economic mechanism and that urban concentrations, from the standpoint of transportation efficiency, are the points of lowest cost in the processes of production and consumption. Note that the core of this explanation is physical, for the concentrations of people and things are the result of efforts to minimize what Haig calls "the costs of friction," that is, the costs of overcoming the friction of space. Space relationships, then, are primary factors in the very existence of our urban organization

[1] R. M. Haig, *Major Economic Factors in Metropolitan Growth and Arrangement* (New York: Regional Plan of New York and Its Environs, 1927).

[2] *Ibid.,* p. 21.

[3] *Ibid.,* p. 22.

and in the location of our urban centers. Cost, an economic factor—and, more specifically, the minimizing of cost—is the controlling force.

We have now established the underlying hypothesis that the locational pattern of urban areas is a reflection of basic economic forces and that this arrangement of people, buildings, and activities in urban concentrations at strategic points on the web of transportation lines is a part of the economic mechanism of society. We may now develop the logical extension of this hypothesis in its application to the internal structure of cities. There are three essential concepts which require statement—location, enterprises as packets of functions, and the dimensions of the cost of friction.

*Location.*—Each of us has a commonsense notion of the meaning of location, but it is important to see clearly the full implications. Location refers to the unique complex of space relationships within which each site is fixed at a given point in time. These are relationships to all other people, to things, and to activities—if the notion be carried to the extreme, relationships throughout the whole world. Of course, not all space relationships have significance with respect to a given site; the significant space relationships are determined by the use to which the site is put. Each relationship will vary in importance to a given use for the site and the pattern of variation may change with time.

*The enterprise as a packet of functions.* —Haig points to the danger of treating each business enterprise as an indivisible unit in locational analysis. "Each business is a packet of functions, and within limits, these functions can be separated and located at different places."[4] Certain of the functions are but loosely tied together; for others, there is a strong cohesive force. Department stores in large cities often separate storage and order-filling functions from the sales floor. Lawyers store their old files in cheap and remote warehouse space.

[4] *Ibid.*, p. 37.

But a small-scale business may find it impracticable to separate physically the packet of functions which the proprietor must conduct himself or closely supervise and co-ordinate.

*The dimensions of the costs of friction.* —Haig starts with the physical problem of overcoming the friction of space. To do so is costly in time and energy. "Accessibility . . . means ease of contact—contact with relatively little friction," that is, at low cost.[5] Transportation is a method of overcoming the friction of space, but since transportation is never instantaneous or effortless, it remains a costly process. Transportation costs are only one of two dimensions of the costs of friction. The other component is site rental.

"Site rentals are charges which can be made for sites where accessibility may be had with comparatively low transportation costs."[6] Thus, an enterprise will pay in rent an amount up to the savings which it can make in transportation costs by reason of the accessibility of a site. Site rentals and transportation costs are complementary and in total represent the cost of what friction remains.

The nature of transportation costs varies with each activity, and the term must be interpreted broadly. For a retail enterprise, the costs are not alone those of assembling the merchandise which stocks the shelves but also the costs of employees' travel between home and work and, most important, the travel costs of the customers who come to shop. The convenience of the customers is the prime determinant in location and the basis for the high rent typically paid for central retail sites.

With these three concepts in mind, we can proceed to explain the internal land-use organization of the city. The basic hypotheses which Haig presents are these:

1. Each activity seeks a site for which the costs of friction are at a minimum.

2. Through a process of competition or

[5] *Ibid.*, p. 38.

[6] *Ibid.*, p. 39.

bidding in the real estate market, that activity which can most successfully exploit the locational attributes of a given site will probably occupy it.

3. By their evaluation of the relative importances of the various conveniences—through their choices, the people of the community determine how they wish the land to be used. For example, the locations of retail stores of various types are conditioned by the buying habits of the potential customers.

4. Efficiency in the layout of the city is inversely proportional to the aggregate of the costs of friction.

One might say that the structure of the city is determined by the dollar evaluation of the importance of convenience.[7] The various potential users of land are concerned with different aggregates of convenience determined by the special combinations of functions in the various enterprises. Each activity seeks to minimize the disutilities and costs of friction by locating where its transportation costs are at a minimum and must be willing to pay site rent up to the amount which, added to transportation costs, is just less than the total of transport costs and site rent for alternative locations. The enterprise will be in competition with other activities which can also use the location to advantage; the successful bidder will be that activity which can most successfully exploit the aggregate of convenience which the site offers to the enterprise for its special combination of functions. In this fashion, assuming perfect competition, each site becomes occupied by that activity which can use it most efficiently. Since the locational attributes of each location are dependent upon the nature of the occupants of every other location and since the bidding for all sites is not simultaneous, in real life there is a constant shifting of land uses as locational attributes change with shifts in the occupancies of other locations. With all the im-

[7] Richard U. Ratcliff, *Urban Land Economics* (New York: McGraw-Hill Book Co., 1949), p. 375.

perfections and distortions of the market, there is an observable tendency for the natural economic forces to create an urban pattern which is relatively efficient in its basic space relationships.

The hypothesis that the people of the community determine how they wish the land to be used is deserving of further elucidation. The location of industrial enterprises within the urban area is a matter in which the citizens have little direct voice except as they are the proprietors. The locational decision of the industry is a dollars-and-cents matter, depending on the total of frictional costs for alternative locations. The retail pattern, however, is largely determined by considerations of convenience for the consumer. Thus the location of stores of various types is conditioned by the buying habits of the potential customers and by the resulting volume of their custom. In the location of home sites, consumers have a strong voice.

In the matter of public land use, the citizens, acting in unison through their elected representatives and the established governmental machinery, determine where parks, schools, streets, and sewerage plants shall be found and enter the market to bid for these locations at a market-determined price. It is true that the citizenry cannot be outbid if the community is willing to pay the necessary price in a condemnation suit, but the decision to proceed with public improvements is, in fact, greatly influenced by the prospective cost of acquisition of the site, whether by negotiation or by condemnation.

Citizens exercise another form of control over the pattern of land use where zoning ordinances are in effect. It is notable that Haig's analysis was in large part a response of the economist to the plea of the confused city planner charged with the responsibility for establishing the land-use control. Haig's answer is that zoning should aim to minimize the aggregate costs of friction. In adopting a zoning ordinance, then, the people decide how, in their opinion, costs of friction can be minimized through the arrangement of land uses to be decreed. The zoning pattern affects the convenience of almost every citizen in one way or another, and his approval, indirect and uninformed though it be, is a part of a democratic determination of the urban pattern.

Haig does not discuss land values as such, but he might have gone on to point out that the pattern of site rentals is the equivalent of the pattern of land values. He does show that a general improvement in transportation or a general reduction in transport costs will mean a reduction in total frictions and thus a reduction in the aggregate of site costs. Conversely, when bus fares are raised, the tendency is to increase the total of land values in the area served, since the costs saved by convenience will be greater. The spread in the use of the private automobile has, in fact, tended to reduce land values in central areas by making outlying retail centers more generally accessible.[8] It further follows that the best-planned city will have the lowest total of land values.

An important corollary to Haig's thesis is discussed under his heading, "The Economic Basis of Zoning." "Zoning finds its economic justification in that it is a useful device for insuring an approximately just distribution of costs, of forcing each individual to bear his own expenses."[9] Haig is something short of lucid in explaining what he means by this statement, but it is possible to derive an explanation from his general thesis.

In an idealized arrangement of land uses with aggregate costs of friction at a minimum, each site occupant would bear a rent burden properly representative of the savings in transportation cost for his enterprise. But let one enterprise be inappropriately located and there are created additional costs of transportation for all other enterprises because the most efficient

pattern of space relationships has been distorted. These extra costs are not borne by the offending enterprise but by the other activities. Thus zoning control, which would prevent such a misplacement, serves to insure a fair allocation of site costs. Haig uses as an illustration the men's garment industry on Manhattan Island which was once appropriately located there but later was destined to give way to more intensive land uses. Its presence created costs of friction arising from spoiling the character of the choice shopping district, blocking the avenues leading to the shopping district with vehicles, and pre-empting the transit facilities.[10] These costs should properly be borne by the industry.

Haig concludes his discussion of the assignment of activities to areas by stating that "the forces of competition do tend to approximate the ideal layout, and trends actually in operation are the surest indication as to what is economically sound."[11] Zoning serves to enforce and facilitate the natural forces and to prevent individual exploitation at the expense of others.

Robert Murray Haig was one of the first economists to respond to the challenge of metropolitan planning—that "broad and virgin field which the economist is called upon to cultivate in connection with modern city and regional planning."[12] Since Haig's early term of service, the social scientist has come into his own in the planning arena in light of the ever growing recognition that the master plan is no better than the social and economic analysis of which it is the final expression. Haig foresaw the "change in the economic character of the plan from that of a 'consumption good' to that of a 'production good.' Where the early plan was once content to be a noble design, the modern plan aspires to qualify also as a productive piece of economic machinery."[13] He believed that the aim of the modern master plan is to maxi-

[8] *Ibid.*, p. 372.

[9] Haig, *op. cit.*, p. 44.

[10] *Ibid.*, p. 43.

[11] *Ibid.*, p. 44.

[12] *Ibid.*, p. 20.          [13] *Ibid.*, p. 19.

mize the productive and consumptive efficiency of the urban area through an arrangement of land uses which will minimize the costs of friction. The underlying economic forces which mold and remold the urban land-use pattern are working toward this same end—how imperfectly we know all too well. The imperfections, lags, and obstacles to the free operation of the forces of adaptation are the origins of those urban problems which limit the efficiency of the land-use structure as an economic mechanism.

## CURRENT PROBLEMS

In recent decades, the rapid growth of urban areas has been accompanied by an equally spectacular rise in the intensity of various urban problems. Most of these problems would have existed in some degree even if the growth of cities had been much less rapid. The congestion of traffic and the shortage of parking are the products of prosperity as well as of size. The matter of political and fiscal integration of central city and suburbs is no new problem. Industrial decentralization has been threatened and studied for decades. The central areas have long been infected with blight and have feared the competition of outlying retail centers since the first grocery store broke away from the first village square. In succeeding sections we will examine certain aspects of these problems with a view to explaining the related phenomena in terms of the basic principles of urban growth. We shall be concerned with the repercussions and impact on urban productivity. We shall want to know whether each problem is the unique product of size or whether it is the continuing accompaniment of a dynamic urbanism in a dynamic society.

### DECENTRALIZATION

It is a bold venture to launch yet another discussion of urban decentralization; so much has been written under this heading that the reader may well turn away in re-

vulsion. Through overuse and misuse, the term has become a vague generalization with a hundred different connotations. It is a most popular fallacy to characterize many of the manifestations of urban growth as decentralization. To clarify this point at the outset it will be well to set forth in plain language just what is happening to our cities.

In the first place, we all know, without statistical confirmation of the fact, that cities of all sizes are growing in most parts of the country. They are growing in population, in number and complexity of activities, and in physical extent. Additions to the housing stock are being made where they must be made—on vacant land at the edge of settled area. Occasionally new communities are founded at some distance from the main body of the city, and new subdivisions for a time may be surrounded by open country. This is a configuration as old as civilization; there is no place for a built-up city to expand but on the periphery. In recent years, with the private auto giving greater freedom of location to the householder, patterns of new growth have been more scattered, irregular, and dispersed. But we can already see, though the auto age is still new, how the interstices are filling in and coalescing with the main body of settlement. Is this decentralization? Is it "the suburban trend"? Or is it simply the geographical necessity of urban growth modified by advancing technology which gives greater freedom in choice of location? Residential decentralization can and does take place under some conditions. But in the past decade there is little evidence of an emptying-out of central areas concomitant with peripheral growth. Where such movement has occurred in some of the largest cities, the volume is small and can account for but a fraction of the new growth.

There are certain kinds of qualitative decentralization which give concern to some. The point is properly made that the upper income groups and the persons who are the most promising potential community leaders are moving to the suburbs. The concern is not founded on this movement as such but on the arrangement of political boundaries which removes these people from the tax rolls of the central city and which bars them from office-holding or from serving on public bodies. A basic problem of decentralization would therefore appear to be the political decentralization which separates the new growth from the main body by creating an artificial governmental galaxy which is functionally inappropriate for the economic and social organism of the metropolis.

But are other functions decentralizing— such as industry and commerce? We logically should have begun our consideration of decentralization by examining the locational behavior of the basic or primary activities of the community—the "city builders" which supply the economic lifeblood. Their location has a powerful influence on urban structure. For years there has been concern about the decentralization of industry. A convenient summary of studies of this phenomenon is provided in the recent publication of the Urban Redevelopment Study.[14] A distinction is made between "diffusion," a redistribution of industrial plants from a major central area to a nearby or peripheral area, and "dispersion," a wider redistribution as from a large city to a number of smaller localities throughout a major economic region. After examining all available primary source material, Woodbury concludes that over the past half-century the chief characteristic of the pattern of industrial location is stability. Until World War II there was a "slow but rather persistent diffusion of industry within the major areas or districts of industrial concentration. . . . Indications of dispersion were less strong and . . . varied considerably with general business and industrial conditions."[15] From 1939

[14] Coleman Woodbury (ed.), *The Future of Cities and Urban Redevelopment* and *Urban Redevelopment: Problems and Practices* (Chicago: University of Chicago Press, 1953).

[15] Woodbury, *The Future of Cities*, p. 286.

through 1947, the tendency toward dispersion was stopped but some diffusion continued. This evidence on industrial movement indicates a species of slow decentralization among primary industrial employers which will ultimately effect some reorientation in the pattern of other land uses. That the effect will be slow and moderate is likely for several reasons. First, there is no compulsion for the American to live near his work. His car gives him mobility, and his job may change more frequently than his home location. Second, for those workers who live in the residential areas of the central city, a shift in plant location from the old industrial core to the edge of settlement may mean but little in travel time one way or another. The lesser congestion may be offset by the greater distance. The private car or car-pool arrangement may be more costly than the public transportation but more pleasant and timely. Thus there is no strong reason for such workers to change place of residence. The rapid rise in homeownership suggests another factor which tends to anchor workers in spite of change of place of employment. Finally, we can expect no rapid mutation in urban structure as a result of industrial diffusion because the shift is small and slow in relation to the total industrial plant. The residential and commercial facilities growing up around new outlying industrial developments are ascribable to decentralization only to a minor extent, for they are mainly a response to new growth of industrial facilities rather than to a movement of existing plants to the outskirts.

There has been much talk of retail decentralization. This topic, to be discussed later in this paper, needs only a few comments here. Briefly, there is no evidence of literal retail decentralization—draining of the central business district—except scattered indications from a few very large cities. There are, of course, many new retail facilities appearing in outlying areas, but that process has been going on for a long time. As cities grow, the proportion of retail trade done in the central area declines; but it is only when the central area suffers an absolute decline that decentralization can be said to have occurred.

There are other shifts, minor in number and effect, which represent true decentralization. Certain office and clerical activities are moving from central areas to the suburbs. Most publicized is the shift of office activities out of New York to Westchester County. This movement has not bulked large in total employment; it has affected those types of activities which have a minimum of local contacts, where business is done largely by mail and telephone, and where, therefore, costs of friction are not increased by the move. It might be said of some of these activities that they were misplaced in the congested central commercial district and that they created extra costs of friction for other land uses, costs which will be reduced when the central site is occupied by an activity appropriate to the central situation.

A main point of this discussion of decentralization is that most of the manifestations of urban change popularly classified as decentralization are not literally such; in most cases they are but responses to basic growth taking place where land is available, at the edge of existing development. There has been very little true decentralization, and what has occurred is a natural readjustment in the locations of certain activities as they adapted to changing locational factors. The effect is to reduce the costs of friction for the enterprise concerned and, where soundly executed, to reduce aggregate costs of friction in the community.

The test of whether decentralization is a symptom of degeneration and decay is whether it leaves a vacuum behind. Or we might say that, where decentralization is the product of centripetal forces, it is healthy. Much of the outward movement of certain urban functions occurs as they are pushed out of the center instead of moving in response to a pull toward outlying locations. For example, many of our cities grew up around centrally located in-

dustries which in time were replaced by retail activities able, in effect, to outbid the industries for the central sites. In the study of the Madison central area referred to in a later section, it was found that in 1925 there were thirteen centrally located auto repair shops but only six in 1950. In the meantime, numerous repair shops appeared in peripheral locations. In effect, more intensive types of commercial uses had pushed out the repair man. The history of the Madison central area is one of a constant replacement of less intensive by more intensive uses. This form of decentralization is the complement of centralization and concentration.

And now to deal briefly with the decentralists who advocate positive means to break up the city and scatter it about the countryside. Their objectives are pure and noble and, like attitudes toward sin and motherhood, are matters of wide agreement. But the question to be raised is whether the "good life" which the decentralists envision is what people really want and what they will really get.

It is our hypothesis of urban growth and structure that the city is a nucleated organism oriented to the center and that the natural force which has produced this conformation as an adaptation to man's needs and preferences is the disutility of space giving rise to a constant effort to minimize the costs of friction. Concentration rather than diffusion is the natural product. Decentralization of certain lower-intensity land uses which are forced out of the center by higher-intensity replacements is a normal and continuing process of urban dynamics which enhances efficiency. But artificially induced decentralization holds the danger of loss in total efficiency and productivity in return for the presumed advantages of the suburban way of life. This paper will not venture far into this argument beyond the warning that if total productive efficiency is to be lowered by increasing costs of friction through decentralization of facilities, there may eventuate a reduction in living standards of a more material nature for which Americans show signs of strong affinity.

## METROPOLITAN INTEGRATION

Many frustrations result from the absence of centralized public control over all the area comprising the organic metropolis. Outstanding are the inability to control all land use in accordance with a master plan designed to minimize aggregate costs of friction and the lack of power to force each part of the area to bear its fair share of the remaining costs of friction. The latter is the main point of discussion in this section.

We must first establish the nature of the metropolitan organism in the context of our present analysis. The arrangement of land uses is broadly independent of the boundaries of the political subdivisions which typically lie in irregular pattern about the central city. That the pattern is modified by their existence is admitted by the recognition of the problem of metropolitan planning. Each political unit, acting in what are presumed to be its own interests, may control the assignment of activities within its own boundaries in such a fashion as to exclude developments which would be appropriately located from the metropolitan standpoint. Lack of land-use control, or poorly directed control, may admit land uses which are badly situated for the community as a whole. But in spite of these and other obstacles to the free play of basic market forces, it is generally true that the over-all pattern of land use in the metropolitan area tends toward the most efficient pattern—that which minimizes the costs of friction. The political boundaries are accidents little related to the pattern of development.

It is clear enough that planning and planning controls must be on a metropolitan basis for a minimum of locational frictions. And it is equally true that, co-ordinated with planning control, a metropolitan fiscal control must exist if all areas and all land uses are to bear their fair share of frictional cost. To understand this point it is necessary that we see the role of the tax system in the equalizing of locational costs.

Transportation costs are reduced by improved streets and traffic ways. The costs of improving streets are either borne on the general tax roll or levied, by special assessment, against the properties which are to benefit most directly. We may assume that Haig's definition of site rent (one of the two components of costs of friction) includes tax levies. Thus the site occupant pays a share of the costs of street improvement from which he benefits in varying degree. There is little probability that he pays his exact and proportionate share, for the tax system is hardly so accurate. And yet, when a street improvement benefits a property, the land value tends to rise proportionately, assessed value for tax purposes will rise in response, and, in effect, a share of the cost of the improvement proportionate to the benefit will be borne by the property. The question of whether the occupant—for example, a retail store—can pass on this tax increase to its customers will be dealt with shortly.

Now let us take the example of a central city and a contiguous residential suburb separately incorporated. The city widens and improves a main artery leading from the vicinity of the suburb to the central business district. The cost of this improvement is paid out of the city's general fund. The benefits are to those who will find this route of travel a speedier and more convenient channel. The businesses in the center benefit from reduced costs of transportation for their employees and customers. The employees and customers who will use the improved route will benefit. Many residents of the residential suburb adjacent to the artery will benefit. Who will bear the cost?

If the cost of the improvement is met by a general increase in the city tax rate, each citizen of the city will share the cost in proportion to the taxable value of his property. Because some properties will benefit directly, their site values will tend to rise; this rise will be reflected in the next assessment, and they will bear an increased burden as a result of the improvement equivalent to the increased value times the total tax rate (including the increase called for because of the improvement). Thus the benefited properties will bear a greater burden than other properties but not necessarily a burden equivalent to the benefit. The residents of the suburb who benefit will bear none of the direct costs. Some of them work in the central area; most of them visit the center frequently for shopping and recreational purposes. Is any share of the cost passed on to them as workers or customers?

Now it is common argument on the part of suburbs resisting annexation that their presence is a great asset to the central city and that the businesses of the city benefit by their trade and by the labor force which is housed beyond the city limits. This is a true statement as far as it goes, but it fails to recognize the mutual nature of the relationship. The suburbs and the inhabitants of the suburbs benefit by the employment opportunities present in the community and by the shopping and service facilities there. In this respect, the suburbanites are no different from the people in the central city; the accident of separation by an arbitrary political boundary has nothing to do with the social and economic relationships of mutual benefit which are the lifeblood of the metropolitan organism.

We can say with certainty, therefore, that the suburbanites bear a lesser burden on account of the new street improvement than the citizens of the central city. Because of the improved access to the center, the values of their homes will rise, and yet they bear none of the direct tax cost of the improvement. However, the next owners of these suburban homes will pay a higher price than did the present owners, this higher price reflecting the reduced transportation cost to the center. Thus they will bear a share of the costs of friction in the increased site rent (Haig's equivalent of land value) related to the saving in trans-portation costs. But the present homeowners will capitalize upon the increased values without bearing a share of the costs which brought about the increase.

If it could be demonstrated that downtown merchants were able to pass on some of the burden of the cost of the improvement through higher prices for their goods, then the suburbanites would appear to bear at least some of the cost, though in no event would they bear as much of the cost as the citizen of the central city who shares the tax load. But in a competitive system, it is doubtful whether merchants could secure higher prices as a result of increased accessibility. For items available in the center only, prices are set with no reference to convenience. For items available in outlying areas as well as in the center, prices in the center might rise some, but the increase is limited by the level of prices in the competing areas plus a differential reflecting advantages in convenience. But rather than increased prices at the center, the more likely reaction is an increase in the volume of sales due to expanded accessibility. For competitive items—items available elsewhere in the city—sales will increase because the center has gained in accessibility relative to other shopping areas. For items sold only at the center, sales will tend to increase as a result of more potential customers brought into the area and exposed to effective merchandising blandishments. If, as a result of increased sales volume, profits are swollen, the forces of competition will tend to bring about a price reduction. Thus it may be that our suburbanites not only bear none of the cost of increased accessibility but benefit from reduced transportation costs (greater convenience), from an increased value of their real estate, and from decreased prices of goods which they buy at the center. The citizens of the central city who use the improved street will benefit in the same fashion but will also carry a share of the cost. The merchants will benefit in increased volume of sales and in increased profits, but they will bear a substantial share of the cost of the improvement. Employers may be able to hire workers at lower wages because of increased convenience, but in a competitive system this saving in labor costs will be passed on to consumers in lower prices.

The case of the street improvement has been used merely as an example of public improvements, paid for out of general taxes, which reduce costs of friction. There are many others, including street lighting and traffic control, which in some instances benefit all members of the community and in other cases benefit some more than others. Those who live beyond the jurisdiction of the taxing body and who, as members of the community, use its facilities of employment and service are not bearing their fair share of the costs of reducing the frictions of space.

### TRAFFIC AND PARKING

To deal in simple fundamentals, let us apply the Haig hypothesis to the problem of traffic congestion. Assume a community in which the ideal pattern has somehow been attained, and the costs of friction are at a minimum. Each land use is space-related to every other land use in a manner which maximizes locational efficiency. Now change the scene to include the extra-heavy use of one artery to the center to a point where the time-cost of travel from outlying areas is increased. Increased travel costs on this route may result not only from traffic congestion but also from removal of public transport facilities, changes in the streetcar or bus schedule, or physical deterioration of the street surface. In the first impact, all persons and activities which are space-related along the congested artery will suffer increased costs. The ultimate tendency, however, is to reduce site rent (land values) at both ends as an offset to increased transport costs. The reduction in site rent will ultimately find its expression in reduced costs of the goods and services and will thus tend to offset the added costs and discomforts of the customers. But this

happens very slowly, and after a long period of adjustment. Some of the activities will act to reduce their costs of friction by moving to a point more convenient to their patrons or employees. Once they have moved, they disrupt the balance in the web of space relationships in the central area of which these uses were component parts. This effect leads to further readjustments and, in the end, to substantial shifts in the land-use structure. This process of adaptation is costly, for the shifts in location involve moving costs, tend to hasten obsolescence of buildings, and may require public improvements or decrease the efficiency of existing public facilities.

As an example of the possibilities, let us again take the case of a centrally located home office operation of an insurance company. Assume that the increased congestion has created hardships for its employees. As a result, a decision is made to move to the outskirts, as is the actual conclusion in a number of specific instances about the country. The removal of a substantial number of clerks and executives from the daytime population of the central area may have a considerable effect on the locational pattern and on central land values. The uses affected are the restaurants which served lunches to the departed office workers and all the shops, stores, and service establishments where they bought goods or services at noon or after hours. In the new location of the insurance company operation, new service uses are bound to appear to serve such a large and concentrated group. The land uses in line of travel between the homes of the employees and the new location will be affected. It is possible, if care is not taken in selecting the new location, to create a cross-stream of employee traffic which may create congestion in yet another place. The aggregate convenience in home-to-work travel for the employees of the insurance company, while greater than immediately before the move, is probably less than before congestion increased to a point where the advantages of centrality were offset.

It is apparent that the repercussions of increasing traffic congestion are sweeping and that they extend far beyond the direct and immediate effect upon the central business area. The self-correcting adaptations are long delayed, and the costs created by the processes of adjustment are not likely to be quickly recovered. The efforts of individual enterprises to reduce frictional costs will create new frictional costs which others must bear. The realignment of the pattern of land values will probably result in a lesser total of land values as a tax base. Because of the accidents of political boundaries and the lower tax level in suburban areas, the process of adaptation may push a significant share of the tax base beyond the city limits.

The movement of functions from the central area resulting from increasing frictions through traffic congestion creates a net loss to the community in productivity or, at least, no gain. The move takes place when, by reason of the increased frictional costs, the outlying location is more favorable that the original central site. But, if the central site were appropriate to the use in the first instance, the total community costs of friction are likely to be greater in the new location as compared with the costs in the original location before the condition of traffic congestion existed. The point is that the costs of congestion cannot be evaded by forced and unnatural readjustments in the location of central activities. In addition, new costs are created through the disturbance of the equilibrium of space relationships involving all central uses.

On the other hand, when more intensive land uses replace less intensive uses and force them out of the central area, there is a net gain in productivity. This is the natural process of adaptation which minimizes aggregate frictional costs by placing in central locations those activities which can best exploit focal sites.

The parking problem is inseparable from the traffic problem; so long as people travel to the center by private automobile, termi-nal facilities are as important as streets. The absence of parking facilities or, better, the degree of difficulty in parking, including the parking fee, is as much a transportation cost as the delays of traffic congestion or the bus fare. Thus, if we are to maximize downtown daytime population density, we must provide parking as well as reduce other transportation costs lest the same repercussions be felt.

There exists considerable confusion on the point of financing parking facilities. Who is responsible for providing them—the community, the merchants who benefit through increased sales, or both? In the first place, let us examine the matter from the standpoint of abstract justice. Let him pay who benefits. Who benefits? The answer is that the community benefits—the producer, the consumer, the merchant. The foundation of our economic system is mutuality of benefit. But is it more important for the merchant to be convenient to the consumer or for the consumer to be convenient to the merchant? It may be that the merchant, as an individual owner of a business, benefits more than any one of his customers whose shopping convenience is enhanced by added parking facilities. But this is no test, for the convenience of *all* shoppers who wish to come into the central area is enhanced. Thus both the community and the merchants benefit, and who shall try to judge which benefits the more? Any excess gain by the merchants is temporary, for two forces are at work to level off any additional profits which may result from improved business. First, there is the increase in his site rent, for the landlord will expect to share in the improved locational qualities of his land. Second, in a competitive system, unusual profits invite competition and lead toward an equilibrium of returns. Furthermore, the merchant will bear the burden of increased taxes (which we have included in the site rent), for as the land value increases, so will the assessed value for tax purposes. Since the cost of the improvement will result in an increased tax rate, he will pay an increase in rate upon an increased tax base. Of course, this is also true of the citizens whose homes are made more valuable by the improved accessibility of the central area by reason of the parking space.

The problem of assessing the costs for parking facilities has a parallel in the problem of assessing the costs of street improvements. In neither case is the benefit solely assignable to the adjacent property owners. Streets—and terminal parking lots—are two-way, benefiting those at both ends. They are rightly a general charge on the community—on all the metropolitan community, not just the central city.

There is an ideological argument to the effect that private enterprise should provide the service of parking, at a profitable price, to be paid by the consumer. This is the toll-road scheme of early colonial days, when transport and transport facilities were strictly private businesses. This approach, unless subsidized by downtown businessmen, is well calculated to drive the shopper away. Facilities under this plan are too few, too expensive, and are used only by those who can afford the luxury of close-in convenience and extra service. There are private profit potentials in parking—but not on a scale commensurate with the public interest.

Against the stand that terminal parking facilities should be a general charge on the community is the argument that individuals do not benefit equally—some people do not own cars, others rarely come to the business districts. This same line of reasoning could be used against our system of supporting public education. But in both cases the benefit to the community as a whole, through enhancing its aggregate productivity, is undeniable.

There are certain practical arguments in favor of at least a small service charge for publicly owned parking. In the first place, where the facilities are intended to serve shoppers, the rate structure can be designed to discourage all-day parking by central area employees. Again, because of the accidents of political boundaries, those who come from beyond the limits of the central city would make no contribution whatsoever to the cost of the convenience which they enjoy. These rationalizations are far from satisfactory but do give a color of justification for municipal parking fees; added to this is the practical consideration that even small fees provide net revenues which, in many cities, support their revenue bonds necessary to finance the parking lots.

## THE PROBLEM OF THE CENTRAL AREA

*The problem.*—The dramatic growth of peripheral "one-stop" regional shopping centers in the postwar era has once more engendered a widespread fear of retail decentralization. Merchants of the central area, property owners, and public officials view with trepidation and dismay the development, in the penumbra of large cities and small, of attractive clusters of stores, complete with parking facilities, giving every promise of draining the central district of its lifeblood of trade. Now decentralization is a familiar bogyman whose finger has pointed at the central area before. But never, in so short a time, has competitive outlying retail growth been so rapid, so well planned, and so effectively executed. The last flurry of anxiety in the hearts of the central area owners and merchants came toward the end of the thirties. Business depression had seriously deflated downtown property values, and business mortality had caused the retail district literally to shrink in area. Assessed values and taxes, with natural reluctance, failed to follow market values to their low estate so that property owners raised their voices in protest and pointed to the apparent decline of the central area as justification for tax reduction. It seemed not unnatural, following an era of retarded city growth and in an atmosphere of gloom and despair, that blight would creep over the center of our cities unresisted by the active forces of growth.

The origins of the present danger which is presumed to face the urban center are popularly associated with traffic congestion and the parking problem. Our streets are overcrowded and there is no place to park —therefore, outlying shopping centers. But the more thoughtful are wondering whether the urban structure is not undergoing some functional change which is altering significant space relationships and giving rise to basic structural shifts in the arrangement of land uses. In terms of efficiency in the locational distribution of uses, the question is whether certain activities are not now more efficiently located outside the central area; in terms of Haig's concepts, the question is whether certain central area uses can reduce costs of friction by locational shifts to outlying areas.

*Functional explanation.*—We shall not understand what is happening to the metropolitan central areas without first understanding their functions. What goes on in the center, and why does it go on there rather than elsewhere in the urban complex? First, what are the central functions?

We have no time or space to recount the historical development of the urban core. Suffice it to say that though the activities which have characterized the center have changed over the centuries, the market place has always been at the focal point. In the modern metropolis both retail and wholesale trade are conducted in the central area, though not exclusively there; in addition, there are all manner of commercial services such as banking houses, investment firms, advertising agencies, and accountants; other professional services such as architects, lawyers, and physicians; administrative activities such as home offices of corporations; non-commercial functions such as centers of government, post offices, and courts of law; there are all manner of eating and recreational establishments and agencies of personal service such as barbershops; there are factories, transportation terminals, and dwelling places. This is no complete list, but it is enough to remind the observer that the central area is not just a shopping district centered upon huge department stores.

A historical analysis of these major categories of central-area functions covering the past hundred years would reveal that in number and variety of activities there has been no diminution. Rather, the opposite is true; as society has become more complex, technology has multiplied the items of consumption, and specialized business functions and services have continued to crystallize in increasing number. There is reason to support a hypothesis that the initial locus of most new activities is at the center; not all of them remain there, but most of them do. It is true that over a period of time certain functions and activities have disappeared from the urban scene for one reason or another, but almost certainly there has been a net gain in variety.

Why should new activities crop up at the center in most instances? Those which sprout from existing activities naturally find fertile soil in the same district. For example, specialized accounting services, an offshoot from a basic business function, locate with a view to convenience to clients. New local services, during an initial period at least, when they must draw upon the entire community for their clientele, find a central location essential in minimizing transportation costs. Other activities, with regional or national markets, find it advantageous to be near a grouping of the agencies which serve them, especially during early life when their organizations are small and dependent on outside agencies for such specialized business services as accounting, financing, and marketing. Not all the new activities remain in the center as they grow to maturity and develop internal specialization, but there is a substantial residuum which creates an ever increasing variety in central activity.

There are two basic reasons why central locations are advantageous to various activities and functions; in many cases both reasons apply. Haig gives the clue to this explanation in his early classic. One virtue of centrality, which is of importance to all types of activity, is in the minimizing of transportation costs. For almost all the usual central types, the center is the place most convenient to the greatest number of employees. For many types, it is the place most convenient to the greatest number of customers. This principle may be illustrated by reference to a crude but significant classification.

Central-area businesses may be roughly divided into four groups on the basis of the geographical location of their clientele:

1. *No local clients.* These are the businesses where contacts are largely outside the community and where the community contacts are a small share of the total. An example is a mail-order house with a regional or a national market, including the community where the home office is located. In this case, centrality is of no great importance from the standpoint of customers but may be important from the standpoint of employee convenience.

2. *Community-wide clientele.* The prime example is the downtown department store which serves the entire community and the hinterland for miles about. Convenience to both client and employee is an important aspect of a central-area situation.

3. *Central neighborhood clientele.* The central area is in a situation most convenient to householders who live on the periphery in the central slums, in the Gold Coast apartment hotels, and in the adjacent modest homes of clerks and workingmen. Their focus is toward the center for many services and commodities which in outlying residential areas are typically provided in neighborhood and regional shopping centers. Grocery stores, drugstores, barbershops, and dry cleaners situated on the fringe of the central area exist primarily to serve the residential districts which border the commercial core.

4. *Central-area clientele.* This group of businesses might be termed "parasitic" except for the fact that they are essential to the productivity of the urban organism. In a sense they feed off the center, but in another sense they serve the center. Examples are the eating establishments which nourish the daytime population of the cen-

ter, both customer and employee. Another type is the business service, the accountant or advertising firm which finds its clients among the businesses located in the central commercial area. Both examples show how a central location is inevitable in light of the nature of the contacts involved.

In examining this first basic reason why central locations are advantageous, the emphasis has been on space relationships between business and client and between business and employee. The importance of a central location in terms of these relationships will of course vary from business to business. The mail-order house has no need for a central location to serve its clients and may be able to recruit enough employees from one sector of the community so that an outlying location is feasible. There are current examples of this situation in the movement of insurance company home offices to suburban locations. The accounting firm serving downtown clients could locate away from the center without much increase in the frictions of its primary services, since much of the actual auditing work is done in the clients' own offices. But the extra convenience of central location for face-to-face contact between principal and client is worth the small premium in rent—small in terms of total operating expenses which are mainly for personal services. Where the clientele is community wide, as in the case of a medical specialist or a department store, the maximizing of customer convenience is of primary importance.

The importance of employee convenience is conditioned by a variety of factors including the tightness of the local labor market, the competitive level of wages, and the proportion of total operating costs which is accounted for by personal services. The pattern of these factors varies from business to business and even from time to time.

We now turn to the second basic reason why certain activities seek central locations. Here we again acknowledge a great debt to Robert Murray Haig for a most useful concept—the cohesion of functions. Haig first developed the notion to explain the force which militates against physical separation of the functions of a given enterprise.[16] He shows that, under certain circumstances, business functions can be separated; for example, the lawyer may store his old files in a separate building at lower space rent than the place where he meets his clients. A department store may warehouse its stock in the wholesale district and fill orders from floor samples. But in a small business, the proprietor must perform a variety of functions and his presence is required to supervise others; thus all functions must be carried on in small compass —the cohesion of functions is strong. Haig goes on to show that fundamental locational analysis must be in terms of functions; each enterprise is to be viewed as a packet of functions with its proper location determined by the proportioning of the components of the packet.

We now move to extend this concept by application to the galaxy of enterprises which make up the central commercial zone. It has long been observed that certain retail store types tend to cluster, and attempts have been made to measure these associative tendencies.[17] The most significant and highly crystallized grouping is that of the women's shopping-goods stores. In every central business district, closely associated with department and variety stores, are found dress shops, shoe stores, hat shops, hosiery stores, and other women's specialty outlets. But there are other less prominent groupings of store types. Outlets serving men are usually grouped in a men's-wear cluster. Restaurants, theaters, and florist shops show a tendency toward clustering. The financial district is a place of banks, investment houses, business services, lawyers, account-

ants, insurance companies. There is often a wholesale district with its warehouses and loft buildings and perhaps a manufacturing and processing area. Thus the central area, no matter how one may choose to delimit it, is a galaxy of constellations, clusters of activities which appear to have a locational affinity one for the other. Nor are the individual clusters or constellations unrelated to other clusters.

When we understand the nature and origins of these various affinities, we shall uncover the fundamental stabilizing force which promises to preserve our central areas with little basic change for decades to come. First, to look at the constellations— related land-use types which are found in groupings generally confined in extent to a ground area which can be comfortably covered on foot. The nature and structure of these groupings are determined by the locational preferences of those whom they serve. "In a very real sense the people of a community decide for themselves, by their expenditures, how they desire the land to be used," says Haig.[18] Others have developed this idea to show that there is a hierarchy of "convenience-desirability" among land-use types and how consumers vote by the amount and frequency of their purchases to establish the retail structure in a pattern which maximizes their convenience.[19] This is the basis of the cohesion of the women's shopping district, for example, for the buying habits of women call for competitive fashion goods outlets to be in close proximity to facilitate comparison and to provide a wide assortment within small compass. In the same shopping district are other types of non-shopping-goods outlets such as variety stores and candy shops which serve the women shoppers, not in any sense as parasites, but providing items which are secondary but nonetheless important objectives of the downtown shopping trip. Even goods bought on impulse, as a

[16] Haig, *op. cit.*, p. 37.

[17] Richard U. Ratcliff, *The Problem of Retail Site Selection* ("Michigan Business Studies," Vol. IX, No. 1 [Ann Arbor: University of Michigan School of Business Administration, 1939]).

[18] Haig, *op. cit.*, p. 43.

[19] Ratcliff, *The Problem of Retail Site Selection*, chap. 4.

box of bonbons, may well yield satisfactions equal to purchases long planned.

There are endless examples to illustrate the "cohesion of functions" that binds together the functional constellations of the central area but in each case the forces are the same—the maximizing of convenience or the minimizing of the costs of friction. These are measurable forces only on a comparative basis, though we can observe, over time, the effect on locational structure of the relative importances of various species of convenience.

The functional constellations of central-area activities are bound one to another by the same kind of force that binds them internally. The financial district is related to the shopping area in ties of convenience for shoppers who may wish to make deposits or withdrawals as one planned activity in the course of a downtown expedition; the convenience of the merchants in procuring banking services is important. The wholesale and retail districts are tied together where the downtown stores comprise a substantial share of the wholesalers' market. The downtown medical arts building is located close to the retail core to house specialists who serve the full community and to offer convenience to shoppers on multiple-purpose visits to the center. Convenient medical service is also available to downtown employees, proprietors, and professionals. In this fashion, then, are the clusters interrelated, and this way they form a nucleated pattern in the central zone of our cities.

This picture of the central area is one of common advantage in location at the focus of transportation and mutual advantage in proximity among the central land uses. In other terms, the central area offers a unique convenience built of two component qualities which we might term *accessibility* and *availability*. *Accessibility* is the ease of movement from some point of origin (the shopper's or employee's home) to the destination area (the central retail district). *Availability* is the number and kind of services and activities within the destination area. The primacy of the central area in accessibility is geographical but also man-made, in the converging transportation facilities. The primacy in availability is a product of the unmatched variety of services and activities, the wide range of choice within each service, and the relatedness, direct and indirect, of most of the central activities.

These dimensions of availability give the central area a tremendous potential advantage in convenience over any other spot in the community, as the following oversimplified illustration will show. Compare two hypothetical areas, A and B. Suppose that A is the locus of ten different types of services compared with five for B. Then in Area A there are forty-five possible combinations of two services while in B there are ten. The larger the possible combination of errands which can be run within a destination area, the greater the aggregate potential saving in transportation costs. Add to this economy of movement the efficiencies of proximity of related businesses and business services and we must credit this intricate web of interdependent functions and significant space relationships with providing the most convenient spacing for a very large share of the activities of a high proportion of the people of the community. In addition it is the most convenient place to get to for the greatest number of people and the most convenient spot to distribute from in serving the whole area.

This analysis of the functional basis for the central area suggests four ways in which the center might lose in advantage in business done and thus in property values: (1) reduced accessibility, (2) reduced availability, (3) reduced interdependence, and (4) reduced employment.

1. *Reduced accessibility.* This is the bogyman of the modern day, for it implies traffic congestion and lack of parking. The usual view is the individual one—that it is now more troublesome to go downtown than it used to be. But, in general, the central area is potentially more accessible than ever, and more people are entering it

than ever before. The pain may be greater but the people still come. For certain purposes the downtown district is *comparatively* less accessible as services of various kinds appear in outlying areas, but this process is in part a natural accompaniment of community growth. As we will show later, the pattern of retail services continually shifts as the city grows, so that a progressively smaller proportion of retail business is done at the center. The unanswered question is whether the traffic and parking problem is to become so serious, in spite of countermeasures, that there will be a basic functional change at the center.

2. *Reduced availability.* So far the central areas have been moving in the direction of greater not lesser availability. The variety of activities has been increasing, and the range of choices offered to the shopper in brand, style, quality, and price has not diminished. Ever increasing specialization in business functions tends to create more, not less, interdependence and thus more not fewer symbiotic relationships where space-convenience is important. Here the danger to the center lies in losing more functions than are gained, or in losing activities of special significance in strength and extent of their relationships with other central activities. The removal of a single activity may create repercussions in many other activities with which it has had direct contact; in turn, the cessation of direct contacts will have secondary effects on enterprises and activities which have had relationships with the activities directly affected. Thus the removal, without replacement, of a single activity will disturb the web of relationships in a series of impacts of diminishing strength, like the ripples from a stone cast into a millpond. The removal of the home office of an insurance company from a central location will diminish many types of convenience—of the employees in their daily travel to and from work; of customers who come to the home office on business; of contact between investment offices and financial houses, between the sales department and advertising

agencies, between the medical department and medical specialists and laboratories, between the personnel department and employment agencies; and the employees of the company will no longer enjoy the convenience of noon or after-work shopping or errand-running in the compact central area where stores and services are within walking distance.

Let the center lose too many functions and the web of mutually advantageous space relationships will weaken and the decline will gain a self-induced momentum which may be seriously destructive.

3. *Reduced interdependence.* If the central area contained only a group of unrelated enterprises each going its separate way and serving a separate group of individuals, the seeds of destruction would find fertile soil. To the extent that intercompany contact is important and frequent, the convenience of the compact downtown arrangement will be a perpetuating factor. In addition, the changes in merchandising which decrease the number of outlets in relation to the variety of the goods tend to reduce the cohesion of the shopping district. As the department store extends its lines or expands its offerings in a given line—in style, model, and price—to that extent it frees itself from the need for close proximity of other outlets which make comparison-shopping possible. To the extent that preselection through advertising and brand acceptance becomes more widespread, so the clustering of competing outlets becomes less necessary. To the extent that business enterprises expand and provide specialized business services within their own organizations through a legal staff, an advertising department, or a research staff, so the close proximity of business specialists is less important.

4. *Reduced employment.* In most cities, the central district is the greatest single point of employment concentration. Historically, cities have grown up around the center of employment, and the homes of the workers have been oriented to this focal point. In a study of the relationship of

home to place of work, Douglas Carroll shows how the demonstrated tendency for workers to seek dwellings near their employment has made the center, in proportion to its importance as a place of employment, a dominant force in determining population distribution.[20] Even off-center places of employment are oriented to the main center in many respects. Thus the whole urban structure is organic with the central area as the primary nucleus. Because of this structural orientation toward employment, the central area is a logical spot for a concentration of services for two reasons: (1) it is most convenient to the greatest number of places of residence; (2) the services are convenient to the employees when at their places of work.

It would seem that a reversal of the historical growth process would have a diluting effect upon the center and its dominance. If primary employers move to peripheral locations or if new local off-center concentrations of employment develop, the ultimate effect will be to modify the orientation of the population distribution and to alter slowly the structure of service activities. The daytime population of the center will be decreased and thus also the potential of convenient customers for downtown establishments.

Up to the present time, the major desertions from the central area have probably been manufacturing activities. This is not a recent trend and, in fact, is well finished in most cities. Of the primary activities around which many cities were built, the residue at the center consists largely of the loft-type industries and the transport terminals. There have developed many other types of primary central employment. The tendency of some activities—for example, offices with relatively few local contacts such as home offices of corporations with widespread interests—to move to suburban locations could have serious effect in some

cities if it should reach large proportions.

*Recorded behavior.*—Most of the cries of pain on the subject of central-area decline are of anticipation rather than realization. There is little recorded fact which supports the view that the decline is under way. In a few scattered instances there have been statements that after the opening of branch stores, downtown "mother" department stores have suffered some loss in volume of sales. But there are also claims of increased business in the central store. It is said that in Los Angeles downtown retail sales volume has dropped 14 per cent since 1948, while store sales in Greater Los Angeles have gone up 18 per cent.[21] On the basis of such limited information it can hardly be said that the death knell of the central area has been sounded. The phenomena are subject to various possible interpretations and much more study is required.

Observation of the recent surge in new outlying shopping developments has led to two hypotheses:

1. The popular hypothesis is that the peripheral retail expansion is taking place at the expense of the central area; that there is occurring a literal decentralization, a dispersal of retail activities from center to outskirts. It is a logical extension of this hypothesis that the central retail district ultimately will decline in volume of business and in land values.

2. The alternative hypothesis is that the peripheral growth of retail facilities is consistent with and proportionate to the population increase and spatial expansion of our urban areas. Under this assumption, it may be expected that central areas will continue to grow in productivity and that business volume and property values will continue to rise as the total population increases, though perhaps at a slower rate than population. This hypothesis explains the recent spectacular spurt in outlying retail development as nothing more than a secular and temporary acceleration of a normal growth

[20] J. Douglas Carroll, Jr., "The Relation of Homes to Work Places and the Spatial Pattern of Cities," *Social Forces,* Vol. XXX (November, 1952).

[21] Marmion D. Mills, "Decentralization," *Mass Transportation,* July, 1953.

process. In connection with this hypothesis, there is no implication that the central area will normally retain a constant or increasing proportion of the total retail business of the community. To the contrary, there is historical evidence that, as cities grow, the central area accounts for a decreasing proportion of commercial activity and that this phenomenon has long characterized urban growth patterns.[22]

There are no adequate data on which these alternative hypotheses can be properly tested. However, by studying the central-area functions over a period of time, some light may be thrown on the matter. The main question is whether the retailing function, where it appears that changes of some nature may be occurring, is changing quantitatively or qualitatively to such an extent that there will be serious effects on basic land values. An analysis of changing central-area functions in Madison, Wisconsin, a midwestern city of about 100,000 population, started with a classification of land-use types represented in the central area.[23] At approximately five-year intervals beginning in 1921, the types present were recorded with the number of each type. In this way it was possible to see which types appeared or disappeared and which multiplied or declined in number. To explain the changes in the land-use pattern, five hypotheses were set up:

1. As the metropolitan area grows in population, those businesses which can most successfully exploit the whole of the expanding trade area will tend to displace

[22] Larry Smith, a real estate and business consultant, states that the ratio of retail business done in the center declines with size as follows:

| Population of City | Per Cent Outside Center |
|---|---|
| Under 250,000 | 30 |
| 250,000–500,000 | 50 |
| 500,000–1,000,000 | 60 |

See *Business Action for Better Cities,* a report on Businessmen's Conference on Urban Problems, June 23, 24, 1952 (Washington, D.C.: Chamber of Commerce of the United States), p. 46.

[23] Richard U. Ratcliff, *The Madison Central Area* (Madison: Bureau of Business Research and Service, University of Wisconsin, 1953).

those with more limited patronage zones in the choice central locations. For example, the grocery store in a central location will benefit little from general population growth of the entire area because its trading zone is limited to but a small section of the community. At the other extreme, the department store, which draws its patrons from the entire metropolitan area and beyond, will benefit directly in increased volume of sales when population increases. Thus, if the number of groceries in the central area declined while the number and size of department stores increased, the interpretation might be that the central area is responding to the growth of the entire community by providing more of the kinds of services which serve the whole area, and that such expansion is displacing services (groceries) of a type which have a smaller zone of patronage.

2. Even though population did not grow, we should expect a continuing readjustment in the central-area business structure in response to social, economic, and technological change. For example, the development of television has brought an increase in appliance outlets and a decline in movie attendance which may result in the closing of some theaters. General prosperity with its high level of family income encourages the appearance of establishments dealing in luxury items; depression and economic stringency may cause their failure and removal. The rapid rise in the birth rate since the war may have its influence on the appearance of specialty shops dealing in children's wear.

3. Changing merchandising methods can influence the central retail structure—for example, the tendency in recent years toward retail outlets with larger frontage and floor area, and offering a more complete and varied stock of merchandise. The result has been the elbowing-out of some small and marginal specialty shops and a net reduction in the number of retail outlets in a given area. An outstanding case in point is the supermarket technique of dispensing groceries, which greatly reduces the num-

ber of stores required to serve a given population.

4. Shifts in the home locations of the clientele of a retail store or other central-area service may induce responsive shifts in store location. As the settled area of the community spreads outward, and as residential occupancy near the center becomes predominantly tenancy, hardware outlets catering to homeowners find it more profitable to be in outlying locations near the suburban homes of their customers.

5. Increasing frictions of interurban movement may force commercial establishments to move closer to their clientele. Traffic congestion, inadequate mass transport, and lack of convenient parking are forms of friction which deter potential customers from trips to the central area and lead to the provision of commercial services in outlying locations.

These five hypotheses concerning change in a central business district do not cover all possible explanations of structural shift. We know, for example, that there is a constant turnover of tenants in retail areas as the result of poor management and inadequate capital. Again, local shifts in economic forces which affect the level and distribution of income or which change the balance between primary and secondary employment will modify the retail and service pattern of the community. But most of the structural change can be explained by one or more of these five hypotheses. To the extent that changes appear to be caused by increasing frictions which generate outlying competition (5) or by a decline in the number of consumers living close to the center (4), there will be a loss in volume of business and a decline in property values. Changing merchandising methods (3) may or may not be destructive of central-area values: if such new methods serve to increase efficiency in the use of floor space in present locations, the effect may be to increase sales and raise values. The displacements caused by the appearance and expansion of commercial land-use types which serve the entire community

(1) is healthy, for these are the basic functions which must continue to thrive in the central area if values are to be sustained. Social, economic, and technological change (2) are so varied in their impact on locational structure that it is impossible to generalize. Certainly, basic social forces may appear which will permanently modify the urban land-use pattern and bring about a decline in the central area. But the opposite may also come to pass, and we may see developments which will strengthen the centripetal forces on which the central area flourishes.

The historical and functional analysis of the Madison central area produced a few findings which bear upon the foregoing hypotheses of change. In the first place, the study reveals that the central area has grown little in extent in the last 30 years, a period in which the metropolitan area which it serves almost tripled in population. The measure of growth was in number of non-residential ground-floor uses or enterprises which make up the central cluster. In 1921, there were 400 such separate land uses; in 1931, 437; 1941, 450; and 1950, 448. In the 20-year period from 1930 to 1950, the increase in uses was small and the physical expansion of the area was correspondingly small, consisting largely of filling in among the existing non-residential uses by replacement of residual housing. There was a small increase in the over-all average frontage per unit, with certain retail classes of use showing substantial increases in size of outlet.

A hypothesis stated earlier to the effect that the variety of central-area activities tends to increase is not strongly supported by the Madison data. In 1921 there were 120 different non-residential ground-floor-use types; in 1931 this had increased to 129 and to 133 by 1950. The limitation of this information is that it does not include the office type of activity, which no doubt showed a greater increase in variety over the period studied.

The Madison central area is a typical situation wherein the extent has remained relatively constant while the community has grown substantially. It is possible to show that such a static situation in areal terms, or even a shrinkage, does not indicate decline, provided that at the same time there are internal changes in the direction of greater predominance of more intensive uses.

There are certain physical limitations which inhibit indefinite expansion of the central retail area—an expansion which would be essential if the central area should be the exclusive locus of retail distribution. One well-known limitation is the distance consumers are willing to walk within a destination area to which they come on a shopping expedition. This human characteristic limits the geographical spread of the retail district and thus the aggregate volume of business which can be done within its borders. This physical limit is not approached in small cities. In large cities, the limit applies to the retail core of the central area but does not directly include the specialized districts such as the financial and wholesale segments.

At an earlier point, we accepted the hypothesis that, as cities grow, the center does a decreasing share of the total retail business. There is no known way of offsetting the fundamental and inexorable forces of city growth which result in a continual scattering of retail stores and in the development of outlying commercial districts to serve the expanding city. There is no expectation in a growing community that the central area will be the exclusive and sole locus of retail distribution—for any class of merchandise. Neither does it follow that a decline in the center's share of total community business is disastrous. As the city grows in population and extent, the number of retail enterprises which can be supported increases in somewhat the same proportion. It is not reasonable to expect all of them to locate in the center. Those types which have relatively small patronage groups such as groceries will scatter through the community, seeking to serve adequate patronage groups at the most convenient points. Other types, serving larger patronage groups, will appear at strategic outlying retail centers in such numbers as to permit each outlet to survive, including some of the original representative types of the center. As a general rule, the smaller the minimum patronage group required to support a given type of store, the smaller the share of such business which will be done at the center.

The fact that the retail center does not grow in extent in proportion to community growth does not imply that the volume of goods and services purveyed there does not grow. To the contrary, in the usual situation, as the city grows beyond a certain size, through greater efficiency in the utilization of space, the center becomes more productive with very little or no increase in area. Many kinds of stores can greatly increase volume of sales without need for increased floor space. It is a not unreasonable guess that the stores which lined Madison's capitol square in 1921 could have tripled the volume of business without increase in floor space. It may be observed that the types of retail outlets which tend to become more predominant in the central area as the city grows are those which use the ground area most intensively. For example, the department store is usually in a multistoried building. Variety stores offer a wide choice of articles in a small space served by many clerks and achieve a high rate of turnover. The parasite types—such as the candy store—use a small floor area with high intensity. Conversely, some of the shopping and specialty types which tend to leave the central area are those which require relatively large areas not intensively used, such as furniture stores.

It is not alone the intensity in the physical use of space which is the measure of productivity. Productivity is finally measured by profitability or rent-paying capacity. It has long been recognized that there is a hierarchy of rent-paying capacities among retail types (assuming appropriate sites) measured by the dollar difference between gross income and costs before rent.

This balance available for rent is therefore affected not alone by volume of sales but by prices, markup, and costs of operation (except rent). Thus a retail type with a low turnover, a high sales price, and a wide markup, such as a jewelry store or a very fashionable women's dress shop, may have a higher rent-paying capacity and thus a higher productivity than another type such as a family shoe store which has a higher turnover and makes a physically more intensive use of the floor area but has a lower price per sale and a smaller markup. Using the term "productivity" as synonomous with rent-paying capacity, as there is an increase in the proportion of central-area space absorbed by the higher rent-paying types, the aggregate productivity of the entire central area may be said to increase without increase in its total extent. Such a rise in productivity would be accompanied by a rise in rental income to landlords and in land values.

The foregoing discussion demonstrates that a static or even declining central-area land coverage is not necessarily a sign of decay even in a growing city. The typical behavior of central retail areas is to grow in intensity of use rather than in extent after an optimum size has been reached. This rule does not bar moderate growth of the whole central area as metropolitan areas expand and the complexity and variety of economic activities grow. The central area of Chicago is larger than that of Milwaukee, which in turn is larger than that of Madison. But the area differences among these cities reflect only a fraction of the differences in population. They also reflect variations in the use of central sites for non-retail purposes, such as offices, and the effects of very large daytime populations which are an important support for retail trade in the central area.

In the Madison study, change in the shopping-goods distribution function was assumed to be the prime indicator of central-area health or decline. This type of activity feeds off the entire community; loss in central-area dominance most certainly will occur when competing shopping facilities bring about a decline in central shopping-goods distribution. With this loss in dominance will come a fall in land values. The Madison data fail to reveal any evidence of central-area decline over the period studied. To the contrary, there was a significant increase in the importance of the shopping-goods group of uses both in the number of outlets and in the extent of frontage they occupied. There was a steady increase in the frontage devoted to shopping-goods outlets and a continuing replacement of less intensive uses with the more intensive uses, of types with lower rent-paying capacity with types of higher rent-paying capacity, and of non-commercial or non-retail uses, convenience and specialty-goods outlets with shopping-goods outlets. These are the indications of healthy growth.

*The future.*—It is the sense of this argument that the cohesion of central-area functions is so strong that disintegration is most unlikely within the foreseeable future. The greatest strength of the central area lies in its unmatched variety, or "availability," as the term was used at an earlier point. Even the most elaborate of the new one-stop regional shopping centers provides but a fraction of the activities and combinations of services which are in the downtown destination area.

Because it is a popular belief that the new regional shopping centers spell the doom of the central area, a few derivative comments are warranted. Developments of this kind, viewed functionally, are a natural adaptation of the urban retail structure to metropolitan growth. This has been going on since the dawn of urbanism. Every large American city has had regional shopping centers for decades, facilities located at major intersections which provide services even more elaborate than the postwar versions. These older regional shopping centers are now buried in the built-up areas of the city, many of them as congested as the center. They were not preplanned and designed in architectural harmony. They originally depended largely on mass transportation and are not well adapted to the automobile age. The postwar regional center is aesthetically superior and functionally modern. It is built all at a time in contrast to the older centers, which grew over the years by accretion and with a succession of use-types and structural internal change reflecting maturity and increasing intensity of use. The real and serious competition is not between new regional center and central area but between new and old regional and neighborhood centers.[24]

Very basic indeed are the various measures now being taken in most urban areas to minimize the costs of movement to and from the center. Improved parking and traffic control, freeways, added parking space, and street-widenings all contribute to increased accessibility and offset, in varying degree, the convenience of outward travel to competing services in regional shopping centers. There is a desperate search for some formula that will induce people to abandon their private vehicles for mass transit. But in prosperous times we do not choose to abandon independence in timing and route for the economy of public transportation. Because the need for solution is so pressing and the ingenuity of man so pervasive, we should not despair of technical or managerial developments which will make mass transit attractive.

But as we devote our energies to making the central area more accessible, we should, if we wish to preserve the efficiencies inherent in the nuclear arrangement of urban land use, strive even harder to maintain the variety of activities and the concentration of employment which are functional essentials. Positive action and promotion by business groups and downtown property owners' associations could induce new businesses to locate in central spots with some selectivity as to types of activity. A refined type of zoning, such as that based on the packet of functions which Haig proposed,

might be developed to adjust activity more suitably to environment and to exclude locationally inappropriate uses from areas where their presence will increase frictions. Every effort should be made to adjust the central structure to social, economic, and technological change so that its physical rigidity—of building and street pattern—will not hamper prompt locational adaptations. In this connection, discouragement should be given to the use of long-term leases and to the erection of special-purpose buildings, for the highest degree of flexibility should be maintained to permit the free and constant rearrangement of land uses in patterns which maintain frictions at a minimum in the face of changing conditions.

The urban redevelopment device is a method of accelerating the natural readjustments of the land-use pattern. This plan should be pushed in full confidence that its initial costs will be many times repaid in increased productivity of the urban structure. A re-use to be ardently sought for areas peripheral to the central business district is the large office-type activity which employs substantial numbers. On cleared land, just out of the congestion at the core, such an establishment, like the home office of an insurance company or other activity with most of its contacts outside the community, could enjoy adequate parking and could utilize the converging lines of transport to carry its employees from all parts of the city. Unless such activities can escape the worst of the congestion, the advantages of central location are nullified—such advantages as centrality in the local labor pool, convenience for employees to the myriad shops and services of the central area, and the convenience of business contacts for the company. The dominance of the central area is basically dependent on the presence of a large daytime population of employed; every effort should be made to preserve and increase this number.

Perhaps we have assumed that the central area is worth preserving without explicitly stating the reasons why. The basic

[24] San Francisco Department of City Planning, *Local Shopping Districts in San Francisco* (San Francisco, 1952), p. 30.

advantage to be cherished is the efficiency or convenience in the arrangement of land uses which is the source of the cohesion of central functions. To break up and disperse the related constellations of interrelated activities which comprise the center is to add greatly to the time, money, and human energy costs of doing the city's work. Only a web of fast, cheap, and strategically located mass transport could begin to substitute for foot travel within a concentrated destination area, and only New York City has anything remotely approaching such transport. We conclude, therefore, that the preservation of the central area is not only desirable in terms of productivity but that it is most likely by reason of the instinctive human inclination to minimize the disutilities of movement and in light of the calculated efforts to overcome the frictions which growth and the automobile age have created.

## CONCLUSION

These more or less integrated commentaries on various aspects of the locational distribution of urban activities sketch the outline of a physical and social structure which is in constant flux. Many of the manifestations of change are popularly assumed to be unfortunate and destructive; actually most of them are natural adaptations to new conditions and move toward higher, not lower, total efficiency. The problems are not problems of size but of imperfect or delayed adaptation, though they are aggravated by size. They are problems of growth and problems of physical rigidities in a milieu of social and technological mutation. With all its problems, the modern metropolis is more efficient, more productive, than its forebears.

Collective efforts to raise urban efficiency through planning, land-use control, taxation, improvements in traffic, transport, and parking, urban redevelopment, and metropolitan integration should be directed toward the facilitation of land-use changes which enhance *total* efficiency, the discouragement of changes which diminish it, the reduction of *total* costs of friction, and the equitable distribution of those costs.

## TRANSPORTATION

Without transportation the functional differentiation of areas into the various specialized types of land uses and, indeed, the existence of cities themselves, in the modern sense, would be impossible. Transportation, by providing a means of moving people and goods to places where they can be more useful, permits the concentration of labor force and materials for the carrying-on of manufacturing and trade and is therefore indispensable to the development of cities. Within cities and metropolitan areas, furthermore, transportation facilities constitute important elements of the land-use and functional pattern, and they serve as nuclei around which other functional differentiations within urban areas take place.

In most modern cities, not only is the extent of the hinterland and consequently the size and character of the city largely a reflection of the transportation connections, but the transportation facilities themselves, in most instances, constitute the most important single category of urban land use. Streets and highways constitute from one-fourth to one-third of the total built-up urban area, the railroad routes constitute the axes of much of the industrial development, and the airport often comprises the most extensive single parcel of urban land devoted to one continuous use. Port areas and facilities are basic components of the urban pattern in many cities.

American cities are undergoing a revolutionary change in their patterns and physical forms as a result of the current accelerated program of highway construction, particularly that of the federal system of interstate expressways, much of which is being built in cities and metropolitan areas. The new expressways, from present indications, will affect the growth and pattern of American cities in the mid-twentieth century to an extent comparable to the effect of the railroads in the nineteenth century. Study of the relationships of the emerging highway system to the structure, growth, and functional organization of cities and metropolitan areas constitutes an outstanding contemporary opportunity for the urban geographer.

This section presents three articles on the relationships of transportation facilities to cities. The first, by a British geographer, describes the railways of certain great European cities. The second describes in greater detail the railroad pattern of one large American metropolitan area in which the ultimate in complexity has been reached. From these it may be possible to draw analogies to the

**325**

new trunk lines of urban and intercity transportation in the form of express highways.

The third article, rather different in character, is not concerned with the internal patterns of transportation within cities but rather with the relations of a form of transportation—commercial airlines—to the generation of intercity traffic. Were the data available, similar studies could be made of both passenger and freight traffic patterns by rail, highway, and waterway.

Transportation geography is a field rather separate from urban geography, and many geographers specialize in it. The two fields have, however, a broad area of overlap and for many reasons are closely related. It is not possible to understand or explain many of the characteristics of urban functions, structure, location, or internal pattern without a knowledge of areal differences in transportation with which such differences in cities are associated.

# THE RAILWAYS OF GREAT CITIES

Rail transport of both passengers and freight forms an integral part of the economic life of any modern town, but in that of the great capital cities it is a vital element, without which the daily life of the city would be quite impossible. The functions of the railway in such an environment are manifold. Dealing first with pas-

to the principal towns or regions of the country. From this point of view, therefore, the railway plan should consist of a series of lines radiating from the city, more closely spaced on the side or sides which lie nearest to the most important regions of the country, and with perhaps a series of tentacles or branches on the outskirts of

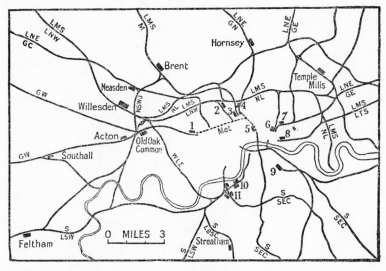

LONDON

The principal marshaling sidings are named. The terminal goods depots are numbered as follows: *1*, Paddington; *2*, Camden; *3*, Somers Town; *4*, King's Cross; *5*, Farringdon; *6*, Broad Street; *7*, Bishopsgate; *8*, Fenchurch Street; *9*, Bricklayer's Arms and Willow Walk; *10*, Nine Elms (north and south); *11*, Battersea (S.R., G.W.R., and L.M.S.R.). (Reproduced by permission of Longmans, Green and Co.)

senger traffic, the railway system of a great city must provide (*a*) adequate means for transporting the suburban-dwelling workers to and from the city daily, and very largely at two specific "rush-hour" periods, thus necessitating spacious terminal facilities and multiple tracks; (*b*) main-line services

Reprinted from *Geography*, XXII, Part 2 (June, 1937), 116–20, by permission of the author and the editor.

the city serving the suburbs. It will also be very desirable for some interterminal transport facilities to be provided; such facilities may take the form of a surface railway actually connected to the terminals, or an underground line without such physical connection. But the presence or absence of such a connecting line may be determined by the relative age of the transport system of the city as a whole, upon which may de-

**327**

pend the existence and importance of inter-terminal tramway and omnibus routes.

As regards freight traffic, the railways of the city must provide, in the first place, for the daily food supply of the vast population. This necessitates the provision of adequate unloading, transshipment, and perhaps also marketing facilities at the terminals, preferably not too close to the passenger terminals, lest congestion ensue. The of the great city, therefore, will be (*a*) sorting facilities, where traffics from all directions can be reassembled for their destinations, and (*b*) adequate connection from one radial main line to another. Thus the belt or girdle line becomes an almost inevitable feature of the railway pattern, and, since the sorting of railway wagons necessitates much open space, the great sorting and marshaling sidings tend to spring up

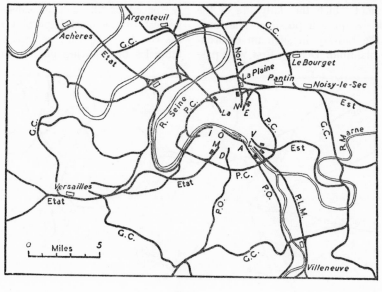

PARIS

| | | |
|---|---|---|
| *La*, St. Lazare | *L*, Lyon | *O*, Quai d'Orsay |
| *N*, Nord | *A*, Austerlitz | *I*, Invalides |
| *E*, Est | *D*, Denfert | *P.C.*, Petite Ceinture |
| *V*, Vincennes | *M*, Montparnasse | *G.C.*, Grande Ceinture |

great city, moreover, and especially the capital city, simply by reason of its position at the focus of a series of radiating railway lines, is almost bound to act as an entrepôt for goods from one part of the country or from abroad destined for another part or another country. It will be more convenient, and probably quicker, to send a small consignment of goods via the entrepôt, where sorting facilities will exist and where the small consignment will become part of a larger consignment for the same destination, than via a somewhat circuitous cross-country route. The main need on the outskirts of the town in close proximity to the belt line.

The ideal railway plan for a large city thus somewhat resembles a wheel: the city is the hub, the main lines are the spokes, and the circumference is the belt line. Naturally, the symmetry of this arrangement will depend on numerous factors connected mainly with the history of the growth of the lines, with the nature and source of the traffics, and, of course, with topographical conditions.

The accompanying maps illustrate how, in a number of the greatest European cities, the major features of the plan enunciated above are present.

*London.*—The radial lines, as becomes a capital city of such outstanding dominance, are particularly well developed, some fifteen main lines leading outward to all parts of the country. Interterminal connection is provided for passenger traffic by the "Inner Circle" underground railway and by several transverse tube lines (not shown on the map); and it should be noted that a certain amount of goods traffic also uses that section of the Inner Circle between Paddington and King's Cross, and an important transverse interterminal goods

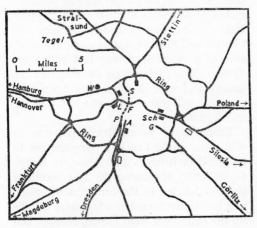

BERLIN

| | |
|---|---|
| *L,* Lehrter Bahnhof | *S,* Stettiner Bahnhof |
| *Sch,* Schlesischer Bahnhof | *P,* Potsdamer Bahnhof |
| *W,* Westhafen (port) | *A,* Anhalter Bahnhof |
| *F,* Friedrichstrasse Bahnhof | *G,* Görlitzer Bahnhof |

line links King's Cross with Farringdon and St. Paul's. Terminal goods facilities are available as shown; it is noticeable that the southern termini, which lie nearest to the heart of London, where little land was available at the time of construction, have no goods stations adjacent to their passenger terminals, facilities being provided in the flat, low-lying Thames-side area, formerly largely waste, between Nine Elms and Battersea. The northern termini, which were on the edge of London when built and which lie in a formerly rather damp and inhospitable clay tract, had

more space available and so tend to have their goods and passenger terminals close together. The most important belt lines for interradial freight traffic are the North London, linking all the northern lines to the Docks; the West London railway, linking the western and southern lines, and the North and South-West Junction, linking the northwestern group with the southwestern. The positions of the great marshaling sidings, where the radials and belt

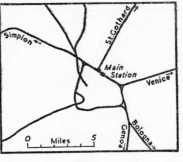

MILAN

lines meet, are shown on the map. It is noteworthy that there are no real belt lines on the southeast, for little interradial freight traffic is likely to occur on this side, and traffic from the northern to the southern lines can be carried by the transverse Farringdon line or the West London line, which in a sense may thus be regarded as part of an inner belt or girdle.

*Paris.*—The railway plan of Paris is rather more symmetrical than that of London. The radial plan is, of course, evident; interterminal passenger traffic is provided for by the roughly rectangular network of underground lines (not shown on the map). The inner circle (*petite ceinture*) is used mainly for local passenger traffic, as well as for numerous through coaches from the Channel ports to central Europe or the Mediterranean. The outer circle (*grande ceinture*) lies well beyond the suburban limits of the city, and is mainly used for freight traffic. The principal terminal goods depots, and outer-suburban marshaling yards, the latter associated mainly with the outer circle, are shown on the map.

*Berlin.*—Berlin has a rather asymmetrical radial plan, the position of the city with regard to the rest of Germany and Europe having necessitated more lines radiating in a west, south, and southeast direction than toward the north. An interesting feature is the presence of a through transverse line from east to west across the heart of the city; a new underground north-south link is under construction (dotted on map). There is a single girdle line (the Ring-

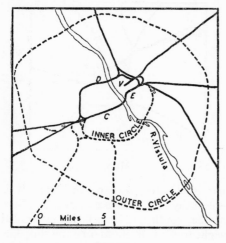

WARSAW

D, Danzig Station          E, Eastern Station
V, Vilna Station           C, Central Station

bahn), well connected by spurs to the radial lines, and there is, in addition, a goods line linking the industrial suburb of Tegel, on the northwest, with the eastern radial lines. Terminal goods stations exist as shown on the map; the two great marshaling yards are located near to the Ringbahn, on the important Dresden and Silesian lines; and extensive sidings exist also at the Westhafen—the inland waterway port of Berlin.

Amongst great cities which are not capitals, Milan provides a good illustration of the same general plan. Bucharest and Sofia have almost perfectly symmetrical patterns,

with a nearly circular girdle in each case. The girdle line of Sofia has only recently been completed; it is encouraging suburban industrial growth.

A most interesting example of the same kind of pattern in the making is provided by Warsaw. Here, until after the Great War, two different gauges were employed, the lines radiating to the west being of standard gauge, those to the east being of the Russian broad gauge. This, of course, hindered the development of the normal plan. After the war the broad gauge lines were converted to standard gauge, and within the last few years a comprehensive series of developments has been in progress, including suburban electrification, the provision of an east-west link between the Central and Eastern stations, and the planning of a complete double belt with marshaling sidings (shown on the map) on the eastern and western sides. New main lines to Silesia will increase the symmetry of the radial pattern.

Examples of asymmetrical patterns in which the girdle line is incomplete are to be found in Brussels and Rome. In Rome, the difficulty of crossing the Tiber north of the city has led to the confinement of the belt line to the southern side, where it links up the main lines from Genoa, Naples, and Florence and several suburban lines. In Brussels, the hilly belt southeast of the city has resulted in the confinement of the belt line to the northwestern side, where it links up the lines entering from Ostend, Antwerp, Cologne, Namur, and northern France. Budapest has a rather one-sided pattern because of the high right bank of the Danube in Buda; but a belt line is provided on the lower Pest side. Vienna is also rather one-sided, because of the position of the city on one bank of the Danube; but there is a well-developed girdle line on the southern side, which is much used for through-passenger and freight traffic passing from west to east or vice versa.

HAROLD M. MAYER

# LOCALIZATION OF RAILWAY FACILITIES IN METROPOLITAN CENTERS AS TYPIFIED BY CHICAGO

Railway patterns are among the most stable structural elements in large American cities. Unlike many other types of land use, railway routes and, to some extent, terminal facilities were already well developed when the large cities burst the bounds imposed upon them by the use of foot and horse transport and spread out to absorb the surrounding countrysides. Railway facilities, unlike most other public utilities of more recent development, cannot be moved as easily as other elements of the urban pattern, for these facilities are integral parts of the larger railway network as well as of the urban complex. Thus they must be localized where they can perform their specialized roles most effectively with relation to other railway facilities as well as to the general urban pattern. The tremendous capital investment and the complex structure of bonds, mortgages, long-term leases, and operating agreements represented by present rights-of-way, yards, and terminals enforce a relatively stable railway pattern.

Because railways are vital foundations of urban growth and because they are relatively fixed in location, the nature and methods of operation of their metropolitan railway facilities are of vital concern to all large cities in the process of planning their future patterns and structures. Some general principles affecting localization of railway facilities are illustrated by study of a typical large center.

Metropolitan Chicago, the world's most important railway center, possesses an ex-

Reprinted from *Journal of Land and Public Utility Economics*, XX (November, 1944), 299–315, by permission of the author and the editor. (Copyright, 1944, by University of Wisconsin, Madison, Wis.)

tremely complex pattern of railway lines, and a multitude of terminal facilities that together constitute a functioning organic unit. The complexity of the pattern, however, becomes less when one understands the relationships among its components. The general pattern is relatively simple; only the details and ramifications are complex. The numerous trunk lines that converge in central Chicago from all directions bring passengers to and from a series of six downtown terminals that have for many years constituted one of the city's major planning problems. Much freight, too, reaches the central area, although in recent years the freight handling has tended more and more to shift toward the urban periphery. The thousands of cars moving to and from many thousands of origins and destinations both within and without the metropolitan area are classified and shuffled into road freight trains and transfer trains at large classification yards mainly on the urban periphery. To and from these yards lead a large number of radial lines, cityward continuations of trunk routes connecting these outer yards, the minor yards, freight terminals, and about 5,000 industrial sidings. Interconnecting the outer and inner yards and also serving many industries along their routes are a number of belt lines that enable freight cars to move between any trunk line and any trackside location within the metropolitan area. Supplementing the belt lines are other switching and industrial lines reaching additional industrial sidings and freight stations. All those freight-handling facilities are fed by a freight tunnel system in central Chicago and by motor trucks that perform pickup and delivery. Finally, there are many acces-

331

sory facilities necessary for the maintenance of the railway service: shops, engine
terminals, coach yards, and offices, all
closely interrelated in location both to each
other and to all features of the urban pattern.

## OUTER RAILWAY APPROACHES

The dominant impression that one ob-
tains upon first inspection of a map showing the railway pattern outside the Chicago
city boundary for 40 or 50 miles in every
direction (Fig. 1) is that of a number of
radial lines intersected by a circumferential
line. The radial lines are here called the
outer railway approaches, and the circumferential line is commonly known as the
Chicago Outer Belt Line. Other than the
general radial arrangement, the outer belt
line, and the concentration of lines around
the southern end of Lake Michigan, no
other pattern is evident. In that respect,
Chicago is in marked contrast to most
other major railway centers where differences in elevation and slope of the land
surface and the existence of water barriers
strongly channel the railway approaches
into a limited number of routes. No mountains, rivers, hills, or valleys restrict the
approaches to Chicago. Only Lake Michigan and, to a very minor extent, the highest of the moraines that partially encircle
the metropolitan area affect the regularity
of the railway pattern. Close to the center
of Chicago, however, the Chicago River
and its branches affect the location of terminals far out of proportion to the small
sizes of those streams.

The absence of major surface features
has had an important effect upon the relationship between railways and the general
land-use pattern of metropolitan Chicago.
The railway routes, not surface configuration as in many cities, formed the principal
axes along which settlement has taken
place and along which urban decentralization has been carried on. Of particular significance is the close relationship between
the railways and the configuration of the
outer boundary of urban development

which took place most rapidly and intensively along the railway lines, thereby
forming prongs of urbanization that extend
far out into the hinterland.

## CHICAGO OUTER BELT LINE

The trunk-line railways enter what is
generally called the Chicago Terminal District at the points where they are intersected by the Chicago Outer Belt Line (the
Elgin, Joliet, and Eastern Railway) at a
distance of 25 to 40 miles from the commercial core of Chicago.

The Chicago Outer Belt Line constitutes
a unique type of facility, distinct from the
other belt railways in function and in location. From Porter, Indiana, to Waukegan,
Illinois, it is 130 miles in length, considerably longer than any other belt line. Its
average distance from the central part of
Chicago is twice that of any other belt line.
It passes for the most part through rural
areas, in contrast to other belt lines which
are located largely in built-up areas. It is
unique further in that it is the only belt
line that crosses and has direct physical
track connection with *all* the trunk lines
serving Chicago.

Like the other belt lines, the Elgin,
Joliet, and Eastern serves as a connecting
link over which through freight traffic
moves between the various radial lines,
and as an intermediate carrier or terminal
line for freight originating or terminating
within the Chicago terminal district. Its
functions and location are greatly affected
by its ownership and control by the United
States Steel Corporation. Although it is a
common carrier, a large proportion of its
traffic moves to, from, and between plants
of the parent company. To a great extent
it is a local inter-plant facility as well as a
belt line. It handles approximately 30 million tons annually, or about 22 per cent of
the total traffic of all belt and switching
railways in the metropolitan area.[1]

[1] Interstate Commerce Commission, *Comparative Statement of Railway Operating Statistics,
Years 1938, 1937, and 1936* (Washington, D.C.,
1939).

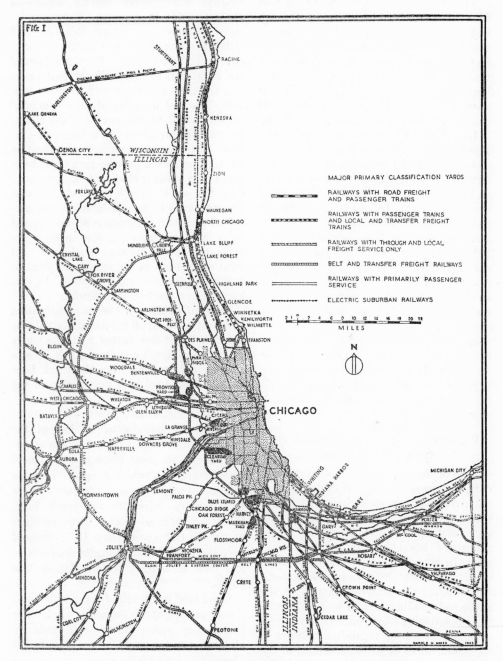

FIG. 1.—Functional pattern of the railways in metropolitan Chicago

The unique function of the Outer Belt Line as a road-haul carrier of through traffic around the outer edge of the metropolitan area is further demonstrated by the fact that in 1938 the average haul per revenue ton was 45 miles, considerably longer than that of any of the other belt lines. The long average haul reflects, of course, the peripheral location of the line.

Interchange of cars between the Outer Belt Line and the trunk lines that it intersects is direct and expeditious. At each intersection an interchange track is provided and, at the most important crossings, there is a small yard. Inbound and outbound freight trains on the trunk lines do not, as a rule, originate or terminate at the Outer Belt crossings because the traffic interchanged there constitutes a small proportion of the cars in most trunk line trains. In every case the Outer Belt intersects the main lines *beyond* their principal Chicago district freight yards. Thus the yards required for interchange of cars between the line-haul carriers and the Outer Belt Line are neither large nor complex and do not require vast areas as do the major classification yards of the trunk lines located closer to Chicago.

## PRIMARY CLASSIFICATION YARDS OF THE TRUNK LINES

Each of the principal trunk-line railways radiating from Chicago operates one or more classification yards in which freight trains are classified in accordance with their destinations and in which freight trains are assembled for further movement. In area they are the most extensive of all railway facilities, and their locations vitally affect the land-use pattern of the entire metropolitan area as well as the efficient functioning of its railways.

On almost all the trunk-line railways of the metropolitan area the outermost of the classification yards are the largest and most important. In those primary yards the road freight trains are assembled outbound or are broken up into transfer trains inbound.[2]

Virtually all the primary or outer classification yards have certain locational characteristics in common. They are located well inside the Outer Belt Line and either just outside or just within the next outermost belt railway. They are beyond the peripheral belt of industry that encircles the city of Chicago and its inner suburbs. The vast majority of the commercial and industrial establishments of the metropolitan area are closer to the center of Chicago than are the primary classification yards. The reason for the peripheral location of the yards is obvious if one considers that the object of all terminal switching movements is to handle inbound and outbound cars with a minimum of mileage and delay and, wherever possible, without reverse movement between road train and local destination or between local point of origin and the road train in which the cars are to leave the terminal district.

Location of the major outer classification yards at or near the intersection of the outermost belt line (other than the Outer Belt Line railway) enables the belt lines to transfer cars to and from the trunk lines without back-haul over any section of the latter (Fig. 2).

Because the Elgin, Joliet, and Eastern handles only one-quarter or less of the total belt-line traffic of the Chicago terminal district, the most efficient operation of transfer trains would not result from the location of major yards at the points where that railway intersects the trunk lines. Were the yards so located, large numbers of transfer trains would have to be operated over the trunk lines for longer distances to and from such more remote classification yards.

Level land is essential for the location of the large freight classification yards. For that reason among others, such yards are all located on the level Chicago plain rather

[2] The term "road train" refers to a train operated between a yard or other location within the terminal district and a distant point as distinguished from a "transfer train," which operates from one yard or point within the terminal district to another within the district.

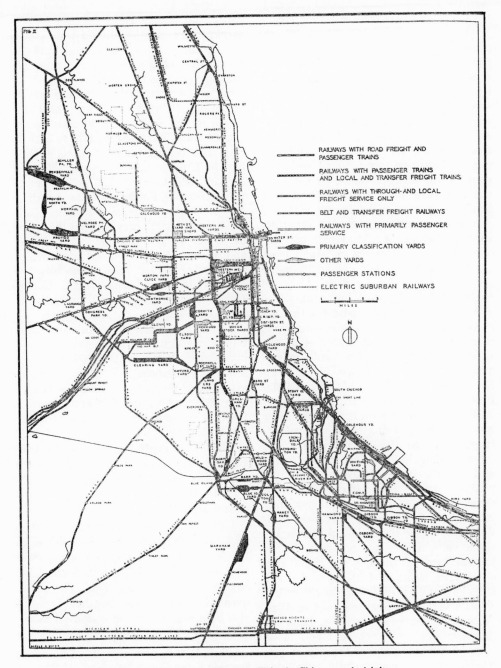

Fɪɢ. 2.—Pattern of railway facilities in Chicago and vicinity

than the rolling morainic upland surrounding the plain a few miles from the city.

The outer major classification yards are provided with a variety of facilities requiring, in some instances, many hundreds of acres. A large classification yard is in reality a group of several yards, each serving a specialized function in relation to the whole. A typical classification yard includes an inbound receiving yard, a hump or throat for inbound movement, an inbound classification yard, an inbound departure yard for the transfer trains, an outbound receiving yard, an outbound throat or a hump for gravity switching, an outbound classification yard, an outbound departure yard, interchange tracks, repair or "bad order" tracks, caboose tracks, roundhouses, coaling facilities, repair and maintenance shops, icing facilities for perishables, and feeding pens for livestock in transit.

An indication of the vast areas that are required for the major classification yards is afforded by the car capacities of the various sections of Proviso Yard, the primary yard of the Chicago and North Western Railway, located west of Chicago. Originally a smaller yard with a capacity of 2,000 cars, Proviso Yard is now one of the world's largest, having been enlarged between 1927 and 1930 to many times the capacity of the original layout constructed in 1902. The inbound classification hump yard at Proviso holds 3,274 cars; the hump repair yard, 187 cars; the forwarding yard, 1,724; the outbound Wisconsin Division yard, 1,889; the outbound Galena Division yard, 1,522; and so forth. In all, Proviso Yard has capacity for 26,000 cars at one time, embraces 1,500 acres, and is 5 miles long and 1.5 miles wide at the widest point. Several other yards in metropolitan Chicago are nearly as extensive. Land for such facilities could not be found in or near the built-up parts of the city at reasonable cost, and, consequently, even aside from the requirements of railway operation which favor a peripheral location, such yards must of necessity be located at or beyond the edge of the urbanized area.

As train lengths increase, classification yards must become longer because the economical maximum length of a train is limited by the length of the longest tracks in the yards, unless expensive and time-consuming "push-pull" switching is used instead of the more efficient hump or gravity operation. Between 1921 and 1941 the length of the average freight train in the United States increased from 38 to over 50 cars. The average train entering and leaving the Chicago area is considerably over 50 cars, and trains of 100 and more are very common. Furthermore, as schedules are speeded up, the number of intermediate yardings of freight cars between the points of shipment and consignment decreases and, conversely, the amount of switching and sorting at the major terminals and gateways such as metropolitan Chicago (other things being equal) greatly increases.

The major classification yards are, therefore, tremendous establishments representing in many instances the culmination of a series of expansions and enlargements. In many cases they are the final result of a long series of removals farther and farther from the center of the city as space requirements have outgrown the areas of land available for expansion and as the land values in the vicinities of the older yards have risen beyond the capacity of the railways to purchase land for expansion of the classification facilities.[3]

Like the classification yards, large industrial plants have also been established on the periphery of the city, where extensive sites are available at low cost. Such plants have located on the belt lines. The consequent rise in traffic on these belt lines has also been a factor in the peripheral movement of the classification yards which are

[3] Cf. C. C. Colby, "Centrifugal and Centripetal Forces in Urban Geography," *Annals of the Association of American Geographers,* XXIII (1933), 1–20 [see above, pp. 287–98]; and Homer Hoyt, "Forces of Urban Centralization and Decentralization," *American Journal of Sociology,* XLVI (1941), 843–52.

now located along belt and trunk-line intersections.

Chicago has a series of old freight yards along most of the trunk-line railways which have more or less outgrown their original functions as major primary classification yards and now serve only industries in their vicinities. In such yards classification of road trains does not commonly take place. They are used for local interchange and switching or for storage of idle cars. In some cases they have been completely abandoned. Many of them are no longer suited to the handling of modern trains.

The establishment of Proviso Yard as the primary classification yard for the C.&N.W. in the Chicago district, of Markham on the Illinois Central, Bensenville on the Chicago, Milwaukee, St. Paul, and Pacific (the Milwaukee Road), and similar yards on many other railways resulted in the abandonment of one or more yards as major yards; and, in every case, the older yards were closer to the city. Along some of the railways (Fig. 2) a series of three, four or more yards may be seen, each once the major outer classification yard of its respective line and each relegated to a secondary function when a newer and larger classification yard was opened farther from the city.

The final stage in the peripheral movement of freight classification outside Chicago is perhaps in the "preclassification" of trains at a division point far outside the metropolitan area. This process greatly reduces the amount of switching required in the metropolitan yards and, in effect, relieves the Chicago yards from the primary classification function altogether. As an example of how the process works, we may point to the Chicago, Burlington, and Quincy Railroad. Unable to expand the Morton Park–Clyde Yard, which was its major classification yard on the western city limits of Chicago, the Burlington, rather than establish another and larger yard nearer the metropolitan periphery, decided to perform the primary classification at the next division points to the west: Galesburg

for its main-line trains and Savanna, Illinois, for its Mississippi River line trains— 162 and 145 miles, respectively, from Chicago. At those points, inbound trains are classified in "station-order"; that is, cars are placed on the trains in the order they are to be dropped in secondary yards, at interchange points with connecting and belt lines, and for spotting at freight stations and industrial sidings in the Chicago area. Thus cars for the Outer Belt are placed at the head end of the train, those for the next yard or junction are placed just behind, and so on. This enables the road locomotive to switch off the cars with minimum delay and eliminates the necessity of reshuffling and classifying the entire train at a yard near Chicago. Similarly, other roads preclassify at division points a hundred or more miles from Chicago; the New York Central at Elkhart, Indiana, the Michigan Central at Niles, Michigan, the Chicago and Eastern Illinois at Danville, Illinois, and the Wabash at Decatur, for example.

## BELT LINES WITHIN TERMINAL DISTRICT

The Chicago terminal district is noteworthy for the magnitude and complexity of its belt-line railways. By the use of belt lines, shipments may be routed to, from, or between any of the trunk-line railways that serve the metropolitan area whether or not the trunk lines involved in the movement intersect. Likewise, shipments that originate or terminate on the industrial sidings or at the freight stations of any trunk line may be routed in or out of the terminal district over any other trunk line. The belt railway lines of metropolitan Chicago are, for the most part, owned and operated by specialized organizations—the belt railway companies which, in turn, are mainly controlled by the trunk-line railways. Several trunk lines also operate circumferential lines without separate incorporation.[4]

[4] The term "belt line" as used in this paper refers to any circumferential line the primary business of which is intermediate hauling of freight to, from, or between trunk lines regardless of the nature of

There are, in the metropolitan area, in addition to the Outer Belt Line already described, three important circumferential routes so located as to form a generally concentric pattern. Each of the three routes is not controlled and operated by a single company but rather is composed of sections of railway under various ownerships and operations.

The circumferential routes are important factors in the localization of industries. The centrifugal trend in industrial location has been greatly accelerated by the operation of the belt lines, which offer to shippers the opportunity to locate beyond the more congested central part of Chicago yet within easy access of all the trunk lines in every direction. Of the 5,735 industries with private switch tracks in the Chicago Switching District just before the beginning of World War II, 1,389, or 24.2 per cent, were located on lines of belt railway companies.[5] Hundreds of additional industries are along the circumferential connecting lines of the trunk railway systems. From all such locations, cars are switched directly to and from the primary classification yards in transfer trains without the intermediate yardings that are required of cars bound to and from more central locations on the trunk lines. Reduction of trucking movements on congested streets, particularly for less-than-carload shipments, results in additional time-saving.

The three major belt routes may, for convenience in discussion, be considered as the peripheral, the intermediate, and the inner belt routes.

The peripheral belt route,[6] approximately 50 miles long and located at an average distance from the Chicago central business district of about 15 miles, carries the heavi-

est traffic of the three routes. The line connects the primary classification yards of the principal trunk-line railways and enables interchange of cars to be made between such yards with minimum delay. In general, the line is located at the outer edge of the built-up urban part of the metropolitan area, from one to five miles beyond the limits of the city of Chicago. Transfer trains are operated on regular schedules to connect at the classification yards with the scheduled "manifest" or fast freight trains of the trunk lines. In addition, local way freight trains pick up and drop cars that originate and terminate at the industries along the belt line. The line is entirely double-tracked.

The northwestern sector of the peripheral belt route differs somewhat from the rest of the route in character of operations and traffic. It is operated by the Chicago and North Western Railway—primarily for through freight moving between Proviso Yard and the north and northwest. It serves a similar purpose for the C.M.St.P.&P., which has trackage rights over the line into Bensenville Yard. By use of this line each of the two railways can route trains to and from its main freight classification yard west of Chicago, even though a large number of such trains operate over lines to the north and northwest.

Most of the peripheral belt route, however, is jointly owned and operated by the Indiana Harbor Belt Railroad and the Baltimore and Ohio Chicago Terminal Railroad. Interchange yards are located at each intersection of the line with radial trunk lines, somewhat similar to the yards along the Outer Belt Line. The route passes close to the west end of the huge Clearing Yard of the Belt Railway and, continuing to the southeast, it crosses several trunk lines at Blue Island and there splits into two separate lines. The first, the line of the B.&O. Chicago Terminal, leads to Barr Yard where

---

its corporate organization. It thus includes, in addition to belt lines proper, circumferential lines operated directly as integral parts of trunk-line-haul carriers.

[5] Tabulation: *Tariff 22-BB, Directory of Industries with Private or Individual Side Tracks in the Chicago District*, Illinois Freight Association, Chicago Switching Committee, June 1, 1939.

[6] The peripheral belt route is not to be confused with the Chicago Outer Belt Line (Elgin, Joliet, and Eastern Railway) which is twice as far from central Chicago.

the B.&O. road freight trains are assembled and broken up. The second, the line of the Indiana Harbor Belt Railroad, leads to the busy East Blue Island Yard, where many road trains of the New York Central System originate and terminate. East of the two yards several lines of both belt railway companies serve plants in the Calumet industrial district of northwestern Indiana.

The peripheral location of the joint double-tracked Indiana Harbor Belt—B.&O. Chicago Terminal route—together with the control of both companies by important trunk-line railways, has encouraged development of fast transfer service on schedules closely coordinated with trunk line road freight trains.

Most shipments originating on belt lines within the Chicago switching district[7] cost the shipper no more than if they were to originate directly on the line of the road-haul carrier by which they leave the district, since the latter railway in most cases absorbs the switching charges of the belt lines. Industries are thus free from the former disadvantage of having to pay additional freight charges on all traffic except that handled directly by the line-haul carrier. Belt-line locations, therefore, cost the shipper no more in freight charges than do locations on trunk lines. At the same time they give access not to one, but to all, of the trunk lines entering the district. A location on a trunk-line route, on the other hand, generally compels the shipper to route his traffic over the railway on which he is located or to pay additional switching charges on traffic moving to or from a competitive road-haul carrier.

The intermediate or middle-belt route, only half as distant from the commercial center of Chicago as the peripheral route, passes through an intensively developed industrial zone within the city. Except for its northern sector, most of the route is operated by the Belt Railway Company of Chicago, a terminal and transfer company

owned jointly by thirteen trunk-line railways. That company serves its owners as a transfer route and as a source of traffic to and from the hundreds of industries along the route, as well as a means of efficient and rapid classification of cars.

The principal classification facility of the Belt Railway of Chicago is Clearing Yard, so named because it was designed to perform for the railways which share in its ownership much the same function that a clearinghouse serves for banks. It receives cars from the various railways, classifies them, and assembles them into transfer trains, delivering them to the line-haul carriers for further movement toward their destinations. Within the yard are 180 miles of track, with a capacity of over 6,000 car classifications per day. Special facilities, such as an icing plant for refrigerator cars and stockyards for livestock in transit, enable the yard to service all types of shipments. Clearing Yard is located just outside the city boundary, about 15 miles southwest of the central business district, in an area that is partly undeveloped vacant land, in part intensively developed with industrial plants, large and small. The yard, five miles long, extends between the Belt Railway Company's line on the east and the peripheral I.H.B.–B.&O.C.T. line on the west. Thus all three of the major belt railway companies of the Chicago district, as well as the thirteen owner trunk lines, have direct access. Clearing Yard is ideally located for the function that it performs. It is near the areal center of the terminal district, is between the two principal belt routes, and is easily accessible from all directions. Furthermore, the numerous industries in the vicinity (including those of the Clearing Industrial District) are well served by switching movements directly to and from the classification tracks of the yard, thereby making intermediate hauling and yarding of cars unnecessary. A shipment from the Clearing Industrial District, for example, southbound over the Illinois Central, is switched directly to the appropriate track in the classification yard at

---

[7] The outer boundary of the Chicago Switching District is generally located just outside the joint I.H.B.–B.&O.C.T. belt-line route.

Clearing, placed in a transfer train that takes it to Markham Yard, where it is classified directly into the Illinois Central train that carries it to its southern destination. Only two yardings, therefore, are necessary between the loading of the car and its final movement out of the metropolitan area.

The inner belt route, third of the concentric routes within the Chicago Switching District, is more complex in function and in operation than are either of the other routes. It is not a single railway line but rather a group of several railways operating on closely parallel rights-of-way over a single elevated embankment. At its nearest point it is less than two miles west of downtown Chicago. For its entire length it is lined with industrial establishments which are served by numerous sidings and small yards. There are also numerous carload and l.c.l. freight stations along the line.

The three belt-line routes (excluding the Elgin, Joliet, and Eastern Railway, which is different in character) and the many radial trunk lines give to the city of Chicago and its contiguous suburbs a cellular pattern. The built-up sections of the metropolitan area are divided into compact units separated by railways and the associated strips of industrial land from neighboring units. Orientation of the railways in conformance with the gridiron pattern of city streets emphasizes that characteristic. Because most of the lines, especially those close to the center of the city, are on elevated embankments, they form physical barriers among neighboring communities. That encourages the development of distinctive neighborhood units with homogeneous economic, social, and ethnic characteristics within each of the cells. This condition is somewhat of a disadvantage to the city in that it impedes free and easy access from one part of the city to another but is an advantage in that it furnishes physical lines of demarcation within which the planner is presented with the opportunity of developing physically integrated neighborhoods. Many such cellular areas are now within the blighted and near-blighted parts

of the city. In the rebuilding and rehabilitation of such areas by utilizing the railway boundaries the planner and developer has the opportunity to create real communities with homogeneous or balanced characteristics. The industries along the railways bordering the communities can furnish employment to the residents who will live in the central parts of each cellular unit.

## TRUNK-LINE ROUTES

Near the commercial core of Chicago the twenty-eight radial routes of the twenty-one railway systems that enter the metropolitan area are crowded into seven major routes. Therefore, the general pattern of the trunk lines, although radial, has dendritic modifications near the metropolitan center. Were each line to retain its separate identity in approaching the center of the city and to operate over its own right-of-way, there would be such crowding and duplication of facilities that little if any land surrounding the central business district would be available for other than railway use.

The seven approach routes to central Chicago are aligned parallel to the north and south branches of the Chicago River, to the shore of Lake Michigan, and to the rectangular street grid of the city. The earliest routes appropriated, in general, the water frontage. They were originally regarded mainly as feeders of traffic to the water routes. Such railway lines (built before the street grid was extensive) do not, in general, conform to it. Later lines, in order to avoid excessive condemnation and the platting of irregularly shaped parcels, were constructed with north-south or east-west alignment parallel to the city streets. Such lines generally were not oriented with regard to water areas because waterfront land was taken up by earlier lines. Later, the rail-water interchange of traffic became relatively unimportant. The general flatness of land in and near Chicago made unnecessary the paralleling of waterfronts to secure favorable grades.

The seven approach routes (Fig. 3), proceeding counter-clockwise from the north, are as follows:

1. The Chicago River North Branch route, used by the Milwaukee and Wisconsin divisions of the C.&N.W.

2. The Kinzie Street route, used by the Galena division of the C.&N.W. (Chicago's earliest railway) and, to a point two miles west of downtown Chicago, by a joint line of the C.M.St.P.&P. and a freight division of the Pennsylvania system.

3. The Sixteenth Street route, used by the B.&O. and its tenants (Chicago Great Western, Soo Line, and Pere Marquette), the Burlington, and a freight line of the C.&N.W.

4. The Chicago River South Branch–Des Plaines River route, utilizing the old "Chicago-Portage" route across the glacial divide, used by the Alton and Santa Fe railways, and, for a part of the distance, the western line of the Illinois Central.

5. The Pennsylvania–Chicago and Western Indiana route, consisting of two parallel rights-of-way used by the Pennsylvania (Pittsburgh, Fort Wayne and Chicago) Railroad, and the C.&W.I., the latter a terminal road leasing trackage rights to the Erie, Wabash, C.&E.I., Monon, and Grand Trunk Western.

6. The New York Central-Rock Island route, consisting of common trackage owned jointly by the New York Central (Lake Shore and Michigan Southern) and the Chicago, Rock Island, and Pacific, and also leased to the Nickel Plate Road.

7. The Lakefront route, owned by the Illinois Central, and also used by the New York Central (Michigan Central), "Big Four" (New York Central System), Chicago, South Shore, and South Bend (South Shore electric), and freight trains of the Chesapeake and Ohio and Nickel Plate Road.

Several characteristics are common to all seven routes of approach to central Chicago. Particularly noteworthy is their width, which in some cases exceeds a city block. In addition to four or more main running tracks, the rights-of-way are also developed with freight houses, team tracks, sidings, interchange freight yards, passenger coach yards, and other accessory facilities. Traffic density on the routes is high, and in some cases each of the running tracks

serves a special function: local freight, suburban passenger, through passenger, and so forth. Most commonly the freight tracks are the outer ones in order to serve sidings and yards without necessity of crossing over other main tracks.

The relations between the seven approach routes to central Chicago and the localization of industry and residential areas is noteworthy and of great importance.

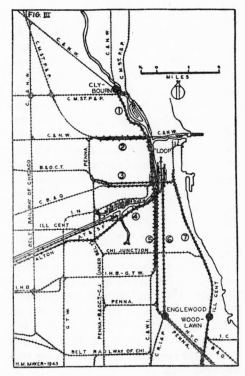

Fig. 3.—The seven railway approaches to central Chicago.

Along each of the routes there has been developed wedges or strips of industry which radiate from the commercial core of the city. Only the Lakefront route is relatively free from industrial development. Two such strips, along the two branches of the Chicago River, had already begun their industrial development before railways came to Chicago, but the railways undoubtedly enabled them to maintain their importance long after waterways became relatively unimportant as a factor affecting industrial location in downtown Chicago. Each of the four remaining routes, however, passes through industrial areas that extend for miles outward from the heart of the city. Thus the general pattern of industry within the city of Chicago, as distinguished from the outer parts of the metropolitan area, is radial and corresponds generally to the routes by which the railways reach the city's center.

The smoke and noise that in the past have accompanied railway operation, together with the advantages of industrial location along the main-line railways prior to the period of belt-line development, have forced residential building mainly to the interstitial areas between the prongs of industry along the railway axes. The requirements for residential use of the land were not so specialized as were those for industrial use; as a result the residential development took place in the areas that remained after the industrial sites had been appropriated. Thus in Chicago a wedge-shaped pattern of residential areas has developed within the city proper, particularly close to the commercial core in the area between Lake Michigan and the innermost belt line, as contrasted to the cellular pattern farther out and the stellate pattern on the urban fringe. Between each pair of railway approaches to central Chicago is a pie-shaped residential area, with its apex close to the commercial core where the railways converge.

### Freight Terminals of Central Chicago

Surrounding the central business or Loop district is a belt of freight terminals, in part obsolete in design and layout, and in part poorly located for efficient railway operation. Some of the freight terminals form serious obstacles to the orderly development of the area surrounding the Loop. In many instances, also, these terminals are a source of excessive operating expense to the railways. They are mainly survivals from the period before the development of

belt lines and motor truck, although there are a few more modern terminals which serve the establishments of the commercial core and the wholesale and light manufacturing district that surrounds it.

In recent years there has been a strong tendency for many freight houses to be located near the edge of the city rather than close to its heart. Notable examples are the huge package freight terminal and transfer house at Proviso Yard and a similar, though somewhat smaller, terminal at the Galewood Yard. Shipments routed to and from such outer freight houses avoid the congested yards and terminals closer to the city. Those shipments that are bound to and from the downtown freight terminals are generally subjected to more or less delay in passing through the terminal district. They are loaded on cars that are switched, in the case of outbound shipments, to the nearby industrial or secondary classification yards. There the cars are put on transfer trains which, in turn, are operated between the secondary yards and the large primary classification yards. At such yards, after additional time is consumed in switching and classification, the cars are finally placed in road trains for movement toward their destinations. In the case of less-than-carload shipments an additional handling is commonly necessary because such shipments from a given siding or freight station are often placed in cars without regard for ultimate destination and are reloaded at "transfer houses" into cars wherein shipments from many origins but bound for the same destination or route are combined. By trucking l.c.l. shipments to and from the freight houses on the urban periphery, much of the intermediate switching and reloading is eliminated and many hours can be saved in transit time.

### Passenger Coach Yards

The areas required for servicing passenger equipment, for its storage while not in use, and for the making-up and breaking-up of passenger trains are very extensive. Obviously, the centrally located land in the vicinity of the major passenger terminals is far too valuable for such uses. As in the case of the freight classification yards, there has been a notable decentralization and peripheral movement of many of the coach yards. Because some operations involved in maintenance of passenger equipment are similar to those for freight cars, several of the railways have located their coach yards near freight yards and shops. However, in view of the short time available for turn-around of rolling stock between incoming and outgoing runs, there is an economic limit to the distance coach yards may be located from the downtown passenger terminals. The expense and time of backing an empty train for several miles from depot to yard and then backing it into the depot for the outgoing run is minimized wherever possible. In some cases, particularly several of the fast streamlined trains making turn-arounds of two hours or less, additional cars would be required to maintain schedules if the coach yards were not located relatively close to the terminals.

As in the case of freight yards, the major consideration in the localization of the passenger coach yards is a reasonable balance between the high cost of the land close to the depot on the one hand and the expense and time of long turn-around back-up runs on the other. A secondary factor is the inertia of locations that were selected many years ago when sites now close in were peripheral.

Although distance of coach yards from depots varies from less than a mile in the case of the Illinois Central to 10 miles in the case of the Nickel Plate Road, most of the railways have located their passenger yards relatively close to the downtown terminals. Formerly the scheduled turn-around time for passenger equipment was much longer than now and it was feasible to locate coach yards at sites that were then on the edge of the city on land of low value and with sparse settlement. As the city expanded, such areas generally remained in railroad use because coach yards, unlike

freight yards, could not be economically removed outward toward the new urban periphery. On the contrary, it became ever more desirable to move them closer to the center of the city but, in general, it was impracticable to do so because of intensive use and high value of close-in land.

The coach yards for the rolling stock used in suburban trains are, in several instances, located closer to the downtown depots than are those that service equipment used in long-distance intercity trains. Such separation of facilities and differentiation of functions is necessitated by the rapid turn-arounds and shorter runs of the suburban trains. Obviously, a train making a 1,000-mile round trip can more conveniently and economically make a 5-mile turn-around run between depot and coach yard than can a suburban train that makes a 20- to 40-mile round trip.

## LOCOMOTIVE TERMINALS

Locomotive terminals, where locomotives are stored and minor repairs made between runs, together with the associated forges, foundries, and other associated facilities, including those for fueling the motive power, are usually found in proximity to the yards where cars are assembled into trains. The pattern of areal distribution of locomotive terminals and their accessory facilities, therefore, closely corresponds to the pattern of major freight and passenger yards.

## SHOPS

Railway shops may be divided into two general classes: first, major shops in which motive power and rolling stock of entire railway systems or large segments thereof are overhauled, repaired, and rebuilt; and, second, smaller shops where light running repairs, ordinary overhauls, and routine maintenance of equipment operating to, from, and within the terminal district are carried out.

Maintenance shops other than the large major shops are located chiefly in or near yards where trains are handled. Each of the larger freight classification yards has as a part of its layout a number of "bad-order" tracks upon which cars found in transit to require minor repairs are placed. Those cars are taken to the shops, usually conveniently located nearby. In association with each passenger coach yard, likewise, is a series of shops where ordinary repairs are made. Running repairs in locomotives are most commonly made at shops located within engine terminal areas which, in turn, are usually associated with yards.

The very large railway shops, on the other hand, are conspicuous by their relative absence from metropolitan Chicago. Of the twenty-one trunk-line systems that serve the area, only one operates its principal shops within Chicago. The explanation is found in the fact that the railways terminate in rather than pass through the metropolitan area. The shops, particularly those of the large systems that extend for hundreds of miles, tend to be located toward the middle rather than at the ends of their respective railway systems because motive power and rolling stock can be moved to such intermediate locations with maximum expediency and minimum mileage. Most railways, rather than operate a number of shops for major equipment repairs each serving a segment of the systems, prefer to centralize such operations at one or a limited number of very large plants, thereby receiving the benefits of economies that result from large-scale mass-production assembly-line methods.

Such large shops are, in general, located at or near the "center of gravity" of their respective railway systems, where there is a balance between distances to extremities of the system on the one hand, and the relative traffic density in both directions from the shop location, on the other. In cases where one end of a large system has much greater traffic density and hence more rolling stock and motive power than the other end, the shops tend to be located near but seldom at the heavy end. Thus the Pennsylvania Railroad centralizes all major repairs at Altoona, somewhat east of that system's central point, because the eastern

portion of the railway has heavier traffic and more equipment than the western portion.

The operation of this principle in location of railway shops is illustrated by the movement of the principal shops of the Illinois Central System, long located at Burnside on Chicago's South Side, to Paducah, Kentucky. The latter city is an important junction point nearly midway between the two ends of the system's main Chicago–New Orleans line. The Burnside shops, once a very important center of railway activity and employment in Chicago, are now used only for maintenance of suburban electric cars, diesel switch engines, and other equipment used locally within the metropolitan area.

The Keeler Avenue shops of the C.&N.W. are the largest in Chicago and the only ones in the metropolitan area that serve as the primary shops of a large railway system. These shops are about one-half square mile in area. The convergence of several of the principal routes of the C.&N.W. at Chicago makes them accessible from many parts of the system. Unlike many other railways, the C.&N.W. is not composed of a single line with branches; it is a complex network the principal lines of which fan out from Chicago to the north, northwest, and west. With such a pattern, the location of the system's principal shops in Chicago is a logical exception to the general rule.

PASSENGER TERMINALS

The passenger terminals constitute the cores of the metropolitan railway pattern and are the points to which practically all the radial trunk lines are directed.

Six major depots located in the central business district handle the great volume of passenger traffic, relieved only slightly by several way-stations in outlying parts of the city—notably at Englewood, on the south side. To the downtown terminals lead the seven avenues of approach to which reference was made above. Associated with the depots is a vast agglomeration of subsidiary facilities including the yards through which the trains are switched in entering and leaving the station tracks, the baggage and express houses, and the mail-handling facilities. Beyond those facilities are many of the principal freight houses which required central locations in the horse-and-buggy age and which now suffer from impaired efficiency through congestion on nearby streets only partially relieved by the tunnel system.

The passenger terminals and their associated facilities form a band of steel around the commercial core of Chicago and form barriers limiting expansion of the urban center. That condition constitutes a large part of the explanation for the unduly high land values resulting from concentration of intensive land uses in a very small area of central Chicago, a problem of acute importance to all who are concerned with the orderly development and functioning of the city.

## SUMMARY

For nearly half a century the consolidation and co-ordination of the railway terminals in the central part of Chicago has been prominent among local public issues. The literature on the subject is enormous,[8] and scores of plans for new terminals have been published; but little has actually been accomplished. The present terminals were located partly in response to the competition of the railway companies, each seeking to secure the most favorable routes into the city and the most advantageous terminal sites. The roads that entered the city first took the best sites; those that arrived later were forced to accept less favorable locations or to utilize jointly with earlier railways the routes and terminals already

[8] For a summary of the more noteworthy Chicago terminal studies and reports see Harold M. Mayer, "The Railway Pattern of Metropolitan Chicago" (Ph.D. diss., University of Chicago, 1943), pp. 128 ff.

developed. Several important co-operative agreements resulted among the railways to avoid duplication of facilities. They form precedents for more comprehensive terminal consolidations in the future, although some of the railways have considerable investments in existing facilities and high-value land in the central area which gives them competitive advantages they would be unwilling to give up.

Most of the plans for rearrangement of railway facilities have been primarily concerned either with the immediate surroundings of the central business district or with the operation of the railways as such. No comprehensive plan has been evolved that considers in detail the relationships between the railway pattern and the other elements of the urban agglomeration in order to insure that the railway facilities will function more effectively as integral parts of the metropolitan area as a whole. The relationships that should be considered include, among others, those between the railways and the location of industrial districts, residential areas, streets, highways, mass transportation routes, neighborhood and community boundaries, harbors and waterways.

Considering railway service and operation only, the pattern of Chicago's railway facilities, which developed in response to the forces of competition without any comprehensive planning, is reasonably efficient. There is need, however, for the improvement of the pattern and its operation in several respects. The classification of freight can be even further simplified and expedited. Traffic can be routed to avoid, in some cases, the more congested facilities near the center of the city. And finally, last but not least, the railway phalanx around Chicago's Loop, particularly the multiplicity of passenger terminals and associated facilities, must be simplified.

EDWARD J. TAAFFE

# AIR TRANSPORTATION AND UNITED STATES URBAN DISTRIBUTION

The dynamic role of transportation in the regional development of the United States is well known and well studied.[1] Canals, railroads, and highways, channeling the flow of traffic, have created urban alignments, hinterlands, and nodal points. Now air transportation promises to become a vital factor. Geography, with its emphasis on spatial relations, represents a particularly effective approach to an analytical consideration of this rapidly growing form of transportation and its possible regional implications.[2]

In its present stage of development United States air transportation is concentrated on the medium- and long-haul carriage of passengers between cities. Its ultimate impact on the urban pattern depends on the relative technological advance of air and surface transport in terms of both freight and passenger traffic. However, even in the present, passenger-oriented stage it is possible to note certain significant relationships between the distribution of United States cities and that of air-passenger traffic. This paper is an attempt to

ascertain some of these relationships from the empirical evidence presented on a series of maps. In particular, the effects on air traffic of such urban characteristics as size, function, proximity of other cities, and railroad services will be considered. The method used is (1) comparison of air-passenger and urban-population maps to determine the urban features of most significance in air-passenger traffic; (2) more detailed analysis of a map of per capita traffic-generation indexes in terms of these features.

## COMPARISON OF POPULATION AND AIR-PASSENGER MAPS

A comparison of Figures 1 and 2 reveals similarities and differences, but on the whole there is an understandably close correlation between air traffic and urban population. The same general group of cities appears on both maps, with roughly the same importance. The first step, therefore, in analyzing the air-passenger map (Fig. 1) is to note the similarities, so as to avoid attributing any unique distributional characteristics to air transportation that are merely inherent in the distribution of urban population.

The most striking similarity is the dominance of the general area of the American Manufacturing Belt. Within this area the axis of most intensive air-passenger traffic in the United States follows the axis of densest population between Chicago and New York, along a line from Detroit to Cleveland, Pittsburgh, and Washington, thence along the eastern seaboard through Baltimore and Philadelphia to New York and Boston.[3]

Reprinted from *Geographical Review,* XLVI (April, 1956), 219–38, by permission of the author and the editor. (Copyright, 1956, by American Geographical Society, New York.)

[1] Walter Isard considered the impact of the principal forms of transportation on United States development as a whole in "Transport Development and Building Cycles," *Quarterly Journal of Economics,* LVII [1942–43], 90–112, and, with C. Isard, the long-run impact of air transportation in "Economic Implications of Aircraft," *ibid.,* LIX (1944–45), 145–69.

[2] E. L. Ullman, "Transportation Geography," in *American Geography: Inventory and Prospect* (published for the Association of American Geographers by Syracuse University Press, 1954), pp. 310–32.

[3] This line also coincides roughly with the ridge of highest market potential defined by Chauncy D.

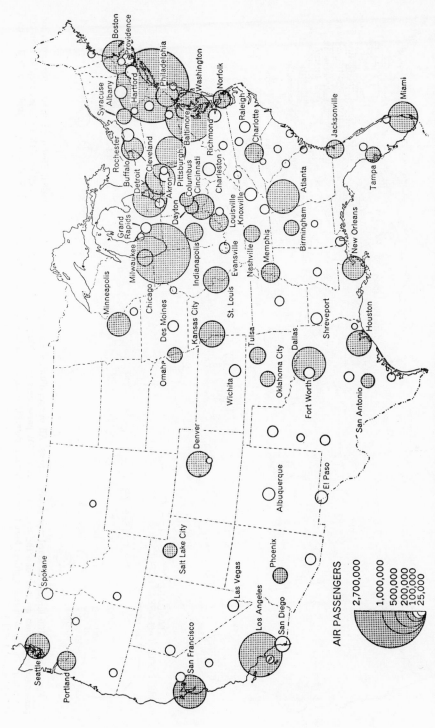

FIG. 1.—The 106 largest air-passenger generators in 1951. All cities shown accounted for at least 21,000 passengers, or 0.1 per cent of total air-passenger traffic. Each named city enplaned 50,000 passengers; each shaded city enplaned 100,000. (Source: *Enplaned Airline Traffic by Community, Calendar Year, 1951* [Washington, D.C.: Civil Aeronautics Administration, 1952].)

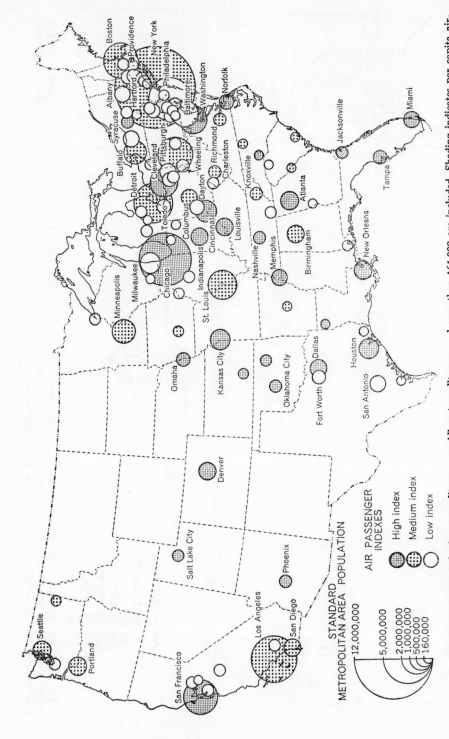

Fig. 2.—The 106 largest standard metropolitan areas. All metropolitan areas larger than 161,000 are included. Shading indicates per capita air-passenger generation greater than the median figure of 201 passengers per 1,000 population. On all other maps cities with an index greater than 201 are referred to as high-index cities; here they are broken down into high- and medium-index cities. (Source: U.S. Census of Population, 1950, Vol. I [Washington, 1952].)

Two groupings within the Manufacturing Belt show the same relative importance on the two maps: Buffalo and the large Mohawk Valley cities; and the cities referred to in this study as the Cincinnati Group (comprising Dayton, Columbus, Louisville, and Indianapolis), which though widely spaced as regards surface transport, may be considered a group as regards air transport.

Outside the American Manufacturing Belt the maps are similar in the prominence of the largest regional centers, particularly in the West and Southwest. These comprise the four large Pacific Coast cities, Salt Lake City and Denver, the Texas centers of Houston and Dallas, and such gateway cities as Kansas City, Omaha, and Minneapolis–St. Paul. In the southeastern and south-central United States the largest cities in such alignments as the Piedmont and the Mississippi Valley are prominent. Thus the similarities between the two maps indicate the importance of the largest cities in air transportation.

The shading on the urban-population map emphasizes the differences between Figures 1 and 2. The unshaded circles should be particularly noted. These are cities that generate fewer air passengers than would be expected from their population totals, cities with an air-passenger index lower than the median value.[4] Their distribution indicates that an important qualification must be attached to the generalization that air-passenger cities are largely concentrated within the Manufacturing Belt. The number of unshaded circles shows that air transportation is much less concentrated within the belt than urban population is.

It will be noted that these unshaded circles occur wherever cities are closely grouped. This is the traffic-shadow effect, the tendency of the largest city in any clus-

ter of cities to act as the traffic-receiving point for the entire cluster. It might be considered one specific illustration of the idea of the primate city, expressed by Mark Jefferson.[5] The outlying location of most airports lessens the inconvenience of a somewhat longer bus ride to another city. This gives a high passenger index, or per capita traffic generation, to the primate city and casts a traffic shadow over all nearby cities in the form of low passenger indexes.

The large number of low-index cities in the eastern United States is due to the facts that the cities are too close to one another for effective air transportation and that New York casts a traffic shadow over the entire area by reason of its fast and frequent air services from all parts of the country. Boston is the only other city on the eastern seaboard north of Washington with a passenger index higher than the median value. Philadelphia and Baltimore are notable examples of traffic shadow because of their position between the two great passenger-generating centers of New York and Washington. Evidence of this is found in Baltimore's current difficulty in attracting air traffic to its large new airport.

Elsewhere within the Manufacturing Belt traffic shadow may be observed in the presence of three groups of low-index cities: the industrial cities between Cleveland and Pittsburgh; the cities of southern Michigan; and Milwaukee and the small cities near Chicago. On a smaller scale traffic shadow is also noticeable outside the belt wherever cities are clustered; for example, Fort Worth, San Bernardino, Tacoma, and the cities around San Francisco.

Another important difference between the air-passenger and population maps results from city function, as will be noted from the high indexes of Washington, D.C., and such resort cities as Miami and Phoenix. In addition, the 106 largest air-passenger generators include a number of resort cities too small to be included among the

Harris ("The Market as a Factor in the Localization of Industry in the United States," *Annals of the Association of American Geographers,* XLIV [1954], 315–48; reference on p. 326).

[4] See Fig. 3 and text footnote 6.

[5] "The Law of the Primate City," *Geographical Review,* XXIX (1939), 226–32.

106 largest metropolitan areas on Figure 2. City function also accounts for the high indexes of such regional commercial centers as Denver, Dallas, and Atlanta, as compared with the low indexes of many eastern manufacturing cities.

A final difference is the relatively greater air-passenger importance of cities beyond the Manufacturing Belt. In part, this is associated with the absence of traffic shadow in the more diffuse urban pattern, but it is also associated with the fact that these cities are so located as to necessitate rather long hauls from the large eastern and midwestern cities.

Thus four factors are evident in the similarities and differences between the air-passenger and urban-population maps: the dominance of large centers; traffic shadow or urban grouping; city function; and length of haul.

### ANALYSIS OF PASSENGER-INDEX MAP

The map of air-passenger indexes (Fig. 3) depicts the relation between air-passenger traffic and urban population as expressed in the number of air passengers per 1,000 inhabitants in 1951. The 106 leading air-passenger generators of Figure 1 are shown, and all the 168 standard metropolitan areas, of which the 106 largest are shown on Figure 2.[6] This map provides a quantitative base for the separate consideration of the four factors noted in the preliminary comparison.

*Dominance of large centers.*—It has been evident for some time that air transportation by the very nature of its development

[6] Figure 3 consists of 174 cities. First, the total of 168 standard metropolitan areas was reduced to 161; seven pairs of standard metropolitan areas were represented by a combined circle, since they are served through a single airport. The number was increased to 174 by adding the 13 cities among the 106 leading air-passenger generators that were not standard metropolitan areas. For purposes of computing the median passenger index as the criterion for separating high- and low-index cities, the sample was reduced to 159 because 15 of the standard metropolitan areas were without scheduled airline service in 1951.

to date has been inordinately focused on the larger cities. The 106 largest air-passenger generators accounted for 90 per cent of the total air-passenger traffic, whereas the 106 largest metropolitan areas accounted for only 51 per cent of the total population. In degree of concentration the two distributions are generally similar. Together with the fact that Figure 3 is fairly uniform despite its exaggerated circle scale, this similarity confirms that the relationship between standard-metropolitan-area population and air-passenger generation is reasonably close and consistent.

However, closer inspection of Figure 3 indicates that the similarity in degree of concentration is most marked for the largest cities and generators. Of the metropolitan areas smaller than 125,000, only 14 per cent have high passenger indexes, as compared with 34 per cent of those between 125,000 and 500,000, and fully 81 per cent of those larger than 500,000. Nearly all cities too small to be included on Figure 3 have very low passenger indexes. Figure 2, the urban-population map, also reflects this tendency in the greater prevalence of low indexes for the smaller metropolitan areas.[7]

The inordinate concentration of air-passenger traffic on the largest centers might also be considered in terms of traffic flow between pairs of cities. This criterion indicates that the routes between the largest centers are dominant.[8] One study of air-

[7] The late-postwar dominance of large cities is somewhat greater than would be indicated by the figures used in this paper, since non-scheduled airlines are important only at the largest air-transportation centers. The addition of non-scheduled passenger figures at such cities as New York, Chicago, and Los Angeles would increase the totals by some 5 to 10 per cent.

[8] For an example of the use of a gravity model to determine traffic potential between a few selected points, see D'Arcy Harvey, "Airline Passenger Traffic Pattern within the United States," *Journal of Air Law and Commerce*, XVIII (1951), 157–65. Chicago's traffic flow is discussed in E. J. Taaffe, "The Air Passenger Hinterland of Chicago," Ph.D. diss., University of Chicago) (*University of Chicago Department of Geography Research Paper No. 24*, 1952).

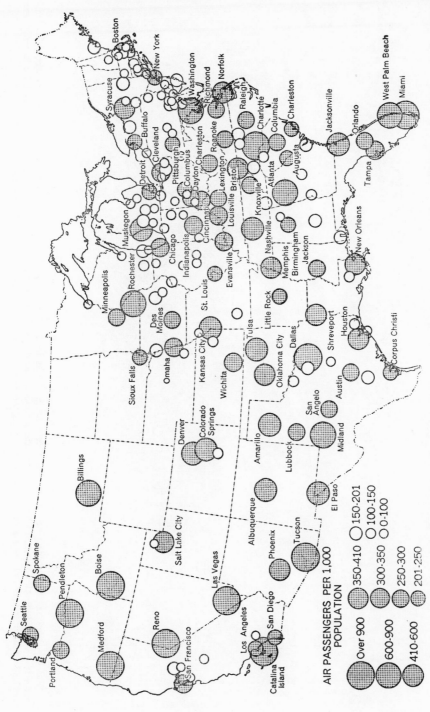

Fig. 3.—Air-passenger indexes. Named cities with shading are those with an index greater than 201, the median figure for the 159 cities that either accounted for 0.1 per cent of the total air traffic or were standard metropolitan areas with scheduled air service in 1951. Because of the relative uniformity of the passenger indexes, the circle scale has been exaggerated and cities are listed in the legend according to separate size categories, the areas of which increase more rapidly than do the index figures.

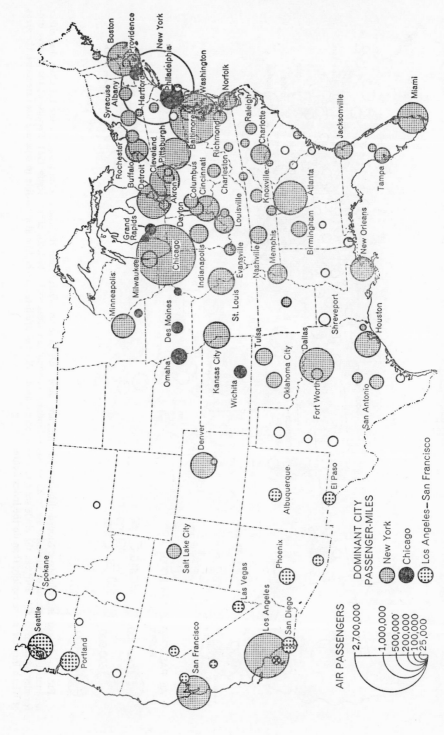

Fig. 4.—Dominant air-passenger-mile generators. Circles are graded in size according to 1951 air passengers. Shading indicates passenger-mile dominance in a selected month (March, 1949). Unshaded cities were dominated by cities other than those indicated in the legend. Miami, for instance, was the leading air-passenger-mile generator at New York during the selected month due to heavy winter resort traffic.

passenger traffic showed that nearly 50 per cent of the total United States traffic is accounted for by less than 1 per cent of the 15,000 city pairs with air service.[9] Maps of regional dominance in air passengers have further indicated that five or six large urban centers dominate the air traffic of the majority of medium-size cities.[10] In number of passenger-miles (a unit proportionate to airline revenue) large-center dominance is even more striking, as Figure 4 illustrates. During a selected month all the 106 cities of Figure 1 were dominated in passenger-miles by just 12 large centers. At 89 of the cities on Figure 4 the leading passenger-mile generator was New York, Chicago, or Los Angeles–San Francisco. New York alone dominated 66 cities. Particularly significant is the number of large and medium air-passenger generators at which New York accounted for the most passenger-miles.

The question could be raised here whether this apparent large-city dominance may not be merely a stage in the general growth and expansion of air services. It might seem that the dominance of large centers will steadily diminish as air transport matures and provides services to more and smaller communities. Other studies, however, indicate that this is not necessarily the case, since air transport has already gone through one phase of expansion to smaller urban centers, which was followed by an irregular tendency toward reconcentration on the larger centers.[11] The early postwar period was one of premature expansion due to great optimism regarding the economic feasibility of providing air services to smaller cities. Heavy losses on lightly traveled routes resulted in the curtailment of many of these services. Among the factors increasing the importance of the larger centers during the later postwar period were the greater use of fast, four-engine planes,

ill suited to short-haul flights, and the concentration of low-fare coach flights on the profitable routes between the large centers. The lack of an economical short-haul aircraft has so far been the principal deterrent to the growth of air-passenger traffic at smaller cities.

*Traffic shadow.*—The traffic-shadow effect evident on Figure 2 is shown by the greater detail of Figure 3 to be a widespread characteristic of air transportation. The concentration of small circles in New England and eastern Pennsylvania is particularly striking. The seven of these cities closest to the large centers of New York, Boston, and Philadelphia had no scheduled airline service whatsoever listed in the *Official Airline Guide* for September, 1951.

Traffic shadow is also apparent in the Southeast, though here it is primarily a contrast between high-index and medium-index cities; poor surface connections tend to reduce the number of low-index cities. Charlotte, for example, acts as a high-index regional focus for the Carolinas. Atlanta, however, is the dominant regional center of the Southeast, both in total passengers and in passenger index. The difference in passenger index between Birmingham and Atlanta indicates that Atlanta's air-passenger primacy is out of all proportion to the difference in population between the two.

Texas provides a contrast with the concentrated urban distribution of the Northeast: it is characterized by a large number of widely scattered, medium-size cities. Thus traffic shadow is at the minimum. There are three Texas cities besides Dallas and Houston with passenger indexes higher than 300 (El Paso, Midland, and Amarillo) and four others with indexes higher than the median 201. However, even within such a diffuse regional hierarchy, traffic shadow is apparent in the low-index cities around Dallas and Houston.[12]

[9] H. D. Koontz, "Domestic Air Line Self-Sufficiency: A Problem of Route Structure," *American Economic Review*, XLII (1952), 103–25; reference on. p. 118.

[10] Taaffe, *op. cit.*, pp. 36–43.

[11] *Ibid.*, pp. 21–24.

[12] Fort Worth has taken vigorous steps since 1951 to escape Dallas' air-traffic shadow. The diversion of a number of airline schedules from Dallas' Love Field to Fort Worth's newly opened Amon Carter Field sparked a renewal of the rivalry between these two Texas centers.

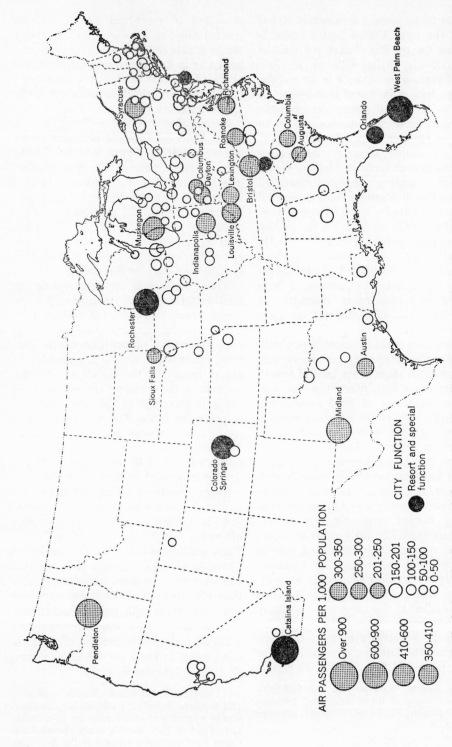

FIG. 5.—Traffic-shadow cities. Passenger indexes of those cities within 120 highway miles of a larger city or metropolitan area. Named and shaded cities are those with high indexes (more than 201). Resort and special-function cities are black; the five named are high-index, the unnamed (Atlantic City and Asheville) low-index cities.

**AIR PASSENGERS PER 1,000 POPULATION**

- 300-350
- 250-300
- 201-250
- 150-201
- 100-150
- 50-100
- 0-50

- Over 900
- 600-900
- 410-600
- 350-410

**CITY FUNCTION**

Resort and special function

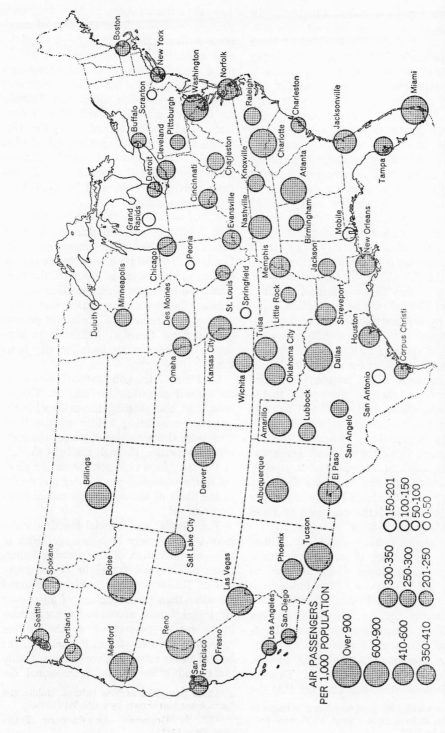

FIG. 6.—Non-traffic-shadow cities. Passenger indexes of those cities which do not have a larger city or metropolitan area within a radius of 120 highway miles. All cities are named, but only high-index cities are shaded.

Figures 5 and 6 represent a more quantitative expression of the traffic-shadow generalization. For the construction of these two maps traffic shadow was defined simply as the condition existing at a city or standard metropolitan area that is within 120 highway miles of a larger city or standard metropolitan area. The passenger index map (Fig. 3) was then split into two maps according to the 120-mile definition. More refined criteria were not deemed necessary in view of the resulting contrast between the two maps. The great number of small circles on the traffic-shadow map (Fig. 5) indicates the prevalence of low per capita passenger generation among the cities within 120 miles of a larger city. The circles on the non–traffic-shadow map (Fig. 6) indicate the prevalence of high-index cities among the cities that are largest within a radius of 120 miles. The correlation is improved by the fact that several of the high-index cities on the traffic-shadow map are resort and special-function cities. The average passenger index for the traffic-shadow cities—exclusive of 15 without scheduled airline service—was 167, as opposed to 405 for the non–traffic-shadow cities.[13] The fact that the non–traffic-shadow map is dominated by high indexes indicates that the two primary factors in air-passenger generation are standard-metropolitan-area population and traffic shadow, since these are the two factors modified by the use of per capita indexes and the exclusion of cities close to large centers.

The 120-mile definition of traffic shadow accounts for nearly all the cities with a passenger index lower than the median value of 201. There are 87 low-index cities among the 108 traffic-shadow cities, only eight among the 66 non–traffic-shadow cities. Most of these eight are located outside the American Manufacturing Belt; namely, Fresno, San Antonio, Mobile, Springfield (Mo.), and Duluth. This location is associated with the fact that the

120-mile criterion seems to have decreasing validity westward from the area of maximum airline activity. Infrequent schedules at the smaller outlying cities not on the more widely separated high-frequency routes tend to widen the traffic-shadow area of the largest on-line cities. San Antonio, for instance, although classified as a non–traffic-shadow city according to the 120-mile definition, is really in the traffic shadow of Dallas and Houston despite its distance from them, since the two larger cities are more conveniently situated for New York and Chicago traffic.

*City function.*—A third factor that was seen from the first two maps to be associated with air-passenger generation is city function. A useful base map for the consideration of this factor is Figure 6, the non–traffic-shadow map, which modifies the two primary factors of population and traffic shadow. The residual differences in passenger index are therefore indicative to some degree of other factors, including city function.

On Figure 7 the non–traffic-shadow cities are shaded according to function. The intensity of the shading increases with the passenger-generating ability of the function, from the unshaded circles of the manufacturing cities, through the light shading of the diversified cities, to the darker shading of the wholesale-retail cities, and finally to the black of the resort and special-function cities.[14]

The resort and special-function cities have the extremely high average index of 679—an indication of the growing importance of personal travel in air-passenger traffic. Business travel, which accounted for more than three-quarters of all prewar air travel,[15] now accounts for an increasingly smaller percentage as the airlines move into the mass-travel market with the help of faster schedules, coach fares, family fares, and other special promotional de-

---

[13] In computing all passenger-index averages in this study, indexes greater than 1,000 were considered to be 1,000.

[14] Such port cities as New Orleans, Mobile, and Norfolk are also shown by unshaded circles.

[15] W. L. Grossman, *Air Passenger Traffic* (Brooklyn, 1947).

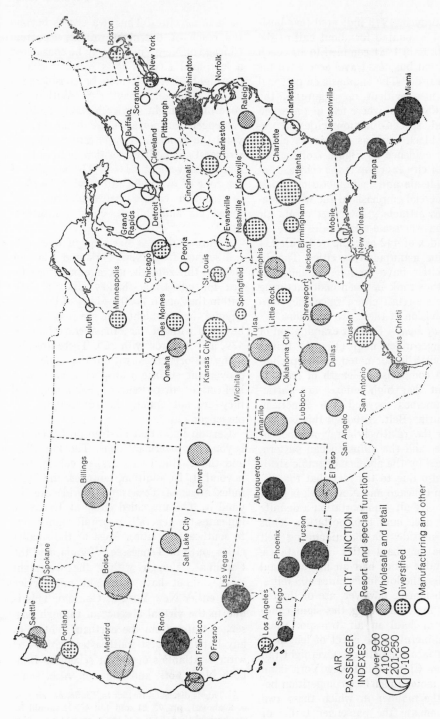

FIG. 7.—City function of non-traffic-shadow cities. The urban classification used as the basis for shading the passenger-index circles of the non-traffic-shadow cities is that used by Chauncy D. Harris ("A Functional Classification of Cities in the United States," *Geographical Review*, Vol. XXXIII [1943] [see above, pp. 129–38]). Many cities with relatively minor resort employment were arbitrarily reclassified as resort cities because of the disproportionate importance of this function in air passenger traffic.

vices. A study in 1948 indicated that business travel accounted for about half of the total; a study in 1951 confined to air coach indicated that business travel accounted for only one-third.[16] The emphasis on personal travel is also evident on Figure 5, the traffic-shadow map, where five of the seven resort and special-function cities represented in black rank as high-index cities.

Another evidence on Figure 7 of the importance of city function is the contrast between wholesale and manufacturing cities. The commercial emphasis of the wholesale-retail cities attracts greater per capita air traffic. The wholesale-retail cities have an average index of 442 as compared with 234 for the nine manufacturing cities. The diversified cities have an average index of 345, and thus rank between manufacturing and wholesale-retail cities, since they represent a division of these two functions.

*Length of haul.*—Further examination of the passenger-index map (Fig. 3) brings out the fourth factor noted in the preliminary map comparison—length of haul. It is apparent that high indexes are particularly numerous beyond the American Manufacturing Belt. Although this is partly due to the relatively large number of resort cities and the diffuse urban pattern, as evidenced by the absence of traffic shadow, it is also due to the fact that the distance from Chicago and New York is great enough to give air transportation a definite advantage over land transportation. Thus the cities outside the manufacturing belt tend to be long-haul cities. For instance, the high-index cities had an average haul of 510 miles, the low-index cities 403 miles. Average distances, however, are of limited usefulness in determining the significance of length of haul in air transportation. More meaningful is the effect of length of haul on surface competition. Overnight rail service from Chicago and New York is an important factor in surface competition because of the manner in which these two centers dominate the passenger traffic of

[16] J. L. Nicholson, *Air Transportation Management* (New York, 1951), p. 357.

most other cities. Thus if a city is beyond the reach of overnight rail service from Chicago or New York, it may be considered a long-haul city; if it is within reach of overnight service, it may be considered a medium- or short-haul city. Within the zone of overnight service highway and rail passenger transportation are dominant; beyond the zone air transportation holds its strongest competitive position, both in fares and in convenient service. The margins of the zone of overnight rail service therefore represent a competitive equilibrium between air and rail passenger transportation.[17]

Figure 8 depicts the zone of overnight rail service from New York and Chicago. Beyond this zone the average passenger index for non–traffic-shadow cities is 497; within the zone it is 307. Many of the cities beyond the overnight zone are resort cities, but even without these the average index is 429, as compared with 306. There are also many resort cities within the zone, but convenient surface transport makes them ineffective air-passenger generators, and they are not among the 106 leading air-passenger cities.

Certain important air-transport areas lie beyond the overnight zone. The Far West and the Pacific Coast are, of course, well beyond it. In addition, however, the high-index areas of Texas and Florida are beyond it. The unshaded circle at Knoxville indicates the generally poor rail connections to southeastern cities. Most of the smaller cities south of Tennessee, Virginia, and the Carolinas, though within the overnight zone, do not have overnight rail service from either New York or Chicago. This is due to the virtual absence of through passenger trains from the northern centers to any but the largest southeastern cities—as witness Atlanta's overnight schedules from both New York and Chicago. Also, some

[17] This is discussed further in Taaffe, *op. cit* (see n. 8 above), pp. 73–81 and 129–49. It should be emphasized that the use of the overnight-zone idea here is primarily to separate an area of definite air advantage from an area of definite rail advantage.

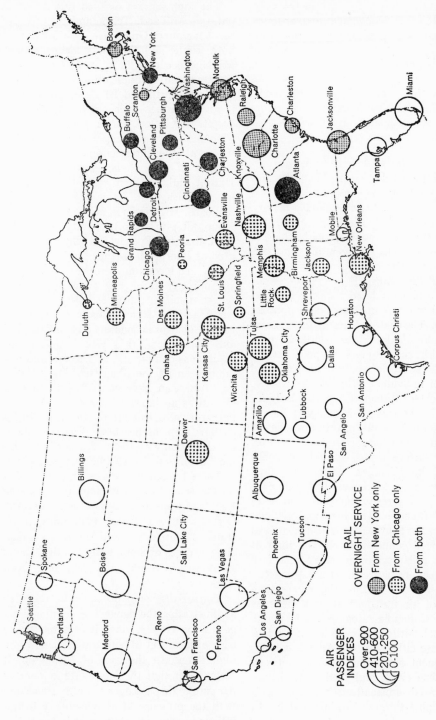

FIG. 8.—Rail overnight zone, non-traffic-shadow cities. Rail overnight service from New York or Chicago, here defined as that service which comes within at least one hour of a 4:00 P.M. departure and a 9:30 A.M. arrival, local standard time. (Source: *Official Guide of the Railway and Steam Navigation Lines of the United States* . . . [New York: National Railway Publishing Co., 1951].)

of the southeastern cities within the overnight zone have inconvenient arrival times, such as two or three o'clock in the morning, since many of the schedules are designed for morning arrivals in Atlanta or Jacksonville. Finally, many high-index cities, although within Chicago's overnight zone, are well beyond New York's and therefore tend to have their air traffic from the East increased.

## OTHER FACTORS

The traffic-shadow map (Fig. 5) now provides the basis for map analysis beyond the two primary and two secondary factors. The 21 high-index cities among the 108 cities on the map should provide clues to certain less obvious factors in air transport. Five have already been identified as resort or special-function cities. Austin, Texas, might also be considered a special-function city in view of its university and political functions. The high indexes of the remaining 15 traffic-shadow cities seem to be associated with such factors as poor surface transport, strategic route situation, and policies of individual airlines.

Poor surface transport is particularly influential in the case of Muskegon: the air routes from Milwaukee, Minneapolis–St. Paul, and even Chicago are much shorter than the surface routes around the south end of Lake Michigan. Avalon, Catalina Island, owes its extremely high index as much to poor surface transportation as to its resort function. The high and medium indexes in the Southeast are also related to poor surface connections, as the map of overnight rail service shows. Poor surface interconnections between southeastern cities tend to improve further the competitive position of air transport at such cities as Augusta, Columbia, Roanoke, Richmond, and Bristol. Airline policy is likewise a factor at these cities. Eastern Air Lines operates frequent short-haul services between southeastern cities, and Piedmont Airlines has operated unusually successful local-service flights through Virginia and North Carolina.

The high indexes of such traffic-shadow cities as Midland, Texas, and the cities of the Cincinnati Group are associated with both route situation and airline policy. Midland occupies an intermediate position on American Airlines' route between Dallas–Fort Worth and El Paso, which gives it an advantage over nearby San Angelo despite the latter's larger population. The Cincinnati Group occupies a strategic position at the intersection of two broad streams of traffic: one between Chicago–Detroit and the Southeast; the other between Chicago–St. Louis and the eastern seaboard. High indexes at the cities of this group, despite their proximity, have also been associated with the different cities used as intermediate stops by different airlines. This has minimized the possibility of any one city developing a marked air-passenger dominance over the others. Eastern Air Lines has focused many of its short-haul Chicago schedules on Indianapolis and Louisville; Trans World Airlines has made considerable use of Dayton and Columbus on its short-haul schedules; Delta and American have concentrated on Cincinnati as an intermediate stop. Route situation is also evident on the non–traffic-shadow map, as has been discussed above in connection with the weakness of the 120-mile definition for off-line outlying cities.

There remain four high-index cities that do not seem to be satisfactorily accounted for by any of the factors cited: Medford, Oregon (an extremely high-index, non–traffic-shadow city), and the three traffic-shadow cities of Sioux Falls, South Dakota, Pendleton, Oregon, and Syracuse, New York.

Sioux Falls could probably be regarded as illustrating the dangers of defining categories too closely, since it is a borderline case with respect to both traffic shadow and high index. In the case of Pendleton, it seems clear that the inordinate amount of per capita air-passenger travel is associated with the presence of atomic-energy installations nearby. In addition, it is located at a point where two United Air Lines routes cross a West Coast Airlines route.

Medford and Syracuse may both be associated with route structure. Medford is the point where United's routes connect with the southern terminal of West Coast Airlines and the northern terminal of Southwest Airways, and Syracuse is located at the point where the north-south routes of Colonial Airlines cross the east-west routes of Mohawk and American. Medford's index may be raised by the resort travel destined ultimately for Crater Lake, Syracuse's index by the unusual traffic-shadow pattern in upstate New York and in New England. Syracuse is in the traffic shadow of both Albany and Rochester and should therefore generate fewer passengers. However, Albany and Rochester are, in turn, in the traffic shadow of larger centers (Hartford–Springfield and Buffalo, respectively).[18] Thus Syracuse, although smaller than the other two, occupies a strategic central position in a rather large blank zone on the non–traffic-shadow map (Fig. 6).

Thus, an analysis of eight maps indicates that the two primary factors in the development of the air-passenger pattern of the United States have been urban population and urban grouping; the two secondary factors have been urban function and overnight rail service. Urban population as a factor has been particularly evident in the concentration of traffic on centers with a metropolitan area population exceeding 500,000, and in the dominance by a few large centers of the passenger traffic of most other cities. Urban grouping as a fac-

[18] The combined populations of Hartford and Springfield were used to determine traffic shadow, since both are served through the same airport.

tor has been evident in the traffic-shadow effect that channels the flow of traffic to the largest single city of any cluster at the expense of smaller cities within a radius of roughly 120 miles. The secondary factors of urban function and overnight rail service were evident in the high per capita traffic of resort–special-function cities and whole-sale-retail cities as well as of cities such as those in Texas and Florida which are beyond the reach of overnight rail service from New York or Chicago. Finally, the importance of such additional factors as poor surface connections, strategic route situation, and airline policy was indicated by certain cases of greater per capita air traffic than would be expected from the above four criteria.

To attempt to predict changes in the United States air-passenger pattern as presented in this study is to attempt to predict the direction of technological development. If this development should have the effect of continuing to increase the airlines' share of the combined air-rail passenger traffic, the circles on the air-passenger map would be markedly enlarged at all cities without much alteration in the pattern, except for the probable greater growth of recreational and other personal-travel centers. Certain technological changes, however, would alter the pattern greatly. The development of an economical short-haul or local-service airplane or helicopter, together with improved airport–central-city access, would modify the effects of traffic shadow and give smaller cities and outlying cities more representative air-passenger totals. On the other hand, a generally increased emphasis on speed in the form of domestic jet or turbo-prop service, which seems a more likely development, would tend to increase the primacy of the large centers.

## PORTS

A great number of the cities of the world are located on navigable waterways. In many of them the port function is dominant, not only as a component of the economic base, but also as a major element in the physical pattern. Ports are the meeting places of water and land transportation, where break-of-bulk occurs and, consequently, where goods are handled. This, in many instances, gives rise to the necessity for a labor force, which, in turn, requires goods and services, thereby creating a "multiplier" effect that is a major stimulus to urbanization.

The study of ports has been of interest to geographers for many years, and there is probably as prolific a literature on that subject as on any phase of transportation in relation to urban development. There are several reasons for the interest which ports hold for geographers. In the first place, ports are the gateways for extensive hinterlands, sometimes involving entire nations and even groups of nations, and therefore the movement of goods at the ports gives a good indication of the economic development of the hinterland region or nations. Second, because most port traffic is international in nature and there are custom regulations and other barriers, accurate statistics on the flow of goods and people are generally more readily available at ports than anywhere else. Third, ports are inherently important not only to their hinterlands but as urban agglomerations in their own right.

The first article in this section is a concise summary of the basic elements of ports which are of major concern to the geographer, with numerous illustrations from specific port situations in many parts of the world.

The second article, from a book on port geography by a British geographer, is primarily concerned with the relations of ports to their hinterlands or to the areas which they serve as gateways. Various types of hinterlands are discussed, as are some of the considerations relating to efforts of ports to obtain the traffic of overlapping or competitive hinterlands. It will be noted that, in relation to its hinterland, a port occupies a situation somewhat analogous to that of central places, discussed in an earlier section of this volume.

The third article in this section summarizes a monograph on a particular type of port institution: the free port or foreign-trade zone, which is a port or portion of a port set aside as an area outside the customs limit of the host country for the purpose of facilitating indirect or transshipment trade. In several of the urbanized and industrialized countries, free ports have been, in the past, important stimuli to commerce and, consequently, to employment and to urban development of the port cities. The situation of a given port with relation to other nations has been a major consideration in the degree of success of free ports, and therefore the relations of existing and potential free ports with their respective hinterlands and forelands are of major concern to geographers who specialize in the study of ports and of maritime trade.

GUIDO G. WEIGEND

# SOME ELEMENTS IN THE STUDY OF PORT GEOGRAPHY

The literature of port geography has become more abundant in recent years, both in the United States and in Europe. The subject matter has been concerned chiefly with certain functions of ports or with the geography of specific ports, but there have also been methodological discussions. In this article the author would like to bring into focus some of the basic elements of port geography—port, carrier, cargo, hinterland, foreland, and maritime space—and analyze them systematically as they apply to seaports.[1] This is not a final and all-inclusive statement but is intended to be another step in the formulation of more definitive general principles in port geography.

## The Port

The port is the place of contact between land and maritime space, and it provides services to both hinterland and maritime organization. It is, therefore, a knot where ocean and inland transport lines meet and intertwine. Its primary function is to transfer goods (and people) from ocean vessels to land or to inland carriers, and vice versa.

Reprinted from *Geographical Review,* XLVIII (April, 1958), 185–200, by permission of the author and the editor. (Copyright, 1958, by American Geographical Society, New York.)

[1] The reader is referred to the following earlier articles by the writer, in which various elements of port geography are discussed: "Bordeaux: An Example of Changing Port Functions," *Geographical Review,* XLV (1955), 217–43; "Les notions d'arrière-pays et d'avant-pays dans l'étude des ports," *Revue de "La Porte Océane,"* II, No. 113 (February, 1955), 5–10; "The Functional Development of the Port of Hamburg," *Tijdschr. voor Econ. en Sociale Geogr.,* Vol. 47 (1956), pp. 113–20; "The Problem of Hinterland and Foreland as Illustrated by the Port of Hamburg," *Economic Geography,* XXXII (1956), 1–16.

Traffic means life and prosperity not only for the port but also for the city and region around it. Thus it is inevitable that a dynamic port will seek to attract as much traffic as possible from wherever it can and will frequently come into competition with other ports. The origin and evolution of a port and its ability to attract traffic of any kind at a particular time are based on a complex of physical and human factors which can be categorized but which must be studied carefully in each case.

Among the physical factors, site is obviously of outstanding significance. Ideally a port, aside from sufficient space for its operations, should have among its attributes easy entrance, deep water, a small tidal range, and a climate that will not hamper port operations at any time of the year. Rarely can all requirements be met, because maritime services may be needed in locations where human considerations outweigh physical. Sites can be modified by man if the need is great enough. For example, in Saudi Arabia crude oil is loaded by means of pipelines in open roadsteads, and ships have no protection against wind and sea. One might even mention the construction of temporary port facilities on the Normandy beaches, where military necessity overbalanced all considerations of cost.

The *World Port Index*[2] recognizes eight types as sufficient to classify all ports of the world. Coastal ports and river ports can each be divided into "natural" and "tide gate" types, the latter being provided with locks or other devices that isolate the port area from the tidal effects of the open sea. Moreover, coastal ports may be of the "breakwater" type and river ports of the

[2] U.S. Hydrographic Office Publication No. 950, 1953.

"basin" type, both of which have protective constructions or excavations that do not close off the port area. Finally, there are the "canal or lake" type and the "open roadstead," the former having a situation on the interior part of a canal or lake connected with the sea by a navigable waterway.

"Situation" is a concept that may have either physical or cultural implications. It is one that has been significant throughout the development of ports. The term "situation" implies a relationship to other factors, of which there may be a large number. Because many of these factors are not static, the relationship, and therefore the meaning of "situation," may be under constant change. For example, the situation of a port is related to the physical landscape; it may be an "interior" port, away from the open ocean, or an "exterior" port, directly on the coast.[3] Historically, most of the great ports have been interior ports, because sailing vessels needed protection from the weather and a few days' difference in travel time was not important. Moreover, ships were small, and estuaries were deep enough to be no hindrance to ocean traffic. Most important, before the building of railroads and adequate roads land transport was difficult and slow, so that a seaport located as far inland as possible was at the same time a regional capital that not only provided maritime and land transport but possibly performed political, economic, and social functions as well.

Modern navigation, however, has brought grave problems to ports not on the seashore.[4] Ships are larger, and operating costs are constantly increasing. Shippers want fast and easy access to ports and a rapid turn-around. Many interior ports are plagued with inadequate depth of channel, sedimentation, and fluctuating water level;

[3] Marcel Amphoux, "Ports intérieurs et ports extérieurs," *Revue de "La Porte Océane,"* VI, No. 61 (May, 1950), 5–7.

[4] See, for example, G. G. Weigend, "River Ports and Outports: Matadi and Banana," *Geographical Review,* XLIV (1954), 430–32.

often approaches and departures can be made only at high tide, and delays are costly. Thus a port such as Le Havre, at the mouth of the Seine estuary, has attracted more ocean traffic than older ports upstream.

It is, however, the never ending and constantly changing patterns of human activity that have had a continuing influence on situation. In the seventeenth and eighteenth centuries Bordeaux was ideally located for trade and traffic between France and its possessions in the West Indies. Port life flourished, as did the entire region. Yet in the twentieth century Bordeaux finds itself in the backwater of ocean transport. There are many reasons for the change, largely beyond the control of the port and its administration. For example, Napoleon decided to encourage the growing of sugar beets in northern France in order to reduce the country's dependence on cane sugar, importation of which was threatened by the British blockade. Bordeaux had been a principal importer of cane sugar, and many refineries were located in and near the port area, most of which were eventually liquidated. Moreover, the Industrial Revolution had its greatest impact in northwestern Europe, and the Channel and North Sea ports became the chief terminals and ports of call for the important sea routes connecting Europe with other continents. The situation of Bordeaux, therefore, is no longer favorable with respect to the major world patterns of ocean trade. The port, once of national importance, has become purely regional.

It appears to be the human factor, then, that is paramount in the rise and decline of ports. This factor may range from world activity over which the port has no control to decisions of local administrators and port planners. Between the eleventh and fifteenth centuries ports on the shores of the Mediterranean became prosperous through shipping and commerce, chiefly as intermediaries between the Orient and northwestern Europe. In the fifteenth century, however, the rise of the Ottoman

Turks and accompanying piracy made the traditional trade routes hazardous if not impossible to use. Moreover, the discovery of the route to Asia around the Cape of Good Hope created a safer and easier seaway connecting northwestern Europe directly with the Orient. As a result, ports in the Mediterranean found themselves in the backwater of world ocean trade and traffic for more than two centuries and a half. An era of rejuvenation began with the opening of the Suez Canal, together with the advent of the steamship, continued industrialization in northwestern and central Europe, and French colonization in North Africa. The Mediterranean again became one of the world's principal ocean highways, benefiting ports located on its shore. Thus, in the case of Mediterranean ports, neither hinterland nor foreland nor the port itself has been able to influence or determine its destiny; rather, the totality of expansion and development in the world at each stage has narrowed or broadened its field of economic activity.

Similarly, policy decisions of national governments may influence ocean trade and transport. As has already been pointed out, the desire for national self-sufficiency in certain imported products may curtail port activity; the reduction or prohibition of export of other goods may have the same effect. Wheat exports from Russia ceased after the Bolshevik revolution, and Odessa lost its principal function; port life and city growth stagnated while many other cities in the Soviet Union doubled and trebled in size under the new regime.[5] Preferential railroad freight rates may favor some ports and cause traffic to flow over lines it would not normally follow. Finally, the movement of a commodity may come under the absolute dictate of the government, so that economically determined patterns of flow are erased. For example, the present French government decides how much coal is to be imported, where it is to be purchased and at what price, which

[5] C. D. Harris, "The Cities of the Soviet Union," *Geographical Review*, XXXV (1945), 107–21.

ships are to carry it, and to which ports it will be shipped.

In the narrowest sense, the human factor in development operates at the local level. Although the port may attempt, often successfully, to influence governmental policy in its favor, it is within the port's own realm of activity that greatest influence can be exerted on its economic well-being. In other words, the aggressiveness and imagination of the port administration and commercial interests are vital to successful port operation. The port must find ways and means of providing services and facilities that will induce maritime interests and shippers in the hinterland to use it in preference to another port. The port and city of Rotterdam were severely damaged by the Germans during World War II. Although the city urgently needed restoration, port facilities were reconstructed first because port traffic meant life, and delay in restoring the flow of ships would have resulted in loss of traffic to competing ports, traffic Rotterdam might not have been able to recapture. Extreme caution and conservatism may have the opposite effect and stagnate the life of a port and its tributary area. Failure to provide certain facilities, perhaps because of overreliance on established reputation, is likely to divert traffic to competing ports that can provide the services and are probably eager to do so.

The study of the human factor in port development can also be approached systematically. Economic, political, and social forces can be distinguished, all operating individually or simultaneously in conjunction. For example, the exceptional enterprise of the merchants and shippers of Hamburg, who early established commercial contacts throughout the world and who succeeded also in local operations, contributed immeasureably to the continued success of the port despite such political setbacks as the two world wars. Politically, the wars were only temporary, though severe, setbacks to Hamburg's development, but other political factors had longer-lasting effects. The fact that Hamburg enjoyed for many centuries a quasi-independent status and later complete political freedom as a city-state made possible full economic exploitation of city and port.

Frequently the economic and political factors are interlocked, as, for instance, in the growth of Marseilles into the largest seaport of France. In the nineteenth and twentieth centuries French colonial expansion in Africa, and especially in Algeria, created close economic and political ties between the two French shores of the Mediterranean, and Marseilles became the principal gateway for French-Algerian traffic. Moreover, the construction of the Suez Canal was motivated by both political and economic considerations of a scope far beyond the local interests of Marseilles. Yet because of the favorable location of Marseilles with respect to French sea transport to Asia by way of the Suez Canal the port benefited enormously when the canal was opened. In addition to being the chief contact point of France with Algeria, it soon became France's threshold to Asia and to French colonial possessions there.

Social forces acting on port development can be as decisive as economic and political forces, but their influence may not be as continuous. Energy and foresight had much to do with Hamburg's evolution as a port, but at certain periods progress was hampered by difficulties emanating from the guild system. Quarrels, jealousies, and intrigues among the guilds postponed or slowed down the growth of manufacturing, even in such basic port industries as shipbuilding. A hostile attitude toward industrialization in the nineteenth century on the part of the policy-making class of merchants and shippers further delayed a general planning scheme for a Greater Hamburg, finally realized in the twentieth century.

Because the analysis of a port can be based on a great variety of criteria, many classifications have been devised and employed. The site factor is the basis for such terms as "river port," "coastal port," or "lake port." World, national, or local patterns of human activity yield a classification of ports as international, colonial, national, regional, or local. With respect to the port's radius of activity, such a classification is based on the extent of its hinterland and foreland. It is economic activity, however, that provides the widest variety in the nomenclature of ports. The name of the principal commodity handled may be applied, such as petroleum, ore, coal, or fish; or what is done with the greater part of the cargo may determine whether the port is industrial, commercial, transit, or transshipment; finally, ports have been named according to the type of carrier that predominates in their traffic patterns, such as passenger, liner, tramp, or tanker. Each of these classifications is based on specific criteria that presumaby characterize the port according to a predominant function. However, the same port can be put into more than one classification. Thus an ore port may also be a local or regional port, and a liner port may be composed of an industrial port, a petroleum port, a lumber port, and a section where commercial activities predominate, perhaps within a free port or foreign-trade zone.[6]

Since the primary function of a port is to transfer goods (and people) from ocean vessels to land or to inland carriers, and vice versa, the classifications discussed above apply to variations of the primary function. As yet it has been impossible to assign a fixed order of importance to the various criteria employed, and no universal classification of ports has been formulated.

## The Carrier

The carrier must be considered in port geography so far as its size or special construction affects port operation—characteristics that also reflect distinctive types of commodity movements and physical conditions of sea lanes. The classical division

[6] For a recent study of free ports and foreign-trade zones, see R. S. Thoman, *Free Ports and Foreign-Trade Zones* (Cambridge, Md., 1956) [see below, pp. 388–91].

into tramps, liners, passenger liners, and so on is of limited value at present, but it is important to note that oil tankers of more than 100,000 dead-weight tons are now under construction. Only a handful of ports, San Francisco among them, can accommodate ships of that size. Although this does not mean that small tankers will disappear from the oceans, large crude-oil importing ports will be forced to modernize their facilities either by deepening the channel approaches or by providing pipelines to stations where the water depth will allow such supertankers to discharge cargo. Thus the port is faced with solving a problem that includes both size of vessel and special equipment needed for loading or unloading. The supertanker is an extreme case, but the problem of larger ships and deeper channels has been with ports for decades. The principal question is whether dredging to certain depths is economically feasible in view of actual or potential flow of traffic through the port.

The evolution of specialized ships has also had to be taken into account by port planners in connection with the provision of specialized equipment. The petroleum tanker is but one of many kinds of vessels for which special facilities must be provided. Bordeaux lost most of its banana imports to Nantes because no unloading facilities were available, and it was in danger of losing part of its vegetable imports until the decision was made to provide the port with an air-conditioned transit shed and modern unloading equipment for fruits and vegetables. Subsequently the port recaptured its importance in this specialized traffic: banana imports rose from about 1,000 tons in 1954 to more than 6,000 tons in 1955, and imports of other fruits and vegetables from 20,000 tons to nearly 24,000.[7]

## THE CARGO

Three aspects of cargo are of basic concern in port geography: volume, nature,

[7] Statistics issued by the Port Autonome de Bordeaux.

and direction of flow. Generally, two large classes of merchandise are recognized. Bulk cargo moves unpacked and can be rapidly transferred from one carrier to another with a minimum of handling if appropriate machinery is available. Such bulk cargoes, therefore, as grain, ore, crude oil, and coal represent the largest tonnages of goods handled in ports, but they are much less significant than general cargo in giving the port viability. For example, in 1955 Hamburg imported 4.3 million tons of crude oil, which was somewhat more than one-fourth of all imports; although this large tonnage boosts the traffic statistics of the port and thus its competitive standing, it affects only a small part of the labor force because of the highly mechanized unloading.

It is the general cargo moving in and out of a port that requires a diverse labor force. This category comprises everything that is not carried in bulk and thus encompasses a multitude of commodities packed or unpacked, which must be handled individually. It is the desire of every port to handle as much general cargo as possible, in order to maximize local employment. This achievement, however, may not result in the maximizing of local or regional income, but the proportion of general cargo to total tonnage is a much more valid measure of port prosperity than total tonnage.

The geographer is also interested in the origin and destination of the cargo, both incoming and outgoing. A port which is a terminus for incoming merchandise obviously has much narrower functions and opportunities for expansion and development than one through which goods move to and from interior areas. Merchandise moving through the port on the landward side can be categorized geographically as (1) goods originating in the port or city or destined for consumption or processing there; (2) goods passing through the port in transit to or from an interior destination; and (3) incoming goods marketed both in port or city and inland and outgoing goods coming both from port or city and inland. On the seaward side no such differentiation can be made. All cargo arrives or leaves the port in vessels, and attention must thus be focused on types of carriers and forelands.

In applying these three categories to a port analysis it is essential to distinguish between imports and exports and, more specifically, between types of merchandise. For example, in the traffic of Bayonne, in southwestern France, none of the major imports belongs in category 2; that is, none is shipped exclusively to an interior destination. The bulk of the imports remains in the immediate port area, where it is consumed by a few large port industries. These imports include phosphates and pyrites for a chemical factory, iron ore for a metallurgical plant, and coal for both these plants and for other local industries. The exports of the port, on the other hand, fall chiefly into the second category. They are products from the Landes pine forests to the north, which move through Bayonne to overseas destinations. Thus the port of Bayonne is a terminus for most of its imports and a transit point for its principal exports; or, in other words, the import hinterland is restricted largely to the port itself and its immediate surroundings, whereas its export hinterland extends into the Landes about halfway to Bordeaux.

### THE HINTERLANDS

The cargo classification brings our attention to the great variety of hinterlands of a port. A "hinterland" can be described as organized and developed land space which is connected with a port by means of transport lines, and which receives or ships goods through that port. A port does not necessarily have exclusive claim to any part of its hinterland, and an inland area may be the hinterland of several ports. For example, ports on the Mediterranean and on the North Sea have competed vigorously for Austria's overseas export. Trieste traditionally has been the sea outlet for Vienna, but between the two world wars, and again since World War II, German

North Sea ports have attempted to capture the traffic. They have met with considerable success. In spite of the fact that Hamburg is more than twice as far from Vienna as Trieste, freight takes as much as five days to move from Vienna to Trieste, and only six days to Hamburg, which has better and more frequent maritime connections with all parts of the world and port fees half those of Trieste.[8] The German policy of attracting goods traffic to German ports by granting preferential railroad freight rates has also been successful and has diverted Austrian merchandise away from Trieste and other Mediterranean ports. Furthermore, industry in Austria has been gradually decentralized. Some industries have moved westward, and many new industries have arisen in western Austria and have increased urban population there. Since western Austria has better transport connections northward than toward Trieste, more of its overseas exports now move toward the North Sea.

A different hinterland problem is presented by the port of St. John, New Brunswick.[9] In winter the port has within its hinterland, in competition with other Atlantic coast ports, most of the populated areas of Canada from the Atlantic to the Pacific and certain areas of the United States north of the Ohio and Missouri rivers. In summer, however, the St. Lawrence and Great Lakes ports take over St. John's interior hinterland, and the tributary area of the port shrinks to the Maritime Provinces, which are economically less important and therefore stimulate much less traffic.

Yet another example is the port of Lobito, on the west coast of Africa, which until the end of 1956 was unable to attract the copper exports of Northern Rhodesia

[8] Herbert Paschinger, Triest als wirtschafts- und verkehrsgeographisches Problem," *Verhandling des deutschen Geographentages,* XXIX (Essen, 1953; Weisbaden, 1955), 240–46.

[9] M. H. Matheson, "The Hinterlands of Saint John," *Geographical Bulletin,* No. 7 (Ottawa, 1955), pp. 65–102.

even though the ocean route from Lobito to the main markets is some 3,000 miles shorter than that from Beira and Lourenço Marques, the area's sea outlets on the east coast.[10] The copper companies of Northern Rhodesia had signed an agreement for shipping all copper by way of the Rhodesia Railways to the east coast; in return the railroad had granted low freight rates for taking copper out and for bringing coal into the Copperbelt from mines it services.

It may be that no area can be claimed as the exclusive hinterland of a port except where special arrangements have been made, as in Northern Rhodesia. It can generally be assumed, however, that the ties of a hinterland with one specific port become closer as the distance from the port decreases. On the other hand, the extent of the hinterland varies with each commodity exported and imported through the port, and the geographical analysis of port traffic becomes more meaningful if totals are broken down into imports and exports, and even into individual commodities.

Thus we speak of import hinterlands as the areas of destination for goods imported through the port, and of export hinterlands as the areas where outbound shipments of the port originate. The terms "import" and "export" in this sense do not refer in any way to the foreign trade of the country in which the port is located. They refer simply to commodities arriving at the port, or moving out of the port, by sea, regardless of whether its foreland is in the same country or continent.

The great range in the areal extent of import hinterlands is well illustrated by the imports of crude oil and fruits and vegetables in Bordeaux. The entire crude-oil import of Bordeaux, about 60 per cent of the import tonnage, in 1955 was discharged at the oil refineries in the Gironde Estuary, and the petroleum hinterland of Bordeaux is the port itself. Fruit and vegetable imports, on the other hand, are dis-

[10] W. A. Hance and I. S. van Dongen, "The Port of Lobito and the Benguela Railway," *Geographical Review*, XLVI (1956), 460–87.

tributed throughout southwestern France, and occasional railroad shipments go to distribution points in all parts of the country in direct competition with other large fruit and vegetable importing ports such as Marseilles, Rouen, and Dunkirk. These other ports also have all of France as their fruit and vegetable import hinterlands, among which the urban concentrations, and especially Paris, are the most important. Marseilles markets Algerian fruit and vegetables even in Bordeaux when the prices are lower than those of the Moroccan products. The fruit and vegetable import hinterland of Bordeaux is therefore interwoven with those of other French ports, in which the details of movement depend largely on season, demand, prices, and, not least, the competitive spirit of the importers.

The export hinterland of a port can be similarly simple or complex. For example, in 1953 refined sugar exported through Hamburg originated in sugar-beet areas of Czechoslovakia and Eastern Germany. The petroleum export hinterland, however, was not only the oil-refining area of Hamburg and western Schleswig-Holstein; petroleum products also came to Hamburg for export by sea from as far as North Rhine–Westphalia and Hesse, and even from a refinery in Bremen, Hamburg's chief competitor. Although those petroleum products which originated in the Hamburg area were shipped to all parts of the world, those which came from refineries in Western Germany had their destination largely in Scandinavia, especially Denmark and Sweden. In order to find reasons for such a seemingly illogical pattern, one must analyze carefully an interrelated complex of factors.

It is evident that both "organization" and "development" of a hinterland are of great importance. The ease and rapidity of connection with the port, freight-rate structure and policy, the economic structure of the hinterland, the facilities of the port and the efficiency of its operations, the maritime organization in relation to the port and its forelands, and the forelands themselves all bear on the selection of the port or ports that are to serve as the hinterland's maritime links.

## THE FORELANDS

Forelands are the land areas which lie on the seaward side of a port, beyond maritime space, and with which the port is connected by ocean carriers. The concept of "foreland," as opposed to "hinterland," can be applied to all situations provided traffic is viewed from the port. Cargo that arrives and leaves by ocean vessels comes from, or is sent to, forelands. If cargo arrives at a port and is transshipped to another ocean vessel, it has come from a foreland and

arrives or leaves—coastal craft or seagoing ships.

The significance of forelands in port analysis has already been suggested. A striking illustration is offered by Iran, which, as a chief producer of crude oil in the Middle East, has been a foreland of many ports, particularly those of Europe. In Marseilles more than 9 per cent of the total import tonnage in 1950 came from Iran, most of it crude oil. In 1951 the percentage decreased to less than 5, and in 1952 and 1953 only a fraction of the port's import came from Iran, none of it crude oil. Then a recovery began, which became pronounced in 1955 (Table 1). The reason

TABLE 1

IMPORTS OF MARSEILLES AND ANNEXES FROM IRAN, 1950–55*
(In Metric Tons)

| Imports | 1950 | 1951 | 1952 | 1953 | 1954 | 1955 |
|---|---|---|---|---|---|---|
| Crude oil.... | 674,419 | 437,139 | .......... | .......... | 34,416 | 578,984 |
| Other....... | 12,219 | 2,359 | 2,255 | 4,184 | 5,681 | 16,100 |
| Total.... | 686,638 | 439,498 | 2,255 | 4,184 | 40,097 | 595,084 |

* Source: *Activité économique de la circonscription,* Chambre de Commerce de Marseille, annuals for the years, 1950 to 1955. The Annexes are the oil ports that belong to Marseilles administratively.

leaves again for another foreland. In this case the port itself is the hinterland for the cargo—it never goes farther inland than the transit shed or warehouse in the port.

If, however, cargo is transferred from an ocean vessel to a coastal craft that cannot operate on the open seas and is taken to another coastal port, that port must be regarded as being in the hinterland of the port where the cargo transfer was made. In the study of port geography there is no difference between this type of shipment and the transport of cargo from the seaport to an inland port by way of inland waterways. Inasmuch as most ports on or near the seashore handle both kinds of shipments, sea and coastal traffic are bound to overlap. The basic distinction between hinterland and foreland lies therefore in the type of carrier in which the merchandise

for this peculiar pattern was the conflict between the Anglo-Iranian Oil Company and the Iranian government. The oil industry was nationalized in 1951, all British staff were withdrawn in the fall of that year, and exports of crude oil from Iran ceased for more than two years. The dispute was settled in 1954, the petroleum industry was reactivated in October of that year, and oil began to flow again.

The study of a foreland can be approached either in terms of the port's shipping connections as expressed by number of shipping lines, number of departures, or net tonnage moving in a certain direction, or in terms of the origin and destination of cargo moving through the port. These approaches do not necessarily yield similar results, and it is clear that net tonnage is least satisfactory. In 1955 more than twice as much net tonnage left Hamburg for French Mediterranean ports as for Finnish ports (respectively 603,570 and 240,712 net register tons),[11] yet Finland received 50 times as much cargo (2,784 metric tons exported from Hamburg to Mediterranean France; 141,343 metric tons to Finland). Also, to judge from the smaller number of departures to Mediterranean France (160; to Finland, 272), ships leaving Hamburg for that foreland were larger on the aver-

lyzing the port-foreland relationship than the number of departures or arrivals either of ships or of net register tonnages. A breakdown of cargo data by type (bulk, general) or nature (ore, oranges, and the like) will contribute further to comprehension of the problem.

For detailed analysis, a division of forelands is desirable. Genoa, in generalizing for its foreland traffic, uses a classification that is appropriate and useful for a port on

TABLE 2

THE FORELANDS OF GENOA, 1938 AND 1955*

(In Metric Tons)

|  | 1938 | Per Cent | 1955 | Per Cent |
|---|---|---|---|---|
| 1. Other Italian ports | 1,142,822 | 20.1 | 2,292,461 | 21.9 |
| 2. Western Mediterranean | 82,483 | 1.5 | 347,198 | 3.3 |
| 3. Eastern Mediterranean and Black Sea | 263,985 | 4.7 | 2,313,256 | 22.1 |
| 4. Ports beyond Suez: |  |  |  |  |
| East and South Africa | 89,577 | 1.6 | 239,866 | 2.3 |
| Persian Gulf–India–Pakistan–Ceylon–Indonesia | 171,563 | 3.0 | 931,106 | 8.9 |
| Far East–Malaya–China–Japan–Philippines | 46,809 | 0.8 | 139,108 | 1.3 |
| Australia and New Zealand | 43,387 | 0.8 | 110,302 | 1.1 |
| 5. Ports beyond Gibraltar: |  |  |  |  |
| Spain and France (Atlantic)–Portugal–Great Britain–Northern Europe | 2,629,402 | 46.3 | 856,397 | 8.2 |
| West Africa | 121,953 | 2.1 | 419,321 | 4.0 |
| North America (Atlantic) | 577,224 | 10.2 | 2,170,784 | 20.8 |
| North America (Pacific) | 30,118 | 0.5 | 46,763 | 0.4 |
| Central America | 253,062 | 4.5 | 162,417 | 1.6 |
| South America (Pacific) | 40,254 | 0.7 | 69,610 | 0.7 |
| South America (Atlantic) | 182,025 | 3.2 | 355,719 | 3.4 |
| Total | 5,674,664 | 100.0 | 10,454,308 | 100.0 |

* Source: *Traffic in the Port of Genoa during 1955* (Genoa Port Authority, Statistical and Traffic Promotion Office, 1956), p. 14.

age than those leaving for Finland. In other words, most of the southbound ships probably used French ports merely as ports of call, delivering an insignificant amount of cargo from Hamburg, and perhaps loading additional cargo for farther destinations.

Similar relationships can be established for arrivals and imports or for the total traffic between the port and a foreland. In view of the primary function of the port, cargo tonnages are more meaningful in ana-

[11] *Handel und Schiffahrt des Hafens Hamburg 1955* (Handelsstatistisches Amt der Freien und Hansestadt Hamburg, 1956).

the central section of the northern Mediterranean coast (Table 2). Further refinements can be made, of course, particularly in the categories "Ports beyond Suez" and "Ports beyond Gibraltar." Table 2 shows a great increase in traffic from 1938 to 1955 between Genoa and the "Eastern Mediterranean and Black Sea" and "North America (Atlantic)." Also evident is a striking decrease in the ties with European ports beyond Gibraltar. It is apparent that changes in the world flow of fuels are largely the reason for Genoa's reorientation with respect to its forelands.

Other ports will devise different groupings of forelands, best suited for their traffic patterns at a particular time. For Japanese ports a division of forelands into those on the "Near Seas" and those on the "Far Seas,"[12] together with their subdivisions, was the most practical before World War II in relation to the then prevailing trade and traffic patterns; but a reorientation of these patterns with the many postwar political and economic changes throughout Asia necessitates re-evaluation and regrouping. Still other ports may find it suitable to distinguish among national forelands, forelands on the same continent, and transoceanic forelands. Whatever classification

Ports on or near these avenues have an advantage over ports in "backwaters." Port competition is keenest in regions of converging sea lanes, where large expenditures for improvement of port facilities and deepening of channels can be justified by expected gains in traffic and trade; in fact, if such outlays are not made, traffic might be lost that could never be regained.

The distribution and nature of shipping lanes have been repeatedly discussed in geographic and economic literature. Suffice it to say here that oceanic ties are strongest among areas economically most advanced unless political doctrine or expedi-

TABLE 3

TRAFFIC OF MARSEILLES AND ANNEXES THROUGH THE SUEZ CANAL, 1955*
(In Metric Tons)

| Foreland | Imports | Exports | Total | Per Cent of Total Traffic |
|---|---|---|---|---|
| France overseas and Indochina..... | 313,759 | 276,637 | 590,396 | 3.3 |
| Africa (east coast)................ | 80,677 | 25,306 | 105,983 | 0.6 |
| Asia........................... | 5,011,962 | 177,533 | 5,189,495 | 28.6 |
| Total...................... | 5,406,398 | 479,476 | 5,885,874 | 32.5 |

* Calculated from statistics of the Chambre de Commerce de Marseille in *Activité économique de la circonscription en 1955* (1956).

is devised and in whatever detail, the basic concept of "foreland" remains valid and useful in port geography.

MARITIME SPACE

Between port and foreland lies maritime space. This space has been organized, not for itself, but as a reflection of economic activity in adjacent land areas. Ships ply the waters of some parts of this space more regularly and with greater frequency than others. They thereby create a pattern of sea lanes that become avenues of traffic; these in turn attract traffic from adjacent land areas and promote economic progress.

[12] N. S. Ginsburg, "Japanese Prewar Trade and Shipping in the Oriental Triangle" (Ph.D. diss., University of Chicago, 1949), pp. 6–7. (Also published as University of Chicago, Department of Geography Research Paper No. 6.)

ency outweighs economic considerations. Blockage of an important ocean highway has repercussions on the economic well-being of all states participating directly or indirectly in ocean traffic. The closure of the Suez Canal in 1956–57 is an outstanding example, though it is not yet possible to make a statistical analysis of the consequences. However, we may take the port of Marseilles as an example (Table 3). In 1955 more than 44 per cent of the imports of Marseilles and 8 per cent of the exports, or about one-third of the total seagoing traffic,[13] moved by way of the Suez Canal. The bulk of the imports from Asia was crude oil from the Persian Gulf producing

[13] In 1955, Marseilles imported 12,181,687 metric tons and exported 5,975,163 tons, a total traffic of 18,156,850 metric tons.

regions. Four million tons of crude oil also came into the port from Baniyas, Tripoli, and Sidon, the three chief pipeline terminals in operation on the Levant coast. When this flow too was discontinued during the crisis, Marseilles lost 77 per cent of its imports, or more than half its total traffic. Before the crisis France—and, in fact, all of Europe—depended on the Middle East for most of its crude oil; even the United States imported petroleum from that area. However, when this vital ocean highway was severed, the oil movements of the world had to be temporarily readjusted, and once again tankers began to move eastward from the United States, and also around the Cape of Good Hope, in an attempt to fill the fuel gap in Europe.

Improvement of sea lanes such as the Great Lakes–St. Lawrence route has far-reaching effects on the shipping and economy of land areas on these lanes. Ocean transport is expected to grow considerably after completion of the St. Lawrence Seaway.[14] Lake ports that heretofore have been chiefly inland shipping ports handling bulk cargo will have to expand port facilities to accommodate more and larger ships and to make possible efficient handling of general cargo and rapid turn-arounds. New vessels will be designed to carry a possible maximum cargo tonnage within the draft limits of the enlarged seaway, and manufacturing and trade are predicted to grow in industrialized areas on the United States and Canadian shores. Even the Port of New York, which stands to lose traffic at

[14] H. M. Mayer, "Great Lakes–Overseas: An Expanding Trade Route," *Economic Geography,* XXX (1954), 117–43.

first, hopes to gain in the long run because of the expected general upswing in economic activity.

It has been demonstrated that in port geography the human factors predominate. Ports have been founded and have evolved despite physical obstacles when economic advantage and political expedience were of overriding importance in surmounting such difficulties. In a free economy port traffic normally flows according to the best economic advantage, but in nearly all ports the political factor enters into the pattern in a varying degree. Political influence may, in fact, be so dominant that a port may be created and may flourish at the expense of a nearby port in a neighboring country on which traffic and trade for the entire region would focus were it not for political boundaries.

It is clear that ports must be studied and analyzed not as isolated phenomena but within the framework of relational patterns. A close relationship exists between port and hinterland, on the one hand, and port and maritime organization and foreland, on the other. Effective organization and utilization of the land exert a powerful influence both on the evolution of ports and port functions and on the organization of maritime space, and the character and growth of a port play a leading role in the development and prosperity of the hinterland and maritime organization. Also, the sea lanes of maritime space have a direct bearing on the economic development of ports and land areas at each end. A change in the organization and function of any or all of these elements affects the entire structure.

F. W. MORGAN

## *HINTERLANDS*

The concept of hinterlands of ports as a simple parceling-out of the country behind them, with areas of overlap where ports compete, and with certain peculiar courses where a mountain range or a frontier affects the flow of trade, is hardly adequate. A port generally has a different hinterland for each commodity which enters into its trade and has thus an enormous number of hinterlands. Sometimes, it is true, the limits or limiting zones of these commodity hinterlands will coincide so that there will be some justification for the idea of a linear boundary. The nature of the structure and the areal extent of hinterlands are subject to variations arising from three main factors: the nature of commodities, the mechanism of sea transport, and the influence of political policies. As a result of the interplay of these factors, hinterlands show variations, not merely in extent, but also in complexity: there are orders of hinterlands, or a hierarchy.

### Primitive Hinterlands

Port hinterlands which are simple in composition and outline may be called "primitive." They lie behind ports on islands or behind ports along coasts where there is no cheap and easy lateral transport communication with the hinterland of the next port along the coast. Then all goods entering into the trade of each isolated community pass through each port, and the hinterland of each port is the entire local inhabited area. Such ports are often served by coasting steamer or small short-sea vessels. Examples are to be found in the Western

Reprinted from *Ports and Harbours* (London: Hutchinson House, 1952), chap. 7, 111–31, with permission of the author and the publisher. (Copyright, 1952, Hutchinson's University Library, London.)

Islands of Scotland, the Norwegian islands and parts of the mainland, many Greek islands in the Aegean, parts of Turkey, e.g., Trabzon (Trebizond), Sinope, or Antalya, much of West Africa, and parts of the west coast of South America. Such ports are nearly always small, although Curaçao and Aruba are examples to the contrary. Where there is a railway running inland from a port but not connected with any other lines, the same principle holds, and each railway merely extends the area of the "island"— examples are Mogadishu (Italian Somaliland), Mocambo Bay (Portuguese East Africa), Mossamedes and Loanda (Portuguese West Africa), Libreville and Douala (French Equatorial Africa), Freetown (Sierra Leone), Abidjan and Lome (French West Africa), Payta, Ferrol Bay, and Pisco (Peru).

Such primitive hinterlands are brought to an end as soon as lateral communications become possible and cheap in relation to neighboring transport costs. In the past the development of a railway network marked this phase and usually took some decades to come about. In the last twenty years or so the multiplication of motor transport has brought about rapid changes in the accessibility of territory some distance from a port. Once lateral communication is established, differentiation among commodities takes place and thus concentration of traffic into certain ports and the aggrandizement of their hinterlands.

### Raw Material Hinterlands

A most important consideration is the nature of each commodity and its weight/value ratio. Sea transport is the cheapest of all forms of large-scale transport. The lower the value of a commodity in relation to its weight the more advantageous it is to carry it as far as possible by sea before trans-shipping it to land transport. In the opposite direction, land transport is cut to a minimum where possible. Thus iron ore will seek the nearest existing port or a port will be built for it. Not only do the Lapland ores travel no farther than Narvik or Luleå for export, but several mines in North Africa, some distance from the general ports like Algiers, Oran, Bougie, Phillippeville, etc., have loading installations built for them nearby. The numerous coal-loading points on the Tyne and northeast coast, in Fife, and in South Wales are other examples.

The case is clearer when we consider the import of coal. The frequency of coal-importing ports in France is proof enough that in a country where distances are considerable, even where there is an excellent network of roads and railways, a heavy material of low value—in relation to its weight—moves as far as possible by sea. Italy, Jutland in Denmark, North Germany with its coasting and Rhine-Sea trade in coal, and eastern United States are other regions with well-developed transport networks and, at the same time, many coal-importing ports. In England and in New England a similar situation long existed, but the railways in both countries have exerted a constant pressure to reduce coastwise coal. The small port of Totton on the River Test, some miles west of Southampton, had a trade in coal until the extension of the railway from Salisbury. It is reported that, beginning in 1950, through a change of policy by British Railways, coal for railways would no longer be taken from Newport to ports in southwest England by sea but would be taken overland by train.

A heavy, low-value commodity which does not move in quite the same way as coal or ores is liquid fuel. Petrol may be transported in cans or drums, when the same factors of economy would operate as in the case of coal, but is carried in bulk much more cheaply, and it requires special equipment on shore, especially storage

tanks. A result is that in the distribution of this product there is a tendency to use a smaller number of unloading points.

The raw material is handled in a quite different way. Petroleum is usually produced on a very large scale if it is produced at all, so that every sizable oil-field can have its port, or petroleum can be concentrated simply by means of pipelines and handled on a large scale. With the import of petroleum for refining, the scale of operations becomes important, for a refinery is so costly an apparatus that it must be operated with a large through-put. There are thus normally fewer petroleum-importing points than petrol-importing points.

These facts may be exemplified by a few regional examples. In France before the war crude petroleum was imported at only nine ports; refined petroleum products were imported at fifteen ports; coal was imported at many more ports. In England west of, and excluding, Bristol and Southampton, there were no ports importing crude petroleum, four importing refined petroleum products, and about ten importing coal.

The same general principles apply to bulky goods of low relative value like stone, fertilizers, and timber. A port exporting stone often has a hinterland consisting of a single quarry, e.g., Porthoustock in Cornwall. In the same county the china clay export is almost confined to Fowey, which has an annual trade of about 500,000 tons. Timber is a more complicated commodity in that it comprises a large number of varieties and qualities. The great majority of softwoods, however, while in part carried by liners, is a raw material of relatively low value in relation to its weight. The export from Scandinavia and Finland passes through a great many small ports which are often little more than timber wharves, and we see a principle operating again—a big export of a bulky raw material seeking an outlet on the coast as near as possible to the source of supply. In the United States the outward movement of timber, largely coastwise, from the Pacific northwest, is conducted through a number of small specialized ports—Everett, Bellingham, Port Townsend, Astoria—and is not concentrated through the larger ports of Seattle, Tacoma, and Portland (Ore.). In the import of timber there is a large number of small importing centers besides the big centers of the trade, usually, though not always, confining their activities to the softwood trade. In the timber trade, therefore, we find that there is a large number of export hinterlands, often very restricted, and

Besides softwoods these ports deal with hardwoods of various kinds, plywood, and other more restricted sorts. But the timber trade is not confined to these main importing ports; softwood is unloaded at a number of smaller ports, like King's Lynn, Ipswich, or Plymouth, thus forming local hinterlands within the greater hinterlands.

The world trade in cereals illustrates the low-value commodity hinterland in part only. This commodity, not by any means

TABLE 1

IMPORTS OF TIMBER (EXCLUDING MINING TIMBER AND CERTAIN OTHER
CATEGORIES) IN THE WEST OF ENGLAND, 1938 AND 1948

|  | HARDWOOD (CU. FT.) (000's) | | SOFTWOOD (STANDARDS) (000's) | | PLYWOOD (CU. FT.) (000's) | |
|---|---|---|---|---|---|---|
|  | 1938 | 1948 | 1938 | 1948 | 1938 | 1948 |
| Barnstaple........ |  |  | 0.2 |  |  |  |
| Bideford.......... |  |  | 0.8 |  | 0.4 |  |
| Bridgwater........ |  |  | 2.9 | 0.9 | 0.3 |  |
| Bristol........... | 884.7 | 848.5 | 29.6 | 23.9 | 134.0 | 121.0 |
| Dartmouth........ | 6.4 |  | 1.5 |  |  |  |
| Exeter........... |  |  | 2.8 | 0.3 |  |  |
| Falmouth......... |  |  | 1.2 | .06 |  |  |
| Fowey............ | 2.5 |  | 0.7 |  |  |  |
| Gloucester........ | 145.1 | 25.3 | 35.8 | 15.9 |  |  |
| Padstow.......... | 0.8 |  | 0.3 |  |  |  |
| Penzance......... | 1.1 | 0.1 |  |  | 0.2 |  |
| Plymouth......... | 30.9 | 21.5 | 17.3 | 15.9 | 7.2 | 63.9 |
| Poole............ |  | 18.0 | 9.0 | 5.3 |  |  |
| Southampton...... | 141.9 | 896.7 | 34.9 | 14.1 | 8.7 | 107.3 |
| Teignmouth....... |  |  | 1.3 | 0.3 |  |  |
| Truro............ |  |  | 1.6 | 0.5 |  |  |
| Weymouth........ | 8.5 |  | 2.1 | 0.1 | 1.2 |  |

a fair number of import hinterlands of all sizes.

In England the leading ports are the leading importers of timber (quite apart from the special trade in mining timber, which not unnaturally concentrates upon the ports nearest the coalfields); in fact, the timber-importing hinterlands of England have a fivefold symmetry around the Mersey, Bristol, Southampton, London, and the Humber ports, leaving the northeast coast to the Tyne and the Tees, an arrangement which resembles the popular notion of port hinterlands in England as a whole.

confined to tramps, enjoys a considerable value as a part cargo or "make-weight" cargo for liners. In North America this fact, together with the fact that most wheat-producing regions are in the interior, has meant that the wheat export usually passes through large well-established ports in liners, although a large quantity passes through Montreal in tramps. In Argentina and Australia, on the other hand, the grain-exporting regions are much nearer the coasts and the specialized bulk cargo port appears, and these ports are as close as possible to the sources of the wheat. Thus, in Argentina, Santa Fé and Rosario share the maize export, and Rosario, Buenos Aires, and Bahia Blanca share the wheat export, each having behind it a grain hinterland comprising, broadly speaking, the region nearest to the port. In Australia the export of wheat shows a tendency to seek the nearest outlet. In Western Australia exporting centers are Geraldton, Albany, and Bunbury, besides Fremantle; in South Australia, besides Port Adelaide, they are Thevenard, Port Lincoln, and Wallaroo.

## LINER PORT HINTERLANDS

Just as liner ports are the largest ports, so their hinterlands are the largest of all port hinterland series, often reaching continental scale. They are, at the same time, much more complicated in structure. Ideally, such a hinterland series will comprise raw material hinterlands first of all—an import coal hinterland perhaps, restricted in size, then a liquid fuel import hinterland of not quite the same outline; then other hinterlands corresponding to cargoes which are both tramp and liner cargoes—wheat and other grains, timber and sugar possibly, spreading over much wider areas; then liner cargoes such as tropical products, frozen meat, fruit and various semi-manufactures such as refined metals, all covering much more extensive hinterlands of distribution. The export hinterlands will again take on widely differing shapes and cover very often great areas for articles such as precision machines, fine quality cloth, or optical glass products.

As a small general port Dunkirk exports and imports for the coal field behind it, and exports steel from the Lorraine district, but not much else; a larger general port like Le Havre serves a great part of France for tropical produce, e.g., coffee, and in its special trades will import raw cotton for the neighboring parts of Europe as well as for all the consuming centers in France. But a general port like Antwerp, of continental scale, serves territories as far away as Paris, Switzerland, and Vienna. To some extent it is enabled to serve this wide area

because of the advantages arising from its connection with the Rhine waterway, but mainly because it is served by more liner sailings than Le Havre. Its frequent liner sailings give Marseilles a number of wide hinterlands, some of them of no great weight or density of traffic but of great value in the aggregate. Thus, for the whole of France and to a lesser extent for Belgium and Switzerland, it serves as an exporting port for manufactures and semimanufactures, destined for points beyond the Suez Canal; in this trade it competes with Genoa. Marseilles enjoys, too an enormous hinterland including the British Isles for the mail and passenger traffic to and from the Indian Ocean and Far East.

This combination type of construction of hinterlands for the big general ports may be likened to the simple relief models which geographers make up from a number of layers of cardboard, except that for hinterlands each smaller layer exists within, and not on top of, the next larger layer. This layer or tier construction of big port hinterlands is fairly general throughout the world. In North America we find the principle quite well illustrated. Vancouver has a compound hinterland; from nearby come the heavy exports of timber, partly tramp and partly liner cargoes. A little more scattered, and sometimes more distant, are the sources of a characteristic liner cargo, packed fruit and fish. Extending a long way eastward is the peculiar wheat export hinterland of the western prairies—again, part tramp and part liner. But much more extensive even than this is the pure liner hinterland of Vancouver, extending as far as eastern Canada and touching at times the northern parts of the United States, the hinterland for which it imports Far Eastern produce, including raw silk, and from which it exports manufactures.

Seattle has a similar "layer" structure, although its pure liner hinterland is of even greater interest. From the Middle West it draws many manufactured products which are exported to the Far East, southwest Asia and Australia, but for many lines of more valuable goods its export hinterland extends as far east as the Atlantic Coast. For one import of particular significance during the 1920's, its import hinterland lay mainly in the cities of the eastern United States; that was for the raw silk from Japan. So valuable a commodity could bear the charges of the long railway haul to the eastern cities. The trade has declined, however, partly owing to the rise of silk-importing centers on the Gulf Coast, through the development of liner services to such ports as New Orleans and Galveston by way of the Panama Canal.

Thus we must conceive of the hinterland of the general port as comprising an entire series of hinterlands, often different in extent from one another: some liner, some both liner and tramp, and some tramp—both import and export. Conversely, a tract of country may lie in the hinterlands of many different ports for the various commodities which enter into its trade. There will be an almost infinite series of frontier zones. Some authorities use the terms "primary" and "secondary" hinterlands. In this usage the primary hinterland is the area in which the port is well established, and the secondary hinterland the area of frontier or fringing zones in which other ports compete with it. But there is no such neat division by which all the primary hinterlands are separate from each other and by which the secondary hinterlands form a general area where rivalry is a "free for all." New England is in the primary hinterland of both Boston and New York; the Ohio Valley is in the primary hinterlands of both Baltimore and Philadelphia, but it is certainly also in the primary hinterland of New York. West Virginia is in the primary hinterland of Newport News and Norfolk for its outward movement of coal, but for most other trades it is in the primary hinterlands of all the big general ports on the Atlantic Coast. For such an important trade as the import of raw wool, West Riding is in the primary hinterlands of London, Southampton, Liverpool, and Hull. All the hinterlands of Manchester lie within the

hinterlands of Liverpool, many lie within the secondary hinterlands of London, and some even within the primary. For some trades the area which can be served from Bristol lies within the primary hinterland of London; for other trades the two ports compete in their secondary hinterlands. To some extent the primary hinterlands of Bremen and Hamburg overlap, e.g., in Thuringia and Brunswick, but for many trades all the hinterlands of Bremen lie within those of Hamburg, which likewise includes many hinterlands of Settin.

A peculiar type of commodity hinterland occurs, more especially in Europe, where some port has built up a leading trade in a commodity. It occurs especially in those commodities which require elaborate marketing arrangements, including facilities for sampling, grading, and testing, and which are commonly composed of many different varieties for the "trade"—although we may call the commodity simply "wool" or "tobacco." Le Havre and Bremen have long-established trades in raw cotton; the German port in peacetime served a great part of central Europe in this commodity, and the import very much exceeded the import into Hamburg. Amsterdam enjoys a long-established trade in the import of colonial produce like tobacco, coffee, spices, and nuts, and the hinterlands to which these commodities are dispatched are frequently more extensive than those generally served by Amsterdam. The important trades of this kind in London are well known and have an extension far beyond the Channel in the form of a re-export to Europe or entrepôt trade. Copenhagen enjoys a similar trade, in miniature, with the Baltic.

Aggrandizement is a characteristic of liner port hinterlands. Such ports have a force of attraction which is the more powerful the larger and more established they are. London and Liverpool dominate the export trade of manufactures. Southampton, Middlesbrough, and Hull, as well as the packet-boat ports, compete most strongly with the two big ports. In some trades, e.g., the export of motor vehicles from the Midlands, London was in the lead, followed by the Mersey with the others far behind. The South Wales ports, in spite of their facilities and heavy trade in coal, timber, and metals, failed to make much headway against the overwhelming dominance of London and Liverpool. Since 1946 the Welsh ports have actually had some encouragement from the government to bring more liners to their quays, not only to attract trade from the Midlands, but also to insure that, of the products exported from the new light industries in South Wales, a proportion should pass through South Wales ports and not, as they had been doing, almost entirely through London and Liverpool. In January, 1947, only 10 per cent of light miscellaneous manufactures from South Wales was shipped through its ports. In January, 1949, however, 28 per cent passed through these ports, and the proportion was expected to increase.

A small but interesting example of the same situation is found with the mining machinery exports from west Cornwall which pass through London and Liverpool and not Plymouth or Bristol—the reason being, as in all the other examples, that the liners are at London and Liverpool and not at any other ports which might be thought more "natural." These, and all other high-grade manufactures, can bear the transport costs to a port which is not the nearest.

Antwerp, with more liner sailings than any other Continental port, draws manufactures from Lille and Roubaix, as well as steel from Lorraine. In Germany both Hamburg and Bremen export machinery; communications to Hamburg from any part of Germany for the transport of machinery are not superior in any way to those leading to Bremen, but Hamburg is a much greater port than Bremen and has many more liner sailings, and this difference is seen at once in its much greater machinery export. It draws more heavily from all the sources of production in Germany, including the Ruhr and Württemberg which are nearer to Bremen than to Hamburg.

Aggrandizement of hinterlands is, of course, but a reflection of the growth of ports; it is an inevitable consequence as well as a cause. It appears in the shape of inequality among ports. New York stunts the east coast and the Gulf ports, and New Orleans in turn stunts the development of the other Gulf ports like Mobile. Le Havre among the northern French ports and Hamburg among the German ports have the same position of absolute primacy. In the United States the factors affecting hinterlands and the currents of trade all operate freely, without the interference of frontiers and national interests. In Europe these same interests exert a powerful influence in modifying the extent of hinterlands, and it is the fringing hinterlands which are most susceptible to them, though it is not only these fringes which suffer changes of great consequence, as with Trieste, Königsberg, or Salonika.

### POLITICAL INFLUENCES

The conscious and determined attempts to extend and maintain hinterlands are seen best in central Europe and take the form of a struggle between northern and southern ports as well as rivalry between ports on the same coast. It occurs mainly in liner traffics but is not confined to them. Broadly speaking, the instrument by which heavy traffic is influenced is the inland waterway, and the instrument by which lighter traffic or the liner cargoes are influenced is the railway or, rather, the railway system.

*Waterways and waterway politics.*—The northern ports in Europe generally have the advantage that the great rivers extend their hinterlands far to the south. Thus, by means of the Seine and associated waterways, the coal imports of Rouen are carried inland to the upper parts of the Saône basin. Antwerp and Rotterdam, through the Rhine and Strasbourg, dispatch their imports of heavy raw materials to the upper Saône basin and Lyons, thus trespassing in the apparent natural hinterland of Marseilles, which suffers in the Rhône an ineffective means of transport for bulk goods to the north. Similar commodities reach

Basel for distribution through much of Switzerland by way of the Rhine. The Swiss hinterlands of Genoa are mainly, though not entirely, of liner traffics. The Elbe extends the hinterlands of Hamburg into Czechoslovakia.

A special problem arose in the interwar period in the competition for the import and export traffic passing between the Rhine and the sea. This lay mainly in the bulk cargo trade—imports for the Ruhr and Rhine districts in Germany, for eastern France via Strasbourg and for Switzerland, exports of potash from Alsace, coal and industrial products from the Ruhr. Of interest to several countries, this traffic amounted to the enormous total of 57 million tons in 1938. Antwerp is the chief competitor of Rotterdam, and at one time, deprived of their hopes of a new and direct big barge canal through North Brabant to the Waal, the Antwerp authorities gave a subsidy to barge traffic from the Rhine to Antwerp. Amsterdam was also a competitor and so was Ghent to a minor extent.

The matter was complicated by the fact that the French government was involved in the Rhine traffic. In an attempt to shelter Dunkirk from the fierce competition of Antwerp it sought to divert certain traffics to Dunkirk, compensating Antwerp by reserving certain French Rhine traffics, e.g., Alsatian potash to Antwerp—Rotterdam being the loser. It was a case of robbing Peter to pay Paul. These, and other points at issue, were settled by the Franco-Belgo-Netherlands treaty of 1939 relating to Rhine navigation, which among other things fixed the limits of the proportion of Rhine traffic passing to the Belgian ports at 18 and 24 per cent.[1] Now, of course, this traffic is much reduced. The waterway hinterlands of the two great ports have not been altered, therefore, in their extent and shape, but they have been regularized, and the erosion of one by the other has been reduced to very narrow proportions.

The German waterways offer a very interesting field for port competition. The Dortmund-Ems waterway, opened in 1892, was an attempt to provide a direct all-German route to the sea for the trade of Dortmund and the eastern Ruhr, and it became available for the whole Ruhr and for Rhine traffic after 1913, when the opening of the Rhine-Herne Canal provided a connection with the Rhine. But Emden never became a serious rival to Rotterdam, and in 1938 as much coal and ore traffic between Emden and the Ruhr went by rail as by waterway. The eventual extension of the Mittelland Canal to the Elbe—the through connection was not made until 1938 at the Rothensee shiplift—threatened to introduce new currents into the trade of central Europe, but the through connection had not been in existence long enough before the war for them to be observed. But even during the early discussions of the Mittelland project the East German landowners had feared that their agriculture would be undermined by the importation of cheap foreign grain through Rotterdam and the canal, and Demangeon[2] drew the logical conclusion that in conditions of freedom of trade and transit the Mittelland Canal could extend the hinterland of Rotterdam eastward. The easy circulation of Dutch tramp barges in prewar days as far as the Oder makes this seem possible (Fig. 1).

As the backbone of a hinterland the Danube is not very important and the ports of Braila and Galatz are of modest size. In the interwar period the river had been made into a vehicle with greater carrying capacity than the needs of the riverine states, under the International Danube Commission. The wheat of Hungary (and the oil of Rumania) as often as not reached its market in the upstream countries by way of the river; seaward movements of oil were made by pipeline to Constantsa, and the outward movement of cereals has declined in recent

[1] League of Nations, *Treaty Series,* Vol. 195 (1939), Nos. 4532–66 (Geneva, 1939).

[2] L. Febvre and A. Demangeon, *Le Rhin* (Paris, 1932), p. 249.

years. Polish coal has at times reached Budapest by way of the Black Sea and the Danube, but in general there has never been a movement of heavy cargoes to compare with that on the lower Rhine. The Danubian countries are poor industrially, and political factors have not been conducive to a greater use of the river.

It is clear that in most instances waterways are "given" factors, though sometimes a determined policy has carried out great engineering works. The Rhône, not easy for barge navigation, would need to be reconstructed as a waterway or replaced by a lateral canal in order to give Marseilles the benefits of a Rhine, and policy in France is not determined enough or the cost is prohibitive in terms of the scale of French economy.[3] The construction of the Albert Canal in Belgium, which goes far to rivet part of the nearby hinterland of Antwerp more closely to the port, was not entered upon without long opposition to a policy of heavy expenditure on a waterway undertaking.

In few other parts of the world are waterways and waterway politics of great importance as factors in the structure of hinterlands. The Great Lakes in relation to the North American ports have a transport geography of their own. The lakes and the St. Lawrence are of prime importance to Montreal in bringing down the Canadian wheat crop, and of some importance to New York insofar as Canadian wheat reaches the port via Buffalo. The Mississippi in the earlier part of the nineteenth century was the great carrier of produce southward, and New Orleans was a rival of New York. The railways, however, drew traffic away from the Mississippi, and the river became relatively unimportant in the life of the port of New Orleans, though it has regained some of its importance under government

[3] A substantial advance has been made toward the amelioration of the Rhône by the application of Marshall Aid funds to the navigation and power development of the Donzère–Mondragon stretch of the river.

encouragement. Relatively and absolutely, New Orleans is no Rotterdam.

The other example of a waterway feeding a port and playing a great part in determining its hinterland is the Yang-tse-kiang, which contributes so much to the activity of Shanghai and extends its hinterlands far into China. The importance of the river has been magnified relatively by the lack of railways in China; the port near the mouth of the greatest transport artery has become established as the most frequented liner

Fig. 1.—Waterways and the hinterland of Rotterdam.

port of all ports in China, a position in which it is by now almost impregnable. The evolution of Shanghai has been exactly opposite to that of New Orleans. The Si-kiang plays some part in feeding Canton. Other rivers, like the Parana-Paraguay may, perhaps in the future, support busy hinterlands in their basins.

*Railway politics and hinterlands.*—Railway hinterlands have been fought over by conscious means much more than waterway hinterlands; through the weapon of railway rates a policy can be pursued much more consistently and usually more effectively than on waterways. The railway is more flexible; it has many more lines to its network over which the traffic is spread; it is frequently able to carry port traffics at special rates and is, therefore, a powerful and widespread influence upon port hinterlands. A good example of railway competition between a northern and a southern port occurred during the 1920's when the Deutsche Reichsbahn, by means of special rates, fought to extend to the south the hinterland limits of Hamburg and Bremen and thus to trespass upon the territory of Trieste. The Germans claimed a dividing line along points equidistant from Hamburg and Trieste: the port authorities, then Italian, claimed a dividing line along the northernmost frontier of the former Austro-Hungarian Empire. German pressure was the stronger, and in the course of several agreements in 1925 and 1927 the dividing line was moved successively southward toward the center of Bohemia (Fig. 2).

With the rise of Gdynia came a new rival to Trieste and Fiume and to Stettin and Hamburg. Favorable rates and accommodating forwarding arrangements attracted both import and export traffic to the Polish port for a region which included Bohemia, Moravia, Slovakia, and Polish Upper Silesia. This entire region is one of overlapping hinterlands of a number of ports, and for a great many rail-borne traffics they are all fringing hinterlands. In conditions of unrestricted trade Trieste would have advantages for many commodities, especially those concerned with its many former liner services to America, Asia, Africa, and Australia. Conditions today are far from unrestricted, and the regimes in the hinterlands of Trieste are mostly protagonists of directed trade. It is now thought that, of the Polish ports, Gdynia will serve mainly Polish requirements and Szczecin (Stettin) will become the chief port for other Slav countries, under the political regimes now prevailing. Achievement of this mission on the part of Stettin would be chiefly at the expense of Trieste.

The aggrandizement of hinterlands through the application of special railway rates has taken place on the largest scale

along the northern coasts of Europe. Up to 1914 the hinterland of Königsberg extended far into Russia for timber and flax exports and for imports of manufactures and fish. It was enabled to do this because, according to a Russo-German commercial agreement, Russia gave no advantages in rates to its own Baltic ports. At the same time, Danzig, the natural outlet for the Vistula Basin, was handicapped because the German railway rates were arranged so as to draw traffic to Königsberg and Stettin.

The chief field of operation for these "seaport exceptional tariffs" lay farther west, however. A large part of the trade of south Germany and Switzerland had its "natural" outlets at Rotterdam and Antwerp, to the former chiefly by waterway, to the latter chiefly by railway. Beginning originally as a means of drawing traffic from the German Rhine ports to Hamburg and Bremen, the "seaport exceptional tariffs" were applied on an increasingly massive scale to divert traffic to the two German ports. Antwerp was the chief sufferer. That there was a great deal of weight in the incidence of these rates was revealed in the summer of 1940, when the Hamburg port authorities were considering the future of the port in the new Europe under German domination which seemed then to be coming into being; it was said that with Antwerp and Rotterdam virtually under German control, Hamburg would not be able to expect a continuation of the shelter which it had enjoyed so long against the competition of the Dutch and Belgian ports in central Europe, and it would have to seek new hinterlands in southeastern Europe. The conditions now prevailing in Europe place the future of all the competing ports in the melting pot. A postwar Swiss estimate put the frontier between the Hamburg–Bremen and Rotterdam–Antwerp hinterlands, in purely economic terms, uninfluenced by policy, as lying along a line between Hamm and Cheb (Eger) in Czechoslovakia.

In countries outside Europe the railways have frequently had a decisive influence in shaping the hinterlands of ports, and railway politics have been closely intermixed with port politics. The western prairies of Canada became part of the hinterland of Vancouver for wheat exports almost solely through a slight reduction of railway rates westward. In the United States, railway rates have long governed the attachment of all the ports from Boston to Galveston to the great interior lowland for the export of wheat and of other products. The railway differentials have been of decisive importance in securing a share of the outward movement for each of several ports; Kansas and Nebraska lie in the fringing hinterlands of Galveston, New Orleans, Baltimore, Philadelphia, New York, and even Boston. Each railway company had an interest in securing traffic for the port or ports which it served. The share of each in this export hinterland, therefore, was largely dependent upon the policy of the railway companies.

In Australia we find almost a separate railway system to each state and, there-

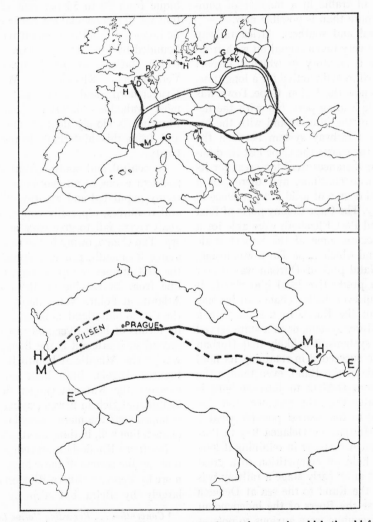

Fig. 2.—Port competition in Europe. The upper map shows the area in which the chief elements of competition are found. In the lower map *EE* indicates the line of equidistance between Hamburg and Trieste; the lines *HH* and *MM* represent the agreements of 1925 and 1927.

fore, to its chief port, owing largely to the existence of differences of gauge. More than this, owing to the exercise of control by each state over its railway system and its refusal to grant "taper" rates on goods carried beyond its rails by another state's rails, each state, port and railway system, forms an "island" and within each "island" a separate set of hinterlands tends to have its being. If there were cheaper through communication in the eastern states, there would probably arise a trend toward concentration of traffic in a number of commodities, more than is possible now.

In central and southern Africa railway politics are very much bound up with frontiers. It is a territory in which transport problems will remain active for a long time. In what is now the Union, Cape Town was for long the leading port, but with the development of the interior and with the beginning of a railway system between the Rand and the coasts the Cape lost its dominance. The distances were too great for its momentum to continue, and there was a pronounced degree of local independence in each colony. The Cape Colony ports of East London and Port Elizabeth were able for a while to secure some of the import trade for the Rand which Cape Town was losing. But the Natal port of Durban was nearer and had a productive local hinterland; it thus had an even better chance to become the port for the Rand. In a state with a unitary railway system, or in a state served by several systems, it is likely that Durban would have succeeded in retaining its hold on the trade of the Rand, even though the distance from Durban to Johannesburg is rather greater than the distance from Johannesburg to the nearest possible rival— Lourenço Marques on Delagoa Bay in Portuguese East Africa—or in retaining it long enough to hold off competition to a great extent. But at an early stage a railway was built from the Rand to the sea at Delagoa Bay because the Boers of the independent Transvaal republic were anxious to possess an outlet which would be free from British control. They built the line, therefore, and

Delagoa Bay at once became a powerful vested interest.

When, after the establishment of the Union, there arose in South Africa an acute need of native labor from the Portuguese colony, a concession to recruit this labor could only be obtained by a promise to maintain the share of the Portuguese port in the trade of the Rand. The Union undertakes, by the terms of the Mozambique Convention last renewed in 1928, "to secure to the port and railways of Mozambique from 50 to 55 per cent of the total tonnage of commercial sea-borne goods traffic imported into the 'competitive area' . . . bounded by lines drawn between the goods traffic stations serving Pretoria, Springs, Vereeniging, Klerksdorp, Welverdiend, Krugersdorp, and Pretoria."[4] Thus the most valuable hinterland of Lourenço Marques is closely defined, and traffic to and from this hinterland is regulated by treaty.

In central and south-central Africa the problem is one of an enormous hinterland, thinly populated and wealthy only in mineral resources, especially copper ores. Two great rivers fail to give easy access to the sea. The Congo, owing to the rapids not far above its mouth, provides opportunity for the first drainer or tap railway, the French line from Brazzaville on the river to the Atlantic at Pointe Noire, designed to drain the Congo hinterland as far as the Katanga by means of both river and rail links. The second such attempt is the Benguella Railway to the Atlantic at Lobito Bay, in Portuguese Angola. Both lines tap in some measure the Katanga copper district, far distant but rich in a well-paying traffic; it is hoped that the more immediate environs of each line will, in time, create more traffic.

Northern Rhodesia is served, to some extent, by the second of these lines, but much more by Beira; Southern Rhodesia is served largely by Beira but also by Lourenço

[4] *Convention . . . Regarding Native Labour from Mozambique, Railway Matters and Commercial Intercourse.* Treaty Series No. 9 (1930). Cmd. 3495 (London, 1930).

Marques and in some degree by the South African ports. From the map, these great territories appear to represent the fringes of several ill-defined hinterlands. Southern Rhodesia may one day achieve an outlet in British territory, at Walfisch Bay; a serious obstacle to the development of this route is the 500 miles of railway construction which would be necessary. The eastern part of the Belgian Congo is served by the East African port of Dar-es-Salaam.

Beira promises to become much the most important outlet for the Rhodesias. Two factors favor Beira, and they are both factors which cannot be deduced from a map showing railway and shipping routes. The first factor is that of railway policy, which adversely affects Lobito Bay. The copper-producing district of Northern Rhodesia is not simply a "watershed" in which the hinterlands of Lobito Bay and Beira overlap, for, as a result of agreements between the Rhodesia Railways and the four main copper-mining companies, the companies undertook to export copper and to import materials via the Rhodesia Railways (and, therefore, via Beira) and to take all fuel requirements from Wankie in Southern Rhodesia; in return, the railways reduced the copper rates to Beira and made certain reductions in coal rates.[5] Such rate arrangements as these frequently have far-reaching effects on port activities. Discussions at the Lisbon Conference (1949), of measures designed to improve transport facilities in southern Africa, showed a certain tendency to refrain from exploring railway rate policies.

The second factor which favors Beira in comparison with Lobito Bay is the greater attraction to shipping companies offered by the South and East African route. The west coast of Africa, south of the Congo estuary, is much more "lean" in its demands for shipping space, both inward and outward. It is not the hinterland of Lobito Bay which affects its fortunes so much as the hinterlands of many other ports.

[5] *The Rhodesia Railways Ltd.*, Report by Sir Harold Jowitt (London, 1946), p. 18.

RICHARD S. THOMAN

# FREE PORTS AND FOREIGN-TRADE ZONES
# A SUMMARY REVIEW

Regardless of location a free port, in its strictest sense, involves a plot of ground wherein merchandise is not subject to customs formalities and, at least theoretically, to customs jurisdiction. This plot of ground is under political authority of the host nation but is separated from customs territory by a fence, the gates of which are guarded by customs officials. Foreign merchandise brought into this zone may be stored and exchanged (the latter almost invariably on a wholesale basis), and may or may not be manipulated, exhibited, or manufactured (depending upon local regulations). In any case it may be re-exported without having been subject to tariffs of the host nation.

The foreign-trade zones of the United States differ from the free ports of northern Europe in name only. Our foreign-trade zones are essentially free ports, whether considered by legal foundation, by form of administration, or by functions performed.

### HISTORICAL DEVELOPMENT OF THE FREE PORT OR FOREIGN-TRADE ZONE

The foreign-trade zones of the United States and the free ports of Scandinavia have been modeled after forms in the once-free cities of Hamburg and Bremen. These, in turn, were indirect offshoots of earlier units that can be traced at least to classical civilizations centered upon the Mediterranean Sea. Traditionally, the device has been a means of facilitating international re-exports, and it was successful in this objective for over 2,000 years. As long as the world was divided into numerous, tiny political units of which each maintained its own customs barriers, certain of these units—particularly the ones blessed with favorable location—sought and benefited from international re-export commerce through the use of some form of free city or free port.

However, especially in the twentieth century, international commerce has been affected markedly by new trends in development of the world pattern of political and economic units. Such trends have been toward large individual nations and toward regional associations, whether political or economic, of the less fortunate political dependencies and smaller nations. In addition, some of these smaller nations have established a measure of economic self-reliance and independent trading capacity. To these trends has been added the reality of a Communist world and a free world that are engaged in political, economic, and ideological warfare along an Iron Curtain. These trends have mitigated free-port activities by reducing the need for international re-export commerce.[1]

### THE ROLE IN THE WORLD ECONOMY OF THE FREE PORT

The free port is found today in all continents but Australia. It necessarily functions in sharply differing segments of the political-economic systems described in the preceding paragraph; and for this reason a generalization concerning its present role cannot be made with fine precision. Ideally, each free port should be considered indi-

Reprinted from *Free Ports and Foreign-Trade Zones* (Cambridge, Md.: Cornell Maritime Press, 1956), pp. 159–64, by permission of the author and the publisher. (Copyright, 1956, by Cornell Maritime Press.)

[1] However, some free ports are temporarily benefitting as liaison portals through the Iron Curtain. Hong Kong is an excellent example.

vidually; but, since this is impossible in a summary, a rather coarse classification can be made as follows: (1) free ports of outlying areas, including (a) those at the foci of major transportation routes and (b) those developed for a particular need; and (2) free ports of highly industrialized, tariff-inclosed nations.

The free port in certain outlying areas gives promise of lasting service. Particularly the units at the foci of major oceanic routes, such as those in Hong Kong, Singapore, and Colon, should fulfil a need for the international re-export commerce for which the free port originally came into being. Single-purpose units which grant land-locked nations access to the sea, such as the free zones in Trieste, Thessalonica, or Beirut, also appear to be performing a fundamental service in easing international borderline tensions by providing to such nations a measure of control over an actual plot of ground at the oceanside.

## FREE PORTS OF HIGHLY INDUSTRIALIZED, TARIFF-INCLOSED NATIONS

This study has been concerned almost entirely with the second of the above categories as epitomized by the free ports in the German Federal Republic, Scandinavia, and the United States.

*German Federal Republic.*—Free ports of the German Federal Republic are found in Hamburg, Bremen, Bremerhaven, Cuxhaven, Emden, and Kiel. Of these, the active units are in the Elbe River seaport of Hamburg and in the Weser River seaports of Bremen and Bremerhaven, which, together with the Hamburg-owned portion of Cuxhaven, are remnants of former free cities that were forced into Bismarck's Customs Union of German States in 1888. The free port is stoutly championed within these one-time free cities that are strongly affected by a sense of re-export tradition. However, it appears to be encountering increasing opposition, particularly from certain inland interests, from authorities of the national government, and from local, normally non-partisan minds. This opposi-

tion is based principally upon the thesis that the Hansa cities are no longer engaged mainly in re-export trade but are almost wholly agents serving the host country—a thesis substantiated by numerical data covering the period 1928 to 1953, the only period for which such data are available. Throughout that period it was seldom that more than 20 per cent, and in 1953 less than 9 per cent, of all foreign merchandise placed in free-port warehouses and bonded warehouses of Germany and the subsequent German Federal Republic was re-exported. Although this decline has been partially due to the proximity of the Iron Curtain, which has tended to isolate Hamburg from much of its prewar hinterland, it has been partially due also to such a factor as the growth of independent shipping lines in Scandinavia, which was formerly dependent in large measure upon transshipment commerce from Hamburg.

Moreover, the bulk of this commerce is comprised of a very few high-duty commodities. In Hamburg, coffee and tobacco accounted for over 50 per cent, and some fifteen commodities for over 90 per cent, of all foreign merchandise placed in free-port warehouses in 1953.

Furthermore, the free ports of Hamburg (size: 3,898 acres), Bremen (396 acres), and Bremerhaven (about as large as Bremen) encompass vital deep-water sections and excellent facilities of their associated seaports. An inestimable portion of commerce coming into each of these is attracted to local facilities and not to the device itself.

Not only customs duties but also certain other taxes are not generally applied within free ports of the German Federal Republic. This is particularly true of the German turnover tax, which is currently responsible for over half the revenue to the national government. Such exemption is based upon the theoretical but only partially true concept that industries of the free ports are operating for purposes of re-export.

Manufacturing is found only in the free port of Hamburg, where the principal op-

erations are shipbuilding, petroleum-refin-
ing, and small metal industries. Theoretically, manufacturing plants and shops are
producing for re-export, but actually a sizable portion of their output now moves into
the German Federal Republic. This has
caused increasing domestic pressure for curtailment of free-port manufacturing, which
currently involves 85 firms and over 16,000
workers.

Administratively, the free port of Hamburg approaches the ideal concept of a free
port more effectively than do other examples of the device in northern Europe
and in the United States. This has been
accomplished by the creation of a single
office that, on the one hand, is responsible
for managing most operations inside the
free port and, on the other, is the chief customs office for the national government regarding most matters of customs procedure
that arise within the free port. This office,
the Hamburg Free Port Administration, is
a part of the executive branch of the state
of Hamburg. One agency has thus been
charged with some customs responsibility
to the national government and with managerial responsibility to the local government. Such an arrangement might well be
given careful examination by those who are
considering the establishment of successful
free ports elsewhere, for it provides a solution to one of the thorniest of free-port
operational problems—the division of authority between local and national governments.

The free ports of Bremen and Bremerhaven are generally similar to that of Hamburg except: (1) the actual areas and volume of free-port warehouse commerce are
much smaller than in Hamburg; (2) these
free ports do not enjoy the privilege of
manufacturing; and (3) the local administration does not have the degree of responsibility for intra–free-port customs procedures that is found in Hamburg.

The remaining free ports of the German
Federal Republic, located in Cuxhaven,
Emden, and Kiel, are comparatively ineffective. Still others that were established
in small seaports during the past half-cen-

tury have ceased to function. The only free
ports now active in the German Federal
Republic involve sizable core sections of
leading seaports.

*Denmark and Sweden.*—Scandinavian
free ports are located in Copenhagen,
Stockholm, Göteborg, and Malmö. The free
port in Copenhagen was initiated shortly
before the turn of this century, and those
in Sweden came into being during the immediate aftermath of the First World War.
All have been modeled after Hamburg and
Bremen but are different in concept from
the originals in that they were borrowed for
purely economic purposes and are viewed
by local administrators with less emotional
traditionalism. They are moderate in size
(72 to 208 acres) but are located in dynamic seaports. Manufacturing, although
limited, is found only in the Copenhagen
unit. All are enjoying a healthy volume of
commerce, and yet there is found in each
an attitude of skepticism on the part of
some administrators concerning the value
of the device to a total port traffic that is
comprised mainly of imports and exports.
The prevailing opinion of these administrators is that much of the free-port traffic is
attracted to the excellent deep-water quay-
side and modern storage facilities found
within free-port limits rather than to the
free-port device itself. In some cases,
bonded warehouse systems or similar alternatives are being given serious attention.

*United States.*—Seven foreign-trade zones
have been initiated in this country during
the past eighteeen years. These were located in New York, Mobile, New Orleans,
San Antonio, Los Angeles, San Francisco,
and Seattle. The largest, in New York, initially encompassed some 92 acres but has
subsequently been reduced in size by about
50 per cent. Most of the remainder were
either single warehouses or groups of warehouses, of which the New Orleans zone,
with about 20 acres, was the most extensive. The Mobile and San Antonio zones
have closed, and the Los Angeles zone has
announced its intention to close. Only those
in New York and New Orleans are operating at a financial profit.

Since the initiation of foreign-trade zones in this country, the commerce of bonded warehouses with which they are in competition has nearly doubled,[2] whereas that of every foreign-trade zone has been erratic and has not indicated a continuous upward trend on a year-by-year basis. In 1954 the value of all materials forwarded from the then active five foreign-trade zones of the United States amounted to 8.6 per cent of that forwarded from all bonded warehouses of this country.

### THE OUTLOOK FOR FREE PORTS AND FOREIGN-TRADE ZONES OF HIGHLY INDUSTRIALIZED, TARIFF-INCLOSED NATIONS

Free ports and foreign-trade zones of highly industrialized, tariff-inclosed nations must demonstrate that they can compete successfully with bonded warehouses or other alternative systems if they are to persevere. So far, they have not evidenced an ability to do this when (1) they have been placed in small seaports or airports, (2) they have been introduced as very small units in active seaports, or (3) they have been inserted into seaports, large or small, of which the commerce is not conducive to free-port operations. The only free ports of highly industrialized, tariff-inclosed nations that are yet strongly defended with justifiable reason are the large, dynamic units located in equally large, dynamic seaports such as Hamburg and Bremen. Even under similar conditions, however, bonded warehouse systems appear to be functioning successfully in such leading European seaports as Rotterdam, Amsterdam, Antwerp, and London. In addition, bonded warehouse systems can and do operate prosperously in smaller places.

The outlook for the foreign-trade zones of the United States does not appear to be too bright at this time. Such a status quo has resulted from our having adopted the device without a clear understanding of the

entire free-port movement. We could have benefited from closer examination of experience in northern Europe, particularly in Scandinavia. Most of the studies conducted prior to our foreign-trade zones legislation in 1934 were centered upon Hamburg and dealt primarily with descriptions of physical facilities instead of actual functions of European free ports. We did not give sufficient attention to Scandinavia, which had borrowed the device for purely economic purposes and which was, even twenty years ago, questioning its utility. In at least one instance we called upon Scandinavian advice: the Port Authority of Boston, considering the establishment of a foreign-trade zone during the early 1930's, financed a detailed first-hand study of possibilities there by the technical director of the Copenhagen Free Port Company, the administrative organ of the Copenhagen free port. The essence of this report is that the free port is obsolete in countries that have an effective system of bonded warehouses.

The results of the research for this book have indicated that the United States should not consider the establishment of any additional foreign-trade zones until the Great Lakes–St. Lawrence Seaway has become a reality and its traffic has stabilized. At that time, studies should be conducted concerning the over-all efficiency of the foreign-trade zone, as compared with our bonded warehouse system, in facilitating such commerce as would normally benefit by a free port in the one or two really major seaports then active. Such studies should be based on the assumption that the greater part of foreign merchandise stored in either the foreign-trade zone or the bonded warehouse system would be eventually imported into this country and that only a small percentage of such merchandise—probably not more than 15 per cent —would be re-exported. If the results of these studies favor continuation of the foreign-trade zone, such a zone should be planned on a scale sufficiently large that it has a valid chance for success. If the results are negative, steps should be taken toward repeal of our foreign-trade zones legislation.

[2] U.S. Bureau of the Census, *Statistical Abstract of the United States, 1955* (Washington: Government Printing Office, 1955), p. 899.

# COMMERCIAL STRUCTURE OF CITIES

The importance of the commercial areas of cities is far greater than the limited extent of such areas would indicate. In most cities and metropolitan areas the central business district is by far the most concentrated center of employment and is the major focus in the systems of intra-city and intercity transportation with which other types of land uses are closely related. Most of the central-place functions are localized in the central business districts. One group of functions, the retail, has been in recent years increasingly decentralized because of the availability of automobile transportation and the consequent decline of public mass transit. Nevertheless, the growth of outlying business centers has not significantly reduced the role of central business districts in most non-retail commercial functions, and in some aspects of retailing the older centers retain their dominance.

In the first article of this section the late Malcolm Proudfoot, a well-known investigator of the commercial structure of cities, examines the retail structure, using data obtained from the Census of Business of 1935. The article was a pioneering effort to describe the patterns of retail activity and land uses. In spite of the fact that it was written before the rise of the modern planned and integrated outlying shopping center based upon accessibility by automobile, most of the basic elements of the pattern which the article describes are still present. The article is here reproduced, not only for its historic interest as a landmark in the development of knowledge on the subject, but as a classic description of one of the most important elements in the urban pattern.

There follow two excerpts from a book on urban land use by a land economist, Richard Ratcliff, which describe and interpret the commercial patterns of cities in terms of the competition for sites and which relate the commercial elements of the pattern to other aspects of the physical and functional specialization of areas within cities.

As the major nucleus in most cities, the central business district has, in recent years, received much attention from land economists, sociologists, and others, as well as from urban geographers. The article by Murphy and Vance is one of the few comparative studies of elements in a number of cities and is indicative of the value of such comparative studies. One of three written on the subject by the same authors, this article deals with nine cities selected for comparative analysis. It is of particular interest because of its detailed discussion of the

393

methods by which criteria for assuring comparability of the areas was achieved.

The usual census statistics on population indicate only the nighttime or residential locations of population and are of little use in the study of patterns of daytime population or localization of employment within cities. Daytime population must be inferred from other sources. The article by Donald Foley, an urban sociologist, is a noteworthy example of the application of a special type of traffic study to problems of urban functional structure. It is important for its methodological as well as for its substantive content.

The final article in this section, by Homer Hoyt, describes and classifies the newer types of outlying shopping centers which have been developed in many urban areas within the past decade and which have produced important modifications of the city structure described by Proudfoot. Hoyt has been an economic consultant in the selection of sites and in the development of many of the largest and best known of the newer outlying shopping centers in the United States and Canada.

MALCOLM J. PROUDFOOT

# CITY RETAIL STRUCTURE

During the past decade there has been marked improvement in the scope and refinement of urban studies undertaken by geographers. However, little attention has been given to urban land used for retail purposes, either as to structure or function in relation to city life. This exposition seeks to classify and characterize the principal types of city retail structure. It is based on a detailed study of Chicago, Philadelphia, Cleveland, Atlanta, and Des Moines, and a reconnaissance study of Washington, New York, Baltimore, and Knoxville.

The principal cities of the United States, for the most part, possess five types of retail structure. These five types have been named: (1) the central business district; (2) the outlying business center; (3) the principal business thoroughfare; (4) the neighborhood business street; and (5) the isolated store cluster. These structural types are distinguished by class of commodities sold, special concentration or dispersion of outlets, and character of customer tributary areas.

The central business district represents the retail heart of each city (Fig. 1). Here, individually and collectively, retail stores do a greater volume of business per unit area than elsewhere within the city. This areal concentration is manifested by the use of multistoried buildings of which retail stores, for the most part, occupy choice street-level frontage, service establishments are concentrated into upper-story offices, and residential occupance is restricted to scattered hotels. Here retail occupance is characterized by large department stores,

Reprinted from *Economic Geography,* XIII (October, 1937), 425–28, by permission of Mrs. Malcolm Proudfoot and the editor. (Copyright, 1937, by Clark University, Worcester, Mass.)

numerous women's and men's clothing stores, furniture stores, shoe stores, jewelry stores, and similar outlets selling shopping goods. Added to these, though of subordinate importance, there are numerous drugstores, tobacco stores, restaurants, and other stores selling convenience goods.

The central business district draws customers from all parts of the city proper and from outlying suburbs and nearby incorporated towns. Many people, besides being customers, are likewise employed in the various commercial and service occupations which constitute the complex of human activity within this district. To serve this movement of purchasing and working population to and from residential areas, all modes of intra-city transportation are focused here. This district, therefore, experiences extreme traffic congestion during the workday and more particularly during the morning and late afternoon "rush hours." The personal inconvenience of this congestion, and the commutation cost in time and money all have favored the development of the outlying business center, catering to the shopping-goods wants of the outlying population.

The outlying business center represents, in miniature, the same type of retail structure characterizing the central business district. The center possesses a marked areal concentration where closely spaced retail stores do a volume of business exceeded only by those of the central district. Here, for the most part, are found shopping-goods outlets such as women's and men's clothing stores, furniture stores, shoe stores, jewelry stores, one or more large department stores, and an admixture of convenience-goods stores. Although individual outlying business centers do not draw customers from all parts of the city, they fre-

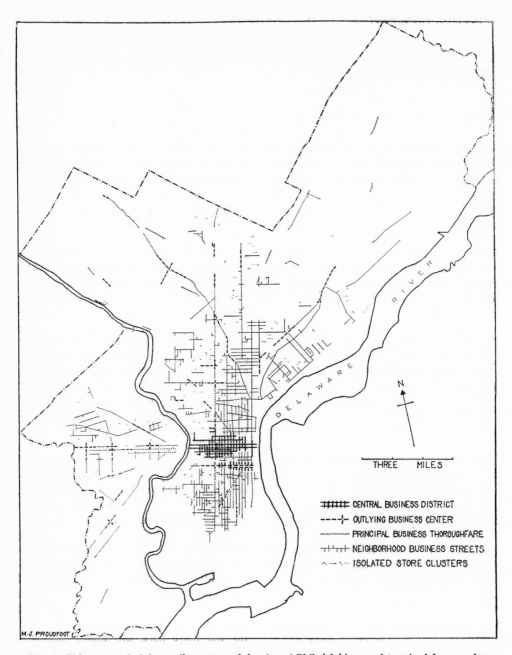

THREE    MILES

┼┼┼┼┼  CENTRAL BUSINESS DISTRICT
----┼-  OUTLYING BUSINESS CENTER
·········  PRINCIPAL BUSINESS THOROUGHFARE
┬┼┬┼┬┬  NEIGHBORHOOD BUSINESS STREETS
⌃⌃⌃  ISOLATED STORE CLUSTERS

M.J. PROUDFOOT

FIG. 1.—This portrayal of the retail structure of the city of Philadelphia was determined from analyses of block-frontage volume of sales. The statistical conclusions were checked in the field. Unfortunately, this field procedure did not provide a complete check because three years had elapsed since the last available census data.

quently attract them from long distances. Since these centers depend on customers drawn from wide areas, they all have developed at focal points of intra-city transportation where pedestrian traffic is increased by passengers of mass and vehicular conveyance.

The principal business thoroughfare is characterized by the co-existence of two related attributes. It is both a business street and a traffic artery. As a business street it possesses large, widely spaced shopping- and convenience-goods stores. As a traffic artery it carries a heavy density of mass and vehicular traffic. This dense traffic primarily results from attractive forces exerted on residential population by the central business district or some outlying business center. Although stores of this structural type cater to, and are primarily dependent on, customers derived from this dense traffic, their presence has little counter effect on the density of the traffic. Offering the special inducement of ample curbside parking space, these stores manage to thrive by attracting customers from a small fraction of the passengers of this intercommunity traffic.

The neighborhood business street is primarily of neighborhood significance. It draws customers, almost without exception, from easy walking distances. This structural type consists of more-or-less continuous rows of grocery stores, meat markets, fruit and vegetable stores, drugstores, and other convenience-goods outlets, interrupted by a minor admixture of shopping-goods stores. These streets extend through residential portions of the city and take the form of a more or less regular network following the principal mass transportation and trucking routes which are undesirable for residential purposes; are extensions to outlying business centers; or are isolated from other retail structures.

The isolated store cluster is the final, and individually the least significant, type of retail structure. These clusters usually comprise two or more complementary rather than competitive convenience-goods stores. Thus there may be a drugstore, a grocery store, a meat market, a fruit and vegetable store, a delicatessen, and possibly a small lunchroom grouped together at a minor street intersection. These stores usually supply a large portion of the immediate convenience-goods wants of residential families located within easy walking distance. Frequently these store clusters develop in sparsely settled fringes of the urban area, but in many instances they are found within densely populated residential areas, restricted, by the chance of occupance or by zoning regulations, to a scant block or even a city lot.

Although they do not constitute a distinct structural type, it is necessary for the sake of completeness, to mention that within any of the principal cities there are numerous instances of single isolated retail stores. Of these the corner drugstore, the grocery store, and the delicatessen are the most numerous, although individually they do a small volume of business. Other less numerous outlets, such as milk distributors, coal and lumber yards, mail-order houses, and the retail stores of mail-order houses, as a rule, do a large volume of business. It is the heterogeneous character of these stores, their relative unimportance when taken in aggregate, and, in many instances, their unusual function (such as a milk distributor serving a wide area with house-to-house wagon delivery) which support the conclusion that they should not be classified as a distinct structural type.

In summary, the retail structure of many principal cities shows a progressive change in type from: (1) the central business district with a marked concentration of shopping-goods stores which serve a substantial proportion of the commodity wants of every city family and which are located within that focal area of intra-city transportation collectively most accessible to the entire city population; (2) the outlying business center, which in miniature form is well-nigh identical to the central business district in concentration and in kind of outlet and in transportational accessibility and which is distinguished by having a more restricted customer tributary area and by the presence of a greater admixture of convenience-goods stores; (3) the principal business thoroughfare which is characterized by heavy mass and vehicular traffic between the central business district and outlying residential areas and by shopping- and convenience-goods stores catering to and principally dependent on customers derived from this heavy traffic; (4) the neighborhood business street which is characterized by dispersed rows of convenience-goods stores along residentially undesirable streets within densely settled residential areas, and by having a customer tributary area restricted, for the most part, to within easy walking distance; and (5) the isolated store cluster characterized by non-competitive convenience-goods stores grouped to serve the immediate wants of families living within an area restricted to easy walking distance.

# DEMAND FOR NON-RESIDENTIAL SPACE

This chapter deals with the forces of demand for urban land that arise in connection with commercial, industrial, recreational, and public service activities. While more area is normally devoted to residential than to non-residential land use, the industrial and commercial uses are of primary significance in the sense that out of them flows the economic lifeblood of the community and that the distributive functions of the retail uses are essential to urban life.

### DEMAND FOR RETAIL SPACE

We have seen that the demand for housing is based on future returns in the form of services and amenities. On the other hand, the demand for retail space is founded on anticipated income from its use to be received in the form of business profits. The geographic pattern of retail outlets grows out of a continuous competition in the real estate market between retail stores of various types, each seeking the most favorable location for its own operations. Our present consideration of the demand for retail space will be confined to a study of those factors which determine space requirements in terms of quantity and to a general treatment of the location specifications of some typical retail types.

#### QUANTITATIVE DEMAND FOR RETAIL SPACE

The portion of an urban area that is actually given over to retail uses is not an exact measure of the current need for retail space in that market. The high rate of mortality among retail stores suggests that not

all the demand that is gauged by land in use is economically sound, although it is effective demand entering into the price-determining processes of the market for retail space.

Retail land use has been analyzed on the basis of area, frontage, and number of stores. In a study covering sixteen self-contained cities, Harland Bartholomew found that about 5 per cent of the privately developed areas of the cities was used for commerce.[1] On the average, there were 63.7 feet of retail frontage for each 100 persons in the population.[2] A similar study in the metropolitan region around Chicago covering fifty-four cities and villages recommended a standard ratio of 50 feet per 100 persons on the basis of the findings.[3] In terms of number of stores, Bartholomew found an average of 2.29 stores per 100 persons.

There are a number of factors that influence the amount of space required by retail services and that account, at least in part, for the variations among cities in the relative extent of retail land use. Bartholomew found that the ratio of store frontage was highest in cities of 50,000 to 100,000 in population, that it was substantially lower in smaller cities, and that the ratio decreased from the high point as popula-

[1] Harland Bartholomew, *Urban Land Uses* ("Harvard City Planning Studies," Vol. IV [Cambridge, Mass.: Harvard University Press, 1932]), p. 72, Table 23. The National Housing Agency reported that commercial use as a percentage of all developed areas ranged from 2.8 per cent in small cities to 5.1 per cent for cities over 500,000 population.

[2] *Ibid.*, p. 76, Table 24.

[3] Chicago Regional Planning Association, *The Relation of Business Frontage to Population in the Region of Chicago*, December, 1936.

tion increased.[4] Size of city is in itself not a basic factor, so that we must look deeper for the possible explanations of intercity variations.

The density of population is one influence in determining the demand for retail space. Where population is concentrated, fewer stores are needed than where the pattern is more diffuse. Well-located outlets in a compact settlement will be convenient to a larger number of customers, and the retailing function can be conducted more efficiently. Another factor is the scope of the trading area of which the city is the focus. For small cities, the proximity of larger centers is a determining factor, since convenience to the larger stores and greater variety of goods available in nearby trading centers reduces the need for certain types of retail stores in the tributary town. In the study of the Chicago region it was found that the ratio of business frontage to population increased as the distance from Chicago increased.[5]

The social and economic characteristics of the population are determining factors, for the expenditure patterns of the people are conditioned by their incomes and their social values. In general, the higher the income level in a community, the greater the demand for retail services. A wider variety of goods and services is consumed, and for some items a greater quantity is consumed, providing support for more stores. A thrifty class of people require fewer retail services than do less frugal folk. The higher the proportion of women in the population, the greater the retail space required, in part because of the female propensity for shopping and the consequent demand for variety in goods offered at retail.

There are no known measures of the importance of the factors mentioned in the foregoing paragraphs, but the direction of the forces that they represent is clear.

Two factors that bring about changes in the demand for retail space within a community are changes in population and changes in the level of family incomes as a result of local or national economic fluctuations. Demand for retail space increases as population grows, but not in direct proportion. Population declines bring a lessening demand, but the readjustment tends to lag behind. It can be demonstrated that the demand for retail space fluctuates with changes in business conditions. The effect of unemployment and reduced incomes on demand for retail space was well illustrated during the last depression by the widespread vacancies in retail areas. For instance, in twenty major outlying business centers in Chicago in 1933, some 15 per cent of the business property was vacant.[6]

It has already been suggested that there is more land in retail use than is economically justifiable. This situation is the result of the misguided optimism of individuals coupled with the relative ease with which a retail business may be started. Overexploitation in retail lines is encouraged by irrational zoning; in many areas zoning ordinances have labeled far too much frontage as potential business property.[7] It has been erroneously assumed that all frontage on major thoroughfares would ultimately be converted to retail use. Property owners have insisted on liberal business zoning, and real estate developers have platted an excess of business lots on the outskirts of our cities because of the speculative premium in price that such lots bring.

In recent years, a more rational approach has been made by some real estate developers to the determination of the amount of space to be allocated to retail use in new subdivisions or in large-scale housing developments. The neighborhood unit is used for the basis of a series of estimates, starting with an estimate of the aggregate retail

---

[4] Bartholomew, *op. cit.*, p. 77.

[5] Chicago Regional Planning Association, *op. cit.*

[6] Malcolm J. Proudfoot, *The Major Outlying Business Centers of Chicago* (private ed.; Chicago: University of Chicago Libraries, 1938), p. 14, Table VI.

[7] Bartholomew, *op. cit.*, p. 71.

purchases of each type for all families who will ultimately inhabit the area. This approximation is based on the level of incomes and the predominant patterns of expenditure as determined by the social characteristics of the families. The next step is to estimate the likely proportioning of expenditures between neighborhood stores and downtown stores, or stores in important existing subcenters. Finally, having determined the approximate volume of sales required for the profitable and efficient operation of retail outlets of the various types, it is possible to estimate the number of stores of each type that can be supported by the area when it has been fully built up.[8]

QUALITY OF DEMAND FOR RETAIL SPACE

The qualitative aspects of a retail site are its location, size, and shape, and by far the most significant of these qualities is location. With some limitations, to be sure, the merchant can adjust his operations to fit the size and proportions of a storeroom, but he is relatively helpless to overcome the handicaps of an inappropriate location.

*Location.*—No two locations are identical, for each site is the focus of a unique combination of social and economic forces. Thus locations differ because of variations in the pattern of geographical relationships with existing land uses and population groups. The value of a site for retail purposes lies in these relationships, for each merchant prefers that situation which is most convenient to the group of potential customers that he seeks to serve. But since there are many retail outlets seeking to serve every group of consumers, it is apparent that all stores cannot be located

with equal convenience. Thus the various retailers enter into competition for preferential locations, and the ultimate retail pattern is determined by the market process of competitive bidding.

For each type of retail store, there is a more or less definite set of location specifications that define the qualities of sites of demonstrated appropriateness. Merchants attempt to secure locations that closely conform to these specifications, for experience has shown that there is small chance of a profitable operation in a location that differs substantially from the standard. We shall not have space to consider the site specifications for all retail types, but it will be illuminating to examine the considerations that guide a number of the large national chain-store organizations in selecting locations for their units.

*Site-selection practice among the chains.*[9] —The steps in the site-selection process are fundamentally similar for all chain organizations. It is customary for chains to follow consistent policies with respect to the acceptability of various zones within the retail structure for their units. Some companies accept only locations in the women's shopping district of the central business area. Other groups will consider any central location or will also consider sites in outlying string streets and nucleations. Some chains locate only in the suburbs. In conformity to the established policy, therefore, the number of potentially acceptable locations is limited to the generally appropriate parts of the retail structure of the city.

The next step is to test the acceptable areas on the basis of whether or not another store of the particular type can be supported. In many cases, a district is eliminated from further consideration when it is apparent that it is already adequately served by units of the same type. Frequently this decision requires a careful analysis

8 This general plan was used in estimating the retail space requirements for Buckingham, a large-scale rental housing development near Washington, D.C., which contains some 1,200 dwelling units. For a more detailed outline of this approach see Bauer and Stein, "Neighborhood Retail Centers," *Architectural Record*, LXXV (February, 1934), 174–87. See also the account of the development of a shopping center near Boston, *Architectural Forum*, June, 1947, p. 84.

9 Adapted from R. U. Ratcliff, *The Problem of Retail Site Selection* ("Michigan Business Studies," Vol. IX, No. 1 [Ann Arbor: University of Michigan School of Business Administration, 1939]).

of potential volume as outlined in the following paragraphs.

The evaluation of a particular site is based upon an estimate of the volume of business that can be done there. A budget for the proposed store is carefully worked out, and a maximum rental is established. The final steps are the negotiation of a lease on the most favorable terms within the limits established by the estimate of volume and the budget. In some cases, several sites may be under consideration, and estimates are worked out for each. In the majority of circumstances, however, only one site is under scrutiny, since it is not often that at any one time more than one or two leases are expiring in a particular district.

The estimating of potential volume in a location, as practiced by the more progressive chain organizations, is based upon a quantitative and qualitative analysis of pedestrian traffic, often supplemented by estimates of the volume of sales of existing competitors in the vicinity of the site. The sales volume of competitors can be closely approximated, according to chain-store officials, by the method of counting the number of persons entering the store during specified periods. The estimate of volume from these data requires facts on the proportion of actual to potential customers entering the store and the average size of purchase. These facts may be determined from the actual experience of the chain making the analysis.

Another method of estimating sales volume in competitors' outlets is by counting the number of clerks. In many lines, the annual volume of expected sales per clerk is a generally accepted figure and provides a basis for a dependable estimate of total annual store volume. A third method is based upon the number of feet of counter in the store.

The analysis of pedestrian traffic varies in practice from a simple count of women passing by the site at certain intervals during the day to a detailed qualitative analysis of the passers-by and the origin and destination of the component currents in the traffic stream. In some cases, this has been done by "shadowing" women shoppers from their homes, downtown, and home again.

The obvious objective of traffic analysis is to determine the number of potential customers who pass the site or who are in the vicinity and might be attracted to a store located there. Traffic counts taken at the site are of greatest value for articles subject to a large measure of impulse purchasing. For shopping goods, the count at various points in the vicinity is needed. For specialties, traffic counts have less meaning than in the other cases.

The first step in traffic analysis is to determine whom to count. Shopping outlets such as women's apparel stores have only to count adult women. Sometimes the count is of women carrying bundles. Cigar stores are interested in both men and women pedestrians, although men are by far the more important group. Men's haberdashery stores count both men and women, since almost half of their sales are to women.

Having determined which group to count, the next step is to decide at what time of day and on what days of the week the most significant counts may be made. For each type of goods, certain hours of the day mark the periods of the largest volume of sales. For women's apparel, the afternoon shopping crowds assay the highest. For articles purchased by men, such as hats, shoes, or sporting goods, the count of men at noon and after working hours is most indicative. The best practice calls for counts at frequent intervals and for short periods throughout the entire day. Greatest weight is given the counts for the most significant periods.

In each city, certain days of the week are, by local custom, the more important shopping days, particularly for women's shopping goods. The Scripps-Howard newspaper organization analyzed the buying preferences of housewives in sixteen cities.[10]

[10] Quoted in *Advertising and Selling,* XIII (August, 1938), 25.

Saturday proved to be the most generally favored day for downtown shopping, leading in preference in thirteen of the cities. Of the remaining days of the week, Monday, Wednesday, and Friday were the important shopping days, with wide variations in importance among the cities analyzed. Counts are taken on both the important and less important shopping days, with more weight given to the results on the best days.

As an aid in the qualitative analysis of pedestrian traffic, some organizations study the traffic stream in the district by counts at various points throughout the area and at transportation terminals. This procedure enables the analyst to chart the currents of traffic in the district with respect to origin and destination and to appraise more accurately the traffic passing any given site at various times of day.

Involved procedures of site analysis and estimation of potential sales volumes for prospective locations are of little avail if a suitable lease does not eventuate for one of the appropriate sites. For this reason, some chain real estate officers claim that site selection is 90 per cent negotiation. The site analysis will reveal the maximum rent that can be supported by a store in a particular location; but if the property owner cannot be induced to accept this figure or a lower one, all the scientific study is in vain. In some cases, as between two locations, that site which will produce the lower sales volume will be chosen because of a rental sufficiently lower to produce a greater net return.

All chains make some attempt to predict the future of the retail district and to foresee any shifts that may affect the traffic stream and the volume of sales at the site under consideration. In some cases, it is apparent that a district is well "anchored." The leading stores are under long leases with many years to run or own their own locations. The transportation system is permanently fixed, and no major changes in it are probable. The better residential areas show no signs of shifting.

Chains avoid districts that reveal any signs of decline. Where shifts in the retail structure are in progress and can be identified, an attempt is made to locate the unit advantageously in the path of the movement. In some cases, pioneering is done in growing outlying nucleations, and stores are installed in anticipation of a substantial development, even though it is known to be an unprofitable site at the time. Some organizations make a practice of leasing locations in growing areas well in advance of intended use. Such sites are subleased until such time as it is profitable to install a store.

There are a number of site characteristics that are regarded as detrimental to all retail outlets. For instance, proximity to undertaking establishments or to land uses that create objectionable odors or noises is avoided. Blocks that are unusually short, or where the shopping continuity is broken by banks, churches, or institutions, are not desirable. Buildings that are dark at night are not congenial neighbors for some types of outlets. Level terrain is preferred to a hillside. Some chains prefer the shady side of the street in summer or the sunny side in winter. Undue traffic congestion may be detrimental if it interferes with the shopping function. Dilapidated or unsightly structures are avoided as well as vacant storerooms. Where the two sides of the street are on different levels, the upper side is considered the better.

As an illustration of site specifications that have been established in a general way, there follow summaries of the site-selection practice of retail chains in a number of fields. These summaries are not inclusive, nor are all retail types considered.

VARIETY.—The great variety chains in America have established site specifications that are both simple and rigid. They insist on sites that are in the very center of women's shopping zones, where there is the maximum traffic count of women shoppers. In the larger cities, in subcenters that have matured to a point where a women's shopping zone exists, stores are located in the "hot spots" of such outlying nucleations. Although there are some exceptions, variety outlets are located in the popular-price shopping zone, in proximity to apparel shops, women's shoe stores, hat and hosiery shops, and department stores. The presence of competing variety outlets is not an important disadvantage in the central retail area. In fact, since women shop among the variety stores for many articles, it is often an advantage. However, in outlying locations, a careful study of the zone of patronage may be required to determine whether there is sufficient business available to support an additional variety outlet. The variety chain is reluctant to pioneer and insists on sites in retail areas that are well established and provided with the essential complement of women's shopping uses. Corner locations are considered more desirable than inside spots, but the advantage is not sufficient to warrant a substantial rental premium.

WOMEN'S DRESSES.—The chains in the field of dresses are mainly in the popular-price field. They are interested only in locations in the shopping zone for popular-price lines. Sites close to department stores, women's shoe stores, hat and hosiery shops, and variety chains are specified. Locations in outlying areas are considered only when the nucleations are well matured and contain other shops dealing in apparel or variety stores.

DRUGS.—The specifications for drugstore sites are perhaps more flexible than for almost any other retail use. The major consideration is convenience to large numbers of people. Consequently, sites near centers of activity that attract crowds of potential customers are in demand. In the central business district, traffic streams attractive to drugstores are found in the shopping area, in the office-building district, and in the vicinity of hotels, theaters, transportation terminals, and streetcar and bus stops. In the outlying shopping areas, favorable locations are found near the major intersections and among the shopping-goods outlets in the higher-grade nucleations. Neigh-

borhood locations are acceptable when at a convenient spot in a well-populated area or in the midst of an apartment-house district. Parking facilities are of some importance in neighborhood locations.

Corner locations for drugstores are not essential in districts of heavy pedestrian traffic but are highly desirable under any conditions. The advantage lies not primarily in the added window display space, but in the fact that the corners mark the point of convergence of two traffic streams, that they are frequently transfer points or stops for streetcar and bus lines, that they are meeting points for people, and that stores on corner locations are used as havens of warmth and comfort on wintry days. The conspicuousness of corner stores is advantageous, particularly in effecting institutional advertising for chains. Finally, the long-time association between drugstores and corner locations—witness the phrase "corner drugstore"—has led the public to expect to find drug outlets on corner sites. In general, competing drug outlets are not welcomed. However, the large drug chains, bolstered by institutional advertising or pursuing a cut-rate policy, can often overcome the handicap of a nearby competitor. Districts favored with heavy pedestrian traffic can often support a number of drugstores in close proximity, but competition is avoided when possible.

RESTAURANTS.—Restaurants and lunchrooms vary widely in the quality of the food and service offered and in the price level of their menus. In general, they try to locate conveniently at points where the economic group whom they serve is located at mealtimes. One large national restaurant chain serving quality food at moderate prices seeks the proximity of office buildings, theaters, hotels, railway depots, colleges, apartment areas, and shopping districts. The downtown area is spotted with eating places ranging from the drugstore lunch counter to the hotel roof garden. Some are located to serve the shopping crowds at midday; others are convenient to the office buildings. In the theater district, the higher-priced restaurants are situated to glean patronage from pleasure-bound crowds. In the wholesale and light industrial area are the cheaper spots—the "hot dog" stands, the foreign cafés, the "greasy-spoon joints." Selection of restaurant sites is based on analysis of pedestrian traffic and neighboring occupancies to provide an estimate of potential customers at mealtimes and at off-peak hours. Competition in the same price range is avoided. In the financial district in New York, it has proved profitable to operate certain restaurants only at noon.

HABERDASHERY.—Included in this category are outlets dealing in men's accessories, such as shirt shops and hat shops. It has been the tendency for these outlets to seek sites of predominantly male pedestrian traffic outside of women's shopping zones, and on corners. Men's shoe stores, men's clothing stores, sporting-goods stores, restaurants, and cigar stores are considered good neighbors. Frequently favorable locations are found in commercial hotel districts and office-building areas. The growing tendency for men's wear to be purchased by women has increased the importance to haberdashery stores of proximity to women's zones. One large shirt distributor reports that 50 per cent of sales are made to women. For this reason, this organization seeks locations where there is an even mixture of men and women pedestrians. Another chain in this field is reported to prefer sites in the midst of the women's shopping zone.

SHOES.—Shoe stores differ in character and hence in site specifications. Women's shoe outlets require sites within the women's shopping zone and seek the proximity of apparel shops, department stores, and variety chains. Outlets dealing exclusively in men's shoes seek locations on the outskirts of the shopping zone, in the vicinity of men's furnishings stores, haberdasheries, sporting-goods shops, or in office-building areas where the male pedestrian count is high. Family shoe chains, which deal in popular-priced footwear, prefer the proximity of the shopping zone, since two-thirds of their customers are women. However, they normally seek sites at the edge of the zone, since they cannot compete successfully with the women's apparel shops for the choicer locations. Popular-price lines frequently find suitable locations in outlying nucleations that are well developed. The higher-priced nationally advertised lines generally seek only central locations. In all lines, proximity to competitors is not avoided. Corner locations are desirable, but not at more than moderate rent differentials.

GROCERIES.—Like the drugstore, the grocery store is appropriate in a wide variety of sites. The great food chains locate their units at sites varying from the isolated neighborhood location to the central business district spot, although there are few instances of this latter location. In the main, convenience to residential districts is the prime consideration. Since but a relatively small zone of patronage is required for the neighborhood unit, locations on major streets in residential districts are sought, provided competitors' stores are not too numerous. Locations in nucleations even in their early stages of development are appropriate. On string streets, spots near important streetcar and bus stops or wherever well-populated residential districts are adjacent are favorable sites. For the smaller outlets, dependence is placed on potential customers within walking distance.

Recently greater emphasis has been placed on larger units and the supermarket type of outlet. The result has been to close many of the smaller stores and to seek locations on major traffic arteries that are central to a larger zone of patronage. Parking facilities are important and in many cases are provided as part of the service. Traffic congestion is avoided with the result that suburban locations are sought. In smaller towns, supermarkets can often be located centrally, though outside of the central business district, and thus draw from the entire community.

Where there exists sufficient business to support more than one grocery, the competing outlets tend to seek one another's company. Some chains adopt a policy of installing stores next to successful competing units. Corner locations are desirable but not necessary. In neighborhood locations they are sought, but in nucleations it is not ordinarily possible for groceries to compete with a number of other uses of higher rent-paying ability for corner locations.

*Shape of parcel.*—The dimensions of the space demanded by various retail types is in part dependent on the nature of the product offered for sale. For the majority of small retail businesses, the predominant demand is for ground-floor units of 15- to 25-foot frontage, a depth of from 40 to 125 feet, storage space in the basement, and a rear door on an alley for deliveries. The present trend is toward larger units, particularly in the apparel line. The advantages include more attractive interior display and the opportunity for carrying an increasing variety of secondary lines of merchandise. Department stores require large areas with ample display windows along the street. They prefer corner locations and usually require multistoried buildings. Variety stores and furniture stores need relatively large inside floor areas and sometimes spread over more than one floor. Other types that seek storerooms larger than the standard 15- to 20-foot frontage are auto salesrooms, banks, grocery supermarkets, the larger restaurants, theaters, and gasoline stations. For shopping-goods outlets, frontage for window displays is more important than for stores dealing in convenience or specialty goods.

There are a few examples of retail types that are not always on the street level. For instance, merchant tailors and an occasional jeweler may be found on second floors in retail districts, and barbershops or shoe-repair shops sometimes locate in basement rooms.

## DEMAND FOR OFFICE SPACE

Among those economic functions which are centered in urban areas, there are a number of business activities that require office space. With few exceptions, this type of space is found in and about commercial areas, in office buildings, and on upper floors above street-level retail uses. Managerial activities of co-ordination and control such as those conducted by the executive branch of a corporation require office space. Offices are used as the headquarters for selling operations; in some instances as the gathering place for a crew of salesmen, as in the case of a life insurance sales agency; and again, as a sales office to which customers may come or telephone, as in those types of marketing in which customers order from samples or on the basis of specifications. Of course, many sales offices, such as those dealing in industrial equipment, provide space for the performance of both functions. A third general type of activity utilizing office space is the performance of business, professional, and personal services. This class includes the services of accountants and lawyers, doctors, and fortune-tellers.

The ratio of office-space requirements to population varies among cities by virtue of the differences in economic character. Small towns that are primarily trading centers require relatively little office space save for personal services and a few lawyers and real estate brokers. Communities that are predominantly industrial likewise exhibit a low office-space ratio. In such areas the managerial functions are generally performed in office facilities connected with the plants. The greatest demand for offices appears in cities that are financial centers or distribution centers. In financial centers are found the offices of investment bankers, security exchanges, security brokers, international bankers, factors, and the myriad professionals who offer business services— accountants, lawyers, engineering firms, investment analysts. Here also are corporate headquarters of large firms to whom banking connections and close contacts with other corporations are important. In cities that are centers of distribution, office space is required by sales offices, transportation companies, purchasing agents, credit agencies, and financial agencies concerned with marketing operations.

There are some cities in which the predominating activity is of a nature that requires unusual office facilities. For instance, in Hartford, Connecticut, are located the home offices of a number of casualty insurance companies and in Washington, D.C., the numberless agencies of the federal government have absorbed acres of floor space in government buildings in addition to a great deal of space in private office buildings. In fact, at times, the pressure for space has forced the conversion of a number of hotels and apartment houses into office buildings. Several large mansions have been taken over for government use and a large auditorium, stage and all, has been packed with desks and files. On the other hand, resort cities like Atlantic City or Miami require relatively little office space for use in connection with their primary industry.

It is not to be expected that all population growth will be accompanied by a proportionate increase in the demand for offices. Such increases come only with the expansion of the office types of activity. On the other hand, the economic maturing of a community may create additional demands for office space that are proportionately greater than population increases. A situation of this kind might arise after a period of rapid industrial expansion during which the establishment of service activities did not keep pace with the tide of immigration. In time, the increased demand for various services leads to the establishment of additional service facilities until a well-rounded assortment is made available.

The aggregate demand for office space fluctuates in response to general economic conditions. In time of depression, business failures reduce the number of enterprises requiring space, branch offices are closed,

office workers are laid off, and the curtailment of space requirements is widespread. Returning prosperity reverses the process. In Table 1 the data for the years from 1930 to 1940, a period when the supply of office space remained virtually unchanged, illustrate the effect of business decline and recovery.

The precise nature of the location is not so important in the selection of offices as in the selection of retail space. This statement applies more truly to some types of business than to others, but in general the differentials between optional locations within the commercial area are narrower for offices

TABLE 1

OFFICE-BUILDING VACANCY*

| Year | Per Cent Vacant | Year | Per Cent Vacant |
|------|------|------|------|
| 1925 | 8.0 | 1933 | 26.9 |
| 1926 | 8.5 | 1934 | 27.4 |
| 1927 | 9.9 | 1935 | 26.0 |
| 1928 | 11.9 | 1936 | 22.7 |
| 1929 | 11.8 | 1937 | 19.1 |
| 1930 | 12.4 | 1938 | 18.1 |
| 1931 | 17.3 | 1939 | 17.8 |
| 1932 | 22.4 | 1940 | 17.0 |

* *Real Estate Analyst*, June 25, 1940.

than for retail stores. On the other hand, the physical characteristics of the space and the services provided by the landlord are more important. Office-space buyers look to the attractiveness of the building, the quality of elevator service, the layout of space as it affects efficient utilization for their purposes, natural light and ventilation, and the artificial lighting. For some types of business, certain street addresses or building names possess a prestige value.

While somewhat less importance is attached to location by office-users than by merchants, this factor can by no means be ignored. Convenience is an important consideration, be it convenience for customers or for employees. Sales or service offices to which customers must come seek locations that are as accessible as possible to the groups that they serve. Offices that are to serve consumers coming from all parts of the city should be situated near the focal point of transportation facilities, although the precise location is not so important. Where the customer group is concentrated in one section of the community, in the downtown business area, for example, the maximum of convenience is more desirable. In general, the greater the distance traveled by customers, the greater the latitude in selecting a location. People who come several miles do not resent the necessity for going an extra block or two off the beaten path to reach their destination nearly so much as persons coming from close by resent the need for going around the corner.

Another consideration in selecting office space is the convenience of employees in getting to and from work. This factor gives an advantage to situations in the central business area, but, in cases where convenience to customers need not be considered, other areas may serve nearly as well.

Organizations that perform management functions prefer locations that are central to the activities that are being controlled or co-ordinated. Thus it is to the advantage of the central office of a local retail chain to be situated at a point most convenient to the greatest number of its units. Of course, other considerations may control, such as the advantage of convenience to banking services, accounting firms, selling agents, and other organizations that do business with the firm.

In some cases, businesses of like nature are found grouped for the purposes of facilitating interfirm communications or transactions. Such groupings often serve potential customers by facilitating shopping among the agencies. Again, the grouping may simply be the outgrowth of the attempts of the individual firms to locate at a point most convenient to their clienteles. Finally, some office buildings provide special facilities and services for one type of occupant. Thus doctors and dentists are often found in concentrations. Other factors that lead to medical groupings are the practice of referring patients from one specialist to another and the prestige that attaches to a location in a building in which prominent members of the profession are practicing.

DEMAND FOR WHOLESALE SPACE

Within our complicated mechanism for the distribution of goods, certain forces are at work that are having the effect of reducing the proportion of the urban area devoted to the wholesale district. In general it may be said that channels of distribution are shifting in such a way as to reduce the importance of wholesalers. Those functions in which the wholesaler specializes are being taken over by manufacturers and by retailers or groups of retailers. One of the underlying factors in these changes is the increasing standardization of commodities. The widespread use of grading and branding supported by national advertising facilitates buying from samples and catalogue descriptions and encourages direct selling to retailers by manufacturers. Other devices that are short-circuiting the wholesaler are selling through manufacturers' agents, public warehousing, wagon distribution, and group buying by retailers. Finally, many chain-store organizations are of sufficient size to assume all the wholesale functions. Thus, not only is a shrinkage occurring to the aggregate space required for the performance of wholesale activities in general, but also there is a geographical diffusion of the locus of these activities into the retail and industrial areas.[11]

The decline of the wholesaler has not by any means led to his extinction. Table 2 presents data on the changes in 1929, 1935, and 1939 in the number of wholesalers in leading lines. It is apparent that the effect upon the wholesale function of shifts in marketing channels has varied among the several lines of merchandise.

[11] For more complete discussions of trends in wholesaling see Beckman and Engle, *Wholesaling* (New York: Ronald Press Co., 1937), chap. 27; and Edmund P. Learned, *Problems in Marketing* (New York: McGraw-Hill Book Co., 1936), Marshall Field case.

Our next step is to consider the general location requirements of wholesalers. Convenience to transportation facilities is important. Railway track service is highly desirable where bulky and heavy goods are to be handled or where the volume of goods is so large that carload lots are dealt in. Where smaller volumes of goods are characteristic and where the items are compact and easily handled, the availability of truck transportation reduces the importance of trackage. The proximity of railway stations is advantageous not only for receiving and shipping goods but also for the convenience of buyers. For some types of business, ready access to public storage facilities is required. Another consideration is convenience to local sources of supply.

In general, wholesalers prefer to locate as closely as possible to the group that they serve. In the marketing of style goods, convenience is of particular importance because of the frequency of contacts with the retailer. For other products considerable storage space is required because of the bulk of the commodity, the great variety of items stocked, or the fact that buyers insist on inspecting the specific goods that they purchase. In such cases, the amount of space required may preclude a central location. Wholesalers who sell from catalogues, by mail, by telephone, or through an outside sales force do not require sites near their customers. Dealers with a national market best serve visiting buyers at points convenient to railroad terminals, hotels, and amusement areas.

The advantage of a location near competitors varies with the scope of the market and the nature of the commodity. In general, the proximity of dealers in the same line is desirable where the market to be served is regional or national, where shopping, comparison, and selection are important steps in the buying process, and where the function of price establishment is performed within the market formed by a cluster of wholesalers. Another advantage of the proximity of competitors is the opportunity such location affords for filling out orders when shortages occur in certain items.

TABLE 2

NUMBER OF WHOLESALERS BY TYPE OF BUSINESS, 1929, 1935, AND 1939*

| TYPE OF BUSINESS | NUMBER OF ESTABLISHMENTS | | |
|---|---|---|---|
| | 1929 | 1935 | 1939 |
| Drugs.......... | 488 | 274 | 297 |
| Dry goods, general line.......... | 848 | 303 | 222 |
| Electrical goods... | 2,182 | 2,437 | 3,072 |
| Hardware, full line | 953 | 630 | 772 |
| Grocery......... | 4,776 | 3,210 | 3,942 |

* U.S. Census of Distribution, 1929 and 1935; U.S. Census of Wholesale Trade, 1939.

Wholesalers find it less advantageous to seek one another's company when their market is local or covers only a part of the city, when the product is bulky, with storage and selling associated, where buyers do not visit the market, and when comparison is not important.[12]

[12] For the study on which this discussion of the clustering of wholesalers is based see Committee on Regional Plan of New York and Its Environs, *Regional Survey of New York and Its Environs, 1B, Clothing and Textile Industries, Wholesale Markets and Retail, Shopping and Financial Districts* (New York, 1928), pp. 65–69.

RICHARD U. RATCLIFF

## INTERNAL ARRANGEMENT OF LAND USES

The land-use pattern of any urban area is a reflection not of the immediate and current space requirements of the community but rather of the cumulative needs over a period of years. It is not the same pattern as might be proposed if the land were all vacant and a new community of the same size and character were being planned. The fixity of the investment of land improvements has already been cited as responsible for the lag in adjusting the physical aspects of the community to new social and economic needs. Thus in most of the cities of the land, the skeleton of the street and utility systems is a relic of earlier times, and a majority of the buildings are representative of generations past. Cities that have grown slowly and steadily are more likely to be adjusted physically to present needs than areas where expansion and internal shifts have been explosive and sporadic.

Early land economists and human ecologists were inclined to describe the distribution of urban land uses in terms of concentric circles of relatively homogeneous utilization, with a core of financial and retail uses at the center. Outside this core was to be found the wholesale and light manufacturing zone, interspersed and surrounded by the homes of the lowest income groups.

Reprinted from *Urban Land Economics* (New York: McGraw-Hill Book Co., 1949), pp. 386–97, by permission of the author and the publisher. (Copyright, 1949, by McGraw-Hill Book Co., Inc., This section owes a special debt to Homer Hoyt, who has been a leader in developing description and theory in the field of city growth and structure and who has summarized his work so effectively in the Federal Housing Administration publication, *The Structure and Growth of Residential Neighborhoods in American Cities* (Washington, D.C.: Government Printing Office, 1939), and in his earlier *One Hundred Years of Land Values in Chicago* (Chicago: University of Chicago Press, 1933).

This description places heavy manufacturing in the next zone, with a tendency to be grouped about the transportation facilities that lead to the outside world. The outer belts of residential land use serve progressively higher income groups as the distance from the center increases. It is apparent that there is a substantial basis of fact and theory to support this concentric-circle conception of urban agglomeration. But even with full recognition of the exceptions that are to be found in individual cities by reason of accident or topography, there are other generalizations of city structure, which in some cases tend to invalidate the circular conception and which, in any event, must be incorporated into any generalized description of urban land-use structure. A separate examination of each of the major functional areas will provide a basis for a modification of some of the earlier concepts of city structure.

### RETAIL STRUCTURE

With very few exceptions, the central retail shopping district is found at the very convergence of all transportation and traffic channels. This spot is the center of the city in terms of being most convenient to the greatest number of people, although it may not be the geographical center of the built-up area. It is the place associated with the highest land values, tall buildings, high-density land use, and the greatest concentrations of people during daylight hours. In only the larger cities is there a sufficient specialization of land use to result in a separation of the retail and financial districts. Where such is the case, the grouping of financial functions is found close to, but at one side of, the central shopping zone. A more detailed examination of the retail pattern is necessary, since a large share of the retail business in many cities is done outside the central district. The focal point of every city is the central shopping area, familiarly termed the "100 per cent district." Here are the great department stores, the incarnadine variety chains, the smart apparel shops, interlarded with restaurants, drugstores, and specialty stores that serve the shopping crowds drawn into the district. This is the area that, by virtue of the ecological organization of the city and the convergence of transportation lines, is the spot most accessible to the greatest number of consumers. Crowding and interpenetrating the area of most intensive retail activity are the lesser retail uses—popular-price department stores, shops that sell men's wear, furniture, pianos, family shoes, sporting goods, and radios, and popular-price restaurants. In one sector there may be a scattering of theaters and at another point the financial and office-building district. As the central business area merges into the wholesale and light-manufacturing district or into the slum and rooming-house area, there appears the lowest grade of central business uses—pawnshop, food store, pool hall and beer garden, burlesque house, automotive supply shop, shoe repairer, cheap photographer, and cheap restaurant. In the direction of the better residential areas, the retail area tapers off in specialty shops, food stores, restaurants, giftshops, small men's and women's apparel stores, and automobile showrooms.

It is a common misconception that the majority of retail trade is done in the central district. Two authoritative studies of retail trade, one covering Baltimore in 1929,[1] and the other Philadelphia in 1935,[2] reveal the relative importance of

[1] I. K. Rolph, *The Location Structure of Retail Trade* (U.S. Bureau of Foreign and Domestic Commerce, "Domestic Commerce Series," No. 80).

[2] U.S. Department of Commerce, *Intra-city Business Census Statistics for Philadelphia, Pennsylvania*, prepared under the supervision of Malcolm J. Proudfoot, Research Geographer (Washington, D.C.: Bureau of the Census, May, 1937), p. 25.

the central area (see Table 1). In Baltimore, the central shopping district contained 6.1 per cent of the city's stores and accounted for 28.1 per cent of the total retail business. In Philadelphia, the corresponding ratios were 9.2 per cent and 37.4 per cent. In only two retail classifications did the central district account for more than 40 per cent of the city sales—the general-merchandise group, with 71.5 per cent, and the apparel group, with 63.2 per cent. In three other groups, the central area

TABLE 1

Per Cent of Total Sales and Total Sales Falling in Central Business District Philadelphia, 1935*

| Business Group | Per Cent of Stores | Per Cent of Sales |
|---|---|---|
| All groups.............. | 9.2 | 37.4 |
| Food stores............. | 2.5 | 5.7 |
| Automotive group........ | 5.0 | 9.5 |
| Filling stations.......... | 1.8 | 2.2 |
| General-merchandise group | 4.9 | 71.5 |
| Apparel group........... | 22.1 | 63.2 |
| Furniture-household group. | 18.0 | 34.9 |
| Lumber-building-hardware group................ | 7.3 | 15.3 |
| Restaurant group......... | 14.6 | 37.4 |
| Drugstores.............. | 5.7 | 25.2 |
| Other retail stores........ | 17.6 | 37.0 |

* *Intra-city Business Census Statistics for Philadelphia, Pennsylvania* (see n. 2).

accounted for roughly one-third of all sales —the furniture-household group, the restaurant group, and the unclassified group. Twenty-five per cent of all drugstore sales, 15 per cent of the sales of the lumber-building-hardware group, and less than 10 per cent for the food stores, automotive group, and filling stations were made in the central area.

The pattern of the outlying retail structure consists of combinations and variations of two basic conformations. The one phenomenon is the retail use of property abutting a traffic artery, stretching out along its length, and rarely sprouting off down intersecting streets. This form is variously called a "string-street development," a "business thoroughfare," or "business street." The nature of the uses comprising this conformation depends upon the extent to which the street is a main automobile artery and the degree to which it is the core of a residential area. The use of the street as a traffic artery attracts retail shops serving the transients—filling stations, accessory shops, automobile showrooms, quick lunches and refreshment stands, food market, and fruit stands. The proximity of residential districts encourages convenience-type outlets —drugstores, grocery stores, laundry and cleaning branches, hardware stores, delicatessens, and pool halls. Since there are infinite variations in the relative importance of major streets as arteries and as the cores of residential districts, the nature of string-street retail development cannot be strictly defined.

The other basic conformation of the outlying retail structure is the nucleation, a clustering of retail uses, which in the higher forms tends to assume a stuctural unity. This form typically appears at the more important intersections and creates a pyramiding of land values to a peak adjacent to the intersection. The nucleation may vary in nature, extent, and intensity of land use from the neighborhood grocery-drugstore combination to a major retail subcenter providing on a reduced scale all the services of the central business district. Frequently, nucleations appear as peaks of development in a string street, and the boundary between the string street and the nucleation is a matter of arbitrary definition. In most cases, the nucleation is concentrated on the primary street, although it frequently sends off short spurs down the major crossstreet. The junction of two string-street developments is usually the locus of a nucleation. The numerous isolated grocery stores and drugstores that spot residential areas are of the same nature as the nucleations proper and often constitute the original germ that develops into a nucleation as the tributary residential area matures.

Attempts have been made to identify and define subclassifications of these two

basic conformations, the string street and the nucleation, which are encountered in the outlying retail structure. Imperfect as these classifications are, they prove useful in providing a rough measure of the relative importance, in the retail trade of the city, of these areas as defined and in characterizing the services found there.

In his study of the retail trade of Philadelphia, Proudfoot identifies the more intensively developed nucleations as "outlying business centers":

Here, for the most part, are found shopping-goods outlets such as women's and men's clothing stores, furniture stores, shoe stores, jewelry stores, one or more large department stores, and an admixture of convenience-goods stores. Although individual outlying business centers do not draw customers from all parts of the city, they frequently attract them from long distances. Since these centers depend on customers drawn from wide areas, they all have developed at focal points of intracity transportation where pedestrian traffic is increased by passengers of mass and vehicular conveyance.[3]

The lower-grade nucleations are termed "isolated store clusters":

These clusters usually comprise two or more complementary rather than competitive convenience-goods stores. Thus there may be a drugstore, a grocery store, a meat market, a fruit and vegetable store, a delicatessen, and possibly a small lunchroom grouped together at a minor street intersection. These stores usually supply a large portion of the immediate convenience-goods wants of residential families located within an easy walking distance. Frequently these store clusters develop in sparsely settled fringes of the urban area, but in many instances they are found within densely populated residential areas, restricted, by the chance of occupance or by zoning regulations, to a scant block or even a city lot.[4]

String-street developments are divided into "principal business thoroughfares," and "neighborhood business streets." With respect to these two classifications,

It is both a business street and a traffic artery. As a business street it possesses large, widely

3 *Ibid.*, p. 3.                     4 *Ibid.*, p. 4.

spaced shopping and convenience-goods stores. As a traffic artery it carries a heavy density of mass and vehicular traffic. This dense traffic primarily results from attractive forces exerted on residential population by the central business district or by some outlying business center. Although stores of this structural type cater to, and are primarily dependent on, customers derived from this dense traffic, their presence has little counter effect on the density of this traffic. Offering the special inducement of ample curbside parking space, these stores manage to thrive by attracting customers from a small fraction of the passengers of this intercommunity traffic.

The neighborhood business street is primarily of neighborhood significance. It draws customers, almost without exception, from within easy walking distances. This structural type consists of more or less continuous rows of grocery stores, meat markets, fruit and vegetable stores, drugstores, and other convenience-goods outlets, interrupted by a minor admixture of shopping-goods stores. These streets extend throughout the residential portions of the city. They either take the form of a more or less regular network following the principal mass transportation and trucking routes, which are undesirable for residential purposes, are extensions to outlying business centers, or are isolated from other retail structures.[5]

In the statistical analysis of retail sales for Philadelphia, the data for outlying stores were grouped into three classifications—outlying business centers, principal business thoroughfares, and community business areas, which include isolated store clusters, neighborhood business streets, and single isolated store clusters, neighborhood business streets, and single isolated retail stores.

Table 2 shows, for each of the types of retail business, what percentages of the total for the city were accounted for in outlying business centers.

More than one-third of the city's purchases in the automotive and furniture-household groups are made in outlying business centers. With the exceptions of the filling-station and general merchandise

groups, which run lower, there is a high degree of consistency in the percentages for the other groups, ranging from 19 per cent to 27 per cent, with a clustering around 20 per cent.

An examination of the character of trade in the individual centers points to a marked diversity.

For example, there are: four centers with over 50 per cent of their individual business derived from sales in the food group . . . ; three other centers have from 50 to 70 per cent of their sales volume accounted for by the auto-

TABLE 2

PER CENT OF TOTAL STORES AND TOTAL SALES
FALLING IN OUTLYING BUSINESS CENTERS
PHILADELPHIA, 1935*

| Business Group | Per Cent of Stores | Per Cent of Sales |
|---|---|---|
| All groups.............. | 18.6 | 19.2 |
| Food stores............. | 13.3 | 22.0 |
| Automotive group........ | 17.5 | 34.8 |
| Filling stations.......... | 8.1 | 10.8 |
| General-merchandise group | 28.5 | 6.7 |
| Apparel group........... | 39.2 | 26.9 |
| Furniture-household group. | 35.7 | 38.6 |
| Lumber-building-hardware group................. | 21.6 | 20.9 |
| Restaurant group......... | 15.5 | 19.4 |
| Drugstores.............. | 14.1 | 20.8 |
| Other retail stores........ | 19.6 | 19.3 |

*\* Intra-city Business Census Statistics for Philadelphia, Pennsylvania.*

motive group . . . ; three centers derived a substantial proportion of their business from sales in the general merchandise group . . . or in the apparel group . . . ; several other centers are as well represented in the furniture group . . . ; and restaurants are outstandingly represented in five centers. In contrast, there is little concentration in the case of any individual center in such enterprises as filling stations and drug stores; and one-third of the centers, those not listed above, show little deviation from the average condition.[6]

These facts suggest that there is a diversity in the character of the tributary areas

[5] *Ibid.*

[6] *Ibid.*, p. 11.

supporting these nucleations and emphasizes the difficulties in constructing an adequate qualitative classification of retail
groupings.

The principal business thoroughfares of
Philadelphia are generally dominated by
either the food or the automotive groups.

Six thoroughfares are outstandingly dominated by stores of the food groups . . . ; and four
are dominated by automotive establishments.
. . . The dominance of these two kinds of business, as shown by the sales volume of these
thoroughfares, amounts to from 50 to 80 per

TABLE 3

PER CENT OF TOTAL STORES AND TOTAL SALES
FALLING IN PRINCIPAL BUSINESS THOROUGH-
FARES, PHILADELPHIA, 1935*

| Business Group | Per Cent of Stores | Per Cent of Sales |
|---|---|---|
| All groups.............. | 2.8 | 3.3 |
| Food stores............. | 2.3 | 3.0 |
| Automotive group........ | 7.0 | 20.3 |
| Filling stations........... | 4.7 | 8.5 |
| General-merchandise group | 3.1 | 0.1 |
| Apparel group........... | 1.9 | 0.5 |
| Furniture-household group. | 3.7 | 4.4 |
| Lumber-building-hardware group................. | 4.2 | 4.0 |
| Restaurant.............. | 2.8 | 2.2 |
| Drugstores.............. | 3.0 | 3.0 |
| Other retail stores........ | 2.3 | 2.2 |

* *Intra-city Business Census Statistics for Philadelphia, Penn-sylvania.*

cent of their totals. Finally, in this connection,
it is to be recalled that 67 per cent of the total
sales recorded for all of these thoroughfares is
derived from these two business groups. These
conditions are the apparent outgrowth of heavy
automobile traffic passing these establishments,
which, with their wide spacing, offer ample
parking space for vehicles, the passengers of
which either make convenience-goods food purchases or buy automobiles and auto accessories.[7]

This explanation fails to recognize the
effect upon retail trade of residential districts adjacent to string-street developments.
The predominance of food sales in some of

[7] *Ibid.*

these thoroughfares cannot be explained
without considering the extent of residential development nearby.

The relative importance of the business
thoroughfare in the various lines of trade
for the city as a whole is shown in Table 3.
It is apparent that, as defined by Proudfoot, the principal business thoroughfares
of Philadelphia play a minor role in the
retail distribution of the city, except in the
automotive and filling-station groups.

The community business areas of Philadelphia are the most important of the four
general classifications of retail areas, containing 69.4 per cent of all stores and doing
40.1 per cent of all retail trade. According
to Proudfoot, the outstanding characteristic
of these areas is

the rather uniformly high proportion of business conducted by stores of the food group.
From a high average of over 42 per cent of the
combined volume of sales recorded for food
stores, it is notable that for fifteen areas over
40 per cent of their business is of this kind. In
only two cases does this proportion fall below
25 per cent . . . and in two other cases nearly
60 per cent of the volume of sales is of this kind.
. . . Outside of this primary dominance of food
stores in most community business areas, there
is a secondary concentration in three areas of
sales in the automotive group . . . and one area
in which the general merchandise group accounts for over 83 per cent of the combined
volume of sales. . . . Therefore, the retail trade
of these community business areas, with minor
exceptions, seems to fit the general description
given for neighborhood business streets and isolated store clusters.[8]

Table 4 reveals the relative importance
of community business areas in the trade of
the city.

Among the other attempts at classification of outlying retail conformations are
those of I. K. Rolph in a study of Baltimore and of the author in a study of Detroit.[9]

[8] *Ibid.*, p. 12.

[9] Rolph, *op. cit.;* R. U. Ratcliff, "An Exami-
nation into Some Characteristics of Outlying Retail
Nucleations in Detroit, Michigan" (Ph.D. diss.,
University of Michigan, 1935).

The Rolph classification recognizes neighborhood developments, string-street developments, isolated units, and subcenters. Subcenters are grouped into four classes.

The . . . extent to which they contain outlets representing commodities necessary to make a community self-contained from a merchandising view point is the basis of the following designations:

Class A subcenter contains minimum requisites in all of nine groups of merchandise.
Class B subcenter contains minimum requisites in any seven groups of merchandise.
Class C subcenter contains minimum requisites in any six groups of merchandise.
Class D subcenter contains minimum requisites in any five groups of merchandise.

The nine commodity groups are similar to those previously cited from the Proudfoot analysis of Philadelphia, with the addition of a jewelry group and the omission of filling stations and the miscellaneous group: food, general merchandise, apparel, automotive, furniture and household, lumber and building, restaurant and eating places, drugs, and jewelry.

In the study of outlying retail structure in Detroit, subcenters were classified on the basis of the presence of high-class retail uses, retail uses having been classified according to relative rent-paying ability.

Regardless of the usefulness of extended subclassification of retail conformation, it does appear that there are two basic forms —the nucleation (which describes the central business district as well as outlying clusters) and the string street. The essential difference between the two is the lack of internal organization in the case of the string street as compared with the more definite pattern in arrangement of uses that characterizes the nucleation.[10]

### WHOLESALE AND INDUSTRIAL AREAS

The wholesale and light-manufacturing zone is not found on all sides of the central retail district, as implied by the concentric

[10] The discussion of the retail structure is adapted from Ratcliff, *The Problem of Retail Site Selection.*

zone conception of the city. Rather, the wholesale area tends to locate on one side of the central retail district, in a location convenient to transportation facilities. This area may contain some of the older residential structures, not yet converted to business use. The area is characterized by the predominance of loft buildings, which are suitable for both the storage requirements of the wholesale function and the operations of light-manufacturing estab-

TABLE 4

PER CENT OF TOTAL STORES AND TOTAL SALES
FALLING IN COMMUNITY BUSINESS AREAS
PHILADELPHIA, 1935*

| Business Group | Per Cent of Stores | Per Cent of Sales |
|---|---|---|
| All groups.............. | 69.4 | 40.1 |
| Food stores............. | 81.9 | 69.3 |
| Automotive group........ | 70.5 | 35.4 |
| Filling stations........... | 85.4 | 78.5 |
| General-merchandise group | 63.5 | 21.7 |
| Apparel group........... | 36.8 | 9.4 |
| Furniture-household group. | 42.6 | 22.1 |
| Lumber-building-hardware group................... | 66.9 | 59.8 |
| Restaurant.............. | 67.1 | 41.0 |
| Drugstores.............. | 77.2 | 51.0 |
| Other retail stores........ | 60.5 | 41.5 |

*\* Intra-city Business Census Statistics for Philadelphia, Pennsylvania.*

lishments such as those engaged in printing, photoengraving, jewelry manufacture, and women's garment or men's-wear production.

The amount of the land area of a community that is devoted to industrial uses varies widely in accordance with the character of the area. Cities that are founded on recreational or political activities may have but a small percentage of land area used in production, mainly for local consumption. On the other hand, major manufacturing centers such as Detroit, Chicago, and Cincinnati have as much as 16 per cent of the privately developed area in industrial use. The forces that led to a concentration of industry at the center of the cities in their early stages of development have shifted until manufacturing is no longer a typically central-area use. This type of activity is now associated with the routes of transportation, notably railroads and waterfronts. Industrial plants string out along railroad lines, rivers, and lake and ocean fronts in long bands. Occasionally this pattern is broken by a concentration of industry in a special industrial district, which has been provided with connections to the major transport routes. Belt lines that connect with the trunk lines also attract industrial use. Recent industrial growth has been found in large part on the outskirts of cities where land is cheaper, taxes lower, congestion less, and plenty of space available for modern one-story plants and for employee parking.

## RESIDENTIAL AREAS

Residential land use accounts for the major area of all cities. In one study of sixteen cities, 80 per cent of the privately developed land was used for this purpose.[11] In these cities, all under 300,000 in population, single-family homes absorbed 74.2 per cent of the privately developed land, two-family structures occupied 4.28 per cent, and multifamily structures took up 2.23 per cent. The 1940 U.S. Housing Census provides a rough measure of the relative importance of different residential types in the land-use structure of urban areas. Eighty per cent of all non-farm residential structures were single family, 11 per cent two family, 3 per cent three and four family, and 2 per cent five or more family.[12] As we shall see, in the urban land-use structure, there is a strong tendency for residential structures of similar type to be found in groupings. There are wide differences in the proportioning of residential structure types among the cities, with a

[11] Harland Bartholomew, *Urban Land Uses* ("Harvard City Planning Studies," Vol. IV [Cambridge, Mass.: Harvard University Press, 1932]).

[12] One- to four-family structures with business uses combined constituted 3 per cent of all residential structures; miscellaneous types were less than 1 per cent.

tendency for the larger cities to have a larger proportion of the multifamily structures. In the metropolitan areas, there is a tendency for the proportion of multifamily structures to diminish with the distance from the center of the city.

An attempt to break down the residential areas for more refined structural analysis shows many physical, social, and economic characteristics which form individual geographical patterns and which might be used as a basis for delineating residential subareas. In the following paragraphs the basis of differentiation is the level of residential rents and values, with the term "rent" used as a general term to indicate the qualitative differences in housing. It has been found that there is a good correlation between the level of rents and values and the level of family incomes as well as the quality of the housing.

The pattern of rental areas that has been found typical of most American cities is not in the configuration of concentric circles or in sharply defined rectangular districts. There are seldom any distinct dividing lines between districts of different rent levels, but rather there are transitional zones, which partake of the nature of both adjoining areas. There is usually found in every community one or more clusters of blocks where the level of rents is the highest in the city. From these poles of high rent and high housing quality, there is a grading down through successively lower rent levels until the meanest housing and the lowest rents are reached. In smaller cities, the high-rent area may be located near the center of the city, but in the larger and more dynamic communities it may be found at the periphery. Often there is more than one high-rent district. Sometimes the high-rent area may take the form of a wedge or a ridge, extending outward from the center to the very edge of development.

Immediately surrounding the high-rent areas or sectors, which are necessarily small in extent, are the zones of intermediate housing. In some cases there will be additional intermediate-rent areas at the periphery of the city at a point removed from any high-rent district.

The low-rent areas of the community usually may be found both at the center and at the edge of the developed area, often in the form of a wedge spreading out from the center to the edge. The traditional association of the lowest rent districts and the central portions of the community is too limited a view. The crowded slums of the older, central districts have their counterparts in the shack towns of the outlying districts. It can be demonstrated that, although the centers of cities have low-rent areas, there is no general upward gradation of rent levels toward *all* parts of the periphery; low-rent areas may form districts extending through the center from one edge to the other; they may take up a half or

more of the city's area unbroken by higher rent districts. In short, a description of the residential districts in terms of wedges or sectors is more realistic than the older, concentric-circle approach.[13]

A recent ecological study of natural areas in a midwestern city has developed a hypothesis that has much merit. It was ascertained that, in this community, the pattern of housing characteristics that were related to economic status, such as rent and value of property, fell naturally into a sector configuration. On the other hand, the characteristics that related to age of structure and the place in the neighborhood cycle followed a concentric pattern. The natural areas, i.e., areas of greatest homogeneity, were best determined by the overlapping of the two patterns.

[13] The sector theory is set forth by Hoyt, *op. cit.*

RAYMOND E. MURPHY and J. E. VANCE, JR.

## DELIMITING THE CBD

The Central Business District, frequently referred to as the CBD,[1] is the heart of the American city. Here one finds the greatest concentration of offices and retail stores reflected in the city's highest land values and its tallest buildings. Here, too, is the chief focus of pedestrian and automobile traffic. By way of the transportation net the remainder of the city and an area of decreasing intensity extending far beyond the city's corporate limits are oriented toward the CBD.

Interest in the district has been increasing rapidly in recent years. Studies have been made of its theoretical shape and of the daily movements to and from this critical area. Planners, with more immediate, practical aims, are working on the problems of routing through traffic in such a way to avoid this congested district, and, at the same time, of providing parking space for the many who work in the CBD or who seek the goods and services it has to offer. And businessmen, who have seen their large investments in the district threatened by the growth of outlying shopping centers, are striving mightily to maintain the supremacy of this central area.

In view of these impinging interests it is surprising that so far no uniform method of delimiting the district has been used, that for each city the limits of the CBD have been largely a matter of local agreement. This is all very well for a planner in an individual city, working on local problems,

Reprinted from *Economic Geography*, XXX (July, 1954), 189–222, by permission of the authors and the editors. (Copyright, 1954, by Clark University, Worcester, Mass.)

[1] Among alternative names by which the CBD is known are Central Traffic District, Central Commercial District, Downtown Business District, and, more popularly, Downtown.

but it is only through the use of a standardized method of delimitation that significant comparisons of CBD's are possible. And it is only through such comparisons that a real knowledge of the content and functioning of this critical area can be attained. The development of a practical technique for delimiting the CBD, essentially a geographic problem, is the central theme of this paper.

### VARIATIONS WITHIN THE CBD

Even a cursory examination of the area we are proposing to delimit brings out the fact that it is far from homogeneous. First of all, there is a variation in what might be called commercial intensity. This is reflected in the tendency of some writers to use the designation "commercial core" for the more highly concentrated central portion of the CBD. In similar fashion the term "hard core" has been used to distinguish this central area from the remainder of the district, and others have spoken of a "primary area" and a "secondary area."

It should not be inferred, however, that sharply defined intensity areas are normal. Generally, there is a point of maximum intensity which is well known locally: the street intersection around which the average front-foot lot value is highest. This *peak land-value intersection,* as it is here called, is likely to be the locality with the maximum pedestrian concentration, and, not infrequently, the point of greatest vehicular congestion. From this center, various measures of intensity ordinarily decline toward the edges of the city, though more sharply in some directions than in others.

This does not mean that there is no observable regionalization within the CBD. Financial, theater, night club, and intensive shopping districts may often be differentiated; and there may be areas devoted to those industrial types that characterize the CBD or to the single-company office buildings of insurance companies and oil companies. Such regionalization varies greatly with individual cities and generally is more striking the larger the city. In addition, there is a vertical zonation, retail stores tending to occupy the choice ground floor positions and offices or sometimes merchandise storage, the higher floors. In smaller cities the upper-floor space may be shared with dwelling units. But in general the tendency is for intensity to decline with distance from the peak value point.

### NATURE OF THE CBD EDGE

It follows from the fact that intensity values decline with distance from a point of maximum concentration that the edge of the district is itself gradational. As Bartholomew says, "It [the CBD] is a somewhat vague area with no definite boundaries."[2] Such obstacles to expansion as a park, or, in the case of a state capital, a group of government buildings, may give the CBD some line boundaries, but such sharp edges are exceptional. Much more often the edge is a belt or zone.

This zonal character of the CBD border has been recognized by various students of the city, partly because the zone is in several respects a problem area. As Dickinson puts it, "the combination of high land values and obsolescent buildings, ripe for demolition, accounts for the dingy-looking 'zone of deterioration' that surrounds the business centre of almost every city."[3] Firey refers to the border area as, "the blighted zone which generally lies between a city's central business district and the surrounding residential districts."[4] The

blighted condition of the zone has been attributed to "slackening in the expansion of commercial and industrial uses near central business districts."[5] Not infrequently it is this zone that has furnished the sites for the redevelopment projects that have been planned in so many cities.

### THE CBD AS A REGION

What we have been saying is, essentially, that the CBD is a region with the normal qualities of a region. It has a core area in which the definitive qualities reach their greatest intensity; it has zonal boundaries, and these boundaries, for the most part, are impermanent.

### THE PROBLEM RESTATED

Though the boundaries of the CBD may be impermanent and zonal, for any particular time it should be possible to draw a line that would approximate this zonal edge. The problem undertaken by the writers of this paper was the development of a practicable method for drawing such a line. If a defensible method could be developed and were widely accepted, it could result in the delimitation of comparable CBD's in various cities. This, the writers believed, was a necessary step to gaining a deeper understanding of the nature and functioning of the CBD.

### DELIMITATION METHODS USED BY PLANNING AGENCIES

Since local determinations so often have been relied upon, it was decided, as an early step in the boundary study, to investigate methods used locally throughout the United States. Accordingly, letters were written to the head planning officials of some twenty-five or thirty medium-sized cities asking, in each case, for a map show-

---

[2] Harland Bartholomew, *Urban Land Uses: Amounts of Land Used and Needed for Various Purposes by Typical American Cities, an Aid to Scientific Zoning Practice* ("Harvard City Planning Studies," Vol. IV [Cambridge, 1932]), p. 12.

[3] Robert E. Dickinson, *City Region and Regionalism* (London, 1947), p. 96.

[4] Walter Firey, "Ecological Considerations in Planning for Urban Fringes," *American Sociological Review*, XI (1946), 411.

[5] Homer Hoyt, *Structure and Growth of Residential Neighborhoods in American Cities* (Washington, D.C.: Federal Housing Administration, 1939), p. 108.

ing the extent of the area regarded as the CBD in their city and for a statement of the methods used in arriving at the CBD boundaries.

Most of those queried sent maps outlining their respective CBD's, but there was little uniformity in methods of arriving at the boundaries. In several instances the planner said that for his city no single answer was attempted; instead, the zoning ordinance might give one CBD delimitation and the traffic ordinance a different one, and the fire department might use still a third. For most cities, however, a single delimiting line was used, in nearly all instances following block boundaries. The area shown was "generally understood locally" to be the CBD; in one instance it was arrived at "intuitively." Barriers such as rivers or railroad tracks were mentioned as forming parts of the boundaries of some CBD's. In general, a knowledge of local land use lay back of the judgments, but in most instances no specific or exact delimiting techniques were used.

In the cases of only two of the cities queried were any definite techniques reported. One of these was in use in Worcester. Charles M. Downe, director of the Worcester Department of Planning and now director of the Division of Planning, Massachusetts Department of Commerce, based his delimitation upon land values. He used assesed land values by lots reduced to value per front-foot at a uniform 100-foot depth, drawing his CBD boundary line at the outer limit of the lots with front-foot land valuations of $300 or more (Fig. 1). In similar fashion he used the area enclosing lots with front-foot land values of $2,000 or more to delimit an inner area that he called the "hard core."

This was a very satisfactory delimitation for one city, but since valuation methods differ markedly from city to city the direct use of land values can hardly be expected to yield comparable CBD's for different cities. The whole matter of the use of valuation data will be considered more fully in later pages of this study.

The second technique reported was used in Denver. The following paragraphs describe the method in detail:

This method requires only the use of an ordinary land-use map. It presumes that you want a brief method which takes account of the characteristics of land use.

1. Base—land-use map.
2. Land use to be included in CBD—business, commercial, and industrial.
3. An "analysis unit" comprising a group of blocks should be selected to serve the following purpose: the group should be wider in radius than the width of a typical business ribbon along a transit street. A diameter of four blocks is suggested.
4. Procedure:
   a) Cut a circle in a sheet of paper, the diameter of which is four blocks at the scale of the land-use map. This template represents the size of the "analysis unit."
   b) Lay tracing paper over the land-use map. Draw a perimeter around the obvious core of the CBD.
   c) Place the center of the template at any point along this perimeter and slide it outward, radially away from the CBD unit until half of the included land uses become residential. At this point business and residential use will be interspersed, but a fairly objective determination can be made of the relative proportion of non-business uses.
   d) Place a dot on the tracing paper in the center of the template. Return the template to the CBD core line, one diameter away from the previous starting point. Repeat the process of sliding the template radially to a point where half of the uses become residential.
   e) After completing the process around the entire CBD, a number of points representing the *margin* of the CBD will encircle the CBD core. Simply connect these points by a line. It may be adjusted to coincide with the nearest streets or other cultural boundaries.[6]

The chief objection to this method is that too much is included in the CBD. Using this technique, areas of solid manu-

[6] Quoted from a letter from W. F. Henniger, Director, Department of Planning, City and County of Denver, July 9, 1952.

facturing development, of wholesaling, and of railroad yards are included—in fact everything out to the point where half or more of the land is used for residences. This, it seems to the writers of this article, is too liberal a definition of the CBD. And the very fact that one city may delimit its CBD on the basis of land values and another on the basis of non-residential land use shows why some standardization of de-limitation techniques is necessary if comparative studies of the district are to mean anything.

## THE LITERATURE OF DELIMITATION

A search of the literature dealing with the CBD revealed little that was pertinent to the present problem. Most geographers, sociologists, and other writers who have focused upon the CBD or dealt with it inci-

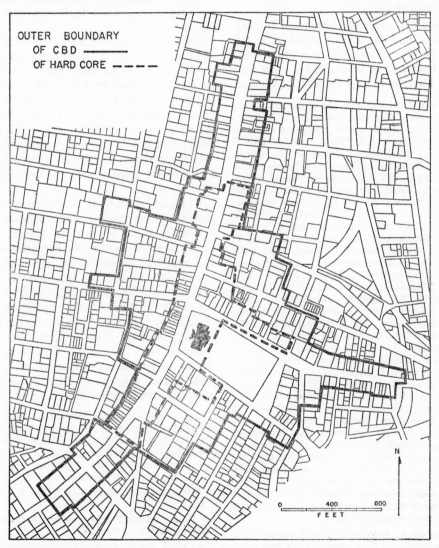

OUTER BOUNDARY
OF CBD ———
OF HARD CORE — — —

N

0        400        800
FEET

Fig. 1.—Worcester's CBD and hard core as delimited by Charles M. Downe. He worked with lots, basing his boundaries on front-foot land values reduced to uniform 100-foot depth. The black area near the center of the hard core is the City Hall.

dentally have relied, in the case of each city, upon local judgment as to the extent of the district.[7] The inadequacy of such locally determined boundaries for any work involving city comparisons is obvious. As Foley and Breese put it, "The areal definition of the CBD has not yet been standardized [but] . . . eventually technicians and scholars may be able to construct a workable definition of the CBD that could be applied to all cities."[8]

Some work done in Sweden and Norway, however, and one study carried on in this country bear sufficiently upon the problem of delimitation to be considered more fully here. First, let us note the work of William-

Olsson on Stockholm.[9] In studying retail trade, which he defined as trade not only in goods but also in meals, amusements, and lodgings, he used a "shop-rent index" (*butikshyrestal*) which he described as the total of shop rents of a building divided by the length of its frontage. This was indicated graphically on William-Olsson's maps by rectangles, the base of each being a building frontage, and the vertical, reaching away from the street, the shop-rent index in kroner.[10]

Sund and Isachsen in a study of dwelling and working places in Oslo[11] point out that they were unable to obtain shop-rent data for Oslo and hence used the total turnover or trade instead. Their "trade index" (*omsetningsverdi*) is plotted on a map in much the same manner as William-Olsson's index except that in this case the vertical dimension of the rectangle (that at a right angle to the street frontage) is proportional to total trade.

It might appear, at first glance, that some minimum shop-rent index or trade index value could be used to delimit the CBD. However, both methods require data that would be difficult if not impossible to assemble for the average American city.

Volume of trade was used in an interesting study of Philadelphia supervised by Malcolm J. Proudfoot.[12] In setting up "intra-city business areas" "block-frontage-volume-of-sales" was used. This term refers to the total annual volume of sales, for each side of a block, of all stores whose addresses indicate that they front on that

---

[7] See A. E. Parkins, "Profiles of the Retail Business Section of Nashville, Tennessee, and Their Interpretation," *Annals of the Association of American Geographers*, XX (1931), 164–76; Earl S. Johnson, "The Natural History of the Central Business District with Particular Reference to Chicago" (Ph.D. diss., University of Chicago, 1941); Gerald W. Breese, *The Daytime Population of the Central Business District of Chicago* (Chicago: University of Chicago Press, 1949); George W. Hartman, "Central Business District: A Study in Urban Geography," *Economic Geography*, XXVI (1950), 237–44; Donald L. Foley, "The Daily Movement of Population into Central Business Districts," *American Sociological Review*, XVII (1952), 538–43 [below, pp. 447–53]; and Richard U. Ratcliff, *The Madison Central Business Area: A Case Study of Functional Change* ("Wisconsin Commerce Papers," Vol. I, No. 5 [Madison: Bureau of Business Research and Service, University of Wisconsin, 1953]). See also such more general studies as Harland Bartholomew, *op. cit.*, esp. pp. 107–9; Malcolm J. Proudfoot, "City Retail Structure," *Economic Geography*, XIII (1937), 424–28; and Richard U. Ratcliff, *The Problem of Retail Site Selection* ("Michigan Business Studies," Vol. IX, No. 1 [Ann Arbor: Bureau of Business Research, School of Business Administration, University of Michigan, 1939]). There are, in addition, numerous studies of individual cities which show the CBD delimited along with other areas of the city. Such delimitations are based on local opinion or upon the author's subjective judgment. In no case that has come to the writers' attention is any systematic delimitation technique used.

[8] Donald L. Foley and Gerald Breese, "The Standardization of Data Showing Daily Population Movement into Central Business Districts," *Land Economics*, XXVII (1951), 348–53, ref. on pp. 349–50.

[9] See W. William-Olsson, "Stockholm: Its Structure and Development," *Geographical Review*, XXX (1940), 420–38. See also William-Olsson's *Huvuddragen av Stockholms geografiska utveckling 1850–1930* (Stadskollegiets Utlåtanden och Memorial, Bihang Nr. 11 [Stockholm, 1937]).

[10] William-Olsson, "Stockholm," Figs. 7 and 8, p. 426.

[11] Tore Sund and Fridtjov Isachsen, *Bosteder og arbeidssteder i Oslo* (Oslo, 1942).

[12] United States Census Bureau, "Intra-city Business Census Statistics for Philadelphia, Pa." (prepared under supervision of Malcolm J. Proudfoot, Research Geographer), May, 1937.

side. Thus any block would have four such totals though the figure might be "0" for one or more sides if no establishments fronted on those sides. "For the outer zone of the central business district . . . a block frontage lower limit of $75,000 was used."[13] An inner zone of the central business district also was delimited; this had a block frontage lower limit of $500,000.

In Proudfoot's study only volume of retail sales was used. This works better for delimiting outlying shopping centers than for the CBD, since in the outlying shopping centers retail trade is more predominant. But much is carried on in the CBD besides retail trade. It would be possible in the case of any city to have the Census Bureau prepare at cost a map showing total volume, not only of retail trade, but of services and wholesale trade as well, for each side of each block in the central portion of a city, and these data could even be totaled by blocks if one preferred to work with blocks. But, aside from the time and cost involved, such a method would still fail to take account of offices (such as the central office of a large oil company), of banks, and of certain other activities that are important in the CBD.

## NUMEROUS POSSIBILITIES

Of course, from the very conception of the current project the authors had certain ideas as to possible means of delimiting the CBD. The correspondence with planning agencies added to this growing list of possibilities and so, too, did the literature survey and conversations with countless individuals. All these possibilities were listed, and each that appeared to have promise was considered, in an attempt to develop a delimitation system that was practicable and, at the same time, could be defended on philosophical grounds. The first several months of research time were spent at Worcester, Massachusetts, home base for the project, and were devoted to the preliminary trying-out of various possibilities

[13] *Ibid.*, p. 7. See also the business-areas map, Fig. 2 in the same report.

and to the laying of plans for further work.

Shop-rent index, trade index, and block-frontage-volume-of-sales have been discussed, and it has been pointed out that their use would be impracticable for work on the average American city. There appeared to be three other principal groups of possibilities: (1) population distribution and related phenomena; (2) valuation of land or of land and buildings; and (3) land use.

### POPULATION AND RELATED DATA

Several delimitation possibilities are based directly upon man. These deal in turn with distribution of population, pattern of employment, movements of pedestrians, and traffic flow.

*Distribution of population.*—Use of population data, either directly as such or through the location of dwelling units, is based on the fact that the CBD is essentially lacking in permanent residents.

One might visualize a map of population per unit of area, with the CBD appearing as essentially empty and a certain density ratio marking its edge. Unfortunately, however, the smallest unit for which direct population data are available, the census enumeration district, is too large to permit any reasonable approximation of the CBD edge. Moreover, the blank area at the center is not necessarily central business; it is merely non-residential. Blocks of factories or public schools might well be responsible for sections of the blank area and yet obviously are non-CBD in character.

Population distribution may be presented indirectly by a map of dwelling units per unit of area based on block housing data from the census. This has an advantage over the population map since data are by blocks. Nevertheless, the dwelling-unit-density map is subject to the same criticism as the population map: though the blank central area is non-residential, it may include blocks of non-central business use.

We must conclude that neither the population-density map nor the dwelling-unit-density map is of much help in precise delimitation of the district. In each case it would have to be supplemented by a land-use map.

*Pattern of employment.*—If it were possible to obtain, and to localize on a map, data on the number of persons employed in offices and retail stores, this might form the basis for a delimitation technique. Sund and Isachsen were able to obtain statistics on the number of persons who worked in each building in Oslo and to break these data down on the basis of general types of employment.[14] But such data are difficult to obtain. Though they might be assembled for any city, the time and effort involved would be entirely too great for employment to be used as the basis for a standardized delimitation technique.

*Pedestrian counts and traffic flow.*—Pedestrian counts and traffic flow, reflecting as they do the activity on the streets, form other possible approaches to CBD delimitation and are used in some cities in establishing land values for commercial property. The edge of the district on each street leading away from the peak intersection might, conceivably, be fixed where certain minimum counts were reached.

Traffic flow may be briefly dismissed, since it has some very obvious flaws as a possible basis for delimitation. For instance, in some cities all through traffic passes the peak intersection; in others, fortunately an increasing number, the modern tendency is to route traffic so as to avoid the peak point. Moreover, many cities prohibit downtown parking during the busier hours of the day; hence traffic bears little relation to volume of business. Since cities have different policies in these respects, it is hard to see how traffic flow could furnish a basis for delimiting districts that would be at all comparable.

Pedestrian counts are somewhat more promising, since movement of people on the streets is essential to the central functions of the CBD. But techniques based on pedestrian counts suffer from the same handicap as those based on population density and dwelling-unit density (or on traffic flow, either, for that matter): pedestrians may include factory workers, and students on their way home from a downtown high school. This difficulty may be partially offset by proper timing of the counts. Another problem is that the same limiting pedestrian count could hardly be expected to prevail in one city as in another. However, if all counts in a city were expressed as percentages of the count for the peak point, a limiting percentage might be found that would be reasonably consistent from city to city.

The possibilities of pedestrian counts were not investigated in the current project. Up-to-date counts are not available for the average city or at least not in a form that could be used for CBD delimitation, and to make such a count requires a considerable force of experienced workers.[15] Nevertheless, the use of pedestrian counts remains a possibility that might be worth investigating.

But it must be pointed out that there is another obvious flaw in the use either of pedestrian counts or traffic flow: they would at best result only in a point on each street. How could these points be connected in a sufficiently objective manner so that the resulting area in one city would be comparable with that in another?

## LAND VALUES AND CBD DELIMITATION

Valuation data are of considerable interest in connection with delimiting the CBD,[16] but unfortunately their use presents many problems to the research worker. For example, the valuation data for a city may be established on either of two bases: appraisal or assessment. *Appraisal* is

[14] Sund and Isachsen, *op. cit.*, pp. 95–101. See also Tore Sund, *Bergens byområde og dets geografiske utvikling 1900–1940* (Bergen, 1947).

[15] The use of properly timed air photos of a large scale as a basis for such counts is an intriguing possibility.

[16] Sund and Isachsen used tax data in differentiating central Oslo but did not attempt to draw a line boundary, *op. cit.*, Fig. 46 and pp. 104–5.

intended to be a close approximation of the market value of the property, in contrast to *assessment*, which represents the legal valuation of a property for tax purposes.

*Basis for assessment* is the percentage of the market value at which the property is appraised. It often is fixed by law and differs from city to city and also regionally. Thus New England and other areas of eastern United States tend to have a higher basis for assessment than do middle western or far western or southern areas.

Since the assessed value is often a stated percentage of the appraised value, it is possible by simple calculation to convert assessed values into appraised values. But the situation is complicated by the fact that the basis of assessment in some areas differs with the major type of land use. This requires further adjustments in converting assessed values to appraised values.

For most cities, data by lots are collected both for land value and for the value of land plus buildings. It can be assembled from the assessor's records, but this is a time-consuming operation. Fortunately for anyone interested in comparing CBD's, the data on land values for the central section of the city frequently have been brought together on maps that are available locally. Less commonly, land and building values have been so assembled.

Frequently the data on land values (not including buildings) are expressed as front-foot values. These data are based on the fact that for commercial property the frontage on the street is of considerably greater value than the land farther to the rear of the lot. For this reason the relative values of lots are more dependent upon their frontages on the business street than upon their sizes. To correct for unevenness in lot sizes, front-foot values may be adjusted to a standard depth. Where land values have been assembled for the central area of a city, they usually have been adjusted in this way, ordinarily to a 100-foot depth.

As part of the current project, valuation data were collected and their potentialities for CBD delimitation were investigated.

*Techniques based on valuation data.*— Land values, it was decided, furnished a more promising basis for delimitation than land and building values. Building values vary essentially in proportion to the size and age of buildings and do not grade regularly from any peak point. Moreover, a large, new apartment house or a factory at the edge of the CBD would result in a marked area of high land and building values, though the uses were obviously not central business uses in type. There was the added practical point that, though most city-planning agencies had assembled land values, land and building values were not so readily available.

The bases for land values differ so much from city to city that direct city comparisons are unreliable. But it may be assumed that the data for any one city are derived in a reasonably consistent manner. Therefore, as far as reliability of data is concerned, land values could form an adequate basis for a CBD delimitation for that city. This was the basis on which Downe delimited the Worcester CBD. But the same limiting values that he applied in Worcester would mean little in another city.

Another possibility would be to use lot land values (not front-foot values) in order to arrive at an average value per unit of block area. By selecting a limiting value, a CBD boundary could be drawn on a block basis. Like the method mentioned in the last paragraph, however, there would be no basis for comparability from city to city.

The authors experimented with a method that seems to be more broadly applicable. This involves the use of a system of index numbers. Thus the front-foot land value at 100-foot depth for the highest-valued lot was represented by the number 100; the value of each other lot was shown by the number corresponding to its percentage of the value of the peak value lot. The line inclosing those lots with indexes of 5 or higher seemed best to represent the edge of the CBD. Since this technique is based on the percentage that each lot value makes up of the highest lot value, it makes no difference whether the land-value data are given as assessed values or as appraised values. Moreover, such an index system allows comparability from city to city. Figure 2 shows the delimitation of Worcester's CBD that results from the use of the 5 per cent land-value line.

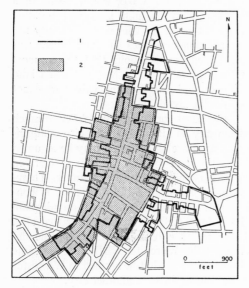

Fig. 2.—The area in Worcester outlined by the 5 per cent land-value line (*1* on map) does not correspond very closely with the CBD based on land use (area *2* on map), the delimitation of which is discussed later in this study. In part this difference results from lots forming the basis for the land-value line and blocks for the CBD based on land use. But there is the added fact that land values do not discriminate among uses. Apartment houses and factories may occur in areas of high land values, and, conversely, stores or other central business uses may extend beyond the 5 per cent land-value line.

The land valuation technique just described requires no field work. Also, since land values are on a lot basis, the delimitation is a fine-textured one.[17] But balanced

[17] Although the technique was tried out only with lot values, there is no reason why it could not be applied to the land values per unit of block area described in an earlier paragraph.

against these advantages are a number of objections to any method based on land values. In some cities the data, though on the assessor's books, have not been assembled. In others, though the data have been brought together, local authorities, for one reason or another, are unwilling to make the information public. When the data are obtained it must be remembered that they represent subjective judgments. Another difficulty is that tax-free property (schools, churches, public buildings) are commonly not assigned a valuation. As a result the actual drawing of a boundary based on land values is sufficiently subjective so that the districts delimited by two different individuals might vary considerably.

But two other objections to any land-value technique are even more serious. One of these is that if the valuation is properly done it does not reflect the height of buildings; yet surely the vertical dimension needs to be considered. The second is a shortcoming that the land-value technique shares with the delimitation methods mentioned earlier: it does not discriminate among land uses. It is entirely possible for a factory block or a block of apartment houses to occur in an area of high land values and hence to be included in the CBD even though not central business in type. This problem is not so likely to arise near the center of the CBD; it is near its edge that these other uses may compete successfully with central business for the land. It is equally true that along the edge of the CBD central business uses may extend into areas of lower land values. And it is at the edge that the problem of drawing the boundary is localized.

LAND USE AND CBD DELIMITATION

Land values are, after all, only a reflection of the use to which land can be put. It would appear, therefore, that land use should furnish a more direct and realistic approach to delimitation of the CBD than land values. There are several possible delimitation methods which, though based on land use, do not require a complete job of land-use mapping. These will be considered first.

*Break in continuity.*—The first and most obvious technique of this sort and the one most likely to be used by the casual observer is a simple break in continuity of central business uses. This generally is thought of in connection with ground-floor use. At some point on every street leading away from the peak land-value intersection the shops and office buildings that characterize the CBD will give way to residences or factories or to some other non-central business use.

But break in continuity has decided limitations as a basis for locating a CBD boundary. For instance, there is the question: How much of a break must there be in order for it to be significant? Moreover, the method results at best in a point along each street. How should the points be connected on the map? Any resulting delimitation must be a highly subjective one, and workers in various cities could hardly be expected by such means to arrive at comparable CBD's.

*Types of establishments at CBD edge.*— Another possible method of determining the approximate position of the CBD boundary is based on the hypothesis that certain types of establishments tend to be concentrated at or near the boundary. Supermarkets, automobile sales rooms, filling stations, furniture stores, rooming houses, and several other types of land use have this reputation. To what degree do these establishments coincide with the boundary? Are they really concentrated at the CBD edge, or is the CBD merely a relatively blank area on a map showing distribution of any one of them?

A graduate student, working under the senior author's direction, attempted to answer these questions for one city: Worcester, Massachusetts.[18] For each type of establishment suspected of marking the

[18] Lane J. Johnson, "The Coincidence of Certain Types of Establishments with the Edge of the CBD" (M.A. thesis, Clark University, 1954).

edge, a separate map of central Worcester was used and each occurrence was spotted on through field work. On each of these maps lines were drawn at regular distance intervals parallel to the CBD edge as determined later in this study. These zones were used to measure degrees of concentration.

It was decided that there were two general types of establishments that might show concentration along the CBD border. One type might be expected to concentrate in a more or less continuous belt. Rooming houses formed the best example of this type. The work in Worcester brought out a very definite concentration of rooming houses along the CBD border.

The second type consisted of such establishments as supermarkets and filling stations that obviously tended to occur chiefly along important streets leading away from the CBD. In Worcester, establishments of this second type showed less concentration along the CBD edge than was expected, though filling stations and automobile sales agencies showed a slight concentration at the edge. The general conclusion regarding the second type was that, though such establishments were rare within the CBD, they showed no marked concentration at its edge. However, there was a definite tendency for the CBD to be a relatively blank area on the map showing any one of these distributions. Though they showed little edge concentration, the beginning of their occurrence along any street leading away from the CBD might serve to mark the edge. Some combination of these establishments—for example, a supermarket and a filling station, or a supermarket, a filling station, and automobile sales rooms—would appear to be a more effective indication of the edge than any one of them alone.

This study of edge establishments would need to be carried further and applied to a number of cities in order to arrive at any worthwhile generalizations. From the standpoint of CBD delimitation, however, it appears that this line of work could be of value only for a preliminary, rough spotting of the boundary of the district on the principal streets leading away from the center.

## LAND-USE MAPPING BASIC TO CURRENT PROJECT

As various techniques were tested, the authors became increasingly convinced that detailed land-use mapping furnished the most practical common denominator for the determination of comparable CBD's. The district is best thought of as an assemblage of land uses, some of which are especially distinctive. Moreover, land-use maps are relatively easy to construct, since they

TABLE 1

POPULATION DATA, APRIL 1, 1950, FOR THE NINE CITIES STUDIED

(U.S. Census of Population)

|  | Incorporated City | Urbanized Area |
|---|---|---|
| Worcester, Mass........ | 203,486 | 219,330 |
| Grand Rapids, Mich.... | 176,515 | 226,817 |
| Salt Lake City, Utah.... | 182,121 | 227,368 |
| Tacoma, Wash......... | 143,673 | 167,667 |
| Sacramento, Calif....... | 137,572 | 211,777 |
| Phoenix, Ariz.......... | 106,818 | 216,038 |
| Tulsa, Okla........... | 182,740 | 206,311 |
| Mobile, Ala........... | 129,009 | 182,963 |
| Roanoke, Va.......... | 91,921 | 106,682 |

do not depend upon the availability of any unusual data. Hence, it was decided to carry out land-use mapping in a number of cities, at the same time collecting all other available information that might prove useful in CBD delimitation. The resulting detailed field mapping in nine cities and more limited observations in many others form the chief bases for this study (Fig. 4).[19]

*Choice of cities for study.*—The nine cities in which detailed field mapping was done were chosen with certain definite con-

[19] The field mapping and other field observations, except in the case of Roanoke, were carried on by the junior author between October 1, 1952, and June, 1953. The Roanoke mapping was done by graduate students as one of the field exercises in the 1953 fall field camp of the Graduate School of Geography, Clark University.

siderations in mind. In the first place it was decided that restriction of the cities to the same general size group would simplify the problem, since it would rule out great differences due to size alone. Moderate-sized cities rather than very large or very small ones seemed best fitted for the study. Very large cities, such as New York or Philadelphia, have so much individuality as to make generalizations mean little; and in very small cities the CBD is not strikingly enough developed to show all of the features that people have come to associate with the district. With this background of thinking it was decided to use cities whose urbanized areas[20] were in the 150,000 to 250,000 population class (Table 1).[21] This size had the further advantage that there were enough such cities to permit some selectivity. Moreover, the sort of mapping contemplated was more practicable for these than for larger cities.

In addition to the factor of size there were other considerations in selecting the nine cities. In order to avoid local regional peculiarities, cities widely scattered in location were chosen. Also, it was considered desirable to select cities that varied in their basic support. Finally, a few cities were ruled out because preliminary correspondence showed that the maps and data available were so limited as seriously to handicap the proposed field work.

Through application of the criteria that have been described, the nine cities were selected for study (Fig. 3). They may be briefly characterized as follows:[22] Worcester is an old manufacturing city of New England. Grand Rapids is a younger, midwestern, manufacturing center. Salt Lake

[20] As defined by the 1950 United States Census.

[21] Roanoke, though it has a somewhat smaller population total than the others, was studied because of adjacency to the Clark University fall field camp.

[22] The following characterizations are based in part on Victor Jones, "Economic Classification of Cities and Metropolitan Areas," *Municipal Year Book,* 1953, pp. 49–54 and 69, and Table IV.

City is primarily a wholesale center but is also the state capital and a religious center. Tacoma is a diversified city with manufacturing predominant. Sacramento is primarily a state capital. Phoenix, a relatively new city, is more predominantly a retail center than any of the others but is also a state capital and winter resort. Tulsa, like Phoenix, a young city, is diversified, though retail trade is outstanding. Mobile is a port, but, like Tulsa, is a diversified city

yond to encompass any land that could possibly be thought of as included in the CBD. Even this, in the size group of cities dealt with, meant the mapping, in the average city, of a total area of somewhat less than one square mile.

*Central business uses.*—It early became apparent to the writers that not all the land uses represented in the CBD were equally at home. There is a considerable difference in this respect between a church,

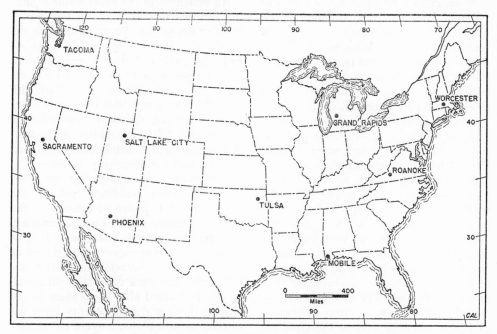

FIG. 3.—Detailed field work in nine cities supplied the data for this study

where retail trade is predominant. And Roanoke, a city created by a railroad, is likewise a diversified city where retail trade is outstanding.

*Only central areas mapped.*—It was obviously unnecessary as well as impracticable to map the entire area of each city. There is in every city a central section where department stores, banks, offices, and the like are concentrated to a greater degree than anywhere else. This is unquestionably part of the CBD. The field mapping in each of the nine cities covered this obvious area and extended far enough be-

engulfed by CBD development, and a department store, which depends upon the advantages that a CBD location has to offer. A decision as to what were and were not typical central business uses was a necessary preliminary to delimitation.

The really essential central business functions appeared to be the retailing of goods and services for a profit and the performing of various office functions. Stores of all sorts that retail merchandise, shops that offer services, and the whole miscellany of offices so often found near the center of a city—all appear to represent characteristic central business uses. Similar stores and shops and offices occur elsewhere in the city, but their area of maximum concentration is the CBD, where they are oriented around the peak land-value intersection and where they serve the city as a whole rather than any one section or any one group of people. These establishments, it was decided, were the ones upon which any delimitation of the CBD should be based.

In accordance with this decision, various types of land use, though found in the CBD, were considered not to represent real central business uses. Wholesaling is one of these. It is not a central business function, since it is localized more by the presence of railroads or other transportation media than by the pull of centrality. Even more obviously, factories and residential units (private dwellings, apartment houses, and rooming houses),[23] though represented in the CBD, are not characteristic elements.

Absence of the normal profit motive excludes from the characteristic CBD list municipal and other governmental buildings and parks, churches and other religious establishments and land, public and other non-profit-making schools, organizational establishments such as the quarters of fraternal orders, and several other types of space occupance. The establishments included in this group perform necessary functions, and they add to the crowding, and hence to the problems, of the CBD. But it is the contention of the writers that these are not the central businesses that give the area its essential character.

It may be argued that certain forms of retailing are non-central business in character, and it is undoubtedly true that supermarkets, filling stations, and automobile sales agencies are rare within the CBD. But if these specific types of retailing are

non-central business, there are others that are only a little less so; and, although wholesaling is considered non-central business, there are certain specific types of wholesaling that profit considerably from a central location. In short, a whole series of centrality judgments are involved that are unnecessary and beyond the scope of this study. In view of these considerations the writers decided not to attempt to split the retailing group.

An exception to the general rule regarding factories may be made in the case of the city newspaper. To a considerable degree getting out a newspaper is a manufacturing operation. Yet the same concern sells newspapers and sells advertising in the newspapers, and is so closely identified with central business activities that the authors have considered the whole operation as part of the CBD assemblage along with stores retailing merchandise, shops offering services, and the miscellany of offices.

A problem is presented, too, by large, specialized office buildings such as the home office of an insurance company or the home or regional office of an oil company, a telephone company, a steamship line, or a railroad. In some respects these do not fit into the group of characteristic CBD establishments, since some of them might equally well be located almost anywhere in the city. Still, they derive benefits from the association with banks, lawyers' offices, restaurants, and the like in the CBD. Because of this and because they are so much like other CBD establishments in type, they are included in the group of characteristic establishments.

In line with the foregoing, it was decided that, for the purposes of this study, certain uses would be considered as non-central business in character. These are listed in Table 2. All of them are found to some degree in the CBD, but they are considered to be either antagonistic to true central business uses, as in the case of permanent residences or industrial establishments, or neutral, as in the case of government establishments.

[23] The residential sequence extends from private dwellings to hotels, and the line between non-central business and central business in this sequence is difficult to draw. In this study the break was considered as coming between rooming houses and obviously transient hotels.

With this background we are in a position to consider in detail the mapping method that was used and the techniques that were based on the mapping.

*The mapping procedure.*—For the central area of the average American city a lot line map on a scale of 1 inch to 200 feet is available. This was the normal map equipment for the CBD mapping described in this paper.[24] The desired results were three maps: one for the ground floor, one for the second floor, and a third that generalized the remaining floors.

In the land-use mapping of the nine cities due cognizance had to be taken of the upper stories. Most planning-agency land-use maps show ground-floor uses only, but the CBD involves three dimensions. Any measures of intensity of land use in the district must take the vertical dimension into acount; in addition, the land use of upper stories is a part of the CBD picture just as is that of the ground floor.

Though maps for each floor can be constructed directly in the field, the profile method was found to be more efficient for recording the desired information. The profiles are made on ordinary lined tablets. The horizontal scale is the same as the scale of the base map, and the space between each two lines on the tablet is considered as one story. On these profiles each non-central business unit (as listed in Table 2) on each floor is indicated by an $X$. Each other space unit is marked with the letter $C$, which indicates the presence of any central business use. To discriminate between the individual central business or non-central business uses requires much more mapping time and is unnecessary if the purpose is merely one of delimitation.[25] Every floor of use is thought of as one story in vertical dimension. A parking lot

is mapped as one story of $C$, and a vacant lot as one story of $X$. Moreover, each building is mapped as if occupying its entire lot, unless the deviation from this situation is extreme. In general, throughout the CBD such deviations are slight, and to map separately the small scraps of land that may be left over around buildings would require more time than the slightly increased accuracy of result would justify. The completed profiles show at a glance the number of floors for each space unit as well as indicating the use.

TABLE 2

GENERAL TYPES OF LAND OCCUPANCE
CONSIDERED TO BE NON-CENTRAL
BUSINESS IN CHARACTER

Permanent residences (including apartment
  houses and rooming houses)
Governmental and public (including parks and
  public schools as well as establishments carrying
  out city, county, state, and federal
  governmental functions)
Organizational establishments (churches, fraternal
  orders, colleges, etc.)
Industrial establishments (except newspapers)
Wholesaling
Vacant buildings or stores
Vacant lots
Commercial storage

In order to make the method clear, the details of profiling for one block in downtown Tulsa are shown in Figure 4. Section I shows a plan view of the block as it would appear on a typical lot line map of the downtown area of any city. Section II shows the profiles of the four sides of the block, and Section III shows the three resulting land-use maps of the block. Note that even the ground-floor map departs considerably from the original lot lines. The lot at the corner of Fourth Street and Detroit Avenue, for example, is divided into seven establishments.

The third map, the "upper-floors" map,

[24] Though the scale of 1 inch to 200 feet is recommended, a larger scale can be used. For two of the nine cities lot line maps at 1 inch to 200 feet were not available, so maps at 1 inch to 100 feet were used instead. With larger scales mapping can be done in greater detail but the time required to do the work increases correspondingly.

[25] The research project on which this paper is based went far beyond delimitation. Therefore, in the basic field work, land use, in both the $X$ and in the $C$ categories, was broken down in considerable detail.

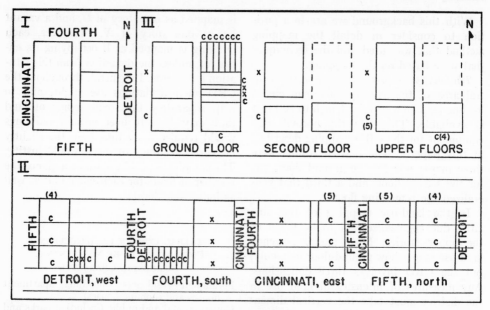

Fig. 4.—A block of downtown Tulsa on a scale of 1 inch to 200 feet. A plan view of the block showing lot lines (*I*) is followed by profiles (*II*) and the three resulting land-use maps (*III*). Each profile is drawn from left to right as the observer faces the block. "Detroit, west" refers to the west side of Detroit Avenue; "Fourth, south," to the south side of Fourth Street; and so on around the block.

TABLE 3

MEASUREMENTS AND CALCULATIONS FOR TULSA BLOCK SHOWN IN FIGURE 4*

| FIRST FLOOR | | SECOND FLOOR | | UPPER FLOORS | | | BLOCK INVENTORY | |
|---|---|---|---|---|---|---|---|---|
| Use | Space | Use | Space | Use | Space | Adjusted Value | Use | Space |
| *C*...... | 0.350 | *C*...... | 0.350 | *C*...... | 0.350×4 | 1.400 | *C*...... | 4.935 |
| *C*...... | 0.385 | *C*...... | 0.315 | *C*...... | 0.315×5 | 1.575 | *X*..... | 2.135 |
| *X*...... | 0.665 | *X*..... | 0.665 | *X*..... | 0.665 | 0.665 | | |
| *C*...... | 0.050 | | | | | | | |
| *C*...... | 0.050 | | | | | | | |
| *C*...... | 0.050 | | | | | | | |
| *C*...... | 0.050 | | | | | | | |
| *C*...... | 0.050 | | | | | | | |
| *C*...... | 0.050 | | | | | | | |
| *C*...... | 0.140 | | | | | | | |
| *X*...... | 0.070 | | | | | | | |
| *X*...... | 0.070 | | | | | | | |
| *C*...... | 0.070 | | | | | | | |
| Total | 2.100 | | 1.330 | | | 3.640 | Total space = | 7.070 |

\* All measurements are in square inches at a scale of 1 inch to 200 feet. Measurements begin with the first land use at the southeast corner of the block and proceed clockwise around the block.

Total Height Index = total space ÷ ground-floor area = 7.070 ÷ 2.100 = 3.4.
Central Business Height Index = *C* space ÷ ground-floor area = 4.935 ÷ 2.100 = 2.4.
Central Business Intensity Index = (*C* space ÷ total space) × 100 = (4.935 ÷ 7.070) × 100 = 69.8 per cent.

is a generalized representation of the third and higher floors. Floors above the second normally are so uniform in use that such a generalization is practicable. On this upper-floors map the letters represent third-floor use only, unless a number is given. If there are more than three stories, then a number is shown. This tells the number of floors of the particular use above the second. Thus, on this map the letter $X$ standing alone shows that the building is three stories in height with the upper floor in non-central business use. And the letter $C$ accompanied by the number $5$ indicates that central business use prevails, or at least predominates, on the third to seventh floors of a seven-story building.

Of course it is possible for sharp differences in land use to exist above the third floor. If these are substantial and obvious, they should be taken into account. Suppose, for example, that a department store occupies the lower three floors of a five-story building and that the upper two floors of the building are occupied by some fraternal organization. The simplest way to take care of the situation would be to show, on the upper-floors map, one-third of the space as $C(3)$ and two-thirds as $X(3)$. In this connection it must be remembered that the three maps are not made to show exact distribution of central business and non-central business establishments on each floor but merely to form the basis for calculations leading to delimitation of the CBD.

Although a single block is used here in order to make the method of profiling and map construction clear, in practice the profile may be made for the same side of a street for a series of blocks. And the end product is not a number of maps of individual blocks but three maps (ground floor, second floor, and upper floors) for the entire central section of the city.[26]

More detail is shown regarding one

[26] Of course, for a city substantially larger than the ones worked with in this study, each map might have to be presented in several sections.

group of non-central business uses—governmental establishments. Though shown with the $X$ designation just as are other non-central business establishments, they are also labeled in some manner on the maps. This is done because, in the delimitation method recommended later in this paper, a special rule is applied to such structures.

It would be possible to make more exact profiles of the upper floors so that detailed maps of the third, fourth, or any number of floors could be made, but this more exact profiling would require an inordinate amount of field time. In the present study the three maps were considered adequate and the profiling was done accordingly.

*Blocks versus streets.*—At this stage a decision had to be made—whether to base calculations upon street frontage or upon blocks. Frontage is admittedly more realistic, since the tendency for land use to differ by streets rather than by blocks is a matter of common observation.

But there were obvious difficulties. Using street frontage would result in certain sides of blocks falling within the CBD and others not. To obtain a continuous CBD area, which seemed desirable from a practical standpoint, it would then be necessary to decide how to split the blocks. Blocks vary so much in shape (see, e.g., the map of Worcester, Fig. 5) as to make such an operation decidedly difficult. At best, subjective judgments would be involved, and the writers were seeking a method that would be sufficiently objective and standardized so that it could be widely used with comparable results. Any division smaller than blocks would imply, too, a precision of mapping which it was felt would be impractical. Working with street frontage had the further disadvantage that it did not lend itself to calculations of the contents of the CBD. After considering the pros and cons at length, the authors decided to work with block units. Even this did not completely solve the problem, as it is sometimes hard to decide what constitutes a block. In general the practice was followed of considering that a block ended only where a named street occurred.

*Office calculations.*—The three land-use maps are by no means end products. The office calculations that follow involve, first of all, finding the area of all floor-space units. For this purpose a pattern of squares 0.1 inch on a side and ruled on transparent paper was used. All measurements are based on floor areas, but, since an assumption of equal height is made for all floors, the relationships between areas is unaltered if the height factor is omitted from calculations. A vacant lot or a parking lot is considered to be one floor in height just as is a one-story building, so that the total ground-floor space in the block is the total of all ground-floor area minus alleys. Streets are left out of the calculations; so, too, are railroad tracks or yards. Second-floor space is the total floor area at the second-floor level of all buildings that are two stories or greater in height; and upper-floor space is the total of all floor areas above the second floor. The system of tabulating the data resulting from the area calculations will be clear from a comparison of Table 3 with Figure 4. To simplify later checking, all measurements begin at the southeast corner of the block and proceed clockwise around the block.

We are now in a position to calculate some interesting ratios for each block.

The first of these is the *Total Height Index* or height in floors if all of the space were spread uniformly over the block. It is obtained by dividing the total floor space (at all levels) by the total ground-floor space (Table 3). (THI = total floor space ÷ total ground-floor space.)

The *Central Business Height Index* is the number of floors of central business uses if these are thought of as spread evenly over the block. It is obtained by dividing the total floor area of all central business uses by the total ground-floor area of the block. (CBHI = central business space ÷ total ground-floor space.)

The *Central Business Intensity Index* is the proportion of all floor space in central business uses. It is the percentage that total floor area of central business uses makes up of the total floor space at all levels. (CBII = [central business space ÷ total floor space] × 100.)

In summary, note that the block shown in Figure 4 has a Total Height Index of 3.4, a Central Business Height Index of 2.4, and a Central Business Intensity Index of 69.8 per cent.

## DELIMITATION TECHNIQUES BASED ON THE LAND-USE MAP

Having described the method of land-use mapping, the construction of the maps, and the measurements and calculations based on these maps, we can now consider techniques of delimitation which the maps make possible.

*Building heights.*—Building heights furnish a simple, approximate method of delimiting the CBD. The district is likely to stand out on an air photo as the area of taller than average buildings. For more exact work a map of building heights can easily be constructed from the land-use maps earlier described, since they show the number of floors for each building. Or, a building-height map on a block basis may be constructed using the Total Height Index. In either case a limiting value must be decided upon to mark the edge of the CBD.

In a general way such maps show the location of the CBD. But building heights have the obvious disadvantage that they take no account of use. Apartment houses, government buildings, factories, and other non-central business uses may rank with office buildings or department stores in terms of height. At best, then, the building-height map can furnish only a rough indication of the extent of the CBD.

*Central Business Height Index.*—Floors of central business uses is a much better basis for delimiting the CBD than building height. Just as in the case of the building-height maps, a map of floors of central business use can be made on a building basis, the height shown for each building being the total height minus the floors of non-central business uses. But the resulting map presents a very uneven pattern and is difficult to work with.

Use of the Central Business Height Index by blocks gives a more valuable picture since many of the irregularities are ironed out. In the present study it was decided that the Central Business Height Index of 1 (the equivalent of a one-story building devoted to central business uses and covering the entire block) gave a good limiting value. Figures 5–13 show which blocks met this requirement in the nine cities studied. This technique has a great advantage over the use of building height since it rules out non-central business. But it has one serious limitation: it fails to show the proportion of space in central business uses. Though central business uses might average two stories for a given block, these two stories might be overlain by three stories of apartments or three stories of manufacturing.

*Central Business Intensity Index.*—The proportion of space devoted to central business uses can be shown on a block basis by means of the Central Business Intensity Index. A limiting value of 50 per cent was decided upon, since it was felt that unless at least half the available space were devoted to central business uses, a block should hardly be considered as belonging in the CBD. Figures 5–13 show the extent in the nine cities of blocks that met this intensity requirement.

A delimitation based on the Central Business Intensity Index by itself has this fault: it takes no account of the gross amount of central business floor space. A block might have a Central Business Intensity Index of 50 per cent, which would place it within the CBD, but this might be achieved by a one-story building which, though entirely devoted to central business uses, occupied only half of an otherwise vacant block.

## THE CENTRAL BUSINESS INDEX METHOD

If both the Central Business Height Index and the Central Business Intensity Index are considered, a more realistic delimitation is achieved. In this combination of techniques a block, to be considered CBD in character, must have a Central Business Height Index of 1 or more and a Central Business Intensity Index of 50 per cent or more. In Figures 5–13 the crosshatched blocks are those that met both criteria.

Although the group of crosshatched blocks around the peak value intersection of any one of the cities is a close approximation of our final CBD, some decisions still have to be made in drawing the exact line. There are crosshatched blocks separated from the main cluster; there are blocks which fail to "make the grade" on one or both indexes but are surrounded by blocks that do; and there are still other irregular cases that have to be taken care of.

To meet the special problems just mentioned the following special rules were set up:

1. To be considered part of the CBD a block must be part of a contiguous group surrounding the peak value intersection. Even though a block touches the others only at one corner it is considered contiguous.

2. A block that does not reach the required index values but is surrounded by blocks that do is considered part of the CBD.

3. A block completely occupied by the buildings and grounds of a city hall or other municipal office building, a municipal auditorium, city police or fire department headquarters, or a central post office is included within the CBD if it is adjacent to blocks meeting the standard requirements. In some cities it will be necessary to add to this list the buildings and grounds of certain other government buildings: the courthouse in a county seat; the state capitol building of a state capital; and occasionally certain federal buildings in addition to the post office, e.g., a federal court building or other federal office building the activities of which are closely

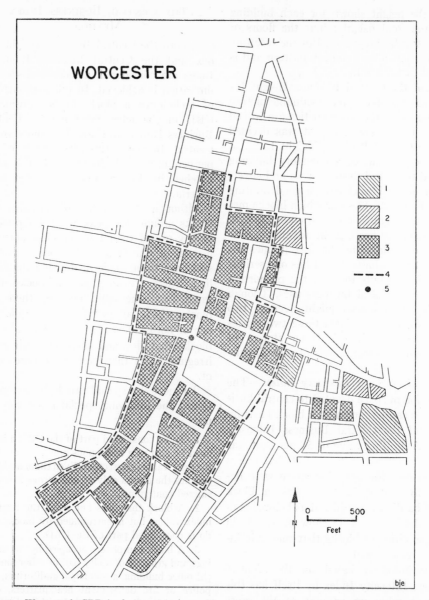

WORCESTER

| | 1 |
| | 2 |
| | 3 |
| ---- | 4 |
| ● | 5 |

0      500
N
Feet

bje

Fɪɢ. 5.—Worcester's CBD is elongated in a roughly north-south direction along its axis, Main Street. Relatively steep slopes to the west, particularly north of the center, and the presence of railroad tracks to the east help to account for this shape. The peak land-value intersection is at the point where Pleasant Street reaches Main from the west and continues southeastward as Front Street. In Worcester as in Grand Rapids the delimitation problem is complicated by a great range of block sizes. Compare this map with Figs. 1 and 2.

Key to legend: 1. Central Business Height Index of 1 or more; 2. Central Business Intensity Index of 50 or more; 3. Central Business Height Index of 1 or more and Central Business Intensity Index of 50 or more; 4. CBD boundary; 5. Peak land-value intersection.

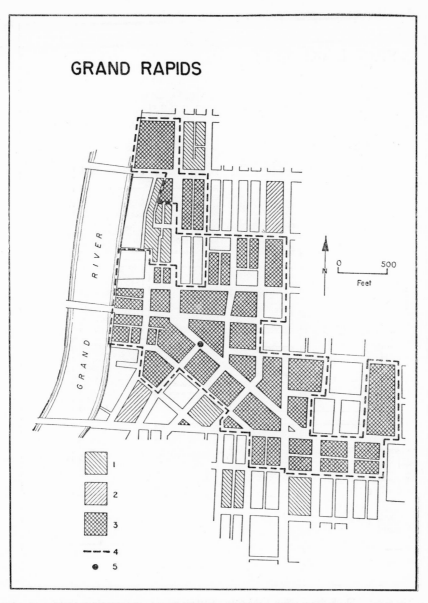

GRAND RAPIDS

Fig. 6.—Irregularity in shape characterizes the Grand Rapids CBD. The district extends in a roughly NW-SE direction, with its peak land values where Market Avenue, coming from the southwest, forms a **T** intersection with NW-SE trending Monroe Avenue. Grand River on the west and a steep rise toward the east help to account for the overall shape of the district. As in Worcester there is a great range in block sizes.

Key to legend: 1. Central Business Height Index of 1 or more; 2. Central Business Intensity Index of 50 or more; 3. Central Business Height Index of 1 or more and Central Business Intensity Index of 50 or more; 4. CBD boundary; 5. Peak land-value intersection.

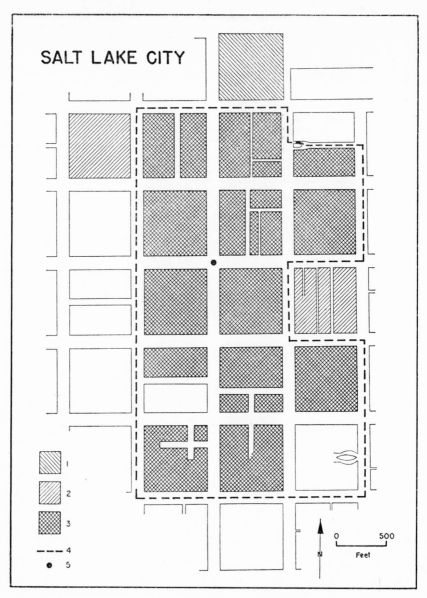

Fig. 7.—The average block size for Salt Lake City's CBD is more than three times that for any other of the nine cities. This is unfortunate for CBD delimitation, since the central portions of each block tend to be less intensively used than the edges. Obviously, however, a delimitation system based on lot lines or on some other system of splitting blocks would be ineffective in dealing with these relatively hollow squares. As it is, a fairly compact and definite district stands out. The peak land values are reached at the intersection of Main Street, running north-south, and Second Street South.

Key to legend: 1. Central Business Height Index of 1 or more; 2. Central Business Intensity Index of 50 or more; 3. Central Business Height Index of 1 or more and Central Business Intensity Index of 50 or more; 4. CBD boundary; 5. Peak land-value intersection.

438

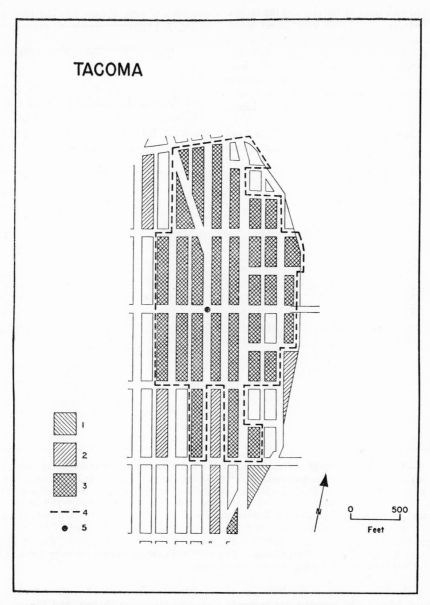

# TACOMA

I

2

3

— — 4

● 5

N

0        500

Feet

Fig. 8.—Tacoma's CBD lies on more steeply sloping land than the CBD of any other one of the nine cities. Though the land in general slopes steeply eastward there is a particularly sharp drop at the eastern edge of the district, and this steep descent is bordered to the east by the Northern Pacific tracks. This site helps to account for the north-south elongation of the district and for the elongated blocks. The peak land values are reached at the intersection of Broadway, which extends in a NNW-SSE direction parallel to the slope, with South Eleventh Street.

Key to legend: 1. Central Business Height Index of 1 or more; 2. Central Business Intensity Index of 50 or more; 3. Central Business Height Index of 1 or more and Central Business Intensity Index of 50 or more; 4. CBD boundary; 5. Peak land-value intersection.

integrated with those of the city and the region. In no instance should such government buildings as those described in this paragraph result in the extension of the CBD for more than one block beyond normal CBD blocks. Thus where there is a group of state buildings occupying several blocks that border the CBD, as in some state capitols, the whole group is considered non-CBD.

4. If the structures mentioned in Rule 3 occupy only part of a block which is contiguous

boundaries were drawn for the nine cities (Figs. 5–13).[27]

### The Boundaries Analyzed

A more careful analysis of each of the boundaries will show how application of the indexes and special rules work out.

*Worcester.*—In Worcester (Fig. 5) a block far to the south and a cluster of three small blocks to the east were omitted from

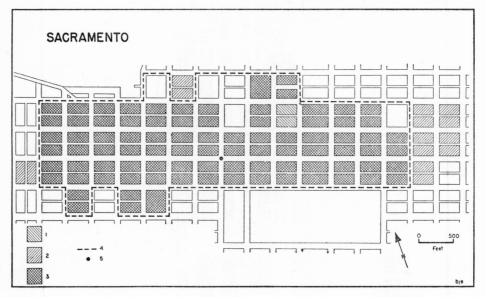

Fig. 9.—The east-west spread of Sacramento's CBD is due in part to the confining influence, at the north, of railroad tracks and, farther east, county buildings, the post office, and the city hall. The state capitol and its satellites to the south (including Capitol Park) serve as barriers to expansion in that direction. The peak land values occur at the intersection of K Street, which runs the full length of the CBD, and Ninth Street at right angles to it. Sacramento and Salt Lake City have CBD's that are approximately the same size, substantially greater in area than those of the other seven cities.

Key to legend: 1. Central Business Height Index of 1 or more; 2. Central Business Intensity Index of 50 or more; 3. Central Business Height Index of 1 or more and Central Business Intensity Index of 50 or more; 4. CBD boundary; 5. Peak land-value intersection.

to other CBD blocks and if the inclusion of these establishments as central business would bring the two indexes of the block to the required totals then the block is considered part of the CBD.

The *Central Business Index Method,* which we are here suggesting, involves the application of the two indexes and the special rules just described. Using this method,

[27] Would it be possible to achieve the same or a close approximation of the same CBD boundaries through air photograph interpretation? If so there would be certain obvious advantages, the chief of which is that it would then be unnecessary to visit a city in order to delimit its CBD.

A definite answer to this question would require complete air coverage for each of the nine cities, and the carrying out of the inquiry in detail would be a major project in itself. It appears to the writers, however, that the chief possibilities lie in

the CBD because of non-contiguity. Special cases of included blocks are the post office block, near the southern end of the district; the block occupied by the city hall and Common just southeast of the peak value intersection; and, farther north, two blocks that reflect in turn Rule 1 and Rule 4. A county courthouse and a municipal building at the northern edge of the mapped area were excluded because they are separated from the main CBD area by several blocks that do not meet the required index values.

*Grand Rapids.*—In Grand Rapids (Fig. 6) as in Worcester several blocks that meet the required index values were omitted because they were not contiguous with the main cluster. One small outlier of this sort lies just southwest of the district and two other outlying blocks occur just southeast of the area shown on the map. Five blocks (blank on the map) were included under Rule 3. A special decision was necessary regarding a hotel property at the northern edge of the district. Hastings Street was considered projected westward to the river in order to include a hotel but exclude land north of it that did not qualify.

*Salt Lake City.*—In Salt Lake City (Fig. 7) the only problems encountered in drawing the boundary involved government buildings. Thus the block occupied by the

---

a building-height map from which various non-central business uses have been eliminated. It should be possible in most instances to identify private homes, rooming houses, and apartment houses; parks, public schools, churches, and some governmental structures such as a post office, city hall, or courthouse; the buildings and grounds of a college or university; most factories, where they occupy independent buildings; and vacant lots. On the other hand, certain types of land occupance which were listed as non-central business in character appear essentially impossible to identify from air photographs. In this group are upper-floor residential use; wholesale establishments; commercial storage; vacant building space; factories when not in a separate building; some governmental establishments; and such organizational space use as the quarters of fraternal orders.

city-county building at the extreme southeast was included under Rule 3; so, too, was the narrow block southwest of the center where the post office is situated.

*Tacoma.*—In Tacoma (Fig. 8) one outlying block at the south was excluded; and several blocks throughout the area were included under Rule 3. In the latter group are the post office block, near the eastern edge of the district, and the blocks at the extreme north occupied by the city hall and the city hall annex.

*Sacramento.*—Sacramento (Fig. 9) presented much the same problems as the other cities. The three open blocks in the northernmost tier of the map correspond, respectively, to the county courthouse, the post office, and the city hall; the municipal auditorium is at the extreme northeast. A park, just south of the city hall, was included because it is surrounded by CBD blocks. One block, a little northeast of the center of the district, fell beneath the necessary index but was included, since it is surrounded by CBD blocks.

*Phoenix.*—In Phoenix (Fig. 10) one block along the northwest edge of the district, where a federal building is situated, was included under Rule 3. The business of the federal building is as much a part of Phoenix's normal activities as that of a city hall or courthouse. The long block toward the north was included under Rule 4: the presence of a post office brings the average for the two indexes up to the necessary levels. A city hall block at the southwest was also included.

*Tulsa.*—Drawing the boundary line for Tulsa's CBD (Fig. 11) presented few problems. A block at the northwest, partly occupied by the post office, was included under Rule 4.

*Mobile.*—In Mobile (Fig. 12) one block that met the required indexes was excluded because it was non-contiguous; and several blocks were included under Rule 3. In this category are those blocks containing the county courthouse and the city hall

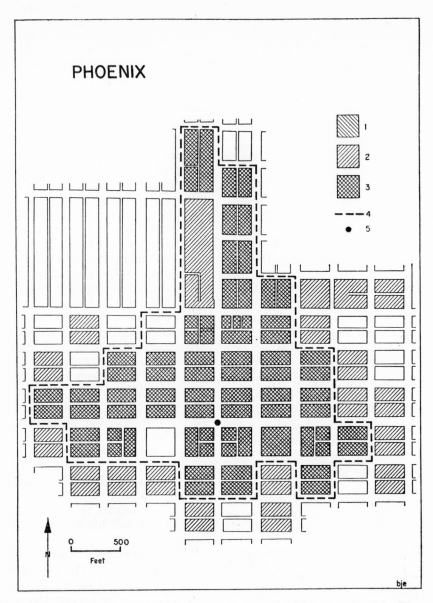

Fig. 10.—The site of Phoenix' CBD is flatter than that of any of the other nine cities. There are no natural barriers to prevent expansion of the district, but the Southern Pacific Railroad line discourages expansion toward the south. The peak land values occur at the intersection of Central Avenue, which extends in a north-south direction, and east-west Washington Street.

Key to legend: 1. Central Business Height Index of 1 or more; 2. Central Business Intensity Index of 50 or more; 3. Central Business Height Index of 1 or more and Central Business Intensity Index of 50 or more; 4. CBD boundary; 5. Peak land-value intersection.

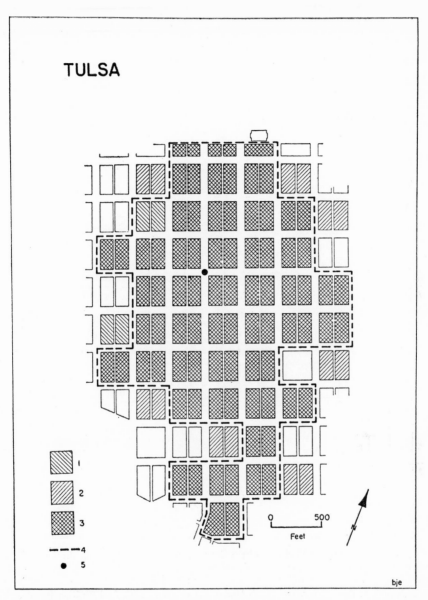

TULSA

1
2
3
---- 4
● 5

0        500
Feet

bje

Fig. 11.—Tulsa's CBD has a rolling site. The peak land-value intersection, at the crossing of Fourth Street (trending ENE-WSW) and Main Street, is on a minor rise of land from which there is a slope outward in all directions. Railroad tracks occur at the northern edge of the district and also just to the east of the CBD.

Key to legend: 1. Central Business Height Index of 1 or more; 2. Central Business Intensity Index of 50 or more; 3. Central Business Height Index of 1 or more and Central Business Intensity Index of 50 or more; 4. CBD boundary; 5. Peak land-value intersection.

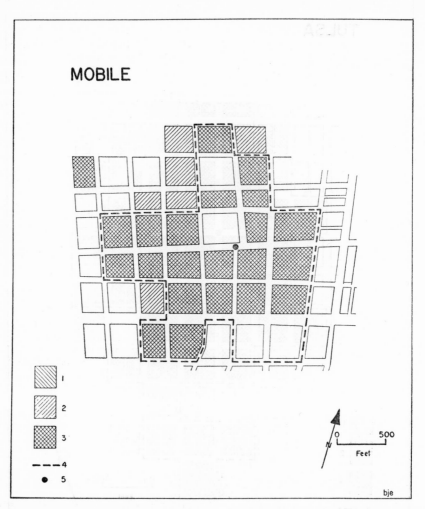

FIG. 12.—Mobile's CBD is limited toward the east by a wholesale district and the Louisville & Nashville tracks, near Mobile River. The peak land values are at the intersection of St. Emanuel Street from the south with Dauphin Street which runs in a WSW-ENE course.

Key to legend: 1. Central Business Height Index of 1 or more; 2. Central Business Intensity Index of 50 or more; 3. Central Business Height Index of 1 or more and Central Business Intensity Index of 50 or more; 4. CBD boundary; 5. Peak land-value intersection.

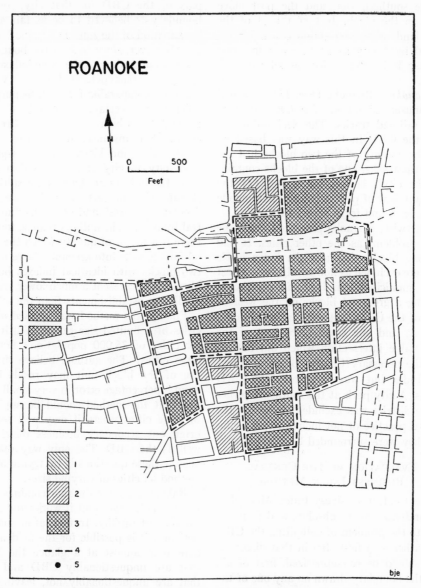

ROANOKE

0      500

Feet

1

2

3

- - - 4

● 5

bje

FIG. 13.—Roanoke's CBD is confined by railroad tracks on the east; at the north two blocks beyond the main line of the Norfolk & Western Railway are included, because of the presence of the city's largest hotel (built by the railroad company) and the N. & W. office building. The peak land values of the district occur at the intersection of Campbell Avenue with Jefferson Street, the latter traversing the CBD in a north-south direction.

Key to legend: 1. Central Business Height Index of 1 or more; 2. Central Business Intensity Index of 50 or more; 3. Central Business Height Index of 1 or more and Central Business Intensity Index of 50 or more; 4. CBD boundary; 5. Peak land-value intersection.

in the southern tier, and the post office block in the north. Just northwest of the peak land-value intersection is a block occupied by a city park; this was included because it is surrounded on all sides by CBD.

*Roanoke.*—Roanoke (Fig. 13) presented the unusual situation of a CBD crossing busy railroad tracks. The decision to extend the CBD in this way was based on (1) the activity of the two blocks just beyond the tracks, one of the blocks containing the city's largest hotel, and (2) the constant flow of pedestrian and automobile traffic back and forth across the tracks.

Otherwise, Roanoke presented much the same problems as the other cities. It had outlying blocks that met the index levels but were excluded as non-contiguous; a post office, municipal building, and courthouse forming a group of blocks on the western edge of the CBD that were included under Rule 3; and one small block east of the peak value intersection which did not attain the necessary Central Business Intensity Index but was surrounded by CBD blocks. A city park at the southeast corner of the district was excluded, following the general practice of not including parks unless they were surrounded by CBD blocks.

### EVALUATION OF THE CENTRAL BUSINESS INDEX METHOD

The Central Business Index Method is not presented as an absolute and final answer to the problem of delimiting the CBD but rather as a first step in that direction.

It should be re-emphasized, first of all, that the boundary drawn on any one of the maps is not *the* boundary of the CBD for that city. To think that it is would be naïve indeed, since the edge of the CBD is a zone or belt of transition. But the area delimited in each case does include the major part of the CBD for that city, and the boundary is believed to be as fair an approximation of the zone as a single line can be. Moreover, since each of the boundaries is drawn according to the same indexes and rules the areas delimited in the various cities are comparable for analysis purposes.

There are certain shortcomings of the method of which the authors are well aware. For instance, delimitation is by block units, and block size varies greatly from city to city and even within cities. Also, the indexes are based on a subjective classification of certain establishments as "central business" and others as "non-central buiness." The authors realize, too, that there is a factor of quality which the method fails to take into account. There may be two blocks with identical indexes but one block may represent a much lower grade or quality of establishments than the other.

Finally, the method was applied only to cities of a limited size range. Will it work for cities of 25,000 population? For very large cities? The authors believe that the use of the block unit may result in too great a percentage error in very small cities, but that the method should be applicable to large cities where it may well serve to bring out secondary business districts as well as the CBD. The only way really to answer these questions is by trying out the method on cities of varying sizes.

Balanced against the shortcomings of the method is the fact that it works and can be carried out rapidly. In fact, after some experience, it is possible for the field man to determine almost at a glance the blocks that are unquestionably CBD and those that are unquestionably not, leaving only a fringe of doubtful blocks to be mapped. And the method is sufficiently objective so that the resulting areas obtained by workers in different cities should be reasonably comparable.

DONALD L. FOLEY

# THE DAILY MOVEMENT OF POPULATION INTO
# CENTRAL BUSINESS DISTRICTS

This paper reports an exploratory study of urban "daytime" population. While we have rather detailed data and a correspondingly mature understanding regarding "nighttime" population—the census, for example, being primarily concerned with where residents sleep—we lack an adequate picture of daytime patterns. There are great gaps in our knowledge of where metropolitan residents are distributed while carrying out their jobs, their shopping, and other daily functions.[1]

Specifically, this study examines the daily movement of persons into the central business districts (CBD's) of middle-sized and large American cities. The guiding question has been: *What proportion of a metropolitan population enters and accumulates in the CBD each weekday?* Two other related questions are also posed: How do these entry and accumulation proportions vary by city size? How have these proportions varied with time?

## SOURCES AND METHODS

Only limited discussion of the daily movement of population into CBD's is available in the literature reporting research by sociologists and population experts.[2] Virtually no empirical information relating to this problem has been collected

Reprinted from *American Sociological Review,* XVII (October, 1952), 538–43, by permission of the author and the editor. (Copyright, 1952, by American Sociological Society.)

[1] Since the present research was started, the U.S. Bureau of the Census has for the first time moved into the daytime population field by undertaking "to prepare, for the Federal Civil Defense Administration, estimates of daytime and nighttime population by zones within specified cities." (News note by Lowell T. Galt, in *The American Statistician,* VI [February, 1952], 5.)

first-hand by social scientists. However, a considerable number of rather comprehensive studies of vehicle movements into CBD's have been conducted, mainly by traffic engineers for traffic analysis and control purposes. In varying degree these studies have also reported the number of entering passengers. It is the findings from these "traffic surveys" that have been tapped by this researcher.

Usable information was assembled for some 63 cities, all but 10 of which had 1940 metropolitan populations of 100,000 or over.[3] The number of adequate counts in each city varied from one statistical measure to the next, leaving more gaps in the findings than would have been desirable.

Three main indexes are used to measure typical weekday population movement:[4]

[2] Gerald W. Breese, *The Daytime Population of the Central Business District of Chicago* (Chicago: University of Chicago Press, 1949), provides the most complete reporting for a single large city. This source also includes a bibliography of previous relevant research (pp. 247–67).

[3] During the summer of 1951 questionnaires were sent to appropriate municipal officials in 158 cities. Replies were received from 107 (or 68 per cent) of this list. (For cities of 100,000 or more population, replies were received from 75 per cent.) From these replies and from the traffic-survey reports sent for analysis, information was secured for about 55 cities. Relevant statistics were obtained for 8 other cities through correspondence and interlibrary loans.

[4] In the original assembly of information from the many traffic surveys examined some additional or alternative measures were recorded. The final selection of the time period, 7:00 A.M. to 7:00 P.M., resulted from this being modal for the cordon counts examined (from which type of count measures *a* and *c* derive). This necessitated the adjustment of most origin-destination survey findings to this same 12-hour basis. For a combination of reasons pedestrian movements were excluded.

447

a) *The total number of persons entering the CBD as passengers during the 12-hour period, 7:00 A.M.–7:00 P.M.* This includes both persons with destinations in the CBD and persons merely passing through the CBD.

b) *The total number of persons with destinations in the CBD during this same period, 7:00 A.M.–7:00 P.M.* This generally includes only passenger entrants in standard vehicle types.

c) *The maximum accumulation of persons in the CBD, typically sometime between noon and 3:00 P.M.* This includes only passengers who entered the CBD after 7:00 A.M.

Each of these measures is then expressed in ratio form—as *the number of persons per 1,000 metropolitan-district population*—thus facilitating comparisons. These three main measures are termed: (*a*) *entrance ratio,* (*b*) *destination ratio,* and (*c*) *accumulation ratio.*

A major problem involves the existence of two quite different traffic-survey systems. The older system, the cordon count, consists of counting vehicles as they cross an imaginary cordon surrounding the CBD. From cordon counts come the data for measures *a* and *c*. The other system, known as the origin-destination survey, has been in effect only since about 1944.[5] Residents are interviewed at home and drivers are interviewed as they enter the metropolitan area or as they park in the CBD. Where this is done on a sampling basis, the results are inflated to provide an estimate of total vehicle and person movements. From this system comes measure *b*.

Generally speaking, these two types of surveys have not been carried out concurrently for the same city, so that the relation between measures *a* and *b* or between measures *b* and *c* could not be studied directly, city by city. Rather, averages for

clusters of cities within given city-size and time-period groupings were computed and compared.

Typically there were at the most only one or two comprehensive surveys for each city. Time series covering four or more years could be developed for only about a half-dozen cities. Hence, again, we must rely on averages from groupings of cities, impeding direct and conclusive interpretations as to time-series trends.[6]

No standard areal definition of a CBD has been followed in carrying out traffic surveys. In one city the district used for traffic-study purposes may have been so small as to represent only the core of a CBD; in another city the district may have been unusually large. An adjustment or standardization procedure at least partially to cope with this difficulty has already been reported, in collaboration with Gerald Breese.[7] In this previous reporting a single and constant "standard" ratio of CBD acreage to metropolitan population was assumed. In the present study this is modified to a varying ratio, based on a smoothed regression curve passed through ratios shown in the final column of Table 1. The standardization procedure consists of statistically adjusting each city's entrance, destination, and accumulation ratios to estimates of what they would have been had that city's CBD acreage been standard for its size. This by no means solves the basic problem of what the areal definition of a CBD *should be.* It merely summarizes what the relative size of the CBD *has been* as defined for traffic study purposes and provides a means of adjusting CBD traffic-survey findings so as to take unusual acreage differentials into account.

[6] For a discussion of a parallel problem see W. S. Robinson, "Ecological Correlations and the Behavior of Individuals," *American Sociological Review,* XV (June, 1950), 351–57.

[5] For a comprehensive review and a definitive bibliography of traffic surveys, especially the origin-destination type of survey, see Robert E. Barkley, *Origin-Destination Surveys and Traffic Volume Studies* (Washington, D.C.: Highway Research Board, Bibliography No. 11, 1951).

[7] Donald L. Foley and Gerald Breese, "The Standardization of Data Showing Daily Population Movement into Central Business Districts," *Land Economics,* XXVII (November, 1951), 348–53.

## FINDINGS

The first set of findings, showing the variation in the ratios by city size, is summarized graphically in Figure 1 (with supporting figures in Table 2).

1. For the middle-sized American city (i.e., from a half to 1 million metropolitan population), about 400 to 500 persons per 1,000 metropolitan population *enter* the CBD during the 12-hour period, 7:00 A.M.–7:00 P.M., on a typical weekday. This entrance ratio varies inversely with city size. For the cities studied there is a spread of entrance-ratio group means from 665 (for cities of 100,000–250,000), to 201 (for cities of 3 million or more population). The largest single entrance ratio is 1,047 (Charlotte, North Carolina, 1950), showing that the number of entrants exceeds the entire metropolitan population. At the other extreme New York City's estimated entrance ratio is only 147.[8]

2. For this same middle-sized group (one-half to 1 million population), about 225 to 240 persons per 1,000 metropolitan population daily have *destinations* in the CBD. This destination ratio also varies inversely with city size, but not to the extent that the entrance ratio varies. In the data collected in this study, the highest mean destination ratio is 253 (for cities in the 100,000–250,000 population group), while the lowest mean ratio (Los Angeles, 1950) is 107. The highest single city ratio of 321 (Phoenix, 1947) is equivalent to nearly 1 out of every 3 metropolitan residents.

### TABLE 1

RATIOS BETWEEN CENTRAL BUSINESS DISTRICT ACREAGE AND
METROPOLITAN POPULATION BY CITY-SIZE GROUPS

| Metropolitan District Population (In 1,000's) | No. of Cities on Which Based* | Mean No. of Acres in CBD as Reported in Traffic Surveys Analyzed | Mean No. of Acres in CBD per 1,000 Metropolitan-District Population |
|---|---|---|---|
| Under 25.................. | 10 | 70 | 4.57 |
| 25–49.................. | 4 | 83 | 2.55 |
| 50–99.................. | 7 | 173 | 2.17 |
| 100–249.................. | 28 | 224 | 1.31 |
| 250–499.................. | 15 | 286 | 0.77 |
| 500–749.................. | 8 | 458 | 0.78 |
| 750–999.................. | 3 | 469 | 0.54 |
| 1,000–1,999.................. | 6 | 752 | 0.54 |
| 2,000 and over............ | 5 | 811 | 0.27 |
| Total................ | 79 | ............ | ............ |

* Findings from the Hitchcock and Burrage study of 34 cities (parking surveys conducted between 1945 and 1948) have been merged with findings for 51 cities (traffic surveys made between 1924 and 1950) in the present study. In reporting the total of 79 cities, all overlap has been eliminated. (See S. T. Hitchcock and R. H. Burrage, "Some Travel and Parking Habits Observed from Parking Studies." *Public Roads*, XXVI [June, 1950], Table 2, p. 26.)

3. The accumulation ratios prove to be even steadier than the entrance and destination ratios. For a rather broad range of

[8] The New York figures were not used in computing any of the mean ratios reported in this study. As surveyed, the entry figures were for Manhattan south of Sixty-first Street. The entrance ratio (mean for the years, 1940 and 1948) for the very large district was 244. Adjusted by the acreage standardization process used in the remainder of the study, this ratio dropped to 147, which because of the magnitude of its adjustment and the uniqueness of New York's situation is an admittedly abstract figure. It is reported here merely because it would seem to represent an estimated minimum entrance ratio for American cities.

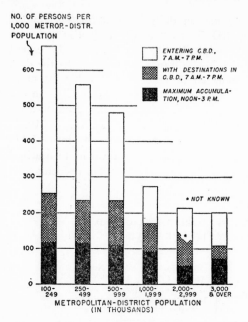

NO. OF PERSONS PER
1,000 METROP.-DISTR.
POPULATION

☐ ENTERING C.B.D.,
7 A.M.-7 P.M.

▨ WITH DESTINATIONS IN
C.B.D., 7 A.M.-7 P.M.

■ MAXIMUM ACCUMULA-
TION, NOON-3 P.M.

• NOT KNOWN

METROPOLITAN-DISTRICT POPULATION
(IN THOUSANDS)

FIG. 1.—Daily population movement into central business districts, by city size. (NOTE: Upper and middle portions of bars to be read as extending to 0 base line. Footnotes in source, Table 2, apply.)

city sizes (from 100,000 to 2 million) *the maximum accumulation of persons within the CBD amounts to between 9 per cent and 12 per cent of the metropolitan population.* The per-1,000-population ratios range from 90 to 115. For cities in the 100,000–250,000 class the ratio averages about 115, and for the very largest cities it drops to about 60 or 70. Excluding cities over 2 million, the range in individual city accumulation ratios is from 63 (Milwaukee, 1948) to 155 (Dallas, 1948).

4. In general, the ratio of persons *entering* the CBD to persons with *destinations* in the CBD to maximum *accumulation* of persons at any one time during the day is about *4:2:1*. This ratio holds most true for cities having from a half to 1 million metropolitan population and varies somewhat for cities smaller or larger than this, as shown in the final three columns of Table 2.

It is not possible to offer very convincing data on *time-series trends*. Figure 2 (sup-

TABLE 2

STANDARDIZED MEASURES OF DAILY POPULATION MOVEMENT INTO
CENTRAL BUSINESS DISTRICTS, BY CITY-SIZE GROUPS*

| METROPOLITAN DISTRICT POPULATION (IN 1,000's) | MEAN NO. PERSONS PER 1,000 METROPOLITAN POPULATION | | | | | | INTERMEASURE RATIOS | | |
|---|---|---|---|---|---|---|---|---|---|
| | Entering CBD, 7 A.M.–7 P.M. | | With Destinations in CBD, 7 A.M.–7 P.M. | | In CBD at Time of Maximum Accumulation | | Dest's to Entrants (Col. 5 ÷Col. 3) | Accum. to Dest's (Col. 7 ÷Col. 5) | Accum. to Entrants (Col. 7 ÷Col. 3) |
| | $N$† | Ratio | $N$ | Ratio | $N$ | Ratio | | | |
| (1) | (2) | (3) | (4) | (5) | (6) | (7) | (8) | (9) | (10) |
| 100–249........ | (8/8) | 665 | (10/10) | 253 | (3/3) | 115 | 0.38 | 0.46 | 0.17 |
| 250–499........ | (11/8) | 558 | (1/1) | 234 | (4/4) | 114 | 0.42 | 0.49 | 0.20 |
| 500–999........ | (7/6) | 481 | (3/3) | 235 | (8/7) | 108 | 0.49 | 0.46 | 0.23 |
| 1,000–1,999...... | (7/5) | 274 | (1/1) | 170 | (2/2) | 90 | 0.62 | 0.53 | 0.33 |
| 2,000–2,999...... | (4/4) | 213 | (0/0) | ........ | (2/2) | 52 | ........ | ........ | 0.25 |
| 3,000 and over.... | (12/2) | 201 | (1/1) | 107 | (3/1) | 71 | 0.53 | 0.66 | 0.35 |
| Total‡....... | (49/29) | 399 | (16/16) | 189 | (22/16) | 92 | 0.48 | 0.48 | 0.23 |

* Traffic surveys for the years 1936–40 and 1946–50 were used as representative of contemporary, reasonably normal conditions. The war years, 1941–45, were excluded, since their ratios tended to be abnormally low. All ratios have been standardized, (1) adjusting for CBD acreage and (2) excluding pedestrian entrants.

† In each pair of figures in the $N$ columns, the first figure represents the total number of traffic surveys used and the second figure represents the total number of cities used. In the total figures for these $N$ columns, overlapping city figures have been eliminated.

‡ The ratio column totals are arithmetic means of the 6 size-group figures, each group weighted evenly. In each of the three cases where there is no figure for the 2–3 million population group, the mean of the three smaller size groups was averaged with the mean of the two available larger size-group figures.

ported by Table 3) summarizes such information as can be reported. It should be noted that the statistics for the period 1931–35 were very incomplete and that even the trend figures for the other periods are tentative in nature.

1. The long-range or secular trend in the *entrance* ratio is slightly downward for cities over 1 million population, falling from 264 in the late 1920's to 235 in the late 1940's. But the ratios for cities under 1 million rose from 411 to 622 during this same period, a gain of over 50 per cent. (These secular trends are most accurately seen in the averages for 1926–30, 1936–40, and 1946–50, considered as a series.)

2. No long-range trend in the ratio of persons *accumulating* in the CBD can be reported with any certainty. It would appear, however, that there has been some tendency for the ratio to stay rather constant in the large cities and to rise slightly in the medium-sized cities.

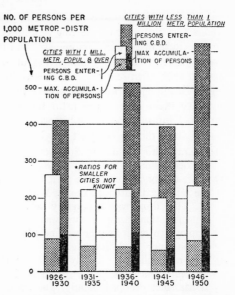

Fig. 2.—Daily population movement into central business districts, for medium and for large cities, by 5-year periods, 1926–50. (Note: Upper portions of bars to be read as extending to 0 base line. Footnotes in source, Table 3, apply.)

TABLE 3

STANDARDIZED MEASURES OF DAILY POPULATION MOVEMENT INTO CENTRAL BUSINESS DISTRICTS, FOR CITIES LESS THAN AND MORE THAN ONE MILLION POPULATION BY 5-YEAR PERIODS, 1926–50*

| TIME PERIOD | PERSONS ENTERING CBD, 7:00 A.M.–7:00 P.M. | | | | MAXIMUM ACCUMULATION IN CBD | | | | RATIO OF ACCUMULATION TO PERSONS ENTERING | |
| --- | --- | --- | --- | --- | --- | --- | --- | --- | --- | --- |
| | Less than 1 Million Metropolitan Population | | 1 Million Metropolitan Population or More | | Less than 1 Million Metropolitan Population | | 1 Million Metropolitan Population or More | | Less than 1 Million Metropolitan Population | 1 Million or More Metropolitan Population |
| | $N$† | Ratio | $N$ | Ratio | $N$ | Ratio | $N$ | Ratio | | |
| 1926–30..... | (6/3) | 411 | (7/5) | 264 | (3/1) | 102 | (1/1) | 89 | 0.25 | 0.34 |
| 1931–35..... | (0/0) | ..... | (3/2) | 223 | (0/0) | ..... | (1/1) | 70 | ......... | 0.31 |
| 1936–40..... | (11/10) | 514 | (13/9) | 224 | (6/6) | 107 | (5/4) | 68 | 0.18 | 0.30 |
| 1941–45..... | (9/7) | 394 | (9/5) | 201 | (4/2) | 62 | (1/1) | 58 | 0.16 | 0.29 |
| 1946–50..... | (14/11) | 622 | (9/5) | 235 | (8/7) | 118 | (1/1) | 85 | 0.20 | 0.34 |
| Total‡... | (40/23) | 485 | (41/10) | 229 | (21/15) | 97 | (9/6) | 74 | 0.20 | 0.32 |

\* As in Table 2, each ratio in the first four ratio columns represents number of persons per 1,000 metropolitan-district population. These ratios have been standardized, (1) adjusting for CBD acreage and (2) excluding pedestrian entrants. Destination ratios were omitted, since they were not available prior to 1944.

† See footnote †, Table 2.

‡ The ratio column totals are arithmetic means of the 4 or 5 separate time-period ratios in each column, each time-period ratio being given equal weight.

3. A complete table of year-to-year trends for specific cities is not reproduced here because of its cumbersome size and its many gaps. A careful examination of the data in such form has suggested the following cyclical, short-range variations in the entrance ratio (the single ratio for which the most information on a historical basis is available) during the past 30 years:

a) The ratio dropped during the lowest years of the depression in the early 1930's.

b) After climbing back in the period 1936–41, the ratio again dropped during World War II. This drop was apparently related to transportation curbs, heavy war industry employment with long hours, and shortages of consumer goods for sale.[9]

c) The ratio climbed sharply following the war, hitting a peak in the period 1946–48. It has since dropped slightly. This marked rise following the war seems to reflect the high level of employment, shopping, and other business activity, both within the CBD, with its consequent drawing effect, and throughout the city, with the result that more persons move through the CBD en route to other destinations.

## DISCUSSION

The findings without question support the fact that the CBD holds a position of vital functional importance. In the broadest terms, we have shown that about 1 person for every 5 metropolitan residents has at least one destination in the CBD during each weekday. And about 1 person for every 10 residents will be found in the CBD in the early afternoon at peak accumulation. These 1-in-5 and 1-in-10 ratios are most accurately descriptive for cities of about 1 million metropolitan population. As cities get larger, the ratios tend to drop. For smaller cities the ratios tend to rise considerably. It is obvious that these ratios would be even higher—for each city-size group—if only active adults were included in the population base figure.

[9] It is also likely that straight line interpolation may have overstated metropolitan population during this war period for many cities, with the net effect of lowering the entrance ratios.

It has become a rather common notion that dispersion has been making strong inroads on American cities. From such an idea one might easily be led to believe that relatively fewer persons have daily business in the CBD now than in former years. The present study, tentative though its findings are, would indicate that the CBD's of our largest cities (i.e., 1 million and over) are holding their own as measured by the entrance and accumulation ratios used as indexes, and that the CBD's of medium-sized cities (from 100,000 to 1 million) are gaining. Whether the level of economic activity in the period following World War II has been abnormally high can be appraised only by future economic historians. The fact remains that the 1946–50 entrance and accumulation ratios were considerably *higher* than the corresponding ratios for 1926–30. Although residential areas, some shopping facilities, and certain employment centers have indeed been dispersed, the CBD today seems to draw more persons per 1,000 metropolitan population than it did twenty years ago.

It does not require profound analysis to account for the fact that entrance ratios are so much larger for medium-sized cities than for the very large ones. The smaller the city, the more likely is the CBD to funnel traffic. But the fact that a larger ratio of persons have destinations in and accumulate in the smaller cities deserves attention. These higher ratios for the smaller cities apparently indicate a relatively greater concentration of functions in the smaller city's CBD. A question can be raised (not answered by the present study) as to how large a city must be before various types of facilities do spread to outlying locations.

Another query: if in the smallest city-size group investigated (100,000–250,000) there are about 250 destinations in the CBD for every 1,000 metropolitan residents and if in larger cities only 170 or so out of the 1,000 have CBD destinations, how is the difference of 80 destinations (per 1,000 residents) to be accounted for? Are these other 80 destinations in outlying sub-centers?

If the findings from this study are to serve as a point of departure for further examination of urban structure and function, it would seem relevant to suggest further courses of research endeavor. Two main directions can be indicated: (1) an analysis of the CBD's place in the contemporary urban community, but at a more detailed level; (2) the identification and description of subcenters outside the CBD—industrial, commercial, educational, etc.—to which persons are drawn during the day.

With respect to the former, the following deserve stress: A breakdown of entry and destination figures by type of transportation and by time of entry; the nature of intra-CBD movements, including those by pedestrians; the purposes for which persons have destinations (employment, shopping, professional office visits, etc.) and the relative importance of each purpose;[10] parking and traffic-congestion problems along with

possible solutions; and the future prospects of CBD's in the face of ongoing facility dispersal to outlying locations.

In studying the various types of subcenters, an initial task is to develop a satisfactory classification—to take into account not only the major single functions, such as manufacturing, retail trade, provision of amusement, governmental administration, and education, but also the various ways by which these diverse functions become nucleated into distinctive outlying centers. A further step would involve study of the daily population movement into and accumulation within such subcenters. We also lack sufficient information on the degree to which different types of facilities are used during any one visit to the subcenter.[11]

---

[10] The origin-destination type of traffic and parking surveys are now providing valuable information on this phase and might well be further tapped by urban sociologists.

[11] Svend Riemer has reported a research investigation relating to this problem and has suggested the term "walking distance area" as applying to the situation in which an urban resident finds a number of different facilities within walking distance of each other. He listed five types of walking distance areas: residential, occupational, educational, commercial, and associational. (See his "Villagers in Metropolis," *British Journal of Sociology*, II [March, 1951], esp. 37–40.) There has also been relevant research by English social researchers, including Tom Brennan, Dennis Chapman, Ruth Glass, and Charles Madge.

# CLASSIFICATION AND SIGNIFICANT CHARACTERISTICS OF SHOPPING CENTERS

In the decade following World War II the universal use of the automobile in the United States and Canada has superimposed a new retail structure upon the retail pattern developed in the previous decades when the horsecar, cable car, elevated railway, suburban railroads, and subways conveyed urban residents from their homes to factories, offices, and shopping centers. The central business district—the Loop in Chicago, Main Street in many cities—was located at the converging point of all mass transit routes.

The tens of thousands of urban dwellers who lived within walking distance of a streetcar line or subway station in apartments, row houses, or closely packed single-family homes on narrow lots, bought local convenience goods—food, drugs, variety items—in small neighborhood stores, and traveled on mass transit vehicles to this central hub for major apparel or furniture purchases. The throngs of shoppers discharged from streetcars, buses, elevated lines, subways, or railroad stations had no automobile to park, and they could move in dense masses along the sidewalks leading to the major stores, with little interference from surface traffic at street intersections.

Department stores like Macy's in New York, Marshall Field in Chicago, J. L. Hudson in Detroit, Wanamaker's in Philadelphia, or Jordan Marsh in Boston occupied, and continue to occupy, entire blocks to a height of 10 to 12 stories, concentrating a great selection of merchandise into a compact area by vertical elevator transpor-

tation. The huge department stores, specialty apparel stores, five-and-ten-cent stores or variety stores in the 100 per cent retail location, and all other stores, were built to the sidewalk line. The world's highest land values, except only for Wall Street in New York, were realized on State Street in Chicago, 34th Street and Sixth Avenue in New York, and Broad and Market Streets in Philadelphia, where the buying power of an entire metropolitan region was brought to stores occupying every inch of land in a five- or six-block retail district.

With the added attraction of concentration of all legitimate theaters, the central offices, banks, courts, law firms, and the leading doctors, dentists, and professional men in this same limited area, it came to pass in 1910 that the land value in the Chicago Loop, covering three-eighths of a square mile, was 40 per cent of the total land value of the 212 square miles of Chicago.[1]

## DECENTRALIZATION AND SUBURBAN EXPANSION

Retail decentralization began in the 1920's in many cities, as the population of urban regions spread farther from the center. Major outlying retail centers with department stores developed in Chicago in areas where streetcar or elevated transportation to the central business district was slow, such as at 63d and Halsted Streets, 92d and Commercial, 111th and Michigan Avenue, Madison and Crawford, and Lincoln and Belmont. This decentralization was facilitated by the rise of the movie

[1] Homer Hoyt, *One Hundred Years of Land Values in Chicago* (Chicago: University of Chicago Press, 1933), p. 337.

theater, which offered the same entertainment in these community centers as downtown, by the establishment of banks in these centers, by the rise of the modern drugstore with elaborate fountains, and by the willingness of national chain variety, apparel, and shoe stores to establish outlets in these outlying centers.[2]

These shopping centers, 7, 10, or 12 miles from the downtown hub, were satellites similar in structure to the central business district. They were located at streetcar intersections, elevated stations, subway stations, or near suburban railway stations, relying on patronage of pedestrians discharged from mass transit vehicles. The buildings were constructed to the sidewalk line and usually covered the entire lot. The peak of value was the transfer corner, the point at which the customers were discharged from streetcars or buses.

Such was the shopping pattern which was dominant in the United States and Canada prior to 1946. Sears Roebuck had pioneered in establishing solitary stores with parking areas. The Country Club Plaza in Kansas City had been established in 1924 as probably the first shopping center outside the central business district which did not rely entirely on mass transit and which provided some off-street parking. These were isolated cases or exceptions to the prevailing retail structure.

After 1933 there was a tremendous outsurge of the American population into suburban areas, beyond the limits of mass transit lines. Cities like Los Angeles and Detroit have had their most rapid growth in the automobile age. New home areas based on septic tanks, water and sewage-disposal systems not connected with the central city system, were developed over a far-flung radius. Families used the private automobile as the chief means of transportation to work and to stores. The journey to the central business district became far more difficult and time-consuming because

[2] *Ibid.*, p. 249.

it was necessary to drive to the suburban railway station or to the end of the subway or elevated lines and park the car there, or drive downtown through congested traffic and then search for a parking space, which also was expensive.

Suddenly the crying need for a new retail mechanism for suburban residents was met by the evolution of a new type of shopping center, which provided for off-street parking, usually in front of and sometimes on all sides of a group of stores set back from the street line.

The simplest form of the new centers consisted of a straight line of stores with a belt of parking from 200 to 600 feet wide in front of the stores and sometimes with parking also in the rear. Frequently stores projecting toward the street at one or both ends formed an L or a U.

In the case of a large regional center of 500,000 square feet of store area or more, however, the arrangement of stores in a line would string them out for 2,000 feet or more, which would be a long distance for pedestrians to walk. To bring the stores into closer compass, the mall type center was developed, first by John Graham at Northgate in Seattle, and it has become the prevailing type for large regional centers. In this type all the stores are grouped around a central mall, surrounded by a belt of parking on all sides. Deliveries of merchandise to the stores are usually made by an underground delivery tunnel.

Now let us examine the extent to which these new shopping centers have been built in the United States and Canada in the last ten years and what their effect has been upon the old retail pattern developed prior to World War II. We will classify these new centers as to type, depending upon their size and the character of their stores. We will analyze their relative importance compared with the central business district and with the older type of outlying business district.

We have classified the new shopping centers into four main categories as follows:[3]

1. The large regional shopping centers with a major department store of 100,000 square feet of store area or more as the principal tenant and a total store area of 250,000 to 1,000,000 square feet, on a 35- to 100-acre site.
2. Community centers, with a junior department store of 25,000 to 90,000 square feet as the principal tenant and a total store area of 100,000 to 400,000 square feet, on a site of 15 to 40 acres.
3. Large neighborhood centers with a variety store or a family clothing store of 10,000 to 20,000 square feet as the largest unit, with a total store area of 50,000 to 100,000 square feet, on a site of 10 to 20 acres.
4. Small neighborhood centers with a supermarket of 10,000 to 20,000 square feet as the largest unit and a total of not over 50,000 square feet including the drugstore, hardware store, and other local convenience shops, on a site of five to 10 acres.

## LARGE REGIONAL CENTERS

In May, 1957, there were thirty-six regional centers in actual operation in the United States, with 400,000 square feet or more of store area each, and at least one major department store of 150,000 square feet or larger, on sites of 40 to 100 acres.[4] These huge centers have an aggregate of 23,215,000 square feet of rentable area, or an average of 645,000 square feet of store area per center. The department stores have an aggregate area of 9,883,000 square feet, or an average of 275,000 square feet per center. There were at least five huge centers with an aggregate of 5,175,000 square feet of store area and 2,140,000 square feet of department store area under construction, and at least seven more with 5,700,000 square feet of total store area and 1,850,000 square feet in major department stores, in which commitments for leases have been

[3] Homer Hoyt, in *Urban Land* (Urban Land Institute, Washington, D.C.), April, 1953.

[4] For a detailed description and statistics on many of these centers see *Technical Bulletin No. 30*, Part One, February, 1957; Part Two, May, 1957 (Washington, D.C.: Urban Land Institute).

made and financing is assured. There will thus be in the United States at least forty-nine leviathans in the shopping center world by 1958. There are fifteen to twenty others in advanced planning stages which may come into existence by 1960, making a total of probably seventy large regional centers.

Among the outstanding operating centers in this group are Hudson's Northland in Detroit with a $100,000,000 sales volume in a 1,000,000-square-foot center; Old Orchard in Chicago with Marshall Field and The Fair department stores in a 1,000,000-square-foot center; Southdale in Minneapolis with Dayton's and Donaldson's department stores in an 800,000-square-foot center; Gulfgate in Houston with Joske's department store in a 700,000-square-foot center; Mid-Island Plaza, Long Island, with a Gertz department store in a 750,000-square-foot center; and Garden State Plaza in Bergen County, New Jersey, with Bamberger's department store in a 1,000,000-square-foot center.

In these largest regional centers, department stores occupy an average of 43 per cent of the total store area and in combination with the clothing, shoe, and variety stores comprise 70 per cent of the total store area.

In addition to these largest regional centers, there are seventeen regional centers in the United States and one in Canada with department stores of 100,000 to 150,000 square feet, and with total store areas in the center of 250,000 to 500,000 square feet. These eighteen medium-size centers have an aggregate store area of 6,079,000 square feet or an average of 338,000 square feet of store area per center and a total department store area of 2,176,000 square feet or an average of 121,000 square feet per center.

Besides these regional centers there are at least six centers in which a large department store occupies an average of 60 per cent of the total store area, such as Parkington and Virginia Square in Arlington County, Virginia; Edens Plaza, northwest of Chicago; Northwood in Baltimore; Cottman-Castor Center in Philadelphia; and Valley Plaza in the San Fernando Valley, Los Angeles. In these six centers there are 1,823,000 square feet of store area, of which 1,110,000 square feet is in department stores.

These large regional centers of 250,000 to 1,000,000 square feet of store area can only be supported where there is a trade area with a population of 200,000 persons or more. The largest centers in the New York, Chicago, Los Angeles, and Detroit metropolitan areas have as many as 1,-000,000 people living in that segment of the trade area from which they draw customers. The trade area for dominant department stores which advertise extensively may extend for 50 to 100 miles if there are no large department stores elsewhere in the trade area. Minneapolis department stores attract customers from a trade area extending as far as Montana. Amarillo, Texas, has twenty-two counties in the Texas Panhandle for its retail trade area.

It is obvious that there should be only one regional center in each segment of a large metropolitan area and only one in smaller cities. However, in the case of Bergen Mall and Garden State Plaza in Bergen County, New Jersey, there is a sufficient population (1,500,000 in the primary trade area) to support two large regional centers.

In the smaller regional centers, department stores occupy 36 per cent of total store area.

## COMMUNITY CENTERS

There are at least 120 shopping centers in the United States with 100,000 to 400,-000 square feet of total store area, which have junior department stores of 25,000 to 90,000 square feet, on 15 to 40 acres. An analysis of some 117 community centers indicates that they have an aggregate store area of 26,041,000 square feet and an estimated 5,200,000 square feet in junior department stores. These small regional cen-

ters have an average of 223,000 square feet each in store areas and the junior department stores an average of 45,000 square feet.

In this type of center, J. C. Penney, W. T. Grant, or a local department store is the leading tenant. In the 117 centers listed, Penney is the leading store in 27 centers, but Penney has a program for 100 stores in shopping centers, of which some are in large regional centers. The Penney stores range from 30,000 to 60,000 square feet in size, averaging 45,000 square feet. W. T. Grant has 25,000 to 40,000 square feet in some of these community centers. In other cases Sears Roebuck may have a B store, or a local department store may be represented.

Centers of this type may be either the largest center in a smaller city or a community center serving one segment of a metropolitan area. There are six centers of this type in Columbus, Ohio. A community center of this type can be supported by a population of 100,000 or even less.

In these community centers, the junior department stores are in a relatively much less important position than department stores in regional centers, occupying only 20 per cent of the total store area compared with 43 per cent for department stores in the largest regional centers. The total area in department, apparel, variety, and shoe stores is less than 50 per cent of total store area, compared with 70 per cent in these stores in the largest centers. These community shopping areas are also local convenience centers, and sales of supermarkets, drugstores, hardware stores, beauty and barbershops often constitute a high proportion of their total volume.

## LARGE NEIGHBORHOOD CENTERS

There are numerous centers of 50,000 to 100,000 square feet of store area, which have a family clothing store, or a variety store in addition to the supermarket, drugstore, and hardware store. No census of these centers has been made, but their aggregate number may well exceed a thousand. The future status of these centers is uncertain because the larger variety store chains—Woolworth and Kresge—are tending to make commitments for larger stores ranging up to 30,000 square feet in size, which they seek to locate in shopping centers with at least 200,000 square feet of store area. This restricts the largest store in this type of center to either a Ben Franklin type variety store or a family clothing store smaller in size than J. C. Penney.

## SMALL NEIGHBORHOOD CENTERS

There are hundreds of neighborhood centers with store areas ranging up to 50,000 square feet, in which a supermarket is the largest unit. Since families spend over $1,000 annually for food, a 10,000 to 20,000-square-foot supermarket with sales of $1,000,000 to $2,500,000 annually would be supported by 1,000 to 3,000 families, if they made all their food purchases at one supermarket; and by 2,000 to 5,000 families or 7,000 to 18,000 persons if they made half their food purchases at the one store. Food stores, drugstores, and hardware stores can thrive on a neighborhood trade.

There is a trend, however, toward larger supermarkets of 30,000 square feet of store area, which will draw trade away from the 5,000- to 10,000-square-foot supermarkets, as these stores attracted business away from the small 1,000- to 3,000-foot grocery store. Even these small centers have their strips of off-street parking in front of the stores.

If there is abundant land area for expansion, a neighborhood center can expand into a community or even a regional center. Southgate in Cleveland started out as a community center with J. C. Penney as the largest store and has expanded into one of the largest regional centers in Cleveland, with a 200,000-square-foot Sears Roebuck store and a 200,000-square-foot Taylor department store. The Village in Gary, Indiana, with J. C. Penney as the largest store,

is expanding into a regional center with a 120,000-square-foot Montgomery Ward store. The Southland Center in Cleveland likewise expanded from a community into a regional center. Southgate in Milwaukee became a regional center with the addition of a 200,000-square-foot Gimbels department store. Thus in a thriving community a small regional center may attract department stores, which transforms it into a full-fledged regional center if it has sufficient ground area to permit expansion.

## RELATION OF NEW CENTERS TO EXISTING RETAIL PATTERN

The new, planned shopping centers, characterized by free automobile parking, do not supplant the retail pattern existing before 1946, which continues to co-exist and to supply many of the shoppers' needs. The largest regional shopping centers do offer a complete selection of both fashion and convenience goods, but in these new centers, built at today's high costs, the most profitable lines are selected, leaving for the older stores, built at lower costs, the types of merchandise that have less rent-paying capacity. Thus, furniture stores, which require large areas for the display of sofas, beds, tables and chairs, etc., and have a low sales volume per square foot, occupy small areas in the new centers. These stores usually occupy older buildings on the fringe of the central business district or buildings on highways where land is cheap. Furniture is sold on the top floors of department stores.

In considering the whole array of retail outlets, we find a wide dispersal of food stores, drugstores, hardware stores, gasoline service stations, automobile salesrooms, and small stores of all types operated by the owners.

While 70 per cent of the total space in the largest regional shopping centers is taken up by department, apparel, and variety stores, only 30 per cent of the entire area devoted to retail uses in Cleveland is devoted to general merchandise or apparel stores. This shows that the new centers compete with the old retail stores only in certain fields and that they do not supply an entirely new merchandising mechanism but only supplement and supplant, in part, one that already exists.

## SPATIAL RELATIONSHIP OF PLANNED CENTERS

It is difficult to define the exact boundaries of a central business district or an outlying shopping district at a streetcar intersection. From the center of the downtown area with the large department stores and specialty apparel and variety stores in the 100 per cent retail location, there is a gradual, block-by-block transition to a lower type of use—furniture stores, cheaper clothing stores, light manufacturing. There is often no sharp, distinguishable break. Similarly, in the outlying sections stores often extend for miles along a streetcar or bus line, or heavy traffic street. There is a concentration of the highest retail uses in department, variety, and apparel stores at main intersections or in certain limited areas, with a gradual decline to lower uses as one leaves these "hot spots."

In contrast to the old retail development with its stores in a string, the new centers are usually clearly defined. A group of stores is set back from the street with a strip of parking in front, or they are grouped around a mall in the center of a huge parking area. Often there are no other stores or retail clusters in the vicinity.

While these planned centers are thus completely integrated and while they constitute a distinct shopping unit, they sometimes become associated with an old-style shopping district or give rise to new stores in areas near them. Evergreen Plaza at 95th and Western Avenue in Chicago, which was a transfer corner under the old-style retail pattern, while set back from the intersecting streets, stimulated building of stores on both 95th Street and Western Avenue. Woodmar in Hammond, Indiana, on 17 acres, started a surge of building on the streets facing it. The mile area between two huge regional shopping centers—Bergen Mall and Garden State Plaza—on Route 4 in Paramus, New Jersey, is filling in with stores until this area may become one shopping district. In Los Angeles some of the new centers such as Broadway Crenshaw have department stores (the May Company and Broadway) on the street line, continuing a strip commercial development on Crenshaw Boulevard, with parking at the rear of their stores. The Broadway Westchester and the Panorama City shopping centers in the Los Angeles area are also of this type. The stores on Wilshire Boulevard in Los Angeles, including Bullock's, the May Company, Robinson's, I. Magnin, are in a strip development with long distances between major stores, and parking at the rear of each store.

## IMPACT ON CENTRAL BUSINESS DISTRICT

There has been much discussion of the effect of the new, planned centers, which are usually in the suburbs, upon the sales of stores in the central business districts.

The central business district long held a predominant position in fashion goods sales. Prior to 1920 it is probable that over 90 per cent of total department store volume was made in central business districts in even the largest metropolitan areas. By 1948 the percentage of department store sales in the central business districts of forty-four of the largest metropolitan areas had dropped to 69.3 per cent and by 1954 it had fallen to 59.7 per cent. In Los Angeles department store sales outside the central business district are already greater than sales in this district and by 1960, when seventy regional shopping centers are in operation, the department store sales in most of the larger metropolitan areas will surpass the sales of the central stores.

In twelve of the largest metropolitan areas, department store sales dropped from $2,586,000,000 in 1948 to $2,359,000,000 in 1954, a fall of 8.8 per cent in dollars and more in physical volume, while they rose from $1,145,000,000 to $1,594,000,000 in the standard metropolitan area outside the central business district, a gain of 39.3 per cent.

The gains outside the central business districts have not been so pronounced in the smaller cities, where there was thought to be not enough business to support a department store outside the main shopping district.

Department stores still remain the bulwark of the downtown area, declining as they are absolutely and relatively compared with outlying areas. There is no known case of a well-known department store's not having a satisfactory volume of sales in the suburban store and it is usually more than expected.

Apparel group sales in forty-four central areas in the largest metropolitan regions declined from 43.4 per cent of the total metropolitan area sales in 1948 to 36.4 per cent in 1954. Shoe store sales declined from 41.2 per cent in the central area in 1948 to 35.2 per cent in 1954. Variety store sales in these forty-four central areas fell from 31.4 per cent of metropolitan area sales in 1948 to 25.32 per cent in 1954.

National apparel and variety chain store operators are making commitments on leases in regional centers; they are renewing leases in central areas only at the same or lower rents with a few rare exceptions. The national chains report a steady increase every year in their sales in the planned centers, with gains as high as 40 per cent in the fourth year compared with the first year of full operation.

We have compiled a list of 190 shopping centers with 70,000,000 square feet of store area of which 25,000,000 square feet is in department stores. These new, planned centers have all been built in the last ten years. This list is not complete and does not include several thousand smaller centers which are already in existence, nor does it include hundreds of others in the planning stages.

The department stores in these new centers have a potential sales volume of $1,-500,000,000, or 14 per cent of 1954 department store sales of $10,558,000,000. Downtown department stores will suffer not only from competition of new department stores but also from competition of J. C. Penney, W. T. Grant, J. J. Newberry, G. C. Murphy, and the variety stores which sell a wide assortment of clothing.

As a result of the impact of the suburban center, a new type of downtown retail area may come into existence, as suggested by Victor Gruen for Fort Worth or as is planned by Charles Blessing for Detroit, in which the main downtown streets are made pedestrian malls, with parking garages on the edges of the downtown area and moving sidewalks to bring shoppers and office workers from their cars to the center of the city.

Such a revamping of downtown areas, accompanied by an improvement in the mass transit facilities which gave these central areas their original importance, would tend to establish a pattern somewhat similar to that of the regional shopping center —namely, a belt of parking surrounding the stores with a pedestrian mall in the center.

This same principle could be applied to major outlying business intersections such as 63d and Halsted Streets in Chicago, as was suggested by Richard Nelson and Frederick T. Aschman.

The new, planned centers, with free off-street parking, will have a decidedly adverse effect upon string-like secondary business districts in outlying neighborhoods with little or no parking. These centers have neither the free off-street parking of the new centers nor the wide selection of merchandise of the central businss districts.

SHOPPING CENTERS IN 1960–70

After the present wave of shopping-center building has passed its crest, there may be a slight lull, but the resumption of the suburban boom in the decade of the 1960's, when the children born just before, during, and after World War II reach marriageable age, will start a new surge of shopping-center building. Practically all the population growth of the next few decades will be in suburban areas. As houses are built in areas beyond the existing settled areas, present regional shopping centers now on the outer edges of the urban growth will be in the center of a dense population.

The new federal highway pattern, with limited-access roads between major cities and belt highways around cities, will be the primary factor in locating the regional centers of the 1960's. Instead of building centers on the edge of the old cities as the first shopping-center promoters did ten years ago, the new centers will be located at a central point between a number of large and small cities like Allied Stores' North Shore Center at Peabody, Massachusetts, 20 miles north of Boston, which can tap a population of 1,500,000 living in numerous towns, cities, and villages by means of the Belt Highway 128, Highway 1, and connecting roads, aptly termed "women's roads" because they are free from the congestion of through traffic.

In the future, as in the past, the means of transportation from home to shopping centers with ample selection of fashion goods will be the governing factor in the location and composition of the regional center. In the automobile age, highway access, ample free parking, and a complete selection of merchandise are and will continue to be the decisive elements in the creation of successful regional shopping centers.

SECTION 14

# INDUSTRIAL STRUCTURE OF CITIES

Industry constitutes a dominant portion of the economic base of many cities, and the structure and pattern of industrial land uses have long been of major concern to the urban geographer. Industrial establishments have many specialized site requirements which limit the potential choices of location. These requirements include certain physical characteristics of sites, relations with other industrial and commercial establishments with which they do business ("linkages"), and accessibility to the labor force, as well as compatibility with their adjacent non-industrial areas.

The first article in this section describes the importance of industrial land and points out that industry must not be regarded as a "lower" use than residence or commerce, a point of view found in many cities in the past. The article indicates some of the ways in which the shortage of suitable land for industrial development may be overcome.

The second article in this section, by an urban geographer and planner, describes the history and characteristics of an institutional form of industrial development which has been responsible for major contributions to the evolving patterns of some of the larger industrial cities. The organized industrial district, which has had probably its most extensive development in Chicago, exists also in many other American cities; a recent study by the United States Department of Commerce lists over three hundred such districts. Such organizations are becoming increasingly popular in planning industrial development.

The study of the location of industry on the national and regional scale, on the one hand, and on the scale of the individual city and metropolitan area, on the other, has been very significant in the growth of urban geography. The literature on the subject is prolific. As in some other branches of urban geography, quantitative statistical methods of analysis are being applied more and more to this field. There is little doubt that our understanding of the principles of industrial location in cities would be greatly facilitated if official statistical sources, such as the census, were to compile and publish information on the daytime location of population and on the localization of employment in cities comparable to the information available on location of population at places of residence.

DOROTHY A. MUNCY

## LAND FOR INDUSTRY—A NEGLECTED PROBLEM

Every manufacturer seeking land for a plant, every local business leader promoting new enterprise for his community, every public official planning community growth compatible with industrial development will be affected by a recent decision of a Connecticut court. By this decision, a community is being shut out from a logical industrial expansion. Here, briefly, is the background:

Newington, a town of 10,000 in Connecticut, wanted to attract industry. This ambition was not unwarranted. Lying between New Britain and Hartford, the town could reasonably expect to share their industrial expansion. So Newington took the first step toward insuring that growth. An area of over 600 acres along the railroad right-of-way was zoned for industrial use.

To protect this land for future industry the zoning code was amended, prohibiting the erection of housing. Furthermore, this land was not to be subdivided into sites too small for plant use. Nor was town money to be spent for residential-size streets or for utility lines whose capacity could not serve future manufacture. Free from such impediments, a new industrial area could be economically and efficiently planned to meet the space needs of modern factories.

But the state Supreme Court of Errors did not agree. A developer who owned a 30-acre parcel, of which 18 acres lay within this industrial tract, wanted to build houses on his land. He brought suit; and on August 4, 1953, the court concurred with the finding of a lower court and decided the case in his favor.[1]

Reprinted from *Harvard Business Review,* XXXII (March–April, 1954), 51–63, by permission of the author and the editor. (Copyright, 1954, by the President and Fellows of Harvard College.)

[1] *Corthouts* v. *Town of Newington et al.,* Supreme Court of Errors, Connecticut, August 4, 1953, 99 A. 2d 112.

### PROBLEM AND PARADOX

This particular decision may have been justified by a technical defect in Newington's zoning code. But the significant point is the court's wording, for it typifies a prevalent attitude toward industry:

The amendment proscribes what has usually been considered as the highest use to which land can be put, namely residential use, in an industrial district where uses regarded as among the lowest and most burdensome are permitted. . . .

The court declared that it was not called upon to decide whether, as a general proposition, a zoning ordinance which prohibits a residential use in an industrial district is valid. However, the only situation it apparently envisaged as justifying such restriction was one calling for protection of residential dwellers, not of industrial users:

. . . where the erection . . . of dwelling houses on land in an industrial area in close proximity to manufactories using highly inflammable or explosive materials or giving off noxious odors or pernicious gases would have a direct relation to the public health, safety and welfare and justify prohibitory legislation against the use of such land for residential purposes. . . .

The implication is that industry operates by sufferance of the community, that industry has no land rights of its own. So long as this attitude prevails, it places undue burdens on productive enterprise, unnecessary inconvenience on workers, and inordinate strains on residential taxpayers.

What a paradox this attitude must seem to the manufacturer seeking a new plant site! Cities large and small, counties rural and urban, pay him ardent court, anxious to win his new factory. Many offer "dowries" of free sites, tax-free buildings, or free rent. Despite these overt gestures to attract industry, most communities subconsciously repel it by ill-concealed prejudice in local zoning and land policy. Unfortunately, little consideration is given to scientifically planning a new industrial area to meet industry's needs.

### INDUSTRIAL LEADERSHIP

Today, however, the industrialist is in a strong bargaining position. Many communities need new factories to strengthen their economic base. This poses the question: What should the businessman demand for his industry before he moves into town with a branch plant or expands a factory in its present location? Or, from the point of view of the community, what should be offered to him?

Modern factories, for all their individuality, have these needs in common: larger sites, desirable locations, good transport, protection from encroachment, unbiased pollution controls, and—most important— a place in the plan for community growth.

Because industry's thinking on these problems is often ahead of the community's, it must speak up. Industry not only has the right but bears the responsibility to ask for those things which will help it produce efficiently. Most towns, once there is awareness of the fact that the community which is efficient to work in will also be pleasant to live in, will be glad to cooperate. Such mutual understanding is particularly important for long-range planning.

It is the purpose of this article to explore ways in which business and community leaders can provide space for efficient industrial growth. The modern factory and its space requirements will be reviewed. Faults in community policy which hinder industrial expansion will be analyzed. Then a prescriptive program of action and research will be offered, illustrated by successful joint ventures on the part of industry and the community.

### INCREASED LAND NEEDS

Basic to a plan for better industrial sites is an understanding of the new factory. Industry today is building plants with far better space standards than towns have required or even anticipated. Several factors have contributed to the need for more land.

*Modern plant buildings.*—Since 1909, when Ford set up his horizontal production lines, there has been a trend toward single-story assembly plants. To cite a recent illustration:

Davis and Geck, the surgical-sutures unit of American Cyanamid, has sold its six-story loft in Brooklyn and built a single-story plant in Danbury. The old building had occupied all of a small city lot, less than 0.3 acres. The new factory in Connecticut, with one-third more floor space, covers only 25 per cent of the 10-acre site.

Along with this trend has come a growing concern for plant appearance. Today's factory is trim, attractive, and built with an eye to community relations and employee morale. Most plants are landscaped; indeed, many of them are rightly called "parks."

*Plant facilities.*—Facilities for employees have been expanded to include not only the usual cafeterias, locker rooms, and dispensaries but often multiroom hospitals, libraries, auditoriums, classrooms, and recreation areas, both indoor and outdoor.

Employee parking lots are a major land requirement. Often the 300- to 350-square-foot area required to park an employee's car is more than the floor space of his work station. Most war plants had good parking facilities (see Table 1), but postwar plants have even higher requirements. General Motors, for instance, figures a ratio of one car for every 1.2 employees.

Modern production practices also increase floor area and land requirements. Few industries now would build a new plant without providing off-street loading for truck and rail, including waiting lanes for trucks and additional rail sidings to avoid bunching. In a study of 240 manufacturing plants built during World War II, only two lacked off-street loading facilities.[2] On-site storage likewise requires additional acreage.

The trend toward self-sufficient plants has added to floor-space needs. Savings in downtime and better quality control are sufficient reasons for tool-and-die shops, paint, carpenter, and maintenance and repair shops to be on factory premises. Since plants at the periphery of metropolitan centers are a considerable time-distance from services in the central city, space for

*Technology and space.*—Technology too has increased industry's land and floor-space needs. The single-story factory, with its need for more land, was made possible by the change in the source of power. When the jungle of line shafts driven by water, then steam, was replaced by the individual motor drive of electric power, horizontal production lines became feasible and desirable.

Another factor has been the evolution of individually operated machine tools into multistation, semiautomatic milling machines. In modern plants, for instance, such

TABLE 1

PARKING RATIOS AT NEW INDUSTRIAL PLANTS, 1941–45

| EMPLOYEES PER PARKING SPACE* | NUMBER OF PLANTS BY DISTANCE FROM CENTRAL BUSINESS DISTRICT | | | | | TOTAL PLANTS | |
|---|---|---|---|---|---|---|---|
| | 0–4.9 Miles | 5–9.9 Miles | 10–14.9 Miles | 15–19.9 Miles | 20 Miles and Over | Number | Percentage |
| Under 2 | 47 | 39 | 24 | 13 | 18 | 141 | 60.0 |
| 2.0–3.4 | 20 | 18 | 11 | 2 | 4 | 55 | 23.4 |
| 3.5–4.9 | 5 | 4 | 2 | .......... | .......... | 11 | 4.7 |
| 5.0–7.4 | 3 | 2 | 2 | .......... | 1 | 8 | 3.4 |
| 7.5–9.9 | 1 | .......... | .......... | .......... | .......... | 1 | 0.4 |
| 10 and over | 9 | 1 | 1 | .......... | .......... | 11 | 4.7 |
| No parking | 4 | 4 | .......... | .......... | .......... | 8 | 3.4 |
| Total | 89 | 68 | 40 | 15 | 23 | 235 | 100.0 |

* Employee count includes major and second shifts.

these facilities must be provided on the site.

*Expansion plans.*—Area for expansion is so essential to some firms that they buy sites considerably larger than needed for immediate use:

U.S. Steel acquired almost 4,000 acres for its Fairless Works at Morrisville, Pennsylvania. Approximately 25 per cent of the site is now in use, and one-half the area is reserved for future expansion.

General Electric's new Appliance Park, near Louisville, has 400 of its 942 acres in active use, the remainder being held for expansion and an arboretum.

Westinghouse follows a rule of thumb that land area should be at least five times the initial building floor space.[3]

[2] Author's original research.

parts as engine blocks, heads, and housings enter these machines as rough castings, and they are piloted through several score of machining operations to finished form by one control employee. This obviously increases the amount of floor space per employee.

Technical advance in one stage of manufacture may, in turn, have far-flung effects in space requirements for subsequent fabricating industries. The heavy-press program sponsored by the Air Force provides an apt example:

[3] Malcolm C. Neuhoff, *Techniques of Plant Location* ("Studies in Business Policy," No. 61 [New York: National Industrial Conference Board, 1953]), p. 37.

The Wyman-Gordon plant in North Grafton, Massachusetts, will soon be forging large structural aircraft parts on a 50,000-ton press, now being built by Loewy-Hydropress. More than 23 acres of industrial floor space will be required to keep this and related presses in operation. The giant press alone will have a pit area of 2,500 square feet.

The products of this press will reduce the number of welders and riveters required in aircraft assembly. Therefore, the floor space per worker, which averaged 300 square feet in World War II aircraft plants, will be increased.

In the near future huge forgings and extrusions will alter floor-space ratios in the manufacture of other equipment—trucks, buses, railroad cars, and earth-moving equipment, to cite but a few.

To anticipate the net effects of automatic controls on industrial space requirements would be premature. However, I have observed, in many of the factories I studied, that where mechanization has replaced a highly manual operation, floor space has been increased for that stage of processing.

Technology has another important effect upon industry's land requirements—the tendency for an industrial complex to develop around certain industries. To illustrate:

During World War II, the synthetic rubber industry was built around refineries. Butadiene and styrene plants received their raw materials by pipeline from the "mother" refinery. Copolymer plants producing buna-S, the rubber crumb, also were located nearby, forming an interdependent industrial group.

Republic Steel is now constructing near Toledo a plant to produce powdered iron by a new process involving the use of hydrogen. The operations will be located next to Sun Oil's high-octane refinery, whose by-product—hydrogen —will be piped to Republic.

The question may arise whether land requirements for industry can be reliably estimated in view of technical advance. Industrial plants now being constructed represent the accumulation of much experiment and long production experience. The lag between technological discovery and appli-

cation allows time to interpret the effects on industrial space. Therefore, we should be able to anticipate with certainty industry's increased land needs at least ten years in advance, and to expect some degree of further increase beyond that time.

## GROWING LAND SHORTAGE

Despite the obvious need for more manufacturing space, most urban areas have not reserved enough land to insure efficient industrial growth. And some of the land once assigned to manufacture is now being taken away for other uses. The shortage exists not only in the older urban-suburban sections but also in rapidly growing new market areas and in the peripheral areas of metropolitan regions where new housing and shopping centers are often preferred to new factories.

This scarcity of good sites especially affects industries that are oriented according to market, labor, and/or transportation, for their efficiency depends on proximity to centers of population. As industries are forced to locate farther from their center of interest, hidden costs mount rapidly—additional movement of goods, longer journey to work, unnecessary cross-area traffic, uneconomical storage and service. This displacement of industry is costly to the community, to industry, to the worker, and, of course, to the consumer. It wastes physical resources and human energy, and it jeopardizes community well-being.

## FAULTS IN LAND POLICY

The underlying cause of industrial-site shortage is the lack of civic understanding of industry's operations. This results in zoning codes and land-use policy hostile to the growth of manufacture.

*Zoning's stepchild.*—While the purpose of zoning is to promote the health, safety, and convenience of the whole community, in practice industry is treated like a stepchild. Not only is industrial land given no protection from residential encroachment, but unrelated commercial structures, and even junk yards, have been allowed to pre-empt the dwindling supply of industrial land near the center of the urban region. This invasion has had tremendous social, economic, and fiscal costs.

Housing built in industrial zones inevitably lacks many of the community services generally provided residential neighborhoods. Normal deterioration is accelerated, and a "problem area" is created, draining municipal coffers and adding little to the tax base. Unrelated commercial uses scattered through an industrial zone likewise add to costs as well as limit development for plant sites. If the utility lines have been installed for industrial service, they cannot be used to full capacity. There are likely to be more public streets than needed, all requiring maintenance; and usually these are narrow streets, inadequate to serve industrial trucking or to carry the heavy employee traffic at opening and closing times. And, of course, both the residential and unrelated commercial uses make assembly of land into the larger sites required by industrial plants difficult and even prohibitively expensive.

Too often, land that is zoned for industry is swampy, subject to flooding, inaccessible, or otherwise undesirable. Poor land requires considerable preparation before it is usable by any type of industry. Is it reasonable to expect industry to bear this cost? Engineering representatives surveying potential sites are quick to check soil conditions, topography, and records of flood levels in the area.

City officials should reflect, as they zone specific land for industrial use, that most companies wanting to build modern, landscaped factories will be attracted only by clean, pleasant locations. Ideally, a site should be high and level, centrally located with respect to both highway and railroad. How many cities can say that most of their industrial sites meet these requirements?

*Inadequate standards.*—Nowhere is the broad gap between community thinking and modern industrial practice more evident than in the space standards enumerated in industrial sections of zoning codes. While most codes do require setbacks and side yards in terms of a few feet, they take no account of the acres of open land for off-street parking, loading, and landscaping that make the modern plant a welcome addition to the community.

The inadequacy of present zoning becomes positively serious when it permits the wilful or misguided exploitation of industrial sites. Some new industrial buildings which are being erected for rental purposes overcrowd the site and provide for no off-street loading or parking. Here is a case in point:

The owner of a 50-acre site proposes to build up to 6 million square feet of floor space for rental to industrial tenants. Compare this ratio with the 475 acres of land used for buildings of six and one-half million square feet at Ford's aircraft engine plant and related facilities in Chicago, or the 600 acres used for buildings of 5 million square feet at Willow Run. These are two of the largest factory installations in the world. The owner of the tract in question proposes to carry 10 or more times as much floor space on roughly the same land acreage.

If this tract were developed at the space standards modern industry has set for itself, several ordinary-size factories could produce efficiently there for many years. But an overcrowded site will soon become a blighted area. The city will have a new industrial slum. The financiers will see their investment depreciate. And the business leaders of that community will have lost an opportunity to strenthen their city's economic position.

When zoning codes permit exploitive space standards in new industrial developments, communities are taking unfair advantage of the vast majority of manufacturers who are improving the appearance and efficiency of industrial areas with well-planned new plants. When responsible management, at considerable private expense, provides off-street parking and loading to lessen congestion on adjacent streets and highways, surely the community should require the same for all new industrial structures.

*Obsolete classification.*—Because the approach to industrial zoning has been restrictive rather than permissive, zoning ordinances have failed to achieve the positive control needed to secure the more desirable types of plants. Most codes provide for only two types of industrial land use—i.e., heavy and light manufacturing. Heavy manufacturing may either be excluded entirely or be restricted to poorer districts; yet some plants of this kind may be far preferable to smaller plants which are built with less careful planning and less concern for community relations.

Light manufacturing zones are usually defined negatively, by a specific list of excluded industries, with a blanket permission of "any other use that is not objectionable because of the emission of dust, odor, noise, excessive vibration, or other nuisances." By specifically naming the industries to be excluded, the code arbitrarily withholds recognition of process improvement in those industries; while new industries, whose processes are not well known, may be unfairly banished to heavy industrial districts. Moreover, since zoning ordinances merely list the kinds of nuisance, without any specific performance standards, a manufacturer is prey to capricious interpretation as to how much dust, noise, or vibration is excessive.

*"Bedroom towns."*—Some communities in metropolitan areas consciously and deliberately make use of zoning to keep out industry. Others, however, are becoming industryless towns by default. The postwar flight of population from the center of the big city often arrived before the suburb or town had quite made up its mind what it wanted to be. The result has been a planless sprawl, rather than a balanced community development with space specifically reserved for industry. Now the few open sections that remain are either too small for industrial use or are surrounded by new houses and narrow residential streets, making access difficult.

A recent zoning incident, involving a rapidly urbanizing town in a rural part of a four-county metropolitan area, illustrates the dissension and hardship that result when a suburb has failed to plan for industrial growth:

In 1948 the planning commission recommended to the county commissioners that some of the remaining open land be zoned for future industry, especially a large tract along a main rail line contiguous to existing industrial development. The county commissioners did not accept this recommendation. In the intervening years, most of this open tract has been built up with small houses, despite a drainage problem.

By the spring of 1953, only a 19-acre tract along the railroad remained vacant. The owner proposed to build a modern factory, to be rented to an unnamed electronics manufacturer. In addition to the rail service, a major north-south highway was only a few blocks from the site. Truck access, however, was only through narrow and poorly graded residential streets. The plant was to be landscaped, with off-street loading and some parking.

Adjacent homeowners, whose houses had been completed only a few months previously, complained. Why had the county permitted their homes to be built if industrial use had been planned for this tract? The complaint was not against the factory, for most of the residents realized that the plant would be clean, the employment opportunities good, and the tax money would pay for needed community facilities. Rather, the criticism was primarily against the public officials whose lack of foresight, just a few years earlier, prevented a compatible development of homes and industry in this new area.

After many stormy hearings, the commissioners denied the owner permission to build the plant. But the problem is not solved. The community still needs a broader tax base. The workers need a wider choice of jobs. And the owner has no market for his land.

*Unprotected sites.*—With all the deficiencies of zoning, industries find even less protection in unzoned areas. In the early postwar industrial expansion, many manufacturers in haste for large sites built in open areas at the periphery of the metropolitan region. Usually these areas were unzoned and unplanned. Since these new plants were being built in open countryside, the lack of zoning hardly seemed a handicap.

But soon these factories found themselves in the whirlwind path of an exploding metropolis. Homes and shopping centers devoured the remaining open space. Country roads, built for lighter service, were soon overburdened. Bars, refreshment stands, loan agencies, and other poorly planned structures, attracted by the plant employment, were built nearby, blighting the surroundings and increasing traffic congestion near plant entrances. Also, without any zoning regulations, "controlled conditions" plants had no protection from the pollution of neighboring activities.

Many industries found that these rural-urban fringe communities lacked the experience, the funds, and the desire to provide the standard of services expected in an urban environment. Rural tax rates soon caught up with city rates. These experiences have resulted in a trend for many market-oriented and labor-oriented industries to locate at the edge of built-up areas, but emphatically *inside* city limits.

### A Positive Program

The remedy for these faults is an industrial land program developed jointly by business leaders and public officials. Such a program must call both for immediate action and for continuing research. Some problems in community-industry growth can be met now; the difficulties have been recognized, effective legal tools are at hand, and the successful experience of many cities furnishes example for corrective action. But other aspects of our accelerated technology and expanding economy require further observation before techniques to insure healthy growth can be confidently applied. Let us look first at some of the areas for action.

*Prohibition of residences.*—One of the first steps to take is amendment of the zoning law to prohibit residential building in the industrial district. Experience indicates

that during public hearings on such a provision arguments against the proposed amendment run along these lines: "What if industry does not build on this land for years?" "What are owners to do in the meantime if they cannot sell it for residential, farm, or commercial use?" Unless the lands affected by the proposal are small islands of open land, surrounded by existing homes, there is seldom strong claim that the land is needed for future homes.

The fact that a number of important cities have adopted such amendments, however, belies the difficulty involved in such an undertaking. More than a score of cities, including Philadelphia, Pittsburgh, Detroit, Cleveland, Milwaukee, Seattle, Los Angeles, Richmond, and Charleston, revised their ordinances to protect industrial land for industrial use. While a few cities adopted such measures before World War II, most of the progress in this respect has been more recent.

The prohibition of residential building usually applies only to heavy industrial districts. The fact remains that this protection is also needed for light manufacturing activities which might require large sites. Philadelphia's revised ordinance is notable in that it excludes residences in light manufacturing as well as in heavy industrial zones:

The specific uses which are prohibited in this District [light manufacturing] shall be the erection, construction, alteration or use of buildings or premises and/or land for:

*a)* Dwellings, except such as are for the residence of a caretaker, watchman or custodian on the same lot with principal use to which it is accessory and are located at least ten feet from any other building.

*b)* Hotels.

*c)* Libraries, art galleries and public museums.

*d)* Hospitals, sanitaria, and eleemosynary public welfare institutions.

*e)* Any use designated for a District having less restrictive regulations.

The passage of a proper provision, however, is only the beginning. The amendment is not in itself sufficient protection against the strong pressures to divert such space to other uses. Soon the restricted land becomes desirable, and the zoning board receives applications for non-conforming use. Before long a landowner seeks a declaratory judgment to determine the constitutionality of the amendment.

In the Connecticut court case described at the beginning of the article, the plaintiff purchased land in a heavy industrial district on December 14, 1951. The zoning revision prohibiting new houses in that industrial area became effective February 1, 1952. The arguments in that case are typical of those used after a zoning code has been revised: "This land is in demand for residential use." "This land is unsuited for industrial development." Thus, arguments which had been settled before the amendment was passed reappear and require refutation. *Those who propose that large, vacant tracts be preserved for industry must be able to substantiate the need.*

To meet these challenges, an industrial land reserve acquired through zoning must be stringently planned:

1. The industrial potential of the community must be carefully, yet boldly, analyzed; for that provides the bench mark.

Before a community can thus establish the amount of land to be zoned for future industry, many careful and varied studies must be undertaken. Planning studies prerequisite to industrial zoning must analyze the community in terms of its physical resources, population trends, labor force, types of industry, manufacturing employment, commercial trends, stability of the economic base, and transport facilities.

2. The quantity of land reserved must be based on modern space standards of those industries whose growth is anticipated, with reasonable allowance for technological advance.

Estimates for future land needs of industry are based on population and labor-force predictions, anticipated growth of specific manufactures, present manufacturing employment per industrial acre, and (a modernization factor) employees per acre in modern plants of related types of industry.

3. The reserved land must unquestionably be topographically suited to industrial development.

Consideration must be given to the natural features of the site, present and proposed transport, and plans for future housing and related services.

4. Procedures to encourage the holding of land beyond a few years must be applied.

The planning commissions of Cincinnati[4] and Philadelphia[5] have made valuable contributions to such industrial land-use plan-

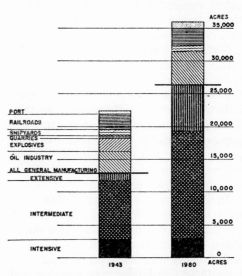

Fig. 1.—Example of land-use planning: Philadelphia metropolitan district, 1943, and proposed for 1980; area of industrial districts by type of district. (Source: Philadelphia City Planning Commission.)

ning. The results of the Philadelphia study are shown in graphic form in Figure 1.

Above all, if an industrial land reserve is to be facilitated through zoning, the pub-

[4] Victor Roterus, *Economy of the Cincinnati Metropolitan Area* (Cincinnati: City Planning Commission, 1946); also City Planning Commission of Cincinnati, *Industrial Land Use, Present and Future* (Cincinnati, 1946).

[5] Maxine Woolston, *Economic Base Study* (Philadelphia City Planning Commission, 1949); also Philadelphia City Planning Commission, *Industrial Land Use for Philadelphia* (Comprehensive Plan Report I) (Philadelphia, 1950).

lic and the courts must recognize that industry not only represents a legitimate land use but has pre-eminent rights in certain physical locations and therefore is entitled to the same protection that is given to residences.

*Industrial foundations.*—While these detailed studies may substantiate the need for land and thereby strengthen the industrial zoning ordinance as a land-reserve instrument, the question of ownership during the fallow years remains critical. Few individual owners, particularly small holders, think—or can afford to think—in terms of long-range investment.

Successful methods of holding land for future industrial development usually involve group ownership. One technique is the industrial district privately financed by industrial realtors, railroads, or specially formed development corporations. The improved site may be leased or sold at a profit; or the area may be intensively developed with buildings and services, available through lease or sale.[6]

In many communities, rather than holding tracts of industrial land as profit-making ventures, business leaders have established industrial foundations to promote and diversify manufacturing activities.[7] In turn, these foundations may purchase and hold land for future industrial growth. For example:

The Kenton Lands Industrial District and Commercial Center, near Covington, Kentucky, was formed four years ago by a group of 10 businessmen who saw an opportunity to gain new industry for their community. The plan was presented by the Chamber of Commerce, and the group bought several hundred acres of potential factory sites. The land is near U.S. routes 25 and 42, and accessible to rail facilities.

[6] For a comprehensive survey of industrial districts in the United States see Milburn L. Forth and J. Ross McKeever, *Planned Industrial Districts* (Technical Bulletin No. 19 [Washington: Urban Land Institute, 1952]).

[7] See Philip Ragan, "Industrial Foundations and Community Progress," *Harvard Business Review* (November–December, 1952), p. 69.

To date six industries have located in the Kenton Lands tract. The most recent, Goodall Palm Beach Company, purchased a 17½-acre site and is building a $2,500,000 clothing plant. Money received from the sale of sites is put back into the development fund to improve remaining land. Not until all improvements are in, and the area is given a parklike appearance, will the backers realize any return. The community, however, has benefited since the first plant began operations.

*Good transport.*—The importance of good rail, truck, water, pipeline, and even air transport to an industrial site cannot be overemphasized. An ideal site for many factories would be near an interregional limited-access highway and within the switching limits of a metropolitan rail-terminal area. Such a location would insure fast truck and rail service. Also the journey to work for many employees would be shortened in time-distance, thereby providing a larger radius for a labor market. And—just to illustrate the significance of some of the little things that often are neglected in planning—if the modern façade of the factory can be visible from the highway, such a site has extra attractiveness in the form of advertising and public relations value.

The economies and conveniences of such industrial siting accrue not only to the factory, its employees, and their families, but to the whole community. An efficiently serviced industry remains in the community, insuring continued employment opportunities.

Those responsible for planning new highways, airports, port development, regional rail or truck terminals, and pipelines can anticipate industrial growth that will come from these improvements. Industrial land reserves should be selected at the same time that routes for any new transport lines are located or sites for terminal facilities planned. For example, when new highway routes are established which parallel rail lines, enough land must be preserved between them for future industrial building.

*Off-street facilities.*—Zoning can accomplish another improvement in industrial space planning—off-street loading and parking. Progressive industrial management voluntarily provides adequate off-street loading facilities and employee-visitor parking in all new plants. To reinforce this trend the community should require off-street facilities, not only in the case of all new industrial plants, but for all new traffic-generating activities.

Without such a required standard, some new construction will lack these facilities—through wilful exploitation by a developer, through negligence, or through inexperience of the designer. The result will be mate-

The parking standards even of these zoning codes, however, are inferior to those of modern factories. In comparison with the requirement of 1 parking space for every 1.2 employees used by the General Motors division referred to earlier, only 4 of these 33 cities stipulate as high as 1 space for every 2 workers. To be effective, zoning standards must be brought up to those of private industry.

Some public officials and transit representatives assert that workers should use public transit for their journey to work. However, most new plants must locate beyond the area of frequent public transport.

TABLE 2

METHOD OF HOME-TO-WORK TRANSPORTATION

(Per Cent)*

| Occupation | Passenger Car | Public Transit | Walk | Other Means | Total |
|---|---|---|---|---|---|
| Professional and semiprofessional | 68.6 | 12.8 | 17.6 | 1.0 | 100 |
| Proprietors, managers, officials.. | 77.9 | 6.6 | 13.3 | 2.2 | 100 |
| Craftsmen, foremen, skilled laborers................... | 73.2 | 12.8 | 10.4 | 3.6 | 100 |
| Operatives, semiskilled, unskilled, and laborers............... | 61.4 | 16.7 | 17.4 | 4.5 | 100 |
| Protective services ........... | 77.6 | 12.1 | 9.6 | 0.7 | 100 |

* Source: *Automobile Facts and Figures* (33d ed.; Detroit: Automobile Manufacturers Association, 1953), p. 67.

rials-handling headaches and costly delays to the manufacturer and his industrial neighbors. By contrast, the entire community benefits from the reduced congestion and freer traffic flow which result from proper facilities.

Progress in this type of zoning has been slower than protection of industrial land from residential invasion. The Highway Research Board in 1950 reported that 33 cities and counties in 12 states, ranging from Clanton, Alabama, to Racine, Wisconsin, required off-street parking in industrial zones. Moreover, two-thirds of these zoning codes rightly recognized that parking requirements for industry should be based on the number of employees and not on ground or floor area. (Factory floor space varies too greatly among types of industry to be a reliable index.)

Still more significant is the fact that the automobile has become primary in the American worker's standard of living; it allows him freedom to choose a place to live and a place to work. The Automobile Manufacturers Association reported that even during gasoline rationing, in 1942, 73 per cent of the employees in 94 war plants drove cars to work.[8] Table 2 shows the continuing importance of the personal car for home-to-work transportation.

The manager of a midwestern factory gave me a good illustration of the way workers insist on using automobiles:

A new plant was built in a sparsely settled area, 8 miles from the central business district of a city of approximately 500,000 population.

[8] *Automobile Facts and Figures* (25th ed.; Detroit: Automobile Manufacturers Association, 1943), p. 20.

Since the plant was not within the regular urban transit area, and the main gate was about one-half mile from a U.S. highway, the manager had arranged with a metropolitan bus company to furnish special morning and evening service for the 2,500 employees. At first four round trips were needed just for the main shift. It was not long, however, before patronage began to fall off. Now, after several years' operations, one round trip each for the main and second shifts is sufficient for this large plant.

The economies of off-street loading facilities are too well understood by cost-conscious management to require further discussion here. But the $1 billion annual loss caused by traffic congestion in New York City streets is indeed a sobering thought![9] Unless prevented by equitable zoning standards, congestion can follow the outward trek of industry and population.

*Subsidiary developments.*—Protection of the high space standards of modern industrial establishments through zoning extends beyond requiring off-street loading and parking for neighboring activities.

Too often, as in the immediate postwar industrial expansion discussed earlier, a new factory is soon surrounded by unpleasant and unrelated land uses. Adjacent sites are quickly occupied by a motley array of refreshment stands, bars, loan companies, small stores, and gas stations, attracted by the ready market of plant employees. These structures seldom achieve the architectural or landscape standards of the modern factory. But aesthetics is not our primary concern. The traffic congestion which such activities cause along the highway and at the entrance gates, however, is a serious problem. With few exceptions, these facilities are poorly planned, with inadequate provision for parking and badly designed entrance and egress.

A different kind of problem arises in connection with such developments as shopping centers. Of the almost 5 million women employed in manufacturing indus-

tries 70 per cent are married and, presumably, have household responsibilities.[10] Moreover, with the changing pattern of family duties, men are doing an increasing amount of family shopping, especially in the suburban shopping centers. So the employment of a large industrial plant, or of a group of small factories, may well warrant a shopping service nearby. For instance:

William Zeckendorf, of Webb and Knapp, has announced a new regional shopping center to be built in Hempstead, Long Island, opposite the industrial development of Roosevelt Field, Incorporated. The industrial district now has four plants with 6,000 workers, and expects new factories with 10,000 additional employees. While the retail center will serve a much wider region, it will be a particular convenience for these industrial employees.

A shopping center close to an industrial development, however, requires especially careful planning to avoid serious congestion at the change of shift. Fortunately this particular kind of development can be controlled without too much difficulty through the zoning mechanism. The critical test of compatibility for shopping centers near an industrial district, or for any other commercial land uses not directly related to the industrial development itself, will be the adequacy of the parking lots, the entrance design, and the highways that will serve such large traffic generators.

At the same time, if industry and shopping centers can be required by zoning to provide high space standards, then the community must also fulfil its responsibility by planning adequate highway capacity.

*Slum redevelopment.*—The major concern in this paper has been the preservation of open land for industrial growth. It is well to digress, however, to discuss the possibilities of profitable redevelopment of slum areas for industrial use. Many industries "incubate" in small facilities near the crowded centers of our cities. Almost al-

[9] This is the conservative estimate made by the Citizens Traffic Board, headed by Percy C. Magnus, after a survey of New York City business and industry representatives, 1953.

[10] U.S. Department of Labor, *Women as Workers: A Statistical Guide* (Washington: Government Printing Office, 1953), pp. 27, 65.

ways they are strangled by not being able to buy contiguous land for expansion, and they usually move outside the city.

If any industrial expansion is to be achieved within the limits of our major cities, the community will have to use its right of eminent domain. Usually these growing industries are located in zones of transition—areas of neglect, surrounded by slum dwellings and dilapidated industrial and commercial structures—in other words, areas ripe for redevelopment. Many cities are submitting plans to the Housing and Home Finance Agency which call for industrial use of slums now being cleared. In most redevelopments the cost of the land is written down. But a successful redevelopment for industry—the Jones and Laughlin Steel Corporation expansion—involved no subsidy of any kind:

> Jones and Laughlin's original 80-acre site along the Monongahela River, across from downtown Pittsburgh, was completely blocked from expansion by a deteriorating area of incompatibly mixed land uses. To expand, J.&L. required 34 acres, which were covered by houses, 1½ miles of streets, church property, a public school, a roundhouse, and several small industrial buildings.
>
> The Redevelopment Authority of Pittsburgh, exercising its right of eminent domain, acquired this land for the steel company. No subsidy of any kind was involved. J.&L. paid for the land and all expenses of the Redevelopment Authority in acquiring the land. Speaking from this experience, Douglas S. Donkin of J.&L. said: "We believe that it is safe to say industrial development on a large scale in metropolitan areas can no longer be accomplished without some form of the right of eminent domain."[11]

Taxpayers and tax collectors will be pleased to hear that, according to a Pennsylvania Economy League report, this redevelopment project has increased the real property values in the city by $5,421,895, with an even greater increase to the county which also assesses machinery.

*Regional planning.*—Obviously planning for new industries cannot stop at the

[11] Walter H. Blucher, "Eminent Domain for Industrial Expansion," editorial in *ASPO Newsletter* (Chicago), October, 1953, p. 85.

boundary of the central city. Large metropolitan regions often include portions of several states; even small cities find their population spreading across county lines. Businessmen can perform a special service to metropolitan planning, for their actions are not circumscribed by arbitrary political boundaries. For example:

> The Greater Philadelphia–Delaware–South Jersey Council is an active group of civic leaders, corporations, public officials, and businessmen from 3 states, 11 counties, and 387 political units—"who recognize the necessity and the advantage of intelligent cooperative planning for the orderly growth and development" of the lower Delaware Valley. Such an organization, through co-operative study and public education, has greatly facilitated the public officials' actions necessary to promote efficient regional growth.

## FURTHER RESEARCH

I have pointed out some of the areas for action by business leaders and by the community. Concurrent with such action is the need for further research on industry's space and location problems.

*Space requirements.*—If industrial land planning is to be more than just broad estimates of space needs, detailed research should be made on land and space requirements by type of industry. Data now available are meager. The Cincinnati study used a single over-all average of 20 workers per acre to estimate future land needs. In Philadelphia the estimating technique was refined to four types of manufacturing districts, with the average number of workers per acre set as follows:

| | |
|---|---:|
| Intensive manufacturing | 147 |
| Intermediate | 40 |
| Extensive | 18 |
| Special (oil refineries) | 3 |

My analysis of 240 plants, representing 14 of the 20 major industrial groups in the Census of Manufactures, indicates that there is enough similarity in plant size by specific type of industry to warrant further investigation. Modern industrial facilities should be surveyed to obtain the following data by type of industry:

Total site area
Area reserved for expansion
Employment—by shift
Total floor space
Ground area of all structures
Distance of plant from center of labor market
Transport service to site
Area for parking and open storage
Employee facilities

From these data, ratios by type of industry can be computed for employees per acre, floor space per employee and per acre, parking space per employee, and so on. Such information will serve many important industrial planning functions as:

1. Evidence to support zoning large land reserves.
2. Criteria for selecting land for industrial zones.
3. Standards for design of planned industrial districts.
4. Information to guide highway, transport, and other land-use planning better to serve industrial activity.
5. Specific data to improve industrial recruitment techniques.

*Performance standards.*—Technological changes and improvements in industrial processing have been so great since zoning criteria were first established that present regulations on nuisance are obsolete. The location of manufacture in urban areas should be based on modern industrial practices. To put it another way, industries should be permitted or excluded solely on the basis of performance.

Considerable research is now being made on the use of performance standards in industrial zoning. Industrial engineers, public health technicians, and city-planning commissions have been investigating methods to detect and measure, and to prevent or reduce, industrial nuisance. Specific standards are being determined for noise, smoke, odor, dust and dirt, noxious gases, glare and heat, fire hazards, industrial wastes, and traffic.[12]

If an industrial plant is designed to meet high performance standards, it should be allowed greater freedom of location in the community. On this basis some light industries would be compatible neighbors in a residential area. And to the extent that any plant can be permitted to locate near homes, both industry and workers benefit from the shortened home-to-work trip.

The important requirement is a realistic approach. Despite much technical advance, some processes will continue to be objectionable, not only to residences but even to other factories. Such operations should be so located as to minimize their effects. Where vibration or noise are the complaints, as in forging and stamping operations, additional space and landscaping are often effective. Prevailing winds are an essential consideration in locating chemical plants which emit irritants. A site downstream may lessen the effect of process effluents.

But the offender is not always industry:

1. Sewage treatment is seriously inadequate in most of our rapidly growing suburbs. Few streams or rivers in our metropolitan areas escape this residential pollution. Industries that depend on this source must often treat water.
2. Armour Institute's study on noise nuisance for the Chicago Plan Commission found that 30 per cent of industrial plants were more quiet than the surrounding residential urban areas; only 6 per cent had noise loud enough to bother nearby residents. The Institute also found that industrial operations generally were not so noisy as the traffic that passed through adjacent streets.
3. With the spreading industrial application of dust collectors, apartment houses and commercial buildings are becoming the major offenders in urban air pollution.

[12] Dennis O'Harrow, "Performance Standards in Industrial Zoning," *Planning 1951: Proceedings of Annual National Planning Conference, Pittsburgh, October, 1951* (Chicago: American Society of Planning Officials, 1952), p. 42; also Louis McCabe (ed.), *Air Pollution: Proceedings of the United States Technical Conference on Air Pollution, Washington, 1951* (New York: McGraw-Hill Book Co., 1952).

Continued research in detection and measurement should lessen the number of charges now unfairly made against industries.

*Linked industries.*—Further research is needed to learn which industries could realize important economies by spatial proximity. If communities reserve large enough industrial tracts, a nucleus of linked activities may have an opportunity to develop spontaneously. But, as more facts about related industries are learned, positive efforts can be made to plan industrial districts specifically designed for serving interdependent factories.

This is too unexplored a field for public policy; yet farsighted industrialists have taken steps in this direction. As noted earlier, synthetic rubber production has already resulted in such "nuclear" developments. The petro-chemical industries, with their multiple by-products, are especially adapted to the economies of physical proximity and of diversified production. For instance:

The new Tuscola, Illinois, plant of National Distillers and Panhandle Eastern Pipeline is located on a 500-acre site at the junction of two natural gas lines, near the Illinois coal fields. The plant will extract hydrocarbon—propane, butane, and natural gasoline being salable without additional processing. Ethane will be converted into ethylene, and manufactured into ethyl chloride and synthetic industrial alcohol. A sulphuric acid plant on the site will provide acid for the alcohol manufacturing process. An ammonia plant will have part of its product converted into nitrogen solutions for the manufacture of fertilizers. A polyethylene plant is also planned.

## CONCLUSION

Industry and the community are not facing this land problem alone. The importance of industrial land needs was recognized at the Mid-Century Conference on Resources for the Future, held in Washington, December, 1953, under the chairmanship of Lewis W. Douglas, with financial aid from the Ford Foundation. The section which studied "Competing Demands for Urban Land Use" reported:

*a*) Residential uses should not be permitted in areas zoned for industry, provided the zoning is based on careful study of anticipated requirements, and the land is actually suitable to industry.

*b*) Performance standards for industry should be substituted for obsolete industrial zoning classifications.

*c*) The planned or organized industrial district, because of its efficiency and compatibility with nearby residential use, should be encouraged where appropriate.

It also recommended further research on:

*a*) Improved techniques for estimating industrial land requirements, and

*b*) Land requirements of various types of industry by size.[13]

The core of our industrial society—the factory—is far ahead of its urban environment. Our task now is to build our cities to be worthy of our industrial plants—to meet the neglected problem of land for industry.

[13] Resources for the Future, Inc., "Competing Demands for Land Use—Urban Lands" (Mid-Century Conference on Resources for the Future Reports [mimeographed, Washington, 1953]), p. 3.

## ORGANIZED INDUSTRIAL DISTRICTS

Manufacturing and similar industries in most large cities are basic activities which employ many workers and use extensive areas of land. It is evident, then, that for these centers one of the most important phases of a comprehensive city plan is the planning of industrial land use.

The need for an industrial plan and the complicated problems involved in preparing it are readily appreciated after seeing the blighted residential areas and industrial districts of these cities and noting the unhappy mixing of various kinds of land use. With few exceptions the manufacturing plants, wholesale establishments, and storage yards located indiscriminately throughout residential neighborhoods are a blighting influence on residential property. Moreover, many of these industries also suffer by being poorly located. On the other hand, many industrial districts with their old industrial structures, storage yards, vacant land and buildings, neglected railroad facilities, and blighted residential and commercial property are unsightly run-down areas detrimental to neighboring land uses, uninviting to new industrial and commercial activities, and a depressing environment for the many people who work in the districts.

Through the years this unfavorable condition has been evolving. With comprehensive plans to guide them, cities might have developed in an orderly fashion and land would have been used more effectively, but without a plan haphazard growth was inevitable. Now, in order to make these cities more efficient and livable, their

Reprinted from the *Journal of Land and Public Utility Economics*, XXIII (May, 1947), 180–98, by permission of the author and the editor. (Copyright, 1947, by University of Wisconsin, Madison, Wis.)

activities must be located in well-planned areas so that land can be put to its best social and economic use.

Considering the need for comprehensive planning of industrial land use, it seems timely to examine the organization and operation of private real estate firms which have been unusually successful in developing planned industrial districts.

### PLANNED INDUSTRIAL DISTRICTS IN GENERAL

Industrial districts, or parts of districts, whose development has been planned in some degree, are found in most large cities. The majority of these industrial areas can be called "planned districts" in a limited sense only; a few, however, have been planned in a thorough manner. Indeed, some industrial real estate firms plan and control the development of their property in such a comprehensive way that they may be called "organized districts."

Several types of planned industrial developments may be noted. Most large manufacturing plants—such as the National Cash Register Company in Dayton, Ohio, for example—are carefully laid out. These plants in themselves are planned industrial districts. Possibly the industrial land use in planned communities developed by large corporations at Longview, Washington, at Kohler, Wisconsin, and at Hershey, Pennsylvania, to name only a few examples, is planned still more carefully. A large loft building or a series of more or less contiguous buildings owned and operated by one organization and furnishing leased space to manufacturers, wholesalers, and warehousemen are still other types of planned districts exemplified by the Starrett-Lehigh Building and the Bush Terminal in New York City. Produce markets, such as the South Water Market in Chicago, Union Stock Yards, and similar facilities, also are planned industrial developments large enough in many instances to constitute a district. Another type of expansion, planned in part, and common to most large cities, is the subdivision improved with paved streets, sewage and water mains, and lighting facilities, and then sold piece by piece to manufacturers and others for industrial development. Certainly this kind of planning is better than none at all, but it must be admitted that a more comprehensive method is necessary in order to develop efficient and attractive industrial districts where both small and medium-sized establishments can build factories and rent space.

Comprehensively planned or organized industrial districts where industrial firms of various sizes can either erect, purchase, or lease buildings have been promoted by a number of private organizations in Great Britain and the United States, but few examples of private development are found in other countries. In the Soviet Union we know all industrial districts are planned by the state. In Great Britain, too, a number of planned developments have been promoted by the government. In most instances the privately owned and highly integrated industrial districts in Great Britain and the United States are organized legally as corporations or common-law trusts and are strongly fortified with large financial resources. They carefully direct virtually all phases of development and in some cases provide the industries with special services and facilities rarely furnished by developers of industrial real estate. In this manner the district is planned as a unit or "community of industries" by an organization working with industrial establishments rather than with families as is the case in so many real estate developments.

Briefly, in comprehensive industrial planning as characterized by organized dis-

tricts, the property is provided not only with streets and public utilities but with architects, engineers, and contractors hired by the district management to supervise the design, construction, and maintenance of buildings. These structures may be bought or leased by the tenants as circumstances warrant. Industries complying with district building regulations also may erect their own plants. To those firms requiring financial help to acquire land and buildings the developers advance funds at favorable terms. If the industrial tract includes many concerns, then public warehouses and other facilities and communal services, such as fire and police protection, may be provided. Moreover, the larger districts, in several instances, have a headquarters building with clubrooms, a dining room, and other facilities where plant and district officials hold business and social meetings. To furnish all these amenities in small tracts, however, is uneconomical. Finally, extensive promotional work aimed at selling the district and its services is another feature of this controlled plan of improvement. From this brief description it is apparent that while in most cases "the interest of an industrial real estate operator and his client invariably ends with the sale of land . . . in [an organized] industrial District, the sale or lease of property often represents merely the first step in the relationship between the District and the client."[1] At all times, though, the district management carefully avoids any interference in the activities of each establishment regardless of whether the industry leases or owns its property. Of course, when all the land and buildings have been sold, the developers have completed their job and the new industrial community is on its own. At this time streets and alleys may be dedicated to the city, or the industries may

[1] Michael J. Jucius, "Industrial Districts of the Chicago Region and Their Influence on Plant Location" (M.A. dissertation, School of Business, University of Chicago, 1932), p. 50. This is an interesting and comprehensive report.

assume responsibility for maintaining them. Complete sale of all property by the district organization, however, has occurred in only a few small tracts.

In Great Britain the Trafford Park and the Slough Trading estates are of special interest. The Trafford Park Estate in Manchester is probably the oldest and largest organized industrial district in the world. Since its establishment in 1896 this estate has expanded to 1,200 acres wherein are located some 200 industrial firms employing almost 50,000 persons.[2] Slough Trading Estate, a 700-acre tract twenty-five miles from London, has about 250 industries and some 25,000 workers. In contrast to the large districts in the United States where no investment has been made in residential property, housing estates of considerable size where plant employees may either purchase or rent units have been built in conjunction with both the Trafford Park and Slough estates. Planning in still a broader sense is illustrated by the noted English communities of Letchworth and Welwyn, where trading estates have been developed in association with housing and social institutions on garden-city lines. Of the other trading estates in Britain some have been promoted by private and some by public interests.

In the United States there are only a few organized industrial districts of any note. The Kansas City area has two important districts incorporating many of the features mentioned above—the Fairfax Industrial District, developed and controlled by the Union Pacific Railroad Company, and the North Kansas City Industrial District. In Minneapolis the Northwest Terminal Company has developed an outstanding industrial subdivision. In Los Angeles a large industrial tract, promoted by the Central Manufacturing District of Chicago, now is controlled by the Atchison, Topeka, and Santa Fe Railroad Company. In the Chi-

cago area, however, the scientific planning of industrial land use in the United States has reached its greatest development. Here an industrial real estate firm, the J. H. Van Vlissingen Company, has promoted the Kenwood Manufacturing District and other developments on land owned by the Phipps Industrial Land Trust. But the pioneers and foremost promoters of organized industrial areas in the Chicago region and in the United States are the Central Manufacturing District and the Clearing Industrial District. The remainder of this paper will describe briefly the development and operation of these districts.

LOCATION AND EARLY DEVELOPMENT OF THE CENTRAL AND CLEARING DISTRICTS

Both the Central Manufacturing District and the Clearing Industrial District have promoted several industrial tracts in the Chicago area.[3] All Central District projects are located in the southern half of Chicago with the two original developments near the city's geographic center. The Clearing District on the other hand has subdivisions within as well as outside of Chicago (Fig. 1 and Table 1).

Although development did not begin until 1905, the Central Manufacturing District actually was organized in 1890 by the Chicago Junction Railways and Union Stock Yards Company. It was formed as an operating unit to develop the many parcels of land which the parent corporation was consolidating in the area directly north of the Union Stock Yards. Owing to its uneven surface and to other factors this area had been largely skirted by the growth of the city. Most of it, therefore, was either vacant or used for non-structural purposes, especially lumber yards, and the lumber trade was an uncertain and declining source of revenue. Officials of the Chicago Junc-

2 "Political and Economic Planning," *Report on the Location of Industry in Great Britain* (London: PEP, 1939), pp. 90–120.

3 Mr. J. L. Hemery, assistant to the general manager of the Central Manufacturing District, and Mr. H. P. Phelps, vice-president, and Mr. D. P. Wells, general manager of Clearing Industrial District, Inc., courteously furnished much of the material used in this report.

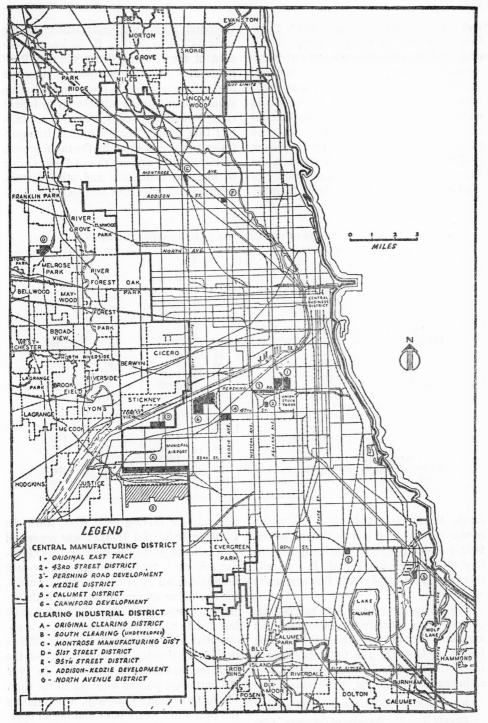

FIG. 1.—Industrial tracts of the Central Manufacturing and Clearing Industrial districts in the Chicago area, 1947.

tion Railways and the Union Stock Yards Company,[4] sensing the possibility of this land for industrial purposes, set out to acquire and promote it as an industrial real estate enterprise. Such a development would furnish the railroad additional freight. As matters stood, the companies' excellent facilities and services, developed to move livestock and perishable packing-house products with great dispatch between the Union Stock Yards area and trunk-line carriers, were not fully utilized. In other

thousand acres, was consolidated in the early 1890's by Mr. A. B. Stickney, president of the Chicago Great Western Railroad. This executive planned to construct and operate outside the city a large clearing yard to facilitate the interchange of freight cars between railroads entering Chicago and thus to help solve a critical transportation problem created by the rapid growth of the country and its railroad net. Owing to financial depression and other factors, however, the plan was suspended in 1893

TABLE 1

INDUSTRIAL TRACTS OF THE CENTRAL AND CLEARING DISTRICTS

| District | Area (Acres) | First Available for Development (Year) | Approximate No. of Firms | Percentage of Tract Developed |
|---|---|---|---|---|
| *Central Manufacturing District:* | | | | |
| Original East Tract................... | 260 | 1905 | 265 | 95 |
| 43d Street District................... | 22 | 1906 | 4 | 85 |
| Pershing Road Development........... | 90 | 1916 | 20 | 85 |
| Kedzie District...................... | 60 | 1919 | 35 | 95 |
| Calumet District..................... | 39 | 1925 | 1 | 35 |
| Crawford Development................ | 380 | 1932 | 11 | 15 |
| *Clearing Industrial District:* | | | | |
| Original Clearing District............. | 530 | 1899 | 105 | 85 |
| South Clearing....................... | 1,300 | 1899 | 0 | 0 |
| Montrose Manufacturing District........ | 18 | 1939 | 8 | 100 |
| 51st Street District................... | 87 | 1940 | 7 | 35 |
| 95th Street District................... | 12 | 1943 | 3 | 33 |
| Addison-Kedzie Development........... | 25 | 1944 | 10 | 100 |
| North Avenue District................ | 118 | 1946 | 2 | 5 |

words, the efficient and rapid service accorded perishable products "could be extended to serve equally efficiently a territory of much greater extent. It was only necessary to find and create this new realm of usefulness."[5]

The utilization of excellent railroad facilities, among other factors, also played an important part in establishing the Clearing Industrial District. The Original Clearing District, the South Clearing property, and additional land totaling in all about four

[4] Now called the Chicago Stock Yards Company.

[5] Richard Hackett, "Speaking of Ourselves," *Central Manufacturing District Magazine,* January, 1941, p. 22.

and was not revived until 1898, when the Clearing Industrial District was organized as a railroad project to complete the classification yard, though not along the same lines laid down by Stickney. Unfortunately, for a number of years there was little activity because the railroads could not be induced to use the yard facilities on a cooperative basis. Finally the Clearing officials decided to develop at least a part of the land for manufacturing purposes. In 1907 the northwest portion was sold to the Corn Products Refining Company, which during the next three years built and began operating an immense plant. Beginning in 1909 a 530-acre tract north of the railroad yards

—the Original Clearing District—was energetically promoted as an organized industrial subdivision; but distance from a labor supply, the absence of utilities, and other factors hindered development. Fortunately though, in 1912 the Belt Railway of Chicago, an important connecting line, organized and jointly owned by thirteen major railroads entering the city, purchased the Clearing District's railroad facilities and rapidly constructed enormous new classification yards. The Original Clearing District, by its proximity to these facilities, profited immensely. Like the Original East Tract of the Central District it now enjoyed door-to-door connections with industries located along all the railroads entering Chicago.

Inasmuch as it was illegal for a corporation in Illinois to own real estate, except for use in its business, the Central District was organized legally as a common-law trust. Three trustees control the organization and function as a board of directors, but a general manager and other officers handle day-to-day operations. Among the commendable features of this type of organization, as compared with a corporation, are ease of transferring control and development of properties to other parties, relative ease in changing the purpose for which the trust was formed, lower fee and taxation charges, and fewer and less-detailed reports, thereby enabling operations to be conducted with greater privacy.

Originally two organizations were formed to handle the Clearing property. The Chicago Transfer and Clearing Company was set up as a holding company to promote and finance industrial development on land owned by the Clearing Industrial District, a common-law trust. After the restrictive Illinois statute had been repealed in 1933 by the General Corporation Act, the Clearing Industrial District, after being incorporated, acquired the assets of the Chicago Transfer and Clearing Company. The new organization is managed in approximately the same fashion as other corporations.

## PROMOTIONAL ACTIVITIES OF THE CENTRAL AND CLEARING DISTRICTS

Since no function influences the success or failure of the organization more than that of selling, the principal job of the officers is to sell the District and its services. Because of this, and the further fact that they are large operators, the promotional work of the Central and Clearing districts is more extensive and thorough than that of the ordinary real estate dealer. In this job they have had valuable assistance from the Chicago Association of Commerce and Industry. In its never ending efforts to bring new industries into the city the association has advertised widely the advantages of a Chicago location. Naturally the Central and Clearing districts benefit from this publicity. On the other hand, the association's task of attracting industry is made easier by the presence of these organized developments.

Various methods are used to contact clients and explain the advantages of a District location, but some lines of approach have proved more successful than others. Advertising in Chicago papers and in *Commerce,* a publication of the Chicago Association of Commerce and Industry, as well as in other trade magazines, has been resorted to with some success. The *Central Manufacturing District Magazine,* which serves primarily as a house organ for the industries, has been published monthly since 1916. It includes descriptions of manufacturing plants, news of the activities and personalities in the District, appropriate scientific and educational articles and other items, in addition to considerable advertising describing the District and its operations. In 1945 the circulation of approximately ten thousand was distributed chiefly in the middle western and eastern states. From time to time brochures and pamphlets, in many cases elaborately illustrated, are prepared and distributed widely. The direct-mail campaign is still another way in which contacts are made. Form letters and pamphlets are sent to selected lists of prospects secured from state chamber of commerce directories and other sources. Feeling that many eastern plants are either moving to, or establishing branches in, the Middle West, the Clearing District has sent letters to prospects in the New England region. The Central District in a single nationwide campaign has mailed letters to almost ten thousand executives. Although this advertising is expensive, one new industry will, in most cases, more than pay for the cost.

By and large, though, personal contact is preferred over the methods listed above. Since each client represents an individual problem and since the average executive is not fully aware of the factors involved in plant location, it is apparent that a district representative—a specialist in the science of locating industries—can present a more convincing case for the District through personal discussion than the general statement used in mass advertising. Yet experience has proved that on the whole the best sources of prospective clients are provided by industries already located in the District and by industrial real estate brokers. Many excellent contacts have been made when satisfied tenants pass favorable impressions of the District on to business acquaintances. Bringing together interested industrial executives and district officials is profitable to real estate brokers because if a sale or lease is consummated, the District, on a purchase contract, will pay the broker a percentage of the total cost of land and buildings and, on a rent contract, a percentage of the total rent paid by the industry over a period of years.

Since from a financial standpoint medium-sized and small establishments fit best into this scheme of development, the districts have solicited and as a rule have secured establishments of this size rather than large plants. In most instances small firms make full use of the District's services and facilities. On the other hand, large corporations do not require this aid. In general they have their own facilities to make

thorough studies of possible industrial locations and to handle other phases of development. Furthermore, a large plant covering an extensive tract should be located on cheaper land than the districts offer.

In their promotional work the Central and Clearing officers stress both the situational and site advantages of a District location. Naturally they play up the "Great Central Market" idea. They describe in some detail that long and familiar list of factors favoring the growth of industry in the Chicago region. Fortunately for them, this list is so formidable that Chicago's situational superiority over virtually all rivals is easy to prove. Certainly this enviable situation has been a major factor contributing to the success of the districts. Within this great manufacturing and commercial area, as their promotional work further outlines, their planned developments, for a variety of reasons, offer better sites to relocated and new industries than the isolated location or the haphazardly developed industrial districts. The value to an industry of an attractive and conveniently laid-out industrial neighborhood, of financial assistance, of building design, of construction and maintenance services, of splendid transportation, and of other services and facilities, is presented in a convincing manner. Frequently noted also is the fact that this whole scheme of development is more akin to sound municipal and regional planning than the usual unguided method of plant location.

## SERVICES AND FACILITIES OF THE DISTRICTS

Some phases of planning in the Central and Clearing districts are common to many real estate projects, but other phases are not. Platting streets and installing public utilities before selling an industrial subdivision, for example, is not an unusual practice, but few real estate promoters design, finance, and erect industrial buildings. These are distinctive services. While other planning services and facilities are important, the utilization of the latter features in particular has enabled the Central and Clearing districts to fashion attractive and efficient industrial developments. It must be noted, though, that the districts did not begin by providing all the services and facilities furnished today but added them as the demand grew.

*Streets and public utilities.*—The method of subdividing land differs in the large and the small districts. Streets in the large tracts are owned by the the District, but in the small tracts they have been deeded to the city as soon as most of the factory sites are sold. More efficient subdividing of land, construction and repair of streets without first having to secure permission from city officials, and the routing of public traffic around the District, are the advantages of private over public ownership in the large developments. In these tracts the districts maintain the streets and then charge each establishment for the cost of repairs along its frontage to the middle of the roadway. If the time comes when all its buildings in the large developments are sold, the Central District may deed the streets to the city; or the industries, through some type of co-operative arrangement, may continue to maintain them. In the smaller districts the entire area may be improved with the necessary streets, alleys, and public utilities before any buildings are erected. Breaking the districts into blocks at this stage of development is practicable because the land may be fully utilized within three to five years. Furthermore, the property likely will be built up with small to medium-sized plants. On the other hand, it is common to develop large districts section by section. Their streets, 60 to 80 feet wide in most cases, are laid out on a gridiron pattern in contrast to some British trading estates where curvilinear streets have been adopted successfully (Fig. 2). Since a decade or more may elapse before the large tract is fully occupied, it is uneconomical to begin development by installing all the streets and public utilities. Moreover, it is also not good practice to divide the entire tract into blocks at this time; it is best to hold one or more sizable parcels in reserve for industries that might want considerable space. How long the land is held of course depends on the speed of development within the District as well as the demand for large parcels.

Water and sewage mains are installed by the District, but power lines and gas mains are installed by the utility companies. The distribution of water and electricity are of special interest, since they are not handled in the same fashion in all the districts. Al-

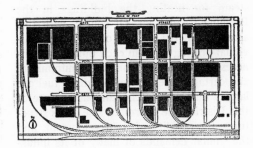

Fig. 2.—The Kedzie District

though part of the water used in the Original Clearing Tract comes from artesian wells located in the District, most of it used in this and the other Clearing and Central subdivisions is purchased from the city of Chicago. In the small tracts all the industries purchase directly from the city, but in the large tracts it is purchased by the District and sold to the individual industries at the same rate as charged by the city. In order to supply greater pressure during the summer months special equipment installed in the Original Clearing District repumps water to the industries at that time of year. To give buildings in this district added protection several group sprinkler systems have been installed. With these independent groups any damage to part of the system may be isolated to one unit with the other groups unaffected. Central sprinkler service has been installed in the Pershing Road and Kedzie developments of the Central District. Thus the erection of unsightly tanks is avoided and industries secure better insurance rates.

All industries in the Clearing District purchase electricity directly from the large power companies serving the territory, but concerns in the Central District are served by the Produce Terminal Corporation, whose generating plant is in the nearby Union Stock Yards which area it also serves. To supplement its capacity this corporation purchases the entire power output of a large plant operating in the Pershing Road Development. However, the primary purpose of the latter unit is to supply steam for heating the buildings in the Pershing Road tract. Of course, with this arrangement the expense of installing individual heating units in each building is unnecessary, the smoke nuisance is minimized, and cartage expenses for handling fuel are largely eliminated. The compact nature of this District, the enormous size of its structures, the rapidity of its development, and the similar demands of many of its industries made the installation of a central heating system practicable. In contrast, the other tracts were developed over a longer period of time and have smaller and more widely spaced buildings. Under existing technical conditions these facts in particular—slow and scattered development and small one- and two-story buildings—militate against central heating units.

Unlike Clearing, the Central District has installed and maintains street lighting paid for by the District.

*Financial arrangements.*—Providing industries with financial assistance, a feature commonly emphasized in their promotional work, is one of the most distinctive characteristics of organized industrial developments as exemplified by the Central and Clearing districts. Certainly this assistance, which may be as high as 80 per cent of the total investment, or more than many financial institutions will advance, especially in the case of small and comparatively unknown firms, has enabled the districts to

attain more quickly their principal objective of selling and leasing their property. It has attracted to the district many firms, and especially new industries, since it enables an enterprise to start with a nominal investment yet with adequate facilities. It is true as a British report states:

The success of many new enterprises depends on the speed with which it is possible to start production. Long delays in the early stages, after the necessary capital has been raised, deplete capital resources and irritate stockholders; meanwhile, there may be radical changes in the outside economic circumstances compared with those ruling when the enterprise was first started. Yet it is equally essential that a new enterprise should not rush into production without a full knowledge of estimated capital and operating costs, nor without a careful choice of site and a sound appraisal of labor requirements. If all the factors involved have to be investigated it necessarily takes time and costs money at a stage when both are particularly precious; [an organized industrial district] can enormously simplify and cheapen this initial investigation.[6]

In order to meet the various requirements of prospective clients, the Central and Clearing districts offer several plans for acquiring and leasing property.

1. Land is sold outright and the purchaser improves it himself within a specified time limit governed by his expansion program. Applying a time limit reduces to a minimum the purchase of land for speculation. All improvements, of course, must conform with District standards.

2. Land with improvements in or about to be installed by the District is sold outright. In this manner the client can submit his requirements and then accept or reject the proposals of the District. Moreover, the District supervises all details of design, engineering, and construction.

3. Land with improvements in or to be put in by the District is sold on a deferred-payment plan. In most cases between 20 and 30 per cent of the cost of land and buildings is paid in cash. The balance is

6 "Political and Economic Planning," p. 91.

amortized over a period of fifteen years or less with interest at 6 per cent. Insurance, taxes, and other costs are paid by the enterprise. In most instances the districts will finance a greater percentage of the cost of a standardized structure than a specialized unit designed for one kind of industry, because the latter building, if it reverts to the District, cannot be converted to other uses easily.

4. Land and improvements built to order by the District may be leased on a long-term contract. The enterprise pays an annual charge of 6 per cent on the agreed valuation of land and 9 per cent for cost of improvements. Of the 9 per cent charge, 3 per cent represents the cost of depreciation charges, and 6 per cent the cost for use of improvements. Taxes, insurance, and other costs are paid by the tenant during the life of the lease.

5. Space in buildings already erected can be leased for a short period at various terms.

With this broad financial policy, suitable contracts can be arranged for most industries desiring a District location. While the interest charges seem rather high, one must remember that it is a "risk" rate, since in many cases the districts are advancing from 75 to 80 per cent of the total investment to small and little-known firms. On the other hand, the borrower, without penalty, can pay off his loan as rapidly as possible rather than in regular instalments over a period of years, as required by some financial institutions. However, before a loan is granted, the prospective client is studied in some detail. As Mr. Richard Hackett, general manager of the Central Manufacturing District, states:

After a thorough analysis of the needs of an industry, based on its present scheme of plant and production, its general record of development, its costs, markets, and future program of sales and distribution, if there is reasonable coincidence between such needs and what we have to offer well and good. If what we can provide cannot be made to tally with the indicated requirements we should be the first to remark

the irreconcilable elements. Since in so many cases we are called upon to finance land and buildings . . . [with] our commitment . . . as great as eighty per cent of the total, our stake in the success of an industry should be perfectly obvious. We could not afford to make the mistake of selling a concern a site in our tracts if it would not qualify because we should incur the hazard of the return of the facilities. Moreover, aside from the financial risk, the presence of an unhappy or unsound industry would present the wrong kind of testimonial for what we have to sell.[7]

*Building design, construction, and maintenance.*—Designing and constructing buildings and then maintaining them as pleasing and attractive units has been an important factor in attracting industry to the districts. This service appeals to prospective clients because it relieves them of the task of selecting an architect, of taking construction bids, and of making arrangements for railroad and utility services. The districts can afford to supply these services more economically than when profits are divided up by the several parties involved. Then, too, large-scale purchases of building materials and considerable standardization of building types do lower construction costs. All these, including the financing, the selection of a site, and other services, can be had by the industry with the signing of one contract or lease. This unified procedure enables the districts to give occupancy in sixty to ninety days after signing a contract. Such speed would be out of the question if it were necessary to negotiate with several parties.

The close supervision of development, including a careful selection of new establishments whose operations are not detrimental to neighboring industries, proper building maintenance, and a general interest in landscaping the front of buildings insures an industry pleasing surroundings and protects the resale value of the property. All the developments, but some more than others, can claim aesthetic merit. Naturally they conform more to sound stand-

[7] Hackett, *op. cit.*, p. 25.

ards of city planning than the unguided industrial development. As the Clearing District states in one of its brochures:

The landscaped vistas and well-tended beds of flowers are in keeping with the inspirational quality of the architecture. Here it has been proved for . . . years that the industrial building may be beautiful and artistic, with limestone and panelled glass design as impressively wrought as in public buildings.[8]

Surely workmen will "come here more willingly than to the dingy type of plant which industry has endured"[9] for many decades. In such a neighborhood an industry can be proud of its address.

Architects, engineers, and other technicians employed full time by each District design all the buildings erected by the Central and Clearing organizations. That specialization has made these people experts in the science of plant design, and that good standards have been established to govern the use of brick, stone, and other building materials are reflected in many fine buildings. These technicians plan each structure as a unit to fit in with other buildings in a comprehensive scheme of development. A profusely illustrated brochure, prepared by the Central District, *Architecture and Design*, gives in chronological order a "visual record of changes and developments in architectural design for industry during more than four decades." Due in part to high land values resulting from its central position in the city and in part to the type of construction commonly used at the time, the Original East Tract, by and large, was built up closely with many multistoried buildings and with virtually no provisions for landscaping. The still more massive and impressive Pershing Road Development is even more of a multiple-story project, with those structures facing Pershing Road and Mc-Kinley Park built to a uniform height of six stories. Because in most instances they occupy cheaper land nearer the periphery

of the city and because more and more industries are using horizontal-line production methods, the majority of buildings erected in the Crawford and Kedzie developments and in the Clearing District properties (in line with modern industrial trends) are of one or two stories.

With the exception of some temporary frame structures, used for a number of years in the Pershing Road Development but now demolished, the districts have not provided limited space at very low rates for infant industries. Such "incubator" plants, of course, are a common feature of most British trading estates.

In building construction the Clearing and Central districts follow different policies. Previous to 1922 the Clearing District hired outside concerns to erect its buildings; but the failure that year of several contractors to complete their jobs at a stipulated time convinced the Clearing management that it should have its own construction department. Today this department—made up of a well-equipped force of key construction men who are employed full time—handles all the District's construction work, including the laying of switch tracks. Only part of a building project—roofing and plumbing, for example—is sublet to other firms. On the other hand, buildings in the Central District are erected by responsible outside contractors who are selected in competitive bidding. All work, however, is closely supervised by the District's engineers and architects. Both districts retain electricians, painters, carpenters, and other building-trade technicians to maintain buildings and equipment. All structures, including those that have been sold, are kept in excellent condition by being inspected periodically and repaired if necessary. Industries are billed for this expense.

The location of new plants within a District is governed by a number of factors. In the oldest and almost fully developed projects, such as in the original tracts, little land is available; hence a new industry desiring to locate there has virtually no choice

8 Clearing Industrial District, Inc., "One-Fourth of a Century of Progress," August, 1934, p. 2.

9 *Ibid.*

of sites. For this reason, as well as because of the trend toward horizontal construction, the District officials have acquired additional land for development (Table 1). In the small and only partly built-up tracts, too, the choice of sites is very narrow. On the other hand, in a large new tract such as the Crawford Development many sites are available.

Expansion in a large District, it will be recalled, begins by improving only part of the land with streets and utilities. Where a new industry locates in this plotted section depends of course on the availability of vacant parcels and the price the prospective client is willing to pay. Naturally, land lying along an important highway that skirts the District is more valuable than a lot located deep within the tract. Since it is the objective of the promoters to sell or lease as much of the land as possible, plants —although they may be widely spaced during the early stages of development—are located in a systematic fashion so that no unusable small or oddly shaped parcels remain unsold after most of the District has been developed. Provisions for landscaping are made by establishing a building line 15 feet back from the sidewalk in some cases, but more especially—at least in recent years —by platting wide streets and then establishing a narrow strip for landscaping between the sidewalk and the roadway. Plants also may acquire an option on additional land and hold it for expansion. Such lots are used for parking automobiles, since the districts provide no such space. Of course streets and utilities will be extended into the unplatted portions of the District to serve a large plant that the already laid-out portion cannot accommodate.

*Railroad and other transportation.*—Excellent transportation, especially railroad service, available in this great Chicago terminal area, has been an important factor contributing to the successful promotion of the Central and Clearing districts. But unlike some of the other services it is not a distinctive feature. Indeed, railroad trans-

portation in the Chicago area is so good that many other industrial plants in the territory enjoy service almost on a par with that available in the planned districts. Motor carrier service is excellent and is used by many firms but water transportation is of negligible importance. Air transport facilities, on the other hand, are improving rapidly.

Laying a railroad spur to the site of most new plants, even before the structure is erected, is common practice in organized industrial tracts. At first the spur is used to transport construction materials to the building site but later of course it can be used by the industry. Even though a new tenant does not require railroad service, the District, in order to facilitate the sale or lease of the property should the original lessee move, usually makes the necessary provisions at the time of construction so that a spur could be provided easily if the demand arose.

Switching and belt-line railroads in the case of some, and trunk-line carriers in the case of other tracts, serve the Central and Clearing Districts. The Central District's Original East Tract, as well as its three other principal developments, was built up chiefly to provide traffic for the short but very important switching line, the Chicago Junction Railway, while the growth of the Original Clearing District has been associated closely with the Belt Railroad of Chicago. These two connecting lines provide rapid and efficient service between each establishment in the large tracts and all the major railroads entering Chicago. The location of the other planned developments along the main lines of such carriers as the Milwaukee and the North Western railroads also has been satisfactory but not as good as a location on the switching and belt railroads. No doubt the trunk lines would provide more frequent service if the districts they serve were larger and more productive of freight, but under the circumstances it is difficult for them to do otherwise.

Since the Chicago Junction and the Belt Railway play a vital part in the success of the older Central and Clearing districts, it is appropriate to examine briefly the principal features of the service they offer. As many as four pickups daily are made by these lines. Carload freight moves out of the city on through trains after being picked up at the industrial siding. Less-than-carload freight, loaded in trap cars at the various establishments in the Central District and hauled to the road's nearby universal freight stations, is classified rapidly and reloaded into appropriate freight cars ready to be hauled by trunk-line carriers to their own freight stations for further classifying. Carload freight is handled in the same manner. In the Original Clearing District l.c.l. shipments are handled by trap truck rather than by trap cars. From the universal freight station merchandise is trucked by the railroad directly to trunk-line carriers. Without this service the shipper would be inconvenienced by having to truck his l.c.l. merchandise, in some cases several miles, to the freight station of the trunk line over which it is to be shipped. Package-car service to certain destination and gateway points also is excellent. Inasmuch as many industries are concentrated in the districts, more pickups can be made than in the case of isolated plants. The trunk lines, too, favor the districts by making more frequent pickups and deliveries of freight. Cars usually are spotted promptly after being requested. Then, too, the movement of cars on the switching and belt lines is facilitated by the fact that the roads handle freight only; hence there is no interference from passenger trains.

In the handling of freight one organized District—the Pershing Road Development—is unique in the Chicago area. In this tract a huge universal freight station centrally located in the District is connected to the industries by a traffic tunnel. Package shipments from each establishment are hauled underground on trailers directly to the freight station or other buildings in the District, hence no trucking to railroad freight terminals is necessary.

An interesting organization in the Central District is the Traffic Bureau of Associated Industries, which was established in 1913 by the plant executives under the auspices of the District. This bureau handles problems and complaints of shippers. Since it represents many establishments in a small area, it has exerted considerable pressure on the railroads for improved service. To facilitate shipments in the Original Clearing District a private traffic bureau has been organized to handle such matters as routing, billing, claims, and rate cases. These traffic bureaus illustrate the value of co-operation. Yet without the District organization to take the lead, and without a concentration of many plants in a small area, these results might not have been attained.

In the Central and Clearing developments, as in all industrial areas, motor carrier service is becoming more and more important. No doubt the enviable location of Chicago at the hub of a great network of trucking routes is a favorable factor attracting industry to the districts, especially in recent years. As in the case of railroad transportation, though, it is not a distinctive feature, since most industries are served by outside trucking firms many of whom have terminals near the districts.

Only the Central District's Original East and Calumet tracts are located along waterways. The latter division is still undeveloped, while the Original East Tract is bisected by the South Fork of the South Branch of the Chicago River, which is not now used for water transportation.

The principal planned developments on Chicago's South Side, especially the Original Clearing District, are close to the municipal airport. Those projects on the North Side, in particular the North Avenue District, are accessible to the huge new air terminal northwest of the city. For rapid travel of executives, salesmen, and others and for the handling of rush orders or perishable or quality merchandise, the splendid air service out of Chicago is an asset.

*Public warehousing.*—Since public warehouses commonly are needed in major industrial districts, it is not surprising that service in the largest Central and Clearing tracts has been made more complete and inviting by the addition of these facilities. Although, as in the case of the Central District, originally promoted by the District organization, the warehouses now are operated by private establishments. The Pershing Road Development in particular has immense storage warehouses in addition to the army quartermasters depot. One structure, built by the Army during the First World War but now operated by the United States Cold Storage Corporation, is among the largest cold-storage units in the nation. These warehouses, used for storage, light manufacturing, and other purposes by outside as well as District establishments, perform a valuable service. Among other things they enable a firm with decided seasonal changes in production to lease extra space during peak months rather than investing in additional plant facilities.

*Other services and facilities.*—The District organization in some cases, and the industries working on a co-operative basis in other cases, provide additional services and facilities in the large tracts, some of which are distinctive.

The subdivisions thus far developed are protected from fire by the Chicago Fire Department. The cost of this protection outside the city in the Original Clearing District is based upon the number of pieces of equipment used and the number of hours it is in service. Payment is made by the industries through their insurance companies. The installation and maintenance of several group sprinkler systems in the Original Clearing District and of a central sprinkler system in the Pershing Road and Kedzie developments is paid for by the industries on a fee basis. The fairly wide spacing of fireproof structures in most of the tracts enables insurance companies to offer favorable rates.

All districts in Chicago are protected by the city police force. In the Central District added police protection and especially night watchmen are also provided on a fee basis. Inasmuch as the Original Clearing District is located outside Chicago, it has been necessary for that development to employ its own police force. To furnish this service is one of the major tasks of the Clearing Industrial Association, a co-operative organization set up by the industries. To employ, full time, nine policemen who have been deputized by the county, each firm is assessed twenty-five dollars per month. In most cases the larger firms in all the districts hire their own night watchmen.

Industries in the original Central and Clearing developments, through their insurance companies, retain an ambulance, a physician, and other medical equipment and personnel to handle emergency cases.

Banking and clubroom facilities located in or near the original developments also are provided by both districts. The club facilities, including dining room service, lounges, game rooms, and activities of a social and educational nature, tend to bring together businessmen with similar interests. Problems and difficulties are discussed, and action is taken when necessary.

No doubt the opportunity of meeting in the clubrooms was a factor of some importance leading to the organization by the industries of four co-operative groups—the aforementioned Traffic Bureau of Associated Industries, the Clearing Industrial Association, the Pershing Road Association, and the Central Manufacturing District Club. The duties and accomplishments of the first-named organization already have been noted. In addition to maintaining a police force, the Clearing Industrial Association maintains men and equipment during the winter months to clear the streets of snow. It sponsors a bowling league, a soft ball league, a golf tournament, and other sporting events. It organizes committees to study taxation, traffic, employment, and other problems relating to the District and industry in general. In these and other ways it is performing a valuable service for the industrial community. The Pershing Road Association was organized primarily to unite the industries in a campaign aiming at widening Pershing Road between Ashland and Western avenues. These efforts have been largely successful, since the city recently widened and paved the roadway along most of the District's frontage. The Central Manufacturing District Club, organized and supported by industrial executives whose plants are located in the District, is primarily a center for social gatherings and business meetings, with its dining room service a major attraction. Certainly the existence of a strong central organization guiding the development of a planned community of industries makes the formation of a co-operative association of District establishments much easier than in the ordinary industrial tract.

*Labor supply.*—The diversity and enormous extent of industrial activity in the Chicago area, resulting in a huge labor pool of skilled and unskilled persons from which industries may secure workers, is a fact emphasized in the promotional efforts of the organized districts. But since establishments in the unorganized industrial sections also draw workers from this labor reservoir the Central and Clearing districts have no advantage other than the fact that their well-built plants and landscaped surroundings offer employees a more attractive environment than does the ordinary industrial plant. However, it must be admitted that the wage rate and the time required in traveling to and from work are even more important considerations in determining a person's place of work.

Securing adequate labor has been less of a problem in the Central than in the Clearing District. Because of their location well within the built-up portions of Chicago the industries operating in the original tracts of the Central District (although facing stiff competition for workers from establishments located outside but near the districts) have been fortunate in securing adequate labor. On the other hand, for a

number of years after the project was launched the firms locating in the Original Clearing District were handicapped by remoteness in terms of distance and inadequate passenger transportation from substantial residential neighborhoods. In view of this condition the Clearing District at first could not be as discriminating as the Central District in selecting new establishments. Gradually, though, the city pushed out, and many residential units have been built adjacent to Clearing since 1940. In spite of this the Original Clearing District, as later figures will show, has had a fairly steady growth. This would seem to indicate that the lower taxes and cheaper land outside the city, the splendid freight service, combined with the many other services of the District organization, more than offset the difficulties of marshaling a labor force. The Clearing District's decision to promote the Montrose and Addison-Kedzie tracts on the North Side rests in part on the fact that this section of Chicago has a dense and growing population with more skilled workers and less competition for them than the South Side. From the labor standpoint, then, these districts are well located. Moreover, they are fairly close to the highly desirable North Shore residential suburbs where many plant executives live.

A recent development, not initiated by the Clearing District but by a war veteran, is the establishment of an employment bureau near the Original Clearing District. This is a valuable service. Among other things it has handled the re-employment within the District of workers formerly employed by Clearing industries.

The distance of most districts from commercial streets made it necessary for many plants to instal some type of cafeteria service. Of course this is an added expense, but since most employees thereby are kept on the premises during the noon hour and rest periods, less time is lost than when they leave the plant.

*Growth of the districts.*—Although the Central and Clearing districts have experienced a rather steady growth, it has been more rapid during some periods than others. By 1917, ten years after actual development began, the Central District's Original East Tract rapidly had grown into a compact industrial community of almost two hundred establishments. Since by this date the Original East Tract was largely built up, the Central trustees acquired the Pershing Road property, then mostly vacant, and began constructing a series of huge loft buildings. The new district grew enormously in 1919 when the Army purchased land and had the trustees erect three immense six-story structures for a quartermaster's depot. As this tract was being occupied rapidly, thereby narrowing a prospective client's choice of sites, and as more and more firms were requesting one- and two-story buildings which profitably could be built only on fairly cheap land, the trustees in 1919 purchased the Kedzie District, still farther removed from central Chicago (see Fig. 1). Rapid expansion during the next five years ran the total number of industries in all the Central District's developments up to 323 by the end of 1924. Although this figure, by the height of the financial depression in 1931, had declined to 288, the district trustees, in order to provide a wider selection of sites on fairly cheap land for new firms and for establishments moving away from the congested downtown sections, signed a contract with the New York Central Railroad enabling the District to promote a vacant tract of 380 acres owned by the railroad company. Today this Crawford Development, although the home of almost a dozen establishments, is still largely vacant. As land there is valued at 45 to 75 cents a square foot compared to values of $1.50 to $2.50 nearer the central portion of the city, it can be held a fairly long period before development. Within the next decade the Crawford tract may become one of Chicago's greatest industrial communities.

It will be recalled that early development in the Original Clearing District was handicapped by inadequate transportation. After the Belt Railway of Chicago was organized in 1912, excellent freight service was available. The purchase that same year, by the Clearing promoters, of a large number of street railway bonds helped to extend streetcar facilities west along 63d Street immediately north of the District. The paving by the city of 63d Street in 1923, after continued efforts by the District, also proved valuable. The splendid freight service, improved transportation for workers, low land values (only 30 cents a square foot in 1945 compared to $1.35 in the Original East Tract), a tax assessment of one-half to one-third the city rate, and no zoning and building regulations other than those established by the District, so appealed to industrialists that the Original Clearing District expanded to forty-three establishments by 1922. During the boom period of the latter 1920's the District grew rapidly, reaching ninety-one concerns by 1928. Many of these were Chicago firms moving away from the congested portions of the city. In line with the majority of establishments that have located in the organized developments they were medium-sized light industries.

Since only a few vacant parcels remained in their original development by 1939, the Clearing management began promoting new tracts both within and outside Chicago. The 51st Street District, like the original tract, is located just outside the city (Fig. 1). Naturally, Chicago benefits more or less from the development of these nearby districts, but it profits more if industries are built within the city. Accordingly, it was a matter of great satisfaction to many Chicagoans when the Clearing District promoted the Montrose Manufacturing District and the Addison-Kedzie Development in the densely populated northern half of Chicago and the 95th Street District on the far South Side. Of these developments the Montrose District is of special interest to city planners, since it illustrates the rebuilding along sound planning lines of a blighted industrial tract of eighteen acres (Fig. 1). Here the Clearing organization, after consulting the Chicago Plan Commission, did a commendable job of rehabilitation. The irregular-shaped Montrose tract, boxed in on all sides by the elevated main-line right-of-way of the Milwaukee and North Western railroads, could be used satisfactorily for industry but for little else (Fig. 3). In this respect it is typical of many tracts in Chicago and

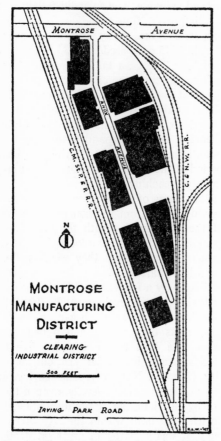

FIG. 3.—The Montrose Manufacturing District

other cities that are so hedged in by railroad facilities, as to be unsuitable for good residential neighborhoods. Within the space of a few months the Montrose District was cleared of several old buildings and improved with a paved street, public utilities, an ornamental gate, and landscaping. Within two years after purchase five modern one-story industrial plants were in operation. The impact of the war favored this

rapid growth. Now the tract is almost entirely occupied by eight attractive industrial buildings. Since all the land and structures have been sold and the street dedicated to the city, the Clearing District has completed its job, but in carrying through the project it profited from both a financial and a prestige point of view. Of course the city, too, benefits in many ways from this planned improvement. The fact that the Clearing District's latest development—the North Avenue District—is located in the far West Side suburb of Melrose Park, brings up the question of industrial planning and the future role in this program of large-scale and well-financed real estate developers similar to the organizations just described.

### THE FUTURE ROLE OF ORGANIZED INDUSTRIAL DISTRICTS IN A REDEVELOPMENT PROGRAM

The Central and Clearing districts have proved by example that they can develop planned industrial communities. However, their ability to do this depends on a number of factors. By and large they have developed vacant land that was held as one parcel at the time of purchase, or at the most in only a few parcels. Also it was fairly cheap land located, with some exceptions, well out from central Chicago. Then, too, for taxing purposes most of it was assessed at a rather low rate at the time of acquisition. In view of these conditions and the further fact that they were prepared to make long-term investments and operate without profit for several years, the districts have been able to succeed in spite of slow expansion. Since the possibility of slow development must be faced, it is doubtful whether organizations like Central and Clearing could successfully redevelop a sizable portion of a long-established industrial area where it may be necessary to purchase old buildings at a high price and then demolish them before new construction begins, and where land is expensive and difficult to assemble into economical units. The industrially-zoned land near the core of large cities costs too much for the growing number of manufacturers desiring horizontal line production housed in one-story buildings. This condition, combined with high taxes, especially personal property taxes and other factors, has caused some Chicago industries with highly-valued inventories to locate in the Clearing District and in other areas near and beyond the periphery of the city. On the other hand, in many instances, higher telephone, public utility, and insurance costs partly offset the advantages of a location outside the city. In general, though, it must be admitted that if taxes and land costs within the cities could be cut to a point where it is economically feasible to build one- and two-story buildings, to provide space for landscaping, and to hold vacant lots for expansion and automobile parking, and if land could be assembled easily into economic units, then organizations similar to the Central and Clearing districts might play an important role in the rebuilding of an industrial area. Under existing conditions their efforts will be confined largely to developing new industrial districts on vacant tracts located in the outer margins of cities and beyond.

## RESIDENTIAL STRUCTURE OF CITIES

Despite the fact that a large proportion of the land in our urban centers is used for residential purposes, geographers have not contributed substantially to generalizations regarding the location and character of urban residential areas. For many of the theories, as well as the empirical data related to the residential structure of American cities, geographers must depend on the work of sociologists, urban ecologists, and those interested in urban land economics. For example, Burgess, in studying the ecology of Chicago, suggested the concentric zone hypothesis as an ideal typical pattern of community growth. His is probably the best-known conception of urban growth patterns among the social scientists. His theory, like all the others which have subsequently been advanced, is based on the assumption that the residential structure of an urban center is an outgrowth of socioeconomic factors operating through time. Land for homes, as for any other use not prohibited by zoning restrictions or local taboos, goes to the highest bidder. Thus the wealthy are able to select the locations within our cities and metropolitan areas which please them. Commonly, high points or sites which provide pleasant views and freedom from nuisances such as smoke, noise, and odor are most highly valued. The poor, on the other hand, are forced to seek shelter in places not considered suitable by those who have achieved a higher economic status.

But wealth is not the only factor determining the location and character of human habitations within our urban settings. Social factors also play their role. Thus the location and character of certain residential segments of our large cities are determined by the status of specific racial, national, or cultural groups. Likewise, time and distance to work are factors influencing the residential development of urban centers and their outlying areas. Some people prefer to live close to their work; others are willing to endure the discomforts of traveling long distances from home to office in order to enjoy the more open spaces of suburban living. The presence of downtown skyscraper apartments on choice sites is evidence of the desire of many to live near their work and near the conveniences and pleasures provided by the central business district.

However, the residential structure of our modern cities cannot be understood solely in terms of socioeconomic factors operating in the present. Residential spaces undergo change, both in location and in character, as a result of obsolescence, city growth, and technological advances. As time goes on, some areas gain in prestige as living areas; others decline. Fringe areas, heretofore inaccessible, are made available for settlement as improvements in transportation facilities take place. These and other developments must be taken into consideration when explaining the residential structure of our modern cities.

The first of the two articles included in this section, Homer Hoyt's "The Pattern of Movement of Residential Rental Neighborhoods," an oft-quoted reference, has given rise to the sector theory of urban growth. According to Hoyt, the American city takes the shape of an octopus with tentacles extending in various directions along transportation lines. Having gathered his data from real property inventories of 142 American cities, he maintains that high-rent areas move outward along one sector as the cities grow. An accompanying chart shows shifts in the location of fashionable residential areas in six American cities from 1900 to 1932 and depicts graphically the sector theory of city growth.

Associated with the location of residential areas of different types is the problem of urban housing. This problem is by no means a new one, for cities have always been hard pressed to provide housing facilities adequate for healthful and comfortable living. With our recent rapid expansion of urban population, areas characterized by deteriorated dwelling units are increasing in extent. Ordinarily, one finds these areas adjacent to downtown business districts, but they are not limited to such locations. They may also be found near heavy industries, along major transportation routes, and in certain sectors of the outlying suburban areas.

The article "Substandard Urban Housing in the United States: A Quantitative Analysis," by George W. Hartman and John C. Hook, makes a significant contribution to a better understanding of the problem. The authors undertook to establish principles that account for areal variations in the proportion of substandard housing in the United States and found that the proportion of families with low income and the proportion of certain family types restricted in choice of residence are relatively good indicators of substandardness.

HOMER HOYT

# THE PATTERN OF MOVEMENT OF RESIDENTIAL RENTAL NEIGHBORHOODS

Of the various shifts that take place in the internal structure of a city as a result of population growth, the movement of the residential rental neighborhoods most vitally concerns the home-owner or the investor in residential mortgages. This study is primarily concerned with residential areas; the other types of land uses are considered because of their influence upon the home sections of the city. Hence the technique for determining the pattern of movement of residential rental areas has unusual importance, and the formulation of the principles defining the path of neighborhood growth is one of the focal points of this study.

From the high-rent areas that are frequently located on the periphery of one or more sectors of American cities, there is a downward gradation of rents until one reaches the low-rent areas near the business center. The low-rent areas are usually large and may extend from this center to the periphery on one side of the urban community. The high, low, and intermediate rental neighborhoods, however, did not always occupy these locations on the urban site. Their present positions are the points reached in the course of a movement taking place over a period of time. It is not a movement of buildings but a shifting and a change in the character of occupants that produces neighborhood change. New patterns of rent areas are formed as the city grows and adds new structures by both vertical and lateral expansion.

There is a need then for a technique for

Reprinted from *The Structure and Growth of Residential Neighborhoods in American Cities* (Washington, D.C.: Federal Housing Administration, 1939), pp. 112–22, with permission of the author.

measuring the movement of the different types of rental neighborhoods so that the pattern of movement may be established. By tracing the course traversed by the residential communities of the various rental grades, principles may be formulated explaining the causes for neighborhood changes.

To measure the movement of rental neighborhoods over a period of time, a series of maps showing the average rent of dwelling units, block by block at different dates, would be desirable. Such maps are available for very recent years for those cities in which real property surveys have been conducted. Unfortunately, however, there is no series of real property surveys that will permit an exact comparison of rental areas at different time intervals. But the question of the shape and direction of movement of different rental areas is of vital importance, and it is necessary to use the best evidence available, even if it is not so accurate as real property survey data.

One method of showing the changes that have occurred is to compare a map showing the various rental areas today with a map showing the entire settled area at a previous period of time. When it is found, as in the case of Washington (Fig. 1), that all the highest rental areas of 1934 lie beyond the limits of the settled area of 1887, it is evident that the best residential section has moved from some point within the area occupied by houses in 1887 to a new area that was entirely vacant at that time.

The use of dynamic factor maps, however, indicates the changes in the location of residential neighborhoods more exactly. These are constructed from evidence gleaned from old inhabitants. Those who have spent their lives in a city are often the only source of information on neighborhood changes. They have been eyewitnesses of the shifting character of neighborhoods. If a number of these residents are consulted independently and if they corroborate each other, much confidence may be placed in their evidence. To secure an accurate picture of the change, however, each of the residents should be asked to draw on a blank map of the city a line around the

blocks in which the average rents of dwelling units were the highest in successive periods of time, such as 1900 and 1915. Similarly, the same residents may be requested to draw, on another map, lines around the blocks in which the average rents of dwelling units were lowest at the same periods of time. Data for recent years are available, for a large number of cities, from real property surveys. In cities not surveyed, recent data may often be secured from local real estate boards. Likewise the

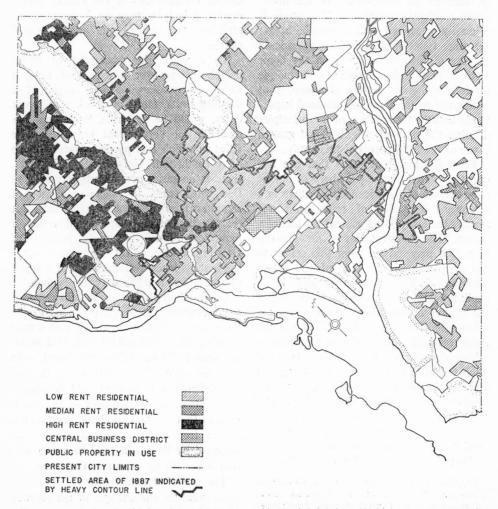

LOW RENT RESIDENTIAL

MEDIAN RENT RESIDENTIAL

HIGH RENT RESIDENTIAL

CENTRAL BUSINESS DISTRICT

PUBLIC PROPERTY IN USE

PRESENT CITY LIMITS

SETTLED AREA OF 1887 INDICATED
BY HEAVY CONTOUR LINE

FIG. 1.—Distribution of rental areas in 1934 compared with settled areas of 1887, Washington, D.C. (Source: Civil Works Administration, *Real Property Inventory for the District of Columbia, 1934* [Washington, D.C.: Federal Housing Administration, Division of Economics and Statistics].)

location of factory and commercial areas may be drawn from the same periods of time.

In securing this type of evidence, it is desirable to ask only for the rental extremes —the most fashionable area on the one hand, the lowest-rent area on the other. Persons depending upon memory might well fail to distinguish between intermediate gradations in rental areas that existed a number of years ago. It is desirable also to select time intervals a considerable number of years apart, so that there will be time for pronounced changes to have occurred that could easily be recalled.

The evidence of such witnesses may be further checked by an examination of the areas outlined. Old fashionable areas usually leave their traces in the form of a few obsolete mansions that are still standing. Frequently old photographic and historical records reveal the character of neighborhoods at an earlier period.

*The high-rent neighborhoods of a city do not skip about at random in the process of movement; they follow a definite path in one or more sectors of the city.*

Apparently there is a tendency for neighborhoods within a city to shift in accordance with what may be called the "sector theory" of neighborhood change. The understanding of the framework within which this principle operates will be facilitated by considering the entire city as a circle and various neighborhoods as falling into sectors radiating out from the center of that circle. No city conforms exactly to this ideal pattern, of course, but the general figure is useful inasmuch as in our American cities the different types of residential areas tend to grow outward along rather distinct radii, and new growth on the arc of a given sector tends to take on the character of the initial growth in that sector.

Thus if one sector of a city first develops as a low-rent residential area, it will tend to retain that character for long distances as the sector is extended through process of the city's growth. On the other hand, if

a high-rent area becomes established in another sector of the city, it will tend to grow or expand within that sector, and new high-grade areas will tend to establish themselves in the sector's outward extension. This tendency is portrayed in Figure 2 by the shifts in the location of the fashionable residential areas in six American cities between 1900 and 1936. Generally speaking, different sectors of a city present different characters according to the original types of the neighborhoods within them.

In considering the growth of a city, the movement of the high-rent area is in a certain sense the most important because it tends to pull the growth of the entire city in the same direction. The homes of the leaders of society are located at some point in the high-rent area. This location is the point of highest rents or the high-rent pole. Residential rents grade downward from this pole as lesser income groups seek to get as close to it as possible. This high-rent pole tends to move outward from the center of the city along a certain avenue or lateral line. The new houses constructed for the occupancy of the higher rental groups are situated on the outward edges of the high-rent area. As these areas grow outward, the lower and intermediate rental groups filter into the homes given up by the higher income groups. In New York City the movement was up Fifth Avenue, starting at Washington Square and proceeding finally to Ninety-sixth Street in the course of a century. In Chicago, there were three high-rental areas, moving southward along Michigan and Wabash Avenues, westward in the band between Jackson and Washington Boulevards, and northward along La Salle and Dearborn Streets to Lake Shore Drive.

Sometimes the high-rent pole jumps to new areas on the periphery of the city, as in the case of the development of Shaker Heights in Cleveland and Coral Gables in Miami, but usually these new areas are in the line of growth of the high-rent areas. In Charleston, West Virginia, the high-grade neighborhood moved from the center of the

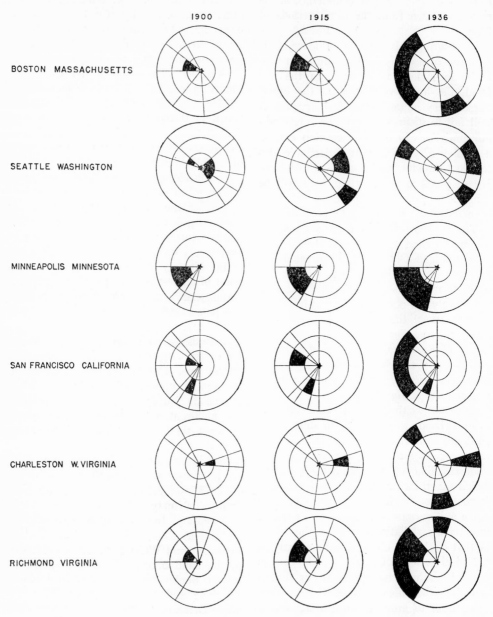

FIG. 2.—Shifts in location of fashionable residential areas in six American cities, 1900–1936. Fashionable residential areas are indicated by solid black. (Federal Housing Administration, Division of Economics and Statistics.)

city along Kanawha Street until it reached the river, and then the new high-grade area jumped to new locations in the hills in the south and north. In Seattle the high-grade neighborhood started near the center of the city and moved northeast in one sector of the city—the location along the lake on the periphery. At the same time the high-grade development sprang up to the northwest, jumping intervening low-grade areas.

In Minneapolis there was a movement of the high-grade neighborhood to the southwest, starting at the center of the city and repeating the same type of growth until it reached the outer edge of the city in a lake region. In Richmond the sector of the city containing Monument Avenue first developed as a high-grade area. The movement of the high-grade neighborhood continued out along the line of Monument Avenue until it reached the city limits and then it expanded, fan shape, in a sector to the north and west. At the same time a high-grade development started to the north in a sector which was bisected by Chamberlayne Street.

In Detroit the growth of the high-grade neighborhood proceeded eastward along Jefferson Avenue out to Grosse Pointe along Lake St. Clair. There was another band of high-grade development west of the axis of Woodward Avenue. In Miami bands of high-grade development followed Biscayne Bay to the north and south and also to Miami Beach.

As a result of the outward movement of the high-rent neighborhoods in American cities, present fashionable areas are mostly located beyond the earlier settled areas of American cities. Thus, Figure 1 shows that in Washington, D.C., practically all the high-rent area of today is located in a section that lies beyond the area occupied by houses in 1887. Similarly, in the fourteen other illustrative cities referred to in this chapter, most of the high-rent areas of today are located beyond the areas occupied by houses at a relatively recent period of time.

High-rent or high-grade residential neighborhods must almost necessarily move outward toward the periphery of the city. The wealthy seldom reverse their steps and move backward into the obsolete houses which they are giving up. On each side of them is usually an intermediate rental area, so they cannot move sideways. As they represent the highest income group, there are no houses above them abandoned by another group. They must build new houses on vacant land. Usually this vacant land lies available just ahead of the line of march of the area because, anticipating the trend of fashionable growth, land-promoters have either restricted it to high-grade use or speculators have placed a value on the land that is too high for the low-rent or intermediate rental group. Hence the natural trend of the high-rent area is outward, toward the periphery of the city in the very sector in which the high-rent area started. The exception to this outward movement is the development of de luxe apartment areas in old residential areas. This will be treated more fully on a following page.

What determines the point of origin of the highest rental areas of the city and the direction and pattern of their future growth? The answer to this question is of vital importance to all students of urban growth, for the high-rent sector is the pole or center of attraction that pulls the other residential areas with it.

In all the cities studied, the high-grade residential area had its point of origin near the retail and office center. This is where the higher income groups work and is the point farthest removed from the side of the city that has industries or warehouses. In each city the direction and pattern of future growth then tends to be governed by some combination of the following considerations:

1. *High-grade residential growth tends to proceed from the given point of origin, along established lines of travel or toward another existing nucleus of buildings or*

*trading centers.* This principle is illustrated by the movement of the high-grade residential neighborhood of Chicago along the main axes of roads like Cottage Grove Avenue leading south around the bend of Lake Michigan to the east, of main roads like Madison Street leading westward, and of roads following the lake northward to Milwaukee. In Detroit there was a trend of fashionable growth along the radial line of Woodward Avenue, the main thoroughfare to Flint and Pontiac, beginning within the Grand Boulevard Circuit and later extending to Highland Park, Palmer Woods, Ferndale, Royal Oak, and Birmingham.

2. *The zone of high-rent areas tends to progress toward high ground which is free from the risk of floods and to spread along lake, bay, river, and ocean fronts, where such water fronts are not used for industry.* The movement of high-grade residential neighborhoods away from river bottoms to higher ground or to wooded hills is illustrated by numerous examples. In San Francisco the wealthy moved from the lowland along the bay to Nob Hill, which was less subject to fogs and smoke. In Washington, D.C., the high-grade neighborhoods moved from the mud flats along the Potomac in the southeast quadrant and from the lowland in the southwest quadrant to the higher land in the northwest section. In Springfield, Massachusetts, the best areas moved from the lowland along the Connecticut River to rising land and to Longmeadow. In Kansas City, Missouri, St. Louis, and Cincinnati, there has been a movement of settlement away from the river bottoms to the higher land.

In cities located on relatively flat land near rivers, bays, lakes, or oceans, the high-grade residential neighborhood tends to expand in long lines along the water front that is not used for industrial purposes. Thus, in Chicago, the lake front on the north side is the front yard of the city and is pre-empted for high-grade residential use for a distance of nearly 30 miles north of the business center. In New York City, a high-grade residential area grew northward along the Hudson River on Riverside Drive from Seventy-second Street to Riverdale in the West Bronx. In Miami the high-rent areas extend along Biscayne Bay to the north and southeast and along the ocean front on Miami Beach. In Detroit a high-grade development extends along Lake St. Clair at Grosse Pointe. On the New Jersey coast, there is a long string of resorts along the ocean front with the highest-paid residential use confined to the strip along the beach. In Charleston, West Virginia, one high-grade residential area extends along the high bank of the Kanawha River.

Thus, where such lakes, rivers, bays, or ocean fronts exist and offer the attractions of bathing, yachting, cool breezes in summer, and a wide expanse of water with its uninterrupted view, rent areas tend to follow the contour of the water front in long, narrow lines of growth.

3. *High-rent residential districts tend to grow toward the section of the city which has free, open country beyond the edges and away from "dead end" sections which are limited by natural or artificial barriers to expansion.* The lure of open fields, golf courses, country clubs, and country estates acts as a magnet to pull high-grade residential areas to sections that have free, open country beyond their borders and away from areas that run into "dead ends." Thus the high-grade neighborhood of Washington, D.C., grows northwest toward expanding open country and estates. Thus the expansion of high-grade neighborhoods to the north of Baltimore, to the south of Kansas City, Missouri, and to the north of New York City in Westchester County is into areas with a wide expanse of country beyond them.

4. *The higher-priced residential neighborhood tends to grow toward the homes of the leaders of the community.* In Washington, D.C., the White House; in New York, the homes of the Astors and the Vanderbilts were the magnets that pulled the members of society in their direction. One fashion-

able home, an outpost on the prairie, standing near Sixteenth Street and Prairie Avenue in Chicago in 1836, gave prestige to the section and caused other leaders of fashion to locate near the same spot.[1]

5. *Trends of movement of office buildings, banks, and stores, pull the higher-priced residential neighborhoods in the same general direction.* The stores, offices, and banks in the central business district usually move in the direction of the high-rent area but follow rather than lead the movement of the high-rent neighborhood. Sometimes, however, when an office-building center becomes established at a certain point, it facilitates the growth of a high-rent area in sections that are conveniently accessible to it. Thus the office-building center in the Grand Central District in New York City has aided the growth of the de luxe apartment area on Park Avenue and also the exclusive suburban towns in Westchester that are served by fast express trains entering Grand Central Station. The establishment of an office-building center at Grand Boulevard and Woodward Avenue in Detroit aided the growth of the high-grade area to the north and west of it. In Washington, D.C., the northwestward trend of the office buildings, while the result of the pull of the high-grade areas to the northwest, also favored the further growth of the northwest area because it made those areas more accessible to offices. Similarly, the trend of office buildings on North Michigan Avenue in Chicago favored the northward growth of the de luxe apartment area.

6. *High-grade residential areas tend to develop along the fastest existing transportation lines.* The high-grade residential areas in Chicago grew along the main plank road, horsecar, cable car, and suburban

---

[1] See Robert S. and Helen M. Lynd, *Middletown in Transition* (New York: Harcourt, Brace & Co., 1937), pp. 81–82, for an interesting example of how the northwest section of Middletown became the outstanding residential section as a result of the movement of the most prominent family to that section.

railroad routes. In New York City, the elevated lines and subways paralleled Fifth Avenue. Fast commuters' trains connect New York City with the high-grade suburban homes in Montclair, the Oranges, and Maplewood in New Jersey, in Scarsdale, Pelham, and Bronxville in Westchester, and in Forest Hills, Kew Gardens, Flushing, and Hempstead in Long Island. In Detroit the high-grade areas are located close to main arteries leading directly to the center of the city—Jefferson, Woodward, and Grand River Avenues. In Washington, D.C., the best areas are on the main transportation arteries—Connecticut Avenue, Massachusetts Avenue, and Sixteenth Street, leading directly to the White House.

7. *The growth of high-rent neighborhoods continues in the same direction for a long period of time.* In New York City, the march of the fashionable areas continued up Fifth Avenue from Washington Square to Central Park for over a century. The high-grade neighborhoods in Chicago moved south, west, and north from their starting points in or near the present Loop to present locations—7 to 20 miles distant—in the course of a century. In the century after the Revolutionary War, the high-grade area of Washington, D.C., moved from the Capitol to the Naval Observatory. The high-rent areas of Detroit moved from points near the present business center to Grosse Pointe, Palmer Woods, and Birmingham, 6 to 10 miles away.

In Miami, Minneapolis, Seattle, Charleston, Salt Lake City, and many other cities, this same continuous outward movement of high-rent areas has been maintained for long periods of time. Except under the unusual conditions now to be described, there have been no reversals of this long-continued trend.

8. *De luxe high-rent apartment areas tend to be established near the business center in old residential areas.* One apparent exception to the rule that high-rent neighborhoods do not reverse their trend of growth is found in the case of deluxe

apartment areas like Streeterville in Chicago and Park Avenue in New York City. This exception is a very special case, however, and applies only to intensive high-grade apartment developments in a few metropolitan centers. When the high-rent single-family home areas have moved far out on the periphery of the city, some wealthy families desire to live in a colony of luxurious apartments close to the business center. Because of both the intensive use of the land by use of multiple-family structures and the high rents charged it pays to wreck existing improvements.

Such apartments can rise even in the midst of a poor area because the tall building itself, rising from humble surroundings like a feudal castle above the mud huts of the villeins, is a barrier against intrusion. Thus, when the railroad tracks were depressed under Park Avenue in New York City and the railroads were electrified, that street, originally lined with shanties, became the fashionable apartment avenue of New York City. In Chicago, the wall of apartments on the sands where Captain Streeter once had his shack is now occupied by the most exclusive social set. In both cases, there was a renaissance of an old neighborhood. It is only where intensive apartment uses occupy the land that such an apparent reversal of trends occurs.

9. *Real estate promoters may bend the direction of high-grade residential growth.* While it is almost impossible for real estate developers to reverse the natural trend of growth of high-grade neighborhoods, even by the expenditure of large sums of money and great promotional effort, it is possible for them to accelerate a natural trend or to bend a natural trend of growth.

Miami Beach, directly on the Gulf Stream in Florida, was favored by nature as the site for high-grade resort homes. When it was a mangrove swamp, separated from the mainland by Biscayne Bay, it was almost inaccessible. Carl Fisher, by building a million-dollar causeway and by pumping up 2,800 acres of land out of the

bay and erecting thereon golf courses and hotels, made it possible for these natural advantages of Miami Beach to be utilized. Similarly, George Merrick acquired a great tract of land at Coral Gables, Florida, and, by spending millions of dollars in laying out streets, in planting flowering trees, and in establishing restrictions, gave the area a high-grade character which it did not otherwise possess. So, likewise, did the developers of Roland Park in Baltimore, Shaker Heights near Cleveland, and the Country Club District of Kansas City take large areas in the line of growth and establish high-grade communities by means of building restrictions, architectural control, community planning, and other barriers against invasion.

In all these cases, the high-rent area was in the general path of growth; but which area of the many in the favored area became the fashionable center depended upon the promotional skill and the money expended by individual promoters.

As a result of some or all of these forces, high-rent neighborhoods thus become established in one sector of the city, and they tend to move out in that sector to the periphery of the city. Even if the sector in which the high-rent growth begins does not possess all the advantages, it is difficult for the high-rent neighborhood to change its direction suddenly or to move to a new quarter of the city. For as the high-rent neighborhood grows and expands, the low and intermediate areas are likewise growing and expanding, and they are taking up and utilizing land alongside the high-rent area as well as in other sectors of the city. When these other areas have acquired a low-rent character, it is very difficult to change that character except for intensive apartment use. Hence, while in the beginning of the growth of the city, high-rent neighborhoods may have a considerable choice of direction in which to move, that range of choice is narrowed as the city grows and begins to be filled up on one or more sides by low-rent structures.

It is possible for high-rent neighborhoods to take over sections which are marred by a few shacks. These are swept aside or submerged by the tide of growth. Negro houses have even been bought up and moved away in some southern cities to make way for a high-grade development. This possibility exists where the houses are flimsy or scattered, where the land is cheap, where it is held by one owner, or where the residents are under the domination of others. It is extremely difficult otherwise. The cost of acquiring and tearing down substantial buildings and the practical impossibility of acquiring large areas from scattered owners, usually prevents high-grade areas from taking over land once it has been fairly well occupied by middle- or low-grade residential uses.

Now that the radius of the settled area of cities has been greatly extended by the automobile, however, there is little difficulty in securing land for the expansion of high-rent areas; for the high-rent sector of the city expands in an ever widening arc as one proceeds from the business center.

The next vital question to be considered is how the various types of high-rent areas are affected by the process of dynamic growth of the city and how the various types are related to one another in historical sequence.

The first type of high-rent development was the axial type with high-grade homes in a long avenue or avenues leading directly to the business center. The avenue was a social bourse, communication being maintained by a stream of fashionable carriages, the occupants of which nodded to their acquaintances in other passing carriages or to other friends on the porches of the fine residences along the way. Such avenues were lined with beautiful shade trees and led to a park or parks through a series of connecting boulevards. Examples of this type of development, in the decades from 1870 to 1900, are Prairie and South Michigan Avenues, Washington and Jackson Boulevards, and Lake Shore Drive in Chi-

cago, Fifth Avenue in New York City, Monument Avenue in Richmond, and Summit Avenue in St. Paul, Minnesota. The fashionable area in this type of development expanded in a long string in a radial line from the business center. There was usually an abrupt transition, within a short distance on either side of the high-grade street.

The axial type of high-rent area rapidly became obsolete with the growth of the automobile. When the avenues became automobile speedways, dangerous to children, noisy, and filled with gasoline fumes, they ceased to be attractive as home sites for the well-to-do. No longer restricted to the upper classes, who alone could maintain prancing steeds and glittering broughams, but filled with *hoi polloi* jostling the limousines with their flivvers, the old avenues lost social caste. The rich then desired seclusion—away from the "madding crowd" whizzing by and honking their horns. Mansions were then built in wooded areas, screened by trees. The very height of privacy is now attained by some millionaires whose homes are so protected from the public view by trees that they can be seen from outside only from an airplane.

The well-to-do who occupy most of the houses in the high-rent brackets have done likewise in segregated garden communities. The new type of high-grade area was thus not in the form of a long axial line but in the form of a rectangular area, turning its back on the outside world, with winding streets, woods, and its own community centers. Such new square or rectangular areas are usually located along the line of the old axial high-grade areas. The once proud mansions still serve as a favorable approach to the new secluded spots. As some of the old axial type high-rent areas still maintain a waning prestige and may still be classed as high-rent areas, the new high-rent area takes a fan-shaped or funnel form, expanding from a central stem as it reaches the periphery of the city.

The old stringlike development of high-

rent areas still asserts itself, however, in
the cases of expansion of high-rent areas
along water fronts like Lake Michigan,
Miami Beach, and the New Jersey coast.
The automobile, however, has made accessible hilly and wooded tracts on which
houses are built on the crest of hills along
winding roads.

The fashionable suburban town, which
had its origin even before the Civil War,
has remained a continuous type of high-
grade area. Old fashionable towns like
Evanston, Oak Park, and Lake Forest near
Chicago have maintained their original
character and expanded their growth. Other
new high-grade suburban towns have been
established. The deluxe apartment area has
been a comparatively recent development,
coming after 1900, when the wealthy ceased
to desire to maintain elaborate town houses
and when the high-grade single-family home
areas began to be located far from the
business center. A group of wealthy people,
desiring to live near the business center and
to avoid the expense and trouble of maintaining a retinue of servants, sought the
convenience of tall elevator apartments.

The high-grade areas thus tend to pre-
empt the most desirable residential land by
supporting the highest values. Intermediate
rental groups tend to occupy the sectors in
each city that are adjacent to the high-rent
area. Those in the intermediate rental group
have incomes sufficient to pay for new
houses with modern sanitary facilities.
Hence, the new growth of these middle-class
areas takes place on the periphery of the
city near high-grade areas or sometimes at
points beyond the edge of older middle-class
areas.

Occupants of houses in the low-rent categories tend to move out in bands from the
center of the city mainly by filtering into
houses left behind by the high-income
groups or by erecting shacks on the periphery of the city. They live in either second-
hand houses in which the percentage need-
ing major repairs is relatively high or in
newly constructed shacks on the periphery

of the city. These shacks frequently lack
modern plumbing facilities and are on un-
paved streets. The shack fringe of the city
is usually in the extension of a low-rent
section.

Within the low-rent area itself there are
movements of racial and national groups.
Until only comparatively recently, the immigrants poured from Europe into the oldest and cheapest quarters on the lower East
Side of New York and on the West Side of
Chicago. The earlier immigrants moved out
toward the periphery of the city. These
foreign groups moved in bands or straight
lines out from the railroad stations near the
central business district. The Italian colony
of Chicago moved westward along the area
in the point between Harrison Street and
Roosevelt Road and northwestward along
Grand Avenue. The Poles proceeded northwest along Milwaukee Avenue and expanded southwest along the stockyards. The
Russian Jews moved west between Roosevelt Road and Sixteenth Street. The Czech-
oslovakians shifted southwest from Eighteenth and Loomis Streets to Twenty-second
and thence westward to Cicero. With the
decline of immigration after World War I,
new immigrants ceased to fill the old houses
in the downtown area and this outward
progression of foreign groups slackened.
Many of the tenements in the lower east
side were boarded up, and some of the oldest quarters near the central business district of Chicago were demolished.

During World War I and after, however,
there was a great influx of Negroes into
the northern cities to take the place of
European immigration. The Negro neighborhood in Harlem, New York, expanded in
concentric circles. In Chicago, the Negroes
burst the bounds of their old area along
State Street and the Rock Island tracks,
Twenty-second and Thirty-ninth Streets
and spread eastward to Cottage Grove Avenue and south to Sixty-seventh Street. In
this movement in Chicago, they spread into
an area formerly occupied by middle-class
and some high-income families. The area,

however, was becoming obsolete and did not offer vigorous resistance to the incoming of other racial groups.

Thus, in the framework of the city there is a constant dynamic shifting of rental areas. There is a constant outward movement of neighborhoods because as neighborhoods become older they tend to be less desirable.

Forces constantly and steadily at work are causing a deterioration in existing neighborhoods. A neighborhood composed of new houses in the latest modern style, all owned by young married couples with children, is at its apex. At this period of its vigorous youth, the neighborhood has the vitality to fight off the disease of blight. The owners will strenuously resist the encroachment of inharmonious forces because of their pride in their homes and their desire to maintain a favorable environment for their children. The houses, being in the newest and most popular style, do not suffer from the competition of any superior house in the same price range, and they are marketable at approximately their reproduction cost under normal conditions.

Both the buildings and the people are always growing older. Physical depreciation of structures and the aging of families constantly are lessening the vital powers of the neighborhood. Children grow up and move away. Houses with increasing age are faced with higher repair bills. This steady process of deterioration is hastened by obsolescence; a new and more modern type of structure relegates these structures to the second rank. The older residents do not fight so strenuously to keep out inharmonious forces. A lower-income class succeeds the original occupants. Owner occupancy declines as the first owners sell out or move away or lose their homes by foreclosure. There is often a sudden decline in value due to a sharp transition in the character of the neighborhood or to a period of depression in the real estate cycle.

These internal changes due to depreciation and obsolescence in themselves cause shifts in the locations of neighborhoods. When, in addition, there is poured into the center of the urban organism a stream of immigrants or members of other racial groups, these forces also cause dislocations in the existing neighborhood pattern.

The effects of these changes vary according to the type of neighborhood and can best be described by discussing each one in turn. The highest-grade neighborhood, occupied by the mansions of the rich, is subject to an extraordinary rate of obsolescence. The large-scale house, modeled after a feudal castle or a palace, has lost favor even with the rich. When the wealthy residents seek new locations, there is no class of a slightly lower income which will buy the huge structures because no one but wealthy persons can afford to furnish and maintain them. There is no class filtering up to occupy them for single-family use. Consequently, they can only be converted into boarding houses, offices, clubs, or light industrial plants, for which they were not designed. Their attraction of these types of uses causes a deterioration of the neighborhood and a further decline in value. These mansions frequently become white elephants like those on Arden Park and East Boston Boulevard in Detroit.

On the other hand, houses in intermediate rental neighborhoods designed for small families can be handed down to a slightly lower income group as they lose some of their original desirability because of age and obsolescence. There is a loss of value when a transition to a lower-income group occurs, but the house is still used for the essential purpose for which it was designed; and the loss of value is not so great. There is always a class filtration to occupy the houses in the intermediate rental neighborhoods. Hence, a certain stability of value is assured.

Since the buildings in low-rent areas are occupied by the poorest unskilled or casual workers, collection losses and vacancy ratios are highest. The worst buildings are condemned or removed by demolition to save taxes. Formerly these worst quarters in the old law tenements of New York or the West Side of Chicago were occupied by newly arrived immigrants. With the decline of immigration, this submarginal fringe of housing is being wrecked or boarded up as the residents filter up to better houses.

Thus, intermediate rental neighborhoods tend to preserve their stability better than either the highest or lowest rental areas.

The erection of new dwellings on the periphery of a city, made accessible by new circulatory systems, sets in motion forces tending to draw population from the older houses and to cause all groups to move up a step leaving the oldest and cheapest houses to be occupied by the poorest families or to be vacated. The constant competition of new areas is itself a cause of neighborhood shifts. Every building boom, with its new crop of structures equipped with the latest modern devices, pushes all existing structures a notch down in the scale of desirability.

GEORGE W. HARTMAN and JOHN C. HOOK

# SUBSTANDARD URBAN HOUSING IN THE UNITED STATES:
# A QUANTITATIVE ANALYSIS

It has been established by American geographers today that the urban geographer
concerns himself with a study of the spatial
characteristics of urban phenomena.[1] Geographic studies of this type usually involve
the use of two separate but related types
of analysis. The first type deals primarily
with the description of the areal arrangement of individual phenomena; the second
involves a comparative study of the similarities or dissimilarities of the individual
distributions. The latter is by nature the
more complex, since it involves analysis of
two or more distributions that may or may
not be associated. The most common comparative technique of study in the past has
been the use of visual comparison of a
series of maps, perhaps as translucent over-
lays, each of which shows only the distribution of one type of data. More recently,
however, a second technique has been gaining favor—that of using certain statistical
procedures that are applicable to testing
spatial associations.

Most urban phenomena in the modern
world are so complex in their associations
and interrelationships that it is necessary
for the geographer to limit himself at any
one time to an examination of a limited
number of variables that have possible associations. The procedural steps in a quantitative investigation under such a limitation at this level of investigation involve
the statement of a problem, the formulation
of a series of hypotheses to be tested, and
the use of established statistical tests to
determine the adequacy of the hypotheses
as related to the stated problem.

The broad problem to be investigated in
this study is concerned with certain geographic considerations of the relative proportion of substandard housing in American
cities. More specifically, three questions are
posed: (1) What is the nature of the variations in the proportion of substandard housing of the 1,262 cities in the United States
with populations of 10,000 or more (1950
Census)? (2) How are the variations in
the proportion of substandard housing areally distributed in the United States? (3)
What is the nature of the areal variations
of possibly associated phenomena?

"Substandard housing" is a term used by
the Public Housing Administration, United
States Housing and Home Finance Agency
(HHFA), to characterize dwelling units
that are deficient in decent safe and sanitary housing facilities, i.e., dwelling units
that are below generally accepted minimum
standards in the United States. More specifically, the term refers to dwelling units
that are either dilapidated or lack basic
sanitary amenities.[2] A unit that lacks sanitary facilities is without hot running water
or without a flush toilet or without bathing
facilities inside the structure for the exclusive use of the occupants of the dwelling.

Reprinted from *Economic Geography*, XXXII
(April, 1956), 95–114, with permission of the au-
thors and the editor. (Copyright, 1956, by Clark
University, Worcester, Mass.)

[1] H. M. Mayer, "Urban Geography," in *American Geography, Inventory and Prospect,* ed. P. E.
James and C. F. Jones (1954), p. 143.

[2] See U.S. Census of Housing: 1950, *Special Tabulations for Local Housing Authorities,* Series HC-6.
The term "substandard" is also referred to and defined for 203 urban real property surveys conducted
between 1934 and 1936 by the Work Projects Administration (Peyton Stapp, *Urban Housing—a
Summary of Real Property Inventories, 1934–36*
[Washington, D.C.: 1938]), Division of Social Research, W.P.A.

If the unit is dilapidated, it is considered to have serious structural deficiencies, is run-down or neglected, or is of inadequate original construction, so that it does not provide adequate shelter or protection against the elements or endangers the safety of the occupants. Quantified data are provided by the Bureau of the Census which make it possible to determine the proportion of substandard housing in each of the cities under study. This is accomplished simply by subtracting from 100 the "Per cent of dwelling units with hot running water, with private

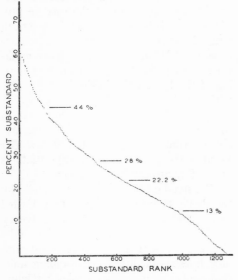

FIG. 1.—Rank in substandardness (every fifth city plotted).

toilet and bath, and not dilapidated" as given in the U.S. Census of Housing, 1950, Vol. I, Table 1, Parts 2–6.

The Bureau of the Census also provides data in the 1950 Census of Housing and Census of Population for a variety of phenomena which have possible associations with substandardness of housing. In this study, all quantified variables considered are taken from housing and population reports of the Census Bureau with the exception of a climatic factor. The source for each variable is indicated in Table 3.

## SUBSTANDARD HOUSING VARIATIONS OF AMERICAN CITIES

Variations in the proportion of substandard housing in the various cities under study are shown graphically in Figure 1 by ranked array. While this graph does not portray the substandard proportions for all 1,262 cities of 10,000 or more population— only the percentage figures for every fifth city have been plotted—the general nature of the variation is clear. The variations range from 0.2 per cent (University Heights, Ohio) to 73.6 per cent (Helena, Arkansas). The median is 22.2 per cent (e.g., Waynesboro, Pa.). The distribution, therefore, is skewed, since there are greater variations among cities with substandard percentages above the median than among those below the median. Breaks or trend changes in the slope of the array line are most noticeable at the values of 28 and 44 per cent as indicated on the graph, and also at 7, 13, 35, 51, and 60 percentage points.

## AREAL DISTRIBUTION OF SUBSTANDARDNESS

In order to determine the characteristics of areal variation in substandardness, individual percentages for the cities under study were first plotted on a map of the United States. Difficulties in visual comprehension of areal variations in 1,262 percentage values as plotted were overcome through generalizations made possible by use of metal pins with colored heads. Since variations in the degree of substandardness of housing appear to fall into eight classes according to noticeable breaks in the ranked array of percentage values as noted previously, pins of a particular color were used separately for each of the following classes: 0.2–6.9, 7.0–12.9, 13.0–27.9, 28.0–34.9, 35.0–43.9, 44.0–50.9, 51.0–59.9, 60.0–73.6.

Inspection of the distribution of the colored pins over the map of the United States indicated that variations in the substandardness of housing have areal differentiation. Cities with the highest percentage of substandardness are concentrated primarily in southeastern United States and along the lower Rio Grande Valley. Cities in most of northeastern United States, in the western two-fifths of the United States, and in peninsular Florida have the lowest percentage of substandardness. Cities in the remainder of the United States have substandardness values that are generally above the median value (22.2 per cent) for all cities in the United States, but they are intermediate

gions of unequal size with their urban housing-quality characteristics are summarized in Table 1.

An attempt to isopleth the 305 cities with substandardness values of less than 13 per cent was not successful. Eighty per cent of these cities are located within the large urbanized areas of the United States as "dependent" urban places. As Figure 4 indicates, these cities with low substandardness

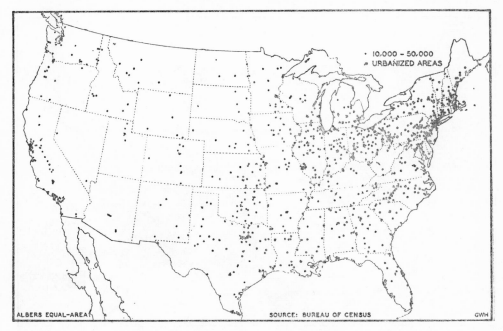

Fig. 2.—Urban places in the United States, 1950. (Source: Bureau of the Census.)

between the areas of high or low values as noted earlier.

If the array-breaks of 28 and 44 per cent are used as isoplethic values, seven regions of substandardness of housing may be outlined. Figure 2 indicates the distribution of the cities under study. Because of cartographic difficulties of showing all the cities in certain of the urban complexes on a small-scale map—72 cities in the immediate New York City area, for example—one symbol is used on this map to represent all cities in an urbanized area. Figure 3 shows the location of the seven regions of substandardness of urban housing. These re-

values are concentrated in the urbanized areas of Boston, New York, Philadelphia, Cleveland, Detroit, Chicago, St. Louis, San Francisco, and Los Angeles. Isoplething is possible in only one area within the northeast region. This area, as outlined in Figure 4, is an elongated one extending from Cleveland to Buffalo to New York City and Philadelphia. Although it contains almost 36 per cent of the 305 cities involved, it was decided not to consider it as a separate or eighth region. The decision was based upon the fact that the area is made up primarily of Lower Great Lakes cities and eastern seaboard cities concentrated around

New York and Philadelphia. The narrow corridor which joins these two groups of cities passes through upper Pennsylvania and southeast central New York, where there are no cities of 10,000 or more population (compare Fig. 4 with Fig. 2).

Cities that do not conform to the substandardness characteristics of the region in which they are located are represented in Figure 5—by a plus sign if a city's substandardness value is above the maximum value of its region or by a minus sign if it is below the minimum value. In addition to the non-conforming cities, ten other cities appear as "erratics" on this map in order to avoid separating the cities composing an urban complex into two regions. All cities in an urban complex are therefore considered as being members of the same region according to the substandardness value of

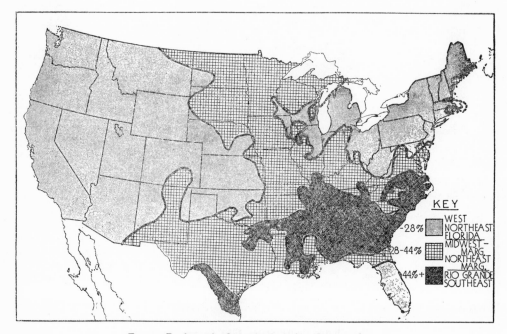

Fig. 3.—Regions of substandardness in urban housing

TABLE 1

REGIONS OF SUBSTANDARD URBAN HOUSING

| REGION | No. OF CITIES | SUBSTANDARDNESS VALUE | |
| --- | --- | --- | --- |
| | | Regional Limits (Per Cent) | Mean (Per Cent) |
| West................... | 228 | Less than 28 | 14.9 |
| Northeast............... | 552 | Less than 28 | 16.5 |
| Peninsular Florida......... | 23 | Less than 28 | 25.6 |
| Midwest-Marginal......... | 302 | 28 to 44 | 33.0 |
| Marginal New England.... | 25 | 28 to 44 | 37.4 |
| Southeast............... | 121 | More than 44 | 49.5 |
| Rio Grande............. | 11 | More than 44 | 55.8 |

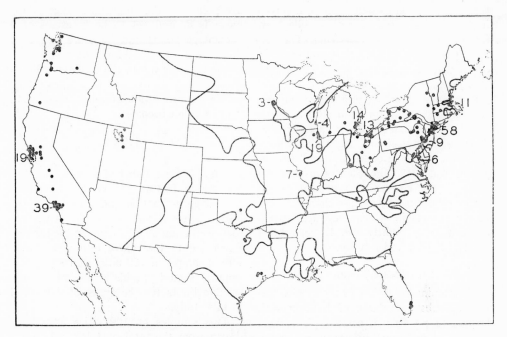

Fig. 4.—Cities below 13 per cent substandardness

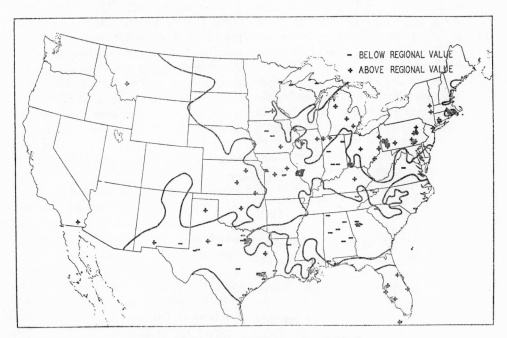

- BELOW REGIONAL VALUE
+ ABOVE REGIONAL VALUE

Fig. 5.—Cities not conforming to regional criteria

the total complex. Urbanized areas involved in this decision are Cincinnati, Mobile, New Orleans, Omaha, and Pensacola. The following combinations of cities, too small to be counted by the Census Bureau as urbanized areas, were also placed in the appropriate region according to a combined substandardness value for both cities: Lafayette and West Lafayette, Indiana; Mishawaka and South Bend, Indiana; Monroe and West Monroe, Louisiana; and Brandon-Judson and Greenville, South Carolina. Altogether, the cities that represent exceptions to the substandardness characteristics of the regions in which they are located constitute only slightly over 10 per cent of the 1,262 cities under study.

## A SELECTION OF SAMPLE CITIES

To examine the nature of the areal variation in substandardness of housing with respect to possible associated phenomena (our third question) by means of recognized statistical procedures is a long and tedious task. For practical purposes the universe of 1,262 cities is simply too large for each city to be included in the computations. Accordingly, a sample of the cities was drawn and used for this purpose.

The question as to the size of the sample is a rather complicated one. Obviously, one wishes to keep the sample size small in order to keep the problem within satisfactory work limits, but a reasonable range of reliability of estimates of the universe also is a necessary criterion. One such determination of sample size is presented by Hagood and Price.[3] It involves estimating the standard deviation of the substandardness values, and the setting of confidence limits of the estimate of the universe mean. According to this source, the standard deviation may be approximated as one-fourth to one-sixth of the range of distributions, and for our study we estimate that the standard deviation is not over 12 percent-

[3] Margaret J. Hagood and D. O. Price, *Statistics for Sociologists* (rev. ed.; New York, 1952), pp. 279–82.

age points. If the confidence range of the mean is desired not to be in excess of 5 percentage points and therefore to set up 95 per cent confidence limits of the estimate of the universe mean, the confidence limits then will be at a distance of 2.5 percentage points on either side of the sample mean. The equation becomes

$$\sqrt{N} = 1.96 \times \frac{12.0}{2.5}$$

where $N$ is the number of cases required in the sample. In this case, it is 89. Since this is a rough estimation and since the distribution is somewhat skewed, it is wise to increase the number of cases in the sample. According to the above estimates, therefore, a sample of 100 cities (an 8 per cent sample) should provide results within reasonable limits for the types of data used in this study.

Two samples of 100 cities each were drawn from the total of 1,262 cities on a random sample basis. In the case of Sample A, the name of each city was typed on a small slip of paper. These names were placed in a container and continuously mixed as 100 cases were drawn at random. For Sample B, the names of the cities in each state, as well as the individual states themselves, were arranged in alphabetical order. The cities then were numbered consecutively from 1 (Anniston, Ala.) through 1,262 (Sheridan, Wyo.). A random numbers table was then employed to select the sample of 100 cities.

There is no question, of course, as to the randomness of the two samples, but it is possible that through pure chance one sample might be more representative of the universe than the other. To test this possibility, the two samples were compared with each other and with the universe as to the estimation of sampling error. This involves a statistical determination of the standard error of the estimate of the mean (substandardness) of the universe. The formula used may be stated as follows:

$$SE = \sqrt{\frac{s^2}{N}(1-f)},$$

where $s^2 = \varepsilon y^2/(N-1)$, the estimate mean square deviation; $N =$ number of sample cities (100); and $f =$ correction factor for a finite universe[4] (1/13 in this study, since one city out of every thirteen is sampled). For Sample A, the standard error of the estimate of the mean of the universe is computed to be 1.343, and for Sample B it is 1.366.

In setting up confidence limits for the estimate of the universe mean of substandardness (in this study the 95 per cent confidence level is used), it is necessary to compute two values. One value becomes the upper limit and the second becomes the

Sample A was selected arbitrarily for use in this study.

## HYPOTHESES AND CORRELATION ANALYSIS

One of the purposes of quantitative geographic research is to establish principles that will "account" for areal variations. A preliminary step in this direction may be made in this study by associating a number of phenomena that present variations from city to city with variations in the proportion of substandard housing. Statistical methods of association involve procedures for determining a number of aspects of association between two or more series of phenomena. The principal summarizing measures used in this study are the Pearsonian product-moment coefficient of cor-

TABLE 2

COMPARISON OF SAMPLE ESTIMATES OF UNIVERSE MEAN

| | S.E.    S.D. | 95 Per Cent Confidence Interval | Mean | Limits |
|---|---|---|---|---|
| Sample A....... | 1.343×1.96= | 2.6 | 22.4 | 19.8–25.0 |
| Sample B....... | 1.366×1.96= | 2.7 | 26.0 | 23.3–28.7 |
| Universe....... | .................. | ............ | 24.2 (actual) | .............. |

lower limit at distances of 1.96 standard deviations from the estimate. Table 2 provides the necessary data for the establishment of confidence intervals—for Sample A it is $22.4 \pm 2.6$, for Sample B, $26.0 \pm 2.7$. This means that if an infinite number of samples were drawn by a random sample procedure, 95 out of every 100 confidence intervals would contain the universe mean. The universe mean has been computed and found to be 24.2 per cent; hence both Sample A and Sample B are in the 95 cases out of 100 wherein the universe mean falls within the limits as set. Furthermore, since both sample means deviate exactly the same amount (1.8 per cent) from the universe mean, one sample appears to be as representative of the universe as the other.

[4] Frank Yates, *Sampling Methods for Censuses and Surveys* (London, 1949), pp. 185–88.

relation (simple and multiple) and the analysis of variance.

Statistical correlations are useful in obtaining a rather precise measure of whether an association exists (i.e., is there a correlation?), the degree of association (how close is the correlation?), and the direction of the association (is the correlation a direct or an inverse one?). They allow, in addition, a regression equation for estimating individual values of one factor by knowing the individual values of the second factor. In the correlation analyses that follow, statistical computations have been made in each case by considering substandardness of housing as the dependent variable (factor $Y$) and the individual factors hypothesized as having possible associations with substandardness as the independent variable ($X$). Each coefficient of correlation has been determined through the use of the standard formula,[5]

$$r = \frac{\epsilon x y}{\sqrt{\epsilon x^2 \epsilon y^2}}.$$

A perfect correlation resulting from the use of this formula would be stated as ±1.00,

a complete lack of correlation as 0.00. For a correlation where 100 individual cases are involved, significance at the 95 per cent level is ±0.20 or greater, and at the 99 per cent level it is ±0.26 or greater.

The correlation results as shown in Table 3 indicate that a number of factors are

TABLE 3

COEFFICIENTS OF LINEAR CORRELATION BETWEEN SUBSTANDARDNESS
OF HOUSING AND OTHER SELECTED VARIABLES

| Variables* | | Coefficient | Universe Confidence Limits† | |
|---|---|---|---|---|
| Family income: | | | | |
| 1   Less than $2,500.............. | Per cent | .80 | .72 | .86 |
| 1   Median.................... | Dollars | −.78 | −.69 | −.85 |
| 5 Overcrowding................. | Per cent | .72 | .61 | .80 |
| 5 No mechanical refrigerator....... | Per cent | .82 | .74 | .87 |
| 5 Non-white families............. | Per cent | .57 | .42 | .69 |
| 5 Renter families................ | Per cent | .43 | .25 | .58 |
| 4 Foreign-born population......... | Per cent | −.44 | −.26 | −.59 |
| Age of structures: | | | | |
| 6   Built before 1920............. | Per cent | .31 | .12 | .48 |
| 6   Built before 1920 and between 1930 and 1940.............. | Per cent | .35 | .16 | .51 |
| 7   Average...................... | ............ | .30 | .11 | .47 |
| 2 Age city one-half 1950 size....... | ............ | .35 | .16 | .51 |
| 2 Population change, 1930–50...... | ............ | .12 | −.08 | .31 |
| Temperature factors: | | | | |
| 5   No central heat............... | Per cent | .52 | .36 | .65 |
| 8   Heating degree days........... | ............ | .14 | −.06 | .33 |
| Civilian labor force: | | | | |
| 3   Unemployed................. | Per cent | .29 | .10 | .46 |
| 3   Employed in manufacturing.... | Per cent | −.11 | −.30 | .09 |

* Source of data for variables:
   1. U.S. Bureau of the Census, U.S. Census of Population, 1950, Vol. II: *Characteristics of the Population* (Washington, D.C., 1952), Table 37.
   2. *Ibid.*, Table 4.
   3. *Ibid.*, Table 10.
   4. *Ibid.*, Table 34.
   5. U.S. Bureau of the Census, U.S. Census of Housing, 1950, Vol. I: *General Characteristics* (Washington, D.C., 1953), Table 1.
   6. *Ibid.*, Table 20.
   7. Based on weighted averages from *ibid.*, Table 20.
   8. U.S. Weather Bureau, *Climatological Data: National Summary*, Vol. III, No. 6 (June, 1952), Table 3A; Clifford Strock, *Heating and Ventilating Engineering Databook* (New York, 1948), pp. 5–63.
   † The probability that the interval between these limits contains the universe value is 95 per cent.

[5] The computations required in correlation coefficient equations may be obtained from any textbook in statistics which deals with the statistics of relationship. See, for example, Margaret J. Hagood and D. O. Price, *Statistics for Sociologists* (rev. ed.; New York, 1952) ; Mordecai Ezekiel, *Methods of Correlation Analysis* (2d ed.; New York, 1941) ; Henry E. Garrett, *Statistics in Psychology and Education* (2d ed.; New York, 1937) ; Charles C. Peters and W. R. Van Voorhir, *Statistical Procedures and Their Mathematical Bases* (New York, 1940) ; George R. Davies and D. Yoder, *Business Statistics* (2d ed.; New York, 1941).

associated with substandardness, but in varying degrees of significance. Each hypothesis under which the factors were selected as possible indicators of substandardness is considered separately as follows:

1. It is hypothesized that for the cities under study the proportion of substandard housing varies directly with the proportion of families with low income and inversely with the median income of families.

If one can assume that family groups are not likely to seek low-quality housing because they desire adverse housing conditions, it may be assumed further that families live in such housing in large measure because of inadequate economic means. In other words, the position may be taken that lack of suitable income forces most people to live in substandard housing. Of course, it must be recognized in this respect that the substandardness of housing in a given city at a given time may be the result of adverse economic conditions existing over a number of years, while in the testing of this hypothesis the income character of families is considered as of a given year. Nevertheless, under the same assumption above, if the income status of families in a city improves, the quality of housing tends to improve, even though there may be a time lag in this association. If the hypothesis is true, housing characteristics should reflect the income characteristics of the occupant families.

There appears to be no generally accepted quantified definition of a low-income family, and for purposes of testing this hypothesis a number of quantified expressions are made, all based upon census-reported family dollar income. The family groups used and the correlation results with substandardness are summarized in Table 4. The results obtained indicate that there is a significantly high association between the proportion of families in the low-income brackets and substandardness of housing and that the highest degree of association in this measure is with the group of families with incomes of less than $2,500. Again with respect to median family income a correspondingly high association is found (—.78), although, as expected, the direction of association is inverse. In the testing of this hypothesis, therefore, it may be stated that cities with a high proportion of low-income families tend to have a high proportion of substandard housing, and, conversely, cities with a high median family income tend to have a low proportion of substandard housing.

In investigating further the association between family incomes and substandardness, median family incomes are used simply because such data for each city are available directly from census reports, while two-step computations must be made in each case in order to determine the percentage of families with incomes less than $2,500. Further, as Table 1 indicates, there is relatively little difference in the coefficients of correlation of these two measures.

The nature of the inverse relationship

TABLE 4

CORRELATION BETWEEN SUBSTAND-
ARDNESS AND INCOME GROUPS

| Per Cent of Families with Incomes | Correlation Coefficient |
|---|---|
| Less than: | |
| $   500 | .60 |
| 1,000 | .69 |
| 1,500 | .76 |
| 2,000 | .78 |
| 2,500 | .80 |
| 3,000 | .72 |
| 3,500 | .67 |

between median family income and substandardness may be described by the regression equation,[6]

$$Yc = 64.25 - 0.01186X,$$

where $Yc$ is the estimated substandardness for a given city and $X$ is the reported median family income for that city. The regression or estimation line is shown graphically in Figure 6 as a straight line superimposed on a background of dots representing census-reported substandard percentages and median family income for the 100 sample cities. The scatter of the dots around the regression line merely confirms our previous finding that the correlation between these two factors, while high, is not perfect. The standard error of the estimate is computed as 8.6 percentage points, which is also indicated in Figure 6 by dashed lines paralleling the regression line.

Brief word need be made here of the use of the standard error of the estimate. It is

[6] For development of such an equation see Hagood and Price, *op. cit.*, pp. 414–19.

a measure of the dispersion or scatter of dots around the regression line. For any given series, the higher the correlation coefficient, the smaller the standard error and the more accurate the estimate. In a normal distribution, roughly two-thirds of all the dots should fall within one standard error equally on either side of the regression line, and 95 per cent should fall equally within two standard errors. In the problem under consideration, 61 out of 100 cases fall within one standard error, with 18 overestimations and 21 underestimations,

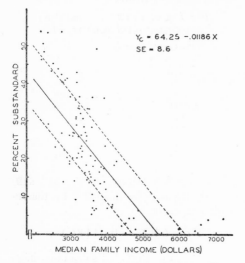

$$Y_c = 64.25 - .01186 X$$
$$SE = 8.6$$

FIG. 6.—Regression of substandardness ($Y$) on median family income ($X$).

and 93 cases fall within two standard errors (3 overestimations and 4 underestimations). The distribution of dots around the regression line, therefore, is skewed, but the skewness is slight and should not materially affect further use of the regression equation.

Thus far the assumption has been made that the association between substandardness and median income is of linear form. The nature of the scattergram in Figure 6, however, would seem to indicate that the association might really be non-linear, and that a curvilinear coefficient of correlation would be materially higher than the linear coefficient. The question may be posed,

therefore, whether the nature of the association between these two phenomena departs significantly from linearity. The answer involves a test of the "correlation ratio."[7] In the application of this test to the nature of this association, however, the difference between the linear coefficient (−.784) and a curvilinear coefficient (−.796) does not constitute a significant departure, and hence further investigation in this direction would not be profitable.

The most marked departures of the estimated substandardness of housing from the reported (actual) substandardness are found toward the extremes of the scattergram. It may be noted, for example, that estimations of substandardness are disproportionately low (beyond one standard error) where median family incomes are below $3,500 and reported substandard values above 40 per cent. Since the cities with high substandard percentages (above 44 per cent) are concentrated in the Southeast and Rio Grande regions, the nature of the scattergram suggests that results from separate regression analyses for these regions would be more fruitful than further investigation of possible curvilinear relationships. Again, the regression equation overestimates substandardness for a number of cities with reported substandard percentages of less than 20 per cent, but in four of the sample cities the equation actually estimates substandardness to be less than 0 per cent. The suggestion is strong that the regions with low substandardness of urban housing (below 28 per cent) need to be analyzed separately from other regions.

The regression equation, then, possibly does not permit a higher degree of accuracy in estimating the percentage of substandard housing from median family income in every case because of *regional* differences in the association between these two factors.[8]

[7] *Ibid.*, pp. 449–56.

[8] Hartshorne asserts that geographers are interested primarily in areal differences in the association between two or more phenomena. "In geography the focus of attention is concentrated, not

The question pertinent here is whether the differences (herein called $d$) between the estimated and census-reported substandardness vary more within the regions of substandardness than between the regions of substandardness. From a statistical standpoint, what is involved here is an analysis of variance—the determination of the variations arising from the varying of differences ($d$) around their respective regional mean, and the variation arising from the varying of region means around the universe mean. "Variation" is a term used in

region" variation is called $F$, and the minimum values of $F$ at various levels of significance are available from prepared statistical tables.[9]

The computations made for the analysis of variance of the differences ($d$) between estimated and census-reported substandardness involve all 1,262 cities in the universe rather than the sample of 100 cities, since the latter, by the nature of its selection, is a sample of the universe rather than a combined sample of the individual regions. The result of the analysis may be

TABLE 5

VARIANCE ANALYSIS OF DIFFERENCES BETWEEN ACTUAL AND ESTIMATED
(FROM INCOME) SUBSTANDARDNESS BY REGIONAL LOCATION

| Source of Variation | Sum of Squares of $d$ | Degrees of Freedom | Mean Square Variance | Ratio of Variance ($F$) |
|---|---|---|---|---|
| Total.................... | 137,931.3 | 1261 | .............. | .............. |
| Between regions.......... | 57,220.9 | 6 | 9,536.8 | 152.0 |
| Within region............ | 78,710.4 | 1255 | 62.7 | |

this instance to refer to the sum of the squares of the deviations of the unit measure ($d$) from the means. The ratio of the "between region" variation to the "within

---

on the phenomenon—one of whose aspects is its distribution—but on the relation of that distribution to the total areal differentiation of the world. . . . The facts concerning the areal differences in these phenomena must be studied in their *areal relations*, that is, their significance to the area as determined by their relations to other phenomena of the same place, and by their spatial connections with phenomena in other areas." Or, taking the liberty of substituting variables in the example given by Hartshorne, ". . . the relation of annual variations of corn production (median family income) to annual variations in rainfall (substandardness) is of great concern to the student of agriculture (economics) but is not of direct concern in geography, whereas the fact that the variations in rainfall (median income) in Nebraska have a greater effect on corn yields (substandardness), than the same degree of variation in Pennsylvania, is a geographic concern" (Richard Hartshorne, "The Nature of Geography," *Annals of the Association of American Geographers*, XXIX [1939], 171–658). Reprinted in book form. Quotations cited above are from the 4th edition (1951), p. 415.

summarized as shown in Table 5. The minimum value of the $F$ ratio required at the various levels of significance is 1.00 where 1,262 cases are involved. Since the ratio of 152 in this instance exceeds the required ratio, it is highly significant. Thus the variation of region means of $d$ is significantly greater than the variation of $d$ units within regions. In other words, the degree of association between substandardness and median family income varies from region to region. For more accurate estimation of substandardness for each city, it would be necessary to compute separate coefficients of correlation and regression equations for each region.

2. It is hypothesized that for the cities under study the proportion of substandard housing varies directly with the proportion of families with low *real* income.

It has been found that cities with a high proportion of substandard housing tend to

[9] Hagood and Price, *op. cit.*, pp. 379–404, and Table F, pp. 562–64.

have a high proportion of families with low incomes. Quantification of the latter has been accomplished through the use of census-reported dollar incomes of families in each city. Certain inadequacies inherent in this quantified measure, however, must be recognized. The dollar incomes of families as reported by the census are based on a 20 per cent sample, so that the correlation results are based on a sample of a sample. More seriously, a refined analysis of the association between the proportion of low-income families and substandardness of housing calls for a measure of *real* income rather than of dollar income. Whether a given family is a part of the low-income group of the city in which it resides depends as much upon the character of the family (number and types of individuals)[10] as upon its dollar income and whether this same family is considered a member of the nation's low-income class depends also upon the relative cost of living in the community in which it resides.[11] In other words, in the association between economic means and substandardness, it is the real income or effective buying income rather than dollar income that is decisive in determining the quality of housing that families can afford.

It is difficult to obtain an acceptable quantified measure of real family income for the cities under study. One such measure is offered in *Sales Management* (June, 1951), wherein estimates of the 1950 effective buying income of families are given for some 1,600 cities in the United States. The precise method of determining estimates is not revealed; hence no estimation of the reliability of the dollar figures is possible. In addition, estimates are not available for

all 1,262 cities under study; in fact, there are no estimates given for about one-fourth of the 100 sample cities.

*Overcrowding.*—Mabel Walker, in describing the characteristics of slum areas, states: "In some of these areas the population becomes so congested that even with low rents the property may yield good returns. This is the strange paradox of the slums—that at the end stage of the deterioration process when the area is populated by the poorest of the poor, the owner may be able to reap a profit through the sheer density of the population forced by necessity to live in the most undesirable surroundings."[12] William-Olsson in his study of the structure and development of Stockholm, Sweden, found that, in 1895, wards that had the lowest income per able-bodied adult in general had the largest number of occupants per room.[13] In personal conversation William-Olsson stated that the same relationship is true today. In the United States for the 100 sample cities under study, a moderately high association (.59) is found between the per cent of families with incomes less than $2,500 and the per cent of dwelling units with 1.01 or more persons per room as reported in the Census of Housing. Thus it would appear that one evidence of low real family income is overcrowding (i.e., forced congestion).

Assuming that low real family income is indicated by some measure of overcrowding and that "1.01 or more persons per room" is an adequate index, then it could be expected that there is an association between the per cent of dwelling units with 1.01 or more persons per room and the per cent of substandard housing. That this association exists is shown by the coefficient of .72 between these two variables.

*No mechanical refrigerators.*—If it may

[10] Eric Schiff, "Family Size and Residential Construction," *American Economic Review*, XXXVI (1946), 97–113.

[11] Chester Rapkin, Louis Winnick, and David M. Blank, *Housing Market Analysis* (Washington, D.C.: Housing and Home Finance Agency, 1953), pp. 66–67, based on Sherman J. Maisel, "An Approach to the Problems of Analyzing Housing Demand" (Ph.D. dissertation, Harvard University, 1948).

[12] Mabel L. Walker, *Urban Blight and Slums* ("Harvard City Planning Studies," Vol. XII [Cambridge, Mass.: Harvard University Press, 1938]), p. 17.

[13] W. William-Olsson, "Stockholm: Its Structure and Development," *Geographical Review*, XXX (1940), 434, Fig. 17.

also be assumed that families with small economic means are not able to buy certain consumer items that are classed as quasi-necessities in modern living, then lack of such an item or items in a household would serve as an indication of low real income. The Census of Housing reports contain statistics for each city on the per cent of occupied dwelling units containing mechanical refrigerators. A high correlation (.86) is found to exist between the latter and the per cent of families with incomes of less than $2,500. Further, a high correlation of .82 is found between substandardness and lack of mechanical refrigerators.

*Overcrowding and no mechanical refrigerators.*—It has been found that cities with

yond one standard error of the estimate of which 17 are overestimated and 16 underestimated.

An examination of the scattergrams of the association between substandardness and overcrowding and between substandardness and no mechanical refrigeration suggests once more that there are regional differences in the multiple association among these three factors. Once again, computations for the analysis of variance of the differences between estimated and census-reported substandardness involve all 1,262 cities in the universe, and the results may be summarized in Table 6.

Since the ratio of 77 exceeds the required ratio of 1, the variation of region means of

TABLE 6

Variance Analysis of Differences between Actual and Estimated (from *OC* and *NMR*) Substandardness by Regional Location

| Source of Variation | Sum of Squares of *d* | Degrees of Freedom | Mean Square Variance | Ratio of Variance (*F*) |
|---|---|---|---|---|
| Total..................... | 93,633.8 | 1261 | 74.2 | ......... |
| Between regions............. | 25,273.4 | 6 | 4,212.2 | 77.3 |
| Within region.............. | 68,360.3 | 1255 | 54.5 | |

a high proportion of occupied dwelling units that are overcrowded and lacking mechanical refrigerators have a high proportion of substandard housing. If the assumptions concerning these factors as satisfactory measures of real income of families are valid, then the two factors may be used in a multiple correlation with substandardness. The correlation coefficient in this case is found to be .87, and the standard error of the estimate is 6.85 percentage points. The regression equation is computed as

$$Y_c = 0.790\,(OC) + 0.934\,(NMR) + 0.60\,,$$

where $Y_c$ is the estimated substandardness of a given city, *OC* is the per cent of occupied dwelling units that are overcrowded in that city, and *NMR* is the per cent of dwelling units that have no mechanical refrigerators. Thirty-three of the 100 sample cities have a reported substandardness be-

the overestimations and underestimations (referred to as *d*) is significantly greater than the variations of *d* units within regions. As in the previous case, more accurate estimations of substandardness for each city require separate coefficients of correlation and regression equations for each region.

3. It is hypothesized that the proportion of substandard housing varies directly with the proportion of population groups restricted in residential choices.

It is a well-known fact that certain minority groups in our society do not have unrestricted freedom in choice of residential neighborhood. "We cannot emphasize too strongly that adequate housing for minority groups represents one of the most important and most difficult segments of the entire housing problem. Generally low incomes, almost universal lack of available sites, frequent lack of mortgage finance and a tradition of neglect of their market complicate the housing problems of minorities."[14] Such restrictions, however, do *tend* to disappear when individual families conform to American social standards of living or rise in the economic scale, except for non-whites.

*Non-white families.*—Traditional neighborhood restrictions, as well as lower economic status, serve to limit housing available to non-white families (for census purposes consisting of Negroes, Indians, and Japanese, Chinese, and other orientals). The following statements, based on the 1940 and 1950 Census of Housing reports, may be offered in evidence:

a) Non-whites comprised 10.3 per cent of the total population in 1950, but occupied only 8.6 per cent of all occupied dwelling units.

b) For non-farm areas, the non-white population rose by nearly 40 per cent while the number of dwelling units it occupied increased by only 31 per cent for the 10-year period ending April, 1950.

c) The proportion of overcrowded units (more than 1.5 persons per room) among non-farm dwellings occupied by non-whites in 1950 was four times as high as that for whites, and the non-farm rate of doubling (married couples rooming with other families) was 2.5 times as high among non-whites as among whites.

d) In urban housing, the proportion of dilapidated homes among non-whites in 1950 was almost six times as high as among whites and, in addition, the proportion of homes not dilapidated but lacking in either running water, private flush toilet, private bathtub or shower was nearly three times as high among non-whites as among whites.

e) The proportion of non-farm homeowners among non-whites during the decade 1940–50 rose by 93 per cent and among whites by 70 per cent; yet nearly two-thirds of the

non-white households in non-farm areas were still renters in 1950 compared with 45 per cent of white non-farm households.

f) The upward shift in distribution of rents paid from 1940 to 1950 in urban areas was such that the increase in median rents for non-white dwelling units was 100 per cent as compared with 50 per cent for white homes.

g) The census estimates of non-farm family incomes for 1949 indicate that approximately half of the non-whites had annual incomes of $1,700 or more, and the other half below that figure. For whites, the halfway mark was about $3,400, twice as great. Approximately 19 per cent of the non-whites, but 60 per cent of the whites, received incomes of $3,000 and over.[15]

For the 100 sample cities under study, a moderately high significant coefficient (.57) is found between the proportion of occupied dwelling units inhabited by non-white families and that of substandardness of housing. The standard error of the estimate of substandardness from the regression line (11.5 percentage points), however, is not markedly below the standard deviation of the reported substandardness values from their mean (13.9). Knowledge of the non-white family proportion for a given city does improve the estimate of substandardness for that city, but not greatly.

The scattergram of these two variables (Fig. 7) around the regression line indicates that for cities with a low per cent of non-white families the per cent of substandardness ranges from 0.7 to 53.5 per cent. Of the 36 cities with substandardness values falling outside one standard error of the estimate, for example, 26 cities (or 72 per cent) have less than 6 per cent of their dwelling units occupied by non-whites. Non-white families apparently constitute too small a proportion of the total families in many of the cities under study to "explain" on a satisfactory basis the pro-

14 "Report of the Subcommittee on Housing for Low-Income Families," *Recommendations of Government Housing Policies and Programs: A Report to the President of the United States* (Washington, D.C.: The President's Advisory Committee on Government Housing Policies and Programs, 1953), p. 257.

15 Housing and Home Finance Agency, *Housing of the Nonwhite Population, 1940–1950* (Washington, D.C.: Office of the Administrator, Division of Housing Research, 1952), pp. 1, 2, 11, Table 11, p. 34, and Table 19, p. 41.

portion of substandard housing. It is to be expected, however, that regional variations occur in the association among the proportions of substandardness, low income and non-white families.

*Foreign-born population.*—Because newcomers to this country can easily be recognized by distinctive homeland cultural ties and language differences and because they are relatively powerless economically and politically, immigrants traditionally have been convenient targets for opposition and aggression.[16] Foreign-born people in urban centers, particularly where they constitute sufficient numbers to be recognized as distinct social groups, have tended to cluster in "immigrant neighborhoods" in the poorer residential districts, although such neighborhoods have been on the decline since about 1924, owing to a marked decrease in immigration and gradual assimilation of the existing foreign-born and their descendants. While only 6.7 per cent of the population of this nation in 1950 was classified as foreign-born white ("other races" add little to the total), 83.5 per cent of the total foreign-born resided in urban places.[17] With voluntary as well as involuntary restrictions in residential neighborhood choices assumed by many foreign-born people, certain characteristics of the association between the proportion of substandardness and that of foreign-born for the cities under study are worthy of consideration.

The assumption of a direct correlation between the per cent of substandardness and the per cent of the population twenty-one years old and older that is foreign-born is found to be incorrect. The scattergram in this case shows that cities with a high proportion of foreign-born (above 20 per cent) have a low proportion of substandardness (below 20 per cent), while cities with a low proportion of foreign-born (below 10 per cent) have substandardness values which

range from the lowest to the highest. The correlation is found to be —.44. Further study of the nature of the nationwide distribution of the urban foreign-born reveals that 64 per cent live in only 14 of the largest urbanized areas,[18] 11 of which are in the northeast substandard region and three on the West Coast. These urbanized areas (all over 500,000 population) have a large quantity of substandard housing, but

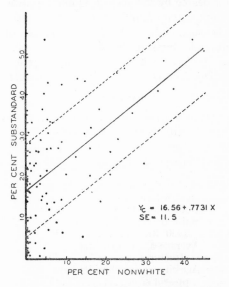

Fig. 7.—Regression of substandardness ($Y$) on non-white proportions ($X$).

the per cent of substandard to total housing is low. The conclusion may be drawn that the details of the association between foreign-born and substandardness must be examined on a regional basis or, probably, on an individual city basis.

*Renter families.*—"One of the outstanding changes in the housing picture over the last sixty years has been the increase in homeownership. In 1890, only a little over one-third of all non-farm homes were occupied by their owners. By 1950 more than one-half were owner-occupied."[19] The rate

---

[16] George E. Simpson and J. M. Yinger, *Racial and Cultural Minorities* (New York: Harper & Bros., 1953), p. 111.

[17] U.S. Bureau of the Census, Census of Population, 1950, Vol. II, Part 1, Table 49.

[18] *Ibid.*, Parts 2–50, Table 34.

[19] Housing and Home Finance Agency, *The 1950 Housing Situation in Charts* (Washington, D.C.: Office of the Administrator, Division of Housing Research, 1951), p. 20.

of increase in homeownership was particularly high during the 1940's. Among white occupants of urban dwelling units, for example, 52 per cent owned their homes in 1950 as against 39 per cent in 1940, and among non-white occupants 32 per cent owned their homes in 1950 against 20 per cent in 1940.[20]

It is entirely probable that in our urban places rental units are occupied to a significant degree by low-income families and by minority-group families restricted in choice of housing. Cities with a high proportion of substandardness of housing, at any rate, tend to have a high proportion of renter families (the correlation is .43). Further,

TABLE 7

CORRELATION BETWEEN SUBSTAND-
ARDNESS AND AGE FACTORS

|  | Coefficient |
|---|---|
| Per cent of dwelling structures: | |
| Built before 1940...... | .31 |
| Built before 1930...... | .28 |
| Built before 1920...... | .31 |
| Built before 1920, and 1930–40............ | .35 |
| Average age of dwelling structures........... | .30 |
| Age city was one-half its present size......... | .35 |

cities with a high proportion of renter families tend to have a high proportion of non-white families, although to a lower degree (correlation, .34). Thus in an analysis of regional differences in the association of certain factors with substandardness, further consideration needs to be taken of the multiple association of rental and non-white status of families with inferior housing qualities.

In summary, the hypothesis under consideration may now be stated more precisely: the proportion of substandard housing in a given city tends to vary directly with the proportion of dwelling units occupied by non-white and by renter families, and inversely with the proportion of the

population over twenty years of age that is foreign-born.

4. It is hypothesized that the proportion of substandard housing varies directly with the age of dwelling-unit structures.

Since it is clear that structural dilapidation is often the result of long-continued use and exposure to the elements and since structures built in an earlier era often lack modernization of plumbing facilities, it may be hypothesized that the older the residential structure of a given city, the greater the proportion of substandardness. Several correlation tests of this hypothesis are summarized in Table 7.

The results of the tests are inconclusive. The direction of association in each case is positive but there is little difference in the results of each age period used. Further, in the sample study, six of the seven correlations are statistically significant, but, when the coefficients are converted to universe limits based on a 95 per cent confidence level of probability, doubt is cast upon the degree of significance of the correlations (see Table 1).

Several difficulties arise in the use of available data relating to the age factor. In the first place, the year built as reported by the Census Bureau refers to the year of the completion of the original construction, without regard to later extensive reconstruction, remodeling or addition, or conversion to housing. Thus age of structures as reported, where considerable renovating is undertaken, is a poor index of "aging-toward-dilapidation" or "lack-of-sanitary-facilities." Second, the Census Bureau warns that data on year built are subject to some inaccuracy because of errors of response and non-reporting.[21] Enumerators relied in most instances upon the memory of the person interviewed as to the year of construction. Third, and perhaps most important, the oldest age category reported, "structures built before 1920," appears too broad for correlation purposes—an average

---

[20] U.S. Bureau of the Census, Census of Housing, 1950, Vol. I, Part I, Table 3.

[21] U.S. Bureau of the Census, Census of Housing, 1950, Vol. I, Part I, p. xviii.

of 44 per cent of the residential structures in the 100 sample cities were built in this period as against an average of 22.4 per cent of all units counted as substandard. The minimum span of 31 years (from 1950 to "built before 1920") probably does not provide sufficient time for substandardness resulting from age to become apparent. The federal Internal Revenue Service, for example, in setting up tables based on reasonable rates of depreciation for buildings of standard construction, considers 60 years as reasonable for the useful life of residential structures.[22] Finally, it must be recognized that the substandardness of dwellings can result from inadequate original construction as well as from aging. In the correlations attempted on age of structures, the highest correlation obtained was arrived at by combining the number of structures built before 1920 with those built during the depression period 1930–40. Since by combining depression-built housing with older housing the correlation with substandardness is improved, the idea persists that it is possible that the faster a city changes in numerical size, the more likely substandardness of housing will appear. A correlation of .12 between substandardness and per cent population change, 1930–50, however, discourages possibilities of significant associations in this respect.

If age is a factor that is significantly associated with substandardness of housing, more precise data are needed. This is particularly true if age and substandardness are to be studied in their regional associations, since age of structures varies considerably from the eastern to the western sections of the United States.

5. It is hypothesized that the proportion of substandard housing varies inversely with normal heating requirements for comfortable living.

The fact that a moderately high significant association (.52) exists between sub-

standardness and the proportion of dwelling units lacking central heat and that cities with the highest proportion of substandardness are concentrated in the South and Rio Grande regions suggests the possibility that substandardness is associated in some significant measure with certain climatic conditions. On the assumption that housing conditions probably vary more with temperature conditions, particularly the severity of winters, than precipitation or other climatic factors, a quantified measure of the effect of temperature on normal living comfort is worthy of correlative consideration. Such a measure can be obtained through the use of the concept "degree day." A difference of one degree per day in the mean daily temperature below 65° F. (considered by heating engineers as the minimum temperature of bodily comfort in the home) is one degree day, and the number of degree days below 65° F. in a normal heating season is the sum of all the daily values for that season. The number of degree days in the heating season for the cities under study can be obtained by interpolating from data provided by the Weather Bureau for selected cities scattered over the United States.[23]

The correlation of this climatic factor with substandardness, however, is .14, with universe limits of −.06 and +.33. The association is deemed not significant for the urban places under study, and hence the hypothesis must be rejected.

6. It is hypothesized that the proportion of substandard housing varies directly both with the percentage of unemployment and with the percentage of the civilian labor force engaged in manufacturing.

*Unemployment.*—In the previous discussion of the association between income and substandard housing, it was pointed

[22] Bulletin "F," *Tables of Useful Lives of Depreciable Property* (Internal Revenue Service Publication No. 173 [1955] [rev. 1942 ed.]), p. 7.

[23] U.S. Weather Bureau, *Climatological Data: National Summary*, III, No. 6 (June, 1952), Table 3A. For additional data and isoplethic map see Clifford Strock (ed.), *Heating and Ventilating Engineering Databook* (New York: Industrial Press, 1948), pp. 5–63.

out that the income characteristics of a city could change rapidly, while the housing characteristics would tend to change more slowly. In other words, one factor is likely to be more dynamic in change than the other. In spite of this contrast, however, it was demonstrated that there is a highly significant association between family income characteristics and substandardness of housing. The percentage of a city's civilian labor force that is unemployed is probably subject to even more rapid changes than the median family income. If, however, a city is subject to long periods of large-scale unemployment, it would be expected that this would be reflected in the income of the people and in turn in the quality of the housing. When the percentage of the labor force that is unemployed is correlated with the per cent of substandard housing, the coefficient is found to be .29. This is statistically significant but indicates only a slight degree of association between the two variables.

*Employed in manufacturing.*—It is a well-known and easily observed fact that residential areas in or near manufacturing districts of the heavy-industry type tend to be of poor quality. From this it is postulated that if a city has a high percentage of its labor force engaged in manufacturing, it will have a high proportion of substandard housing. This is, however, an erroneous assumption. Figure 3 indicates that northeastern United States, which is highly industrialized, is for the most part a region of low substandardness of housing. The coefficient of correlation between the two variables is —.11, which is not statistically significant, indicating that, for the nation as a whole, one is just as likely to find high proportions of substandard housing in cities with a low proportion of their labor force in manufacturing as in cities with a high proportion in manufacturing. Further, an analysis of the 152 metropolitan areas with populations of 100,000 or more indicates that there is a slight tendency for the median family income to increase as the

percentage of workers engaged in manufacturing increases (.39). No concrete conclusions can be presented at this point, however, because of the rather crude nature of the data used. The original hypothesis uses a mechanism based on heavy industry (a term difficult to define), and the test of the hypothesis utilizes data on the percentage of workers in all types of manufacturing. A refinement using the percentage of workers in certain of the census industry groups would perhaps provide more fruitful results, particularly in a regional framework of study.

## Summary and Conclusions

Attention in this study has been focused on a comparative analysis of the proportion of substandardness of urban housing. Three specific aspects of substandardness have been investigated: the nature of the variations in the proportion of substandard housing of 1,262 cities with populations of 10,000 and over, the characteristics of the variations in substandard proportions as areally distributed in the United States, and the nature of the areal variations in substandardness with respect to the areal variations of certain selected phenomena.

It has been demonstrated that there is considerable variation in the proportion of substandard housing of American cities, that there is regional differentiation in substandardness, and that there are a number of factors associated in significant degree with substandardness. Factors which appear to be relatively good indicators of substandardness are the proportion of families with low income (monetary and "real") and the proportion of certain family types restricted in choice of residence. Age of residential structure and unemployment appear to be relevant factors, although no real significance can be attached to them, possibly because of certain difficulties inherent in the use of the types of data available. While no attempt has been made to "explain" on a statistical basis the total variation among substandardness in terms of other variables,[24] it is hoped that in the formulation of the problem and in the selection of variables guided by hypotheses based on current theories in the systematic social sciences, the foundation is laid for possible future retesting of results. A word of warning is necessary here: the "explanations" of substandardness do not necessarily imply direct cause-and-effect relationships. No one can be certain that the associated variables will maintain a stable or predictable relationship in the future or that these variables have been relevant or irrelevant in the past. Repeat studies based on later census years will be necessary for the verification or rejection of findings.

Since the degree of association between substandardness and a number of the variables studied appears to vary from substandard region to substandard region, more accurate estimations of substandardness for individual cities appear to require a determination of separate coefficients of

correlation and regression equations for each region. In a correlation between substandardness and "no mechanical refrigerators" in the southeast region, for example, where a sample of 40 out of 121 cities is used, the coefficient obtained (.52) is substantially lower than for a sample of the entire universe (.82).

Furthermore, in the use of separate regional regression equations to identify specific cities that are highly overestimated and underestimated in substandardness, it is within the realm of possibility that a disproportionate number of these cities are located along the margins of regions. If such be true—and this possibility is worthy of investigation—then a revision of regional boundaries could be based on multiple associations of independent variables with substandardness rather than on one criterion alone (i.e., percentage substandardness). In other words, in continuing the study of the geographic characteristics of substandard housing along the lines outlined above, an investigation of regional differences in the association of substandardness with variables selected within a theoretical frame of reference might possibly lead to a discovery of substandard-complex regions based on multiple associations.

[24] An excellent presentation of multiple regression analysis techniques is found in Donald J. Bogue and D. L. Harris, *Comparative Population and Urban Research via Multiple Regression and Covariance Analysis* ("Scripps Foundation Studies in Population Distribution," No. 8E [Oxford, Ohio, 1954]).

## THE URBAN FRINGE

An important development in urban settlement during the past several decades has been the rapid expansion of population into the unincorporated areas surrounding our large cities and into their incorporated suburbs. Throughout the United States most of the growth in the fringe areas of cities since 1940 has been greater than that within the central cities themselves. One outstanding example of this trend is Buffalo, New York, which from 1940 to 1950 increased by only one-half of 1 per cent, while its suburbs increased in size by 33 per cent. In Wilmington and Charleston, South Carolina, the population within the limits of both cities actually decreased, while their suburbs increased by 45 and 90 per cent, respectively.

This twentieth-century expansion of urban population into fringe areas was made possible by the development of automobile transportation and expressways. Other technological developments, such as the extension of light, sewers, and water mains into the urban fringe areas, have also made it possible for people to live in the open countryside and in suburban places and still be able to depend upon the central city for employment and services.

Geographers and others have been interested primarily in the structure and function of the urban fringe development and in its relation to the character of the entire locality. Geographers have also become concerned with the problems brought about by the growth of suburban areas—problems of land use, of urban transportation, of the multiplication of administrative units, and of the failure of these units to work together for the good of the whole.

One of the early articles to appear in the geographic literature on the topic of suburban development was the late George S. Wehrwein's "The Rural-Urban Fringe," published in 1942. The author recognized the railroads as among the first decentralizers and levelers of urban rents and values and as factors in establishing settlements or agglomerations of population outward in a rather continuous band projecting from the city. The transformation of the agricultural zones about the city went on at a more rapid rate, however, after the appearance of the automobile and hard-surfaced roads.

Chauncy D. Harris, writing in 1943, recognized the need for a study of suburban types and trends. His map of the percentage of population living in suburbs for each of the nation's metropolitan districts shows a zone, which he calls a "climax area," containing cities and metropolitan districts in which over 60 per cent of the population live in suburbs. He advances the generalization that the extent of development of suburbs in metropolitan districts varies according to location with respect to this climax area; according to location with respect to rivers, bays, and associated state boundaries; to functional type of cities; and to size of cities. He classifies suburbs into six types: industrial fringe; industrial; complex with industrial more important; complex with residential more important; dormitory; and mining and industrial.

During recent years the growth of suburbs has been especially rapid, but uneven, throughout the urban fringe area. Clyde F. Kohn found that from 1950 to 1955, suburbs in the Chicago area grew at varying rates. Those which grew at less than average rates (31 per cent) included the older municipalities in which there was no longer room for extensive development of single family homes; industrial municipalities; and small settlements which were still considered too far from the central city for daily trips to work. Those which grew at extremely rapid rates were for the most part dormitory suburbs along major expressways.

Charles R. Hayes, in his article "Suburban Residential Land Values along the C.B.&Q. Railroad," points out several spatial correlations of residential land values and railroad development. Residential land values, he concludes, (1) slope away from the rail land and (2) dip between each station. Many of his findings bear out earlier generalizations advanced by Homer Hoyt and others interested in the development of urban fringe areas.

GEORGE S. WEHRWEIN

# THE RURAL-URBAN FRINGE

Land problems appear in their most acute form on three fringes or transition zones: (1) the area between arable farming and grazing; (2) the zone between farms and forests; and (3) the suburban area lying between the built-up city and farms. In recent years much attention has been given to the two former "fringes"; the "Dust Bowl" and the "cut-over" areas are familiar figures in land-utilization literature. Much less has been done by research agencies and administrators in the other twilight zone—the rural-urban fringe. Students of agricultural land problems stop when they come to "city land" and urban land economists and planners usually stay within the city limits, unless they are studying the region and making regional plans. Meanwhile, residences are spreading into the fringe, industries are "decentralizing," and commercial establishments in the form of traffic-attracted industries are locating themselves along major highways, reaching many miles beyond the residential or the industrial invasion. Urban problems, crying for direction, planning, and social controls, are thrust upon rural governments; yet these units of government are not designed for or are incapable of furnishing direction, plans, or controls. Unguided "settlement," premature subdivisions, and unwise expansion of public utilities with increased expenditures for local government have resulted in tax delinquency and suburban slums. Pathological conditions of this kind have focused attention on this transition zone just as they did on the cut-over regions and the High Plains.

It is the purpose of this article to

Reprinted from *Economic Geography*, XVIII (July, 1942), 217–28, with permission of the author and the editor. (Copyright, 1942, by Clark University, Worcester, Mass.)

examine the land-use structure of the rural-urban fringe, which may be defined as the area of transition between well-recognized urban land uses and the area devoted to agriculture. That this is not a hard and fast, well-defined area is evident from this description. The "built-up" city is not necessarily coterminous with the political city. In many cases the economic and sociological city, the area within which people live the urban way of life, has extended far beyond the city limits; in other cases farms on which people live the rural way of life are found within the political boundaries of cities. The 1940 Census reported almost 260,000 *urban*-farm population. Likewise, the city and the rural-urban fringe may or may not cover the same area as the metropolitan district defined by the United States Census. The fringe area is much smaller than the trade area and usually smaller than the commuting area of a given city. It can better be identified in terms of land uses or modifications of land uses than in any other way.

## Von Thünen's Scheme of Land Utilization

In reviewing the literature which throws light on the land utilization of the fringe the student will find von Thünen's *Isolated State* a good beginning. Von Thünen eliminated all natural features, climate, soil, topography, or anything else which might affect the utilization of land except the presence of a single city in the center of a uniform plain with an agricultural economy. Given only wagon transportation, with no well-defined highways, the cost of bringing farm products to the city is equal for all points equally distant from the market. The result is a system of concentric belts or zones about the central city (Fig. 1).

In the first zone only high-priced, perishable, and bulky products can profitably be grown and marketed, such as milk, eggs, berries, and vegetables. Under the conditions of 1826 (when the first edition of von Thünen's book was published) the presence of a belt of forests as the second zone was not so incongruous as it might seem. Practically all building material, fuel, and other bulky forest products had to be brought to the city by wagons or even on

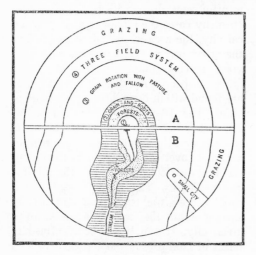

Fig. 1.—Land utilization as determined by location. Modified from diagrams in Von Thünen's *Isolated State*. (From Ely-Wehrwein, *Land Economics* [Macmillan Co., 1940].)

the backs of peasants. Agricultural zones reappear beyond the forest belt; gradually, farming becomes less and less intensive, until grazing merges into the wilderness which surrounds the "state" and shuts it off from the rest of the world.

In this oversimplified scheme of land utilization there is no rural-urban fringe as we know it today. The city boundary sets the limit of the "urban way of life"—beyond it are farms and agricultural land uses. Nevertheless, the intensive use of land, small farms, high-priced land, dense population, and almost daily contact with

the city in marketing their crops means a way of life for the farmers intermediate between that of the city dweller and the general farmer or forester. It is the kind of life and type of agriculture that are often pictured as still existing on the outskirts of our cities but which have been metamorphosed beyond recognition by the forces which have produced the "fringe problems." It is the kind of land utilization, way of life, and occupations hoped for in the "greenbelts" around the "Greenbelt Towns," a girdle of permanent open space intended "to protect the town forever from overcrowding and undesirable building on neighboring land." This belt was designed to contain not only parks, playgrounds, and the gardens of the urban inhabitants but also full-time farmers "who can bring their produce to market by crossing their own fields."[1]

Park and Burgess in their study of city structure conceived of a similar system of concentric zones within the city itself, beginning with the commercial and industrial core and ending with the dwellings of the wealthier "classes" at the periphery of the city. Coupled with von Thünen's scheme for the area beyond the city, the two together form an idealized scheme of land utilization which, however, has so many exceptions that it is sometimes difficult to prove the rule! This orderly arrangement rules out the influence of natural factors which are often predominant. It also presupposes a static population, which, indeed, was the basic assumption of some of the Garden Cities. It is only with a static population that the greenbelt of parks, playgrounds, gardens, and farms can be maintained against the invasion of a growing city or, if the city is permitted to expand, plans must be made for the gradual

[1] *Greenbelt Towns: A Demonstration in Suburban Planning* (Washington, D.C.: Resettlement Administration, September, 1936). The distribution of the land uses in a typical community was planned as follows: community and store buildings, 100 acres; homes, 1,000 acres; parks, 1,800 acres; farms, 2,100 acres.

expanding core, the expansion of the residential area, and the shifting of the rural land uses to urban land uses.

However, few cities have been static; all of them expect to grow, and, with this expectation in mind, they make their plans accordingly when they plan at all. Growth does not take place equally on the periphery of the city and probably never has, in spite of the concentric circles of the "isolated state." Transportation has always followed definite routes; even the camel, pack horse, and oxcart followed certain paths and entered the ancient and medieval city at city gates. The "isolated state" itself must have a system of "farm-to-market" roads which gives the farms adjacent to such roads a locational advantage over those not so situated. Fruit, vegetable, dairy, and poultry farms could be located farther away from the city if situated on a direct road to the city than if not so placed. Von Thünen recognized this when he introduced the river in his diagram and the circles became distorted by projections following the stream (Fig. 1, *B*).

### CHRISTALLER'S SCHEME OF URBANIZATION

The von Thünen scheme of a single city in a large, uniform hinterland of an agricultural economy is of course highly theoretical and is useful primarily for isolation of the economic from the natural and other factors determining land utilization. More realistic is the scheme of Walter Christaller.[2] Assuming once more a uniform agricultural economy, it is evident that not all non-rural functions will be centralized in one city. The farmer needs the services of the blacksmith and other craftsmen, the store, the church, the school, and a tavern, dance hall, or other recreational centers, depending on the customs and mores of the people. Christaller suggests that these services would grow up at certain centers and form hamlets evenly distributed over an

[2] Walter Christaller, *Die zentralen Orte in Süddeutschland* (Jena: Gustav Fischer, 1933).

area assumed to be as uniform as that of the "isolated state." Each hamlet tends to serve an area hexagonal in shape as shown in Sector 1 of Figure 2. However, the hamlet cannot furnish all the services the farmer wants, so some of the villages become the center for doctors, lawyers, hospitals, let us say, serving the rural people in a larger area and those living in the neighboring hamlets as well. This larger

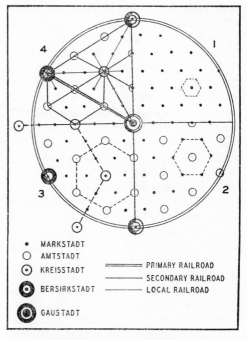

FIG. 2.—Theoretical distribution of trade centers. (Based on diagrams made by James A. Barnes, after W. Christaller.)

area is shown in Sector 2 of the same figure. In this way Christaller builds up a hierarchy of urban centers of which the most important is the "central" city of Von Thünen's *Isolated State* (Sector 3).

The even distribution of cities of various characteristics, sizes, and "hinterland areas" is disturbed by natural factors, locational advantages for manufacturing and "through lines" of transportation. Iowa, because of its agricultural economy, might have come close to furnishing an example of Christal ler's principle. However, the Missouri and Mississippi rivers on its borders, the three important rivers within the state, and the transcontinental railways influenced the location and later the growth of the cities of Iowa so much that their distribution is far from uniform over the state.

Christaller's contribution has significance for the rural-urban fringe in that every one of these urban concentrations will become the basis for a series of belts and zones just as the central city does, and the larger cities will tend to develop "fringe areas." This was recognized by Von Thünen when he introduced another city in his diagram (Fig. 1). More important still is the fact that the distribution of urban centers will determine the transportation system. According to Christaller each hamlet is connected with the rural area it serves, and in turn it is linked with the village or city next in rank, resulting in a system of primary, secondary, and local roads and railways. This is indicated in Sector 4 of Figure 2. Thus a hierarchy of highways is unfolded bearing a volume of traffic in proportion to the size of the cities connected. Moreover, the large urban centers are linked, not only with the cities of a system such as this, but with other metropolitan centers and their "systems." Thus transportation becomes channelized and certain railways, roads, waterways, and air lanes become the main arteries for quick, uninterrupted traffic for passengers and goods. Such railways are double-tracked and roads are made into two-, three-, or four-lane highways to carry the heavy traffic; in fact, some of these main highways are merely a connection of the "Main Street" of one city with the "Michigan Avenue" or "Broadway" of another.

### Railways as "Decentralizing" Factors

Not only the agricultural zones but the city itself tends to follow the lines of transportation. However, as long as animal power was the usual means of transporta-

tion, the city dweller who had business or sought pleasure in the "downtown" part of the city was constrained to live as "close in" as possible. (In 1866 New York had a well-organized system of coach, omnibus, and horse-railway transportation, yet their range was so limited that the outlying districts were undeveloped, while the central streets were badly congested. "The most desirable parts of the island, the sections abreast of and above Central Park, were largely given up to pigs, ducks, shanty squatters, and filth, while lower Broadway was so jammed that a man in a hurry almost lost his reason."[3] This tended to keep the city structure compact, and the competition for accessible sites raised rents and site values. "The expenses of living in the city are increasing every year. Rents are higher now than ever before and there is no prospect of their coming down for many years." This has a distinctly modern tone but was said of New York in 1865 by George E. and F. W. Woodward.[4] Railways were among the first decentralizers and levelers of urban rents and value. "The remedy for this," continue these writers, "is to go into the country. Along the lines of our railroads and navigable waters there are localities where land is abundantly cheap—beautiful healthy regions, where the comforts of a rural home may be secured. . . . We know of localities which can be reached from Wall Street in as many minutes as would be required to go to 50th Street. . . . In the direction we have now specially in mind, there are at least 20 railroad trains which stop at convenient stations between early morning and ten o'clock at night."

The fact that railway trains stop only at definitely located stations no matter how "convenient" tended to produce settlements or agglomerations of population strung along the railway lines rather than a con-

[3] Allan Nevins, *The Emergence of Modern America, 1865–1878* (New York: Macmillan Co., 1927), pp. 81–82.

[4] *Woodward's Country Homes* (5th ed.; New York, 1865), p. 12.

tinuous band of residences projecting from the city. The early streetcars rarely went outside the city's limits, but when these were transformed into interurban electric lines, projected into the rural areas, or connected with nearby cities, the boundaries of the city were stretched still more. Interurbans could be "flagged" at any crossroad, which tended to eliminate the islands of residential areas and make the areas linear in structure. This once popular form of transportation is now almost forgotten, but Figure 3 shows that Indianapolis had almost as many electric interurban railways as steam railways in 1914. The map also shows the characteristic pattern of lines of transportation radiating from a "central" city cutting the rural-urban fringe into wedge-shaped tracts between the lines.

### HIGHWAYS AND THE "METRO-POLITAN INVASION"

However, the real exodus of residences and of commercial establishments generated by traffic did not come until the automobile and hard-surfaced roads provided means of swift, unchanneled, individual transportation as compared with the previous channeled mass transportation. The rural-urban fringe then became penetrated by streaks of urban land uses also radiating from the center like the spokes of a wheel. The primary roads, carrying the heaviest traffic, were most affected. This Benton MacKaye termed the "metropolitan invasion."[5] He noted the development of various traffic-attracted establishments—billboards, "hot-dog" stands, filling stations, garages, stores, taverns, as well as the residences of people with jobs in the city, and part-time farmers. Farmers and others found it profitable to sell from wayside stands, build tourist cabins, advertise "rooms for tourists," or start a "soft drink" stand. The metropolitan invasion not only engulfed the land adjacent to the main highways but transformed the outlying

[5] *The New Exploration* (New York: Harcourt, Brace & Co., 1928).

rural villages. MacKaye deplored this invasion and hoped to regulate it and confine it to certain areas so as to maintain the rural indigenous landscape everywhere else:

This invasion would take its start from the central community. Its movements here as elsewhere we may liken to a glacier. It is spreading, unthinking, ruthless. Its substance consists of tenements, bungalows, stores, factories, billboards, filling stations, eating stands, and other structures whose individual hideousness and

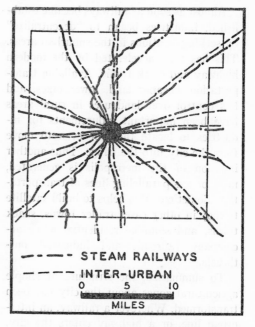

- - - - STEAM RAILWAYS
- - - - INTER-URBAN

0    5    10

MILES

FIG. 3.—Radiating pattern of steam railways and electric interurban lines, Marion County, Indiana, 1914. (From *The Library Atlas of the World*, Vol. I, *The United States* [Chicago: Rand McNally & Co., 1914].)

collective haphazardness present that unmistakable environment which we call the "slum." Not the slum of poverty, but the slum of commerce. This substance, conceived as a projecting, crawling glacial flow, makes its journey along each of the radiating highways. The twenty rural villages of our locality are penetrated one by one. They are welded together into a common suburban mass without form or articulation; the integrity of each former village (each former human unit) is ironed away; its local government is merged in general administration; its "personality" evaporates. Beyond the villages, the lines of flow, growing thin and puddly, continue their inroad toward the hinterland. In this wise the 63,000 souls become distributed in one continuous mass of straggling lines emanating from an overgorged center. These souls live all in a single environment: not city, not country, but wilderness—the wilderness not of an integrated, ordered nature, but of a standardized, unordered civilization. We have named this the metropolitan environment.

Almost as soon as railways became established, industries began to "decentralize" by seeking locations in the suburban areas. This has been accelerated by the modern highway and truck traffic. Available transportation, cheaper land, lower taxes, and less control over land uses in rural areas have been important inducements for industries to locate there or even to move from the city into the fringe. Thus another invasion of the metropolis is generated, more or less paralleling lines of transportation. Sometimes this helps to build satellite towns; in other cases trailer towns, shack towns, and slumlike residential areas accompany railroads and industrial outthrusts.

To summarize, the structure of simple agricultural zones about the city has been transformed. Wherever a railway, an interurban line, or a highway enters the city, residences, commercial establishments, and industrial plants follow, like water flowing through a break in a reservoir, an apt illustration used by MacKaye. Since these means of transportation radiate in all directions whenever physical features do not interfere, the rural-urban fringe consists of rural territory pierced by finger-like projections of urbanized land uses. It has long been observed that cities have become star-shaped. Between the arms of the star, agriculture and other non-urban land uses continue but in more or less modified form.

## RESIDENTIAL EXPANSION INTO THE FRINGE

Motor transportation has released man from the necessity of living in places where mass transportation is available. According to *Automobile Facts* of March, 1941 (published by the Automobile Manufacturers' Association), there are 2,130 places in the United States with a total population of 12,000,000 people, ranging in population from 2,500 to 50,000, that depend exclusively on private cars. In other words, these cities have no streetcars or buses at all. Added to these are the millions in other cities, who, though mass transportation is available, nevertheless depend largely upon private automobiles. These dwellers of the city and the fringe are independent of trains, streetcars, and buses. As a result, cities not merely expanded, they "exploded." "Realtors" began to lay out subdivisions. The open-country features of suburban living, lower taxes, fashion, and prestige not only attracted the "surplus" population but began to invite and allure the established residents of the city itself. This has tended to leave behind empty houses, if not "blighted areas," certainly lower and lower land values. This almost self-evident trend has only recently attracted the attention of planners, lending agencies, and city officials. It was noticeable before 1930, but the 1940 Census showed that while the 92 largest cities of the United States gained 1,600,000 people between 1930 and 1940, the remainder of the counties in which they are located gained almost the same, or 1,500,000 people. While the central cities gained 4 per cent, the suburban areas of these cities gained 14 per cent. Some of our largest cities, including Philadelphia, Boston, and Kansas City, actually lost population.

The wild expansion or "explosion" of the cities has also produced wildcat and premature subdivisions, overexpansion of residential sites, miles of sidewalks running through weed-covered vacant land, and clouded titles on thousands of vacant lots. Moreover, much of this "developed" area has been supplied with streets and sidewalks, water, sewers, gas and electricity, schools, and other public facilities at private or public expense. As long as this land is part of a rural unit of government, farms and other non-urban land are taxed as well as the "urban land" for these services, either by the regular taxing machinery or through specially created districts. Unsold and unused lots often failed to pay taxes, and then the burden for the support of unused facilities has fallen on the remaining taxpayers. The rural land instead of gradually ripening into urban uses has been "forced" into urban uses prematurely and "frozen" there. Only rarely can such land be restored to agricultural use; thus we have created an "institutional desert." Land which according to its location should be growing the crops of von Thünen's first zone is lying as idle as the cut-over lands on the farm-forest fringe. It is reported that a farmer wishing to establish a poultry farm in the New York–New Jersey area had to go 80 miles from the city before he could find a tract of land not blighted by tax delinquency and clouded titles.

Residential developments in the fringe area must rely on rural forms of government to furnish urban services such as streets, sidewalks, fire protection, water, and sewage disposal. Usually rural towns, counties, and precincts have no legal powers to do so. Sometimes the statutes are amended to give these rural units of government, unincorporated villages, or special districts the necessary authority to cope with these problems. In most cases, however, whenever residential areas have sufficient population, they incorporate as separate villages or cities in order to handle their own affairs and to raise and spend their own tax money for services they need and desire. In this way satellite and neighboring villages and cities arise in the fringe. Some of them are of the manufacturing type, with residences surrounding a factory, others are simply residential, "bedroom," or "dormitory" cities where people live who work in the city. These villages and cities depend not only on the main city for jobs but for most of their shopping, pleasures, and educational facilities, thereby generating a daily stream of traffic between the central city and its satellites in the fringe area. Thus another set of urban centers is created, not contemplated in von Thünen's or Christaller's schemes but definitely modifying the land uses and the transportational system of the fringe. The relations of the urban residents living in the fringe (whether living in the unincorporated places or in incorporated villages and cities) to the central city, are very complex and must be omitted from a discussion limited to the physical structure of land uses in the fringe.

## THE RURAL-URBAN FRINGE AROUND INDIANAPOLIS, INDIANA

The metropolitan district of Indianapolis may be used to illustrate many of these points. The district consists of seven of the nine townships which make up Marion County (Fig. 4). The metropolitan district includes "the central city or cities, all adjacent and contiguous civil divisions having a density of not less than 150 inhabitants per square mile and also, as a rule, those civil divisions of less density that are *directly* contiguous to the central cities, or are entirely or nearly surrounded by minor civil divisions that have the required density." Using the same area for previous census periods the change in population of Indianapolis, of the other incorporated places, and of the unincorporated area may be traced as shown in Table 1.

In 1870 Marion County had only one incorporated place—Indianapolis, a city of 48,000, located in Center Township. (Indiana incorporated places are called *towns* or *cities;* unincorporated area is divided into *townships*.) By 1880 four other places had

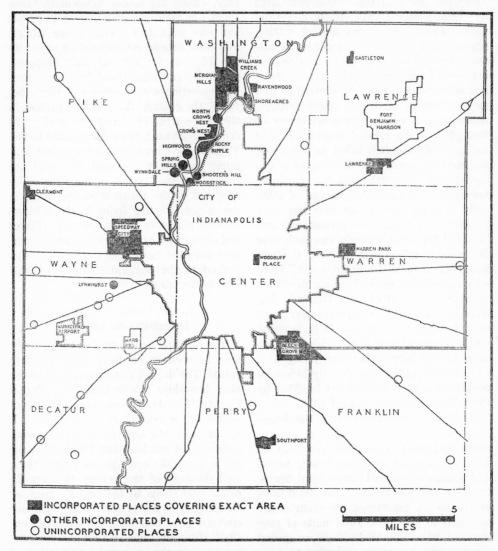

FIG. 4.—The metropolitan district of Indianapolis, Indiana. The district embraces all of Marion County except Pike and Franklin townships. The highly irregular boundary of Indianapolis and projections, such as the one into Perry Township, indicate the manner in which the city has annexed territory from the rural-urban fringe. The municipal airport is a legal part of Indianapolis. The area of some of the incorporated places is so small as to be lost on a map of this size; they are indicated by circles. The larger towns and cities are shown by the areas occupied; unincorporated places are shown by open circles, except Mars Hill. Only the main highways are placed on the map. (Based on the "Map of Marion County, Indiana" by Paul R. Brown, County Engineer, March 1, 1941, who also furnished information on the boundaries of incorporated areas.)

incorporated, including Woodruff Place, situated in the heart of Indianapolis, which has maintained its separate existence to this day. The other incorporation of this period, Southport, is typical of several other towns located some distance from Indianapolis; all of them have grown rather slowly. Southport had 388 people in 1880 and 549 in 1940. Most of the incorporations, however, took place in the immediate rural-urban fringe, and since 1890 Indianapolis has annexed and absorbed seven of them. Eleven incorporations took place between 1920 and 1930 and two in the last census decade, practically all of them just outside

Figure 4. Traffic maps prepared by the Indiana Highway Commission in co-operation with the United States Bureau of Roads in 1937 list 15 unincorporated places with a total population of 12,738, 2,806 dwellings, and 241 business places; also, 18 subdivisions with 1,297 dwellings. Some of these unincorporated places have more population than the incorporated towns and villages. Mars Hill, for instance, had 2,580 people in 1937, more than any town or city except Beech Grove and Indianapolis. These figures are not complete. In a few cases either the population or number of dwellings was not given. Only dwellings

TABLE 1

GROWTH OF POPULATION IN THE INDIANAPOLIS METROPOLITAN DISTRICT
AND MARION COUNTY, INDIANA, 1910–40*

|  | 1910 | Per Cent† Gain | 1920 | Per Cent Gain | 1930 | Per Cent Gain | 1940 | Per Cent Gain |
|---|---|---|---|---|---|---|---|---|
| Indianapolis................. | 233,650 | 38.1 | 314,194 | 34.5 | 364,161 | 15.9 | 386,972 | 6.3 |
| Incorporated areas........... | 3,024 | − 4.2 | 5,557 | 83.8 | 8,863 | 59.5 | 11,462 | 29.3 |
| Unincorporated areas........ | 22,709 | 9.6 | 24,117 | 6.2 | 44,661 | 85.2 | 56,923 | 28.9 |
| Total metropolitan district.... | 259,383 | 34.4 | 343,868 | 32.6 | 417,685 | 21.5 | 455,357 | 9.0 |

* *Metropolitan Districts* (Washington, D.C.: Bureau of the Census, 1932) and other U.S. Census publications.
† Gain or loss, 1900–1910.

the city limits. According to Figure 4 several more places have incorporated since 1940. Some of them are very small, having in 1940 as few as 19, 21, or 30 people. (Small areas and population groups may no longer incorporate. The 1941 legislature of Indiana in Chapter 69, Section 1, now provides that not less than 250 people with at least one person for each four acres may incorporate.) Because of annexation to Indianapolis, incorporated places actually lost population from 1890 to 1910; after that the gain was remarkable—84 per cent from 1910 to 1920, over 59 per cent in the next decade, and 29 per cent between 1930 and 1940.

However, these figures do not give a complete picture of urbanization of the district. Many people are living in densely settled but unincorporated places, as shown in

were reported for the subdivisions. All subdivisions within Indianapolis or other incorporated places and the two townships not in the metropolitan district are not included in the above.

The unincorporated area increased but slowly in population until 1920, in fact actually decreased from 1900 to 1910. Figures of this type are deceptive, however. As soon as an agglomeration of people appears they may incorporate as a town or may be annexed to an existing town or city and the remainder of the area is left with fewer people than at the previous census enumeration. Indianapolis has consistently annexed unincorporated territory, at first only from Center Township, but, as Figure 4 shows, the city has invaded every bordering township. In spite of losses by annexation or incorporation the result of decentralization into the unincorporated area has been remarkable since World War I. Population increased 85 per cent between 1920 and 1930 in the unincorporated area and 29 per cent during the next decade. Even the two townships not included in the metropolitan district, which in 1920 actually had fewer people than in 1870, gained appreciably in the past 20 years. The unincorporated places, subdivisions, and single residences strung along the highways are responsible for most of the increase.

The urbanization of Marion County is interestingly indicated by the fact that in Warren Township the east and west country roads all bear the name of those streets of Indianapolis with which they connect, while the north and south roads in the eastern part of the town still bear rural names such as Mitthofer, German Church, and Fort roads. City street names are found in the unincorporated areas of most of Washington, Wayne, and even in Pike Township but to a less extent in the three southern townships.

### RECREATIONAL FEATURES IN THE "FRINGE"

The land uses of the fringe are also conditioned by the recreational needs of the urban people and by the people living within the region as a whole. Planners envision parks, playgrounds, beaches, parkways, golf grounds, and forests within driving distance from the central cities to provide part of the indigenous environment contemplated by Benton MacKaye. The Forest Preserves of Chicago are a modern adaptation of von Thünen's forest zone but for recreational purposes entirely. "It has been suggested that an area equal to that occupied by urban developments should be accessible for public recreational activities within 100 miles of each great city," or a total of over nine million acres for the United States, "part of which is already available in city, metropolitan, and state parks or reservations."

To carry out this ideal means large-scale metropolitan regional planning and the allocation of land to public recreational uses, most of it lying in the nearby fringe area so as to be accessible to people who can afford only a few hours' or a day's outing. However, land available for this purpose lies in the jurisdictions outside the cities, and the rural governments are in no position to furnish and maintain public recreational facilities for the benefit of the hordes from the cities. Metropolitan districts, counties, the state, and perhaps even the federal government must share in providing these recreational lands.

Unfortunately most of the natural features suitable for recreation within the fringe area have long been pre-empted for private use. Riparian land along lakes and streams is covered with summer cottages, resorts, taverns, dance halls, and "Coney Islands." Roads leading to such resort areas are lined with the same type of amusement places. Private farm land is overrun by city "sportsmen" who claim the right to roam over the farms in the fringe within easy driving distance of the city. Nowhere are the conflicts between landowners and the alleged rights of the public more acute than in the areas adjacent to our cities. Farmers have posted their lands, and towns and counties have found it necessary to prohibit shooting entirely.

### INSTITUTIONAL FACTORS CONDITIONING FRINGE LAND USES

Finally, the land uses in the rural-urban fringe are also the result of institutional and legal factors. It has long been the practice of cities to "dump" unwanted yet necessary industries into rural territory by ordinances excluding them from the cities per se. Slaughter houses, wholesale oil storage, noxious industries of all sorts, junk yards, trailers and trailer camps, taverns and dance halls, substandard dwellings, carnivals, and the sale of firecrackers have all been the subject of restrictive city legislation at one place or another. Such establishments or land uses escape urban restrictions by locating in the country where rural governments are too feeble, or too apathetic to do anything about it. Some of the city's own public utilities are likewise placed in the fringe area or beyond; recreation, water supplies, radio towers, sewage disposal plants, airports, cemeteries, are among urban necessities found in the suburban areas. There is a bit of poetic justice in the Jefferson County, Wisconsin, zoning ordinances which prohibit most of these uses in the "conservancy districts" and some of them even in the "agricultural districts." The only place left for them is in the incorporated places without zoning ordinances of their own! Using such maps as were available, the writer noted forty-three "facilities" of various types in the Indianapolis metropolitan district located in the unincorporated area, most of which are associated with the activities of those living in Indianapolis, although some are state institutions such as the Indiana School for the Blind, or federal, as Fort Benjamin Harrison. The most numerous were country clubs, schools, airports, cemeteries, and "institutions." Eleven were situated right on the edge of Indianapolis, nine within one mile, eight within one to two miles, another eight were located more than two but less than four miles from the city limits and the others were farther out. It was interesting also to find eighteen institutions, golf courses, parks, and cemeteries just inside the present boundaries of the city absorbed from the rural-urban fringe by annexations. The Indiana State Fair Ground is an example. In some cases such factors become the nucleus for urbanization. The famous Indianapolis Speedway is now part of Speedway City, incorporated in 1921.

In conclusion, the rural-urban fringe is really an extension of the city itself, actual and potential. It is an area where most of the land uses are in flux and therefore subject to planning, direction, and control. A considerable proportion of the land in the built-up city is already dedicated to various uses, planning can be little more than replanning, and zoning must recognize the existing industrial, commercial, and residential districts. Unfortunately, much of

the land in the rural-urban fringe is already "frozen," with lot sizes, streets, and public utilities the result of haphazard growth or the decision of a speculative subdivider.

Since the city or cities of a metropolitan area and the suburban or fringe area are a unit economically and sociologically, the entire area should be thought of and planned as a unit. Within this region there should be a proper place for every structure and land use needed by people living therein. The lowly and despised junk yard has become a vital element in national defense and deserves a place in the regional plan just as much as the "high-class" residential area. This place is not found by zoning it out of "higher" land-use districts. Much of our planning and zoning has been inadequate because it sets up a hierarchy of land uses leaving farm land and other nonurban land as a residual or as an unrestricted area upon which everything may be unloaded.

County zoning has made a beginning in directing and controlling the land uses of the rural-urban fringe; in fact, the first enabling acts were designed for this particular purpose, notably in California and Wisconsin. In the latter state the zoning statute has been amended to permit the restriction of the use of land for agriculture, forestry, and recreation and the control of all forms of riparian land. Twenty-five counties have "rural zoning" ordinances of this type. Planners have felt that this was a distinct contribution to the zoning of the rural-urban fringe, since it gives power over all types of land and not only the urbanized forms of land use. Combined with other directional measures, such as subdivision control, platting control, health and sanitary codes, many of the cities and counties of the United States now have the power to prevent haphazard, unharmonious, and incompatible land uses in the rural-urban fringe. However, mere power does not carry with it the desire, courage, or the wisdom necessary to make for a well-planned rural-urban region and the proper structure of land uses in this transitional area.

## SUBURBS

The strong suburban trend in American cities calls for a study of suburban types and trends.[1] In view of the need for studies of cities with their suburbs, the Bureau of the Census has recognized some sort of metropolitan district since 1910.[2] The Six-

Reprinted from the *American Journal of Sociology,* XLIX (July, 1943), pp. 1–13, with permission of the author and the editor. (Published by the University of Chicago at the University of Chicago Press.)

[1] See Louis Wirth, "Urban Communities," *American Journal of Sociology,* XLVII (May, 1942), 829–40, especially pp. 833–35; and Anonymous, "The Growth of City Suburbs," *Federal Home Loan Bank Review,* VII (August, 1941), 373–75, 387.

[2] U.S. Bureau of the Census, *Thirteenth Census of the United States, 1910,* Vol. I: *Population, 1910, General Report and Analysis* (Washington, D.C.: Government Printing Office, 1911), "Cities and Their Suburbs," pp. 73–77. In this census 25 metropolitan districts were recognized; each contained a city of more than 200,000 population.

*Idem, Fourteenth Census of the United States, 1920,* Vol. I: *Population, 1920, Number and Distribution of Inhabitants* (Washington, D.C.: Government Printing Office, 1921), "Cities and Their Suburbs," pp. 62–71. In this census 29 metropolitan districts are recognized; each contained a city of more than 200,000.

*Idem, Fifteenth Census of the United States, 1930, Metropolitan Districts, Population and Area* (Washington, D.C.: Government Printing Office, 1932). This census defined 96 metropolitan districts, each of which had a population of more than 100,000. Significant studies based largely on this census include R. D. McKenzie, *The Metropolitan Community* (New York: McGraw-Hill, 1933), especially pp. 39–49, and U.S. National Resources Committee, *Our Cities, Their Role in the National Economy* (Washington, D.C.: Government Printing Office, 1937).

Population figures for metropolitan districts and their suburbs for 1940 as used in this paper have been taken from the U.S. Bureau of the Census, *Sixteenth Census of the United States, 1940,* Press Releases, Ser. PH-1, Nos. 1–140, and Summary (Washington, D.C.: U.S. Bureau of the Census, various dates between February 13, 1941, and June

teenth Census provides data on 140 metropolitan districts. Each contains at least one city of more than 50,000 population and includes contiguous minor civil divisions with a density of population of 150 or more per square mile. Mere density is only a moderately good indicator of the limits of cities, but the figures on metropolitan districts have the great virtue of uniformity. The following study includes only those areas which lie within metropolitan districts but outside the chief cities.

### POPULATION IN SUBURBS

The suburbs of the 140 metropolitan districts have a population of 22,369,432, which is 35.5 per cent of the population of these urban units and 17.0 per cent of the population of the entire country.[3] Of the

_____

11, 1941). The same figures are found in *ibid., Population, First Series, Number of Inhabitants, United States Summary* (Washington, D.C.: Government Printing Office, 1941), pp. 71–75. Detailed figures on each district are contained in the bulletins issued for each state. It is planned also to have a Vol. VIII, *Metropolitan Districts.*

[3] Large cities which are clearly subordinate to the main city either in terms of size or trade relationships are grouped with suburbs in this study, even though they are considered part of the "central cities" by the census. Without these changes the suburbs would have a population of 20,169,603, or 32.0 per cent of the population of the metropolitan districts.

Fifteen of the 23 metropolitan districts with more than one central city have been altered. The following "central cities" are grouped with suburbs: Elizabeth, Jersey City, Newark, and Paterson (New York); Oakland (San Francisco); Niagara Falls (Buffalo); Kansas City, Kan. (Kansas City, Mo.); New Britain (Hartford); Schenectady and Troy (Albany); Holyoke (Springfield, Mass.); Haverhill (Lowell–Lawrence); Bethlehem and Easton (Allentown); Portsmouth and Newport News (Norfolk); Council Bluffs, Iowa (Omaha, Neb.); Rome (Utica); Rock Island and Moline,

1,077 urban units in the United States with more than 10,000 population in 1940, slightly more than one-third (383) were suburbs in metropolitan districts.[4] In 10 metropolitan districts more than 60 per cent of the total population live outside the political boundaries of the chief city. Of this group, Boston and Pittsburgh are particularly striking in having more than a million people in suburbs. Other cities are Providence, Springfield (Massachusetts),

habitants; the only large city of this group is New Orleans.

The extent of development of suburbs in metropolitan districts varies according to location with respect to a climax area, according to location with respect to rivers, bays, and associated state boundaries, to functional type of cities, and to size of cities.

The principal factor in amount of suburbanization appears to be location with

Fig. 1.—Percentage of population in each metropolitan district living in suburbs. The line incloses the climax area.

Hartford, Albany, Scranton, Allentown, Wheeling, and Davenport. On the other hand, there are 9 cities with less than 10 per cent of their population in suburbs, but most of these have fewer than 100,000 in-

Ill. (Davenport, Iowa) ; Ashland, Ky. (Huntington, W.Va.) ; and Superior, Wis. (Duluth, Minn.).

The 9 metropolitan districts in which two central cities are recognized as either co-ordinate or relatively independent are: Beaumont–Port Arthur, Fall River–New Bedford, Hamilton–Middletown, Lowell–Lawrence, Minneapolis–St. Paul, Racine–Kenosha, Saginaw–Bay City, Scranton–Wilkes-Barre, and Tampa–St. Petersburg. (Lowell–Lawrence falls in both groups.)

respect to a small area, hereafter called simply the "climax area," which covers only the eastern part of the Manufacturing Belt

[4] Of this number, 317 were incorporated and 66 were unincorporated but defined as urban under a special rule of the United States Census. The 352 suburbs classified in the Appendix include the suburbs with more than 10,000 population in 1930. Together with 5 unincorporated suburbs not classified for lack of sufficient data and 153 in central cities (130 single central cities, 18 centers in 9 double districts, and the 5 boroughs of New York City) they make up the 510 urban units within metropolitan districts for which employment data were available in the 1935 censuses of trade and manufactures.

and includes southern New England, the middle Atlantic states, and the industrial area near the Appalachian coal fields (Fig. 1). Within the climax area are 9 of the 10 metropolitan districts with more than 60 per cent of their population in suburbs and 15 of 18 with more than 50 per cent. The 31 metropolitan districts in this area average 49.2 per cent of their population in suburbs, compared to 23.9 per cent for the

TABLE 1

PERCENTAGE OF POPULATION OUTSIDE CENTRAL CITY IN METROPOLITAN DISTRICTS BY SIZE GROUPS IN CLIMAX AREA AND IN REST OF COUNTRY*

| Size Group | Climax Area | Rest of United States |
|---|---|---|
| 1,000,000 or more........ | 50.8 | 34.7 |
| 500,000–1,000,000..... | 65.1 | 26.6 |
| 300,000–  500,000..... | 55.2 | 24.1 |
| 200,000–  300,000..... | 33.2 | 21.6 |
| 150,000–  200,000..... | 51.0 | 28.4 |
| 100,000–  150,000..... | 42.2 | 24.4 |
| 50,000–  100,000..... | 38.8 | 19.4 |
| All sizes.............. | 49.2 | 23.9 |

* Each metropolitan district is given equal weight.

other 109 districts in the United States (Table 1). Stated another way, in this area 48 per cent of the metropolitan districts have more than half of their population in suburbs, compared to but 3 per cent of the districts in the rest of the country. Tables 1 and 2 show that in this area all functional types and all sizes of cities are well above the national average in percentage of population in suburbs.

The sharp localization of the climax area appears to be related to two factors. (1) In the East, extensive urbanization and a high density of population associated with manufacturing have been superimposed on an older pattern of small towns and townships. Although engulfed by the spread of population from the larger centers, these small units have maintained their political independence. Urban growth has not been con-

spicuous in the part of the East that lies outside the climax area. (2) In the western part of the climax area the high degree of suburbanization appears related rather to the nature of the steel and coal-mining industries, which have fostered the development of suburbs in western Pennsylvania, eastern Ohio, and West Virginia. Except locally, other types of industry have not given rise to marked suburbanization in other parts of the Manufacturing Belt in the Midwest.

Location with respect to rivers, bays, and state boundaries is important in the suburban development of a number of cities.

TABLE 2

PERCENTAGE OF POPULATION OUTSIDE CENTRAL CITY IN METROPOLITAN DISTRICTS BY REGION AND FUNCTIONAL TYPE*

| FUNCTIONAL TYPE | REGION | | | | TO-TAL‡ |
|---|---|---|---|---|---|
| | Climax Area | Mid-west† | South | West | |
| Manufacturing (M) | 48.1 | 25.7 | 26.6 | 31.0 | 34.4 |
| Diversified (D).... | 51.7 | 20.7 | 22.9 | 28.9 | 24.9 |
| Political (P)....... | 57.2 | 15.3 | 25.2 | 33.4 | 27.2 |
| Transportation (T). | 29.7 | 35.8 | 26.2 | ..... | 27.8 |
| Wholesaling (W)... | ..... | 14.2 | 16.6 | 29.2 | 20.8 |
| Retailing (R)...... | ..... | 9.7 | 14.8 | 28.4 | 19.3 |
| Resort (X)........ | ..... | ..... | 32.0 | 33.5 | 33.4 |
| Mining (S)........ | 64.0 | ..... | ..... | ..... | 64.0 |
| Av............. | 49.2 | 22.4 | 23.5 | 30.1 | 29.5 |

* Each metropolitan district is given equal weight, regardless of size.
† Excluding 7 cities in the climax area.
‡ Including cities in the East not in the climax area.

San Francisco, Davenport, and Norfolk, the only three cities outside the climax area having more than 50 per cent of their population in suburbs, fall into this group.

Six metropolitan districts include parts of three states; all lie on rivers which form state boundaries. Twenty-two metropolitan districts include portions of two states; all except six of these districts lie on rivers forming state boundaries. Suburbanization due to political division thus results from the dual function of rivers as political boundaries and as once-important highways of commerce along which large cities became aligned. State boundaries associated with the Mississippi River and its tributaries form the basis for the political separation of suburbs in the midwestern cities of Wheeling, Huntington, Cincinnati, Louisville, Davenport, Omaha, Kansas City, and St. Louis. (See the Appendix for the names of the larger suburbs.) Other

ever, 24 of the 31 cities have been classified as manufacturing, and the suburban development in the others is due almost exclusively to industry. Manufacturing centers include most of the metropolitan districts already mentioned as having more than 60 per cent of their population in suburbs. Other industrial centers with important suburbs in the climax area are Lowell–Lawrence, New Haven, Binghamton, Youngstown, Canton, and Huntington.

Fig. 2.—Functional types of cities (*M*, industrial; *D*, diversified; *P*, political; *T*, transportation; *W*, wholesaling; *R*, retail; *X*, resort; and *S*, mining).

examples are New York, Philadelphia, and Columbus, Georgia. Bays and associated rivers (but without state boundaries) have been important in Boston, Norfolk, and San Francisco.

Among the various functional types of cities recorded in Figure 2, manufacturing cities show the greatest development of suburbs, averaging 34.4 per cent of their population in suburbs.[5] This type of city shows above-average suburban development in all regions except the climax area and in all size groups except the largest (Tables 2 and 3). In the climax area, how-

Examples from the less-suburbanized Midwest are Peoria, South Bend, Cincinnati, and Louisville. The mining district of Scranton–Wilkes-Barre includes scores of suburban mining boroughs.

Resort cities show above-average suburban development. In the South and West, where such cities are most numerous, they have a higher proportion of population in suburbs than any other type.

[5] For a list of cities in each category and a discussion of the criteria of classification see Chauncy D. Harris, "A Functional Classification of Cities in the United States," *Geographical Review*, XXXIII (January, 1943), 86–99 [see above, pp. 129–38].

Diversified, political, and transportation cities as groups show moderate suburban development. Some political centers, such as Albany, Harrisburg, and Charleston, have strong suburban development associated with industry. Similarly, the diversified cities of New York, Boston, and Chicago have many industrial suburbs.

Wholesale and retail centers show the weakest suburban development of any functional types. Trading centers as a group have few suburbs.

In general, the larger cities exhibit

11 mining). Retailing and distribution wholesaling are seldom of more than local importance in suburbs; such functions cling tenaciously to the central city. Several diversified suburbs, although subordinate to the central city, serve as trade centers for lesser suburbs in addition to having moderate industrial development: Hammond (Chicago), Oakland (San Francisco), and East St. Louis (St. Louis).

Some residential suburbs contain remarkable concentrations of professional or clerical workers who commute to the cen-

TABLE 3

PERCENTAGE OF POPULATION OUTSIDE CENTRAL CITY IN METROPOLITAN DISTRICTS
BY FUNCTIONAL TYPE AND SIZE GROUPS*

| SIZE GROUP | FUNCTIONAL TYPE | | | | | | | | ALL TYPES |
|---|---|---|---|---|---|---|---|---|---|
| | M | D | P | T | W | R | X | S | |
| 1,000,000 or more....... | 39.2 | 35.7 | ...... | ...... | 55.3 | ...... | ...... | ...... | 40.6 |
| 500,000–1,000,000.... | 46.4 | 25.4 | 27.0 | 8.4 | ...... | ...... | ...... | 64.0 | 37.1 |
| 300,000– 500,000.... | 41.2 | 26.5 | 43.0 | 55.4 | 17.7 | ...... | ...... | ...... | 38.0 |
| 200,000– 300,000.... | 28.2 | 16.9 | 26.1 | ...... | 18.8 | ...... | 26.0 | ...... | 24.5 |
| 150,000– 200,000.... | 40.5 | ...... | 32.7 | 23.6 | ...... | 24.6 | ...... | ...... | 36.7 |
| 100,000– 150,000.... | 29.1 | 14.3 | 31.6 | 32.4 | ...... | 12.9 | 41.2 | ...... | 27.5 |
| 50,000– 100,000.... | 21.8 | 16.8 | 18.0 | 21.9 | 13.8 | 22.8 | 32.8 | ...... | 20.0 |
| All sizes............ | 34.4 | 24.9 | 27.2 | 27.8 | 20.8 | 19.3 | 33.4 | 64.0 | 29.5 |

* Each metropolitan district is given equal weight.

stronger suburban development than the smaller cities, but the relationship is rather irregular (Tables 1 and 3).

## FUNCTIONAL TYPES OF INDIVIDUAL SUBURBS

Suburbs are highly differentiated segments showing much greater specialization in function than characterizes the urban unit as a whole. The commonest types of individual suburbs are housing or dormitory suburbs (H) and manufacturing or industrial suburbs (M).[6] Of the 352 suburbs which have been classified in the Appendix, 174 are dominantly residential, 149 dominantly industrial, and only 29 fall into other categories (3 assembly wholesaling, 4 retailing, 10 diversified, 1 government, and

tral city. This concentration can be measured by occupation figures which record occupations by place of residence rather

[6] The types of *individual* suburbs designated by the letters H and M discussed in this section and again referred to in Table 4 and in the Appendix are not represented on the maps. The symbol $M$ on Fig. 2 should therefore not be confused with suburb type M. For the study of residential areas a valuable source with suggestive techniques, useful maps, and extensive references is Federal Housing Administration, *The Structure and Growth of Residential Neighborhoods in American Cities* (Washington, D.C.: Government Printing Office, 1939). An excellent study of a suburban area is Robert C. Klove, *The Park Ridge–Barrington Area, a Study of Residential Land Patterns and Problems in Suburban Chicago* (Chicago: Private edition, distributed by the University of Chicago Libraries, 1940). Examples of planned suburbs of various types are given in Arthur S. Comey and Max S.

than by place of work. Of the 19 cities in the United States which had the highest percentage of their gainfully occupied workers in professional occupations, 16 were suburbs in metropolitan districts.[7] Similarly, of the 21 cities with the highest percentage of the gainfully occupied in clerical occupations, 18 were suburbs.[8] Transportation workers show a high degree of concentration in 3 suburbs.[9]

There are three good measures of intensity of industrialization in industrial suburbs. The Appendix lists the principal suburbs indicated by each index. One measure is the percentage of the total gainful

workers who are engaged in manufacturing and mechanical occupations. Of the 16 cities in the United States with the highest percentages, 13 are suburbs and 3 are co-ordinate members of central cities. Particularly notable are Hamtramck (Detroit), with 74 per cent; Garfield (New York) and Aliquippa (Pittsburgh), with 72 per cent; and Central Falls (Providence), with 71 per cent. Occupation figures are by place of residence and do not necessarily indicate a large industrial employment within the suburb.

A second and closely related measure of industrialization is the percentage which industrial employment forms of the total employment in industry and trade.[10] A high percentage indicates that a suburb leans heavily on other suburbs for trade, since a relatively insignificant number of people work in stores within the suburb. (Employment figures are recorded by place of work.) Unusually high percentages in industry are found in Dearborn (Detroit), Campbell (Youngstown), and Munhall (Pittsburgh), with 98 per cent, and Ecorse (Detroit) and Lodi and Harrison Township (New York), with 96 per cent.

A third measure of industrialization is the ratio of employment within a suburb to the population of the suburb. A high ratio indicates a strong daily movement of people who work here but who live in other suburbs or in the central city. The outstanding example of such a suburb is Dearborn (Detroit), in which 70,635 people were employed in 1935, although the entire population of the city was only 63,584 in 1940. Other suburban units with unusually high ratios are Hamtramck and Highland Park (Detroit) and Johnson City and Endicott (Binghamton). Also worthy of mention are

---

Wehrly, "Planned Communities," Part I in *Land Planning and Land Policies,* Vol. II of *Supplementary Report of the Urbanism Committee to the National Resources Committee* (Washington, D.C.: Government Printing Office, 1939), especially pp. 51–55, 67, 83–92, and 101–9.

[7] In Berkeley (San Francisco), Glendale, Pasadena, and Santa Monica (Los Angeles), Evanston and Oak Park (Chicago), Cleveland Heights, East Cleveland, and Lakewood (Cleveland), Wilkinsburg (Pittsburgh), Lower Merion Township (Philadelphia), East Orange, Montclair, and White Plains (New York), and Brookline town and Newton (Boston), more than 14 per cent of the gainfully occupied were in professional occupations in 1930. (Calculated from U.S. Bureau of the Census, *Fifteenth Census of the United States, 1930, Population,* Vol. IV: *Occupations by States,* Tables 3 and 5. Figures were available for cities of more than 25,000 population only. Detailed occupation figures for 1940 are available for metropolitan districts as units and for all cities of more than 10,000 population in *Sixteenth Census of the United States, 1940, Population, Second Series, Characteristics of the Population* [Washington, D.C.: Government Printing Office, 1942] [bulletin for each state], Tables 33, 42, and 51.)

[8] In Alameda (San Francisco), Oak Park, Berwyn, Cicero, and Maywood (Chicago), Norwood (Cincinnati), East Cleveland and Lakewood (Cleveland), Wilkinsburg (Pittsburgh), Upper Darby Township (Philadelphia), Jersey City, East Orange, Kearney, Bloomfield, and Irvington (New York), and Somerville, Arlington town, and Medford (Boston), more than 18 per cent of the gainfully occupied were in clerical occupations in 1930. The three cities not suburbs are Washington, D.C., Hartford, and Topeka.

[9] Council Bluffs (Omaha), Covington (Cincinnati), and Superior (Duluth).

[10] Figures are calculated from figures of the 1935 *Biennial Census of Manufactures* and the 1935 *Census of Trade* as assembled in U.S. Bureau of Foreign and Domestic Commerce, *Consumer Market Data Handbook,* 1939 ed. ("Domestic Commerce Series," No. 102 [Washington, D.C.: Government Printing Office, 1939]), lines 18, 20, and 22 for each city.

East Chicago (Chicago), Lawrence (Low-ell–Lawrence), and Passaic (New York). Such suburbs are similar to city cores such as the Loop in Chicago or Manhattan in New York City in being the focal points of commuting; they differ, however, in the relative dominance of industrial employment.

many factories but relatively few people. Commuting is not from suburbs to city but from city to suburbs to work in factories located outside the political limits of the city. Some factories are so located to avoid taxes or legal restrictions; others, to find large blocks of cheap land; and yet others, to be away from the city because of their

| ▲ | A |
| ● | B |
| ◨ | C₁ |
| ◻ | C₂ |
| ○ | D |
| ◪ | E |

FIG. 3.—Suburb types (*A*, industrial fringe; *B*, industrial; *C*-1, complex with industrial more important; *C*-2, complex with residential more important; *D*, dormitory; *E*, mining and industrial).

## GENERALIZED SUBURB TYPES

The study and classification of individual suburbs is a fascinating business; but, in order to facilitate generalizations, all suburbs in each metropolitan district have been grouped and treated as a unit. On this basis the suburbs have been classified into six types.[11] The classification includes only 104 metropolitan districts with more than 100,000 population. Statistics are not definitive for 4 districts of this size or for the 32 smaller metropolitan districts with populations between 50,000 and 100,000. Figure 3 shows the distribution of these suburb types.

Industrial fringe suburbs, designated by the letter "A," are those in which there are

[11]The various types have been recognized and separated by a rather complex set of statistical criteria. With a few exceptions the principal types may be recognized, however, by rather simple indices. A-type suburbs are found only in metropolitan districts in which the central city is relatively dominant, having over 75 per cent of the population. The ratio of people employed in industry and trade in the suburbs to the population in the suburbs is at least .12, and exceeds the ratio for the central city by at least .02. In B-type suburbs the central city is relatively less dominant, and the ratio of people employed in the suburbs is sometimes higher and sometimes lower than in the central city, but the ratio employed in industry alone is considerably higher. In C-type suburbs the ratio employed in industry and trade in the suburbs is considerably less than in the central city, but the ratio employed in industry alone may be either more or less. In C-1 suburbs the ratio in industry in the suburbs is at least .08, and in C-2 suburbs

own fire hazards, odors, or other nuisances. Sometimes the city line has even been redrawn to exclude large industrial properties from the city tax base. A-type suburbs are most numerous among smaller metropolitan districts in the South, where several cities have large oil refineries or other factories just outside city limits. Wichita, Tulsa, and Oklahoma City are examples. New Orleans is the largest city of this group. Fort Wayne is the best example within the Manufacturing Belt.

B-type suburbs are industrial suburbs containing not only factories but also a large proportion of the people who work in them. These suburbs lean heavily on the central city for wholesale and retail trade and professional services. B-type suburbs are found in the Manufacturing Belt, particularly in the climax area, which alone accounts for 11 of the 17 cities with this type of suburb. Reading, Allentown, Binghamton, Utica, Albany, Springfield (Massachusetts), and Providence are outstanding examples in the climax area. Davenport is the leading example outside this area.

D-type suburbs are dormitory or residential suburbs. Industries in them are relatively insignificant, and such retail trade as is carried on is merely to serve the people who live there. D-type suburbs are well distributed except in the climax area, where they are overwhelmed by industrial suburbs. In resort and political centers this is the most common type. Although dormitory suburbs characterize the large cities of Los Angeles, Washington, and Cleveland, such suburbs are more common among smaller cities, such as the political centers of Austin, Lansing, and Des Moines; among resorts, such as Phoenix, San Diego, and Miami; among industrial centers, such as Winston-Salem, Evansville, and Flint; and among other types, such as Portland (Maine), Jacksonville, Omaha, and San Antonio. It is probable that most of the

metropolitan districts with populations between 50,000 and 100,000—not here classified for lack of data—would fall into this group.

Many cities have a complex group of suburbs among which both industrial and residential suburbs are important. Suburbs in such cities have been classified as C-type. "C-1" is used to designate urban areas in which industrial suburbs appear to be the more important, and "C-2" those in which dormitory suburbs predominate. C-1-type suburbs are most common among manufacturing cities on the southern and western edges of the Manufacturing Belt. It is the suburb type of the great centers of Boston, New York, Philadelphia, and Chicago, four of the five largest cities of the nation. C-2-type suburbs, the most numerous type, are well distributed both regionally and among different functional types of cities. Cincinnati, St. Louis, San Francisco, and Columbus are examples from industrial diversified, wholesaling, and political centers. Both complex types are proportionately more common among large than among small centers.

A mixture of coal-mining and manufacturing suburbs has been designated by the letter "E." E-type suburbs are best represented in the anthracite region of eastern Pennsylvania (Scranton–Wilkes-Barre) but are also found in the Appalachian bituminous field (Johnstown, Pittsburgh, Wheeling, and Charleston) and in its southern extension (Birmingham).

The percentage of the population in suburbs shows close correlation with suburb types. The percentage ranges from 56.6 per cent for E suburbs (mining and industry) through 50.3 per cent for industrial suburbs (B), 35.5 per cent for C-1 suburbs, 28.5 per cent for C-2 suburbs to 25.1 per cent for D suburbs; thus, with decreasing relative importance of the industrial function there is a decreasing percentage of total population in suburbs. The relationship holds reasonably well for all regions and for all functional types of cities. The most sig-

---

.04–.08. In D-type suburbs the figure is usually considerably below .04. In E-type suburbs the employment in both mining and industry is high.

nificant single group is the B-type suburbs in the East, which average 57.5 per cent of the population of their metropolitan districts.

## THE SUBURBAN TREND

The decade 1930–40 was one of marked suburbanization. If each metropolitan district is given equal weight regardless of size, the average increase of population in suburbs was 29.7 per cent, compared to only the suburban trend was relatively weaker than in the larger cities.[13] The percentage increase in population in suburbs varied directly with the general rate of increase of the district and inversely with the percentage of population of the district living in suburbs.

Although suburban development has been closely associated with industry, the chief growth during the last decade was in residential suburbs. Among individual suburbs

TABLE 4

AVERAGE PERCENTAGE INCREASE IN POPULATION, 1930–40, FOR SELECTED
METROPOLITAN DISTRICTS AND THEIR SUBURBS

| METROPOLITAN DISTRICT | WHOLE DISTRICT | CENTRAL CITY | OUTSIDE CENTRAL CITY | SUBURBS OVER 10,000 POPULATION* | | |
|---|---|---|---|---|---|---|
| | | | | All | Industrial (M) | Residential (H) |
| New York......... | 7.2 | 7.6 | 6.7 | 7.4 | − 0.6 | 11.6 |
| Chicago........... | 3.1 | 0.6 | 11.5 | 5.1 | − 0.2 | 7.7 |
| Los Angeles........ | 25.3 | 21.5 | 29.6 | 25.0 | ......... | 28.9 |
| Philadelphia........ | 1.8 | − 1.0 | 7.9 | 7.2 | 0.4 | 11.8 |
| Boston............ | 1.8 | − 1.3 | 3.5 | 4.5 | − 0.6 | 7.5 |
| Detroit............ | 9.1 | 3.5 | 25.4 | 7.0 | 4.2 | 9.8 |
| Pittsburgh......... | 2.1 | 0.3 | 3.0 | 1.7 | 3.3 | − 2.0 |
| San Francisco...... | 10.7 | 0.0 | 20.8 | 20.6 | 17.7 | 21.1 |
| St. Louis........... | 5.8 | − 0.7 | 17.0 | 5.1 | − 0.5 | 13.8 |
| Milwaukee......... | 6.3 | 1.6 | 22.8 | 10.6 | 5.0 | 21.8 |
| Providence........ | 3.0 | 0.2 | 4.6 | 4.8 | 0.3 | 12.0 |
| United States†..... | 10.8 | 6.5 | 29.7 | 6.6 | 1.7 | 11.7 |
| United States‡..... | 8.2 | 5.0 | 15.8 | ......... | ......... | ......... |

\* Each suburb is given equal weight. For list of suburbs included under each classification in each district see Appendix.

† Each metropolitan district is given equal weight (percentage increases for each district are added and this total is divided by the number of districts).

‡ Cities weighted by size (total numerical increase is divided by the total 1930 population of identical units).

6.5 per cent for the central cities. It is notable that, whereas the total population of the United States increased 7.2 per cent, the total urban population 7.9 per cent, and the population in 133 metropolitan districts 8.2 per cent, the total population in central cities increased by only 5.0 per cent but that in suburbs by 15.8 per cent.[12] Rapid increases in population in suburbs characterized all sections of the country, all functional types of cities, and all sizes of cities, although in cities of less than 100,000

[12] The figures of 9.3 per cent increase in metropolitan districts, 6.1 per cent for the central cities, and 16.9 per cent for areas outside central cities given in the census, include in the increases the total 1940 population of the 7 metropolitan districts for which 1930 figures are not available (622,021 total population—445,174 in central cities and 176,847 outside). The only metropolitan districts in which central cities grew more rapidly than suburbs were New York, Scranton–Wilkes-Barre, Allentown, Oklahoma City, Jacksonville, Savannah, Altoona, Lincoln, Cedar Rapids, and Corpus Christi.

[13] Analysis of rate of increase of population in suburbs failed to reveal significant differences re-

of more than 10,000 population (which incidentally grew less rapidly than the smaller suburbs and unincorporated areas), those classified as residential averaged 11.7 per cent increase in population, compared to 1.7 per cent for those classified as industrial.[14] Table 4 shows that in nearly all large metropolitan districts industrial suburbs either lost population or gained only slightly, whereas residential suburbs showed rapid growth. In the New York metropolitan district the City of New York increased more rapidly than did the suburbs, for, although the new residential suburbs of Long Island grew rapidly, the more numerous and populous industrial suburbs of New Jersey stagnated.

Three factors contributed to the rapid growth of suburbs: (1) increasing use of the automobile, which facilitated commuting to distant but pleasant residential suburbs, many of which had cheaper land and lower tax rates; (2) decreasing size of the family and the consequent increase in number of housing units needed for a given population; and (3) a tendency for changes in some city lines to lag behind the expansion in the built-up areas.[15]

## APPENDIX

### FUNCTIONAL TYPES OF SUBURBS

This list includes the 352 suburbs of more than 10,000 population for which figures were available. Of these, 310 are incorporated, and 42, mostly in Massachusetts, Rhode Island, New Jersey, and Pennsylvania, are unincorporated.

Letter symbols for functional types of sub-

___

lated to size of city (above 100,000), function of city, or regional location, except differences due to correlation of the above with rate of increase of population for whole metropolitan districts or with percentage of the population living in suburbs.

[14] The metropolitan districts classified as industrial also grew slowly during 1930–40. Their average rate of growth was 6.1 per cent, compared to 10.8 per cent for all metropolitan districts and 34.4 per cent for resorts, 28.2 per cent for retail centers, 16.0 per cent for political centers, 13.2 per cent for transportation centers, 12.1 per cent for wholesaling centers, and 11.8 per cent for diversified cities. See Chauncy D. Harris, "Growth of the Larger Cities in the United States, 1930–40," *Journal of Geography*, XLI (November, 1942), 313–18.

The slower rate of growth of industrial centers extended back into the 1920 decade. Daniel O. Price ("Factor Analysis in the Study of Metropolitan Centers," *Social Forces*, XX [May, 1942], 450, Table I) found a negative correlation of .2758 between percentage of increase in population 1920–30 and the percentage of the gainfully occupied in non-service industry in the 93 cities of more than 100,000 population in 1930.

[15] For fuller analyses see Charles C. Colby, "Centrifugal and Centripetal Forces in Urban Geography," *Annals of the Association of American Geographers*, XXIII (1933), 1–20 [see above, pp. 287–98], and Homer Hoyt, "Forces of Urban Centralization and Decentralization," *American Journal of Sociology*, XLVI (May, 1941), 843–52.

urbs are as follows: M for manufacturing or industrial suburbs; H for housing or dormitory suburbs; D for diversified suburbs having both important trade and manufacturing; R for suburbs in which retail trade appears to be the chief function; W for suburbs in which wholesaling is important.

A letter in parentheses indicates a secondary function. Danvers town (Boston), principally a dormitory suburb but with large industrial employment also is listed: "H: Danvers (M)."

Since figures refer to political boundaries, a suburb is classified as H if its industrial workers are employed in a factory just across the line in another suburb or in an unincorporated area.

*Akron, Ohio.*—M: Barberton; H: Cuyahoga Falls

*Albany, N.Y.*—M: Cohoes, Rensselaer, Schenectady, Troy; H: Watervliet

*Allentown, Pa.*—M: Bethlehem, Pa., Phillipsburg, N.J.;[1] D: Easton, Pa.

*Atlanta, Ga.*—H: Decatur

*Atlantic City, N.J.*—H: Pleasantville

*Baltimore, Md.*—Government: Annapolis

*Binghamton, N.Y.*—M: Endicott,[1, 2] Johnson City[1, 2]

[1] One of the 32 industrial suburbs which lean heavily on other suburbs or on the central city for retail trade, as evidenced by the very high percentage which industrial employment forms of the total employment in industry and trade—more than 90 per cent, compared to the national average of 59 per cent and about 80 per cent for several of the highest metropolitan districts.

[2] One of 19 suburbs to which there is a large daily movement of working population from other

*Birmingham, Ala.*—M (and mining): Bessemer; H: Fairfield

*Boston, Mass.*—In Essex Co., M: Beverly, Gloucester, Lynn, Peabody,[1, 2] Salem; H: Danvers town (M), Saugus town, Swampscott town

In Middlesex Co., M: Cambridge (also university), Everett, Framingham town, Waltham, Watertown town; H: Arlington town, Belmont town, Malden, Medford, Melrose, Matick town, Newton, Somerville, Stoneham town, Wakefield town, Winchester town, Woburn (M)

In Norfolk Co., M: Norwood town, Quincy; H: Braintree town, Brookline town, Dedham town, Milton town, Needham town, Wellesley town, Weymouth town

In Plymouth Co., M: Brockton

In Suffolk Co., M: Chelsea; H: Revere, Wintrop town

*Bridgeport, Conn.*—M: Shelton[1]

*Buffalo, N.Y.*—M: Lackawanna,[1] Niagara Falls, North Tonawanda, Tonawanda; H: Kenmore

*Canton, Ohio.*—M: Alliance, Massillon

*Chicago, Ill.*—M: Chicago Heights, Cicero, Harvey, Melrose Park, Waukegan, Ill., East Chicago,[1, 2, 3] Gary, Whiting,[1, 2] Ind.; H: Berwyn, Blue Island (M), Brookfield, Calumet City, Elmhurst, Elmwood Park, Evanston (also university), Forest Park, Highland Park, La Grange, Maywood, Oak Park, Park Ridge, Wilmette, Winnetka, Ill.; D: Hammond, Ind.

---

areas in the metropolitan district, as evidenced by the fact that the ratio of people employed to the total population is .300 or more, compared to an average of .138 for all metropolitan districts, .243 for Flint, the highest metropolitan district, and .348 for Manhattan, the commuting heart of New York City. The employment figures are from the 1935 *Census of Trade* and the 1935 *Biennial Census of Manufactures,* as conveniently assembled in U.S. Bureau of Foreign and Domestic Commerce, *Consumer Market Data Handbook,* 1939 ed., lines 18, 20, and 22.

[3] One of the 16 suburbs of more than 25,000 population in which an unusually high percentage of the residents are engaged in manufacturing and mechanical occupations—more than 60 per cent of the gainfully occupied, compared to the national average of 28.9 per cent and 58.3 per cent for Flint, the highest single central city in a metropolitan district. Three members of central-city clusters are also marked. Employment is not necessarily in the same suburb. (U.S. Bureau of the Census, *Fifteenth Census of the United States, 1930, Population,* Vol. IV: *Occupations by States,* Tables III and V).

*Cincinnati, Ohio.*—M: Norwood, Ohio; H: Covington, Fort Thomas, Newport, Ky.

*Cleveland, Ohio.*—M: Euclid; H: Cleveland Heights, East Cleveland, Garfield Heights, Lakewood, Parma, Shaker Heights

*Columbus, Ga.*—H: Phenix City, Ala.

*Davenport, Iowa.*—M: East Moline,[1, 2] Moline, Rock Island, Ill.

*Detroit, Mich.*—M: Dearborn[1, 2, 3] Ecorse,[1] Hamtramck,[1, 2, 3] Highland Park,[2] Pontiac, Wyandotte,[3] H: Ferndale, Grosse Pointe Park (?), Lincoln Park (?), Mount Clemens, River Rouge, Royal Oak

*Duluth, Minn.*—H: Superior, Wis. (also transportation)

*Evansville, Ind.*—W: Henderson, Ky.

*Fall River[3]—New Bedford,[3] Mass.*—H: Fairhaven town

*Harrisburg, Pa.*—M: Steelton[1]

*Hartford, Conn.*—M: Bristol,[1, 2, 3] Meriden, Middletown, New Britain

*Huntington, W.Va.*—M: Ashland, Ky., Ironton, Ohio

*Kansas City, Mo.*—M: Kansas City, Kan. (H); H: Independence, Mo.

*Lancaster, Pa.*—M: Columbia

*Little Rock, Ark.*—H: North Little Rock

*Los Angeles, Calif.*—H: Alhambra, Belvedere Township, Beverly Hills, Burbank, Compton, Gardena Township, Glendale, Huntington Park, Inglewood, Long Beach, Monrovia, Pasadena, Pomona, Santa Ana, Santa Monica, South Gate, South Pasadena, Whittier; D: Ontario; W: Anaheim, Fullerton

*Louisville, Ky.*—H: Jeffersonville, New Albany (M), Ind.

*Lowell-Lawrence,* [2, 3] *Mass.*—M: Amesbury town, Haverhill, Newburyport; H: Methuen town (M)

*Milwaukee, Wis.*—M: Cudahy,[1] South Milwaukee, Waukesha, West Allis; H: Shorewood, Wauwatosa

*Minneapolis–St. Paul, Minn.*—M: South St. Paul

*New Haven, Conn.*—M: Ansonia, Wallingford; H: Derby (M)

*New York, N.Y.*—In Nassau Co., N.Y., H: Freeport, Floral Park, Glen Cove, Hempstead, Lynbrook, Rockville Centre, Valley Stream

In Westchester Co., N.Y., H: Mamaroneck, Mount Vernon, New Rochelle, Ossining, Peekskill, Port Chester (M), White Plains, Yonkers (M)

In Fairfield Co., Conn., M: Norwalk, Stamford

In Bergen Co., N.J., M: Garfield,[1, 3] Lodi[1, 2]; H: Cliffside, Park, Englewood, Hackensack (R), Lyndhurst Township, Ridgefield Park, Ridgewood, Rutherford, Teaneck Township

In Essex Co., N.J., M: Bloomfield, Newark; H: Belleville, East Orange, Irvington (M), Maplewood Township, Montclair, Nutley, Orange (D), South Orange, West Orange (M)

In Hudson Co., N.J., M: Bayonne, Harrison,[1] Hoboken, Kearny,[1] Union City, West New York; H: Jersey City (M), North Bergen Township, Weehawken Township

In Middlesex Co., N.J., M: Carteret,[1, 2] New Brunswick, Perth Amboy, South River;[1] H: Woodbridge Township

In Monmouth Co., N.J., H: Long Branch, Neptune Township; D: Red Bank; R: Asbury Park

In Morris Co., N.J., R: Morristown

In Passaic Co., N.J., M: Clifton, Hawthorne, Passaic,[2] Paterson

In Union Co., N.J., M: Elizabeth, Linden, Rahway; H: Cranford Township, Hillside Township, Roselle, Summit, Union Township, Westfield; D: Plainfield

*Norfolk, Va.*—M: Newport News; H: Portsmouth

*Omaha, Neb.*—H: Council Bluffs, Iowa (also transportation)

*Peoria, Ill.*—M: Pekin

*Philadelphia, Pa.*—M: Bristol, Chester, Conshohocken Township, Phoenixville, Pa., Burlington, Camden, N.J.; H: Abington Township, Cheltenham Township, Haverford Township, Lower Merion Township, Norristown, Upper Darby Township, Pa., Collingswood, Gloucester (M), Pensauken Township, N.J.

*Pittsburgh, Pa.*—In Allegheny Co., M: Clairton,[1] Coraopolis, Duquesne,[1] McKeesport, McKees Rocks,[1] Munhall;[1] H: Bellevue, Braddock, Carnegie (M), Dormont, Homestead, North Braddock, Swissvale (M), Turtle Creek, Wilkinsburg

In Beaver Co., M: Aliquippa,[3] Ambridge

In Fayette Co., R: Uniontown

In Washington Co., M: Canonsburg, Charleroi, Donora; D: Washington

In Westmoreland Co., M: Jeannette, Latrobe, Monessen,[1, 2] New Kensington; H: Arnold,[1] R: Greensburg

*Portland, Me.*—H: South Portland, Westbrook

*Portland, Ore.*—M: Vancouver, Wash.

*Providence, R.I.*—M: Bristol,[1] Central Falls,[3] Cumberland town, Pawtucket,[3] West Warwick town, Woonsocket,[3] R.I., Attleboro, North Attleboro town, Mass.; H: Cranston (M), East Providence (W), Newport, North Providence (M), Warwick, R.I.

*St. Louis.*—M: St. Charles, Mo., Alton, Belleville, Granite City,[1, 3] Ill.; H: Maplewood, University City (also university), Webster Groves, Mo.; D: East St. Louis, Ill.

*San Francisco, Calif.*—M: Richmond; H: Alameda, Berkeley (also university), Burlingame, Palo Alto (also university), San Leandro, San Mateo, Vallejo; D: Oakland

*Scranton–Wilkes-Barre, Pa.*—M: Kingston; mining: Carbondale, Dickson City, Dunmore, Hannover Township, Nanticoke, Old Forge, Olyphant, Pittston, Plains Township, Plymouth, Taylor

*South Bend, Ind.*—M: Mishawaka[1]

*Springfield, Mass.*—M: Chicopee,[3] Easthampton town, Holyoke, Northampton, Westfield, West Springfield town

*Tulsa, Okla.*—H: Sapulpa

*Utica, N.Y.*—M: Rome; D: Herkimer

*Washington, D.C.*—H: Arlington Co., Va.; D: Alexandria, Va.

*Waterbury, Conn.*—M: Naugatuck[1, 2]

*Wheeling, W.Va.*—M: Moundsville, W.Va., Bellaire (H), Martins Ferry, Ohio

*Worcester, Mass.*—M: Clinton town, Marlborough

*Youngstown, Ohio.*—M: Campbell,[1, 2] Niles, Warren, Ohio; Farrell,[1, 2] Sharon, Pa.; H: Struthers (M), Ohio

CHARLES R. HAYES

# SUBURBAN RESIDENTIAL LAND VALUES
# ALONG THE C.B.&Q. RAILROAD

The lobate pattern of the suburban communities extending outward from Chicago along the railroads is well known. Homer Hoyt described the pattern in 1933,[1] and Harold Mayer compared these urbanized extensions to beads on strings,[2] an analogy which is obvious from an examination of any large-scale map of the Chicago Metropolitan Area.

The purpose of this investigation is to describe the pattern of one of these urbanized extensions as reflected in residential land values and to relate the value of the residential land to lines of public transport, to industrial areas, and to any topographic features which seem to affect the value of the nearby residential property.[3]

Figure 1 indicates the lobate pattern of suburban Chicago. The lobe comprising the string of suburban communities from Cicero west through Downers Grove is the one with which we are concerned. It is the so-called west suburban urbanized area served by and to a large extent dependent on the Chicago, Burlington, and Quincy Railroad from Cicero to Downers Grove, a distance of about fifteen miles.

Reprinted from *Land Economics*, XXXIII (May, 1957), pp. 177–81, with permission of the author and the editor. (Copyright, 1957, by the University of Wisconsin, Madison, Wis.)

[1] Homer Hoyt, *One Hundred Years of Land Values in Chicago* (Chicago: University of Chicago Press, 1933).

[2] Harold M. Mayer, "Moving People and Goods in Tomorrow's Cities," *Annals of the American Academy of Political and Social Science* (November, 1945), pp. 116–28.

[3] Data are from Olcott's various Land Values Blue Books for the Chicago Area for the year 1953 or adjusted to 1953. Values have been spot checked with records of real estate transactions in Western Springs, La Grange, and Riverside.

The Burlington suburban service is the only public transportation serving the entire area, but even in parts of the area where it competes with other forms of public transportation it is certainly the fastest and, owing to recent modernization, it is generally conceded to be the best.[4]

Residential land values along the C.B.&Q. lobe are rather high relative to other extensions. It is an area of high-grade, dormitory suburbs with several small but well zoned and developed industrial areas, principally along the Indiana Harbor Belt Railroad.

The area of high residential land values at the north edge of the block diagram (Fig. 2) north of the C.B.&Q. Railroad but within the diagram is where residential land values have risen as a result of the location of the Congress Street Expressway now under construction. It would be interesting, though it is not within the scope of this paper, to trace the development of the area adjacent to the Congress Street freeway to determine the point in construction or the point in local political history that residential land values began to rise as a result of the proposed highway. Or, more speculatively, what would happen to that lobe of high residential land values if construction of the highway were suddenly stopped and the entire project dropped?

The block diagram (Fig. 2) embraces the suburban communities served by the C.B.&Q. and overlaps to the north the area to be served by Congress Street and part of the area served by the Chicago and North Western Railroad suburban service. Each cube on the diagram represents a quarter-section of land the height of which is pro-

[4] "Are Commuters Worth It?" *Railway Age*, February 8, 1954, pp. 61–64.

portional to the value per front foot of the residential land contained in the quarter section.

It is obvious that the railroad rides a ridge of residential land values. That is, the value of the residential land slopes away from the rail line parallel to the right of way, in this case to the north and to the south. The Douglas Park and the Garfield Park elevated lines (marked C.T.A. on Figure 2) also ride value ridges. The rising

residential land values at the north edge of the diagram indicate the location of Congress Street and the C.&N.W. Railroad just to the north of the area embraced by the diagram. This evidence seems sufficient to assume that each line of public transport rides a residential land-value crest of its own making.

An inspection of Figure 2 reveals that residential land values not only slope away from the rail line but dip between each

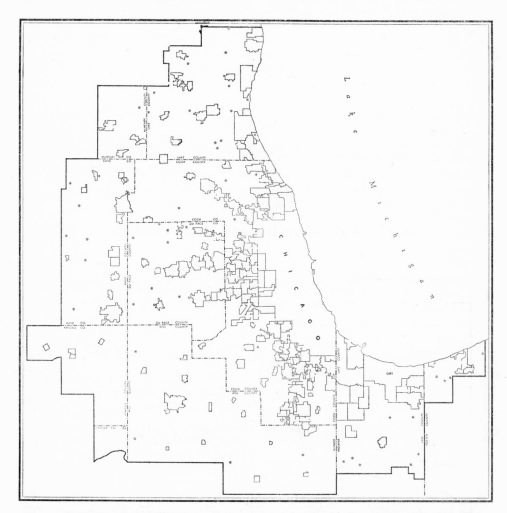

FIG. 1.—Metropolitan Chicago. The above area embraces a population of more than 5,500,000. Extending some 40 miles from the city's center, the area embraces hundreds of places besides Chicago itself. The map shows only the 195 incorporated places and 50 unincorporated places, which latter, because of their size, merit inclusion.

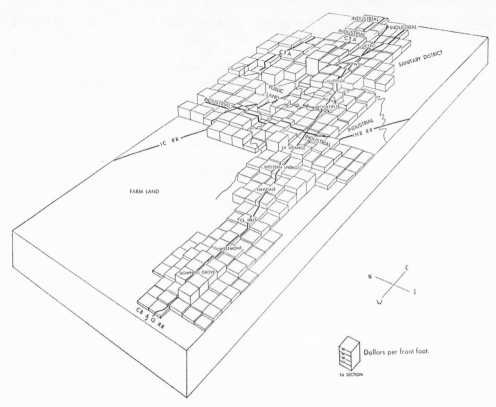

FIG. 2.—Suburban residential land values along the C.B.&Q. R.R.

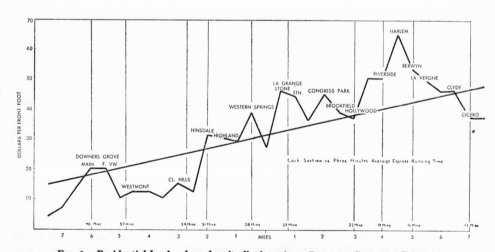

FIG. 3.—Residential land values, longitudinal sections, Downers Grove to Chicago

station. Values form a modified cone or pyramid around each station but with each successive cone tending to be a little higher than the last as one approaches the city. The *longitudinal sections* graph (Fig. 3) reveals this concept with the stations at the high points on the graph and the areas between the stations at the low points on the graph.

phasizes the pyramid effect of residential land values referred to previously, and it reveals other value configurations lost in the smaller scale of the block diagram (Fig. 2). The railroad actually runs in a value trough or valley extending about one-quarter mile on each side of the tracks. Residential land values rise sharply to plateaus on both sides of the rail line about one-half

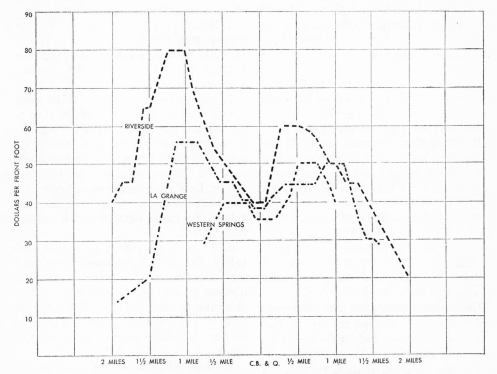

FIG. 4.—Residential land values, cross-sections, along the C.B.&Q. R.R.

The stations without well-developed commercial cores or good shopping centers (Westmont, Clarendon Hills, Highlands, and Hollywood) are in general below the average or trend line for other centers but are, nevertheless, higher in residential land values than areas without stations adjacent to them.

The *cross-sections* graph (Fig. 4) is a block-by-block representation along one street in each of the villages of Western Springs, La Grange, and Riverside. It em-

mile from the railroad then drop sharply about one to one-and-one-half miles from the tracks. It would seem that people are willing to pay a premium to live at least one-quarter mile but not more than one-and-one-half miles from the railroad.

The *longitudinal sections* graph (Fig. 3) has been compiled from quarter-section average residential land values one-and-one-quarter miles on each side of the railroad integrating a reasonable cross-section into each point on the graph. When a straight line is adapted to this graph by statistical methods the downward trend in residential land values from east to west, from the city outward, is evident. The vertical lines on the graph each represent three minutes' running time, on the average, for all suburban express trains serving those stations. If the value at each intersection of the trend line with a three-minute-section line is picked off the graph and all these values averaged, it is discovered that residential land values decrease, on the average, one dollar a front foot for every minute of average suburban express train running time from Cicero to Downers Grove.

The areas marked industrial on Figure 2 are developed factory centers or industrial areas. Almost without exception residential land values are depressed within about one-half mile of these industrial centers. There is, however, an apparent advantage in that again almost without exception residential land values are higher than normal about one-half to one-and-one-half miles distant from the factories. Apparently people wish to live at least one-half mile but not farther than one-and-one-half miles from work. This phenomenon is strong enough to negate locally the effects of public transportation lines on residential land values.

Homer Hoyt points out that shorelines and higher points of land are preferred as places of residence.[5] Patterns revealed by this investigation bear this out. On Figure 2 note that the areas immediately adjacent to stream valleys are depressed in residential land values while the areas about one-half mile distant are higher in value than is normal for their location with respect to public transport. Very likely it is the banks above the stream or river valleys that as-

sume the higher values as preferred residential lots while the lower swampier land in the valleys is shunned as a site for residential building.

This is not an attempt to generalize on the basis of an investigation covering only one small geographic area. However, the conclusions reached here may very well be adaptable to any continuous urbanized suburban area connected to its metropolis by efficient rail service. For example:

1. Suburban rail service connecting continuous urbanized areas runs in an area of high residential land values relative to areas without such service or some distance away from such service.

2. The actual point-to-point values form, however, a jagged line with peaks close to the stations and dips between the stations. Residential land values, then, are in the form of a rough pyramid around each station with the apex at or near the suburban station. Land values are, however, depressed for about one-quarter to one-half mile each side of the tracks parallel to the railroad right of way.

3. There is a trend in residential land values. The trend is downward going away from the city and is proportional to the distance (time) from the city in an observable ratio (in this area one dollar per front foot, on the average, for every minute of average suburban express train running time).

4. Residential land values are depressed within about one-half mile of industrial areas but are elevated from one-half to one-and-one-half miles distant from the industrial areas.

5. Residential land values tend to be elevated along stream or river banks but tend to be depressed in the stream or river valleys.

[5] Hoyt, *op. cit.*

CLYDE F. KOHN

# DIFFERENTIAL POPULATION GROWTH OF INCORPORATED
# MUNICIPALITIES IN THE CHICAGO SUBURBAN REGION

Like most metropolitan centers in the United States, Chicago is being surpassed in population growth, both numerically and percentage-wise, by its suburban region. This is not a new trend, however. In terms of rates of increase, it has been true since the turn of the century; in terms of absolute growth, it has been true since 1930.

Studies completed in January, 1956, indicate, moreover, that the city is continuing to gain fewer people and to grow at a slower rate than its suburban region. It is generally agreed that during the past five years, the city has grown at a rate of 5.5 per cent. This gives it a population today of about 3,800,000; an increase of 200,000 since 1950. In contrast, it is estimated that its suburban region has gained approximately 446,000 inhabitants since 1950, or at a rate of 28.3 per cent. If continued at this rate for the next five years, the suburban growth for the decade 1950–60 will match that of the 1920's; the city's rate, however, will have fallen far behind.

Centers of population growth within an area are as significant to the geographer, however, as rates of increase. Problems of education, housing, integration, and transportation are dependent on the area as well as on the rapidity of growth. It is the purpose of this paper to present rates of population growth of incorporated municipalities in the Chicago suburban region for the past five years, and to note differences in their growth patterns.

Reprinted from *Illinois Academy of Science Transactions*, XLIX (1956), 85–91, with permission of the author and the editor. (Published by the Illinois State Academy of Science, Springfield, Ill.)

## THE AREA STUDIED

As outlined on Figure 1, the area included in this study is limited to Lake, Cook, and DuPage counties in northeastern Illinois, to that part of Lake County Indiana, which lies to the north of Crown Point, and to Crete Township in Will County, Illinois. The area so delimited is hereafter referred to as the Chicago suburban region. It includes the entire urbanized area of Chicago as defined by the Bureau of the Census in 1950, with the exception, of course, of the city itself. It does not include, however, all of the "Standard Metropolitan Area" as defined by the census.

Within this region are 155 incorporated municipalities. Although a number of these had their origins more than 100 years ago, substantial growth has taken place only since 1890. Since then, and especially in the 1920's and the past ten years, a large proportion of these municipalities have experienced rapid growth.

Estimates indicate that in 1955, the 155 incorporated municipalies of the Chicago suburban region had a population of nearly 1,750,000. This represents a numerical increase since 1950 of nearly 415,000, or an average growth of 31 per cent. An additional 273,000 live in unincorporated areas. It is estimated that the Chicago suburban region has a total population today of more than 2,000,000, compared to the city's population of 3,800,000. The ratio of population in the city to that of the suburban region is now less than 2 to 1.

## BASIS OF ESTIMATES

The population estimates presented in this paper are based on data collected from a number of sources late in 1955. For that year supplemental United States Census counts were made for 40 municipalities located within the Chicago suburban region. These data were used, wherever possible, to determine the rate of growth. Estimates of population for those municipalities for which there were no supplemental United States Census counts were based on: (1) field mapping of new dwelling units; (2) comparison of aerial photographs taken in the 1940's and in 1955; (3) examination of records of building permits; (4) forecasts by other groups and organizations; (5) studies of recent birth rates and school populations; and (6) records of family service agencies. Great reliance was placed on correlations which were established between number of residential building permits and population increases. Correlations were established for suburban communities for which the United States Census Bureau made supplementary census counts in 1955; these were then applied to other communities having similar characteristics.

It was difficult to estimate population growth for the areas of unincorporated land within the region studied. Late census counts have not been made for such areas, and building permits are not recorded on a township basis. As a result, their 1955 population was projected by means of a straight "least-squares" trend line. It should be

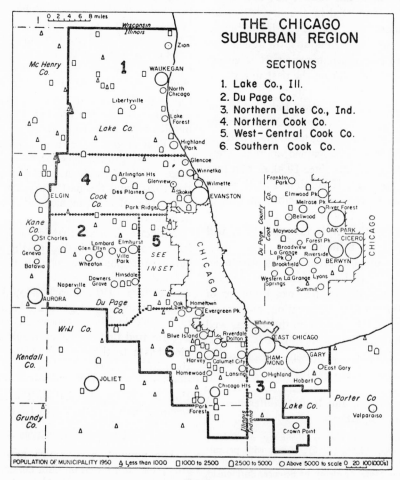

FIG. 1

noted that such projections are likely to err on the conservative side because of the statistical technique employed. This is certainly true for DuPage County, where growth in unincorporated areas is certainly much higher than indicated by the statistical technique used.

### ANALYSIS OF DATA

In analyzing the differential population growth of incorporated municipalities in the Chicago suburban region, attention is directed to: (1) population growth by sections; (2) growth of the large municipalities; (3) municipalities of less than average growth; (4) municipalities of more than growth;

average growth; and (5) municipalities of very rapid growth.

*Population growth by sections.*—The several sections of the Chicago suburban region are growing at different rates. Northern Cook County (Fig. 1, Sec. 1) has gained the largest number of people but ranks second to southern Cook County in rate of increase. West-central Cook County and northern Lake County, Indiana, rank third and fourth, respectively, in terms of numerical increases, but fifth and sixth in terms of rates of growth. DuPage and Lake counties have gained fewer people than any of the other sections but rank third and fourth in terms of percentage increases.

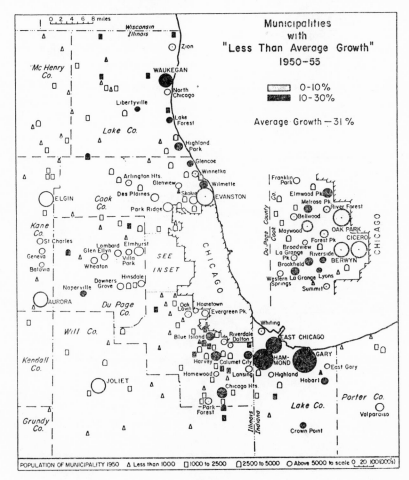

FIG. 2

*Growth of the large municipalities.*—In 1950 there were 30 municipalities in the Chicago suburban region which had a population of more than 10,000. Seven exceeded 50,000, and one, Gary, exceeded 100,000. From the standpoint of numbers, growth in these large municipalities has been outstanding. Altogether, the 30 cities account for nearly 41 per cent of the total increase registered for all the suburban municipalities. Two cities, Skokie and Gary, have each gained more than 20,000 residents during the past five years.

On a percentage basis, however, the large cities of the Chicago suburban region have not equaled the population growth experi-enced by some of the smaller municipalities. As a whole, the 30 larger municipalities have gained at a rate of only 18.4 per cent. Only 7 of the 30 have gained at rates faster than the average for all the suburban municipalities. All of the first 10 have increased at rates lower than the 31 per cent average. Of these, Evanston, Cicero, Oak Park, Berwyn, and Maywood have registered very small rates of increase since 1950.

*Municipalities with less than average growth.*—The municipalities which have grown at rates lower than the area's average of 31 per cent are indicated in Figure 2. These include: (1) all North Shore municipalities, except North Chicago and Zion;

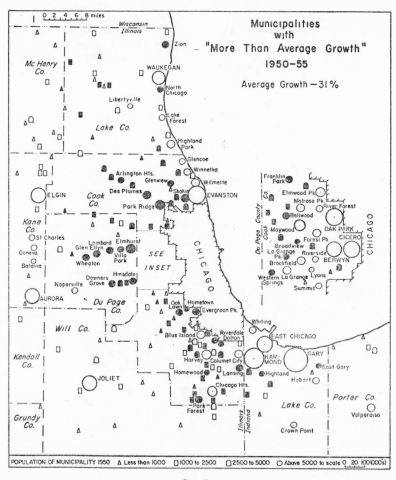

Fig. 3

(2) a cluster of municipalities along the west-central limits of Chicago, including the large and long-established centers of Oak Park, Berwyn, and Cicero, and several nearby residential suburbs; (3) four small industrial centers, Blue Island, Harvey, Chicago Heights, and Calumet City, together with a few very small suburbs; (4) large industrial cities of northern Lake County, Indiana; and (5) a number of small communities located near the fringes of the Chicago suburban region, principally in the lake region of western Lake County, western DuPage County, and southwestern Cook County.

In general, it appears that the suburban

municipalities which have grown at less than average rates include: (1) older municipalities in which there is no longer room for extensive development of single-family homes; (2) industrial municipalities which may have experienced large numerical increases but because of size do not register high rates of growth; and (3) small settlements which are still considered too far from the central city for daily trips to work.

It may be predicted that rates of growth in the older suburbs will continue to decelerate unless single-family homes are replaced by multiple dwelling units or the suburbs annex additional land. Small settlements now located near the fringes of the

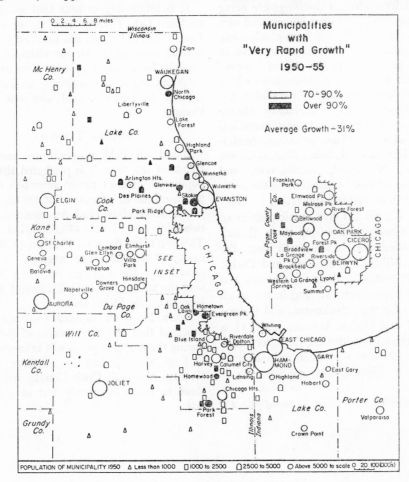

Fig. 4

Chicago suburban region will grow more rapidly if the present widespread demand for single-family homes, located in the open country, continues. Finally, it may be predicted that present industrial centers will grow at a more rapid rate when strong attractive forces, such as the St. Lawrence Seaway and the deepening of the Sag Channel, cause industrial location in the Chicago suburban region.

*Municipalities with more than average growth.*—Eighty-nine municipalities in the study area (Fig. 3) have added more than 31 per cent to their population in the past five years. These include: (1) scattered small settlements in western Lake County in which former resort dwellings are being converted into year-round homes, and new dwellings being built, and from which many workers commute to Waukegan and North Chicago as well as to the city of Chicago itself; (2) a string of municipalities which lie inland from and roughly parallel to the North Shore suburbs, including Skokie (which has achieved the largest numerical increase of any Chicago suburban municipality), Lincolnwood, Niles, Morton Grove, Glenview, Northfield, Northbrook, and Wheeling—all more dependent on the automobile than on rail transportation for commuting; (3) all but five municipalities of DuPage County, comprising three distinct string settlements: in the north along the Chicago, Milwaukee, St. Paul, and Pacific Railroad; centrally, along the Chicago and North Western Railroad; and in the south along the Chicago, Burlington, and Quincy Railroad and Ogden Avenue; and (4) a large number of residential, dormitory suburbs located on or near main railroad lines and major highways in southern Cook County.

*Municipalities of extremely rapid growth.*

—Since 1950, 29 municipalities have more than doubled their populations (Fig. 4). A third of them are in northern Cook County. They include Skokie, Niles, Northbrook, Lincolnwood, Morton Grove, Wheeling, Northfield, Glenview, Mt. Prospect, and Rolling Meadows, which now has an estimated population of more than 5,000. It is a dormitory suburb which has been built since 1950.

The second largest area of rapidly growing municipalities lies to the south of Chicago. Here may be found such suburbs as Evergreen Park, Hometown, and Park Forest, all residential developments of recent years.

It is interesting to note that no city in northern Lake County, Indiana, or in DuPage County, Illinois, has doubled its population since 1950. All the cities in these counties have grown at more than average rates but not so phenomenally as have the suburbs in northern and southern Cook County.

## FUTURE TRENDS

Based on field observations and the trends of the time, it is predicted that the population of the Chicago suburban region will continue to increase at about the same rate as it has since 1950. An expected additional increase of some 440,000 is indicated. This will bring the total 1960 population to nearly 2,460,000. The average rate of growth for the Chicago suburban region over the ten-year period will amount, therefore, to nearly 56 per cent.

Again, based on empirical evidence, it is expected that the higher rates of increase during the next five years will take place in DuPage County and in southern Cook County. Northern Cook County will continue to gain numerically but at a lower rate.

## THE CITY'S WATER SUPPLY

The principal utility systems required by a city are water, sewerage, gas, electricity, and telephone. Geographers do not ordinarily deal with these utilities per se, but they are concerned with them as factors in urban land-use development. For example, there is the problem of the areal association of industrial and residential land use and water supply; of flood control during periods of heavy rainfall; and of the relation between water supply and the recreational uses of watersheds. Geographers, working on more detailed problems of land use, are properly concerned with the location and size of such facilities as pumping stations, reservoirs, and flood-control dams.

Of particular importance to the growth of urban areas is the city's water supply. In meeting their needs, urban places must consider quantities of water required, quality desired, various sources of supply, the treatment required of each source, and the system to be developed for storing and distributing the necessary water. To determine the quantity of water needed by municipalities, estimates are generally made for domestic, commercial, and industrial purposes. To assure an adequate amount to meet peak demands, especially in areas of rainfall variability, storage facilities need to be constructed. To meet the desired standards of quality, water supplies must be free from bacteriological and other contamination. The water should also be as clear, colorless, odorless, as pleasant to the taste as possible, and not too highly mineralized.

The development of an adequate water supply is a growing problem confronting many municipalities, especially in this age of rapid metropolitanization. In many urbanized areas, supplies of ground waters are becoming exhausted or insufficient to meet the needs of rapidly expanding suburbs. Ways and means are being sought, in some metropolitan areas, to develop unified water systems requiring the co-operation of central cities with their outlying suburbs.

Municipalities obtain their water supply either from subterranean sources by means of wells or from surface waters, such as lakes, creeks, or rivers. In most instances the source is nearby, but some cities must build aqueducts to convey their water supplies from distant sources.

Another phase of the water-supply problem involves the storage systems required to supply cities with adequate amounts at all times. Large quantities are required by our cities, and sufficient amounts must be stored in a reservoir or a series of reservoirs. If properly controlled, the land surrounding reservoirs may be used for recreational purposes.

Many of our urban places are facing a serious shortage of water, confronted as they are with a fast-growing population and industrial expansion. In some places depletion of the water supply has become a dominant political issue.

John R. Borchert, in his study "The Surface Water Supply of American Municipalities," analyzes the location of American municipalities using surface water in terms of the geographic patterns of surface water supply. He finds that the average yield of water from the land in relation to existing municipal demand is abundant in all parts of the country except southern California. The belt from east-central Kansas to south Texas also presents problems. The municipalities which have the greatest leeway for increased water use are in the southeastern states, especially in the southern Appalachians, in the Pacific Northwest, along the Great Lakes, and along the large rivers of the agricultural Midwest.

JOHN R. BORCHERT

# THE SURFACE WATER SUPPLY OF AMERICAN MUNICIPALITIES

The water which United States municipalities take from lakes, streams, and reservoirs in an average year constitutes about
6 per cent of the total withdrawal use of
water in the nation for all purposes. It is
approximately 11 per cent of the total withdrawal for public and private-industrial
water systems in the nation's urban areas.[1]
Surface-supplied municipal systems serve
nearly two thousand communities with approximately one-half the population of the
United States.[2] And these surface supplies
are highly susceptible to problems created
by pollution, sedimentation, and seasonal
fluctuations of climate. Thus the following
analysis deals with an important aspect of
the United States water supply, although
it is only one of several major interrelated
parts of the total problem. It is hoped that
this study will help to define the geographical limits of some of the generalizations
which have been made from isolated water-
supply problems in various parts of the
country.

## THE LOCATION OF SURFACE-SUPPLIED MUNICIPAL SYSTEMS

City and county governments which can
be directly concerned with problems of
municipal supplies of surface water are

Reprinted from *Annals of the Association of
American Geographers*, XLIV (March, 1954), 15–
32, with permission of the author and the editor.

[1] From data in Kenneth A. MacKichan, *Estimated Water Use in the United States—1950* (U.S.
Geological Survey Circular 115, May, 1951).
"Withdrawal use" here applies to all water used
for domestic purposes, stockwatering, manufacturing, and irrigation.

[2] From data in *Inventory of Water and Sewage
Facilities in the United States,* U.S. Public Health
Service (1948).

confined mainly to parts of thirty-three
states in the Appalachians, the southern
Midwest and mid-continent areas, the
Rocky Mountains, and along the Pacific
Coast (Fig. 1). Within most of the states,
different sections vary widely in the proportion of their cities which use surface
water. A few notable examples occur in the
Carolinas, Georgia, Alabama, Texas, Oklahoma, Kansas, and Illinois.

Most of the large cities of the country
appear on the map (Fig. 1). They use surface supplies because of the high rate at
which they require water. Among the thirty-
nine cities of over 250,000 population in
1950, only three—Houston, Memphis, and
San Antonio—depend upon wells alone.[3]
Of the 106 cities with more than 100,000
inhabitants, only 16 do not appear on Figure 1; 9 of those are on the Gulf coastal
plain, and the rest are scattered widely
about the country.

But Figure 1 does not have simply the
pattern of large cities. It includes over 450
cities in the 10,000–100,000 class and nearly 1,400 places of 1,000 to 10,000 population. The latter group of towns are using a
surface supply even though their requirements are not large and the supply often
needs heavy treatment. Nearly half of the
American city people supplied from surface
water sources are in municipalities of less
than 100,000 population. And over two-
thirds of the surface-supplied public water
systems are in communities of less than
10,000 people. Down to a population level
around 100,000—with a few major exceptions—the geographic pattern of surface-

[3] Houston has completed a reservoir to supplement its ground water supply with surface water
from the San Jacinto River.

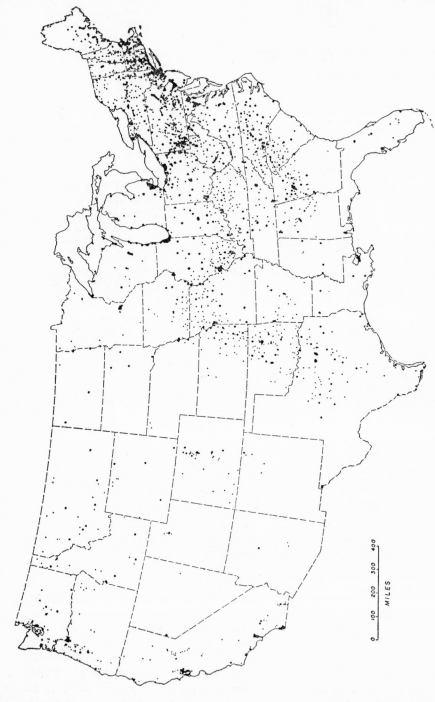

Fig. 1.—Distribution of cities whose municipal water supplies are pumped from a lake, stream, or impounding reservoir. A few cities shown draw a part of their supply from subsurface sources; and systems using infiltration galleries along or beneath surface streams are included. Small dot symbols indicate cities in the 1,000–10,000 population class; large dots, 10,000–100,000; cities shown to scale, over 100,000. Data from *Inventory of Water and Sewage Facilities in the United States, 1945*, Federal Security Agency, U.S. Public Health Service, Cincinnati, 1948.

supplied water systems correlates closely with the pattern of cities. In smaller population classes most places have to use surface water in some regions; in other regions, most places avoid using it. Thus, the problems associated with the use of surface water are not primarily characteristic of large cities, and they are not equally likely in all parts of the country.

*Location in the pattern of ground water availability.*—There are four areal concentrations of cities using surface water supplies in areas where ground water supplies are poor (Fig. 2).[4] In the Appalachian upland region there is a major use of surface water supply in areas of tightly folded and faulted sedimentaries or of dense crystalline rock in New England, in much of New York and northern New Jersey, and in the Blue Ridge and Piedmont provinces. There is also major use of surface sources in parts of the Appalachian "plateaus" and in some belts of the ridge-and-valley province. In those areas there is often much shale in the underlying Carboniferous rocks, with much salt water and few high-yielding aquifers.[5]

The belt of cities through the Ohio–central Mississippi–lower Missouri basins and southward through the mid-continent region is underlain generally by Paleozoic formations—mainly Carboniferous—which contain large amounts of shale and tight limestone. Where there is overlying glacial drift, it is thin and relatively high in clay.[6] These conditions produce low recharge and low rates of yield of ground water. In addition to these widespread ground water problems, excessive salinity is associated with Silurian

formations underlying many of the cities of southeastern Michigan. In parts of western Kentucky, cavernous limestones produce very rapid subsurface drainage and, hence, a highly variable ground water supply. Locally in the mid-continent area cities are underlain by aquifers which have been contaminated by saline water from deeper formations through oil wells.[7]

The concentration of surface-supplied cities in the northern Great Plains of Montana and the Dakotas is less dense because of the relatively small urban development in that region. It is related to the relatively low permeability of the Creataceous and Eocene formations on the plains and the high salinity of the underlying sandstone aquifers.[8] The large number of cities in the mountain west which use surface supplies are in extensive areas of dense, crystalline rocks which are poor aquifers; most of the notable exceptions to these generally poor ground water conditions are in the areas of the porous Columbia lava flows and the major alluvial fans.

There are three other regions in which there is a notable concentration of surface-supplied municipalities notwithstanding generally good ground water conditions. One of these concentrations is in the Puget Sound–Willamette lowland; a second is on the shores of the Great Lakes. In those two areas the surface supply is unusually free of sediment and organic matter and is easier to recover than ground water. A third concentration is in the alluvial fan areas of the Los Angeles–San Bernardino plain, where the demand for water far exceeds the available supply from all local subsurface sources.

Three areas of the country have few surface-supplied municipal water systems although they have a relatively high density of towns. Those are the major alluvial plains at the base of the Sierra Nevada and

---

[4] Explanations of these poor ground water conditions are summarized from *Geologic Map of the United States* (U.S. Geological Survey, 1932); *Tectonic Map of the United States* (American Association of Petroleum Geologists, 1940); and U.S. Geological Survey Circular 114, *The Water Supply Situation in the United States with Special Reference to Ground Water* (1951). The author is indebted to Mr. Robert Schneider, U.S. Geological Survey, Minneapolis, Minnesota, for his criticism of this portion of the paper.

[5] See Geological Survey Circular 114, pp. 102–5.

[6] *Ibid.*, pp. 102–3, 107.

[7] See Stuart L. Schoff, "Salt Water Intrusion in Oklahoma" (U.S. Geological Survey mimeographed report, 1951).

[8] See Geological Survey Circular 114, pp. 108–9.

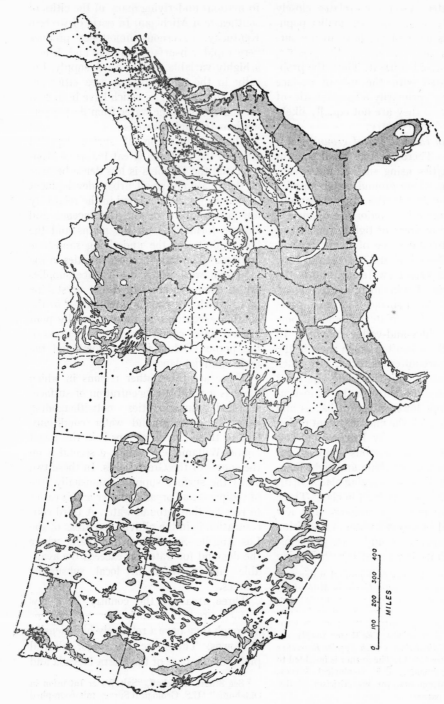

Fig. 2.—The pattern of surface-water-using municipalities compared with the pattern of sub-surface water availability. Shaded areas indicate where ground water containing less than 2,000 parts per million of dissolved solids is available at rates exceeding approximately 72,000 gallons per day (i.e., a fresh water supply adequate for a small town of about 1,000 people). Subsurface pattern adapted from map prepared by Dr. Harold E. Thomas, U.S. Geological Survey, for the Conservation Foundation, Fig. 17, U.S. Geological Survey Circular 114, 1951. The same map appears as Figure 8 in *A Water Policy for the American People*, Vol. 1, Report of the President's Water Resources Policy Commission, 1950, and as a plate accompanying E. E. Thomas, *The Conservation of Ground Water*, New York, 1951.

0    100    200    300    400

MILES

Wasatch Mountains; the areas of eastern Minnesota, Wisconsin, Michigan, northern Indiana, and northern Illinois, in which the glacial drift overlies important sandstone aquifers; and the South Atlantic Coastal Plain, where thick, loose sands with broad catchment areas in the rainy southeast provide the greatest reservoir of ground water in the United States.[9]

It is apparent that most of the municipalities that use surface water supplies are located in regions where ground water conditions are poor as a result of high salinity or low permeability of the underlying rock. The striking positive correlation between areas of surface water use and poor ground water conditions is particularly interesting because it was produced mainly by word-of-mouth information and experience passed among individual well-drillers. The two patterns in Figure 2 existed together, after all, many years before any systematic, comprehensive water studies existed. The correlation is a remainder of the vast store of unassembled, unanalyzed data that rests in the records and recollections of "non-professional" technical tradesmen and businessmen in our society.

Where ground water conditions are suitable to meet local demands, surface water is a second choice, usually because of its greater seasonal fluctuation in temperature and hardness together with its comparatively high content of sediment and organic matter.[10] Thus half the population of the United States is served from surface water sources because, in most cases, there is evidently no suitable alternative.

*Location in the pattern of surface water availability.*—The average daily runoff map in Figure 3 actually shows the pattern of water yield from the land to surface streams through both direct and indirect runoff.[11] Although the pattern is that of average daily yield, it is identical with the pattern of average annual yield or of total yield during a given period of record. The available yield to streams is a remnant of the precipitation after loss by direct evaporation and "consumptive" use by plants and animals. Consequently regional differences in runoff are much greater than regional differences in precipitation. For example, many areas in the high Sierra Nevada yield 900 to 1,000 times as much water per square mile as the nearby Mojave; runoff from southeastern Kansas areas averages 50 to 100 times that from equal areas of southwestern Kansas.

Most of the country has an average daily runoff which is either greater than 250,000 gallons per square mile or less than 20,000 gallons. The Great Plains region is the only wide zone which lies between those two values. On this map (Fig. 3) the areas of over 250,000 gallons runoff are referred to as "high-runoff" regions. The largest number of cities in Figure 3 are within an area of high runoff. A second group includes those cities which are tied to a high-runoff area by a major stream. For example, in the northern Rockies the surface-supplied systems are on the Missouri or its upper tributaries, the Snake or its major upper tributaries, or the main upper tributaries of the Columbia. In the Colorado Rockies and Colorado Piedmont they are on the upper tributaries of the Colorado, Rio Grande, or Platte. A third group of cities is neither within a high-runoff watershed nor naturally tied to one. This group includes cities on the eastern edge of the northern Great Plains, in the James and Red River basins; cities on the southern Great Plains of central Oklahoma and Texas; and cities in southern California. The last comprise the only major cluster of surface-supplied cities in the arid southwest which is not tied by

[9] *Ibid.*, pp. 100–101.

[10] Water temperature Fahrenheit on main streams ranges commonly from the 30's or 40's in midwinter to the 60's, 70's, or 80's in midsummer. (See *Quality of Surface Waters in the U.S.*, U.S. Geological Survey Water Supply Paper, published annually.) Examination of the *Inventory of Water and Sewage Facilities in the United States* shows generally far more elaborate treatment of the water supplies which are drawn from surface sources.

[11] "Indirect runoff" refers to the water returned from precipitation to streams and lakes and reservoirs via ground water percolation and springs.

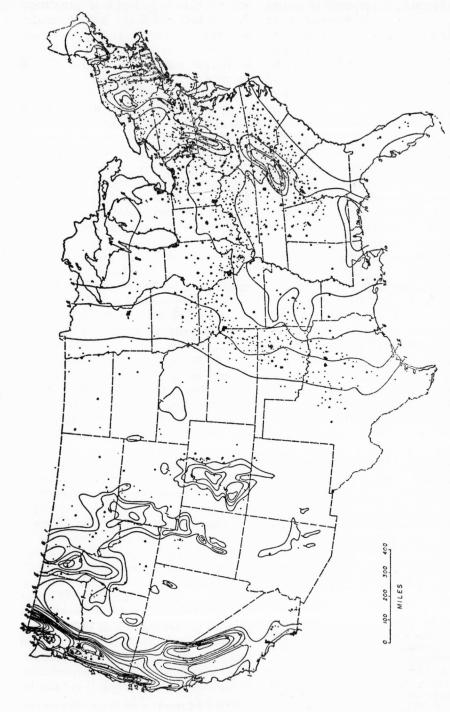

FIG. 3.—The pattern of water runoff in the United States. Numbered isarithms indicate average daily runoff in hundreds of thousands of gallons per square mile. The map is adapted from Walter B. Langbein *et al.*, *Annual Runoff in the United States*, U.S. Geological Survey, Circular 52, 1949. Runoff figures for the original map were computed from stream discharge data and measurements of drainage basin area above each gaging station.

MILES

0  100  200  300  400

a natural stream to a high-runoff watershed region.

Figure 3 shows that in the high-runoff regions small areas yield a quantity of water sufficient for large cities or large industrial plants. Where the mean daily water yield is 250,000 gallons per square mile, an "average" ten-mile-square area (100 square miles) will yield enough water for an average municipality of 125,000 inhabitants in the mountain and Pacific states, and of 250,000 in New England or the southeastern states.[12] Or the same average daily yield of water would cover the average daily demands of—for example—a 30,000 barrel-per-day oil refinery or a thermal-electric station producing 300,000 kwh. daily.[13]

Although surface water is used for municipal supplies in 1,135 counties, Figure 4 shows that cities in only 15 counties withdraw, on the average, more water than the land of their county yields. The local "deficit" of water in these counties would be greatly increased if industrial pumpage were added to the municipal use. Figure 4 shows, further, that in 30 more counties municipal systems use annually a quantity of surface water equal to more than 20 per cent of the yield from their respective counties. It may be assumed that most or all of these counties would also be in the "deficit" category if industrial withdrawal uses were added to municipal figures.[14] In

the remaining 1,000-odd counties in which surface water is used by municipalities, withdrawal is less than one-fifth the yield of the land. In fact, in 830 counties it is less than 1 per cent of the yield. Thus in most counties in the lowest class group in Figure 4 it is almost certain that total surface water withdrawal for all municipal and industrial purposes is far less than total runoff.

This map does not show where the municipalities in each of the 1,135 counties get their water. It does attempt to show the geographic pattern of the relationship between supply and demand within a framework of relatively small areal units. Many communities whose demand could be met from a small drainage basin within the county actually use water from large basins and remote areas. This is especially true in the agricultural Midwest, where a very high proportion of the land is in cultivation, and it is virtually impossible for a municipality to acquire several hundred, or even several score, square miles of land upon which to develop and preserve a forested watershed and small reservoir. Nevertheless, it is obvious from Public Health Service records that most of the municipalities shown in Figure 1 do actually withdraw their water supply from local, small drainage basins.[15] This is indicated by the fact that in the entire country only 86 lakes or main streams are tapped by more than one municipal system. These sources supply about 380 communities. On the other hand, nearly 1,000 systems are supplied by lakes and impounded reservoirs in the upper parts of small basins. These latter systems range in size from the largest to the smallest of those included in this study. Most of the remaining systems use streams discharging from small, local basins. It is also noteworthy that among 26 "large rivers" named by the Geological Survey, the main courses of only 16 are sources of surface water for more than one supply; those streams are pumped by only 185 of

[12] Based on per capita water production data from George J. Schroepfer *et al.*, "A Statistical Analysis of Waterworks Data for 1945," *Journal of the American Waterworks Association*, XL (October, 1948), 1067–98, ref. p. 1074.

[13] From data in *Water in Industry* (National Association of Manufacturers and Conservation Foundation, 1950).

[14] Industrial data parallel to the municipal data used in this study are not available. However, the U.S. Geological Survey estimated the total industrial use of surface water from private sources in 1950 to be 7 to 8 times the total municipal use. (See K. A. MacKichan, *op. cit.*) Analysis of data presented in *Water in Industry* (Appendix 13, Table 5, p. 32) indicates that in most of the standard metropolitan areas of the country the ratio of industrial to municipal pumpage would be of some similar order.

[15] *Op. cit.*

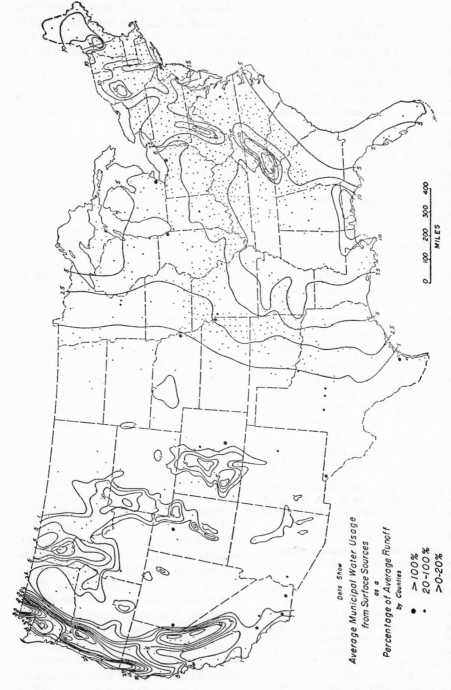

Dots Show

Average Municipal Water Usage
from Surface Sources
as a
Percentage of Average Runoff
by Counties

● >100%

● 20-100%

• >0-20%

0   100 200 300 400
MILES

Fig. 4.—Average annual withdrawal use of surface water in municipal systems in relation to average annual runoff, by counties. Based on water use data from U.S. Geological Survey map of average annual runoff in the U.S. For cities for which Public Health Service had no data, estimates were made on the basis of census population data and regional per-capita water use figures from George Schroepfer *et al*, *op. cit.*

the nearly 2,000 surface-water-using municipal systems in the country.[16]

Thus it appears that, with the exception of the major urbanized areas of the northeast and southwest quadrants of the country, the mean annual supply of surface water in local basins exceeds the mean annual local demand for surface water at the present time. There are, however, notable differences in the degree to which this supply must be stored. These differences are related to patterns of stream discharge during times of low water.

*Location in the runoff pattern of drought periods.*—The map (Fig. 5) attempts to show the pattern of daily average runoff which could be expected during the low-flow months of major drought years. The pattern would occur if there were the "normal" low-month proportion of the annual runoff during a drought comparable to the worst which occurred during the period 1921–45. Actual daily flow is often lower than that indicated in Figure 5, even in a "normal" year. Comparison of Figure 5 with Figure 2 will identify the major regional differences in dependability of yield from the nation's watersheds during its worst droughts.

Most of the country lies, under these conditions, in an area with an average daily water yield either greater than 100,-000 or less than 20,000 gallons per square mile. On this map (Fig. 5) the three major areas with over 100,000 gallons runoff may be referred to as "high-runoff" regions.[17] One high-runoff area is the western high-mountain realm, the crests of the Cascades and northern and Colorado ranges of the Rockies. There meltwater from winter snow is supplemented to a greater extent by summer rains than elsewhere in the western highlands, and glaciated terrain provides many natural reservoirs to stabilize the runoff. The lower runoff of the Sierra Ne-

vada in Figure 5 reflects the greater summer drought in that area. A second large, high-runoff region includes the area of late Wisconsin glaciation in the Great Lakes region as far west as the belt of steep climatic gradients in Minnesota.[18] This is a region in which relatively dependable summer rains and a large spring snow melt are trapped and stored in lakes, ponds, swamps, and extensive areas of coarse sand or gravel terrain. The third large, dependable watershed region is the Appalachian hill country, Piedmont, and southern Alabama–south Georgia–Florida coastal plain. This is a region of high precipitation amount in all seasons, low variability, and relatively low evaporation. In the northern Appalachians runoff and stream flow are stabilized by glacial landforms assisted in many cases by men's wiers or larger dams. The higher general elevation and associated very high annual and minimum monthly rainfall in the southern Appalachians more than compensate for the natural storage features found in the northeast. This third main watershed region, in its extent and in the magnitude of both its low-water and total yield, is the greatest in the country.

If Figure 5 is compared with Figure 2, it is apparent that during times of great drought the surface-water-using municipalities of the country are still in one of three kinds of location in relation to the relative-

---

[16] *Large Rivers of the United States* (U.S. Geological Survey Circular 44, 1949). This brief paper ranks the 26 U.S. rivers with the largest average discharge at their mouths. Those discharges range from 12 billion (Delaware River) to 400 billion (Mississippi River) gallons per day.

[17] J. R. Barnes has noted that a major drought superimposed upon an emergency period when peak industrial production was essential could be disastrous. Viewed against that idea these three watershed regions rank among the country's most basic physical resource concentrations. See "Water for United States Industry," *Report of the President's Materials Policy Commission*, V (1952), 83–98, for Barnes's excellent summary and projection of the over-all U.S. urban and industrial water supply situation.

[18] See maps in C. W. Thornthwaite, "An Approach toward a Rational Classification of Climate," *Geographical Review*, XXXVIII (January, 1948), 55–94; S. D. Flora, *The Climate of Kansas* (Report of the Kansas State Board of Agriculture, June, 1948), p. 302, Fig. 2; maps in J. R. Borchert, "Climate of the Central North American Grassland," *Annals of the Association of American Geographers*, XL (March, 1959), 1–39.

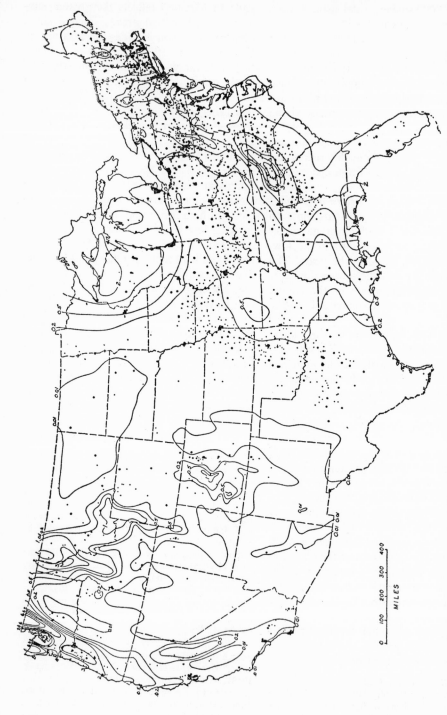

FIG. 5.—Projected mean daily runoff during the low-flow month of major drought years. Isarithms show hundreds of thousands of gallons per square mile per day. The map is derived from a combination of data of median runoff during the normal low-water month and the minimum annual runoff over the twenty-five year period, 1921–45. Data are for 113 "representative gaging stations," from G. E. Harbeck, Jr., and W. B. Langbein, "Normals and Variations in Runoff, 1921–45," *Water Resources Review*, Supplement No. 2 (Washington, 1949), pp. 20–25.

ly high runoff regions. Within the high-runoff areas are those cities in the Pacific Northwest, the upper Great Lakes region, and the Appalachian–Piedmont–Coastal Plain area roughly inside the 100,000-gallon isarithm. To the second group, these places tied to a high-runoff region by a major stream, must be added those systems which use the south margins of Lakes Erie and Michigan, the middle and lower Missouri, middle Mississippi, Ohio, Cumberland, Tennessee, and other streams which pass from the northern Rockies, glaciated upper Lakes region, or Appalachians into the much droughtier central part of the country. This list includes Cleveland, Toledo, Detroit, Milwaukee, Chicago and the Calumet district, the Twin Cities, Omaha, Kansas City, St. Louis, Nashville, Charleston, and the principal cities of the Ohio Valley, as well as some three dozen smaller places which use Lake Erie, the Ohio, Cumberland, Missouri, and Kanawa rivers.[19] To the third group, those neither within a high-runoff area nor naturally tied to one, must be added in a dry period several hundred systems spread mainly across Kentucky, Ohio, Indiana, Illinois, Iowa, Missouri, Kanasas, Oklahoma, Arkansas, and east Texas. These communities draw their water supply from local impounding reservoirs or from streams which originate in this comparatively drought-risky part of the central United States.

The number of counties in which city systems withdraw more surface water than the land yields increase from fifteen under the average conditions depicted in Figure 4 to fifty-one under the drought conditions depicted in Figure 6. The number of counties whose municipal pumpage exceeds 20 per cent of the runoff increases from 30 to 117. There remain, even under these low-flow conditions, nearly 1,000 counties in which city water production from surface sources equals less than twenty per cent of the runoff, and more than 700 counties in which it is less than 1 per cent. If private industrial withdrawals and the effect of

seasonal fluctuations in public use of water could be added, the number of communities in the first two categories would be increased.

The sharpest increase in the number of deficit counties occurs in that belt extending from the western slope of the Alleghenies across the Midwest to Kansas, thence southward through the mid-continent region to central Texas. Over half the deficit counties in the country are there. Thus the largest concentration of surface-supplied cities in an area of very low minimum runoff in drought years is not in the arid west, but in the midwestern and mid-continent area. There also is the group of cities whose local drainage basins are most nearly completely under cultivation. Yet, the midwestern section lies in the heart of the Mississippi basin and touches the south margin of the Great Lakes. Hence the major storage problems which could otherwise beset the large cities of the area are avoided by using the natural import of large streams. However, a large basin has a greater likelihood of pollution and siltation of its discharge. In the mid-continent area even lower runoff and lack of natural access to any of the country's major watersheds, in contrast with the Midwest, makes large storage reservoirs imperative for cities of all sizes.

The only part of the country's high-runoff areas in which water is required beyond available runoff during a major drought period is the urban-industrial belt between Boston and Washington. There storage and careful management is obviously necessary to utilize the large local-basin supplies. And for the city which turns instead to the use of a master stream the risk of pollution is far greater than that which faces midwestern cities because of the smaller drainage basins and greater urban and industrial density.[20] This is illustrated by the fact that the entire public water supply of

---

[19] U.S. Public Health Service, *op. cit.*

[20] *Water Pollution in the United States*, U.S. Public Health Service (1951), esp. pp. 18–19, 28–33; and Drainage Basin Summary Reports on Water Pollution (15 basin reports covering U.S.), U.S. Public Health Service (1951).

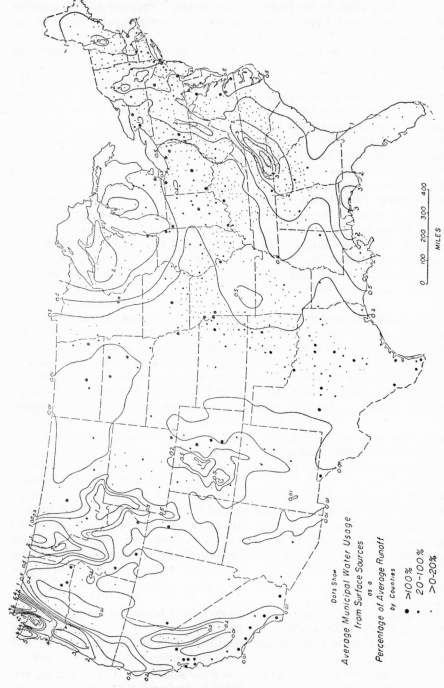

Dots Show

*Average Municipal Water Usage*
*as a*
*Percentage of Average Runoff*
by Counties

● >100%
● 20-100%
· 0-20%

FIG. 6.—Average withdrawal of surface water by municipal systems in relation to approximate average runoff during the low-water month of a major drought year. Based on water use data from U.S. Public Health Service, *op. cit.*, and runoff data from U.S. Geological Survey (see explanation of **Fig. 5**).

metropolitan New York, if it were drawn from the Mississippi at St. Louis, would use and return less than 1 per cent of the mean flow of the river at that point.

## THE MAJOR CONSUMERS AND THEIR SUPPLIES

The foregoing generalizations have been derived from an analysis of all cities of over 1,000 population which use a surface water supply. Those cities are in 1,135 counties and account for practically all of the municipal withdrawal use of surface water in the country. However, about 80 per cent of the total municipal production of surface water is concentrated in the 70 counties were total pumpage averages in excess of 20 million gallons per day. About 75 per cent of the total pumpage is used in 46 counties where consumption averages more than 30 million gallons per day. The 37 counties which use over 40 million gallons per day account for about two-thirds of the national total. Indeed one-fourth of all the municipal supply of surface water in the country is pumped by three systems—New York, Chicago, and Los Angeles.

Figure 7 illustrates the extent of the drainage basins which supply these top water consumers among America's municipal systems. Comparison of Figure 7 with Figures 3 and 5 shows the average annual and average low-month, dry-year runoff in these basins.

It is apparent that the major cities in the high-runoff areas of the Appalachian region and the Pacific Northwest generally use the impounded water of small local basins in which the city can maintain a high degree of control over land use, cover, and settlement. Intensive, careful development of small basins to supply very large requirements is especially characteristic of the major cities of the middle Atlantic seaboard and the northern glaciated Appalachian region. These local basin developments are not spectacular, and they have generally been carried out by local governments without federal subsidy. But they develop

very large water resources.[21] Somewhat larger watersheds in the Sierra Nevada are tapped by the San Francisco, East Bay, and Los Angeles systems. But these watersheds, too, are on land which is devoted primarily to the production of clean water. Typical treatment of all these supplies involves two to four steps.[22]

Notable exceptions to the general pattern of small reservoirs used for the major eastern systems are the Delaware basin above Philadelphia and the Potomac basin above Washington. The two cities involved, unlike their metropolitan neighbors, have not developed the water resources of small local basins. They use the natural flow of large streams to import water from extensive, populous, busy watersheds. They have, therefore, a more serious pollution problem than do the other large cities of the northeast.

It is also apparent from Figure 7 that metropolitan southern California has a water import problem which is unique in the country.[23] One of the major water sources, the Colorado River, is unique among the rivers which supply the country's metropolitan centers. Because of its physiographic setting the Colorado's waters run almost unused for urban or agricultural purposes to the reservoir above Parker Dam. The water withdrawn from the river at that point is not returned because the using communities are remote from the river and in another drainage basin. The

[21] See Edward Higbee, "Three Earths of New England," *Geographical Review*, XLII (July, 1952), 437.

[22] From data in U.S. Public Health Service, *op. cit.*

[23] Only the upper basin of the Colorado is shown as the contributive watershed for southern California in Figure 7; that section of the basin yields more than 99 per cent of the Colorado River water available for California. The Southern California Metropolitan Water District uses about 2 per cent of the Colorado flow from the upper basin, but other consumptive uses, evaporation, and channel loss take another 79 per cent of the flow. (Metropolitan Water District of Southern California, *op. cit.*, p. 67.)

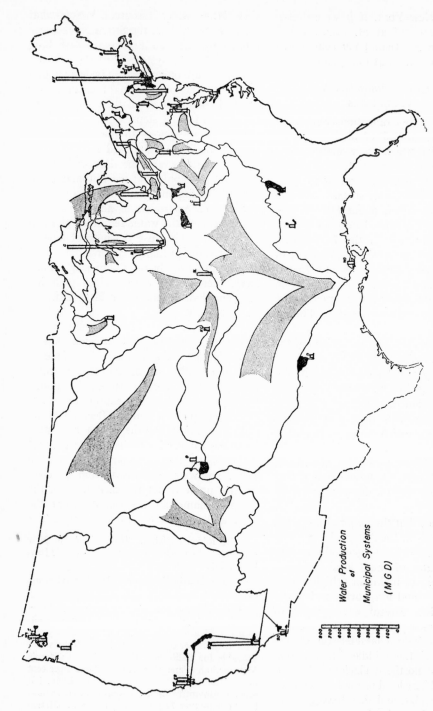

FIG. 7.—The location of major metropolitan systems, the extent of their contributive watersheds, and their average daily water withdrawal. Small basins are indicated by pattern showing their area to scale; basins of large rivers are outlined, and arrows within each basin indicate general direction of flow. Withdrawals by systems shown on this map account for about 50 per cent of the total national water consumption by city systems. Map derived from data in U.S. Public Health Service, *op. cit.; River Basin Maps Showing Hydrologic Stations*, Washington, U.S. Weather Bureau, 1949; *13th Annual Rept.* of the Metropolitan Water Districts of Southern Calif., Los Angeles, 1951; and various topographic maps. Temporary withdrawal from the Hudson River and proposed withdrawal from the upper Delaware River Basin for New York City are not shown.

river's climatic setting presents further difficulties. Evaporation and channel loss below Lee's Ferry is equal to almost seven times the total delivery of water to the Southern California Metropolitan Water District. Thus the Colorado, the master stream of the Southwest, in addition to being a stream whose average flow is not much greater than that of the Delaware and less than that of the Wabash, is a less efficient and more expensive source of water for its municipal users than the other large rivers of the country.[24] Treatment of the Colorado River supply for southern California municipal systems involves from five to thirteen steps, mainly because of the high salt and silt content of the lower river.

In the central United States most large surface-water-using cities pump very small fractions of the major streams or Great Lakes upon which they are situated.[25] For example, the municipal systems at St. Louis, Kansas City, and Cincinnati withdraw less than 0.1 per cent of the river flow at those places. The others impound the upper-basin discharge of tributary streams, such as the Scioto or White (Indiana), in areas which are rather heavily populated and generally cultivated. Those upper basins are in areas of persistently low runoff in the mid-continent setting exemplified by Dallas. Compare, for example, the areas of the contributive drainage basins for Dallas and Syracuse, New York (Fig. 7). Municipal water production is about the same at both cities; runoff per square mile in the small basins above Syracuse averages

[24] Estimated average discharge from Lake Mead with present upper-basin depletion is about 19,000 second-feet (Metropolitan Water District of Southern California, *op. cit.*, p. 65); average Wabash River discharge at New Harmony, Indiana, is 27,500 second-feet; Delaware River discharge at Trenton, New Jersey, averages 14,900 second-feet (U.S. Geological Survey Circular 44, p. 2).

[25] (From data in U.S. Public Health Service, *op. cit.*, and U.S. Geological Survey, *Surface Water Supply of the U.S.*, published annually.) If all other demands were added to the municipal requirements these cities would still use a small fraction of their available supply of river water.

about six times that above Dallas (see Fig. 3). Treatment of these supplies in the central United States involves typically from eight to thirteen steps because of the high sediment and organic content and, often, high acidity from industrial waste. Treatment is generally less for cities along the Great Lakes.

On the Gulf Coastal Plain wells supply cities which use as much water as many of the municipalities shown in Figure 7. Those places include San Antonio, Houston, Memphis, and Miami. The latter three cities do not use the relatively abundant surface water supply of the humid southeast because of the large, available subsurface supply of the coastal plain aquifers. San Antonio is able to avoid the surface water storage problems of Dallas and other cities of the mid-continent, low-runoff region by its use of the coastal plain ground water reservoir.[26]

Thus analysis of Figure 7 illustrates with specific major cities the regional characteristics of surface water supply of American municipalities which have been drawn from Figures 3–6.

## SUMMARY AND CONCLUSION

Analysis of the location of American surface-water-using municipalities within the geographic patterns of surface water supply shows that the average yield of water from the land in relation to existing municipal demand is abundant in all parts of the country except southern California. The use of these local supplies involves the greatest storage problems in (1) the semi-arid and arid regions of the country because of low runoff, and (2) the agricultural Midwest because of large year-to-year variability of runoff coupled with a high proportion of open-tilled crop land in the drainage basins. Greatest development of

[26] For an excellent bibliography on these areas, see H. E. Thomas, *The Conservation of Ground Water* (New York, 1951), pp. 307, 309, 311, 317; see also W. H. Goines *et al.*, *Water Supply of the Houston Gulf Coast Region* (Texas Board of Water Engineers Bulletin 5101, 1951).

small basins to meet major municipal demands is in the northeastern states, with the notable exceptions of Washington and Philadelphia, and few much smaller cities. The greatest use of surface water in areas of low runoff—and potentially most serious actual supply problems if present trends are to continue—are in southern California and the belt from east-central Kansas to south Texas. The municipalities which utilize available supplies to the smallest degree, have the greatest leeway for increased water use, and have access to the largest flow in drought periods are in the southeastern states, especially the southern Appalachians, in the Pacific Northwest, along the Great Lakes, and along the large rivers of the agricultural Midwest.

Perhaps because in most parts of the country the supply is abundant in relation to past and existing municipal demands, no other physical resource has been developed with so little regard for regional differences in its concentration as water for our urban areas. Yet the pattern of these differences is of major importance. This limited study points to a number of major regional and national water supply and utilization characteristics which require further geographical analysis. The words of H. E. Thomas— ". . . the exhaustive analysis and scientific interpretation lag far behind the collection of the basic data for all phases of the hydrologic cycle . . ."[27]—apply no less to geographical than to other methods of analysis.

[27] *Op. cit.*, p. 233.

# BLIGHT AND RENEWAL

Research by students of urbanism is concerned with the qualitative aspects of urban land use as well as with the quantitative aspects. In recent years much attention has been focused upon the physical deterioration of cities and the social and economic conditions of the so-called blighted areas which, in some cities, include a substantial proportion of the urban area and within which live a major proportion of the inhabitants. Concern with urban blight extends far back into the nineteenth century, and much of the literature of Charles Dickens, as well as of later socially conscious authors, such as Lincoln Steffens, Jacob Riis, and Jane Addams, was concerned with the portrayal of urban deterioration and its consequences. Until the 1930's a few attempts were made to clear some of the worst slums, by means of philanthropic housing schemes and limited-dividend housing corporations. During the Great Depression of the 1930's, public housing for low-income families represented a limited attempt to deal with the problem. The concept of "slum clearance" was broadened into "urban redevelopment" as defined by the Federal Housing Act of 1949, which not only provided for an extension of the concept of public housing but also, in Title I, provided a mechanism by which public and private capital could collaborate in the elimination of certain forms of urban blight and the redevelopment of older sections of cities with more adequate housing.

In the first of the two articles in this section, Malcolm Proudfoot describes briefly the history of the various legislative approaches to the problems of urban redevelopment in the United States. Subsequent to that article, the concept was broadened by the Federal Housing Act of 1954, which provides for public participation, under certain circumstances, in the process of rehabilitation and improvement of areas of cities which are not sufficiently deteriorated to justify complete demolition and rebuilding, in order to arrest the encroachment of blight into such areas.

The second article describes another form of urban blight: vacant land which has not been developed but which is surrounded by urban area and which constitutes a detriment to the balanced and proper development of a city and metropolitan region. Much of the so-called dead land resulted from premature subdivision during the boom period of the 1920's, and a typical situation is described—the Chicago area. Actually, much of the former area of arrested development has subsequently been subjected to partial or complete development under the pressure of urban decentralization and expansion in recent years, but in the vicinities of some cities and metropolitan areas the problem remains.

Urban renewal is one of the many socially useful fields where the concepts of urban geography may be applied with the help of the geographer's knowledge and experience. A significant number of urban geographers, as employees of city planning and urban renewal agencies and as private consultants, are finding satisfying careers in the applied aspects of city development.

MALCOLM J. PROUDFOOT

# PUBLIC REGULATION OF URBAN DEVELOPMENT IN THE UNITED STATES

Since the first decennial census of the United States (1790), the proportion of urban population has increased from 5 per cent of the total to 64 per cent. The rapid growth of large cities has been characteristic and, during the last three decades, the even more rapid growth of their suburbs and unincorporated fringes. In 1950 the census recorded 168 standard metropolitan areas, with a total of 84.5 million inhabitants. The population of these areas had increased 22 per cent during the preceding decade, as compared with 14.5 per cent for the total population, but the central cities had increased only 13.9 per cent, as compared with 35.5 per cent for the outlying parts. Some 44.4 million, or more than one-half of this population, were concentrated in 14 areas with one million inhabitants or more. The New York–Northeastern New Jersey Standard Metropolitan Area alone recorded 13 million persons.[1] This rapid urban growth was a response to increased economic opportunity within cities. It was made possible by a chain of improvements in public sanitation, mass and vehicular transport, rapid forms of communication, public utilities, and governmental services, supported by greatly increased productivity on the farms and in the mines.

The change from dispersed rural to concentrated urban living has resulted in a high degree of efficient specialization and mutually beneficial interdependence, but there can be no doubt that it has also greatly intensified human friction. Inexorably, the freedom of the city dweller has been curtailed and subordinated to the public interest. Many personal rights have been replaced by new responsibilities under public regulation, justified by and undertaken to promote the general welfare. Thus after a hundred years of unregulated urban growth, in which each city reflected the relatively unimpeded choice of the individual property owner to use his land as he saw fit, urban development since the turn of this century has been increasingly regulated.[2] Comprehensive zoning ordinances have been generally adopted. Federal, state, and municipal legislation has been directed toward slum clearance and redevelopment, and toward neighborhood conservation. All these regulatory means have obtained legal sanction from a broadening interpretation by the courts of the

Reprinted from *Geographical Review*, XLIV (July, 1954), 415–19, by permission of Mrs. Malcolm Proudfoot and the editor. (Copyright, 1954, by the American Geographical Society of New York.)

[1] Seventeenth Decennial Census of the United States, Census of Population, 1950, Vol. I, *Number of Inhabitants* (U.S. Dept. of Commerce, Bureau of the Census, Washington, 1952), pp. xv–xviii, xxvii–xxviii, and xxxiii–xxxv.

[2] To be sure, the property owner has been, and still is, regulated by individual ordinances concerned with building construction, access streets, and hazards of fire, disease, immorality, and vice, and as in Chicago, by a maze of overlapping governmental taxing and regulatory bodies, but the multiplicity and conflicting character of these precluded comprehensive public regulation of urban development. Mention should also be made of the privately imposed restrictions, especially those written into property deeds by owners, which are passed on with the conveyance of title and become binding upon successive owners. These restrictions most commonly refer to the use of buildings, to their cost and character, to their distance from the street and their height; there are also prohibitions against business use, especially the sale of liquor, and against occupancy by, or sale to, non-Caucasians.

general meaning of public welfare[3] and of the sovereign right of the states to delegate to their municipalities the right to use police power to enforce these regulations. Further change has been brought about by the Supreme Court's nullification of the discriminatory racial covenants contained in property deeds.[4]

## ZONING ORDINANCES

The comprehensive municipal zoning ordinance, with its antecedents in piecemeal regulatory ordinances, had its beginnings in France in the nineteenth century and was first used in the United States in 1916 by New York City. Today, in a majority of our cities with more than 10,000 inhabitants, comprehensive zoning ordinances, based on detailed development plans, have been adopted. These ordinances seek to regulate the use, and more especially the future use, of every parcel of land in a well-ordered development for each municipality. Most of them were enacted at about the same time and conform to a general pattern. They consist of detailed maps showing use and volume districts accompanied by textual material specifying permitted and prohibited action relating to property within each district. Use districts are commonly differentiated as for family residences, duplex residences, group houses, apartment houses, specialty shops, businesses, commerce, and manufacture; volume districts regulate the ground area,

height, and volume of buildings, as well as building lines.

Since zoning ordinances, with few exceptions, were adopted after the functional structure of the municipalities had crystallized, the districts designated were superimposed more or less arbitrarily, and many "nonconforming uses" existed in each new district. Furthermore, as the administrators of most cities soon found, the comprehensive development plans were out of date almost as soon as the zoning ordinances had been adopted, as a result of population growth or decrease or other highly variable dynamic factors effecting structural change. Hence, in view of the many nonconforming uses and the constant need to make accommodations to fit normal, and often desirable, change, most zoning ordinances have been kept flexible, through the medium of appeal boards that permit both general and specific amendments. But the zoning ordinance has not provided the instrument to protect the general welfare against the highly variable, not to say "selfish," interest of the property owner. Quite aside from abuses of non-enforcement and haphazard amendment and variation permitted through political malpractice, zoning ordinances have notably failed in regard to the serious urban problem of residential blight, and the associated problems of industrial, residential, and commercial decentralization that threaten to cripple many large cities through loss of tax revenue.

## HOUSING AND CONSERVATION ACTS

Urban residential decay went largely unchecked until the 1930's. Before then, only sporadic and inadequately financed local efforts had been made, which provided little more than limited examples of what might be done. The Roosevelt administration, using principles of public housing developed during the depression, passed the United States Housing Act of 1937.[5] The

[3] The "public welfare" has been interpreted to mean health, education, peace, morals, convenience, comfort, tranquillity, and safety—in essence, any consideration shown to be "in the public interest" as opposed to the "selfish interest" of the individual.

[4] Those seeking further information, especially on the legal side of this subject, are referred to the excellent work by Harold L. Reeve (of the Chicago bar), "The Influence of the Metropolis on the Concepts, Rules, and Institutions Relating to Property," prepared for the bicentennial celebration of Columbia University and presented to the first conference on "The Metropolis in Modern Life," January 8, 1954 (Chicago, 1954).

[5] Approved September 1, 1937, Ch. 896, Sec. 30, 50 Stat. 899.

act was primarily intended to provide for low-rent public housing, but it also provided for incidental slum clearance financed by federal loans to public housing agencies. This policy was continued under subsequent acts, but it was not until the Housing Act of 1949[6] that the federal government set itself the goal of "a decent home and a suitable living environment for every American family" and authorized loans and grants specifically to permit local public agencies to eliminate slums and blighted areas by the assembly, clearance, and preparation of land for sale to private enterprise for redevelopment.[7] Largely in response to this federal legislation, thirty-four states, the District of Columbia, and four territories[8] took steps to pass legislation to assist their municipalities in clearing and redeveloping slum areas.

In Illinois, for example, during the 1930's and the period of the war, the state legislature provided for slum clearance as a subordinate part of various public housing programs,[9] but it was only after the passage of the Blighted Areas Redevelopment Act of 1947[10] that substantial progress was made toward facilitating municipal clearance and redevelopment of slums.

[6] 63 Stat. 413.

[7] Undoubtedly rent control, instituted as part of the federal Emergency Price Control Act of 1942, accelerated urban blight, since landlords, faced by rising costs of labor and materials, often failed to make essential repairs.

[8] Alabama, Arkansas, California, Colorado, Connecticut, Delaware, Florida, Georgia, Illinois, Indiana, Kentucky, Louisiana, Maine, Maryland, Massachusetts, Michigan, Minnesota, Missouri, Nebraska, New Hampshire, New Jersey, New York, North Carolina, Ohio, Oregon, Pennsylvania, Rhode Island, South Carolina, South Dakota, Tennessee, Texas, Virginia, West Virginia, and Wisconsin; and Alaska, Hawaii, Puerto Rico, and the Virgin Islands.

[9] The Illinois State Housing Act of 1933 (Ill. Rev. Stat. Ch. 32, par. 504–50); the Illinois Housing Authorities Act of 1934 (Ill. Rev. Stat. 1951, Ch. 67½, par. 1–27e, adopted March 19, 1934); and the Neighborhood Redevelopment Corporation Act of 1941 (Ill. Rev. Stat. Ch. 32, par. 550.1–550.44).

[10] Ill. Rev. Stat. Ch. 67½, par. 63–91.

This act, passed primarily to cope with problems of slums and blight in Chicago, provided for the creation by municipalities of independent public land-clearance commissions. It authorized these commissions to use the power of eminent domain to acquire slum and blighted areas and to clear, or otherwise reduce, these areas to usable land for resale to private redevelopers or for conveyance to public authorities for use as streets, parks, schools, or playgrounds.[11] For the purposes of this act, slum and blighted areas were defined as "any area of not less in the aggregate than two acres located within the territorial limits of a municipality where buildings or improvements by reason of dilapidation, obsolescence, overcrowding, faulty arrangement or design, lack of ventilation, light and sanitary facilities, excessive land coverage, deleterious land use or layout, or any combination of these factors, are detrimental to the public safety, health, morals or welfare."

Thus in Illinois and, in response to the federal Housing Act of 1949, in thirty-three other states the public regulation of urban development has progressed to a high degree. Again, municipal police power, using the right of eminent domain, had been extended to supersede the rights of yet another class of urban property owner. Again the extension of public regulation was taken for "public safety, health, morals or welfare" under the ever broadening concept of public welfare. The cities of the United States acquired the right to refashion their deteriorated or blighted residential areas in a manner considered appropriate by their public officials, and with no more than "fair monetary compensation" to the property

[11] This act was subsequently amended to make it conform to the federal Housing Act of 1949, permitting, among other things, the acceptance of federal financial assistance by the land-clearance commissions; and it was further extended by the passage of the Blighted Vacant Area Redevelopment Act of 1949 (Ill. Rev. Stat. Ch. 32, par. 550.1–550.44), which makes comparable provisions applicable to vacant urban land, particularly tax-delinquent "dead land."

owners whose land was condemned. Such public regulation provided a major means for the redevelopment of urban areas, and a curtailment of free enterprise far beyond that provided by the rather passive zoning ordinances.

In Illinois, the regulation of urban development has gone even further by providing that municipal police power may be used to require property owners under penalty to improve or repair their buildings and keep them in a prescribed condition to prevent blight and the development of slum areas. This extension of urban regulation, though not yet tested in the courts, is contained in the Illinois Urban Community Conservation Act of 1953,[12] which briefly prescribes the following procedures to achieve community conservation. A municipality may create a five-man Conservation Board to designate Conservation Areas[13] of more than 160 acres possessing a combination of conditions that might result in the development of slum or blighted areas:[14] an average age of 50 per cent of the structures of 35 years or more; obsolescence, deterioration, dilapidation, or illegal use of individual structures; overcrowding of structures and community facilities; conversion of residential units into non-residential use; and a general decline of physical maintenance. When the board designates a Conservation Area, it appoints an advisory Conservation Community Council composed of residents of the area, of whom a majority are property owners. Each council is expected to assist the board in the preparation of a conservation plan for its area, and to approve the plan by a majority vote before it is submitted to the municipal

council or other legislative body for adoption. If adopted, the board acts to implement the plan, with the assistance of its council. Each property owner in the area is notified if his property does not conform to minimum standards. If he does not make the required improvement, the municipal authorities are to obtain a court order permitting them to make the improvement at the cost of the property owner, to be guaranteed either by a lien on his property or, if necessary, through its forced sale.

## FURTHER ASPECTS

Finally, one remaining major aspect of the public regulation of urban land development in the United States should be considered, namely, the recent Supreme Court decisions nullifying the restrictions in property deeds which compel purchasers of urban land to enter into covenants specifying that they will not sell or lease to Negroes or other non-Caucasians. In the now famous cases of *Shelley* v. *Kraemer* and *Mc-Ghee* v. *Sipes*,[15] supplemented by that of *Barrows* v. *Jackson*,[16] the Supreme Court in effect found certain restrictive covenants pertaining to race to be in violation of the Fourteenth Amendment of the Federal Constitution and restrained the state courts from enforcing these covenants. By this action, the Supreme Court undermined the continuation of a major characteristic of urban structure in the United States—the ghetto-like areas of Negro segregation resulting from restrictive racial covenants preventing Negroes from living in all but the most undesirable urban residential areas. This action will also have the effect of breaking down the segregation of Jews, Puerto Ricans, Japanese, Chinese, and other so-called non-Caucasian ethnic or racial groups.

Public regulation of urban development, to judge by recent action, not only is here to stay but in all likelihood will be extended. Only by such means can municipal

12 Ill. Senate Bill 524, 1953 Session, approved July 13, 1953, Ill. Rev. Stat. 1953, Ch. 67½, par. 91.8–91.16.

13 The term "Renewal Area" is now being used in some quarters in a context similar to that of "Conservation Area."

14 But which are not yet a slum or blighted area as defined in the Illinois Blighted Areas Redevelopment Act of 1947.

15 (May 3, 1948), 334 U.S. 1.

16 (1953), 346 U.S. 249.

government cope with the intricate problems of human relationships consequent on concentrated urban living. The danger, of course, is that the regulations, though desirable in themselves, may strait-jacket individual freedom, and that this may in the long run negate the economic advantages of concentration and thus cripple future urban development. From this standpoint the Illinois Urban Community Conservation Act of 1953 must be viewed as a marginal development. A further consideration is that in many instances these regulations will be administered by ignorant or corrupt local officials. Such administration will not only defeat the purpose of the regulations; it will create new opportunities for political and legal malpractice, which will add further burdens to individual enterprise and serve still more to accelerate costly and debilitating decentralization to the suburbs and unincorporated fringes.

HERMAN G. BERKMAN

# DECENTRALIZATION AND BLIGHTED VACANT LAND

Increasing municipal costs and declining revenues facing American cities pose severe threats to local autonomy. More and more, cities are turning to centralizing units of government, the state and federal level, for help. Analysis of problems of municipal finance reveals the contribution of decentralization, urban sprawl, and tax delinquent vacant land to this unhealthy condition. It is obvious that tax delinquent vacant land means loss of revenue and that decentralization means removal of the tax base. The objective of this paper is to trace the relationship of decentralization commonly resulting in urban sprawl to what has been described as "dead land," unmarketable in fact because of excessive tax delinquency and other complications. More particularly, this paper will deal with a case study in the solution of the problem of dead land.

## THE EVOLUTION OF DEAD LAND

A brief historical sketch of the evolution of dead land may help focus the problem such land presents. Our tale centers around the processes of city development under an enterprise system. The processes occur at the fringe. At the fringe of urban communities lie areas into which urban uses, through the principles of marginalism, expand. This penumbral land is withdrawn from agricultural uses as demand for urban land outbids non-urban uses. Frequently, as cities have expanded, the value of such lands and hence taxes on them tend to increase in anticipation of high rewards in the face of a steadily encroaching urban population.

The advance of urban uses invading rich agricultural land is not steady or uniform. Encroachment may leap over stretches of undeveloped areas leaving empty spots in the future city structure. Indeed there appear to be two phases in such city growth. One is that of initial expansion and the second is the filling-in process. The entire process has been estimated to take as long as from fifteen to thirty years.[1] Further, such subdividing takes place only slowly, lots being sold to individuals who many times hold them for development or speculation themselves. If, after an area has been platted and perhaps some improvements installed, demand for land should suddenly decline or shift direction, or if there should be an excess of subdividing activity in relation to effective demand, there occurs what has been variously called "dead land," arrested subdivision, excess subdivision, or the latest term—blighted vacant land.

Because such land is thrown out of productive agricultural use, the community suffers in the first instance. As time passes and the lots platted are not developed, taxes accrue, titles become clouded and complex, subdivision designs become obsolete, and whatever utilities have been installed fall into disrepair, if usable in the first instance. Action by a public body becomes necessary.

A case in point is the process of subdividing activity in Chicago. Since 1830 Chicago has had five land booms, reaching peaks in 1836, 1856, 1869–72, 1890, and 1926, the present boom—not yet completed and its results not yet known—not included.

Between 1853 and 1857, 9,295 acres

Reprinted from *Land Economics*, XXXII (August, 1956), 270–80, by permission of the author and the editor. (Copyright, 1956, by the University of Wisconsin, Madison, Wis.)

[1] Richard U. Ratcliff, *Urban Land Economics* (New York: McGraw-Hill Book Co., 1949), chaps. 7 and 13.

were subdivided and the city had to triple its population to absorb the lots. From 1866 to 1874, another 20,500 acres were added. Yet even though the city more than tripled its population from 1870 to 1890, some of these lots are still vacant. Despite the slow absorption, another boom from 1875 to 1892 added an additional 17,000 acres within the corporate limits of the city. The scope of the subdivision activity can be realized by the fact that in the seven years between 1886 and 1893, 390,000 lots were subdivided, more than enough for the growth of Chicago in the following twenty years, and some of these lots also are still vacant. Added to these activities were some 8,600 acres subdivided within the city between 1910 and 1916 and some 170,000 in the metropolitan area. Finally, the last boom preceding the current one occurred between 1919 and 1929, with a peak in 1926 when, because most of Chicago city had been subdivided, some 288,000 new lots were added in Cook County and some 650,000 in the metropolitan area. Since between 1930 and 1950 the number of families in the Chicago metropolitan area increased by approximately some 300,000, it is clear that in 1950 the majority of the lots created in the boom of the twenties were still vacant.[2]

Yet current subdivision in the wake of pent-up housing shortage and higher consumer incomes rolls along on its merry way, again stretching farther west, north, and south of the city of Chicago, while much of the area originally subdivided in the 1890's lies idle.[3] Some subdivisions platted as early as 1872 remain unoccupied.

The necessity of solving the problems posed by these tax delinquent lands may be summarized as follows:[4] (1) Cities have an investment in these properties through back taxes, interest, and penalties which represent payments out of past levies. (2) Cities already have heavy investments in utilities and other public improvements accessible to such areas. Fuller use of these means revenue; and fuller use means less need to extend such utilities, services, and improvements to even more outlying areas. (3) The redevelopment of denser portions of the central city can be accelerated through the provision of residential units on these now vacant lands. (4) Development of such areas would reduce charges in handling the collection of taxes. Such costs in Cook County have been estimated at more than one million dollars per year.[5] (5) Delinquent vacant properties are in a "no-man's state." Unused, grown over with weeds, they constitute hiding places for criminals and hazards to the community. (6) Tax delinquent vacant lands swell the tax base and inflate the budget. As long as these lands are counted as part of the tax base, cities must pile on deficits for the taxpayers to pay. Municipalities must remit state and county levies even if properties are delinquent, so that they are left "holding the bag." (7) By not paying taxes, owners of tax delinquent vacant properties force their share of the tax burden on taxpayers. If taxpayers know that they can get away with tax delinquencies, many may refuse to pay their taxes. (8) Tax delinquent vacant land recorded as uncollected general taxes affects tax collection records and hence municipal credit. Bad tax collection records "operate, almost without question, to increase the cost of borrowing money. . . . The extra cost of interest rates . . . could easily become a considerable item in municipal budgets."[6] This is the direct

[2] Homer Hoyt, *One Hundred Years of Land Values in Chicago* (Chicago: University of Chicago Press, 1933), pp. 477–78. Also estimated from *Growth and Redistribution of the Resident Population in the Chicago Standard Metropolitan Area* (Chicago: Chicago Community Inventory, 1954).

[3] Based on field checks by the writer.

[4] A. N. Hillhouse, and Carl H. Chatters, *Tax Reverted Properties in Urban Areas* (Chicago: Public Administration Service, 1942).

[5] Housing Authority of the County of Cook, Illinois, *Dead Land* (Chicago: Housing Authority of the County of Cook, 1949).

[6] *Ibid.*, p. 21. Quotation from Dr. Frederick L. Bird, Director of Municipal Research, Dun and Bradstreet, Inc.

effect on borrowing. Indirect borrowing effects come via the need for borrowing propelled by decreased revenues and relatively increased costs. (9) Tax delinquent vacant land is a factor in neighborhood property value deterioration. The existence of such areas prevents new building, particularly if the original subdivision design is outmoded. The interspersion of vacant lots among built-up ones may even prevent the completion of community facilities necessary to stabilize values. (10) Tax delinquent vacant lands increase costs of land by shortening supplies of land more freely available, thereby increasing housing costs. (11) Since non-residential uses bear a great part of the local tax burdens, if tax delinquent vacant lands do not bear their share, taxes on non-residential areas are affected. The increased taxes may impede the location of tax-paying industry in areas of heavy delinquency. (12) Sound community growth requires harmonious relationships between land uses throughout a metropolitan area; balance between employment and population; development sufficiently compact to constitute an economical and efficient use of space; adequate space for community facilities and activities in proportion to population needs; an environment conducive to safety and to physical and mental health; sufficient shelter, adequate in amount and kind for the population; and adequate tax revenues to support necessary public services. (13) Tax delinquent vacant lands impede sound community growth.

## Stumbling Blocks to Development

Why are these areas, some platted almost a century ago, still lying idle? The answer lies in legal and economic difficulties lying withing the building sites themselves as well as with the laws governing the elimination of these difficulties.

With respect to the sites themselves, we have already mentioned some of the factors. These include diversity of ownership or lost ownership, obsolete platting, exces-

sive tax delinquency combined with special assessment delinquency, penalties, and interest, at times exceeding the fair value of the property, and inadequate utilities. One of these factors would be sufficient to discourage private development, but the existence of more than one absolutely defeats it.

In a group of areas in Chicago studied by the writer, for every hundred lots there are at least fifty different owners, many of whom have either died or cannot be found.[7] Divided or split ownerships (estates), judgments, changes in marital status—all complicate obtaining title. Before 1926 a twenty-five- or thirty-foot lot was considered ample; the majority of the areas studied had lot widths of thirty feet or less. Current insurance by the Federal Housing Administration will not be issued on lots less than thirty-five feet. These areas usually contain excessive areas zoned and platted for business uses, only twenty-five feet wide. Because of anticipations, areas so zoned are generally overpriced in present residential markets and unsuitable for non-residential markets. Such lots are particularly undesirable for residential purposes, being bounded generally by heavily trafficked streets. In Chicago today there are enough lots zoned and platted for commercial uses to satisfy the needs of a city of 10,000,000. Miles of such vacant strips run along Chicago's major streets. The obsolete character of these subdivisions is accentuated by platted or even existing streets of equal width and connecting with equally wide arterial streets which would invite through traffic if these areas were developed but discourage development as well. No provision was made in many of these subdivisions for necessary parks or recreational areas necessary for neighborhood stability. Alleys pervade the original subdivision plats, wasting land area. In many of these areas there are no paved streets; some have partially paved streets; some have sewer but no water grids, some water but no

[7] Chicago Plan Commission, *Blighted Vacant Land* (Chicago: Chicago Plan Commission, 1950).

sewer grid. Most have sidewalks, though in disrepair. If title to all lots cannot be readily acquired, a single owner can only with difficulty obtain necessary utilities.

Only public activity of some kind can make lots in such areas marketable by assisting in their assembly and resubdivision, and helping to make their economic development feasible. Until recently the condition of such lots, despite their high public cost, has impeded action by the public body. One writer lists the following obstacles to the adequate development of these areas:[8] (1) The high cost of foreclosure suits or other actions to acquire title. (2) The difficulty, under present laws and attitude of the courts, to secure a good and merchantable title that will be guaranteed or insured. (3) The lack of proper governmental organization for tax enforcement and the failure of the charter or statutes to place responsibility on a central tax enforcement agency. (4) The antiquated condition of tax sale machinery. (5) Complicated relationships between governmental units having tax liens or special assessment liens on the same parcels. (6) Many officials consider it unwise to bring tax foreclosure suits. (7) Direct-lien special assessments bonds which require the city to satisfy bondholders by payment or compromise before foreclosure.

Basically, solution to problems of "dead" land today require more than tax reform and revision of collection procedures. For, by now, as we have noted, problems of relatively large-scale assembly, replanning, and replatting are involved as well as other economic and land development problems. A review of changes in the laws or procedures dealing with tax delinquencies in blighted vacant land as defined would thus be irrelevant to the problem. Since Chicago is already launched on a program to eliminate such areas within the framework of the laws enacted, the following portion of this paper will be concerned with a case study of what Chicago is doing about this problem.

## THE LEGISLATION

The federal Congress and the state of Illinois recognize the need for assembling lots in these "dead" subdivisions. The legislators are aware of the social nature of past mistakes which led to the development of "dead subdivisions" and the need for replatting, replanning, and restoring the values of such areas where the housing market could absorb them. Title III, Section 110 (C) of the United States Housing Act of 1954, as amended,[9] and previous to this the United States Housing Act of 1949, provided that "land which is predominantly open and which because of obsolete platting, diversity of ownership, deterioration of structures or of site improvements, or otherwise substantially impairs or arrests the sound growth of the community and which is to be developed for predominantly residential uses, constitutes a project" within the meaning of that act. For such a project federal grants-in-aid are available to legally constituted local authorities up to two-thirds of net project costs. As in connection with all projects under Title I of this act, constituted local agencies legally authorized by their respective state legislature and local governing bodies to purchase or through powers of eminent domain to acquire such dead subdivisions are eligible for these.

The philosophy of the program involves the concept of public assembly of the land at fair market prices. Back taxes have first claim when the areas are sold back to private developers for housing construction in conformance with an approved plan of development. With the passage of the federal act of 1949 the state of Illinois amended its Blighted Areas Redevelopment Act of 1947 to enable local agencies within the state to engage in predominantly open land projects which in the state statute are called "blighted vacant areas."

The state statute specifically sets forth

[8] Hillhouse and Chatters, *op. cit.*, pp. 11–12.

[9] Public Law 560 signed by the President, August 2, 1954.

in detail the concept of "blight" as applied to predominantly vacant land. In legislative findings the statute refers to the unmarketability of such vacant areas for housing purposes, the characteristics existing in such areas, the retardation of community development caused by this, and the necessity for governmental financial assistance in the development of such areas by private capital. Thus, the statute states that "predominantly open platted . . . land" to be acquired shall be that which "substantially impairs or arrests the sound growth of the community because of obsolete platting, diversity of ownership, deterioration of structures or site improvements or taxes or special assessment delinquencies exceeding the fair value of the land."

## SITE SELECTED

On August 8, 1951, the Chicago Land Clearance Commission designated its first "Blighted Vacant Land Project"—Seventy-ninth Street and Western Avenue.[10] The character of the site selected well illustrates the difficulties of privately developing such "dead" areas without public assistance. The forty-acre site is located in the extreme southwestern portion of the city and is surrounded by a heavily built up single-family area. Being interstitial in character, it is bounded on two sides by major arterials. The site was subdivided and the plat recorded in 1925. Before the commission designated the area, there were no housing improvements on it. Though ideally situated with respect to community facilities already existing and employment sources, the site remained undeveloped. All basic utilities stretched on the boundaries of the site, readily accessible to site use. Within the site is an old sewer grid originally installed in 1926. An air view would show cracked sidewalks, the unimproved street right-of-way overgrown with weeds, and unused utility poles running through the

[10] Chicago Land Clearance Commission, *Report to Commission on Project No. 2* (Chicago: Chicago Land Clearance Commission, 1950).

site. What impeded the development of this area?

*Diversity of ownership.*—Before commission designation, in order to acquire 264 lots, a developer would have had to contact 157 different owners. The number of different lots per owner averaged 1.7. In 4 of the 10 blocks, the average fell between 1.2 and 1.4 lots per owner. The diversity of ownership by block revealed the scattered nature of the holdings. Twelve of the owners held 46 of the 264 lots and the holdings of these 12 owners were so scattered throughout the site and among the 115 lots held singly, or 44 per cent of the total number of lots, that assembly of a group of contiguous lots would be well-nigh impossible.

*Availability of lots.*—A study of lot transactions in the area indicated, before commission designation, that from 1940 to 1951 there was activity on only 84 of the 264 lots. Where transactions did occur, 28 were by quit claim or tax deeds, not actually resulting in actual, bonafide transfer of fee title under Illinois law. An examination of tax records revealed that 100 of the 264 lots were being carried as "no name parcels," an indication that, although tax bills were sent, the owners could not be found. Thirty-one of the lots were affected by adverse interests and many lots were held under split ownership by heirs of estates.

*Tax delinquency and tax revenues.*—In the entire area 80 per cent of the lots were delinquent one year or more; on over one-half of the lots taxes had not been paid for five or more years, and on one-third of the lots taxes had not been paid for twenty years or more. The number of lots tax delinquent had been increasing at varying rates from 1927 to 1951. The pattern of this delinquency showed no consistent spatial concentration and the wide scattering of tax delinquency in the area left no one part of it free from tax delinquency. In five of the ten blocks, the tax delinquency exceeded the total assessed valuation and, in the area as a whole, delinquencies exceeded assessed value by almost $6,300. In the area as a whole, in 45 per cent of the lots, delinquencies exceeded the assessed value. The amount of tax delinquencies in the area was almost twice as much as the revenue for the entire area, and in one block the ratio was five dollars in delinquent taxes to one dollar of revenue. In only one block did revenues exceed delinquencies. And this block was located closest to available utilities.

*Obsolete platting.*—Only 9 per cent of the lots were over thirty-five feet in width, two-thirds were between thirty and thirty-five feet and the remaining quarter, strip business frontage, were only twenty-five feet. Although a developer could try to obtain wider lots by purchasing adjacent lots, the diversity of ownership, tax difficulties, and difficulties of locating owners made this difficult if not impossible. Even if sufficient lots could have been assembled without government assistance, there would have remained a residual of single lots lying idle between improved lots, thus leading to underutilization of the area and the utilities which would have to be installed.

The platted street pattern of the area, gridiron in nature and of equal width, was tied directly to the major arterials bounding the site, thus inviting through traffic into the area. About 35 per cent of the area was platted in streets compared to an adequate planning standard of 20 per cent.

*Lack of utilities.*—The existence of only a sewer grid and disrepaired sidewalks impeded the development of the area, especially in the light of the other conditions noted. On the one hand, the sewer grid would set the obsolete pattern of development for any developer who would try to avoid the cost of relocation. On the other, the absence of a water grid and paved streets deter private development. Since a bond has to be posted in Chicago for the installation of the water grid, the inability to assemble a sufficient number of lots prevented private developers from risking losses on repayment. Similarly, since subdivision developers must install paved streets, if such a developer is not assured of being

able to assemble the entire area because of the conditions noted, it would hardly have been economically possible for him to provide paved streets. Thus, although the demand for housing was present and although the area was ripe for development, it did not develop, while the new residential construction pushed beyond the city into raw land, raising costs and extending services and utility lines.

An original plan for development, submitted by a private developer to the commission, provided for the construction of 160 single-family homes on typical lots of 50 feet by 110 feet selling for some $12,000 each.

The developer was prepared to pay $32 per lineal front foot of unimproved land or a total price of $287,000 in 1951, a price agreed upon by the Federal Housing Administration. Utility costs alone were estimated at $267,045. Under these conditions, government loss would have amounted to $267,495 since the land cost to the commission was estimated at $278,450. Although it was estimated that tax revenue from the area to the city would have amounted to a minimum of $32,000 a year, the city would gain as much revenue in two years as it had in the past twenty-five, and although this subsidy would have been repaid in taxes in less than ten years, the write-down costs appeared higher than warranted.

Obviously, the development of the area was uneconomical, for otherwise the area might have developed. Yet, despite the public willingness to absorb such losses as expressed in the legislation, the write-down appeared too great and the commission set about reinvestigating.

## THE JUDICIAL PROCESS

While the project was restudied as to ways of bringing costs down, the constitutionality of the statute covering this type of project, first of its kind in the country, was being reviewed in the courts. On August 8, 1951, the commission designated the site and filed a quo warranto suit with the circuit court of Cook County. After almost a year in the courts (on May 14, 1952) the lower court found that the act does "not violate any provision of the constitution of the State of Illinois or of the Constitution of the United States . . . but is in all respects valid and constitutional." The court further declared that the area described above is a " 'Blighted Vacant Redevelopment Project' as defined in said blighted areas Redevelopment Act of 1947, as amended by said amendatory act."

Not content with the decision of the lower court, the state's attorney appealed to the Supreme Court of Illinois, which reversed the decision of the lower court on November 20, 1952. Immediately, the Chicago Land Clearance Commission filed a petition for rehearing, which was granted. And in March, 1953, the Supreme Court reversed its previous decision and upheld the legality of the project and the law. Thus, between August of 1951 and March of 1953, the new procedure for dealing with dead lands was legally established in the United States. It remained to complete a project under this law.

### REINVESTIGATION OF THE SITE

Fearing that between its original site designation in 1951 and the Supreme Court decision of 1953 the essential character of the site had changed, the commission reinvestigated the site. On reinvestigation, it was discovered that the character of the site remained essentially the same. However, on the periphery of the site, close to major and readily accessible utility lines, some residential units had been built. Other than this, the vast majority of lots remained in the same relative condition, except that much of the delinquency had been cleared up in anticipation of commission action.

Of 264 lots studied, 89 were still delinquent as compared to 142 when the site was originally studied. Eighty-seven lots were delinquent both in 1948 and in 1951, and their location was such as to still impede development. Eighteen of the lots were un-

dergoing foreclosure, thus leaving 70 tax delinquent lots scattered through the site. It was concluded on the basis of this reinvestigation that over one-fourth of the lots scattered through the site were still heavily tax delinquent. The foreclosures were concentrated in the most desirable portions of the site. Further, it was found that 36 of the 100 "no name parcels" persisted.

If over one-fourth of the lots remained heavily tax delinquent, the installation of necessary utilities was still impeded because of the economic risks involved, and even if the area were developed except for the 25 per cent, only haphazard and uneconomical development could result—leading to a future blighted area.

Finally, with respect to diversity of owners, reinvestigation revealed that instead of 157 different owners there were 142. Some consolidation had taken place. Yet the average diversity throughout the site had increased only from 1.6 to 1.7 lots per owner, and in 6 of the 10 blocks no change in diversity had occurred at all.

The largest holder held 26 lots and appeared to be a "scavenger," acquiring the lots for resale to the commission rather than for private development. Despite other apparent concentration of ownership, the fact remained that 150 lots of the total of 264 were held by 120 different owners! And these 120 owners comprised 85 per cent of the property holders. On the basis of such considerations, it appeared that the following conclusions were warranted.

In essence, the simplest formulation of the problem of the development of so-called blighted vacant areas appears to be primarily a question of timing as related to the various cost factors involved in the development and as related to the economics of development. With a strong demand and a limited supply of desirable in-lying vacant areas, and assuming profitable and sound economic conditions, there may be a question as to whether eminent domain is necessary unless the cost of such areas over the time it would take to see them developed were more than the public could afford. The use of eminent domain would doubtless result in earlier reduction of municipal costs, earlier increases in municipal revenues, earlier housing construction, and sounder planning.

The review of site conditions indicates that the rate of utilization averaged slightly more than one house per year. The re-examination reaffirmed the blighted vacant status of the site and the commission then considered the questions of cost and the site plan. On reinvestigation, it was found that by increasing the residential density of the area through a combination of single-family and garden type apartments costs could be reduced. And in February, 1955, the federal government approved the project involving the private construction of 269 units in a setting which included a three-acre park and a playground.

Under current conditions it is estimated that the gross project cost would equal some $903,394, that the reuse value of the land would equal $626,957 or a total write-down of $276,437, of which the federal government will pay $184,291, and the city of Chicago, through the installation of utilities, $152,762. This will permit the Chicago Land Clearance Commission to make an immediate profit of over $60,000 for use in other projects. And the city of Chicago will recoup its initial contribution, both directly through assessments on future property owners for the costs of installing utilities and indirectly through stabilized, increased assessments and revenues. And the federal government, through its aid via local determination, does its part toward strengthening American cities and supports local autonomy and decentralized decision-making.

## Dead Land and Urban Sprawl

We have presented the problem of "dead lands" and shown one approach to solving this problem. We have witnessed a case study in municipal problem-solving which has taken almost five years in evolving from theory to practice. Yet, within approx-

imately two years the "test case" will have become a reality. Within two years the precedent and institutional framework will have been firmly established. A new institution for municipal problem-solving, seven years in the making, will have emerged. Too soon to form a judgment about, the completion of the project itself will provide 269 families with homes in an integrated, well-planned modern community, perhaps as impervious to future blight, future tax loss, and municipal costs as man can now accomplish under existing institutions and

TABLE 1

Per Cent Distri bution of Resident Popula tion by Distance Zones from Center of City, 1860–1950*

(Zones in Miles)

| Year | 0–2 | 2–4 | 4–6 | 6–8 | 8 or Mor | All |
|---|---|---|---|---|---|---|
| 1860 | 71.4 | 28.6 | 0.0 | 0.0 | 0.0 | 100.0 |
| 1870 | 58.5 | 35.1 | 6.4 | 0.0 | 0.0 | 100.0 |
| 1880 | 45.8 | 42.7 | 10.9 | 0.6 | 0.0 | 100.0 |
| 1890 | 29.5 | 44.6 | 15.0 | 7.3 | 3.6 | 100.0 |
| 1900 | 21.5 | 43.2 | 16.6 | 12.9 | 5.8 | 100.0 |
| 1910 | 16.5 | 32.6 | 28.4 | 13.3 | 9.2 | 100.0 |
| 1920 | 10.2 | 26.5 | 31.5 | 18.5 | 13.3 | 100.0 |
| 1930 | 6.6 | 19.6 | 28.4 | 24.4 | 21.0 | 100.0 |
| 1940 | 5.9 | 18.6 | 28.5 | 25.1 | 21.8 | 100.0 |
| 1950 | 6.1 | 18.5 | 27.5 | 23.9 | 24.3 | 100.0 |

* Source: Chicago Community Inventory, *Growth and Re-distribution of the Resident Population in the Chicago Standard Metropolitan Area*, p. 18.

concepts. Out of what seems to be the conflicting morass of ideas and institutions, one more tool, however minute, has been added to man's ability to cope with his environment.

As a result of this precedent, municipalities will have one more tool to combat the forces of decentralization. For decentralization grows out of obsolescence of the city plant and consequent undesirable environments. The cancer of obsolescence spreading from the core of American cities and depopulating vast areas in its wake is well illustrated by Chicago. Table 1 shows what has happened to that city. The waves of population movement as obsolescence encroached are clear. But what, one may ask, happened to increase the population in the 0–2 mile zone between 1940 and 1950? Table 2 provides the answer.

If one problem is on its way toward solution, another problem exhibited in Table 2 has arisen. For the non-white population has increased 80.5 per cent in the city of Chicago and the white population has declined. The non-white population in 1940 numbered 282,244. By 1950 it had increased 80.5 per cent to 509,437, an increase of

TABLE 2

PER CENT CHANGE IN POPULATION BY ZONES
FROM CENTER OF CITY, BY RACE, 1940–50*

| DISTANCE OF ZONE FROM CENTER OF CITY | PER CENT CHANGE | |
|---|---|---|
| | Non-Whites | Whites |
| Within 1 mile . . . . . . . . . . | 196.1 | 9.2 |
| 1 to 2 miles . . . . . . . . . . . | 204.1 | − 5.8 |
| 2 to 3 miles . . . . . . . . . . . | 166.3 | − 9.9 |
| 3 to 4 miles . . . . . . . . . . . | 80.9 | − 6.6 |
| 4 to 6 miles . . . . . . . . . . . | 46.2 | − 4.9 |
| 6 to 8 miles . . . . . . . . . . . | 62.7 | − 3.2 |
| 8 to 10 miles . . . . . . . . . | 92.6 | 9.9 |
| 10 miles or more . . . . . . . | 235.5 | 25.9 |
| City of Chicago . . . . . . . . | 80.5 | − 0.1 |

* Source: Chicago Community Inventory, *Growth and Redistribution of the Resident Population in the Chicago Standard Metropolitan Area*, p. 10.

227,193. The white population of 3,114,564 in 1940, however, decreased by 0.1 per cent and between 1940 and 1950 the number fell to 3,111,525, an absolute decrease of 3,039 white persons.

Though the problem of race has been focused sharply in the last ten years, the forces of decentralization sustained by blight will affect even this population. Through reclaiming of blighted areas and the elimination of obsolescence perhaps the forces of decentralization can be mitigated within the city structure; increases in housing supplies will operate to relieve pressure for housing by all groups. Reclamation of worn-out areas involves population displacement and a thinning out of the inner core of our cities, creating perhaps greater urban sprawl and the undesirable consequences we have noted.

Thus, as Table 3 shows for the Chicago area, the flood to raw outlying land continues. The thrust into the rural areas begun in the twenties and thirties has become increasingly greater. Redevelopment and reclamation activities sustain existing market pressures making for the chewing-up of the "countryside." The forces of the land market sustained by pressure from "renewal" activities spill out over the open lands unchecked in many instances by adequate zoning, building, or subdivision regulations. While the spilling-over occurs, in-lying pockets of vacant land have remained unused and incorporated areas have lost their tax base. The resulting misuse of land creates a costly land-use pattern, and sound community growth becomes impossible.

TABLE 3

INCREASE OF POPULATION IN CHICAGO
STANDARD METROPOLITAN AREA
BY DECADES, 1900–1950*

| | 1900–1910 | 1910–20 | 1920–30 | 1930–40 | 1940–50 | 1900–1950 |
|---|---|---|---|---|---|---|
| Chicago SMA | 31.5 | 27.9 | 32.8 | 3.2 | 13.9 | 162.6 |
| Central city . . . . . | 28.7 | 23.6 | 25.0 | 0.6 | 6.6 | 113.2 |
| Fringe . . . . | 43.9 | 44.5 | 58.5 | 9.9 | 31.2 | 375.4 |
| Urban . . . . | 77.5 | 69.5 | 78.0 | 7.2 | 27.2 | 630.0 |
| Rural . . . . . | 10.8 | 5.0 | 8.6 | 21.4 | 46.1 | 123.9 |

* Source: Housing and Home Finance Agency, *Population Growth in Standard Metropolitan Areas, 1900–1950* (Washington, D.C.: Government Printing Office, 1953), p. 62.

While the "dead lands" remained undeveloped, growth has been and is extending into areas not yet ripe for development instead of those ready for residential use. While sound community growth calls for the development of land in a sufficiently compact manner so as to result in an economic and efficient use of space and so as to assure that utilities and public services be provided with reasonable economy free from excessive investment and maintenance costs, the thrust of sprawl leaves vacant, already basically serviced pockets undeveloped. Good planning means the provision of adequate community facilities, but the thrust of sprawl leaves vacant some areas already so serviced for areas not yet serviced. While sound community growth calls for adequate tax revenue to support public services, urban sprawl leaves interstitial tax delinquent vacant pockets depriving areas of tax base and tax revenues. As these forces of sprawl then leave behind the vacant, interstitial areas, local autonomy is jeopardized. These vacant areas thus constitute a threat to local government.

The existence of such areas, ripe for development within city limits but unavailable under reasonable conditions to private builders, has come to be nationally considered a form of urban blight. The concept of blight has been broadened to include such vacant lands because their existence tends to perpetuate forces of urban sprawl.

Building expansion in undesirable locations and under undesirable conditions tends to be perpetuated by the number of units which come forth to supply the needs of families displaced by urban renewal activities. If "dead land" retards community growth and "stimulates" unsound growth, then making such areas available for private residential use constitutes a step forward in blight prevention, in attaining well-planned and integrated residential communities, and in aiding renewal programs. At the same time, making such areas available helps retard "urban sprawl." By impeding urban sprawl, assisting in the execution of urban renewal programs, and by providing close-in areas in desirably planned neighborhoods, the development of such areas can help impede the processes of decentralization.

As renewal activities proceed and dedensification is brought about, effective housing demand is added to demand created by natural increase. Past evidence shows the sprawling nature of much of the new construction beyond incorporated limits, often in uncontrolled areas and in undesirable ways, thus creating new blighted areas in a semirural setting. Likewise, incorporated areas suffer as this new construction proceeds beyond incorporated limits. Opening up the interstitial vacant areas for housing development thus can encourage and indeed is a necessary part of any urban renewal program.

Although the program described in this paper is not the complete solution to the problem of decentralization, it does tend to impede it by permitting city improvement to proceed and by encouraging new construction to stay within the city and so channels it as to take place in an orderly, well-planned manner. A program of "unfreezing" in-lying vacant areas can go far even by itself in building strong tax bases. When coincident with other urban renewal activities, it is particularly desirable.

# INDEXES

# INDEX TO AUTHORS

# INDEX TO SUBJECTS